Pioneer Records
of
Trinity County
California

A Century of Facts
1850–1950

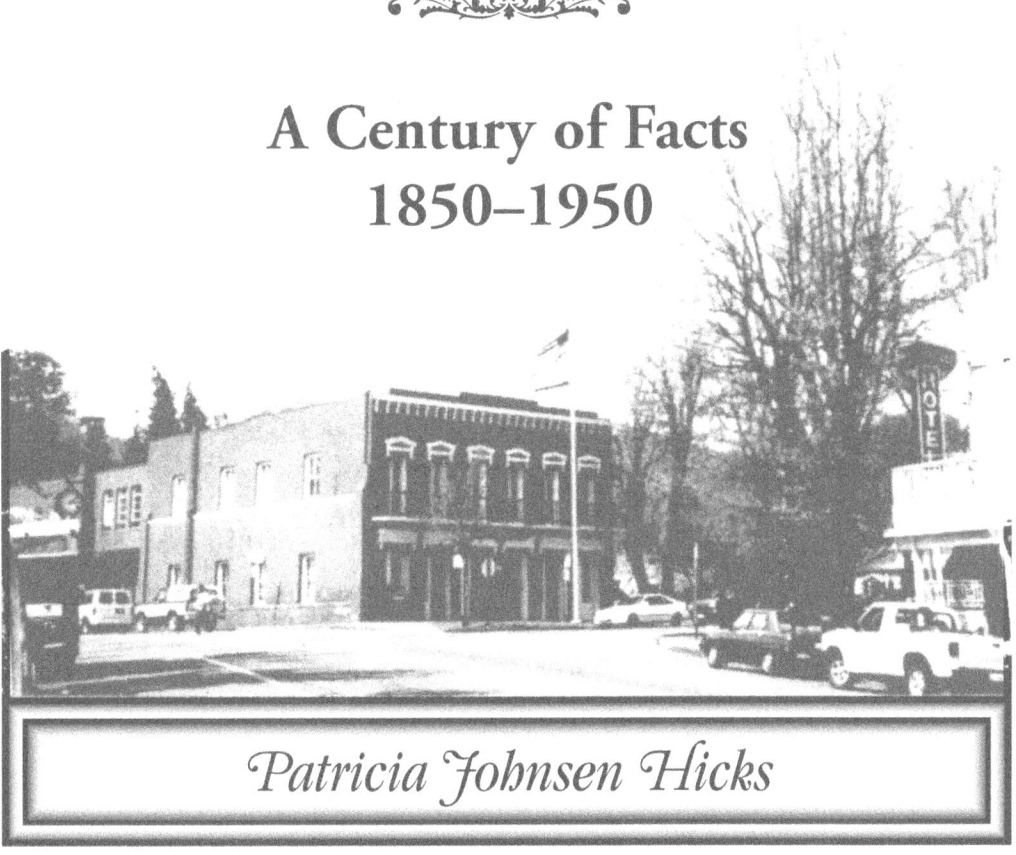

Patricia Johnsen Hicks

HERITAGE BOOKS
2012

HERITAGE BOOKS
AN IMPRINT OF HERITAGE BOOKS, INC.

Books, CDs, and more—Worldwide

For our listing of thousands of titles see our website
at
www.HeritageBooks.com

Published 2012 by
HERITAGE BOOKS, INC.
Publishing Division
100 Railroad Ave. #104
Westminster, Maryland 21157

Copyright © 1998 Patricia Johnsen Hicks

All rights reserved. No part of this book may be reproduced or transmitted in any form or by any means, electronic or mechanical, including photocopying, recording or by any information storage and retrieval system without written permission from the author, except for the inclusion of brief quotations in a review.

International Standard Book Numbers
Paperbound: 978-0-7884-1028-4
Clothbound: 978-0-7884-9147-4

DEDICATION

To my husband,
FRANK ENOCHS HICKS, Jr., R.Ph.,
who shared his love of Weaverville,
and Trinity County, California, with a city girl.

Patricia Johnsen Hicks
Weaverville, Trinity County, California
1998

TABLE OF CONTENTS

DEDICATION iii

TABLE OF CONTENTS v

PREFACE vii

LEGEND ix

Chapter 1   DEATHS 1850 - 1900 1

Chapter 2   INDEX TO DEATHS 1900 - 1950 127

Chapter 3   INDEX TO MARRIAGES 1850 - 1900
       HUSBANDS 161
       WIVES 174

Chapter 4   INDEX TO MARRIAGES 1900 - 1950
       HUSBANDS 187
       WIVES 197

Chapter 5   INDEX TO BIRTHS 1850 - 1900 207

Chapter 6   INDEX TO BIRTHS 1900 - 1950 259

Chapter 7   ADDENDUM 287

About the Author 299

BIBLIOGRAPHY 300

PREFACE

John Sutter obtained a very large Mexican land grant near the American and Sacramento Rivers in California and built what he called "Sutter's Fort" in 1839. In 1847 Sutter decided to build a sawmill. The place chosen was about 45 miles from the Fort, on the American River at Coloma. James Wilson Marshall became Sutter's partner; he was to build and operate the sawmill.

On January 24, 1848, Marshall went to inspect the tailrace, which carried the water back into the river. He saw a glittering particle in the bedrock of the channel, and then some more of the shiny flecks. Marshall and Sutter used every test they knew, and decided that the particles were of gold. The news leaked out, but the Rush for Gold in California did not begin until the beginning of 1849.

Pierson B. Reading, through the friendship and influence of John Sutter, had also obtained a Mexican land grant on the upper Sacramento River. Hearing the news about gold, he visited Sutter and was taken to Coloma. Returning to his rancho, Reading crossed the mountains to the west and found much gold in what is now Trinity County, California, at a place known as Readings Bar on the Trinity River. This was in July 1848.

In the Autumn of 1849, William McKee and a man named Weaver also found gold in Trinity County. When they returned to the Sacramento Valley for the winter, Weaver took his gold and was not heard from again. In the Spring of 1850 McKee took a group of men back to Trinity County where they found gold. In the Summer of 1850, Matthew Stewart built the first building, assisted by James Howe, and named the town Weaverville. California became a State September 9, 1850. Weaverville soon became the County Seat of Trinity, one of the original counties. The first records in the Trinity County Courthouse are dated Oct. 1851.

PIONEER RECORDS OF TRINITY COUNTY tells of the Pioneers in records of their marriages, births and deaths. The records for 1850-1900 are from all available sources, with an Index for the years 1900-1950. Many Pioneer families still have descendants living in Trinity County, California, where people continue to find gold in the streams and mountains of the place known as "The Northern Mines" of the California Gold Rush.

PIONEER RECORDS OF TRINITY COUNTY, CALIFORNIA
A Century of Facts 1850-1950

LEGEND:

TT - TRINITY TIMES, published in Weaverville, Trinity County, California Dec. 1854-1857; available copies: Dec. 1854-Sept. 1855.

TJ - TRINITY JOURNAL, published in Weaverville, Trinity County, California January 1856 - present. (TJ Sat. July 18, 1863) refers to the TRINITY JOURNAL for that date.

DCG - DOUGLAS CITY GAZETTE, later TRINITY GAZETTE, published in Douglas City, Trinity County, California May 1861-April 1862.

1900-1945 Births, Marriages & Deaths are from the Vitals Summary in the TRINITY JOURNAL for January of the following year. The actual reference will be found in the paper for a week or two following the date given.

1946-1950 Births, Marriages & Deaths are from Trinity County Official Records, Recorder's Office, Trinity County Courthouse, Main & Court Streets, Weaverville, Trinity County, California.

Delayed Certificates of Birth were filed during the 1940s and 1950s as people needed proof of citizenship and proof of birth. Some were filed in Official Birth Records, some were filed in separate books labeled "Delayed Certificates of Birth". These records are in the Addendum, together with information from miscellaneous sources, such as family records.

CAUTION! For records for 1900-1950, check the actual listing in the TRINITY JOURNAL and Official Records, if available. The Indexes for 1900-1950 are just a place to start your search.

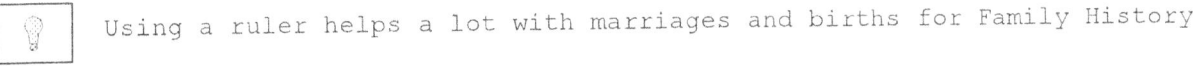 Using a ruler helps a lot with marriages and births for Family History.

PIONEER RECORDS OF TRINITY COUNTY, CALIFORNIA
A Century of Facts

Researched and Compiled by
Patricia Johnsen Hicks

Deaths from all available sources 1850-1899. Index 1900-1950.

[Note: Canon Creek was originally printed with a ~ over the n. It is pronounced Canyon Creek, and is near Junction City. The same is true for Canon City, up Canon Creek, which is pronounced Canyon City. Entries have been copied as they were written: "Canon Creek".]
For people of Chinese descent, please see the listing in the Addendum.

ABER, FRANCES. Died at Ridgeville 14 July 1856, daughter of Elizabeth and Thomas Aber, aged 5 years. (TJ Sat. July 26, 1856). [Buried Ridgeville Cemetery; marker 1980].

ABER, WALTER F. Died at Ridgeville Aug. 24, 1857, only child of Thomas and Elizabeth Aber, aged 1 yr 3 mo 4 days. (TJ Sat. Aug. 29, 1857, p 2). [Buried Ridgeville Cemetery; marker 1980].

ABBOTT, BENJAMIN FRANK. Died in Weaverville Apr. 14, 1880; aged 48 years; native of North Carolina. (TJ Sat. Apr. 17, 1880 p 2). [prob. buried Weaverville Cemetery; no marker 1980].

ABBOTT, JOHN. Died in Weaverville Aug. 13, 1861; formerly from Maine; aged 37 yr. (TJ Sat. Aug. 17, 1861). prob. bur. Weaverville Cem.; no marker 1980.

ABRAHM, SAMUEL. Died New York City, July 31, 1866, aged 68 years; father of Isaac Abrahm of Weaverville. (TJ Sat. Sept. 8, 1866, p 2).

ABRAHM, CHARLIE. (exact copy:) "Died Weaverville Nov. 3, 1875, Charlie Abrahms, aged 7 mo 15 days, son of Isaac and Paulina Abrahams". (TJ Sat. Nov. 6, 1875).

ABRAHMS, CAROLINE K. Died on South Salmon River, Siskiyou County, Aug. 13, 1879; wife of James Abrahms, aged 42 years 11 month 27 days. (TJ Sat. Aug. 30, 1879). Born 16 June 1837.

ABRAHMS, HAZEL MAY. Died Weaverville Aug. 24, 1895; inf. dau. of Mr. and Mrs. F. S. Abrahms, aged 6 mo. (TJ Aug 31, 1895).

ADAMS, ALTA MAY. Died Dedrick Nov. 2, 1898; daughter of Mr. and Mrs. J. Q. Adams; only child, aged 3 yr 5 mo 15 dy; bur. Foresters Cem. Junction City Nov. 4, 1898. (TJ Nov 5, 1898).

ADAMS, HAZEL M. Died Jan. 10, 1908 Hayfork, CA; age 3; female; white; born Calif. [Index to Deaths 1890-1908].

ADAMS, JOHN. Died Weaverville Feb. 5, 1873; native of Mass. aged 70 yr; Pioneer of Trinity County; left Taunton, Mass. in 1849, arrived San Francisco summer of 1849 in bark "Anne", Cobb, Master; came Weaverville 1852; remained, repairing watches; early days of Weaverville, he taught school; left wife, family, 2 sisters in Mass. (TJ Sat. Feb. 8, 1873). On both 1860 and 1870 census, but with no family in Trinity County. [Index to Deaths 1873-1890 adds "watchmaker"].

ADAMS, ST. CLAIRE. Died Weaverville Dec. 1, 1886; native of Ireland, aged about 61 years; buried Thurs. Dec. 2, 1886, public cemetery, Weaverville; Justice of Peace of Long Ridge Township; grown son, daughter, and a brother, all residents of Humboldt County. (TJ Sat. Dec. 4, 1886).

AGAN, WILLIAM. Died Oct. 6, 1858 on Trinity River, aged about 35 years. (TJ Sat. Oct. 9, 1858, p 2). no further information.

AHRENS, HENRY. Died Weaverville Nov. 5, 1884; native of Holstein, Denmark, aged 65 years; came to Trinity County 1851; brother D. D. Ahrens, Junction City. (TJ abt. Nov. 5, 1884). Prob. bur. Weaverville Cem; no marker 1980.

AINSWORTH, EVA. Died Weaverville Feb. 27, 1869; daughter of L. and B. H. Ainsworth, aged 12 yr 6 mo. (TJ Sat. March 6, 1869). Born 27 Aug. 1856. Family not in 1860 or 1870 census. Buried in I.O.O.F. section Weaverville Cemetery. Marker 1980: "Ainsworth, Eva R. daughter of Lewis and Persis H. Ainsworth. Her last words were `I see the angels coming for me, Papa'". Stone carved by J. H. Lee, Chico.

AKERMAN, (sic) JOHN. (TJ Sat. Dec. 7, 1872). See **ALCOMAN**. Correction made in TJ Sat. Dec. 14, 1872.

ALBEE, J. P. Probably murdered; of Redwood Creek, 8 miles from Hoopa and Arcata trail; house burned by Indians Nov. 6, 1862; buried at site of house. Wife and 8 children living "at the Bay" (probably Humboldt Bay); not safe at the farm. (TJ Sat. Nov. 15, 1862; confirmed Sat. Nov. 22, 1862, p 2).

ALBIEZ, FRED. Died Hay Fork Nov. 15, 1899; son of Erhard Albiez; native of Calif., aged abt 18 yr. (TJ Nov 25, 1899).

ALCOMAN, JOHN. Died in Weaverville Dec. 4, 1872, a native of Germany, aged 45 years. (TJ Sat. Dec. 7, 1872 as "Akerman"; corrected TJ Sat. Dec. 14, 1872).

ALDRICH, JAMES E. Died Oct. 29, 1906 Minersville; age 25; male, white, miner. Body sent to Los Angeles. Birthplace unknown. [Index to Deaths 1890-1908].

ALEXANDER, NELL. Died Woods Hole, Mass. Dec. 27, 1886, age 55 yr; native of Killingly, Conn.; formerly engaged in business at Worcester, Mass. Old time resident of Trinity County. (Note: one source gives place of death as Manchester, New Hampshire). (TJ Jan. 22, 1887 pg 3). Not in 1852, 1860, or 1870 census as "Nell".

ALLEN, CYRUS E. Died Weaverville Aug. 28, 1865; son of E. F. and D. J. Allen, aged 4 mo 6 days. (TJ Sat. Sept. 2, 1865 p 2). Buried Weaverville Cem; marker 1984. Born 22 Apr 1865. Family not in 1860 census. 1870 census: Allen, Egbert F. age 33, lawyer, b. New York; Allen, Diantha Joy, age 31, housekeeper, b. Michigan; Allen, Susie, age 1, born California. Weaverville 6-16-1870, page 12. (See also Allen, Ralph M.)

ALLEN, EGBERT F. Died Chicago Mar. 26, 1893; uncle of Mrs. D. G. Reid and Mrs. G. W. Tinsley of Trinity County. Trinity pioneer, District Attorney in 1863; left county in 1860s. (TJ Sat. May 20, 1893 p 3 col 3).

ALLEN, ELLEN ELIZA. Died near Weaverville Dec. 9, 1866; daughter of William and Mary Ann Allen, aged 17 yr 3 mo 12 days; born Marquette County, Wisconsin (28 Aug 1849); buried Weaverville Cemetery. (TJ Sat. Dec. 15, 1866). No marker 1984.

ALLEN, HENRY. Shot by Harry Benckley, Last Chance, Trinity County, California Aug. 1, 1888. (TJ Sat. Aug. 5, 1888, p 2). No further information.

ALLEN, MARY ANN. Died near Weaverville July 8, 1881; wife of Wm. H. Allen; native of England; age 51 years 9 months 16 days (born 22 Sept 1829); funeral Sun. July 10, 1881; buried Weaverville Cem. (TJ abt July 8, 1881). No marker 1984. See also Ellen Eliza Allen.

ALLEN, MORTIMER C. Died at the Empire Hotel, Shasta abt Jan. 18, 1891. Native of Missouri, aged 69 years. Came to Shasta & Trinity County 1852. Bur at Shasta Tues. Jan. 20, 1891 with Masonic services. He was a Knight Templar of Red Bluff Commandery. [*Redding Democrat*]. (TJ Sat. Jan. 24, 1891).

ALLEN, RALPH M. Died Hay Fork Sept. 9, 1867; aged 27 yr 4 mo 19 days (b. 20 Apr 1840); resident here nearly 8 years; born Cattaraugus County, New York; came Calif. from McHenry County, Illinois in 1859 with brother, Egbert F. Allen, D.A. of Trinity County; leaves wife, child, sister, brother, and other relatives here to mourn him, and aged parents in Illinois. (TJ Sat. Sept. 14, 1867, p 2). Buried Kellogg's Cemetery, Hay Fork; marker 1980. Journals of Probate Court 1852-1877: "Ralph M. Allen, probate filed Sept. 12, 1867 Book C page 216". Trinity County Marriages Book H page 133: "Married near Douglas City Apr. 20, 1865 by Rev. George W. Henning, Ralph Allen of Hayfork and Miss Emma Mabie of Douglas City". Mrs. Allen m2) Amos H. Marshall at Douglas City Aug. 31, 1870 (Book H page 225). 1870 Census: Allen, Emma age 24, b. Illinois; Nellie, age 4, b. Calif; Elizabeth, age 2, b. Calif. Douglas City, June 18, 1870, page 9.

ALLEN, WILLIAM HENRY. Died Weaverville Sept. 14, 1891; born Jan. 21, 1825 Waltenundridge, Gloucestershire, England; m 1847 Miss Mary Ann Brown in Gloucestershire; came to US with wife 1848; Calif. 1853; Trinity County 1859; 5 daughters, 4 surviving, also an adopted daughter, Alice Warren; dau. Mrs. Minnie Williams lost her husband just over a year ago. I.O.O.F. funeral Tues. Sept. 15, 1891; bur. I.O.O.F. cem. Weaverville. (TJ Sept. 19, 1891 pp 2 & 3; see also TJ Sept 12, 1891 p 3 col 1 for story of the accident that led to his death.)

ALLISON, EDWARD, Mr. Died The Dalles, Wasco County, Oregon March 3, 1888; aged 79 yr 4 mo 13 days (b. 21 Oct 1808); formerly an old resident of Nevada and Trinity County; born Madison County, Kentucky 1809 (sic); came California with family to Nevada City, etc. Leaves wife, 3 sons; 3 daughters; one, Lucy, is Mrs.

William Vollmers of Trinity Center; 14 grandchildren. Buried near daughter-in-law, wife of son Charles, at The Dalles. (TJ. Mar. 17 and 24, 1888).

ALLISON, JANE, Mrs. Died recently (abt Aug/Sept 1890) in Kellogg, Iowa, age 70, while visiting daughter, Mrs. C. Owings. Remains taken to The Dalles, Oregon, by son Charles Allison; buried by the side of her husband (Edward Allison); Deceased was a resident of Trinity Center for many years. Mother of Mrs. Wm. Vollmers of Trinity Center. (TJ Sat. Sept. 27, 1890 p 3 col 6).

ALVERSON, CHESTAIN. Died MAY 19, 1900, age 50 yr; b. Kentucky. (TJ Jan 1901).

AMARILLAS, SACRAMENTO. Died Weaverville April 19, 1876; native of Mexico aged 42 years. (TJ Sat. Apr. 22, 1876 p 2). [Prob. bur. Weaverville Cem.; no marker 1980].

AMES, EMILY BALCH. Died Weaverville Dec. 13, 1892; born Lubec, Maine 1820, aged 72 yr 4 mo 5 days; dau. of Dr. H. G. Balch. A Balch ancestor settled Danvers, Mass. 1623. Bur. Dec. 14, 1892 Weaverville Cem; leaves bro. J. R. Balch. Married J. J. Ames in Lubec, Maine, came to Trinity Co. 1872. long obit p 3; worth copying. (TJ Sat. Dec. 17, 1892, pp 2 & 3).

AMES, P. Died New River Oct. 11, 1889, a native of Maine, aged abt 58 years. (TJ Sat. Oct. 26, 1889). [Index to Deaths 1873-1890 has similar information]. [Not in 1880 Census].

ANDERSON, JAMES T. Died Dec. 19, 1907 Weaverville; age 76; male, white; born Tennessee; rancher. [Index to Deaths 1890-1908].

ANDERSON, JOHN. "He was killed on Rush Creek mountain by a band of Indians in May 1852"; buried near McKenzie Gulch; body removed last week (August 1857) and interred in Weaverville burial grounds. (TJ Sat. Aug. 22, 1857, p 2). [No marker 1980]. Journals of Probate Court, abt April 1852; Probate Book A-3.

ANDERSON, JOE. Died May 13, 1907 Canon City; age about 29; male, white, miner; birthplace unknown. [Index to Deaths 1890-1908].

ANDERSON, LARS. Died Weaver Creek March 5, 1886; native of Sweden; aged about 64 years; buried Weaverville Cemetery Sat. Mar. 6, 1886; resident Trinity County for over 27 years, living most of his time at Douglas City; miner. (TJ Sat. Mar. 13, 1886). No marker 1980.

ANDERSON, MARY ELLEN. Died at Red Bar, Trinity County, July 24, 1860; daughter of William and Clara Anderson, aged about 14 months. (TJ Sat. July 28, 1860 p 2). Buried Weaverville Cemetery; marker 1980 "aged 13 mo 17 days". [Born 7 June 1859].

ARGUELLA, FRANK L. Died Jan. 24, 1907 Weaverville, age 20, male, white, born Calif. reported by Margaret Arguella. [Index to Deaths 1890-1908]. (should be Arguello; see below).

ARGUELLO, JOSE. Died Weaverville Nov. 23, 1888; son of Mr. and Mrs. J. Aguello (sic) aged 4 yr and 7 mo. (TJ Sat. Dec. 1, 1888). Born 23 April 1884. Possibly buried Catholic Cem. Weav; no marker 1986.

ARGUELLO, JOSE. Died Weaverville May 24, 1899; b. Las Vegas, New Mexico; aged abt 68 yr; came to Trin. Co. 1859; m. Margaret Boler Nov 23, 1876; 4 surviving children: Mrs. Lillie Armstrong, Irene, Frankie and Harry Arguello; bur. Catholic Cem. Weav. (TJ May 27, 1899, pp 2-3). **ASHBROOK, T. B.** Drowned while skating alone at Honey Lake near Susanville, Lassen County Dec. 27, 1878. (no age). Ashbrook taught Public School in Weaverville seven years ago (1872). (TJ Sat. Jan. 4, 1879). No further information.

ATHERTON, DANIEL RITTER. Died Weaverville Jan. 4, 1889; native of New York, aged 66 yr; born Ticonderoga, NY 29 Mar 1821; married Mary A. Atkins (prob. in Vermont); came Calif. 1873; wife survives him. (TJ Jan. 5, 1889). Prob. bur. Weaverville Cem; no marker 1980. 1880 Census: Atherton, Daniel R. age 57; printer; b. NY; parents b. NY; Atherton, Mary, age 56, b. Vermont; parents b. New Hampshire. No children listed. Weaverville page 1, June 2, 1880. [Brief information in Index to Deaths 1873-1890].

ATHERTON, MARY ANN, Mrs. Died Weaverville Jan. 3, 1891; native of Waterbury, VT, aged 71 years 4 mo 19 days; maiden name Atkins; born 14 Aug 1819; married Daniel R. Atherton 1849; no children; came Calif Sept. 1873; bur. Mon. Jan. 5, 1891 next to deceased husband in Weaverville cem. Brother Capt. Geo. H. Atkins of Shasta came for the funeral. (TJ Sat. Jan. 10, 1891 pp 2 & 3).

ATKESON, JESSIE, Miss. Died at Hoaglin Jul 20, 1899; daughter of Mr. and Mrs. W. E. Atkeson; native of Calif., aged 17 yr 11 mo 5 dy. (TJ Aug 5, 1899 p 2 & p 3, col 2).

ATKESON, JOHN. Died at Hoaglin Jul 23, 1899; inf. son of Mr. and Mrs. W. E. Atkeson, native of Calif., aged 3 weeks. (TJ Aug 5, 1899 p 2 & p 3 col 2).

ATKESON, KATE, Miss. Died Hettenpome Mar 6, 1899; dau. of Mr. and Mrs. W. E. Atkeson; native of Calif., aged abt 13 yr. (TJ Apr 1, 1899 p 3 col 2).

ATKESON; WM. E. Died Nov 10, 1900; age 63 yr 8 mo 25 dy; b. Ohio. (TJ Jan 1901).

ATKINS, GEORGE H., Capt. Died at the Odd Fellows Home at Thermalito, Butte Co. Jan 20, 1897; native of Mass., about 70 yr; came to Trin. Co. 25-30 years ago; leaves widow, and 2 daughters, Mrs. T. A. Selby and Mrs. James Bissett of Oakland. (TJ Feb 6, 1897 p 3). [see also Atherton].

ATTERBURY, ARTHUR. Died Weaverville Oct. 10, 1888; native of Kentucky, aged about 51 years; partner of Col. B. B. Money of Lewiston early 1850s. (TJ abt Oct. 10, 1888). Prob. bur. Weaverville Cem; no marker 1980.

ATWOOD, SYBELLA, Mrs. Died Brockton, Mass. Mar 12, 1897, aged 88 yr 4 mo; sister of Mrs. A. Everhart of Weaverville and Mrs. J. A. Bachelder of San Francisco. (TJ Sat. Mar 27, 1897 p 3 col 1).

BACHELDER, W. H. Died Napa City, Napa Co. CA Jan. 5, 1895; native of New Hampshire, aged 64 yr. Harry Bachelder lived in Trinity Co. for a number of years; left Weaverville in 1875 for Napa City. (TJ Sat. Jan 12, 1895 p3 col 2).

BACHMAN, ALOIS. Died Hay Fork Oct. 2, 1882; native of Austria, aged 68 yr. (TJ Sat. Oct. 7, 1882, p 2).

BACON, MARY K. Died North Yakima, Wash. Mar 11, 1896; nee Morris; b. Indian Creek, Trinity Co., CA; m. in Weaverville 1883 to E. W. Bacon, who survives her, with four children; sister of Mrs. E. L. Newman of Hay Fork and William, John, and Henry Morris of Trinity County. (TJ Sat. Mar 13, 1896 p 3 col 2).

BADGLEY, ROBERT BLACK. Died Canon Creek Jun 2, 1898; native of Illinois, aged abt 33 yr; leaves a bro. Geo. E. Badgley, Canon Creek; relatives in Oakland and the East. Funeral at Dedrick Jun 5, 1898; body was taken to Ohio for final interment. (TJ Jun 4, 1898 p 2; Jun 11, 1898 p 3 col 2).

BAILEY, ANNIE MERIEN. Died Dedrick May 17, 1893; infant daughter of Mr. and Mrs. G. L. Bailey, aged 1 day. (TJ Sat. May 20, 1893).

BAILEY, MARY HELENE. Died Weaverville Oct 20, 1897; native of Calif. aged 10 mo 21 dy; inf. dau. of Mr. and Mrs. Geo. L. Bailey of Canon Creek. (TJ Oct 30, 1897).

BAILEY, WILLIAM. Died Weaverville Nov 11, 1897; native of Mattock, Canada, aged abt 63 yr; came to Trinity Co. from Humboldt in 1883; unmarried. (TJ Nov 13, 1897).

BAILEY, WILLIAM M. Died near Redding, Shasta County, Oct. 12, 1884; known as "Billy Bailey"; native of Iowa 27 yr; employed here 3 years; leaves parents, brother and sister in Shasta County. (TJ Sat. Oct. 18, 1884).

BAKER, RICHARD SAMUEL. Died Weaverville Nov. 18, 1888; native of England, aged about 59 yr; unmarried; no relatives in Trinity County; came Calif. 1850; Trinity County 1851. (TJ Sat. Nov. 24, 1888).

BALBACH, JOHN. Died San Jose, Santa Clara Co., CA Aug 3, 1896; b. Mergenthem, Germany Feb 13, 1820; age 76 yr; came to U.S. age 28; started for Calif. Mar 28, 1849; leaves widow, Charles, John, William, Arthur, George and Louis (well known in Weaverville), Mrs. Charles Cleal, Mrs. M. D. Baker, and Mrs. James Traill. (TJ Aug 8, 1896 p 3 col 4).

BALCH, ALICE. Died Weaverville Jan. 19, 1872, infant daughter of James R. and Margaret Balch, aged 14 days; b. 5 Jan 1872. (TJ Sat. Jan. 20, 1872). I.O.O.F. Cem., Weaverville; marker 1976.

BALCH, EDDIE (EDWARD). Died Weaverville Feb. 5, 1885; son of James Ripley and Maggie R. Balch, aged 6 yr 9 mo 12 days; b. 24 Apr 1878. Buried Odd Fellows Cemetery Feb. 6, 1885. (TJ Sat. Feb. 7, 1885).

BALCH, H. G. Died Yountville, Napa Co., CA Mar 7, 1894; brother of J. R. Balch of Weaverville; served in Civil War from 1861; 6th Marine 3 yr; Navy until close of war on frigate Vanderbilt. (TJ Mar 10, 1894 p 3 col 2).

BALCH, JAMES HORATIO. Died Weaverville March 11, 1869; only son of J. R. and Margaret Balch, aged 7 months. b. 30 July 1868. (TJ Sat. Mar. 13, 1869 p 2). I.O.O.F. Cem., Weaverville; marker 1976.

BALCH, JAMES RIPLEY. Died Weaverville Apr 18, 1895, aged 63 yr 4 mo 27 dy; bur. I.O.O.F. Cem., Weaverville Sat. Apr 20, 1895; born Lubec, Maine 1832; m. in Weaverville Miss Margaret Robb 1867; 7 children, 3 living; obit. worth copying. (TJ Sat. Apr 20, 1895; obit TJ Apr 27, 1895 p 3 col 4). ["BALCH, JAMES RIPLEY. Nov. 22, 1831 - Apr. 10, 1895". IOOF Cemetery, Weaverville, Trinity Co., California; marker 1980].

BALCH, RAY. Died Weaverville Feb. 10, 1887; youngest son of Mr. and Mrs. J. R. Balch, aged 5 yr 3 mo 27 days; b. 14 Oct. 1881. (TJ Sat. Feb. 12, 1887).

BALLEAU, LOUIS F. Died Deadwood Apr 21, 1897; native of Canada, aged 71 yr; one of the pioneers of the Deadwood Mining District; bur. Lewiston Cem. (TJ Apr 24, 1897; see also TJ May 1, 1897 and May 8, 1897 p 3 col 2).

BARBER, HARRY S. Died Dec. 9, 1907 Weaverville; age 21; born Calif. (at Dixon, Solano Co). [Index to Deaths 1890-1908].

BARGAS, ROSA. Died Oakland, Alameda Co. May 6, 1893; age 15 yr 3 mo 14 days; daughter of Mr. and Mrs. M. Bargas, formerly of Douglas City. (TJ Sat. May 27, 1893 p 3 col 1).

BARKER, _____. Inf. dau. of Mr. and Mrs. D. Barker; b.d. Dec 03, 1900. (TJ Jan 1901).

BARKER, DAVID EDMUND VALENTINE. Died Hay Fork April 6, 1887; native of Vermont, aged about 66 years. Came to Trinity County 1851; leaves a large family. (TJ Sat. Apr. 9, 1887). 1880 census: David, age 60, b. Vermont; parents b. Vermont; Jane (Indian), 52, b. Calif.; Dwight, 19, b. CA; Don, 18, b. CA; William, 16, b. CA; James, 12, b. CA (d. Dec. 30, 1895); Louisa, 9, b. CA; Edward, 6, b. CA; (d. May 1893); Henry, 3, b. CA; Flora, 6 mo, b. CA (d. July 4, 1895).

BARKER, EDWARD. Died Weaverville May 2, 1893; native of Calif. aged 19 yr. (TJ Sat. May 6, 1893).

BARKER, FLORA. Died Hay Fork July 4, 1895; native of Calif. aged 15 yr 7 mo 9 dy. (TJ July 13, 1895).

BARKER, H. M. Died May 1905 near Carrville, age 59, male, white. [Index to Deaths 1890-1908].

BARKER, JAS. Died Hay Fork Dec 30, 1895; native of Calif. (no age given). (TJ Sat. Jan 4, 1896).

BARKER, JANE, Mrs. Died Hay Fork July 4, 1890; widow of D.E.V. Barker, dec.; native of California, aged 48 yr; mother of 10 children, all living. Bur. Sat. July 5, 1890. (TJ Sat. July 12, 1890). [Similar information in Index to Deaths 1890-1908].

BARKLA, MARY EMMA. Died Weaverville Oct. 26, 1875; aged 21 days; daughter of James and Elizabeth Barkla. (TJ Sat. Oct. 30, 1875). [I.O.O.F. Cem. marker 1976].

BARLEYCORN, JOHN HENRY JAMES. Died Weaverville Feb. 21, 1890; native of Sassendorf, Germany, aged about 75 yr; (b. Dec. 10, 1813). Naturalized Shasta County 1858; Bur. Sunday Feb. 23, 1890 Odd Fellows Cem. Weaverville, beside S. S. Garwood. (TJ Sat. Mar. 1, 1890). IOOF cem. marker 1976. [Index to Deaths 1890-1908 adds single].

BARNES, GEORGE W. Died Jul 05, 1900; age 71 yr 5 mo 18 dy; b. New York. (TJ Jan 1901).

BARNHART, ALLEN VEACH. Died Cox Bar May 24, 1881; native of Calif., aged 25 years; half-brother of Mrs. J. A. Tinsley. (TJ Sat. May 28, 1881).

BARNICKEL, JOHN JACOB. Died Weaverville May 1, 1884; native of Nuremburg, Bavaria, aged 59 yr 2 mo 5 days; born 26 Feb 1825; came Trinity County 1856; purchased Weaverville Book and Drug Store 1870; widow Anna (Junkans); 4 children, 3 girls, 1 son. Bur. Masonic Cem. Weaverville May 2, 1884. (TJ Sat. May 3, 1884). [see also Deaths 1900-1950].

BARNUM, ALICE, Miss. Died Jun 16, 1896 Bridgeville, Humboldt Co., CA; native of Trinity County, age 22 yr; bur. I.O.O.F. Cem. Rohnerville, Humboldt Co. Dau. of Mr. and Mrs. E. B. Barnum. (TJ June 27, 1896 p 3 and July 4, 1896 p 3).

BARNUM, LOTTA MARIA. Died at Cox's Bar Sept. 19, 1879 of diphtheria; aged 13 yr 4 mo 7 days; daughter of E. B. and Alzina Barnum; b. 12 May 1866. (TJ Sat. Sept 27, 1879).

BARRETT, JAMES. Died Weaverville Sept. 8, 1886; native of Ireland, aged 71 years. (TJ Sat. Sept. 11, 1886).

BARRY, DAVID ST. CLAIR. Died Hettenshaw, Nov. 17, 1893; only son of E. R. and Rose Barry, age 12 yr 1 mo 11 days. (TJ Sat. Nov. 25, 1893).

BARRY, EDW. R. Died Jan 05, 1900; age 51 yr; b. New York. (TJ Jan 1901).

BARTHOLOMEW, AUGUSTA MANA. Died Weaverville April 10, 1869; daughter of M. O. and Lucy Bartholomew of Canyon City (no age given); (TJ Sat. Apr. 7, 1869). She may be the daughter born at Canon Creek July 4, 1867 to the wife of Mitchell Orland Bartholomew. (TJ abt July 4, 1867).

BARTHOLOMEW, LUCY. Died Hydesville, [Humboldt Co.] Calif, July 18, 1872; wife of M. G. (sic) (should be M. O.) Bartholomew, native of Vernon County, Missouri, aged 28 yr 6 mo 20 days. (TJ Sat. Aug. 3, 1872). (Not in 1860 or 1870 census). [m. in Weaverville Sept. 9, 1866 by Judge John Murphy, Mitchell O. Bartholomew of Canon Creek and Miss Lucy J. Morris of Weaverville. Trin. Co. Mar. Book H page 168].

BARTHOLOMEW, M. O. Died Napa County about 3 weeks ago; formerly of Canon City. (TJ Sat. Jan. 18, 1873). (Note: Mitchell Orland Bartholomew and Lucy J. Morris Bartholomew had a son, born at Canon Creek Jan. 7, 1869. TJ after Jan. 7, 1869).

BARTLETT, CHAS. H. Dropped dead at his home at Red Hill (Junction City) Fri. morning Mar. 11, 1887. Bur. Mar. 13, 1887, Weaverville Cemetery; Native of Dover, New Hampshire, 61 yr 10 mo 8 days; b. 3 May 1825. (TJ Sat. Mar. 12 and Mar. 19, 1887); (Cox's Annals, Bartlett, James W. Annotations, 1940, says the wife of Chas. H. Bartlett was Mary B. Kennedy Bartlett.)

Bartlett, James W., Judge (of Trinity County Superior Court), son of Charles H. Bartlett and Mary B. Kennedy; b. Junction City May 15, 1862; died March 15, 1936. (Cox's Annals, 1940).

BASSHAM, ALICE E. Died Trinity Center Feb. 19, 1884; daughter of G. B. and E. A. Bassham; born Weaverville; aged 15 yr 9 mo 12 days; b. 7 May 1868. (TJ Sat. Feb. 23 and Mar. 1, 1884). [1880 Census: Bassham, Green B., age 44, b. Alabama; parents b. Alabama; Eliza, age 37, b. Missouri; fa. b. KY: mo. b. Ohio; Annie, 16, b. CA; Gertrude, 14, b. CA; Alice, 12, b. CA; Albert b. Oct. 26, 1874 Weav.; Florence, b. Nov. 19, 1874 Weav.; Ida, 3, b. CA (d. Apr. 15, 1891); William 9 mo. b. CA.]

BASSHAM, GREEN BERRY. Died Trinity Center Oct 29, 1899; native of Alabama, aged 63 yr 11 mo; came to Calif. across the plains with his brother in 1858; m. in Shasta County Eliza Conway, who survives him; ten children, six living; moved from Shasta County to Weaverville in 1869; to Trinity Center in 1882. (TJ Nov 14, 1899 pp 2 & 3, col 2). [see also Freethy].

BASSHAM, IDA, Miss. Died at the home of her parents in Trinity Center Apr. 15, 1891. She was a native of California, aged 14 yr 3 mo 15 days. (TJ Apr 18, 1891 p 3 and TJ Apr 25, 1891).

BASSHAM, KATIE. Died near Weaverville March 22, 1874, daughter of Mr. and Mrs. W. P. Bassham, aged about 2 yr 6 mo; b. 22 Sept 1871. (TJ Sat. March 28, 1874).

BATES, FORDYCE. Died Worthington, Mass. Jan 12, 1900; long obit. (TJ Feb 3, 1900 p 3 col 4). [see also Addendum)]

BATES, FRANK HARRILL. Died Weaverville Sept. 8, 1862; son of John G. and Mary J. Bates of Shasta, aged about 7 months. (TJ Sat. Sept. 13, 1862 p 2).

BATES, NELDA ARLETA. Died Shasta County Jan 2, 1899; inf. dau. of Mr. and Mrs. O. D. Bates; grandchild of Ran Bates who formerly lived at Lowden Ranch, Trinity Co. (TJ Jan 7, 1899 p 3 col 6).

BATES, NELSON. Died Steiner's Flat near Douglas City Dec. 8, 1871, native of New York, aged about 54 yr. (TJ Sat. Dec. 9, 1871 p 2).

BATH, JAMES. Died Douglas City Jun 4, 1899; native of Cornwall, England, aged abt 58 yr; lived Trinity County 30 years; bur. Weaverville Cem. (TJ June 10, 1899.)

BAUMGARTNER, DANIEL. Died Watson Gulch Shasta County "last Tuesday" (prob. Nov. 22, 1881). (TJ Dec. 3, 1881, p 3; from Shasta *Courier*; try Shasta County Library, Redding, CA).

BAUMGARTNER, GOTLIEB. Died at Waxahachie, Texas Dec. 10, 1879; resident Junction City, Trinity County 1869-1870; Brother Blassius Baumgartner, of Trinity County; brother Lawrence Baumgartner, resident of Waxahachie, Texas. (TJ Sat. Dec. 27, 1879, p 3).[see also Wasmer].

BAYLES, ADAM DARLING. Died Hay Fork Apr. 21, 1871; native of Setauket, Long Island, age 21 yr 11 mo 14 days, son of A. D. and Antoinette Bayles; b. 7 May 1849. (TJ Sat. April 29, 1871).

BAYLES, ADAM DARLING. Died Hay Fork Oct 4, 1894, aged about 82 yr; b. Setauket, Long Island, New York May 8, 1813; came to Calif. 1849; left New York Jan. 18, 1849 on the bark *Olivia*, came to Calif. via Magellan Straits. Arrived San Francisco July 3, 1849; worked as a carpenter, then went to mines on Feather River; came to Weaverville 1852; with Albert Shephard, built a sawmill at the junction of East and West Weaver Creeks; went to Hay Fork 1855; built a sawmill & grist mill; brought his family to Hay Fork 1859; only son died in 1871; wife died 1892. Leaves a daughter, Mrs. Mary E. Young, of Weaverville and a sister in New York. (TJ Oct 6, 1894 p 2). [see also Young].

BAYLES, ANTOINETTE, Mrs. Died Hay Fork July 14, 1892; native of New York, aged 79 yr 6 mo 28 days. Came Trinity Co. 1859; lived Hay Fork. Mrs. Mary Young of Weaverville only child still living; husband is strong at nearly 80. Bur. Hay Fork Sat. July 16, 1892. (TJ Sat. July 16, 1892 p 2 & p 3 col 6). Tribute from husband, Adam D. Bayles (TJ Sat. July 30, 1892 p 3 col 3).

BEAL, PERRY. Died Weaverville May 12, 1858; formerly from Athens, Athens Co., Ohio (no age given). (TJ Sat. May 15, 1858 p. 2).

BEAN, PETER. Died at Hetten Jan 22, 1898; native of Virginia, aged abt 65 yr; leaves a daughter Mrs. Hanson and 3 sons; wife died about 4 years ago; stock raiser. (TJ Feb 5, 1898).

BEARDON, JAMES. Died Lewiston Dec. 24, 1886; native of Tennessee, aged 34 yr; leaves wife and young daughter. Wife daughter of Mr. and Mrs. M. R. Newman. (TJ Sat. Jan. 1, 1887). Married in Weaverville Dec. 27, 1880 by Judge T. E. Jones, James P. Bearden and Miss Hattie V. Newman. Trin. Co. Marriages Book H page 400. Note: Mrs. Beardon m2) Willis E. Baker in 1888.

BEATTY, JOHN. Died at Sidney Hill July 11, 1859; a native of Eniskillen, County Fermanagh, Ireland, and late of Brooklyn, N.Y., aged about 27 years. (TJ Sat. July 16, 1859, p 2). (Probate filed July 25, 1859, Probate Book A page 122.)

BEBEAU, JOSEPH. Died about Jan. 18, 1908 Hayfork; age 71; born Canada; farmer; murder; buried Weaverville. [Index to Deaths 1890-1908].

BECK, _____, Mrs. Died Junction City Jan. 6, 1877; aged about 40 yr. Daughter of J. A. Sturdivant; came Calif. 2-3 months ago with husband; left family in Arkansas; buried Weaverville Cemetery Jan. 7, 1877. (TJ Jan. 13, 1877, p 2 & 3).

BECKER, HENRY. German, died Sunday August 27, 1871 in Hay Fork; age about 40. (TJ Sat. Sept. 2, 1878, p 3).

BECKHART, CHAS. Died abt May 24, 1853. Probate Book A page 24 (Journals of the Probate Court, Trinity County, Cal. 1852-1877).

BEHME, MARY ELIZABETH. Died Weaverville Aug. 25, 1869; age 3-1/2 years; daughter of Nicholas and Margaret Behme. (TJ Sat. Aug.28, 1869 p 2).

BEHME, ROBERT L. Died Weaverville Aug. 18, 1869; aged 5 yr 5 mo; son of Nicholas and Margaret Behme. (TJ Sat. Aug. 21, 1869 p 2).

BELCHER, GALITZAN. Died San Francisco May 1, 1870; formerly of Weaverville; aged 48 years. See also Edwards. (TJ Sat. May 14, 1870 p 2).

BELL, R. F. Citizen of Tehama County, drowned in Sacramento river at town of Tehama Jan. 3, 1867. He was crossing with others; the boat capsized; all reached safety except Bell, who couldn't swim. (TJ Sat. Jan. 19, 1867 p 2 col 3).

BELT, HANNAH, Mrs. Died Red Hill (near Junction City) at home of brother R. C. Wilson May 22, 1894; native of Virginia, aged 70 yr 22 dy; came to Calif. across the plains in 1852; husband died in 1890; came to Trinity Co. 1893; leaves 3 brothers in Trinity Col: R. C. Wilson, B. B. Wilson, Geo. Wilson; bur. North Fork (Helena) May 23, 1894. "Stanislaus papers please copy." (TJ May 26, 1894, pp 2 & 3).

BENDER, HENRY. Died Nov 01, 1900; age 60 yr; b. Germany. (TJ Jan 1901).

BENJAMIN, E. M. Died Napa City Nov. 22, 1895; lived Trinity Co. 1880-1893; leaves wife and 5 children. (TJ Sat. Nov. 30, 1895 p 3 col 4).

BENJAMIN, PAULUS. Died Weaverville Sept. 27, 1881; native of France; age 58. (TJ Sat. Oct. 1, 1881, p 2).

BENN, MARGARET. Died San Francisco Jan. 21, 1877; wife of James Benn, aged 22 yr 9 mo 12 days; born San Francisco; daughter of T. O'Niel of Weaverville. (TJ Jan. 1877).

BENNER, Infant. Infant child of Mr. and Mrs. H. W. Benner, late of Weaverville, died recently at Etna, Siskiyou County; aged about 6 months; died of diphtheria. (TJ Sat. Mar. 19, 1881 p 3). (Note: try Siskiyou County Library, Yreka, CA for Scott Valley News before Mar. 19, 1881.)

BENNETT, ALEXANDER G. Died Weaverville Apr. 20, 1869; age 27 yr; formerly of Mineral Point, Wisconsin; wife had recently joined him; buried Apr. 21, 1869 Weaverville Cemetery. (TJ Sat. Apr. 24, 1869 p 2 & 3).

BENNETT, DANIEL. Died Weaverville March 25, 1868; funeral from residence on Taylor Street Sat. March 28, 1868; leaves widow and child. Born Feb. 4, 1825 in Fairhaven, Mass.; came Weaverville 1852. "Fall River and New Bedford, Mass. papers please copy." (TJ Sat. March 28, 1868). Probate filed Apr. 18, 1868 Probate Book C page 256.

BENNETT, JAMES. Died Weaverville Dec. 16, 1868; native of Ireland, aged about 46 years. (TJ Sat. Dec. 19, 1868 p 2).

BENNETT, JEREMIAH. Died Weaverville Nov 15, 1895; aged about 67 yr; native of Fall River, Mass. obit. p 3 col 2. (TJ Sat. Nov. 23, 1895). See Hicks, Patricia J., SOME CALLED IT WEAVER, for a biography of this Trinity County Pioneer and his family.

BENNETT, REUBEN M. Died at Taunton, Mass. Feb. 3, 1860; aged 39 yrs. Dec'd was the elder brother of Jeremiah and Daniel Bennett of this place (Weaverville). (TJ Sat. Mar. 10, 1860 p 2).

BENNING, AUGUSTA, Mrs. Died Nuremberg, Bavaria, Aug 6, 1895, aged 62 yr; sister of Mrs. Henry Junkans, Weaverville; J. M. Einfalt, Gilroy, CA; mother of Mrs. Fred Haas, of Junction City, and late Mrs. Anna Burger. (TJ Sat. Aug 24, 1895 p 3 col 4). (see also Berger).

BENTON, JAMES. Died Weaverville May 12, 1896; native of Scotland, aged 66 yr 1 mo 23 dy; came to Trinity Co. 1856; blacksmith; serving as a juror in the Littlefield case; I.O.O.F. fun. Thursday May 14, 1896; jury attended in a body. Leaves four children: Emerson, Mary, Ella, Barbara. (TJ May 16, 1896 pp 2-3).

BENTON, WILLIAM HENSLEY. Died Weaverville Oct 22, 1895 aged 21 yr 1 mo 2 dy; b. Weaverville Sept. 20, 1870; bur. I.O.O.F. Cem. Weav. (TJ Sat. Oct 26, 1895).

BENTLY, H. A., aka "Dick" Bently. Died Elko, Nevada May 21, 1875 with F. & A.M. ceremonies; Dick used to call at the May Feasts in Trinity County. (TJ Sat. June 12, 1875 p 3).

BERBERICH, FRANK. Accidentally killed at Deadwood March 5, 1892; native of Minnesota, aged about 28 yr. Bur. French Gulch, Shasta County Mon. Mar. 7, 1892; worked at Brown Bear Mine. Story of accident p 3 col 2. (TJ Sat. Mar. 12, 1892).

BEREGIN, CATHARINE. Died Oregon Gulch, Trinity County Apr. 9, 1869; daughter of John and Margaret Beregin, aged 9 yr 3 mo. (TJ Sat. Apr. 10, 1869 p 2 & 3).

BERGER, ANNA, Mrs. Died Jan. 16, 1895 at New Orleans, LA; bur. Greenwood Cem, New Orleans; native of Germany, aged about 32 yr; former resident; m.n. Fleischman; adopted by Mr. and Mrs. Henry Junkans; m. Robt. Berger 1882; leaves husband & daughter & aunt, Mrs. Henry Junkans of Weav. (TJ Sat. Feb 2, 1895 p 3 col 3). (see also Benning).

BERGIN, CHARLES EDWARD. Died Weaverville Mar 22, 1900; native of Calif., age 32 yr 10 mo 28 dy. (TJ Mar 24, 1900 p 2).

BERGIN, HELENA. Died Oregon Gulch Sept. 25, 1885; daughter of John and Margaret Bergin; native of Trinity County, aged 11 yr 11 mo 8 days; buried Sunday Sept. 27, 1885, Catholic Cemetery, Weaverville. (TJ Sat. Oct. 3, 1885). (see also White, Hannah Bergin.)

BERGIN, JOHN. Died Weaverville Jan. 3, 1894; born Cashel, County Tipperary, Ireland Aug. 7, 1834; came US 1848; m. Margaret Hannan in Boston Sept. 9, 1855; came to Trinity Co. 1861. long obit p 3. (TJ Sat. Jan. 6, 1894).

BERGIN, NELLIE. Died on Oregon Gulch June 24, 1871; daughter of John and Mary Bergin, aged about 2 years. (TJ, prob. July 1871.)

BERKLEY, _____. Died Junction City March 14, 1873, infant son of Richard L. and Mary J. Berkley, aged 7 days. No name given. (TJ Sat. March 22, 1873). [Index to Deaths 1873-1890 says Berkeley, R. L.].

BETTENCOURT, M.A.L., Mrs. Died Nov. 11, 1906 Weaverville, age 81; born Azores Islands; buried Weaverville. [Index to Deaths 1890-1908].

BIDDIN, JAMES S. Died Weaverville Sep 30, 1896; native of Virginia, aged about 62 yr; came to Trinity Co. about 25 years ago; had a ranch at Burnt Ranch; moved to Weaverville 1893; graduate of West Point. Fun. Thurs. Oct 1, 1896, Weaverville. (TJ Sat. Oct 3, 1896, pp 2-3).

BIGELOW, AVILLA MASON. Died Douglas City Nov. 5, 1889; infant daughter of Mr. and Mrs. W. R. Bigelow, aged 2 months 5 days; buried Odd Fellows Cemetery, Weaverville Nov. 7, 1889. (TJ Sat. Nov. 9, 1889). [Index to Deaths 1873-1890 says "age 2 yr 5 mo; female, single, born Calif."].

BILAY, PAULINE, Mrs. Died San Francisco, CA "on the 6th inst". (Sept. 6, 1895). Deceased was a native of Germany, aged 68 yr. Her husband, A. F. Bilay, who at one time was a merchant at North Fork (Helena, CA), died in the above city several years ago. (TJ Sat. Sep 14, 1895 p 3 col 1).

BINGAMAN, JOHN K. Died Red Oak, Iowa Apr 17, 1893, age 72; of Lewiston, CA; resided Trinity Co. since 1852. (TJ Sat. May 13, 1893 p 3 col 3).

BIRCH, CHARLEY (??) Died Trinity Center June 14, 1876, "unknown robber", probably Charley Birch, native of America aged 28 or 29 years; resisted arrest for robbing the store of Rumfeldt & Loring at Trinity Center; inquest June 16, 1876. (TJ Sat. June 24, 1876.)

BLACK, EUGENE P. Died Denver, Colorado Mar 6, 1894, age 49; leaves widow and 3 sons, including Harry Black of Trinity Co. (TJ Mar 10, 1894 p 3 col 5; TJ Mar 17, 1894 p 3 (obit).)

BLACK, PETER P. Died near Jacksonville, Oregon Jun 27, 1896; native of Missouri; formerly of Trinity Co; left Calif. in 1890; bur. F & AM Cem. Jacksonville Jun 29, 1896; Civil War veteran - Confederate. (TJ July 4, 1896 p 3 col 2).

BLACKWELL, _____. "Mrs. (Catherine) Blackwell dropped dead at her residence on Taylor Street, Weaverville, Thursday afternoon Apr. 3, 1862. (TJ Sat. Apr 5, 1862 p 3). Bur. Old Pub. Cem, Weaverville; age 36 yr 5 mo 5 days.

BLACKWELL, GEORGE W. Died Nov. 10, 1905 Weaverville; age 57; born Ohio; laborer. [Index to Deaths 1890-1908].

BLACKWELL, JOHN. Died Weaverville Feb. 3, 1887; native of Ireland; aged 64 yr 1 mo 9 days; born North of Ireland Dec. 25, 1822; came Calif. 1850; night watchman Weaverville for many years; funeral Sat. Feb. 5, 1887; bur. Weaverville Cemetery. (TJ Sat. Feb. 5, 1887).

BLACKWELL, JOHN, Jr. Died Red Bluff Feb. 26, 1882; native of Weaverville; age 25 yr 3 mo 18 days; b. 8 Nov 1856; bur. Weaverville Cemetery 8 Nov 1856. (TJ Sat. Mar. 4, 1882, p 2).

BLACKWELL, LIZZIE. (Elizabeth Ellen). Died Weaverville Feb. 19, 1859, aged 9 yr 5 mo 4 days; daughter of John & Catherine Blackwell. "Sunday Feb. 20 the church was crowded to hear the funeral sermon on the death of Lizzie Blackwell, delivered by Rev. Mr. Myers at the Union Church." bur. Old Public Cemetery, Weaverville. (TJ Sat. Feb. 26, 1859 p 3).

BLACKWELL, ROBERT EMMET. Died Weaverville July 18, 1884; native of Weaverville; aged 23 yr 4 mo 25 days, from cannon explosion July 13; b. 23 Feb. 1861; bur. Sunday July 20, 1884, Weaverville Cemetery. (TJ Sat. July 26, 1884.)

BLAGRAVE, MILLICENT. Died at Bolt's Hill, Trinity County, Jan. 7, 1871, Millicent, wife of B. Blagrave, aged 23 yr 10 mo. (TJ Sat. Jan. 14, 1871 p 2).

BLAGRAVE, VESTA. Died at Bolt's Hill, Trinity County, March 12, 1874; daughter of William and Elizabeth Blagrave, age 1 month 19 days. (prob. TJ March 1874).

BLAKEMORE, ARCHIBALD HOMER. Died Deadwood Dec. 16, 1889; infant son of Mr. and Mrs. A. J. Blakemore, aged 3 mo 4 days; buried Lewiston Pioneer Cemetery. (TJ Sat. Dec. 21, 1889). [Index to Deaths 1873-1890 says "age 3 yr 4 mo; male, single, born Calif."]

BLAKEMORE, J. A. Died Oct 03, 1900; aged 32 yr 10 mo 28 dy; b. California. (TJ Jan 1901).

BLAKEMORE, MINNIE VENTURA. Died Deadwood Feb. 21, 1888; infant daughter of Mr. and Mrs. A. J. Blakemore, aged 2 mo and 11 days; buried Lewiston Pioneer Cemetery. (TJ Sat. Feb. 25, 1888).

BLAKEMORE, THOMAS JEFFERSON. Died near Lewiston Jan. 13, 1892; native of Hendricks Co., Indiana, aged 54 yr 8 mo 23 days. Died at his home some four miles above Lewiston. Trinity Pioneer; left Hendricks Co. Indiana in 1849; arrived Calif. 1850, a mere boy. He went to Nevada in the early 1850s, returned to Calif. 1854, and in company with John H. Smith came to Trinity Co. Returned to States in 1865; m. Miss Zela Kelly 1869; came back to Trin. Co. in 1876 with family; ranch on Trinity River; leaves widow, 6 children; 2 brothers; one, J. M. Blakemore lives at Ferndale, Humboldt Co. Uncle James A. Blakemore lives at Paulsen ranch near Lewiston. Buried near home; roads impassable; moved to Weaverville Cem. Sun. Mar. 6, 1892. (TJ Sat. Jan. 16, 1892, pp 2 & 3; TJ Sat. Mar. 12, 1892 p 3 col 2.)

BLAKEMORE, URSULA. Died Aug. 17, 1906 Weaverville, age 56; female, born Germany; buried Weaverville. [Index to Deaths 1890-1908].

BLAKEMORE, VENICIA VETURA. Wife of A. J. Blakemore; native of Calif. aged 30 yr 6 mo 7 day; dau. of Mr. & Mrs. W. A. Blagrave; leaves 5 children. (TJ Sat. Aug 22, 1896 p 2 & p 3, col 3).

BLALLAN, HENRY. Died May 15, 1888 San Francisco; resident of Trinity County 20 years ago; brother-in-law of P. M. Paulsen; no age given. (TJ Sat. May 19, 1888 p 3). (Not in 1860 or 1870 census.)

BLANCHARD, JOSEPH. Died Trinity Center Tuesday July 24, 1877, aged 27 years; prob. buried Trinity Center Cemetery. (TJ Sat. July 28, 1877 p 3 col 3).

BLOCK, BERNARD. "We see by last week's CHRONICLE (San Francisco) the announcement of the death of Bernard Block (abt Sept. 20, 1888), who was a former resident of Weaverville, having clerked here for Greenwood's bank sometime in the 1860s." (TJ Sat. Sept. 29, 1888). [Might be the Block on the 1860 Census, Weaverville, page 111 #1063, 8-21-1860, age 26, clerk, b. Austria.]

BLYTHER (or BLYTHEN), DANIEL. Died Wood's Ranch, lower Trinity, Mr. Daniel Blyther (sic), formerly of Calais, Maine, aged about 30 years; Mrs. Wood is reported to have attempted suicide immediately afterwards. (TJ reference prob. Nov. 1860). Index Journals of Trinity County Probate Court 1852-1877: "Daniel Blythen (sic) died abt Oct. 29, 1860." Probate Book A page 168ff; Book C p 22.

BOCH, RUDOLPH. Old time resident of Trinity County, died San Francisco Oct. 6, 1876; leaves wife and 3 children. (TJ Oct. 14, 1876). (1860 Census: Boch, Rudolph, East Fork, page 73 #1025, 8-1-1860, 31, Trader, b. Mechlenburg.) (Not married in Trinity County; not in 1870 Census).

BOEHM, NICHOLAS. Drowned in Trinity River near Junction City June 8, 1884; native of Prussia, aged about 58 years; raised a family on the Trinity River below Douglas City; children left; wife died. Buried Weaverville cem. June 12, 1884. (TJ Sat. Jun 14, 1884).

BOGAR, SAM. Killed by Indians near Mineral Park, Mojave County, Arizona 1876. No age given. (TJ Sat. May 3, 1879 p 3). (Not in 1860 or 1870 Census).

BORDES, JOHN. Died Oct. 24, 1907 Weaverville, age 80; born France; miner. [Index to Deaths 1890-1908].

BOSWORTH, M., Mrs. Died Dec 27, 1900; age 27 yr 1 mo 1 dy; b. Calif. (TJ Jan 1901).

BOWERMAN, JACOB RAY. Died Minersville Dec. 30, 1879; son of Jacob and Annie Bowerman, aged 4 yr 5 mo 14 days. (TJ Sat. Jan. 10, 1880 p 2). [Buried Bowerman Cemetery].

BOWERMAN, JOHN. Died Bowerman Ranch, near Minersville, Jan. 18, 1895; native of New York, aged about 69 yr; bur. Jan 19, 1895 in "graveyard at the ranch"; leaves brother Jacob Bowerman and family and sister, Mrs. Jessie Tourtellotte and family of Minersville. (TJ Sat. Jan. 26, 1895 pp 2 & 3).

BOWIE, JAMES. Died Oct. 20, 1901 Weaverville; age 56, male, white, American; buried Weaverville. [Index to Deaths 1890-1908].

BOWLER, ALBERT. Died Weaverville May 21, 1888; native of Lincoln County (?) Maine; aged about 66 hr; buried Odd Fellows Cemetery, Weaverville Tues. May 22, 1888; never married; brother Rev. J. R. Bowler of Franklyn, Maine; (he visited Weaverville in 1886). (TJ Sat. May 26, 1888).

BOWLER, ALLEN. Died Rockland, Maine Dec. 1, 1884; only brother of Albert and J. R. Bowler of Weaverville, aged 66 years. (TJ Sat. Nov. 8, 1884).

BOWLER, J. RILEY, Rev. Died Portland, Maine Jan. 19, 1891, aged 65 yr 9 mo 6 days. He belonged to the Aurora Lodge of Masons, Chapter & Knights Templar; bur. Ingraham's Hill burying ground, Portland, Maine. From the Rockland, Maine *Free Press*, Jan. 28, 1891. (TJ Feb. 21, 1891 p 3). TJ Feb. 28, 1891 p 3 col 4 adds: served as Pastor in Weaverville 3 years. He was born July 10, 1825 in Palermo, Maine. He m1) Miss Adaline Turner of Union, Maine. They had 2 children. He m2) Miss Amanda Watson, of South Hancock, Nov. 10, 1883. A son survives from the first marriage.

BOYCE, WILLIAM S. Died Trinity Center Apr 11, 1898; native of Shasta Co., Calif., aged abt 27 yr; bur. Catholic Cem, Centerville, Shasta Co; leaves mother Mrs. John Grattan, Centerville; sister Mrs. Harvey of Igo, and 2 bro., John Boyce of Trinity Center and Charles Boyce of Placer County. (TJ Apr 16, 1898).

BOYLE, HENRY. Died at New River Jan. 27, 1892; native of Wisconsin, aged about 67 years. (TJ Sat. Feb. 6, 1892).

BOYNTON, W. N. Died at New River (Trinity County) May 14, 1891; native of Vermont, aged about 61 years.

BRADBURY, JOSEPHUS. Died Red Bluff, Tehama County Nov. 6, 1884; son of Josephus and Theresa Bradbury, aged about 2 years. (TJ Sat. Nov. 8, 1884).

BRADLEY, ALFRED. Died July 1, 1869. See Martha.

BRADLEY, JOHN S. Died at Grass Valley, Trinity County, May 10, 1866; youngest son of R. H. and Catharine Bradley, aged 1 yr 29 days. "Humboldt (Nevada) Register please copy". (TJ Sat. May 19, 1866 p 2).

BRADLEY, MARTHA ANN and ALFRED. Died Weaverville July 1, 1869, aged 6 months 7 days; twin children of R. H. and Catharine Bradley. (TJ Sat. July 3, 1869 p 2). (Born Lewiston Dec. 23, 1868).

BRADLEY, SERENE. Died Lewiston June 23, 1869 aged 2 yr 4 mo; twin daughter of R. H. and Catharine Bradley. (TJ Sat. June 26, 1869 p 2). (Born Lewiston June 23, 1869). (Bradley family not in 1870 Census).

BRADY, ANNE TERRESSE. Died Weaverville Sept. 10, 1862, daughter of Bernard and Anna M. Brady, aged about 6 months. (prob. TJ Sept. 1862).

BRADY, BERNARD. Died Weaverville Dec. 19, 1867; of Morris & Brady; native of Pottle, County Craven, Ireland, aged 43 yr 9 mo; came to California 1854 from Albany, New York; leaves wife and 3 children; funeral Dec. 21, 1867; buried Catholic Cemetery, Weaverville. (TJ Sat. Dec. 21, 1867 and Dec. 28, 1867). [Wife: Anna Morris Brady; came to Weaverville 1857; parents of Lavina B. Brady Bartlett. (Cox's Annals of Trinity County [1940]: Bartlett, James W. biography.)

BRADY, DOROTHEA AUGUSTA. Died Weaverville Nov. 20, 1891; native of Weaverville aged 11 mo and 3 days; infant daughter of Mr. and Mrs. M. A. Brady. Fun. Sun. Nov. 22, 1891; probably buried Weaverville Cem. (TJ Nov. 21, 1891, pp 2 & 3).

BRADY, JOHN, Major. Died Red Bluff, Tehama County, Wed. Mar. 26, 1890; had a livery stable in Weaverville from 1854; no age given. (TJ Sat. Mar. 29, 1890). (Not in 1860 Census).

BRAGDON, CAROLINE. Died Trinity Center Jan. 17, 1893; aged 66 yr 3 mo; wife of H. H. Bragdon. (TJ Sat. Jan. 21, 1893).

BRAGDON, CARRIE B. Died near Trinity Center Nov. 11, 1886; daughter of Mr. and Mrs. H. H. Bragdon; native of Maine, aged about 19 years. "Gilroy papers please copy." (TJ Sat. Nov. 20, 1886). (Prob. buried Trinity Center Cemetery).

BRAGDON, H. H. Died Santa Cruz, CA Jan 27, 1897; native of Maine, aged abt 75 yr; bur. Trinity Center Cem. Jan 28, 1897; leaves two sons in Trinity Center; was Principal of Weaverville Schools for several years. (TJ Feb 6, 1897).

BRANNAN, JAMES. Died March 4, 1907 Weaverville, age 82; American; miner. [Index to Deaths 1890-1908]. He was born at sea off the Delaware coast in 1825; came to California in Dec. 1848; to Trinity County 1850; m. Mrs. Nancy Puterman at North Fork in 1857; miner; daughters: Mrs. H. Dix, Mrs. T. J. McNamara, of Weaverville, Mrs. C. C. Gage of Lincoln, Placer Co., and H. W. Brannan, of Weaverville, plus 14 fourteen grandchildren and 3 great-grandchildren. (TJ Mar 9, 1907 pg 3, col 5).

BRANNAN, NANCY, Mrs. Died Weaverville Nov 9, 1894; born Ohio Oct 23, 1824, aged 70 yr 9 dy; wife of James Brannan; bur. Nov 10, 1894 I.O.O.F. Cem. m. at early age Mr. Puterman; moved to Iowa; 2 children born in Iowa: Mrs. Merinda Hughes of San Francisco and Mrs. Sarah J. Jones, who d. 1868 in Sacramento; (1st wife of T. E. Jones). Family came to Calif. 1852, Trinity Co. 1854; went to Humboldt Co. She and Mr. Puterman separated; she and children returned to Trinity 1856. She and Mr. Brannan m. 37 yr; 5 children; Olive died in infancy, bur. North Fork; 4 survive. (TJ Nov 10, 1894 pp 2 & 3; Nov. 17, 1894 pg 3 col 2). (see also Puterman & Jones).

BREEN, JOHN. Died Weaverville July 27, 1858, aged about 38 years. (TJ Sat. July 31, 1858 p 2).

BRETT, _____. "Wife of Thos. Brett" died Oak Ranch, 27 miles from Arcata, Thursday of last week. (d. May 20, 1880); no other name available. (TJ Sat. May 29, 1880 p 3) (probably died in Humboldt County). (Not in Trinity County Marriages.)

BRIGGS, JOHN. Died Oregon Gulch July 12, 1863; native of Pembroke, Gennessee County, New York aged 26 yr. (TJ Sat. July 18, 1863 p 2).

BRIX, HENRY. Died Sat. Sept. 22, 1860; bur. Sun. Sept. 23, 1860 in Weaverville Cemetery; native of Hamburg, Germany, age 42 yr 10 mo 5 days; came to Weaverville less than a month ago (abt August 1860); leaves a young daughter. "San Francisco and New York City papers please copy". (TJ Sat. Sept. 29, 1860). Probate filed Oct. 29, 1860: Probate Book C p 168.

BROOKS, SAMUEL GILBERT. Died Weaverville Mar 30, 1898; native of Penn., aged abt 57 yr; bur. Masonic Cem, Weaverville Thurs Mar 31, 1898. (TJ Apr 2, 1898).

BROOKS, SARAH. "Mrs. Sarah Brooks, wife of Joseph Brooks, formerly of Douglas City and later of Canon City in this county, died recently at Silver City, Idaho. We did not learn any particulars." (TJ Dec. 22, 1877 p 3).

BROOKS, SMITH B. Died July 25, 1907 Weaverville, age 75; born Ohio; miner. [Index to Deaths 1890-1908].

BROWDER, ALFRED. Died Weaverville Feb. 28, 1884; native of Missouri, aged about 65 years; (colored) (sic). Came Trinity County 1851, a slave from Missouri; bought his freedom and that of Harriet, later his wife; 2 sons and daughter, all grown; funeral Sat. Mar. 1, 1884; buried Weaverville Cemetery. (TJ Sat. Mar. 1, 1884 pg 2 & 3).

BROWDER, JAMES O. Died Weaverville May 29, 1894; native of Calif, aged 35 yr 8 mo 2 dy; bur. pub. cem. May 31, 1894. (TJ June 2, 1894).

BROWDER, JESSE. Died Mon. May 11, 1863 (probably Weaverville); son of Albert (sic) and Harriet Browder aged 4 years. (TJ Sat. May 16, 1863 p 2).

BROWDER, LIZZIE (Elizabeth). Died Weaverville May 8, 1888; native of California, aged 26 yr 5 mo 13 days; buried Weaverville Cemetery Thurs. May 10, 1888. "Of seven children of Mrs. Browder, only 2 survive." (TJ Sat. May 12, 1888).

BROWDER, MINERVA. [b. 16 May 1867 d 18 March 1870. Grave marker Old Public Cemetery, Weaverville. All of the Browders have markers except Harriet and Nelson (d. 1912)].

BROWDER, REBECCA BROWN. Died Weaverville March 31, 1870; daughter of A. and H. M. Browder, aged 4 yr 6 mo. (TJ Sat. Apr. 2, 1870 p 2).

Other children of Alfred and Harriet:

Browder, William Thatcher [b. Feb. 1849 Texas; Died at Red Bluff Nov. 24, 1876. He was a Drover in the 1870 census.]

Browder, James Oliver [b. Weaverville 1858; died Weaverville May 29, 1894].

Browder, Nelson Isaac [b. Weaverville Aug. 1863; died Wv. (sic) Aug. 31, 1912.]

[See TRINITY JOURNAL Sat. June 8, 1901 - Death of Mrs. Browder].

The Browder story from several sources: Alfred came to Trinity County as a slave in 1851. Working in the mines, he was able to save some money, and was also assisted by some white miners so that he could buy his freedom. He borrowed the money to buy the freedom of Mrs. Anna Maria Harriet Thatcher, whom he married April 9, 1856. Every penny was repaid. They had seven children, and were treated with respect by the townspeople. A large number of people attended the funeral of "Old Al" in 1884. Mrs. Browder died in 1901, mourned by many. She was affectionately known as "Aunt Harriet", and was survived by one son, Nelson I. Browder, who died in 1912.

BROWN, _____. Died abt Nov. 8, 1853. Probate Book A p 37; Index, 1852-1877. No further information.

BROWN, CATHARINE. Died Weaverville April 12, 1884; native of Wisconsin, aged 33 yr 6 mo 12 days; wife of Richard Brown; married 5 years ago; resident Weaverville 12 years; sister of Mrs. David Taylor; funeral Sun. April 13, 1884; buried Weaverville Catholic Cemetery. (TJ Sat. Apr. 19, 1884). (See baby, Morris Ambrose Brown, also.)

BROWN, CARRIE P. Died at Mount Pleasant, Iowa, March 15, 1861; daughter of H. N. and Maria L. Brown, formerly of Weaverville; (no age given). "We recollect little Carrie as one of the prettiest and most amiable of children and like others who knew her, regret her loss." (TJ Sat. May 18, 1861).

BROWN, CAROLINE. Died May 13, 1900; age 70 yr; b. Nova Scotia. (TJ Jan 1901).

BROWN, CHARLES L. Died Jan 25, 1900; age 71 yr; b. Austria. (TJ Jan 1901).

BROWN, EDWARD. Died Weaverville Aug. 29, 1867; native of Sweden, aged 45 years. Buried Catholic Cemetery, Weaverville; leaves wife. (Tj Sat. Aug. 31, 1867 p 2).

BROWN, FLEMING H. Died near Weaverville Oct. 14, 1892; born Rock County Virginia 1811; aged 80 yr 2 mo 3 days. Bur. Oct. 15, 1892 Odd Fellows Cem. Weaverville; moved to Saline Co. MO 1840; 1850 came overland to Calif. arriving Placer Co. Sept. 28, 1850; came to Douglas City July 21, 1851. (TJ Sat. Oct. 15, 1892 and TJ Sat. Oct. 22, 1892, p 3 col 1).

BROWN, GEORGE WASHINGTON. Died Weaverville Sep 25, 1898; native of Penn, aged abt 79 yr; came to Trinity Co. 1855, lived in Lewiston; leaves wife and 2 adult children; bur. Weaverville Cem. (TJ Oct 8, 1898).

BROWN, IRENE MABIE. Died Deadwood May 10, 1897, aged 17 yr 3 mo 17 dy; born Douglas City Jan 23, 1880; m. Jerry Brown Oct 21, 1896; bur. Clement Ranch Cem. on Indian Creek. (TJ May 15, 1897). (TJ Aug 7, 1897: "monument in place over grave of late Mrs. Jerry Brown in the private cemetery at Clements Ranch, by W. J. Masterson of Red Bluff Marble Works").

BROWN, JAMES. Died Red Hill Mine, Salmon River, Siskiyou Co. Dec. 22, 1894; miner; bur. Fork of the Salmon; lived Trinity County many years. (TJ Dec. 29, 1894 p 3).

BROWN, JULIA ANN. Died April 8, 1908 Weaverville; age 83; born New York; buried Weaverville. [Index to Deaths 1890-1908].

BROWN, LEMUEL. Died Weaverville Nov. 25, 1896; native of North Carolina, aged about 64 yr. (TJ Sat. Dec 5, 1896).

BROWN, MATILDA. Died Weaverville Aug. 12, 1866, Matilda, infant daughter of Wm. B. and Matilda Brown, aged 5 months. (TJ Sat. Aug. 18, 1866 p 2).

BROWN, MORRIS AMBROSE. Died Weaverville Apr. 17, 1884; infant son of Richard and Catherine Brown, aged 9 days. Funeral Apr. 18, 1884; bur. Catholic Cem. Weaverville. (TJ Sat. April 19, 1884; TJ Apr 12, 1884 says "born April 8, 1884").

BROWN, "Old Man". Died Dec. 7, 1875, Weaverville, aged about 50 years; wife and family living in London, England. (TJ Dec. 11, 1875).

BROWN, WM. Died at Searles Ranch, Indian Creek (Trinity County) Aug. 17, 1857, from Lee County, Virginia, age 23. (TJ Sat. Aug. 29, 1857, p. 2).

BRYANT, ANN W., Mrs. Died Weaverville Sept. 22, 1876; native of Pennsylvania aged 66 yr 11 mo; funeral Sat. Sept. 23, 1876; bur. Odd Fellows Cem; mother of Judge T. E. Jones. (TJ Sat. Sept. 23, 1876 p 2 & 3).

BUCK, JENNIE M., Mrs. Died Seattle, Washington Jan 19, 1899; pioneer resident of Weaverville; born Bucksport, Maine 1838; came to Weaverville 1854; husband Frank A. Buck arr. Weaverville 1852, conducted a general merchandise business with Capt. John Cole in store now occupied by D. Hansen; 2 children, Arthur and Emma L., were born in Weaverville; moved to Chico 1866; much later moved to Seattle; leaves husband, 2 sons, Arthur B. Buck of Seattle, and Rufus Buck of Alaska, and 2 daughters, Mrs. Emma L. Norton and Mrs. Mary S. Carr of Seattle. (TJ Feb. 4, 1899, pg 3 col 3). [Note: Franklin A. Buck was the author of A YANKEE TRADER IN THE GOLD RUSH, Houghton Mifflin Co., 1930.] [see also Trufant and Cole.]

BUCKMAN, GEORGE. Killed by Indians at Mad River, Trinity County, Nov. 14, 1868; bur. Nov. 17, 1868 (prob. Mad River; no age given). (TJ Sat. Nov. 28, 1868 p 2).

BUCKS, DAVID A. Died abt June 14, 1852. Probate Book A p 6; Index to Journals of Probate Court 1852-1877. No further information.

BUDD, JOSEPH A. Died at Little Prairie, Trinity River, in the 32nd year of his age; formerly of Turin, Lewis Co., New York; left St. Louis in 1849 for California, and long resided on Trinity River. (TT June 2, 1855).

BUDDEN, GEORGE W. H. Died Weaverville Aug. 11, 1883; aged about 53 yr; bur. Weaverville Cemetery Sun. Aug. 12, 1883; photographer; leaves wife and four children in destitute condition in Reno, Nevada; nephew Harry Calvin of Camptonville, Yuba County. (TJ Sat. Aug. 18, 1883). [There were notices in Trinity Journal about his work a few weeks before his death].

BULLEN, EDWARD. Drowned at Long Package, Dutch Bar, British Columbia (near Yale) abt Jan. 1862; aka "Dutch Jake"; from New Sheron, Franklin Co. Maine; "Mr. Bullen was for several years a resident of this county, residing most of the time either at Douglas City or Steiner's Flat and was highly esteemed by all who knew him. In common with the many friends he possessed in this vicinity, we deplore his untimely fate." (DCG Wed. Jan. 22, 1862).

BUNKER, HENRY. Died Los Angeles Sun. July 12, 1885; born Big Flat, Trinity County, March 11, 1862; father, Geo. H. Bunker, lives in Oakland; brother, Clark Bunker, of Weaverville. (TJ Sat. July 18, 1885).

BUNKER, HENRY L. Died Springfield, Mass. Jan. 6, 1865; the father of Geo. H. Bunker of this county, aged 67 yr. (TJ Sat. Apr. 8, 1865).

BUNKER, SOPHIE C. Died San Francisco June 5, 1878, aged 40 years. Wife of George H. Bunker; former resident of Trinity County. (TJ Sat. June 15, 1878 p 3).

BURCH, JOHN CHILTON. Died San Francisco Aug. 31, 1885; native of Missouri, age 59; came Trinity County 1851; graduate of law in Missouri; County Clerk, District Attorney [1853], Assemblyman and Senator from Trinity County; member of Congress from this district; code commissioner for California. Leaves behind him "a noble, pure and devoted wife." (TJ Sat. Sept. 5, 1885 p 3. col 2, top.) (TJ Sat. Sept. 19, 1885, p 3: "Mrs. Martha L. Burch, widow of late Judge John C. Burch; Will dated at Sacramento July 21, 1873 names her as Executrix.") (Cox's Annals of Trinity County [1940]: biography of Burch: born 1820; m. 24 Dec 1857 in Sacramento, Miss Martha Gordon.)

BURGER, GEORGE. Died Coumbs Springs (now Deer Lick Springs), Trinity County Jul 20, 1899; native of Calif. age 19 yr 1 mo 24 dy; son of late John Adam Burger, one of the Pioneers of Trinity County; born Canon Creek 1880; leaves 2 sisters, Mrs. Paris Markwell and Miss Julia Burger; 1 bro. John Burger of Canon Creek; 1 half-sister Mrs. John Bartlett, of New River. (TJ Jul 22, 1899).

BURGER, JOHN. Died May 27, 1878 Canon Creek, age 34. Buried Odd Fellows Cemetery, Weaverville, May 29, 1878. Cousin J. A. Burger. (TJ Sat. June 1, 1878 p 3). (Age from Trinity County Great Register of Voters, 1877; Naturalized 1873; born Alsace; miner).

BURGER, JOHN ADAM. Died Jan. 15, 1895 at Canon City, aged about 64 yr; born Alsace, France 1831; came to Trinity Co. & Canon Creek early 1850s; m. Mrs. Mary A. Smith, widow of Sidney Smith, 1874; 4 children: John A., George, Margaret, Julia Burger; step-dau. Mary Smith m. John H. Bartlett of Canon Creek; Mrs. Burger d. 1884; bur. I.O.O.F. Cem. Weav. (TJ Sat. Jan 19, 1895 pp 2 & 3).

BURGER, MARY A. Died Cañon Creek Dec. 4, 1884; bur. Odd Fellows Cem. Weaverville; native of Cincinnati, Ohio aged 31 yr 8 mo; wife of John Adam Burger; leaves husband and 5 children. (TJ Sat. Dec. 6 and Dec. 13, 1884).

BURKE, THOMAS. Killed by Indians in Hay Fork Valley Oct. 13, 1868; native of Feddens, County Waterford, Ireland, aged 56 yr 9 mo 13 days; house burned; wife and three children will return to Illinois; bur. Catholic Cem. Weaverville. (TJ Sat. Oct. 17, 1868 p 2 col 1 & 4).

BURNETT, JAMES A., Mrs. Died Quartz, Calaveras Co., CA, age 27, in childbirth; child survives; bur. Jamestown Cem., Tuolumne Co, CA; former resident of Weaverville; maiden name Harriet Willard, sister of late Mrs. Wm. Matthews, Mrs. L. P. Castner of Trinity Center, and Mrs. Lucy Hoskins of French Gulch, Shasta Co.; m. Mr. Burnett in Trinity County. (TJ Dec 17, 1898 pg 3 col 3).

BURNS, ANNIE. Died Hay Fork Feb. 11, 1888; native of Calif. aged 21 years. (TJ Sat. Feb. 25, 1888).

BURNS, GEORGE. Died Indian Creek, Trinity County, July 28, 1862; native of Wexford County, Ireland, age 31 yr. (TJ Sat. Aug. 9, 1862 p 2).

BURNS, HENRY. Died Weaverville Mar 16, 1897; native of Union, Maine, aged 65 yr 8 mo 13 dy; b. Jul 3, 1832, son of John & Margaret B. Burns; came to Calif. 1861, Trin. To. 1876; one of the best miners in the county. M. at Marysville, Yuba Co.

Apr 5, 1867, Mrs. E. W. Brown, who survives him; he leaves 2 nephews, 3 brothers, a sister. Bur. Masonic Cem, Weav. Mar 18, 1897. (TJ Mar 20, 1897). (TJ Nov 27, 1897: "handsome tombstone erected over the grave of the late Henry Burns. The stone is the product of the Pacific Granite and Marble Works of San Francisco.")

BURNS, WILLIAM D. Died Pawtucket, Rhode Island Dec. 28, 1864; son of John and Alice Burns, aged 11 yr 10 mo. (TJ Sat. Feb. 25, 1865 p 2).

BURT, WARREN E. Died Mayfield, San Mateo, Calif. Jan. 9, 1870; late of Orleans Bar, Klamath County, Calif; native of Mass, aged 38 years. (TJ Sat. Feb. 12, 1870).

BUSCH, CHARLOTTE. Died Minersville Mar. 18, 1866; native of Bavaria, Germany; aged 34 yr 4 days. (TJ Sat. March 24, 1866 p 2).

BUSCH, LEWIS E. died San Francisco Sat. March 22, 1879 age 43 yr. Brother of Julius Busch of Weaverville. (TJ Sat. Mar. 29, 1879).

BUSH, _____. Died Weaverville Oct. 4, 1891, the infant daughter of Mr. and Mrs. H. T. Bush, aged 5 days; born Weaverville Sept. 29, 1891. (TJ Oct. 3, 1891; Oct. 10, 1891).

BUSH, ABRAHAM S. Died Hay Fork May 7, 1883; native of New Jersey, aged 76 yr. (TJ Sat. May 12, 1883 p 2).

BUSSELL, FRANK. Died Willow Creek, Humboldt Co. Oct 8, 1895; former resident, and old partner of W. A. Pattison; native of Bangor, Maine, in his 66th year. (TJ Sat. Oct 19, 1895 p 3 col 3).

BUTLER, ALLEN. Died Jul 24, 1900; age 81 yr 9 mo 26 dy; b. England. (TJ Jan 1901).

BUTTS, LOUIS. Died Reddings Creek Oct. 30, 1890; native of Calif.; no age given. (TJ Sat. Nov. 1, 1890). [Similar information Index to Deaths 1890-1908].

CABANISS, T. T., Dr. Died abt July 14, 1887 San Francisco, CA; buried Monday July 17, 1887. Born 1826 Williamsburg, VA; graduate in medicine from University of Maryland 1847; came to California 1849; well known by residents of this county. [See San Francisco *Examiner* July 20, 1887.] (TJ Sat. July 23, 1887).

CAFFATO, PETRO. Died Weaverville Feb. 10, 1880; native of Italy aged about 59 yr; buried Weaverville Cem. Feb. 11, 1880. (TJ Sat. Feb. 14, 1880 p 2).

CAHALAN, MARGARET. (Widow of John Colbert; m. Michael Cahalan Oct. 22, 1865). "Died in Weaverville Jan. 24, 1880, Margaret, wife of Michael Callahan (sic), native of Ennis, County Claire, Ireland, aged 49 yr." Old resident, came here 1855; lived Oregon Gulch; lived Weaverville 10 years; buried Mon. Jan. 26, 1880, Catholic Cem. Weaverville. "Adult children: Mrs. Mary Morris, Miss Maggie (Colbert) and James, John and Daniel Colbert." (TJ Sat. Jan. 31, 1880, p 2 & 3). [Note: her gravestone in the Catholic Cemetery was buried for many years; it was uncovered in 1992.]

CAHILL, JOHN. Died San Francisco Nov. 3, 1878; Member Genoa Lodge, I.O.O.F., State of Nevada; in Weaverville several weeks last summer. (TJ Sat. Nov. 16, 1878).

CALL, JOHN. Died Nov. 1856; probate filed Dec. 1, 1856, Probate Book B page 30 (from Index; Book B had not been located as of 1987). No further information.

CAMBRIDGE, HENRY. Died Weaverville Dec 3, 1897; native of England, aged abt 70 yr. Leaves a son Walter Cambridge of Fort Bidwell; the body of Henry Cambridge will be taken to Cedarville in the Spring. (TJ Dec 4, 1897 p 2; Dec 11, 1897 p 3 col 1).

CAMP, ALEXANDER. Died Lewiston Jul 19, 1896; aged 80 yr. (TJ Sat. July 25, 1896).

CAMPBELL, ELMER T. Died Feb. 9, 1907 Hayfork, age 4 months, born Calif; bur. Hayfork. [Index to Deaths 1890-1908].

CAMPBELL, EMMA DORRIS. Died at Lower Trinity Jan 16, 1898; aged 5 mo 11 dy; dau. of Mr. and Mrs. Wm. Campbell. (TJ Feb 5, 1898 p 2).

CAMPBELL, JAMES. Died Eureka, (Humboldt Co.) CA Feb. 11, 1888; recently from New River (Trinity Co.); nephew of Thomas Campbell, pioneer of Trinity County. (TJ Sat. Feb. 11, 1888 p 3).

CAMPBELL, JAMES C. Died Weaverville Oct. 16, 1884; Native of Kanawha County, West Virginia; age 58 yr. Came to Trinity County 1869, Junction City; Weaverville 1881; Justice of Peace Weaverville 1882. Father, age 87, resides Washington D.C. (TJ Oct. 18, 1884).

CAMPBELL, JOHN. Broke his leg at Oregon Gulch a short time ago; died of the wound March 13, 1859; buried Tuesday March 15, 1859 in the Catholic Cemetery Weaverville; formerly resided Pawtucket, Rhode Island; no age given. (TJ Sat. March 19, 1859).

CAMPBELL, JOHN. Died Indian Creek August 25, 1868; native of Ireland; late of Pawtucket, Rhode Island, age 39 yr. (TJ Sat. August 29, 1868 p 2).

CAMPBELL, N. H. Died June 27, 1905 Hayfork, age 26, born Calif; bur. Hayfork Cem. [Index to Deaths 1890-1908].

CAMPBELL, PATRICK. Died Junction City Sep 19, 1896; native of Ireland, aged about 68 yr. Came from Nevada Co. over 20 years ago; employed at the Cie Fse company at Junction City; fell into Trinity River; Coroner's report p 3 col 3. (TJ Sat. Sept 26, 1896). [see also Saladin in Appendum].

CAMPBELL, THOMAS GUSTAVE. Died at Lower Trinity June 24, 1891; native of Kentucky, aged about 62 yr; merchant and rancher. (TJ Sat. July 11, 1891).

CANTWELL, PATRICK. Died Red Hill (near Junction City) March 5, 1882; aged about 44 years; native of Ireland. (TJ Mar. 11, 1882).

CANWELLE, JOHN P. Died Jan. 8, 1908 Mooney Gulch, near Lewiston, about 46, miner, born New York, unmarried; bur. Mooney Gulch; shot. [Index to Deaths 1890-1908].

CARAWAY, VIRGIL. Died at Raymond Ranch, South Fork (of the Trinity River); native of Virginia, age 56 yr. (TJ Sat. Apr. 17, 1875).

CARDOZA INFANTS (twins), both male, premature birth; b. Calif. Died March 3, 1908 Indian Creek, Trinity County, California, both buried Weaverville. [Index to Deaths 1890-1908].

CARISCH, CHRIS. Died May 27, 1906 Trinity Center, age about 45; buried Trinity Center. [Index to Deaths 1890-1908].

CARLSEN, JAMES. Died Weaverville Feb. 9, 1871; native of Norway; aged 41 years. (TJ Sat. Feb. 11, 1871 p 2).

CARMER, REUBEN. Died Seattle, WA Dec. 1920, aged 84 yr; freighted between Red Bluff and Weaverville "in the early days"; 1870s lived in Redding; Charter member of Redding Odd Fellows lodge - last of the Charter members. (TJ Jan. 8, 1921).

CARNES, JOHN. Died Weaverville Sept. 4, 1855, age 32; from Pennsylvania, leaves wife and 2 children. Funeral Wed. Sept. 5, 1855; buried Weaverville Cemetery. (TT Sept. 8, 1855).

The CARR family of John Carr who wrote Pioneer Days in California in 1891.

CARR, AGNES HAYNES. Died Eureka (Humboldt Co.) July 26, 1870; daughter of John and Delilah Carr, aged 7 mo 20 days. (TJ Aug. 6, 1870 p 2).

CARR, KATIE. Died Eureka May 24, 1873; daughter of John and Delilah Carr, aged 5 yr 5 mo 17 days. (TJ Sat. June 7, 1873).

CARR, WELLINGTON S. Died Eureka, Humboldt County, Nov. 13, 1872; son of John Carr, aged 16 yr 8 mo. (TJ Sat. Nov. 23, 1882).

1860 Census, Hay Fork, Trinity County, Cal. page 43 #995, 7-8-1860
Carr, John, age 31, farmer, b. Ireland.
    Delilah, age 28, b. New Jersey.
    Wellington G., age 4, b. California.
    Lewis, age 3, b. California
    Thomas, age 2 months, b. California.

CARR, THOMAS. Died Eureka, Humboldt County, CA Feb. 6, 1884; resident of Eureka 16 years; came to California 1852 [with brother John Carr, Mrs. Thomas Carr, and Mrs. John Carr.]; leaves widow, 4 daughters, & son Edward B. Carr, of the Ferndale Enterprise. (TJ Sat. Feb. 23, 1884, p 3).

CARR, _____. Died abt. May 1873. "Death of a little daughter of Thos. Carr reported by Humboldt Expressman Clifford." (TJ May 31, 1873 p 3).

1860 Census, Weaverville, Trinity County, Cal. page 119 #1071, 8-23-1860.
Carr, Thomas, age 35, teamster, b. Ireland.
    Ann, age 28, b. Ireland.
    Elizabeth, age 6, b. California.
    Mary Ann, age 4, b. California.
    Catherine, age 2, b. California.
    Emaline, age 3 months, b. California.

CARRS of Carrville, near Trinity Center, Trinity County, California

CARR, CECELIA LORING. "Daisy Carr". Died Trinity Valley Mar. 26, 1881; age 14 yr 5 mo 21 days; only daughter of J. E. and S. J. Carr. (TJ Sat. Apr. 2, 1881). (Buried Carrville Cemetery).

CARR, _____, and **CARR,** _____. "Two youngest sons of J. E. and S. J. Carr have died of diphtheria; ages and names unknown. (TJ Sat. Apr. 16, 1881, p 3). Grave markers in Carrville Cemetery (1980) read: CARR, WILLIAM HENRY CHARLES, "In memory of, born Carrs Ranch, CA Oct. 1, 1875; died at Carrs Ranch Apr 4, 1881, aged 5 yr 4 mo 3 days. CARR, JOHN JAMES. "In memory of, born at Carrs Ranch, Cal. Sept 6, 1870, died Apr. 7, 1881 at Carrs Ranch, aged 10 yrs 7 mo 1 day". "Daisy" Carr also died from diphtheria.

CARR, JAMES ERASTUS. Died Trinity Center Feb. 12, 1894; native of Ireland; aged about 81 yr. (TJ Sat. Feb. 17, 1894). [see below].

CARR, JESSE. Died Carrville Oct. 28, 1889, aged 21 years; native of California. (TJ Sat. Nov. 9, 1889). [Gravemarker in Carrville Cemetery (1980) reads: CARR, JESSE E. d. Oct. 28, 1889 aged 20 yrs 10 mo 2 days, "In loving remembrance of". His grave and stone are next to the graves of 2 babies.] [Similar Information Index to Deaths 1873-1890].

Other members of the CARR family of Carrville, Trinity County (aka Carr's Ranch) buried in the Carrville Cemetery are:

CARR, AGNES MacILWAINE. 1894 - 1933.

CARR, CLARENCE. Dec. 14, 1892 - Dec. 28, 1959. (Temporary marker, 1980). (Son of late George Carr and wife Juanita. TJ Dec. 31, 1959 p 1; lists descendants).

CARR, GEORGE JAMES. 1891 - 1917.

CARR, GEORGE LEE. 1863 - 1910. (Obit. TJ May 12, 1910 p. 2 & 3.)

CARR, JAMES ERASTUS. "In loving remembrance of, died at Carrville Feb. 12, 1894 age 81 years." (Obit. TJ Feb. 17, 1894). Came to Calif. 1849, Trinity County 1855, Carrville 1860.

CARR, JUANITA L. 1904 - 1965 (Temporary marker 1980). Widow of Clarence Carr. [See Trinity County Deaths July 1960 - June 1971, page 186, and TJ Sept. 9, 1965.]

CARR, MARGARET JANE. "In memory of, born at Carrs Ranch, Cal Sept. 1, 1873 and died at Carrs Ranch Sept. 5, 1873 aged 5 days." Monument and headstone with M. J. Carr. (1980). No birth or death notice in Trinity Journal Sept. 1873.

CARR, MARY ALICE URSHER. 1868 - 1936. Widow of George Lee Carr, m. June 1, 1890 Trinity Center.

CARR, SARAH J. "In loving remembrance of, died at Carrville Nov. 2, 1902 aged 64 yrs 8 mo 3 days. MOTHER. O.E.S. star." (Obit. TJ Nov. 15, 1902. Born Ireland Feb. 29, 1838.) [see also Feeny].

Members of other CARR families:

CARR, ANNIE, Mrs. Died Douglas City Jan 2, 1897; native of Calif, aged 34 yr 8 mo 22 dy; m. A. C. Carr in 1881; seven children, including a baby 11 days old; dau. of late Richard Gribble and Mrs. Jane Gribble of Junction City; bur. Weaverville Cem. Jan 4, 1897. (TJ Jan 9, 1897 pp 2 & 3). [see also Addendum].

CARR, ELLA M., Mrs. Wife of Thomas H. Carr, d. Nevada City, CA May 9, 1896; dau. of Mr. and Mrs. C. W. Huson; b. Illinois, came to Calif. age 2; raised in Nevada Co.; m. at Weaverville 1874; moved to Smartsville, Grass Valley, then Nevada City about 16 years ago (1880); leaves six children, husband, mother & brother A. S. Huson, all of Nevada City. (TJ Sat. May 9, 1896 p 3). [see also Huson].

CARR, FRANCIS. Died suddenly in Redding, Shasta Co, Sep 20, 1896; well-known lawyer of Shasta County. (TJ Sept 26, 1896).

CARR, HYRAM HENRY. Died Evans Bar Nov 14, 1899; native of Ohio, aged 79 yr 9 mo 25 dy; born Franklin Co., Ohio Jan 19, 1820; married in Valparaiso, Indiana Nov 15, 1849, Mary E.; bur. Weaverville Cem.; family info in obit. (TJ Nov 18, 1899 p 2 & p 3 col 3).

CARR, JEREMIAH H. Died Weaverville Oct. 8, 1877, aged 53 yr, native of Pennsylvania; came from Trinidad, Humboldt County, "recently". (TJ Sat. Oct. 13, 1877 p 2 & 3). [Note: no apparent relationship to any of the above CARR families.]

CARR, WILLIAM CORIDON. Died Evans Bar, Trinity River, Jan. 22, 1894; born Decatur, Iowa Jan. 1, 1859; aged 35 yr 22 dy; came to Calif. 1875; thanks to neighbors from H. H. Carr and family of Douglas City. (TJ Jan. 27, 1894).

CARRAWAY, VIRGIL. Died abt April 1875; probate filed Apr. 13, 1875: records of Probate Court D page 18 (Index to Probate Journals 1852-1877). No further information.

CARROLL, DENNIS. Died Weaverville May 21, 1862; killed by John Bailey; native of Ireland, County Cork, age 31; leaves wife and babe. Funeral May 23, 1862; prob. bur. Catholic Cemetery, Weaverville. (TJ Sat. May 24, 1862 p 3). Probate filed May 24, 1862, Probate Book B p 314. [1860 Census: Dennis, age 30, Saloon Keeper, b. Ireland. Elizabeth, age 26, born Ireland. Weaverville, p. 113 #1065, 8-22-1860; not married in Trinity County.]

CARROLL, ELIZA. Died Weaverville Jan. 4, 1863 of Scarlet Fever; daughter of Eliza Carroll, aged 5 mo 11 days.

CARROLL, JAMES. Died Weaverville Nov. 18, 1887; native of Ireland, aged about 80 years. (TJ Sat. Nov. 19, 1887).

CARROLL, THOMAS. Died Weaverville Dec. 27, 1862 of Scarlet Fever; son of Eliza Carroll, aged 1 yr 7 mo 6 days. (TJ Sat. Jan. 3, 1863 p 2).

CARROLL, WILLIAM. Died Coleridge, Trinity County Oct 27, 1897; native of Canada aged abt 32 yr. (TJ Oct 30, 1897 p 2).

CARSON, J. T., Prof. Died Simcoe, Ontario Aug 19, 1893; no age given; Principal of Weaverville schools 1882-3. (TJ Sat. Sept. 28, 1893 p 3 col 1).

CARSON, JAMES. Died Nov. 10, 1906 Weaverville; age 84, born Ireland, miner. [Index to Deaths 1890-1908].

CARTER, A. M. Died Redding, Shasta Co. June 1898; pioneer citizen of Trinity County; native of Iowa, aged 57 yr; arr. Trinity County 1861; resided 25 years on Coffee Creek; leaves widow and 8 children, 6 sons, 2 dau. Bur. Coffee Creek. *(Redding Free Press, June 29, 1898).* (TJ Jul 2, 1898 p 3 col 3).

CARTER, EFFIE CLARA. Died Hay Fork May 18, 1898; b. Colusa Co. Dec 30, 1876; aged 21 yr 4 mo 18 dy; wife of George W. Carter; dau. of Mr. and Mrs. C. W. Robertson. m. Mr. Carter June 26, 1895 at Hunters, Tehama Co.; 2 children of tender age. (TJ May 21, 1898 pp 2-3).

CARTER, JOHN W. Died March 11, 1907 Hayfork, age 80; hotelkeeper; bur. Public Cemetery, Hayfork. [Index to Deaths 1890-1908].

CARTER, R. J., Mrs. Died Apr 27, 1900; age 61 yr 3 mo 21 dy; b. Indian Territory. (TJ Jan 1901).

CASE, NATHAN P. Died near Minersville Feb. 15, 1872; native of Pennsylvania, aged 52 yr 2 mo and 15 days. (TJ Sat. Mar. 9, 1872).

CASEY, D____. Died Dec. 1854. Probate filed Jan. 2, 1855, Probate Book A page 55. No further information.

CASS, JOHN M., Mr. Died Apache Pass, Arizona Feb. 18, 1869, aged 38 yr; native of Hallowell, Maine, formerly a resident of Weaverville. (TJ Apr. 3, 1869 p 2).

CASTILLO, MICHAEL. Killed at Big Bar Tues. June 14, 1859 by a bank cave; buried Big Flat abt June 16, 1859. Also killed was Thos. Donovan. (TJ June 18, 1859 p 2; June 25, 1859 p 3).

CATON, JOSEPH, Mrs. Died near Weaverville June 12, 1881; aged about 52 years. (TJ Sat. June 18, 1881 p 2.) (Not in 1870 or 1880 Census).

CATON, MARGARET. Died Weaverville Feb. 9, 1890; born Indian Creek, Trinity County, Calif; aged 14 yr 10 mo 8 days; daughter of J. Caton. Buried Catholic Cemetery Thurs. Feb. 13, 1890. (TJ Sat. Feb. 15, 1890). [Index to Deaths 1873-1890 adds "single"].

CHADBOURNE, HOMER LYMAN. Died Trinity Center Sept. 27, 1860; son of Moses and Diana Chadbourne aged 2 yr 3 mo. (TJ Sat. Oct. 6, 1860 p 2).

CHADBOURNE, JABEZ. Died Alameda, Alameda Co. July 1, 1897 at home of dau. Mrs. Alfred Scott; [see note below]; admitted to state bar of Illinois 1848; came to Weaverville June 1853; opened a law office; removed to Red Bluff, then Alameda, then Redding; leaves widow, daughter, and brother, Matthew Chadbourne, of Alameda County. (TJ Jul 10, 1897 p 3 col 4).
[Note on CHADBOURNE, JABEZ. Born Bushire, Franklin Co. Vermont 15 Sept. 1819. Came to Calif. June 1853. Built at Trinity Center 1853-4 a hotel and saw mill. Cox's Annals [1940] p. 111.]

CHADBOURNE, MOSES. Died San Jose, Santa Clara Co., Calif. Jan. 8, 1887. Former resident of Trinity Center. Brother of Matthew Chadbourne of Trinity County and Jabez Chadbourne, Esq. of Alameda. (TJ Sat. Jan. 22, 1887 p 3).

CHADWICK, E.C.M., Capt. Died San Francisco April 15, 1865; Commander of the Steamer Chrysopolis, California Steam Navigation Company. (TJ Apr. 22, 1865).

CHAMBERLAIN, JOS. C. Died Feb. 3, 1907 near Trinity Center, age 60; carpenter; buried Trinity Center. [Index to Deaths 1890-1908].

CHAMBERLAIN, PAUL REONARD. Died Lewiston Feb 9, 1898; b. Kentucky 1835, aged 63 yr 1 mo 8 dy; came to Trinity County 1860; one bro. V. M. Chamberlain of Lewiston, and one in Idaho. Bur. Masonic Cem. Weaverville. (TJ Feb 12, 1898).

CHAMBERLIN, MARY S.H., Mrs. Died at the residence of her son, G. W. Huestis, at the Don Juan Mine, Trinity County, Jan. 15, 1886; native of New Jersey, aged 77 yr 5 mo 20 days. Married George D. Huestis 1834 (younger brother of late Judge A. J. Huestis). Huestis died 1852 San Francisco; m2) Dr. Wm. B. Chamberlain (sic), who died about 2 years ago. She arrived in San Francisco 1861 and learned of death of eldest son, Chas. A. D. Huestis at the hands of Indians near Redwood Creek, Humboldt Co. Leaves 3 grown sons, Geo. W., Wm. P. and Theodore F. Huestis. (TJ Feb 6 and 13, 1886; see also Eureka *TIMES TELEPHONE*, Humboldt Co., Calif. abt Feb. 6, 1886).

CHANCE, CORA, Miss. Died Lewiston Apr 16, 1900; native of Ohio, aged nearly 20 yr. (TJ Apr 21, 1900 p 2).

CHANDLER, FLEMING. Died Weaverville Jan 16, 1898; native of Kentucky, aged abt 86 yr; came to Trinity County in the early days; bur. Friday Jan 21, 1898 in Weaverville Cem. under auspices of Old Settlers Assn. (TJ Jan 22, 1898).

CHAPMAN, CAROLINE RICE, Mrs. Died Utica, Michigan Oct 30, 1899, aged 85 yr 7 mo; b. Jewett, Green Co., NY Mar 1814; local members of family include Geo. P. Chapman and Mrs. W. C. Given of Junction City, Cal., and Mrs. G. O. Williams of Rockford, Ill. (TJ Nov 18, 1899 p 3 col 4).

CHAPMAN, JOHN. Died Eureka (July 1889) aged 67 years. Resident of Blocksburg, Humboldt Co; former res. of Trinity County; known as "Kentuck". (TJ July 20, 1889).

CHAPMAN, JOHN, Deacon. Died Utica, Michigan, Dec. 31, 1883, age 83; father of Geo. P. Chapman and Mrs. C. A. Given of Junction City, Trinity Co. Calif. Native of New York; married there 1833; golden wedding 3 years ago. 8 children; all survive, and aged widowed mother. See also Utica *SENTINEL* Jan. 9, 1886.

CHAPMAN, JULIETTE R. Died near Junction City Mar. 16, 1890; aged 1 yr 2 mo 16 days; daughter of George P. and Sarah Chapman. Buried Weaverville Cemetery Tues. Mar. 18, 1890. (TJ Sat. Mar. 22, 1890).

CHAPMAN, SARAH S. Died near Junction City Dec. 3, 1894; beloved wife of George P. Chapman; a native of Bath, Maine, aged 46 yr 4 mo 1 day. Came to Calif. 1870s; married to Geo. P. Chapman of Junction City; 3 children; girl died; 2 boys living. Buried Weaverville Cem. "Bath papers please copy." (TJ Sat. Dec. 8, 1894 pp 2 & 3).

CHAPMAN, WM. B. Chapman, shot by Eoff in San Francisco several days ago, is dead; native of Connecticut. (TJ Sat. Jan. 31, 1863).

[Note on **CHAUNCEY, HARVEY.** Born Saratoga, N.Y. 1821; studied medicine in 1839; came to Oregon, then Calif. 1851; Trinity Co. 1852; built Chaunceyville 1851, with a dwelling house, saw mill, packet line of 25-30 mountain clippers between Weaverville and Shasta; built a lime kiln; Medical Doctor in Weaverville. (Cox's Annals, 1940).]

CHERRY, JAMES. Died Oregon Gulch Aug. 15, 1861, age 34; unmarried; native of County Clare, Ireland. (TJ Sat. Aug. 24, 1861 p 2 col 1).

CHINERY, CHARLES. Died Weaverville July 24, 1894; native of New York, aged abt 78 yr. (TJ Sat. Jul 28, 1894, p 2).

CHRISTIANSEN, CHRISTIAN. Died Weaverville Aug. 2, 1878; native of Denmark, aged about 51 years. (TJ Sat. Aug. 10, 1878 p 2).

CHRISTIANSON, NELS. Died Redding, Shasta Co abt Jan 23, 1897; native of Norway, aged abt 35 yr. (TJ Jan 23, 1897 p 3 col 4).

CHRISTIANSON, OLE. Died Oct 3, 1896 Alsen, Germany; old res. Trinity Co, came here 1852; partner with P. M. Paulsen in Turner Bar Company; also partner of Jacob Paulsen; left here 1878. One brother, Fred Christianson, lives at Hayward, CA. (TJ Sat Sept 5, 1896 p 3).

CHRISTOPHER, HENRY. Died May 1858; probate filed May 17, 1858. Probate Book B p 69 (from Index to Probate 1852-1877). No further information.

CHURCH, JOHN E. Died Red Bluff, Tehama Co. (prob. Jan. 18, 1886); funeral Tues. Jan. 19, 1886, Presbyterian Church, Red Bluff. (Prob. buried Oak Hill Cem., Red Bluff.) Arrived Calif. 1849; pioneer resident and merchant of Weaverville, Shasta, Red Bluff. Born Providence R.I. July 4, 1824; wife and 2 children: daughter Mrs. J. H. Pryor; son Charley Church; brother and sister in Providence. (TJ Sat. Jan. 23, 1886; see also Red Bluff *Cause*.

CHURCH, RUTH, Mrs. Died Adamsville, Rhode Island. (no date; prob. died abt Jan. 1861). Parent of J. E. Church, Esq. of this village (Weaverville), aged about 80 years. (TJ Sat. March 23, 1861).

CLAIRE, RICHARD, Mr. Died Sept. 25, 1881 at his residence, 17 Grattan Parade, Drumcondra, Dublin (Ireland); aged 65 years; father of Rev. James J. Claire, Catholic Pastor, Weaverville. (TJ Sat. Oct. 22, 1881, p 3).

CLANCY, SARAH. Died at Oregon Gulch May 27, 1862; wife of Mr. John Clancy; aged about 30 years. Deceased was a native of Balymegan, County Donegal, Ireland. "San Francisco and Philadelphia papers please copy." (TJ Sat. May 31, 1862 p 3).

CLARK, ABNER LELAND. Died Weaverville Oct 13, 1897; native of Maine, aged abt 67 yr; leaves 2 daughters in Humboldt Co.; came to Weaverville 2 years ago. (TJ Oct 16, 1897 pp 2 & 3).

CLARK, ADELLA. Died Red Bluff, Tehama County Nov. 16, 1878; younger daughter of L. D. and Matilda Clark, aged 3 yr 5 mo 21 days. (TJ Sat. Nov. 23, 1878).

CLARK, D. C. Died October 1855; probate filed Oct. 29, 1855; probate book B page 10. (Index to Probate 1852-1877). No further information.

CLARK, JOHN. Died April 14, 1880, Walla Walla, Washington; ex-Judge of Lewiston, Idaho. Left Trinity about 1862. (TJ Sat. April 24, 1880 p 3).

CLARK, JOSEPH CURTIS. Died near Weaverville July 17, 1899; native of San Francisco, age 20 yr 4 mo; bur. Mt. Olivet Cem., San Francisco. (TJ Jul 22, 1899 pp 2 & 3).

CLARK, RALPH. Died Nov. 21, 1905 Canon Creek; 7 months; male, white, born Calif. [Index to Deaths 1890-1908].

CLAY, T. C. Died April 14, 1904 LaGrange Mine; age 32, born Missouri; buried Public Cemetery, Weaverville. [Index to Deaths 1890-1908].

CLAYTON, ELBRIDGE. See "Ellbridge".

CLEMENS, NANCY JANE (sic). Died June 28, 1906 Weaverville age 80. [Index to Deaths 1890-1906].
[Note: this is Nancy Jane Swett **Clement**, wife of William Clement. She was born June 26, 1826 New Hampshire, the daughter of John Swett; died June 28, 1906. Buried in Clement Cemetery on R K Ranch, Reading's Creek. Clement family history, researched by Patricia Johnsen Hicks 1978.]

CLEMENT, MOSES H. Died Weaverville Nov. 7, 1884; native of New Hampshire, aged 73 yr. Brother of William Clement. (TJ Nov. 8, 1884). (Buried in cemetery on Clement Ranch, Readings Creek; known as R K Ranch in 1978.)

CLEMENT, WILLIAM. Died July 13, 1894; b. New Hampshire, 69 yr. Buried Clement Cemetery, Readings Creek. (TJ July 14, 1894). (Also gravemarker in Clement Cemetery, R K Ranch, Reading's Creek.)

"CLIFFORD", _____. "Step-son of John Clifford". Died Weaverville July 22, 1880, between 12 and 13 years of age. (TJ July 10, 1880; Aug. 14, 1880 p 3).

CLIFFORD, RICHARD. Died Weaverville Oct. 19, 1879, aged 52 yr 8 mo 17 days; native of County Cavan, Ireland. Obituary page 3 -- one column long. (TJ Sat. Oct. 25, 1879).

COCHELL, ISABELLA. Died at her father's residence, Weaverville, July 20, 1860; eldest daughter of Absalom and Maria Cochell; aged 15 yr 4 mo 2 days; funeral at Union Church July 21, 1860; buried Weaverville cemetery. "Louisville, KY and New Albany, Indiana, papers please copy." (TJ July 1860).

COCHELL, MARIA. Died San Francisco, CA May 9, 1893 age 80 yr 11 days; lived Weaverville many years; husband A. Cochell, of Weaverville and 4 children survive. (TJ Sat. May 13, 1893.)

COCHRAN, EDMUND O. Died April 26, 1890 Weaverville; white, age 23, male, single, b. Calif. [Index to deaths 1873-1890].

COCHRAN, JAMES. Sheriff of Trinity County. Killed at Red Bluff March 17, 1868 by an insane man whom he was conveying to Stockton. Native of Ballindrait, parish of Lifford, County Donegal, Ireland; aged about 33 years 3 months; leaves widow and 3 children. (TJ Sat. March 21, 1868 p 2 & 3). [Family not in 1860 Census.]

COCHRAN, EDMUND O'CONNELL. Drowned in South Fork (of Trinity River) Apr. 26, 1890; native of Weaverville, aged about 23 years; employed by A. H. Marshall at cattle ranch on Mad River; body not found yet (p 3). (TJ Sat. May 10, 1890; Sept. 20, 1890 "no trace".)

COCHRAN, ROBERT, Mr. Died near Benton, Lafayette County, Wisconsin Feb. 28, 1861; deceased was father of Mr. James Cochran, of Weaverville. Mrs. Sarah Cochran requested publication. (TJ Sat. Nov. 2, 1861).

CODDINGTON, WILLIAM. Died San Francisco Jan 4, 1874 aged 63 years; formerly a member of the firm of Bowles & Coddington at Big Bar.

CODY, PETER. Died at Hawkins Bar Oct 27, 1895, aged abt 71 yr; b. St. Charles, Missouri; crossed plains in 1850; mined first at Grass Valley, Nevada Co., later Trinity Co. (TJ Sat. Nov 9, 1895 p 2 & 3).

COFFEY, MAHALA, Mrs. "An Aged Negro Lady" died Sept. 24, 1891 at her home on Elder Creek, Tehama County. She was born Mahala Tinsel, in Buckingham Co. Virginia May 10, 1820; moved to Missouri with parents 1832; married A. A. Coffey, who survives her, Oct. 9, 1842. He came to Calif. 1849 with permission of his Master, worked hard, saved his money and returned to Missouri 1852; "bought himself", paying his "old master" $1000. He worked as a free man, then returned again to Missouri and paid $2500 for his wife and five children and they crossed the plains in 1857, settled in Shasta County until Feb. 1871 when they all moved to Tehama County and located land on Elder Creek. She leaves her husband & seven children: Mrs. Mary Prindle of Boston; John W., Charles L. and Alvin A. Coffee, of Red Bluff; Levinia Snaden, of Corning, and Mrs. Orifina Williams of Red Bluff survive the deceased. [*Red Bluff Sentinel*]. (TJ Sat. Oct. 3, 1891 p 3 col 2). Note in Trinity Journal: "Mrs. Coffey was the mother of Charley Coffey, who has been driving teams to this town for many years."

COFFIN, FREDERICK. New River miner; lost in snow Sat. evening before Christmas near North Fork, or drowned in Trinity River, also his partner, a Frenchman known as "Louis"; Coffin was a native of New York; leaves a brother in San Francisco. Died abt Dec. 1861. (TJ Sat. Jan. 11, 1862 p 3).

COHN, MORRIS. Died San Francisco Nov. 25, 1869; age 17 yr; recently of Weaverville, son of Philip and Ereke Cohn. (TJ Sat. Dec. 11, 1869 p 2).

COLBERT, DANIEL. Died Weaverville July 30, 1885; born Oregon Gulch, Trinity County Feb. 4, 1858; age 27 yr 5 mo 26 days. Bur. July 31, 1885, Catholic Cem. Weaverville. (TJ Sat. Aug. 1, 1885).

COLBERT, JOHN. Died Oregon Gulch March 5, 1864; native of Youghal, County Cork, Ireland, aged 38 yr. (TJ Mar. 12, 1864 p 2). Probate filed Mar. 18, 1864, probate book C page 90. (Index to Probate 1852-1877).
[See Walker for mother of Mrs. John Colbert].

COLBERT, NELLIE. Died Oregon Gulch Feb. 19, 1863; daughter of John and _____ Colbert, aged 3 yr 1 mo 26 days. (TJ Feb. 1863). 1860 Census: Oregon Gulch, page 56 #1008, 7-19-1860: Colbert, John, age 33, Saloon Keeper, b. Ireland. Colbert, Margaret, age 33, b. Ireland; Mary, age 12, b. Mass; John, age 9, b. Mass; Margaret, age 3, b. Calif.; Daniel, age 2, b. Calif. Ellen (Nellie), age 7 months, b. Calif. Note: Margaret Colbert, Mother, m2) Michael Cahalan. [see also Cahalan].

COLE, _____. Died Weaverville July 15, 1858, son of John and Sarah Cole. (Typhoid fever). (TJ Jan. 1858).

COLE, HANNAH. "Little Hannah Cole, formerly lived in Weaverville, died New York a short time ago (abt July/August 1861). (TJ Sat. Aug. 24, 1861 p 2 col 2, bottom.)

COLE, JOHN, Capt. Died Weaverville March 21, 1859; formerly of Bucksport, Maine; age 40 yr 4 mo. "San Francisco, New York, and Maine papers please copy." (TJ Sat. March 26, 1859 p 2 & 3). Probate filed March 29, 1859 Probate book B page 105. (Index to Probate 1852-1877). Born Nov. 20, 1818 Bucksport, Maine. Master of ship at age 20; arrived Calif. fall of 1849; family came to Weaverville fall of 1852; mercantile store [Buck & Cole]. (Cox's Annals, [1940]). See also Buck, Franklin, *A Yankee Trader in the Gold Rush*. Buck and Cole were partners. [COLE note: I.O.O.F. Section, Weaverville Cemetery, has three stones (1976): "Capt.

John Cole, d. March 21, 1859 40 yr 4 months (F. & A. M emblem). "Little Eddie" and "Infant son of J & S Cole"].

COLE, SARAH, Mrs. Died Portland, Maine Dec 28, 1898 at the age of 81 yr; home was in Bucksport, Maine. Pioneer resident of Weaverville. Husband, Capt. John Cole, died Weaverville 1859; buried Masonic Cem. Mrs. Cole returned to Bucksport in 1860 with 2 daughters, who survive her.

COLEMAN, W. G. Died Minersville Nov. 18, 1893; native of Mississippi, aged about 40 years. Coleman was born a slave in Mississippi about 41 years ago; he ran away as a boy of 10 and joined the Union Army; came to Calif. 17 years ago, Minersville 15 years ago; nice obit. by his friend John Skewis. (TJ Sat. Dec. 2, 1893 p 2 & p 3 col 3).

COLL, JOHN. Died Nov. 19, 1856 age 35; formerly of Melbourne, Australia; brothers and sisters reside in Australia; arrived California 1850. (TJ Sat. Nov. 22, 1856.

COLLINS, JAMES. Killed by a land slide near Burnt Ranch Jan. 9, 1880; native of Ireland, aged about 52 yr; buried near Burnt Ranch. (TJ Sat. Jan. 17, 1880 p 2 & 3). (See also Kearnan).

COLLINS, THOMAS. Died Canon Creek (Canyon Creek) April 12, 1856, about 25 yr, from St. Louis, MO. (TJ Sat. April 19, 1856 p 2). Probate filed April 28, 1856; probate book B page 16 (Index to Probate 1852-1877).

COLLINS, WM. Died Weaverville June 13, 1861; native of Parish More, County Roscommon, Ireland, aged about 30 years; funeral Friday June 14, 1861; prob. buried Catholic Cemetery, Weaverville. (TJ Sat. June 15, 1861 p 2). Probate filed June 15, 1861, probate book B page 217. (Index to Probate 1852-1877).

COLLINS, WILLIAM L. Died Nov. 8, 1890 Eureka, Humboldt Co., pioneer resident of Trinity County; native of Ireland, aged 77 yr; 2 grown sons in Humboldt Co; wife died several years ago. (TJ Sat. Nov. 22, 1890 p 3). 1860 Census, Trinity County, Calif. Weaver Basin, page 102 #1054, 8-16-1860: Collins, William L., age 38, miner, b. Ireland; Mary, age 38, b. Ireland; George, age 4, b. California. Not married in Trinity County. Not in 1870 Census.

COLLOPY, JOHN AUGUSTUS. Died Lewiston June 4, 1869. Son of John and Bridget Collopy. (TJ June 26, 1869 p 2).

COLLOPY, DANIEL. Died Lewiston June 20, 1869, age 2 yr 4 mo; son of John and Bridget Collopy. (TJ June 26, 1869 p 2).

COLLOPY note: Stone in Catholic Cemetery, Weaverville (1976) says: "John Gustas, d. June 1870 age 9 yr; Danna d. June 1870 age 3 yr. Children of John and Sarah Colopy (sic).

COLLOPY, SARAH, Mrs. Died Lewiston Apr. 29, 1888; native of Ireland, aged about 56 years; wife of John Collopy; married nearly 30 years; 3 children: one living: Otis J. Collopy, lives Montana. Bur. Catholic Cem. Weaverville Mon. Apr. 30, 1888. (TJ Sat. May 5, 1888).

COMSTOCK, ISRAEL. Died Red Bluff, Tehama County, Sept. 9, 1868, aged 39 yr. (TJ Sat. Sept. 19, 1868).

CONDON, JOHANNA, Mrs. Died Oct. 20, 1887 at Harvard, McHenry Co., Illinois, age 75 years. Mother of William Condon of Weaverville. (TJ Sat. Nov. 12, 1887 p 3).

CONDON, KATIE. Died Weaverville Sept. 28, 1873; daughter of William and Mary Condon, aged 10 months. (TJ Sat. Oct. 4, 1873). [Index to Deaths 1873-1890 adds "single"].

CONDON, MAURICE. Died San Francisco Feb. 5, 1876, aged 38 yr; brother to William Condon of Weaverville. (TJ Sat. Feb. 12, 1876 p 2).

CONDON, MARY. Died Weaverville Nov. 1, 1881, aged 46 years; native of Kinsale, County Cork, Ireland. Wife of William Condon, m. Nov 4, 1862; 6 children. Bur. Nov. 3, 1881, prob. in Catholic Cem. Weaverville. (TJ Nov. 5, 1881 p 2).

CONDON, TOMMY. Died French Gulch, Shasta Co. March 1, 1885, aged 14 yr 3 mo 13 days. Visited family of his uncle Mr. T. Madden. Bur. Catholic Cem. Weaverville Tues. Mar. 3, 1885. (TJ Mar. 7, 1885).

CONDON, WILLIAM, Sr. Died Chicago, Illinois, Dec. 31, 1876; father of William Condon of Weaverville; aged 84 yr 8 months. (TJ abt Jan. 1877).

CONDON, WILLIAM. Died Weaverville July 17, 1888; native of Ireland; born May 1830, aged 58 yr 2 mo. bur. Catholic Cem. next to wife July 18, 1888. Married Miss Mary Desmond of French Gulch 1863; 7 children, 5 survive: William, John,

Mary, Nellie, and Annie. (TJ Sat. July 21, 1888; long obit. p 3). [see also Madden].

CONDON, WILLIAM SPENCER. Died Weaverville Feb 04, 1900; aged 3 mo 27 dy; inf. son of Mr. and Mrs. William Condon; grandfather William Spencer Lowden. (TJ Feb 10, 1900 p 2).

CONLON, MARY, Mrs. Died Weaverville Aug. 6, 1878; native of Ireland, aged about 38 yr; sister of Mrs. Frank O. Conner. Husband resides in San Francisco. Buried Catholic Cemetery, Weaverville Aug. 7, 1878. (TJ Sat. Aug. 10, 1878 p 2).

CONNELL, JOHANNA DESMOND. Died Weaverville Sept. 30, 1879; wife of John Connell; sister of Mrs. Wm. Condon of Empire Hotel; native of County Cork, Ireland, aged 43 years. Buried Catholic Cemetery, Weaverville. (TJ Sat. Oct. 4, 1879).

CONNER/CONNOR, DANIEL. Died Douglas City April 15, 1871; native of Belfast, Ireland, age about 61 years. (TJ Sat. Apr. 22, 1871 p 2). Probate filed Apr. 28, 1871 "Dan'l Connor (sic)" County Court Book B page 275. (Index to Probate 1852-1877).

CONNORS, NEWTON. Died Oregon Gulch Mar 17, 1896; native of Ireland, aged about 56 yr; bur. Cath. Cem. Weaverville Mar 19, 1896. (TJ Mar 21, 1896).

CONNOLLY, DENNIS. Killed by a bank cave in the claim of Thomas Foley on Five Cent Gulch (Weaverville) on Thursday December 22, 1859; 22 years of age; formerly of South Boston, Mass. (TJ Sat. Dec. 24, 1859 p 2).

CONWAY, JOHN. Died Stuart's Fork Dec 10, 1897; "native of America", aged abt 40 yr. (TJ Dec 18, 1897 p 2).

CONWAY, JOSEPHINE. Died Trinity Center Dec. 27, 1893; native of Ohio, aged about 52 yr 10 mo 13 days; Shasta Co. papers, please copy. (TJ Jan. 6, 1894).

CONWAY, WILLIAM P. Died Etna, Siskiyou County, Cal. April 20, 1878, aged 16 yr 9 mo 7 days. "Shasta, San Joaquin and Butte County papers please copy." (TJ Sat. Apr. 27, 1878 p 2).

COOK, BENNET. Died July 23, 1877 at Stone Bridge, Mass; came to Trinity County in the early days (early 1850s) with uncle, Pardon Cook, bought Point Bar Ranch; 1861 flood of Trinity River ruined business; sold property to Robert Stillwell; had Challenge Saloon in Weaverville, sold to Dan Bennett, returned East. (TJ Sat. Aug. 11, 1877 p 3, col 1; see Fall River (Mass) NEWS July 26, 1877.)

COOPER, ROBERT E. Died Weaverville Aug. 8, 1861; aged 31; formerly from Napanee, Canada West; funeral Friday Aug. 9, 1861; bur. Weaverville Cemetery. (TJ Sat. Aug. 10, 1861 p 2). Probate filed Sept. 23, 1861, probate book B page 249. (Index to Probate 1852-1877).

COPELAND, WILLIE A. Died Weaverville Dec. 29, 1868; son of Emeline Copeland; aged 6 yr 6 mo 9 days. (TJ Sat. Jan. 2, 1869).

COPELAND, RICHARD. Died Ridgeville Dec. 1, 1856; aged about 23 yr; formerly of Reynolds County, Missouri; accidentally shot by Mr. L. Osgood 5th September (thought he was a deer). (TJ Sat. Dec. 6, 1856 p 2).

CORAZZO, ALEXANDER. Died Lewiston Jan 28, 1894; native of Italy, aged about 73 yr; came to Calif. 1855; bur Jan 30, 1894 Lewiston Cem. (TJ Sat. Feb 10, 1894, pp 2 & 3).

COSHOW, SARAH E., Mrs. Died Weaverville Aug 25, 1894; native of Indiana, aged 45 yr 5 mo 21 dy; leaves husband and son 4 years old. Family came here 1 month ago from Montana. The Ladies of Weaverville took charge of the remains and prepared them for burial. Bur. Weaverville Cem. Aug 26, 1894. (TJ Sept 1, 1894 pp 2 & 3).

COUMBS, ALICE. Died Weaverville Sept. 18, 1893; native of Canada; aged 17 yr 3 mo 8 days; (typhoid fever); bur. Wed. Sept. 20, 1893, Odd Fellows Cem., Weaverville. (TJ Sat. Sept. 23, 1893).

COUMBS, ANNIE, Miss. Died Browns Creek Mar. 15, 1887, age 23 yr; daughter of Thomas Coumbs; niece of John Coumbs, both residents of Brown's Creek. (TJ Sat. Mar. 26, 1887).

COUMBS, ELIZABETH, Mrs. Died Weaverville Sept. 28, 1893; born Montreal, Canada, 1842; aged 51 yr 4 mo 24 days. (typhoid fever). Married Thomas Coumbs 1862; good obit. (TJ Sat. Oct. 7, 1893 pp 2 & 3).

COUMBS, MABEL. Died Weaverville Oct. 24, 1893; native of Calif; aged 10 yr 7 mo 20 days; adopted dau. of John Coumbs. (TJ Sat. Oct. 28, 1893 p 2 & p 3, col 6).

COUMBS, MAUD FRANKLIN. Died Browns Creek, near Douglas City, Apr 6, 1899; b. Browns Creek Sep 30, 1881, aged 17 yr 6 mo 6 dy; dau. of Thomas Coumbs; mother d.

abt 6 years ago. Leaves father, 5 sisters: Mrs. S. M. Gibson of Weaverville, Mrs. M. W. Dockery of Hay Fork, Mrs. Curt. Clements of Indian Creek, Misses Lizzie and Jennie Coumbs, and 2 brothers: Thomas and Walter of Browns Creek. Bur. Weaverville Cem. (TJ Apr 8, 1899, p 2 & p 3, col 3).

COVVEY, ABRAHAM M. Died Weaverville Oct. 29, 1883; native of New York, aged 58 years. (TJ Nov. 3, 1883 p 2).

COWAN, ALEX. Died Feb. 21, 1850 near Weaverville. May be buried next to W. W. Cowan, at "Kine Gold-Weber Village; 1/2 mile East of Weaverville, above forks of road, North side of road. Reported by Larry Moore 1981. No further information.

COYLE, JOHN. Died Sat. June 6, 1885 Happy Camp; bur. Fort Jones Cem. (Siskiyou Co.) June 7, 1885; mother resides at Trinity Center. (TJ Sat. June 13, 1885 p 3 col 2; see Yreka *Journal* for June 10, 1885).

COYLE, MARY, Mrs. Died Trinity Center Oct. 19, 1889; native of County Roscommon, Ireland, aged 95 years. (TJ Oct. 1889). [Similar information in Index to Deaths 1873-1890].

COYLE, THOMAS. Died Trinity Center Sept. 5, 1871; native of Ireland, aged 44 yr. Born Roscommon County, Ireland; came Trinity County 1858; buried Coffee Creek-Trinity Center Cemetery. (TJ Sept. 9, 1871; Sept. 16, 1871). Will Book A, ages 85-86. (see same).

COYLE, THOMAS EDWARD. Died at the Albemarle Mine in New Mexico Dec 20, 1899; native of Trinity Center, age 36 yr 2 mo; leaves mother, 3 sisters, 2 brothers. (TJ Jan 27, 1900 p 3 col 3).

CRABELL, F. Died Aug. 1858; probate filed Aug. 31, 1858; probate book B p 89. (Index to probate 1852-1877).

CRAIG, CORA WINIFRED. Died Redlands, San Bernardino Co. Mar 2, 1897, age 19 yr 6 mo 11 dy; native of Weaverville; dau. of C. W. Craig, formerly editor and proprietor of the TRINITY JOURNAL. (TJ Mar 13, 1897 p 3 col 5).

CRAIG, ELIZABETH, Mrs. Died Riverside, CA Dec. 1, 1929. Born Weaverville, age 80 years. Wife of late C. W. Craig, for many years owner and editor of the TRINITY JOURNAL. Sold paper Jan 1887 and moved to Inyo County, then San Bernardino; after Craig's death, Mrs. Craig lived with her daughter Mrs. Nellie Densmore in Riverside. (TJ Jan. 2, 1930). [see also Norwood & Lockhart.]

CRAIG, JOSEPH. Died San Bernardino, Cal. abt Apr 5, 1899. One of Trinity's pioneers, he lived 14 years in Weaverville; b. Westmoreland County, England Mar 13, 1822; came with family to US 1831; m. Dec 18, 1845, Miss Eliza Delavan, who survives him; had 3 daughters & 2 sons born in Pittsburgh, PA; came to Calif 1857; brought family in 1859; much family info. in obit from *Redlands Citrograph* Apr. ___ 1899. (TJ Apr 15, 1899 p 3 col 4).

CRAIG note. "C. W. Craig is now a grand dad. On Feb 20, 1898, a daughter was born at Independence (Cal) to the wife of Frank E. Dinsmore, who was formerly Miss Nellie L. Craig." (TJ Sat. Mar 5, 1898).

CRAWFORD, B. T. Died Jun 03, 1900; age 28 yr 6 mo 3 dy; b. California. (TJ Jan 1901). (see Mayme, below).

CRAWFORD, MAYME S., Miss. Died Sacramento Dec 11, 1898; bur. Sacramento Dec 12, 1898; born in Weaverville, youngest dau. of late Dr. M. T. Crawford and Mrs. Selina Crawford; age 19 yr 7 mo 26 dy; left Weaverville 2 years ago; leaves mother; 2 sisters: Mrs. F. S. Abrahms, of Abrahms, Trinity Co.; Mrs. C. W. Hutton, of Sacramento; bro. B. T. Crawford of Weaverville; 2 half-brothers, Edward Treloar of Junction City and Thomas Treloar of Cox Bar. (TJ Dec 17, 1898 p 3 col 2).

CREAMER, CAMILIA MAY CRUTHIS. Died Weaverville Jan 27, 1896; native of Calif. aged 14 yr 4 mo 19 dy; dau. of Mr. and Mrs. Chas. N. Creamer; bur. Weaverville Cem. (TJ Sat. Feb 1, 1896).

CREIGHTON, _____. Died Indian Creek May 10, 1889; infant daughter of Mr. and Mrs. John Creighton, aged 10 days. (TJ Sat. May 25, 1889). [Index to Deaths 1873-1890 says "Creighton, Baby; d. May 20, 1889 Trinity Center; white, 10 days, female, b. Calif."].

CRISSEY, ABRAHAM. Killed by Indians abt May 27, 1868 at old Fort Baker on Van Dusen Fork of Eel River. He was herding stock for Tom Middleton. (no age). (TJ May 30, 1868 p 2 col 1).

CROFTEN, GEORGE, Mrs. Died San Francisco Mar. 13, 1885; native of Ireland, aged 78 years; former resident of Weaverville. (TJ Sat. Mar. 21, 1885 p 3). [1860 Census, Trinity County, Calif., Weaverville page 115 #1067, 8-22-1860: Crofton, George, age 50, Miner, b. Ireland; Julia age 50, b. Ireland. Also in 1870 Census, 6-13-1870, age 60 each. No children listed. Not in 1880 Census.]

CRONIN, PATRICK. Died on or about the 28 of November 1886, near Lewiston; aged 63 years; native of Ireland. Disappeared Nov. 2, 1886; murdered; buried near spot by Trinity River where found August 8, 1887. (TJ Sat. Aug. 13, 1887; see also Nov. 13, 1886, and Dec. 25, 1886). "The remains of Patrick Cronin that were interred in the Lewiston Cemetery were exhumed and brought to Weaverville Nov. 1, 1889 to be interred in the Catholic Cemetery, Weaverville." (TJ Sat. Nov. 1, 1889 p 3).

CRORK, ISAAC. Killed at Point Bar by a bank cave Dec. 19, 1867; native of Pennsylvania, aged about 32 years. (TJ Sat. Dec. 21, 1867).

CROUCHER, WILLIAM, Dr. Died Weaverville Nov. 22, 1884; native of England, aged 61 years; physician; came Weaverville 1855. (TJ Sat. Nov. 29, 1884).

CROW, JAMES. Died Weaverville March 21, 1865; native of County Clare, Ireland, aged about 35 years. (TJ Mar. 25, 1865).

CRUTHIS, EARNEST. Died Douglas City Jan 21, 1896; native of Calif. aged about 17 yr; bur. Weaverville Cem. Jan 23, 1896. (TJ Sat. Jan 26, 1896 pp 2-3).

CRUTHIS, JAMES. Died Douglas City Oct 4, 1894; native California, aged about 11 years. (TJ Sat Oct 6, 1894 p 2).

CRUTHIS, JESSIE ELONA. Died near Douglas City Aug. 30, 1892; native of Calif, aged 1 yr 7 mo 21 days.

CULLEN, PATRICK. Died San Francisco Jan. 6, 1884; native of Ballycahill, County Tipperary, Ireland, 55 years of age. A former resident of Trinity County; left Oregon Gulch about 12 years ago. (TJ Sat. Jan. 19, 1884 p 3).

CULVER, DANIEL. Formerly of Junction City. Died recently (abt Dec. 1875) near Olympia, Washington Territory. (TJ Sat. Dec. 25, 1875).

CUMMINGS, EMMA E., Mrs. Died Sacramento Nov. 28, 1887; buried Redding (Shasta County) Wed. Nov. 30, 1887. Wife of J. W. Cummings; daughter of Mr. and Mrs. J. M. Estes, all of Redding; formerly of Weaverville. (no age given, but prob. 30; see below). (TJ Sat. Dec. 3, 1887). 1860 Census, Trinity County, Calif. Douglas City, page 29 #980, 6-28-1860: Estes, John M., age 27, miner, b. Missouri; Mary Eliza, age 21, b. New York; **Emma Eliza**, age 3, b. California; Catherine M., age 1, b. California. 1870 Census, 6-24-1870 adds Ella K., age 8 b. Calif.; Lillie M., age 5, b. California, and John T., age 2, b. Calif. (No Catherine M. in 1870 listing). Not in 1880 Census. Not married in Trinity County.

CUMMINGS, JOHN. Died Minersville Dec. 1, 1888; aged 93 yr 3 mo 19 days; native of Scotland. Married 64 years; leaves wife, 5 sons, 1 daughter; 15 grandchildren, 4 dead; 4 great-grandchildren, 4 dead. Came Calif. 1866. "Stockton and Vancouver papers please copy". (TJ Sat. Dec. 8, 1888). 1880 Census, Trinity County, Calif., Minersville page 14, 6-12-1880: Cummings, John, age 84, farmer, b. Scotland; Agnes, age 81, b. Scotland. Also in 1880 Census are sons: James (age 50, single, farmer, b. England); John S., age 55, single, farmer, b. England); Thomas A., age 49, farmer, b. England (with wife Alafaire, and children Mary, Dora, John, Lee, and Thomas, all in Minersville.)

CUMMINGS, JOHN C., Mrs. Died Minersville May 9, 1890, aged 91 yr. Husband died a little more than a year ago at 93; oldest couple in County for many years; buried Minersville. (TJ Sat. May 17, 1890). (Note: Minersville is now under Trinity Lake. All known graves were moved to Trinity Center-Coffee Creek Cemetery about 1959.) Trinity Center-Coffee Creek Cemetery (1980) Cummings markers: John d. 1888; Mrs. John d. 1890. Infant 1892-1892. John S. d. 1904. [Cummings, Raymond E. 1896 - 1967; may not belong to this Cummings family; not in 1900 or 1910 Census, Trinity County.] [Similar information Index to Deaths 1890-1908].

CUMMINGS, LAURA H. Died at Ridgeville, Trinity County, Sept. 5, 1857; daughter of Thos. and Alafaire Cummings, age 10 mo 5 days; probably buried at Ridgeville Cemetery; no marker. (TJ Sat. Oct. 3, 1857).

CUMMINGS, THOS., Mrs. Died near Minersville Oct 11, 1894; native Maysville, KY; no age given; maiden name Alaferie Jones; came to Ridgeville, Trinity County, in

1853; 6 children, 5 survive: Mrs. Frank Cadermartori; Dora, John, Lee and Thomas Cummings. (TJ Oct 13, 1894, p 2; Oct 20, 1894, p 3.)

CUNNINGHAM, LULU, Mrs. Died Junction City May 15, 1889; native of Belmont, Maine, aged about 22 yr; came Trinity County 8 years ago; married Morris Cunningham May 4, 1887; daughter of Mr. A. A. Flagg of Junction City. Buried Weaverville Cemetery May 17, 1889. (TJ Sat. May 18, 1889). [Index to Deaths 1873-1890 has similar information.]

CUNNINGHAM, MORRIS FRANCES. Died Junction City Dec. 26, 1892; native of Maine, aged 28 yr; bur. Pub. Cem. Weaverville Dec. 27, 1892 beside wife, died a few years ago; son-in-law of A. A. Flagg. (TJ Dec. 31, 1892).

CUNNINGHAM, SARAH E. Died at Bolt's Hill, Trinity County Sept. 15, 1870; wife of Benjamin Cunningham, aged about 40 years. (TJ Sept. 17, 1870 p 2). 1870 Census, Trinity County, Calif., Lewiston page 2, 7-8-1870: Cunningham, Benjamin, age 39, miner, b. Alabama; Sarah, age 38, b. Maine; Bennie, age 2, b. Calif.

CUNNINGTON, BENJAMIN. Died Weaverville Oct 20, 1896; native of Alabama, aged about 65 yr; came to Calif. 1854, Trinity Co. 1856; lived at Lewiston; moved to Weaverville a few years ago; son Benjamin now living in Siskiyou Co. (TJ Sat. Oct 24, 1896).

CURLY, EDWARD. Died Mar 17, 1900; age 51 yr; b. New York. (TJ Jan 1901).

CURRIE, MARY ELLEN. "In memory of Mary Ellen, daughter of Algernon S. and Rebecca Currie August 29, 1865 - August 29, 1866". Gravestone, Helena Cemetery, standing in 1984; no notice in Trinity Journal found.

CURRIE, ROBERT. Died Weaverville Oct. 16, 1885; native of Scotland, aged 71 years. Resident of Canon Creek (Canyon Creek). (TJ Sat. Oct. 24, 1885).

CURRIER, DAVID. Died Jan. 19, 1886 Willow Creek, Humboldt County, Calif. Born 1813 Clinton County, New York; Came from Humboldt Bay to Big Bar on Trinity River in June 1854 and has lived since on Lower Trinity. (TJ Sat. Feb. 6, 1886 p 3). 1880 Census, Trinity County, Calif. Martinville page 6; 6-7-1880. Currier, David, age 67, widower; Millwright; b. New York; parents b. New Hampshire. (No family listed on 1860, 1870, or 1880 Census in Trinity County.)

CUSSINS, WM. Died latter part of November 1892 Dewitt, Nebraska; son-in-law of H. H. Carr of this county; former resident Trin. Co.; leaves wife and several children. (TJ Sat. Dec. 10, 1892).

DACK, ISABEL. Died at Anderson, Shasta Co. June 11, 1890, aged 34 yr 6 mo; Mrs. Elisha R. Dack; daughter of Thomas Baker of Lewiston; brothers Walter & Willis Baker. Buried Redding Cemetery Thurs. June 12, 1890. (TJ Sat. June 14, 1890 p 3).

DACK, MARY ANN. Died Feb. 3, 1870 in Lewiston, Trinity County, CA, aged 53 yr 8 mo 10 days; wife of John Dack. (TJ Sat. Feb. 12, 1870 p 2). [Bur. Weaverville Cem. see Feour.]

DAHL, NILS. Died April 24, 1903 Chloride Mine, Dedrick; age about 38; born Sweden; buried Dedrick Cemetery (Canyon Creek, Trinity County, California.) [Index to Deaths 1890-1908].

DALY, JAMES. Died Inyo County, CA July 4, 1894; old resident; mined at Indian Creek. (TJ Aug 11, 1894 p 3 col 1).

DANIELL, JAMES FRANCIS. Killed accidentally near Lewiston Apr. 22, 1892; native of Penn, aged 55 yr; drowned in Collopy's ditch; bur. Lewiston Cem. Sun. April 24, 1892. (TJ Sat. Apr. 30, 1892).

DANN, F. P. Died Prescott, Arizona abt Sept. 28, 1884; resident and attorney in Weaverville July 1880 - July 1882; son Fred P. Dann, 922 34th St. Oakland, CA; (bro?) Charles H. Dann, Warsaw, N.J. Bur. Sept. 28, 1884 Prescott Odd Fellows Cemetery. (TJ Oct. 4, 1884.)

DANNENBRINK, CHRISTIAN WILLIAM. Died Feb. 8, 1866 Canyon City; son of Conrad and Augusta Dannenbrink, aged 18 days. (TJ Sat. Feb. 17, 1866 p 2).

DANNENBRINK, CONRAD. Died Canon Creek Mar 26, 1895; aged 72 yr 7 mo 16 dy; b. Hanover, Germany Aug. 13, 1822; came to U.S. age 22, Calif. 1850; m. Augusta Junkans, sister of Henry Junkans, in 1863; ten children; Mrs. Dannenbrink d. Aug 12, 1891; bur. Masonic Cem., Weaverville Thurs. Mar 28, 1895; leaves children: Henry, August, Mrs. M. A. Brady, William, Augusta, Johanna, Carl & Nora; son (Christian) William and daughter Dora, dec'd. TJ Sat. Mar 30, 1895 pp 2 & 3).

DANNENBRINK, DORA. Died Anderson, Shasta County, Nov. 28, 1887, aged 17 yr 7 mo 15 days; daughter of Mr. and Mrs. Conrad Dannenbrink of Canon Creek; measles; born Trinity County; buried Dec. 1, 1887, Weaverville Cem. (TJ Sat. Dec. 3, 1887).

DARLING, WM. H. Died Weaverville Aug. 15, 1860; formerly of West Lincklaen, N.Y; aged 34 years; buried Weaverville Cemetery Wed. Aug. 15, 1860; leaves aged father. (TJ Sat. Aug. 18, 1860 p 2). Probate filed Mar. 28, 1861, Probate Book B page 204.

DARRELL, FAY. Died Junction City Apr 7, 1899; native of Calif. aged abt 28 yr. (TJ Apr 8, 1899 p 2). Verdict of Coroner's Jury: Maud Melvin, known as Fay Darrell. (TJ Apr 15, 1899 p 3 col 3).

DATES, JOHN. Died Trinity Center Sept. 6, 1883; native of Bavaria, aged about 53 years. (TJ Sat. Sept. 15, 1883 p 2).

DAUGHERTY, JAMES. Died at St. Mary's Hospital, San Francisco May 29, 1869, aged 47 yr. (TJ abt June 1, 1869).

DAVIDSON, LYDIA J., Mrs. Died at Colebrook, New Hampshire on Thanksgiving day at the advanced age of 86. Four children now living, son living in Illinois, dau. in New Hampshire, and a son, Austin J. Davidson and a dau. Mrs. H. G. Jordan, of Trinity County. (TJ Sat. Dec 12, 1896 p 3 col 4).

DAVIS, _____. Died at Bullychoop, Trinity Co. Oct 9, 1894, inf. son of Mr. and Mrs. Oliver Davis, aged 10 mo. (TJ Oct 20, 1894 p 2).

DAVIS, ALEXANDER. Died Weaverville Thurs. Feb. 26, 1857; crushed by rock in Garden Gulch; funeral Fri. Feb. 27, 1857; buried Weaverville Cemetery; from Louisville, Kentucky, about 22 years of age. (TJ Sat. Feb. 28, 1857 p 2).

DAVIS, ALVIN W. Died Trinity Center Oct. 18, 1868; aged 5 yr 1 mo 3 days. (TJ Sat. Oct. 31, 1868 p 2).

DAVIS, CHARLES. Died Minersville May 26, 1882, aged 51 years; buried Shasta, Shasta County Calif. abt May 28, 1882. (TJ June 3, 1882 p 2).

DAVIS, CHARLES, Mrs. Died near Minersville Jan. 12, 1880 aged about 50 yr; found in deep snow by Jack Blackwell, mail rider; husband with cattle in Sacramento Valley; 3 children. (TJ Sat. Jan. 17, 1880 p 2). "Mrs. A. Davis, native of Dublin, Ireland, aged 48 years". (TJ Jan. 24, 1880 p 2). 1870 Census, Trinity Co. Calif, Minersville page 2, (no date): Davis, Charles, age 37, miner, b. Ireland; Ann, age 40, b. Ireland; John, age 10, b. Calif.; Sarah, age 3, b. Calif; James, age 1, b. Calif; Daniel, age 1, b. Calif.

DAVIS, "DAN". Killed last Wednesday (abt Sept. 11, 1889) at Soda Springs, Shasta County, by a log rolling on him; no age given; brother of John McCall of Trinity Center. (TJ Sat. Sept. 14, 1889 p 3).

DAVIS, DAVID P. Died Sept. 9, 1906 Red Bluff, Tehama, Calif; age 46; blacksmith. Buried Weaverville. [Index to Deaths 1890-1908].

DAVIS, ED. Killed at Rohnerville, Humboldt County, Jan. 30, 1888; shot by Ed Canman (no age given). Lived Weaverville a number of years ago. (TJ Sat. Feb. 11, 1888.) (Not in 1860, 1870, or 1880 Census, Trinity County, CA).

DAVIS, ISAAC. Died Portland, Oregon May 6, 1870, aged 52 years, formerly of Trinity County. (TJ Sat. June 11, 1870 p 2).

DAVIS, JAMES. Died Weaverville Dec. 27, 1857; native of Ireland, aged about 32 years. (TJ Jan. 1, 1858).

DAVIS, JAMES. Died Minersville Feb. 29, 1880, aged about 11 years. (TJ Sat. Mar. 13, 1880 p 2). (1870 Census: son of Charles and Ann Davis.)

DAVIS, ORRAN F. Died Mar 7, 1899 San Francisco at home of bro-in-law C. H. Dettmar; born East Orange, Vermont; m. Miss Emma Osgood in Sacramento Feb 28, 1889; old resident of Trinity Co; no age given. (TJ Mar 18, 1899 p 3 col 4). [probably the Davis, "Orange" F., age 31, b. Vermont, Weaverville, reg. to vote Aug 12, 1875. (Great Register of Voters, 1877).]

DAVIS, ROBERT. Died Long Ridge Mar 31, 1899; native of Calif. aged 12 yr 4 mo 12 dy. (TJ Apr 15, 1899).

DAVISON, HENRY B. Married Miss Dolores Zenteno of San Francisco 1854; founder of Weaverville Drug Store, July 1852; on Special California Census July 1852, East Side Main Street, Weaverville. Died after 1896. See biography in Cox, Isaac, Annals of Trinity County [1940], pages 182-183.

DAWSON, THOMAS FRANKLIN. Died Junction City Aug. 27, 1887; native of Ohio, aged 62 years; came Trinity County 1852, worked at Arkansas Dam; leaves large family; buried Weaverville Cemetery Mon. Aug. 29, 1887. (TJ Sat. Sept. 3, 1887. 1880 Census, Trinity Co. Calif., Junction City page 4, 6-2-1880: Dawson, Thomas, 54,, married, Teamster, b. Ohio, parents b. Virginia; Lucy (Indian) age 36, married, b. Calif. parents b. Calif.; Mary age 19, b. Calif.; Ann, age 17, b. Calif.; Lizzie, age 8, b. Calif.; Thomas age 4, b. Calif.; Frank, age 1, b. Calif.

DAY, _____. Died near Weaverville Dec. 2, 1880, aged about one month; infant son of Mr. and Mrs. J. L. Day. (TJ Dec. 11, 1880). 1880 Census, Trinity Co. Calif., Weaverville page 14, 6-8-1880: Day, James L., age 46, married, Teamster, b. Illinois; father b. Virginia; mother b. Illinois.
Mary, age 42, married, b. Scotland, parents b. Scotland. Mary, age 18, b. Calif. William, age 15, b. Calif. Grant, age 13, b. Calif. John, age 10, b. Calif. Levi, age 6, b. Calif. Walter, age 4, b. Calif. [Probably George; see father's obit.]

DAY, ANN, Mrs. Died Dec. 12, 1886, Hampton, Franklin County, Iowa; born Oct. 4, 1796, aged 90 yr 2 mo 8 days. Mother of J. L. Day (James Levi Day) of Weaverville. (TJ Sat. Jan. 1, 1887).

DAY, CHARLES WILLIAMSON. Died Weaverville Sept. 13, 1899; native of Wayne Co., Illinois, aged 64 yr 8 mo 16 day; of Junction City, Pioneer of Trinity County; came to Trinity Co. 1852; bur. "Foresters Cemetery", Junction City; interesting obit. (TJ Sept 16, 1899 p 2 & p 3 col 3).

DAY, JAMES LEVI. Died San Francisco Feb 3, 1899; old resident of Trinity Co.; b. Shellsburg, Illinois Mar 1, 1834, aged 64 yr 11 mo 2 dy; came to Calif. 1855; m. in Gibsonville, Sierra Co. Jan 14, 1860, Mary Andrews; 7 children (2 are dead: William I. and George); Mrs. Mary Partridge of Bodie, Mono Co; Ulysses G.; Joseph D.; James L.; and Walter A. Day of Trin.Co.; came to Trin.Co. 1863; abt 1898 m. Mrs. Emma Campbell of San Francisco; lived at the [Day] ranch at East Weaver; bur. Weaverville I.O.O.F. Cem., Feb 7, 1899. (TJ Feb 11, 1899 p 3 col 2).

DAY, JOHN HOOVER. Died East Fork Nov. 30, 1893; native of Missouri, aged 49 yr 2 mo 29 days; bur. Helena Cem. Came to California in the early 1850s and Trinity County 15 years ago. He was one of the party that discovered the first quartz mines in the East Fork district. (TJ Sat. Dec. 9, 1893).

DAY, MARIANA, Miss. Died San Francisco Aug. 31, 1893, age 33 years; former Trinity County teacher. (TJ Sept. 9, 1893 p 3 col 6).

DAY, WILL J. Died North Fork Nov. 2, 1885; native of Trinity County, aged 21 yr 2 mo 18 days; Son of Mr. and Mrs. Jas. Levi Day of Weaverville; buried Odd Fellows Cemetery, Weaverville Wed. Nov. 4, 1885; father member of that order. (TJ Sat. Nov. 7, 1885). [father's obit. says "William I."]

DAYTON, _____, Mr. Died abt July 1890 in Iowa; old resident of Trinity County. Married Martha Mathews, well known in Weaverville. (TJ July 12, 1890). Trinity County Marriages Book H page 212: Married at East Weaver, October 3, 1869 by C. B. Crowninshield, J.P., William H. Dayton and Miss Martha J. Mathews. (Not in 1870 Census. 1860 Census, Trinity Co. Calif., Weaver Basin, page 103 #1055, 8-17-1860: Dayton, William H., age 23, miner, b. Maryland. Mathews family not in Trinity County 1860.)

DAYTON, MARION. Died Eureka, Humboldt Co. Jan. 31, 1871, aged 32 yr; wife of H. B. Dayton. (TJ Feb. 11, 1871 p 2).

DEAN, ALFRED LARKEN. Died Trinity Center May 8, 1891; native of Fall River, Mass. aged 55 yr 6 mo and 17 days. "Sutter County papers please copy." (TJ Sat. May 16, 1891 p 2).

DEAN, WALTER. Died Trinity Center Feb. 3, 1888, age 10 yr 2 mo 6 days; Beloved son of Mr. and Mrs. A. L. Dean. "Sacramento and Wheatland papers please copy." (TJ Sat. Feb. 11, 1888).

DEGEN, CHAS. Died San Francisco last Sunday, Mar. 26, 1865; Prussian; formerly of Weaverville. (TJ Sat. Apr 1, 1865 p 2).

DEINER, EMMA. Died Delta (Shasta County), Nov. 28, 1889, age 21 yr. Wife of Isaac Deiner. Reared in family of Mr. John Hindley who died here a few years ago. (TJ Sat. Dec. 14, 1889 p 3). (See also Diener). (Not married in Trinity County.)

DELONG, GEO. S. Died Jan. 11, 1908 Hayfork; age 79; born England; farmer; buried Hayfork; reported by Minnie Lowden. [Index to Deaths 1890-1908].
DENETTE, FRED. Died near Lowden Ranch (near Lewiston) Aug 24, 1898; native of Calif. aged abt 40 yr; obit. p 3 col 5 tells of accident. (TJ Aug 27, 1898 pp 2 & 3).
DENNIS, C. C. Died near Ferndale, Humboldt Co. "last week". Worked at New River mines two years ago; old resident of Humboldt Co. (TJ Sat. Mar 3, 1894).
DENT, CARRIE A. Died at Sacramento May 25, 1868, aged about 24 yr; relict of the late John E. Dent. (TJ Sat. June 6, 1868 p 2). (Note: relict = widow).
DENT, JOHN E. Died Sacramento Apr. 10, 1868, aged 38 yr; formerly of Shasta. (TJ Apr 18, 1868 p 2).
DENVER, J. W. b. Frederick County, VA 1817; arrived Sacramento 1 Sep 1850; ran a pack train in Trinity Co. Cox's Annals [1940].
DEPINETT, JOSEPH. Died Weaverville Dec. 9, 1878; native of Canada, aged about 52 years; early life in New York State; res. Canon Creek 25 years. (TJ Mar. 30, 1878 p 2).
De REIS, ROSA. See REIS.
DE SHIELDS, BRIT. Died Belle Mills, Tehama County, June 27, 1874, aged 32 yr 6 mo 3 days. (TJ July 11, 1874).
DESOY, FRANK. Died Weaverville Feb. 27, 1868; native of Island of Goa; aged 34 yr. (TJ Feb. 29, 1868 p 2).
DIARKS, HERMANN. Drowned at Evan's Bar, Trinity River (near Junction City) Aug. 17, 1861; born Hanover, Germany; aged about 45 years. (Douglas City Gazette Aug. 21, 1861; also spelled Dierck, Diercks.)
DIBBINS, JANE. Died Weaverville July 17, 1892; native of England, aged about 72 yr. (TJ Sat. July 23, 1892).
DICKERSON, DAVID W. Died Lewiston Jan. 24, 1883; native of New York, aged 66 yr; bur. Weaverville Cem. Jan. 27, 1883; res. Lewiston 7 years. (TJ Jan. 27, 1883 p 2).
DICKERSON, LOUIS. Died Lewiston Apr. 7, 1882; native of New Jersey, aged 77 yr 7 mo; bur. Weaverville Cem. Sunday Apr. 9, 1882; lived New York, came Calif. about 12 years ago; children: Mrs. W. H. Berber, Mrs. H. B. Hays, Mrs. John Ralph, all of Lewiston. (TJ Apr. 15, 1882 p 2 & 3). (Stone in Old Section, Weav. Cem., says "Lewis" [1978])
DICKEY, SAMUEL. Died Lowden Ranch (Lewiston) Mar. 29, 1880; native of Indiana, aged 60 yr 17 days; came about 2 years ago from Ashland, Oregon; leaves wife, 1 or 2 children; father, aged 82, lives with a younger son, J. C. Dickey, on Grass Valley Creek (Trinity County, also near Lewiston). (TJ Sat. Apr 3, 1880 p 2).
DIDAWICK, ANNIE. Died Hydesville, Humboldt County Sept. 7, 1866, aged 10 mo 20 days; youngest daughter of Stephen J. and Annie Didawick. (TJ Sat. Sept. 22, 1866 p 2). 1860 Census, Trinity County, Calif.: Steiners Flat, page 47, #999, 7-17-1860: Didawick, Stephen J., age 29, blacksmith, b. Virginia. (Not married in Trinity County.)
DIDDY, MARGARET. Died at residence of John M. Owing in Trinity Valley July 9, 1896; beloved wife of Wm. M. Diddy, aged 75 yr 2 mo 7 dy. (TJ Sat. Aug 1, 1896).
DIDDY, WILLIAM. Died Trinity Center Aug 20, 1899; b. New York 1815, aged 84 yr 1 mo 24 dy; leaves 3 sons in Iowa and John Diddy and Mrs. J. M. Owings of Trinity Center. (TJ Aug 26, 1899 pp 2 & 3).
DIEMART, BERTHA EMMA. Died Weaverville Sep 16, 1899; b. Solingen, Rhine Province, Germany Jun 7, 1852; aged 47 yr 3 mo 9 dy; came to US 1862, Calif. 1870; leaves 2 sisters & 3 brothers. Bur. Weaverville Cem. (TJ Sep 23, 1899 p 2 & p 3 col 3).
DIENER, GOTTLEIB FREDERICK. Died San Francisco June 29, 1881; native of Wurtenburg, Germany, aged 63 yr 10 days; bur. Masonic Cem. Weaverville; came U. S. age 13; came Trinity County 1853; unmarried. (TJ Sat. July 2, 1881 p 2 & 3; (see also Deiner).
DIENER, ISAAC. Died Redding this week (Feb 1900); (no age); nephew of late Fred Diener of Minersville. (TJ Feb 10, 1900 p 3).
DIERCK, HERMANN. (see also Diarks, above). Drowned Trinity River at Evans Bar Aug. 16, 1861, age about 36; born Kingdom of Hanover; not married. Buried by

moonlight Wed. night Aug. 21, 1861. (TJ Sat. Aug. 24, 1861). Probate filed Oct. 18, 1861, "Herman Diercks", probate book B page 261.

DILLER, CLIFF. Died May 12, 1908 Peanut, age 21; mail carrier; born Calif. buried Hayfork. [Index to Deaths 1890-1908].

DIMOCK, FLORA IDA, Mrs. Died Trinity Center Mar 19, 1899; born Trinity Center Dec 27, 1865; age 23 yr 2 mo 22 dy; dau. of Louis and Ellen Olsen; m. May 14, 1892 Frank L. Dimock; one child Charles age 6; leaves husband, child, mother, and 3 married sisters: Mrs. J. W. Shuford, of Junction City; Mrs. Robt. A. Skinner and Mrs. R. J. Laird of Coleridge. [Trinity County Historic Sites says that Coleridge was 7.2 miles above Helena (North Fork).] (TJ Mar 25, 1899 p 2 & p 3 col 2; TJ Apr 1, 1899 corrects age from "33 yr 2 mo 22 dy" to 23 yr 2 mo 22 dy).

DINI, FELIDI. Died July 26, 1906 Lewiston; age 44, female, born Italy; buried Lewiston; reported by D. Dominica. [Index to Deaths 1890-1908].

DINKLE, FRANCES, Mrs. Died Mar. 12, 1908 Douglas City; age 46; buried Weaverville Cemetery. [Note: should be DINKEL.] [Index to Deaths 1890-1908]. [Note: daughter, Jane Dinkel White, lives in Red Bluff, Tehama Co. 1998.]

DIRKS, LAWRENCE OTTJES. Died Junction City Oct 31, 1897; native of Germany aged abt 68 yr. (TJ Nov 6, 1897 p 2).

DIXON, CHARLES. Died Douglas City Nov 18, 1895, aged about 74 yr; native of Norway; became U.S. citizen 1861; bur. Weav. Cem. obit. worth copying. (TJ Sat Nov 23, 1895; obit. p 3 col 3).

DIXON, JAMES. Died Virginia City, Nevada Sept. 24, 1877; formerly of Douglas City; no age given. (TJ Sept. 29, 1877 p 3 col 2). 1870 Census, Trinity Co., Calif. Douglas City page 12, 6-30-1870: Dixon, James, age 45, miner, b. Ireland.

DIXON, W. H. Died Oct. 1853, Trinity County; Probate filed Oct. 20, 1853, Probate Book A p. 33. (no further information).

DOBROWSKY, ERNEST. Died Redding, Shasta Co. Feb. 5, 1892; at one time resident of Trinity Co.; age 53, native of Bohemia, came US as a boy with brother Adolph Dobrowski of Redding; had a store at Douglas City 1861; moved to Weaverville 1863; mined with T. E. Jones at Trinity River below Garden Bar, with poor success; m. Mary Bystle 1868, eldest dau. of old Shasta pioneer D. P. Bystle; nine children, eight surviving; bur. Feb. 7, 1892 Redding. (TJ Sat. Feb. 6, 1892; Feb. 13, 1892).

DOBY, J. Died near Hetten Apr 13, 1897; native of Calif., aged abt 38 yr. (TJ May 15, 1897).

DOCK, ELMER. Died April 26, 1908 Poker Bar, Trinity County, CA; age 5, male, black; born Calif. buried Salt Flat. [Index to Deaths 1890-1908].

DOCKERY, CECELIA M., Mrs. Died Weaverville Jul 2, 1899; b. County Roscommon, Ireland Aug 1, 1823, aged 75 yr 11 mo 1 dy; m.n. Cecelia Marie Mulvihill; came to US 1846; m. John Henry Dockery, who died in 1884, Dec. 1846 in New Jersey; 5 children, 2 living: M. W. Dockery of Hay Fork and Mrs. Henry Weinheimer of Weaverville; bur. Catholic Cem. Weaverville. (TJ Jul 8, 1899 p 2 & p 3 col 2). (see also Weinheimer, esp. 1900-1950).

DOCKERY, EDWARD. Died Weaverville Feb. 11, 1893; born County Roscommon, Ireland Dec. 25, 1826; aged 66 yr 1 mo 16 days; came US Aug. 1846, married in Ireland Margaret Monahan May 1846; came Calif 1854, Weaverville June 10, 1856; leaves wife and 4 of 6 children; bur. Catholic Cem., Weav. Mon. Feb. 13, 1893. (TJ Sat. Feb. 18, 1893 p 2 & p 3 col 2).

DOCKERY, ELIZABETH ELLEN. Died Weaverville Aug. 14, 1892, infant daughter of Mr. and Mrs. M. W. Dockery, aged 2 mo 15 days. (TJ Sat. Aug. 20, 1892).

DOCKERY, JOHN J. Died Austin, Nevada Sept. 3, 1874; native of New Jersey, aged 22 yr 10 mo 12 days. (b. 22 Oct 1851). (See TJ Sept. 5 and Sept. 12, 1874 for complete info.)

DOCKERY, JOHN, Sr. Died Weaverville March 16, 1884; native of County Roscommon, Ireland, aged 70 yr 2 mo; bur. Catholic Cem. Weaverville Tues. March 18, 1884; came Weaverville 1854; leaves wife, daughter Mrs. Kate Weinheimer, 2 sons, Patrick and Edward. (TJ Sat. Mar. 22, 1884). (b. 16 Jan 1814).

DOCKERY, MARGARET, Mrs. Died Weaverville Nov 14, 1899; b. County Roscommon, Ireland May 4, 1832, aged 67 yr 6 mo 10 dy; parents Patrick and Mary Monahan; m. Edward Dockery (deceased) May 20, 1846; seven children, 4 living: James E. and Mary Jane Dockery of Weaverville; John W. Dockery of Deadwood; and Mrs. Joseph

Britton of Hay Fork; bur. Catholic Cem. Weaverville; family info in obit. (TJ Nov 18, 1899 p 2 & p 3 col 3).
DOCKERY, NANCY. Died San Francisco, CA Apr 15, 1896; wife of Roger Dockery; family left Weaverville in the fall of 1870. (TJ Apr 25, 1896 p 3).
DOCKERY, RICHARD. Died Weaverville March 24, 1878, aged 12 yr 8 mo 21 days. Son of Edward and Margaret Dockery. (TJ Mar. 30, 1878 p 2). (b. 3 July 1865).
DOCKERY, WILLIAM. Died Weaverville Oct 21, 1894; inf. son of Mr. and Mrs. M. W. Dockery, aged 7 mo 15 dy. (TJ Oct 27, 1894 p 2).
DODGE, FLORA E. Died Weaverville Jan. 23, 1869, aged 4 yr 9 mo 23 days; daughter of J. C. and D. P. Dodge. (TJ Sat. Jan. 30, 1869). (Dodge family not in 1870 Census).
DODGE, HARRY H. Died Eureka, Humboldt Co. Nov. 15, 1870, aged 8 yr 1 mo 15 days; son of John C. and D. P. Dodge, formerly of Weaverville. (TJ Nov. 26, 1870 p 2). (Trinity County, Calif. Marriages, Book H page 68: Married at Minersville, Dec. 11, 1861, by Rev. J. S. Jordan, John C. Dodge and Miss Diana Prudence Gardiner.)
DODGE, INEZ B., Mrs. Died Long Ridge Aug. 3, 1890; native of Butte County, Calif., aged 26 yr 1 mo 12 days; daughter of Mr. and Mrs. C. Duffield. (TJ Aug. 23, 1890). [Index to Deaths 1890-1908 adds white, single, "male"].
DODGE, LAURA M. Died Weaverville May 7, 1868, aged 1 mo 14 days; fun. Sat. May 9, 1868. (TJ Sat. May 9, 1868 p 2) ("Born to the wife of John C. Dodge, in Weaverville March 23, 1868, a daughter." TJ abt March 1868). (Note: this couple also had a son, b. Sept. 19, 1862; no name given; see TJ for Sept. 1862).
DODGE, LEVI W. Killed in his mining claim at Cox's Bar Feb. 1, 1866; native of New Boston, New Hampshire, aged about 37; fun. from late residence, Court St., Weaverville, Feb. 3, 1866; buried Weaverville Cem. (TJ Feb. 3 and Feb. 10, 1866). (Query: brother of John C. Dodge?)
DODGE, MARY E. Died Eureka, Humboldt Co. Nov. 25, 1870 of diphtheria; aged 11 mo; only child of J. C. and D. P. Dodge. (TJ Sat. Dec. 24, 1870 p 2).
DODGE, SAMUEL. Died New Boston, New Hampshire June 29, 1866, aged about 74 years; deceased was father of John C. Dodge, of Weaverville. (TJ Aug. 11, 1866 p 2).
DODGE note: 1860 Census Trinity County, California:
DODGE, A. N., Weaver Basin page 103 #1055, 8-17-1860, age 25, miner, b. New Hampshire.
DODGE, John C., Minersville, page 15 #967, 6-14-1860; age 28, miner, b. New Hampshire.
DODGE, Levi W., Weaver Basin page 103 #1055, 8-17-1860; age 31, b. New Hampshire.
It looks as though A. N., John C., and Levi W., were brothers, sons of Samuel Dodge of New Boston, New Hampshire. There were no residents named Dodge in the 1870 Census.
DOIG, JOHN. (no date). Died Snow Gulch, near Carrville, age about 52; born Scotland; buried Public Cemetery Trinity Center. [Index to Deaths 1890-1904]. [Trinity Journal and grave marker say "died June 21, 1904".]
DOLAN, PETER. Died on Canon Creek below Canon City July 8, 1856; no age given. (TJ Sat. July 12, 1856 p 2 col 1).
DOOLITTLE, _____. Died Long Ridge, Trinity County, April 1, 1890, aged one year; youngest child of Mr. Frank Doolittle [sex not given]. (TJ May 10, 1890 p 3.)
DOOLITTLE, FRANK, Mrs. Drowned in the North Fork of the Eel River at the Willburn Crossing; body not found yet. (TJ Feb 3, 1894 pg 3 col 1 "Long Ridge Letter").
DOMINICI, JOHN FRED. Died Lewiston Dec 4, 1898; b. Sonoma Co, CA, age 13 yr 5 mo 27 dy; came to Trinity County with his parents when he was a baby. Buried Lewiston Cem. (TJ Dec 10, 1898 p 2 & p 3 col 3).
DOMINICI, TERESA. Died near Lewiston Dec. 20, 1891; native of Italy; aged 39 yr 7 mo 13 days. (TJ Sat. Dec. 26, 1891).
DONNAVAN, DANIEL. Killed by a mining accident on Oregon Gulch Apr. 9, 1885; native of Ireland, aged 57 yr; buried Catholic Cem. Weaverville Apr. 10, 1885; unmarried. (TJ Sat. Apr. 11, 1885).
DONNELLY, JIMMY. Died Trinity River "28 Feb 1855" near Texas Bar, a miner named Donnelly (sic); worked with Charley Soule and Tibbets. (TJ Oct. 20, 1877). See also Trinity Times reference and story by Theodore Eldon Jones below.

DONELLY (sic), JAMES. Miner, drowned in Trinity River near Union Bar Feb. 16, 1855 while attempting to cross the river in a skiff; about 30 years of age; native of Londonderry, Ireland; lived Trinity County for 3 years; many years a resident of Philadelphia. Body found on Ferry Bar on March 1, 1855. (TT Mar. 10, 1855 p 2).
DONNELLY note: TJ Sept. 7, 1889, pages 1 & 4: Early Days Along the River, by T. E. Jones. Page 4 tells about finding the body on Ferry Bar, building a box from lumber from wheels and sluice boxes broken in the flood of Feb. 28, 1855, and burying him in a thicket of yellow pine on or near Ferry Bar. (See also Hicks, Patricia Johnsen, STORIES OF A GOLD MINER).
DONNELY, PETER. Drowned Dec. 20, 1860 Canon Creek; no age given. (TJ Sat. Dec. 22, 1860).
DONNELLY note: 1860 Census, Trinity County, CA,
Donnelly, Peter, Canon Creek, page 61 #1013, 7-25-1860 age 25, miner, b. Ireland.
Donnelly, Robert C., Weaverville, page 124 #1076, 8-24-1860, age 28, miner, b. Ireland.
Donnelly, William, Lewiston, page 11 #963, 6-12-1860, age 47, miner, b. Ireland.
DONNELLY, ROBERT, Mr. Died Weaverville Sept. 26, 1860; resident here 2 years or more; native Omar, County Tyrone, Ireland, aged about 29 yr; bur. Catholic Cem. Weaverville, Thurs. Sept. 27, 1860 by Rev. Fr. Florian, who was on a visit here; leaves a brother, Mr. E. C. Donnelly, formerly of Weaverville, now of Boston. (TJ Sept. 19,, 1860 p 2, col 1 and col 4.)
DONNELLY, WILLIAM. Died near Trinity Center abt Nov. 1, 1883; native of Ireland aged 66 yr; old resident of Trinity County. (TJ Sat. Nov. 17, 1883 p 2).
DONOVAN, THOS. Killed at Big Bar Tues. June 14, 1859 by a bank cave; buried at Big Flat; no age given. See also Michael Castillo, killed in same cave. (TJ June 18 and 25, 1859).
DORR, ADA AMES. Died at Pilot Creek, enroute for Humboldt County, Sept. 26, 1870, aged 3 mo 10 days; infant daughter of Dr. J. C. and Ellen R. Dorr. (TJ Oct. 8, 1870 p 2).
DORR, JAMES C., Deacon. Died South Norridgewock, Maine July 30, 1869; no age given; father of Dr. J. C. Dorr of Trinity Center. (TJ Sat. Aug. 21, 1869).
DORSEY, DANIEL JAMES. Accidentally killed in a mine at Pine Grove, Nevada Dec. 4, 1886; bur. Pine Grove, Nev. Dec. 5, 1886; born near Douglas City March 1857, aged 29 yr 8 mo 16 days; brother of Mrs. Isaac Woodbury; half-brother of Frank Dougherty; leaves mother, brother and sisters in Humboldt County. (TJ Sat. Dec. 11, 1886 p 2 & 3).
DORSEY, LAWRENCE. Lost on the steamer "Central America" Sept. 12, 1857; from Illinois and Weaverville; no age given. (TJ Sat. Oct. 31, 1857).
DORSEY, MICHAEL. Died Weaverville Nov. 24, 1862; native of County Tipperary, Ireland, aged 42 yr; leaves wife and 5 children. (TJ Sat. Nov. 29, 1862 p 2). 1860 Census Trinity County, Calif. Lewiston page 9 #961, 6-11-1860:
Dorsey, Michael, age 39, laborer, b. Ireland; Catherine, age 26, housekeeper, b. Ireland; Mary L., 10, b. Louisiana; Elizabeth, 5, b. Calif.; Daniel James, 2, b. Calif.; Catherine, 1, b. Calif. Trinity County Marriages Book H page 100: "Married in Weaverville November 26, 1863 by Father P. O'Reilly, James Dougherty and Mrs. Catherine Dorsey."
DOTTKER, ADAM HENRY. Died Weaverville Dec. 12, 1886; native of Hanover (Germany); aged about 57 years.
DOUGHERTY, FRANK XAVIER. Died Weaverville Feb. 3, 1888; native of Weaverville, age 23 yr 2 mo; born Dec. 4, 1864 Weaverville; bur. Sat. Feb. 4, 1888 I.O.O.F. Cem. Weaverville; leaves sister Mrs. Isaac Woodbury [Trin.Co Mar. Book H page 142, Isaac Woodbury married Miss Mary Louise Dorsey Sept. 23, 1865]; leaves mother and 3 sisters in Humboldt County. (TJ Sat. Feb. 4, 1888). (see also Dorsey).
DOUGHERTY, JAMES V. Drowned in the flood of the Trinity River Dec. 7, 1861, near Lewiston; age 26 years; born Virginia; father and sister reside in Yuba County, Calif. (TJ Dec. 14, 1861). Probate filed Jan. 20, 1870, probate book C page 379.
DOUGHERTY, THOMAS. Died Mar 12, 1857, age 34 yr. Buried in St. Patrick's Catholic Cem., Weaverville. Elaborate headstone and footstone within an iron fence, still standing 1998. The headstone has firmly carved: "Gloria in Excelsis

Deo/ Erected by Neil Dougherty/ in memory of his brother THOMAS DOUGHERTY/ a native of the townland of Ballykilkash/ Parish of Kill McShaRigan/ County of Sligo, Ireland/ late of the City of New York/ Who was accidentally killed on Sidney Hill while at work by a bank caving on him/ on the 12 day of March AD 1857/ aged 34 years. May he rest in peace Amen./ In life respected, in death regretted." The footstone is the size of most headstones. It is firmly carved: "Erected by John Dougherty in memory of his brother Thomas Dougherty." [note: Sidney Hill is near Weaverville. No other record of the death of Thomas Dougherty has been found].

DOWELLS, GEORGE M. Died Eureka, Humboldt Co. Aug. 25, 1869; late of Weaverville; no age given. (TJ Sat. Sept. 4, 1869 p 3). [Not in 1860 census].

DOWLING, MICHAEL. Drowned in his mining claim near Trinity Center Jan. 18, 1866, aged 33 yr. "San Francisco papers please copy." (TJ Sat. Feb. 3, 1866).

DOWLING, MICHAEL. "Died abt Jan. 1868; probate filed Feb. 9, 1868 Probate Book C page 239."

DOWLY, or **Dovely, JAMES.** Probate filed Apr. 30, 1855 Probate Book A p 55. [no further information].

DOWN, MARY S., Mrs. Died at Prairie Cottage, Clark County, Missouri Sept. 6, 1864, aged 54 years. Mother of Mrs. Dr. Thomas of Weaverville. (TJ Sat. Oct. 29, 1864 p 2). [Note: R. A. Thomas, physician to German Hospital, office at the Weaverville Drug Store. (adv)]

DOXEY, HENRY. Died Santa Cruz, [Santa Cruz Co.] Calif. Jan. 28, 1880 in 80th year; former res. Trinity County; came U.S. 1828; Ohio, married 1834; daughter, Mrs. C. D. Holbrook, born Ohio; moved to Beloit, Wisconsin; moved Weaverville 1853, Santa Cruz 1866; wife died 1869 (probably in Santa Cruz). (TJ Sat. Feb. 7, 1880 p 3). [see also Vincent].

DOZIER, JOHN B. Died Stuart's Fork (near Minersville) Jun 18, 1897, John B. Dozier of Redding, aged 19 yr 5 mo 18 dy; b. Dec 25, 1877 Solano Co, Calif; buried in Redding; (TJ June 26, 1897 p 3 col 2).

DRAKE, GEORGE. Died Weaverville Aug 13, 1897; b. County Mead, Ireland, abt 79 years ago; came to Trinity Co. 1854; m. in New York to Sarah Wilse, who joined him in Weaverville 1866; four children: Sylvester, William & James, now living in Colorado, and Francis, who d. in the Civil War, fighting for the Union in a New York regiment. Bur. Catholic Cem., Weaverville. (TJ Aug 14, 1897 p 2 & p 3 col 2).

DRIVER, JOHN R. Died near Junction City May 4, 1880; native of Scotland, aged 41 yr 3 mo. (no obit.) (TJ May 8, 1880 p 2). [Note: pronounced "Dreever"] [Trinity Co. Marriages Book H page 259: "Married at Canon City Dec. 11, 1872 by A. M. Rosborough, District Judge, John R. Driver and Miss Mary E. Gilzean."] [Mrs. Driver married 2) Geo. W. Leavitt in 1887].

DRIVER, WILLIE. Died near Berkeley, Alameda County, May 14, 1877, aged 3 yr 8 mo 7 days. Son of John R. and Mary E. Driver. (TJ Sat. May 26, 1877, p 2).

DUNCAN, ALFRED B. Died Hay Fork May 20, 1897, native of Arkansas (b. 1845), aged 47 yr 6 mo 13 dy; came to Calif. 1849 with parents; leaves 2 bro. R. L. Duncan, of Hayfork, John Duncan of Siskiyou Co.; 3 sisters, one in Idaho, 2 in Trinity County: Mrs. L. Shock of Hay Fork and Mrs. Emma Bragdon of Trinity Center, his wife and five children. (TJ May 29, 1897 pp 2 & 3).

DUNCAN, MAHALA. Died Hay Fork June 4, 1864, aged about 62 yr; wife of Charles G. Duncan. (TJ June 11, 1864 p 2).

DUNCAN, THOS. W. Died March 6, 1907 Hetten Valley, age 71; half-Indian; American; farmer; reported by L. P. Duncan, Sr. [Index to Deaths 1890-1908].

DUNCAN, VIOLA. Died Hettenchow Valley, Trinity County, Calif. Apr. 24, 1887 aged 2 yr and 13 days; daughter of L. P. and Mary Duncan. "Shasta County papers please copy". (TJ Sat. May 14, 1887).

DUNLAP, JAMES M., Dr. Died Hay Fork Dec. 27, 1874; native of Ohio, aged 41 years. (TJ Jan. 2, 1875). [Not in 1870 census.]

DUNN, E. C. Died August 1853; probate filed Aug. 22, 1853, probate book A page 31.

DURICK, J. R. Died Feb. 1, 1866 Shasta; native of Buffalo, NY aged about 40 yrs. (TJ Sat. Feb. 10, 1866).

DYER, MATTIE S. Died Douglas City March 23, 1860; late of Rockland City, Maine, aged 23 years; funeral at the Union Church, Weaverville, March 24, 1860; buried Weaverville cemetery; married "half a year"; no children. "Boston Journal and Portland Transcript please copy." (TJ Sat. March 31, 1860). (not married in Trinity County). [Note: Mrs. George Dyer; prob. married at Shasta; reference: TJ Oct. 12, 1889 p 1].

DYER, O. S. Died Hoboken (New River area), Trinity Co. July 4, 1894; native of Maine, aged abt 72 yr. (TJ Sat. July 28, 1894).

DYER, WILLIAM JOHN. Accidentally killed on Canon Creek Nov. 14, 1879, aged 46 years, native of New York. (TJ Nov. 22, 1879 p 2 & 3).

EARL, ALBERTO R. Died Douglas City Oct. 23, 1877; native of New York, aged 58 yr 10 mo; bur. Weaverville Masonic Cemetery; wife Maria dead; daughter Mrs. Underwood; (TJ Sat. Oct. 27, 1877 p 2; long obit. p 3). Probate Court Book D p 49. "Alberto Rudolpho Earl". (bur. I.O.O.F. Cem. Weav. marker 1976).

EASTMAN, CHARLES BROOKS. Drowned in Trinity River at Eastman's Crossing above Lewiston Feb. 26, 1881; born Bristol, New Hampshire Jan. 15, 1815; body not found; married in Charleston, South Carolina Jan. 11, 1841 to Miss Josephine Dellamote; she died Feb. 10, 1880. (TJ Mar 5 & 12, 1881).
1860 Census Trinity County, Calif. Lewiston page 7 #959, 6-10-1860: Eastman, Charles B., age 45, farmer, b. New Hampshire; Josephine, age 45, school teacher, b. S. Carolina; Mary J., age 16, student, b. Alabama; Elbridge G., age 8, b. Tennessee. (Son Elbridge in 1870, 1880 Census, Lewiston; not in 1900 Census.)

EASTMAN, HAGEN B. Died Eastman's ranch, Trinity River, Jan. 15, 1864, aged about 38 years; native of New Hampshire. (TJ Sat. Jan. 23, 1864 p 2). Probate filed March 6, 1866, Probate Book C page 172.

EASTMAN, JOSEPHINE DELLAMOTE. Died "Eastman's", Trinity County, Calif. Feb. 10, 1880, aged 71 years 8 months 16 days; native of Charleston, South Carolina. Wife of Charles B. Eastman. (TJ Sat. Feb. 14, 1880).

EDDINGER, F. G. Died Cottonwood (Shasta Co.) June 15, 1894; bur. "Potters Field", Redding; citizens of Cottonwood refused him burial at Cottonwood; (killed E. W. Jose). (TJ Jun 16, 1894 p 3 col 4; Jun 23, 1894, pg 3 col 2). [see also Jose].

EDDY, ALEX. Died Jan. 30, 1865; (no place given; Calif.) formerly of Weaverville. (TJ Sat. Feb. 11, 1865). (Not in 1860 Census).

EDDY, J. F. Died Red Bluff, Tehama Co. May 2, 1864; formerly of Weaverville; no age given. (TJ Sat. May 21, 1864 p 2). (Not in 1860 Census).

EDGAR, ORDELIA E. Died Hyampom Apr. 4, 1893, aged 12 yr 9 mo 15 days; daughter of Mr. and Mrs. S. Edgar; bur. Hyampom Thurs. Apr. 6, 1893. (TJ Sat. Apr. 15, 1893). 1880 Census: Edgar, Sydney, Hyampom, 6-17-1880 pg 14; age 48, stockraiser, b. NY; fa Vermont; mo Scotland; Ellen (Indian) age 30, b. CA; Elizabeth, age 8, b. CA; Lewis, age 6, b. CA; Nancy, age 3, b. CA.

EDGECOMBE, JAMES. Died Aug. 12, 1873 Weaverville; native of Massachusetts, aged 45 years. Masonic funeral; buried F. & A.M. Cem. Weaverville Aug. 12, 1873; member Trinity Lodge #27, Weaverville. (TJ Sat. Aug. 16, 1873 p 2). Probate filed Nov. 8, 1873, County Court Book C page 378. [Index to Deaths 1873 - 1890: adds saloonkeeper; white, age 45, male, single].

EDWARDS, F. T. Died July 2, 1858 Weaverville; age 34; formerly of Jackson, Mississippi; "Jackson, Miss. papers please copy". (TJ Sat. July 10, 1858 p 2). Probate filed July 10 1858, Probate Book B p. 81.

EGAN, ELIZA JANE, Mrs. Died Sept. 14, 1860 Milltown (later Junction City), aged about 35 years. (TJ Sat. Sept. 15, 1860 p 2). Probate filed Nov. 10, 1860, probate book B p 175. 1860 Census, Trinity Co. Calif., mouth of Canon Creek, page 59 #1011, 7-24-1860: Egan, Eliza Jane, age 40, b. Ireland; Mary E., age 2, b. Calif. (Not in Trinity Co. Marriages; dau. not in 1870 census).

EGAN, ELLEN. "alias Jenny Miller". Died abt Oct. 1861, prob. Weaverville. Probate filed Oct. 19, 1861, probate Book B page 263.

EHRMAN, GEORGE H. Died March 31, 1908 Lewiston, age 75; born Germany; butcher; buried Lewiston. [Index to Deaths 1890-1908].

EHRMAN, LENA. Died Mar. 25, 1870 Junction City, Trin. Co., daughter of H. and C. Ehrman, aged 20 months. (TJ Apr. 2, 1870 p 2). [Parents: Henry Ehrmann and Miss

Kathrina Bellig, m. June 27, 1863, North Fork, Trinity County. Trinity Co. Marriages, Book H pg 92.]

"ELBRIDGE". Should be CLAYTON, ELBRIDGE. Died Clayton's Ranch on Trinity River, near Lewiston, aged about 1 yr 9 mo. Son of George H. and Mary Clayton; youngest child. Bur. Weav. Cem. Aug. 10, 1883. (TJ Aug. 1883).

ELIASEN, MATHILDE O., Mrs. Died Weaverville Aug 4, 1899; b. Christiania, Norway Jan 26, 1844, aged abt 57 yr; m.n. Iverson; m. 1864 in Christiania the late P. G. Eliasen; came with him to Trinity Co. 1879; fun. Aug 5, 1899; bur. Weaverville Cem. (TJ Aug 12, 1899 p 2; Aug 19, 1899 p 3 col 2).

ELIASEN, PETER GOTFRIED. Died Steiners Flat near Douglas City Oct 11, 1897; b. Christiansand, Norway Jun 18, 1840, aged 57 yr 3 mo 23 dy; m. Matilda O. Iversen Oct 26, 1864 in Christiania (Oslo); came to Trinity Co. July 10, 1874; bur. I.O.O.F. Cem. Weaverville. (TJ Oct 16, 1897 pp 2-3).

ELIGH, JAMES. Died Oct 12, 1900, age 89 yr; b. Canada. (TJ Jan 1901).

ELLERY, JAMES. Died Aug. 27, 1876 near French Gulch, Shasta County; native of England, aged 41 years. (TJ Sept. 2, 1876 p 2). Probate filed Sept. 7, 1876, Probate Court Book D p 31 lists minor children: Elias Ellery and Levi James Ellery. Richard Clifford appointed guardian Sept. 26, 1876, Probate Court Book D p 33.

ELLIS, JOHN, Mr. and Mrs. Drowned in Cow Creek near Millville, Shasta County, Dec. 10, 1881. "Mr. and Mrs. John Ellis and team." (TJ Sat. Dec. 17, 1881 p 3). (Not in 1880 Census Trinity County).

ELLISTON INFANT. Died Apr. 23, 1908 Weaverville; age 3 days; male, white, born Calif; bur. Weaverville; reported by Wm. P. Elliston. [Index to Deaths 1890-1908].

ELSASSER, L. Died Mar. 30, 1867 New York City in the 80th year of his age; father of M. L. Elsasser of Weaverville. (TJ Sat. Apr. 13, 1867 p 2). (No Elsasser in 1870 census).

ELSON, ASA. Died Cinnabar (Trinity County) Feb 5, 1895; native of Illinois, aged about 60 yr. (TJ Sat. Mar 9, 1895).

ELTON, DAVID. Found dead in his drift on Canyon Creek Tues. Aug. 11, 1868; aged 40 years; native of Dutchess County, N.Y. Bur. Aug. 12, 1868. (TJ Sat. Aug. 15, 1868 p 2 col 1).

ELYEA, JACOB. Died Mar. 9, 1860 Stockton, San Joaquin Co., Calif; no age given. (TJ Sat. Mar. 17, 1860 p 2).

ENFIELD, THOMAS. Died Apr. 12, 1866, Forks of New River, Trinity County; native of England, aged about 45 yr. (TJ Apr. 21, 1866 p 2).

ENGASSER, ANTONIO . Drowned Dec. 3, 1861 "in attempting to cross the North Fork of Trinity River in a small boat. He was a German, and had lived at Rattlesnake." (TJ Dec. 14, 1861 p 2). 1860 Census, Rattlesnake (New River area), Trinity Co. Calif. pg 77 # 1029, 8-4-1860, Engasser, Antone, age 27, miner, b. France. Also, Engasser, Gallus, age 19, b. France. Gallus Engasser not in 1870 Census.

ENOS, LOUISA. Died Feb. 24, 1873 Indian Creek; age 1 yr 10 mo 15 days; female; single; born U.S. [Index to Deaths 1873 - 1890].

ENOS, MANUEL. Died Douglas City Aug. 4, 1878 aged 4 years; son of Joseph and Maria Enos. (TJ Aug. 10, 1878 p 2).

EPLER, CYRUS K. Died Sept. 3, 1873 Canyon City, Oregon; buried by I.O.O.F.; formerly of The Dalles; former resident of Weaverville.

ERICKSON, GEORGE. Murdered on Mad River Sept. 7, 1886; born Norway; no age given. (TJ Sept. 11, 18, 1886; Oct. 30, 1886ff). 1880 Census, Trinity County, Calif., Hettenchow, page 15, 6-19-1880: Erickson, George, age 32, married, sheepman, b. Norway; Dena, age 19, mar. b. Wisconsin.

ERSKINE, GEORGIE. Died Feb. 4, 1865 Steiners Flat, Trinity County, aged 2 yr 8 mo 18 days; son of Abial and Hattie J. Erskine. "Portland and Augusta, Maine papers please copy." (TJ Feb. 11, 1865).

ERSKINE, _____, Miss. Died Nelson's Station in Butte County, abt Nov. 1877, age 18 years. Daughter of Abial and Harriet J. Erskine. (TJ Nov. 24, 1877 p 3). Not in 1870 Census. 1860 Census says "female child, no name, age 1".

ESPERON, LOUIS. Died Coleridge (near Helena) Mar. 31, 1893; native of Cannes, France, aged about 69 yr; pioneer of Trinity Co. "Humboldt and Siskiyou papers please copy". (TJ Sat. Apr. 8, 1893).

ESSICK, BELTY. Died Weaverville Nov 12, 1894; native of Penn, aged about 67 yr; came to Calif in early days; miner, worked for Hupp & McMurry; never married; bur. Nov 13, 1894 with F. & A.M. ceremonies; also member of the Old Settlers Asso. (TJ Nov 17, 1894 pp 2 & 3). (First registered to vote in 1866, age 40.)

ESTES, _____. Died Nov. 11, 1879 Weaverville, infant son of Mr. and Mrs. John M. Estes. (TJ Sat. Nov. 15, 1879 p 2).

ESTES, HARRIET N. Died suddenly at Douglas City Aug. 27, 1861, aged nearly 38 years; wife of Wm. C. Estes. (DCG Aug. 28, 1861; TJ Aug. 31, 1861).

ESTES, JOHNNIE T. Died Douglas City Oct. 4, 1875 aged 7 yr 11 mo 20 days; son of Mr. and Mrs. John Estes. (TJ Oct. 9, 1875 p 2 & 3).

ESTES, KATE M. Drowned at Douglas City June 17, 1861; youngest daughter of John M. and Eliza Estes, aged 2 yr 2 mo 2 days. (DCG June 19, 1861; TJ Sat. June 22, 1861 p 2 adds: "buried Weaverville Cemetery Tues. June 19, 1861; drowned same place as Willie Hough last year.") [see also Hough.]

ESTES, LILLIE M. Died Douglas City Sept. 21, 1875 aged 10 yr 7 mo 21 days; daughter of Mr. and Mrs. J. M. Estes. (TJ Sat. Sept. 25, 1875).

ESTES, WILLIAM C. Died at Douglas City Aug. 1, 1886; born July 10, 1810 Kentucky, aged 76 years 9 days. Bur. Tues. Aug. 3, 1886 (prob. Weav. Cem.); Came to Calif. from Missouri in 1850, arrived March 10, 1851 in Trinity County with son John M. Estes. Late County Clerk of Trinity, now a resident of Redding. He leaves his widow, son John Estes, and 2 daughters who live in Missouri. (TJ Aug. 1886). Estes Note: (TJ Sat. Oct. 16, 1886): "Left us - Mrs. Hannah Estes, widow of the late W. C. Estes of Douglas City, left on Monday's stage for Rohnerville, Humboldt County, where she will reside in future. She will make her home with her daughter Mrs. Thos. Middleton."

ESTES, WILLIE C. Died Douglas City Oct. 6, 1875 aged 4 yr 2 mo; son of Mr. and Mrs. John M. Estes; scarlet fever; "3 children in 2 weeks". (TJ Oct. 9, 1875 p 2 & 3).

ESTES note: 1860 Census Trinity Co. Calif. Douglas City, page 29 #980, 6-28-1860: Estes, John M., 27, miner, b. Missouri; Mary Eliza, 21, b. New York; Emma Eliza, 3, b. Calif.; Catherine M., 1, b. Calif. 1870 Census, has John M., Eliza, Emma E., age 13; Ella K., age 8; Lillie M., age 5; John T., age 2.

ESTES marriages: "Married in Weaverville May 28, 1856 by Hon. Judge Pitzer, John M. Estes and Miss Elsie Turot (sic) (Tourot). Trin. Co. Marriages Book E (sic) p 640."

"Married in Weaverville July 18, 1859 by Hon. R. T. Miller, William C. Estes and Mrs. Harriet Breen, both of Kanaka Bar" (later Douglas City). Trin. Co. Marriages Book H page 168. [Harriet widow of John P. Breen].

"Married at Hay Fork Oct. 27, 1867 by Rev. George Childs, William C. Estes of Douglas City and Mrs. Hannah Cowen of Hay Fork". Trin. Co. Marriages Book H page 186.

ESTERLEE, _____, Dr. (dentist). Died March 9, 1869 Shasta, Shasta County; F. & A.M. transported remains to Red Bluff, Tehama County. (TJ Mar. 13, 1869 p 3).

EVANS, DAVID. Died Red Hill (near Junction City) Sept. 7, 1892; native of Wales, aged about 76 years; came to Calif. from Australia, Trinity County "early in 1850"; former partnership with Mr. C. H. Bartlett in mining which lasted for nearly 35 years. Mr. Evans bought Mr. Bartlett's interests in mines, water rights and ditches when Mr. Bartlett died in 1887; family moved to Alameda. Bur. Thurs. Sept. 8, 1892 at 2:30PM at Red Hill, in a spot which we understand was selected by himself. Mr. Evans was a man of kindly instincts, but eccentric in many respects. He employed white labor only, and always paid as good wages as were going. He never married; no known living relatives. (TJ Sat. Sept. 10, 1892 p 2 & 3).

Lone grave near lake at Junction City, CA; private property; grave marker in excellent condition June 23, 1978: "David Evans, born Sept. 24, 1816; died Sept. 7, 1892; native of Wales. `As you are now once was I; As I am now you soon shall be; Now you prepare and follow me.'"

EVANS, JAMES. Died May 24, 1860 at Chellis' Mill, Trinity County; of West Middlebury, Ohio, aged 30 years. (TJ Sat. May 26, 1860).

EVANS, JOSEPH. Died Redding, Shasta Co. Aug 1898; of Minersville; only known relative: bro. W. H. Evans of Lincoln, Illinois. (Redding *Searchlight* Aug 9, 1898). (TJ Aug 13, 1898 p 3 col 3).
Everhart: see Masterson.
EWING, JOSEPH. Died Hay Fork Mar. 8, 1877, aged 55 yr, native of Scotland. (TJ Mar. 10, 1877 p 2 & 3). Trinity Co. Wills A 1851-1877, p 114; executed at Hay Fork 14 Oct 1874; filed and recorded Apr. 5, 1877; wife Henrietta Ewing executor, and receives property. [Note: had hotel in Weaverville until fire of 1855; moved to Hay Fork, farmed on Big Creek.]
EWING, HENRIETTA (Gibson). Died Eureka, Humboldt Co., CA Apr. 5, 1910, age 83 years. Mausoleum in Eureka has "Henrietta Ewing 1827-1910" (photo courtesy of Allen Campbell 1995). See also Emma E. Walker 1854-1941 in next crypt. Known as "the first lady of Weaverville".
EWING, MARGARET J. Died Hay Fork May 13, 1876, age 24, dau. of Joseph Ewing. "Maggie, the pioneer baby of Weaverville, if not of Trinity County, born 1851". (TJ May 20, 1876 p 2 & 3).
EWING, _____. Son, born Hay Fork Nov. 25, 1856 to Joseph and Henrietta Ewing; died a few days before Jan. 30, 1858. (TJ Dec. 1856, Feb. 1858). (Also a daughter, Emma, b. 1854).
FADER, CHRISTIAN E. Died Oct. 27, 1872 Trinity Center, aged about 41 yr; native of Nova Scotia. (TJ Nov. 2, 1872). Probate filed Oct. 31, 1872 County Court Book (B?) page 327.
FADER, FRANK CHRISTIAN. Died Oct. 9, 1863 St. Andrews, New Brunswick, aged 5 mo. Son of Christian and Anne K. H. Fader. (TJ Sat. Dec. 12, 1863 p 2).
FADER, JOSEPH. Died Aug. 11, 1865, Pioneer City, Idaho Territory, aged 25 years; native of Robbinston, Maine. "Maine papers please copy." (TJ Sept. 9, 1865 p 2).
FAGG, LILY. Died July 8, 1858 Weaverville, aged 2 yr 6 mo; buried Weaverville Cem; procession from residence of parents at Faggtown (Mill Street at Main Street, Weaverville). (TJ July 10, 1858 p 2). [Note: stone still legible in 1984].
FAGG, R. A. Died July 23, 1874, Gold Hill, Nevada; native of Ohio; aged 50 years. Pioneer of Trinity County. (TJ Sat. Aug. 1, 1874). [Partner in the City Drug Store, 1850s; "Faggtown" area of Weaverville named for him. Faggtown was the area on Main Street between the J. J. Jackson Museum and East Weaver Creek, and Mill Street, from Main Street to Weaver Creek, where East and West Weaver Creeks come together. The Forty-Niner Motel occupied the site of Fagg's residence in 1998. See also Frost].
FAKES, LEROY POPE. Died Dedrick June 4, 1893; native of Tenn. aged about 72 yr; story about Fakes p 3 col 4. (TJ Sat. June 10, 1893 p 2).
FARMER, WILLIAM. Died Hay Fork Apr 29, 1895; aged 70 yr 1 mo 19 dy; b. Hamilton Co., Ohio 1825; came to Weaverville 1853, Hay Fork 1856; m. Miss Bellzora Kester in Weaverville 1862 (she was a native of Salem Co., Missouri); 3 children: Charles H., George H., and William G. Farmer. (TJ Sat. May 11, 1895 p 2 & p 3 col 2). [see also Kester.]
FARRALMANN, JOHANN. Died near Douglas City abt Jan. 12, 1890, native of Bremen, aged about 64; Crushed by snow; roof collapsed on him; came to California and Trinity County 1856. (TJ Feb. 1, 1890). [Index to Deaths 1873-1890: died Jan. 12, 1890; white, 65; male, single; born Germany].
FARRELLY, _____, Rev. Father. Died Red Bluff, Tehama Co. abt Jan. 20, 1877. (TJ Sat. Jan. 20, 1877).
FARTADO, MANUEL CASCO. Died Lewiston May 28, 1887; native of Azores Islands, aged 41 yr 7 mo; res. Trinity Co. 14 years; leaves one sister and 3 brothers in Trinity Co.; others in Azores Islands; nephew of Mr. Manual Grant and Mr. Michael Joseph of Indian Creek. (TJ Sat. June 4, 1887).
FASSEN, _____. "A Frenchman by the name of Fassen was drowned in the Trinity River near Cox's Bar on Friday Feb. 2, 1855. (TT Feb. 10, 1855 p 2).
FECTEAU, MARY. Died Red Hill (near Junction City) Aug. 16, 1874, aged 1 yr 10 mo 7 days; dau. of Peter and Adez Fecteau. (TJ Aug. 22, 1874).
FEENATY, EDWIN. Died Hydesville, Humboldt Co. Nov. 4, 1885, age 18; son of Mr. and Mrs. H. Feenaty, formerly of Hay Fork. (TJ Sat. Nov. 21, 1885).

FEENATY, JOHN HIRAM. Died Nov. 30, 1873 Hay Fork, age 2 yr 1 mo 22 days; b. Calif. [Index to Deaths 1873-1890]. Son of Henry and Hiza M. Feenaty. (TJ Dec. 6, 1873). (b. Oct. 9, 1871, Weaverville TJ Oct. 14, 1871).

FEENY, RICHARD HENRY. Died French Gulch, Shasta Co., Feb 7, 1899; b. Dec. 11, 1825 Westmeath, Ireland; m. Weaverville Aug 1875 Sarah Doole, niece of Mrs. Sarah Carr; former partner of late James E. Carr; lived Carrville for a number of years; bur. French Gulch Cem. (TJ Feb 11, 1899 p 3 col 2). [see also Carr].

FELCH, ANNA LUCINDA. Died Dec. 6, 1861, age 4 yr 6 mo; daughter of Horace and Cornelia Felch. Trinity Center Cem., Trinity Co. Calif. Stone legible Nov. 1976.

FELIX, ANTONE. Died Jun 10, 1900; age 35 yr; b. Portugal. (TJ Jan 1901).

FELTER, FRANKLIN. Died Oregon Gulch (between Weaverville and Junction City) Aug. 2, 1858; infant son of A. J. and Mary Felter. (TJ Sat. Aug. 7, 1858 p 2 col 1).

FELTER, LAWRENCE. Died San Bernardino Feb. 8, 1875, aged 15 yr 1 mo 20 days; son of A. J. and Mary W. Felter.

FEOUR, MACIE J. Died Apr. 19, 1880 "Eastman's" (Eastman's Ranch, near Lewiston), aged 25 yr 10 mo 10 days; native of Wisconsin; wife of James C. Feour, m. June 1879; father: Mr. John Dack; sister Mrs. O. E. Lowden; bur. Weaverville Cem. next to mother. (TJ Apr. 24, 1880 p 2 & 3).

FERNANDE, _____. Probate filed Oct. 11, 1852 Book A page 17. [not on 1852 census; no further information].

FERNIOUGH, WILLIAM. Died Weaverville Aug 23, 1897; native of New York aged about 52 yr; bur. Weaverville Cem. (TJ Aug 28, 1897, pp 2-3).

FERRY, BARNEY C. Shot and killed near Trinity Center Nov. 4, 1892; native of Vermont, aged about 53 yr; of Etna, Siskiyou Co. (TJ Sat. Nov. 12, 1892; p 3 col 2,4). Bur. Trinity Center Cem., Trinity Co. Calif. Legible marker Nov. 1976.

FIELDS, J. N. Died Oct 18, 1900; age 85 yr 9 mo 6 dy; b. Michigan. (TJ Jan 1901).

FINLEY, JOSEPH W. Died Yale College, Connecticut; native of Calloway County, Missouri, aged about 29 yr; late a resident of Weaverville. No date, but abt Feb. 1863. (TJ Sat. Feb. 28, 1863 p 2).

FISCHER, C. F. W. Died Canon Creek Dec. 4, 1902; aged 61; native of Switzerland. (TJ Dec. 13, 1902).

FISH, I. B., Rev. Died last week (1st week of Jan. 1885) at Watsonville, Santa Cruz Co., aged 60 years. "Last resident Protestant Minister at Weaverville, ME (Methodist-Episcopal) Church." (TJ Sat. Jan. 10, 1885 p 3).

FISH, JOHN. Died Mar. 1, 1873 Burnt Ranch; native of New Jersey, aged 41 yr. Came from Humboldt County; raised in Penn.; served in Army 5 years; served aboard a Man of War 3 yr 8 mo. (TJ Mar. 1873). [d. McWhorters Ranch; Index to Deaths 1873-1890].

FISHER, DAVID. Died Dec. 8, 1875 Washington, Iowa, aged 75 years; father of J. S., J.H., and T.S. Fisher, of Trinity County. (TJ Sat. Feb. 12, 1876 p 2).

FISHER, JAMES GUILD. Died Jan. 6, 1867 Canyon City, aged 38 yr 8 mo 1 day; native of Tennessee; came to Canyon Creek 1852; leaves wife and four children. "Tennessee & Missouri papers please copy." (TJ Jan. 12, 1867 p 2). Probate filed Jan. 16, 1867 Probate Book C page 205. [1860 Census Trinity Co. Calif. pg 60 #1012, 7-24-1860: Fisher, James Guild, age 32, miner, b. Tenn.; Sarah E., 20, b. Missouri; J. E. (male) age 1 b. Calif; family not in 1870 Census].

FISHER, JAMES HARVEY. Died May 22, 1896 Junction City; b. near Portersville, Butler Co., Penn 1832; aged abt 64 yr; came to Calif. 1852, Trinity Co. 1859; family had 11 sons, no daughters; two married; 3 survive him: John Fisher, Junction City (oldest); Robert Fisher, Washington, Iowa; David Fisher, Butte City, Montana. Bur. Masonic Cem., Weaverville Sun. June 1, 1896, by the side of late brother "Potter". (TJ Sat. May 30, 1896 pp 2-3.) (see also Thomas S. Fisher and John S. Fisher).

FISHER, JEREMIAH. Died Mar. 9, 1866, North Fork, aged about 70 yr; native of Tennessee, late of Missouri. (TJ Sat. Mar. 17, 1866 p 2).

FISHER, JAMES H. June 1832-May 23, 1895. "Aged 64 yr Native of Portersville, Butler, Penn." [Grave marker F. & A.M. Cem., Weaverville; legible 1976.]

FISHER, JOHN S. Died Mar. 20, 1906 Weav., age 85; miner; bur. Weaverville. [Index to Deaths 1889-1908].

FISHER, SARAH L. Died July 24, 1869 North Fork, age 6 yr 2 mo; dau. of J. M. and N. A. Fisher. (TJ July 31, 1869 p 2). [1860 census, Canon Creek, pg 60 #1012,

7-24-1860 says: Fisher, James Morgan, 38, miner, b. Tenn.; Nancy A. age 17, b. Missouri.]

FISHER, THOMAS S. Died Mar. 22, 1877 at residence on Court St., Weaverville; native of Butler Co., Penn, aged 39 yr; fun. Sat. Mar. 24, 1877; bur. Weaverville Cem. Brothers John S. and James H. Fisher of Arkansas Dam. (TJ Mar. 24, 1877; see also Mar. 14, 1862, for story about T. S. Fisher, known as "Potter Fisher".) Bur. F. & A.M. Cem. Weaverville; "native of Portersville, Butler Co., Penn." Legible marker 1976 "Potter S. Fisher". Buried next to John Hagelman. James H. Fisher has next plot.

FITCH, _____. Died May 29, 1866 Trinity Center; infant daughter of Horace Y. and Cornelia Fitch. (TJ Sat. June 9, 1866 p 2). [Names of parents from 1860 census].

FITCH, CORNELIA E. Died Aug. 23, 1871 San Francisco, aged 39 yr 8 mo 20 days; wife of H. Y. Fitch, formerly of Trinity Center. (TJ Sept. 2, 1871).

FITZGERALD, PATRICK. Died Lewiston Jan. 6, 1888, native County Cork, Ireland, aged about 67 years. (TJ Sat. Jan. 14, 1888).

FLAGG, A. A. (see also Cunningham). [Amasa Artemus Flagg; d. 1932; see Deaths 1900-1950.]

FLAGG, EBEN. Died at Belmont, Maine Oct. 30, 1891, aged about 83. Deceased was the father of J. R., A. A., and E. S. Flagg of Trinity County. (TJ Sat. Nov. 14, 1891 p 3 col 1). [Note: the 1890 Great Register of Voters gives the following names: Jacob Redding Flagg, Weaverville; Amasa Artemus Flagg, Junction City; Eben Sauze Flagg, Weaverville.]

FLAGG, JAMES H. Died at You Bet, Nevada Co., Calif. Feb. 16, 1884; native of Maine, aged 50 yr 3 mo 16 days; res. Nevada County nearly 25 years. Brother of J. R. and E. S. Flagg of Weaverville, and A. A. Flagg of Oregon Gulch. (TJ Sat. Feb. 23, 1884).

FLAGG, J. R. [see also Mills].

FLAGG, WILLIAM. Died Dec. 30, 1903 Junction City; age 18, born Calif; bur. Public Cem. Weaverville. [Index to Deaths 1890-1908]. [1900 Census lists William as son of Amasa Artemus Flagg & Fedelia Flagg, of Junction City; William was born Aug 24, 1885 at Oregon Gulch.]

FLESHMAN, G. F. Died at his home in Bear Valley, San Diego Co., Apr. 6, 1892, aged 64; former resident of Lewiston, Trinity Co; left with family about 1875. *Escondido Times*. (TJ Sat. Apr. 23, 1892).

FLINN, BENJAMIN FRANKLIN. Died Weaverville Dec. 3, 1882; native Lexington, Kentucky, aged 63 yr. Known as "Doc Flynn" (sic). (TJ Sat. Dec. 9, 1882, p 2 & 3). [1880 Census, Trinity Co. Calif. Weaverville, page 11, 6-7-1880: Flinn, Benjamin Franklin, age 62, widowed, Dep. Co. Clerk, b. Kentucky, parents b. Virginia]. [Note: had son and daughter living in Iowa in May 1872; returned there for a visit after 20 years; returned soon to Trinity County. Wrote articles for the TRINITY JOURNAL under the pen name of "Jacinto".]

FLINN, HATTIE. Died at Clarksburg, Indiana "recently" (bef. Feb. 28, 1885), at home of parents; wife of L. M. Flinn of Lewiston. [not in 1880 Census]. [Note: married in Clarksburg, Indiana Aug. 15, 1881, Mr. L. M. Flinn to Miss Hattie M. Bartolet; returned to Lewiston this week. (TJ Sat. Aug. 27, 1881 p 3)].

FLLIGE (sic), ANTONE. Died June 10, 1900; native of Portugal. (TJ June 16, 1900.)

FLORAINCE, JOHN A. Died Weaverville Sept. 11, 1902, native of Nova Scotia, aged about 83 yr. (TJ Sept. 20, 1902).

FLORIAN, _____, Father. Died July 27, 1868 Marysville, Yuba Co., CA; native of Austria, aged 60 years. (TJ Aug. 8, 1868 p 2 & 3). [First Catholic Priest in Weaverville, known as "Father Florian". He was born Martin Schwenninger in 1809 at Innsbruck, the capitol of Tyrol. He arrived at New York 1844, San Francisco, Calif. Aug 1852 on the steamer Golden Gate. He was sent to Shasta, Shasta County at Pentecost, May 29, 1853, and left for Weaverville after Sep 20, 1853. Father Florian left Weaverville in Feb 1857, succeeded by Rev. Father John Ingolsby. (see also Satorius, Veronica, Between the Lines, pp 1 & 6, and TJ Feb 28, 1857, Mar 21, 1857.) Trinity County Land Claims Index 1851-1866 and Deeds Book D page 623, dated Dec 27, 1854 has a "claim of lot in Weaverville occupied by Catholic Church; Fr. Florian Schweininger, agent for

Archbishop Alemani of San Francisco, claims a town lot lying and being in the town of Weaverville and on the Court House Hill and south of the same, being the lot on which the Catholic Church now stands."]

FLOWERS, _____. Died Dec 21, 1900; inf. son of Mr. and Mrs. Wm. Flowers, age 1 mo 7 dy; b. Calif. (TJ Jan 1901).

FLOWERS, ELLIS. Died Canon Creek Jan. 20, 1893; born Georgetown, Brown Co., Ohio Dec. 19, 1828, aged 64 yr 1 mo 1 day; bur. Jan. 22, 1893 Masonic Cem. Weaverville; came to Calif. 1852, Trinity Co. 1853; m. Miss Amanda M. Frey 1862, prob. in Ohio; 8 children; full column obit. p 3 col 2. (TJ Sat. Jan. 28, 1893).

FLOWERS, ELLSWORTH. Died Aug. 6, 1870 Canon City, aged 7 years; eldest son of Ellis and Amanda Flowers. (TJ Aug. 13, 1870). [Name of mother from 1870 census.]

FLOWERS, NELLIE F., Miss. Died at Napa City, Napa Co., Cal. July 14, 1887, aged 20 yr 8 mo 21 days; daughter of Ellis and Amanda M. Flowers. (TJ Sat. July 23, 1887).

FLOWERS, WM. F., Mrs. Died San Francisco Jan 2, 1897; b. Junction City Apr 30, 1875, dau. of Mr. and Mrs. W. C. Given, Miss Carrie E. Given; became a teacher 1893, taught in the Red Hill School; m. two weeks ago; bur. Foresters Cem. Junction City. (TJ Jan 9, 1897 p 3).

FLYNN, JOHN. Died Weaverville Sept. 6, 1855, age 32. Rev. P. Florian conducted Catholic burial service. (TT Sept. 8, 1855).

FOGARTY, EDWARD. Died Nov. 11, 1866 Louisville, KY, age 41 yr; formerly of Weaverville. (TJ Sat. Dec. 29, 1866 p 2).

FOGG, EDWIN. Died Dec. 19, 1864 Douglas City, aged 5 mo 14 days; son of Calvin P. and Lizzie C. Fogg. (TJ Sat. Dec. 24, 1864). [Note: "Married at Smith's Flat (near Douglas City) on July 3, 1861 by M. W. Personette, J.P., Mr. Calvin P. Fogg to Miss Elizabeth C. Hood, both of Smith's Flat. Maine and Missouri papers please copy." (DCG July 10, 1861).

FOLEY, DAVID. Died Weaverville May 20, 1897; native of Ireland, aged abt 65 yr; b. abt 1832; became US citizen 1854 in New York City; unmarried; fun. May 22, 1897. (TJ May 22, 1897 pp 2-3).

FOLEY, THOMAS. Died Feb. 10, 1908 Weaverville; age 85; b. Ireland. Trinity Co. [Index to Deaths 1889-1908]. Came US 1841, settling in Boston where later he was married; came to Calif. 1852, later to Trinity; Mrs. Foley joined him in Weaverville, returned East where she died about 10 years ago; miner; bur. Catholic Cem. Weaverville Feb. 12, 1908. (TJ Feb. 15, 1908).

FOLLANSBEE, JOHN S. Died Nov. 26, 1875 San Francisco, aged 52 years; formerly of Shasta. (TJ Dec. 4, 1875 p 2).

FORAN, C. J., aka "Happy Jack" Died June 27, 1877 at James Howe's place in Shasta County; (no age given); went to Shasta County over a year ago from Canyon City. (TJ June 30, 1877 p 3). [Not in 1860 or 1870 census].

FORBES, GEO. D. Died Jan. 5, 1867 Shasta, [Shasta Co.] aged 34 yr. (TJ Jan. 19, 1867 p 2).

FORD, BRIDGET. Died Aug. 14, 1867 Weaverville, age 38 yr; wife of Bartholomew Ford. Bur. Catholic Cem. Weaverville. (TJ Aug. 17, 1867 p 2). Grave stone Cath. Cem. "Bridget O'Brien, wife of Bartholomew Ford, d. Aug. 12, 1867 aged 38 yr." legible 1980.

FORSYTH, BOB. Died May 12, 1873 Virginia City, Nevada, aged 47 yr; formerly of Weaverville; native of Elizabethtown, New Jersey; leaves mother, aged 72, 2 sisters and a brother in Elizabethtown, N.J. (TJ Sat. May 17, 1873 p 3).

FORT, SPEAR. Died Jan. 16, 1871 Arcata, Humboldt Co., aged 39 yr. (TJ Sat. Jan. 28, 1871 p 2).

FOUNTAIN, THOMAS THOMSON. Died Weaverville Jan. 7, 1888, native of New York, aged about 53 yr. (TJ Jan. 14, 1888).

FOWLER, JOHN. Died July 29, 1863 Trinity Center; native of Hillsgate, Franklin Co., Vermont; came to Calif. from Princeton, Illinois. (no age given). (TJ Aug. 1, 1863 p 3). Not in 1860 census.

FOWLER, WILLIAM H. Died Red Bluff, Tehama Co. Jun 23, 1899; age abt 62 yr; lived in California since 1852. (TJ July 1, 1899 p 3 col 6).

FOX, ELIZABETH. Died March 28, 1908 Weaverville; age 75; female, born Ireland; bur. Weaverville. [Index to Deaths 1890-1908]. [widow of Orson.] b. Jan 15,

1833, in County Fermanagh, North Ireland, the dau. of William Irving and Luscinda Hetherington Johnston. Mother died in Ireland. Came to U.S. with father. Left New York on Sept 20, 1859 on the steamer, Star of the West, arriving in San Francisco Oct. 19, 1859; arrived in Weaverville 8 days later. Married Orson Fox Aug 15, 1861 in Weaverville; four daughters: Mrs. M. W. Loveridge of Victoria, B.C., Miss Elizabeth H. Fox, Miss Annie Fox, and Mrs. Isabella J. Tourtellotte of Weaverville, and one son, William O. Fox, of Los Angeles, and other relatives. (TJ Sat. Apr 4, 1908 page 3 col 2). [see also Johnston.]

FOX, HARRISON. Died French Gulch, Shasta Co. Feb 17, 1894; of French Gulch; res. of Lewiston for many years; b. Elkville, Jackson Co., Illinois Dec 23, 1832, aged 61 yr 1 mo 24 dy; came Trinity Co. 1860; left for French Gulch 1886; member Trinity Lodge No. 27, F. & A.M.; bur. French Gulch Dec 18, 1894; obit worth copying. (TJ Feb 24, 1894, pg 3 col 2).

FOX, ORSON. Died Weaverville March 15, 1897; born 31 Oct 1824 in Duffield, Conn.; aged 72 yr; obit. says he was buried next to his twin brother Oscar in the Weaverville Cemetery. He moved to Syracuse, New York in 1846; started for California in Jan.1849, arriving in California 26 May 1849. He arrived in Trinity County, CA March 1, 1851, one of the earliest of the Old Settlers; m. Miss Elizabeth Johnston in Aug. 1861. leaves 1 son, 4 dau. (TJ Mar 19, 1897). [see also TJ Sat. March 18, 1933 p 1 col 5.]

FOX, OSCAR. Died Feb. 20, 1872 Weaverville, aged about 47 yr; native of Connecticut. (TJ Feb. 24, 1872). [twin brother of Orson Fox].

FOX, SOLOMON. Died Aug. 4, 1907 Weaverville, age 43, born Ohio, miner. [Index to Deaths 1890-1908].

FOX, WILLIAM L. Died Weaverville Feb. 10, 1873; aged 64 yr; native of North Carolina. (TJ Sat. Feb. 15, 1873). [Bur. old section, Weaverville cem.] [Index to Deaths 1873-1890 has: died Feb. 10, 1873 Lewiston; grocery keeper; white; 64, male, married, born North Carolina.]

FRANCIS, EBENEZER. Died residence of brother in Hay Fork Valley Oct. 6, 1882; native of Missouri, aged 53 yr 5 mo 3 days. (TJ Dec. 14, 1882).

FRANCIS, JOSHUA JAMES. Died Weaverville Nov 14, 1896; native of England, aged abt 78 yr; came to US 1828, Calif 1849, Trin. Co. 1851 at Ca_on Creek; Weaverville 1882; bur. Nov. 15, 1896 Weav. Cem, "under auspices of the Old Settlers Assn." (TJ Sat. Nov 21, 1896).

FRANKLIN, JOHN. Died last week (May 1888) near Weaverville, aged about 55 years. Claimed to be a descendant of Benjamin Franklin. (TJ Sat. June 2, 1888 p 3 col 3, bottom).

FRANKS, ALPHEUS. Died Hyampom Dec. 3, 1881; native of Virginia, aged about 46 yr. (TJ Dec. 17 & 24, 1881).

FREETHY, ANNIE. Died French Gulch, Shasta Co. June 23, 1895; wife of R. Freethy; native of Calif. aged 31 yr 11 mo 6 dy. (TJ Sat July 6, 1895). [see also Bassham].

FREETHY, RICHARD ELLIS. Died Trinity Center Aug 23, 1898; native of England, aged about 43 yr; m. Miss Annie Bassham, dau. of late Mr. and Mrs. G. B. Bassham; bur. Trinity Center Cem. with I.O.O.F. ceremonies. (TJ Sep 3, 1898 pp 2 & 3).

FREITAS, ANNIE F., Mrs. Died Redding, Shasta Co. Apr 21, 1900; mother-in-law of Mrs. M. J. Freitas, nee' Rule, formerly of Weaverville. (TJ Apr 28, 1900 pg 3 col 2).

FRICK, CHRISTIAN. Died Apr 30, 1900; age 77 yr; b. New York. (TJ Jan 1901).

FRICK, CHRISTIAN, Mrs. Died Lewiston May 11, 1898; b. Schleswig-Holstein 1829, aged 69 yr 3 mo; Came to US age 17; m. Mr. Frick 1850; of 4 children, only Jesse Frick is now living; resided in Lewiston since 1853; bur. Redding Cem. (TJ May 21, 1898 p 2 & p 3 col 1).

FRICK, EDWARD C. Died Arlington, Oregon Feb. 14, 1888; bur. Weav. I.O.O.F. Cem. Mon. Feb. 20, 1888. Born Lewiston, Trinity Co. Calif. Aug. 3, 1860, son of Mr. and Mrs. Christian Frick of Lewiston; leaves parents and brother Jesse. (TJ Sat. Feb. 25, 1888 p 3).

FRICK, EMMA CALIFORNIA. Died Apr. 8, 1858 at Mud Valley (Lewiston), Trinity County, aged 1 yr 10 mo 8 days. (TJ Sat. Apr. 10, 1858 p 2). [Daughter of Christian and Caroline Frick, lived Grass Valley, in 1860 Census].

FRICK, CHARLEY. Died Mar. 8, 1866 "at Mud Valley ranch near Lewiston", aged 8 yr 4 mo 1 day; son of Christian and Caroline Frick. (TJ Sat. Mar. 10, 1866 p 2).
FRICK note: Eddie Frick, of Lewiston, graduated State University at Berkeley, Class of 1883. (TJ June 9, 1883 p 3).

FRATES, _____. Died Apr. 5, 1874 Steiners Flat (near Douglas City) aged 10 days; infant daughter of Jos. and Anna Frates. (TJ Apr. 11, 1874).

FRATUS, MARY. Died May 1, 1907, Indian Creek; age 42; b. Calif. Bur. Weaverville. [Index to Deaths 1889-1908].

FREY, FREDERICK. Died Feb. 23, 1908, Lowden's Ranch, about 83; b. Germany; bur. Lowden's ranch (near Lewiston). [Index to Deaths 1889-1908].
FREY note: Frederick Frey "Fritz", b. Jan. 13, 1825 Newstadt, Wurtenberg, Germany, d. Weaverville Feb. 24, 1908. Lucas Frey, b. 1822, Attenstadt, Wurtenberg, Germany, d. Dec. 3, 1894. "Buried on old Leas property, Lewiston, owned by Al Mills in 1979. Frederick's dates are on the Abstract of Title." (Marion Karch of Lewiston, Apr. 15, 1979).

FREY, LUCAS. Died Lowden Ranch (near Lewiston) Dec. 3, 1894; born Attenstadt, Wurtemburg, Germany, 1822; aged 71 yr 7 mo 10 dy; came US 1850; crossed the plains; arrived El Dorado Co. CA Sep 5, 1850; arrived Weaverville Sep 3, 1852; brother Fred Frey; younger brother died of cholera while crossing the plains. (TJ Dec 8, 1894, pp 2 & 3).

FRIEND, ASHBY. Died March 17, 1904 Hay Fork; age 19; b. Calif; rancher; buried Public Cem. Hayfork. [Index to Deaths 1890-1908].

FRIEND, HENRY W. Died Sept. 6, 1907 Hay Fork; age 66; born Missouri; rancher; buried Hay Fork.

FRIETAS, MANUEL. Died Monday Oct. 6, 1856 aged 25 yr; native of Portugal. "Killed at claim on Deadwood Creek by caving of a bank; partner James Sylvia injured; recently arrived in California from Boston, Mass." (TJ Sat. Oct. 11, 1856 p 2). [Note: Deadwood Creek empties into the Trinity River at Lewiston.]

FRONTA, LOUIS. Died Weaverville May 23, 1890; native of France, aged 72 yr; came Calif. from France 1849, Trin. Co. 1862; no relatives in U.S. (TJ May 24, 1890). [Index to Deaths 1890-1908 adds "single"].

FROST, GEO. F. Died Chico, Butte, Calif. July 3, 1887; native of Maine; no age given. One of early residents of Trinity County; blacksmith with Frank Trask; deceased left Trinity County abt 1867; leaves wife and 6 children. (TJ Sat. Aug. 20, 1887 p 3). [1860 Census Trinity Co. Calif. Weaverville, pg 111 #1063, 8-21-1860, age 27, blacksmith, b. Maine]. [Not married in Trinity County]. [see also Trask.]

FROST, NETTIE, Mrs. Died Reno, Nevada Dec 1, 1894; dau. of R. A. Fagg after whom Faggtown was named; born Weaverville, aged 36 yr 11 mo 22 days; leaves aged mother, husband, and 2 children. (TJ Sat Dec 16, 1894 p 3 col 4). [see also Fagg].

FRUTIGER, JACOB. Died Weaverville Apr. 11, 1887; native of County Bern, Switzerland, aged about 65 years. Came Calif. 1851, Sonora, Tuolumne Co.; to Trinity Co. 1856 at North Fork. Brother Samuel Frutiger d. Apr 7, 1887 Forest Home, Amador Co., Calif; lived Trinity County until about 1869. (TJ Sat. Apr. 16, 1887). [1860 census, Trinity Co., Calif. Canon Creek pg 66 #1018, 7-27-1860: Froetiger, Jacob, age 34, miner, b. Switzerland. Prob. the Jacob Fritinger at North Fork 8-3-1870, age 45, miner, b. Switzerland]. [1877 Great Register of Voters: **Froetinger**, Jacob, age 41, b. Switzerland, miner, North Fork, reg. June 8, 1867; naturalized Sept. 29, 1864 in Trinity County].

FRUTIGER, SAMUEL. Died Apr. 7, 1887 Forest Home, Amador Co. Calif. (see Jacob, above). (TJ Sat. Apr. 16, 1887).

FURTADO-CASEO, ANTONE. Died Lewiston Feb. 25, 1892; native of Azores Islands, aged about 19 years; bur. Catholic Cem. Weaverville Sun. Feb. 28, 1892. (TJ Feb. 27, 1892, Mar. 5, 1892, p 3 col 1).

GALL, ALEXANDER. Died Weaverville Jan 12, 1897; native of France, aged abt 49 yr. (TJ Jan 16, 1897 p 2).

GARCIA, ALVINO. Died Red Bluff, Tehama Co. Apr 17, 1896; native of Mexico, aged about 55 yr; horse fell upon him at Wildwood, Trinity Co; fun. Catholic Church, Red Bluff; leaves son George. (TJ May 2, 1896 p 3 col 2).

GARDINER, LOUIS. Died July 15, 1864 Weaverville, aged 10 weeks; son of William and Betty Gardiner. "Boise, Idaho City, News please copy." (TJ Sat. July 16, 1864 p 2).

GARDNER, CHRISTIAN. Died Lewiston Jul 2, 1897; native of Germany, aged abt 62 yr. (TJ Jul 10, 1897 p 2 & p 3 col 4).

GARDNER, WILLIAM. Died Apr. 11, 1870 "at the Warm Spring ranch, Alturas County, Idaho", a native of Bremer Haven, Germany, aged 42 yr; formerly of North Fork, Trinity County, CA; leaves a wife and three children to mourn his loss. (TJ June 4, 1870 p 2).

GARWOOD, JOHN L. Died May 26, 1869 Canyon Creek, age 37 yr; born Butler County, Ohio; came to California from near South Bend, Indiana; brother living at Canyon Creek. (TJ May 29, 1869 p 3).

GARWOOD, SOLOMON SCHLABACH. Died Weaverville June 24, 1888; native of Ohio, aged about 62 yr; bur. I.O.O.F. Cem. June 26, 1888. (TJ June 20, 1888).

GARRATY,-----. Died Oct. 10, 1858 Red Hill, Trinity River (near Junction City), aged about 25 years. (TJ Sat. Oct. 16, 1858 p 2). (no further information.)

GASS, PHILEMAN. Died Dec. 13, 1867 near Trinity Center, aged 62 yr; native of Massachusetts. (TJ Dec. 21, 1867 p 2).

GATES, AARON KELLUM. Died Weaverville Aug 3, 1895, aged 57 yr 8 mo 6 dy; native of New York; came Calif. 1852, Trinity Co. 1887, Weaverville 1893; m. August 1867 Miss Agnes F. Borges; leaves children: James, Mrs. Hattie Gilzean, Agnes, Aaron, Flora, Louis, and Birdie; served in Civil War, Company 1, California Volunteers; received a pension; bur. Weav. Cem. Aug 4, 1895. (TJ Aug 10, 1895 pp 2 & 3). [see also Gilzean.]

GATES, D. V. "Shot at Big Lake between Burnt Ranch and Hyampom Dec. 1877, aged about 36 years"; native of Wisconsin. (TJ Dec. 29, 1877 and Jan. 5, 1878 pages 3). "D. V. Gates, killed last month on Lower Trinity, has 2 cousins, Justin Gates and Dan Virgil Gates and a sister in Sacramento." (TJ Jan. 26, 1878).

GATES, KATE, Miss. Died Red Bluff, Tehama Co. Jan. 20, 1889, age 18 yr; prob. bur. Oak Hill Cem. Red Bluff; parents live Hay Fork, Trinity County; from *Red Bluff News* Jan. 26, 1889. (TJ Feb. 2, 1889).

GAUM, THEODORE. Died Nov. 30, 1868 Weaverville, aged 6 yr; son of Magdalena Gaum. (TJ Sat. Dec. 5, 1868 p 2).

GEGGIS, JOHN. "Died in the snow between Minersville and Trinity Center Jan. 20, 1872"; native of Baden, Germany, aged about 56 years. (TJ Feb. 3, 1872 p 2).

GEIGER, E. M. W., Mrs. Died San Francisco Jan. 27, 1893; of Weaverville; bur. San Francisco Jan. 29, 1893. Sister, Mrs. Henry Junkans of Weav., two nieces, Mrs. F. G. Haas of Junction City and Mrs. Robt. Berger of Anderson, and a bro. John Einfalt, of Gilroy. (TJ Sat. Feb. 4, 1893 p 3 col 2; no age given.) [not in 1880 census].

GEMMELL, ALEXANDER. No date; died Snow Gulch near Carrville, age 36; born Scotland; buried Trinity Center. [Index to Deaths 1890-1908].
Grave marker in Trinity Center Cemetery with John Doig. Trinity Journal Feb. 13, 1904 says "died Jan. 21, 1904; bur. Feb. 10, 1904 Trinity Center Cem."

GEMMILL, ROBERT J. Died Wildwood (nr Hayfork) Apr 17, 1899; native of Indiana aged abt 50 yr. (TJ May 20, 1899 p 2).

GENTRY, HENRY. Died March 25, 1903 Weaverville; age 36; American; caught in snow slide; body shipped to relatives in Indiana. [Index to Deaths 1890-1908].

GEORGE, BEMIAH MONROE. Died Hay Fork July 7, 1893; native of Vermont, aged about 78 yr; bur. Hayfork near his home. "Cox's Annals says that George went to Hay Fork in 1850". (TJ Sat. July 15, 1893). [1880 Census: farmer, single, parents b. Vermont].

GERARD, MARGUERITE. "a native of France, died at Gold Hill, Nevada Territory last week at age of 74 years." "Madame Marguerite", a resident of Weaverville for over 7 years in saloon and restaurant business. (TJ Jan. 2, 1864 p 2). (Died abt Dec. 1863).

GERAUGHTY, DANIEL. Died March 18, 1855 Weaverville; leaves wife and child in San Francisco; no age given. (TT Mar. 24, 1855).

GEULER, CHRISTIAN. Died Apr. 9, 1857 at claim of Owens & Dougherty on Sidney Hill (near Weaverville); I.O.O.F. services Apr. 10, 1857; bur. Weaverville Cem.; no age given (TJ Apr 11, 1857).

GIBSON, DAVID. Died Hydesville, Humboldt Co. July 3, 1885, aged about 60 years; leaves wife, 6 children, 2 sisters in Eureka; former resident Trinity County. (TJ July 4, 1885).

GIBSON, DAVID, "Wife and Eldest Daughter died within last 4 months (Sept. to Dec. 1885)." (From Rohnerville Herald; see TJ Jan. 9, 1886). "Mrs. Tydd, adopted daughter of late David Gibson and son Fred, age 5, drowned in Eel River, Humboldt Co. 1 April 1886; sister and nephew of Wm. Tromback of Rohnerville." (TJ Apr. 17, 1886).

GIBSON, MARY ELLEN. Died Apr. 16, 1863 Weaverville, aged 1 yr 9 mo 4 days; daughter of James B. and Margaret Gibson. (TJ Apr. 18, 1863).

GILBERT, WILLIAM. Died nr. Weaverville Mar 4, 1894; native of Arkansaw (sic), aged abt 46 yr; cook at LaGrange ditch camp; family in Vina, Tehama Co. (TJ Sat Mar 10, 1894 pp 2 & 3).

GILDAY,_____,Pvt. Drowned in the Trinity River at Fort Gaston, Humboldt County, May 20, 1864; native of Denegal, Ireland, aged 29 years. His body was recovered on May 25th; buried May 26, 1864 with military honors. Member of H Company, 2d Infantry, California Volunteers; enlisted at San Francisco. (TJ June 25, 1864).

GILLAN, JOHN. Died North Fork Dec. 1866; no age. (TJ Jan. 12, 1867).

GILLELAND, JACOB S. Died between Sept. 26-30 1905; age 62; buried at New River. (Denny area). [Index to Deaths 1890-1908].

GILLETT,_____, Mrs. Died in Eureka, Humboldt Co. Apr 21, 1896; wife of J. N. Gillett, Esq. (no age given). (TJ Sat. May 2, 1896 p 3 col 1).

GILZEAN,_____. Died Weaverville Jan 24, 1895, inf. son of Mr. and Mrs. C. E. Gilzean. (TJ Jan 26, 1895). [Trin. Co. Mar. Book I page 199: Married in Weaverville Feb. 13, 1894 by Judge T. E. Jones, Charles E. Gilzean and Miss Rebecca Harvey, both of Weaverville; Rebecca born Sept 1873 Calif; father England, mother Ohio].

GILZEAN, ALEXANDER. see Deaths 1900-1950; see also Gates.

GILZEAN, C. E., Mrs. [Born at Trinity Center Feb. 15, 1891 to the wife of C. E. Gilzean, a daughter.] Died at Trinity Center Feb. 15, 1891, native of California, aged 24 yr 10 mo 18 days. Trinity Center News: "buried at Trinity Center Cem. Feb. 17, 1891; she was the daughter of Mr. and Mrs. Ursher of Trinity Center." (TJ Sat. Feb. 21, 1891, pp 2 & 3). [Trinity County Marriages Book I page 108: Married at Trinity Center Feb. 24, 1889 by Judge T. E. Jones, Charles E. Gilzean and Miss Rose A. Ursher; Charles, b. March 13, 1863 at Canon City, residence Deadwood; Rose, age 23, native of California].

GILZEAN, ISABELLA. Died Canyon City Mar. 15, 1869 aged 7 yr 9 mo 10 days; daughter of James and Margaret Gilzean. Born May 1, 1861 Canon City. (TJ Sat. Mar. 20, 1869 p 2). [buried Canon City Cemetery with father and others.]

GILZEAN, JAMES. Died at Canon (Canyon) City June 28, 1891; native of Elgin, Morayshire, Scotland; aged 76 yr 9 mo 14 days; came to US age 17, to New Orleans, LA; married Miss Margaret Waldron 1848; settled on Canon (Canyon) Creek, Trinity County 1853. (TJ Sat. July 4, 1891, pp 2 & 3). [Note: buried in the Canon City Cemetery, near Junction City.]

GILZEAN, JAMES HENRY. Died April 28, 1902 Weaverville; age 45; American; miner; buried Weaverville. [Index to Deaths 1890-1908].

GILZEAN, MARGARET W. Died Oct. 29, 1905 Weaverville, age 77; born Ireland. Informant: Mrs. Mary E. Leavett. [Index to Deaths 1890-1905].

GILZEAN, MOLLIE A. Died Junction City, May 18, 1885; native of Trinity County, aged 18 yr 24 days; buried Weaverville Cem. May 19, 1885; wife of Charles E. Gilzean; daughter of Mr. and Mrs. Barthel Jacobs. (TJ Sat. May 23, 1885).

GIRARD, LOUIS ALTOONA. Died Trinity Center Oct. 25, 1888; aged 4 yr 4 mo 24 days; son of Louis and Annie Girard. "Lakeview Examiner please copy".(TJ Nov. 3 and Nov. 10, 1888).

GIVEN, ALICE. Died Junction City June 9, 1895, aged 19 yr 5 mo 23 dy; wife of Jas. E. Given; b. near Evanstown, Wyoming 1875, m.n. Miss Alice Buys; sister of Mrs. W. E. Richards of Red Hill (near Junction City); bur. Helena Cem. June 11, 1895; has infant baby. (TJ June 15, 1895 pp 2 & 3).

GIVEN, JOSEPH C. Died Feb. 1, 1880 Brunswick, Maine, aged 65 yr; brother of W. C. Given of Junction City; funeral Feb. 4, 1880. (TJ Mar. 20, 1880 p 3).

GIVEN, THOMAS W., Mrs. Died Brunswick, Maine Apr. 9, 1893, age 60 yr; bur. Brunswick, Maine Apr. 11, 1893; dau. of Capt. Charles Thomas; GF a Revolutionary soldier, and husband had a Revolutionary GF; leaves 3 sons and 1 dau; 3 sisters & 3 brothers; mother of Jas. E. Given of East Fork, Trinity Co., CA. (from a Brunswick, Maine paper). (TJ Sat. Apr 15, 1893 p 3 col 5).

GLASS, WILLIAM. Died Canon Creek, Trinity Co. May 1, 1894; b. Candor, Washington Co., Penn 1851; aged abt 43 yr; res Trinity Co. 20 years, at Hayfork. Mar. Nov 12, 1889 Mrs. Sarah Kester; bur. Weaverville May 4, 1894. (TJ Sat May 5, 1894 pp 2 & 3). [see also Kester].

GLASSON, JAMES. Died Aug. 1, 1908 Weaverville; age 71; born England; miner; buried Weaverville. [Index to Deaths 1890-1908].

GLENISSON, EUGENE. Died Weaverville Jan. 23, 1892; native of France, aged about 71 yr. (TJ Sat. Jan. 30, 1892).

GLENN, SAM. Died July 10, 1907 Bonanza King Mine; accident; about 40; born Nova Scotia; miner; buried Trinity Center. [Index to Deaths 1890-1908].

GLOVER, ROBERT. Died Junction City Feb 22, 1897; native of Indiana, aged 69 yr 3 mo 10 dy; came to Trinity Co. 1852; miner; leaves a brother in the east, last of a large family; 3 bro. have died during the past year. Nephew John B. Glover was with him at time of death. Bur. Junction City Cem. Feb 24, 1897. (TJ Feb 27, 1897 pp 2 & 3).

GODWIN, AB. Died recently (abt Nov. 1882) in Humboldt County; known as "Big Ab", an old time resident of Junction City. (TJ Nov. 25, 1882). [Note: may be "Goodwin"--1860 census Canyon Creek.]

GOERING, CHARLES. Died July 21, 1871 Weaverville, aged 3 yr; son of Charles and Louisa Goering. (TJ Sat. July 29, 1871 p 2).

GOERING, JOHN AUGUSTUS CHARLES. "Killed by a caving bank" in Weaverville Nov. 20, 1879; native of Germany, aged about 54 yr; funeral Nov. 22, 1879, bur. Masonic Cem. Weaverville; came Calif. 1850; long obit. (TJ Nov. 22, 1878 p 2-3). [Note: he was the father of children Charles and Louis; born Oct. 23, 1826. Wife Louisa b. Mar 4, 1834; d. Aug. 25, 1894].

GOERING, LOUIS. Died Aug. 31, 1871 Weaverville, aged 10 months; son of Charles and Louisa Goering. (TJ Sept. 2, 1872 p 2).

GOERING, LOUISA, Mrs. Died Weaverville Aug 25, 1894; born Kellinghusen, Germany; aged 60 yr 5 mo 21 days; came Calif. 1859; married in San Francisco June 4, 1859 J. A. C. Goering; 5 children; husband d. Nov. 1879; bur Aug 26, 1894 Weaverville Cem., with Eastern Star services. (TJ Sep 1, 1894 pp 2 & 3).

GOEWEY, JAMES M., Mrs. Died at San Francisco Jan. 3, 1887; born District of Columbia 1846; wife of Judge James M. Goewey; youngest daughter of Nelson Bates, pioneer merchant of Trinity County; lost her eldest daughter some months ago and never recovered from the shock. See *San Francisco Alta* Jan. 4, 1887. (TJ Jan. 8, 1887).

GOGGER, MARTIN. Died Nov. 14, 1860 Weaverville; native of Bavaria, aged about 40 yr. (TJ Sat. Nov. 17, 1860 p 2).

GOLDTHORP, GEORGE. "Died at his home, Elizabeth, Illinois", abt July/August 1860; late of Weaverville. (TJ Sept. 1, 1860 p 2).

GOODBERG, FRANK W. Died abt 28 Jan. 1874, French Gulch, Shasta County; native of Sweden, aged abt 46; buried by F. & A. M. at Shasta Monday Feb. 1, 1874. (TJ Feb 7, 1874 p 3).

GOODYEAR, _____. Died Weaverville Jan 23, 1894; inf. dau. of Mr. and Mrs. C. E. Goodyear, aged about 6 hours; born Jan 22, 1894. (TJ Sat. Jan 27, 1894).

GOODYEAR, MERWIN. Died Weaverville Jan. 6, 1892; infant son of Mr. and Mrs. C. E. Goodyear; native of California, aged 29 days. (see also Paulsen). (TJ Sat. Jan. 9, 1892).

GORDON,-----. Died Humboldt County Apr. 17, 1890; son of D. Gordon; thrown from a wagon at Blue Lake and killed. See *Humboldt Mail* Apr. 19, 1890. (TJ Sat. April 26, 1890 p 3).

GORDON, BURR. Died recently (abt Dec. 1889) in Southern California age 61 yr 10 mo; early settler in Trinity County; son of late John C. Gordon of Jefferson City, MO; brother of late Dr. James B. Gordon of Sonoma County; buried beside brother James in Santa Rosa Cemetery; last of 4 brothers, leaving 2 sisters, Mrs.

John C. Burch, formerly of Weaverville, and Mrs. T. J. Wilburn of Sacramento. (TJ Sat. Dec. 21, 1889 p 3 col 1).

GORDON, CHARLES E. Died Rohnerville, Humboldt Co. Mar. 10, 1893; born Weaverville 1862, son of David E. Gordon, proprietor of the Trinity Journal. (TJ Sat. Mar. 18, 1893 p 3 col 5).

GORDON, DAVID EVERETT. Died Apr 18, 1913, age 82. (TJ Apr 26, 1913). For a biography of Gordon, first publisher of the TRINITY JOURNAL, see TJ Sep 3, 1987, "People in the News", by Patricia J. Hicks.

GORDON, GEORGE. Died Apr. 1855; probate filed Apr 12, 1855 Probate Bk A.

GORDON, GEORGE POPE. Died May 1851 Texas Bar, Trinity River. Buried McKenzie Gulch 1851; body removed "last week" (August 1857) and interred in Weaverville Burial Ground; left family in Atlantic States. (TJ Sat. August 22, 1857 p 2).

GORDON, JOHN C., Capt. Died June 7, 1863 Weaverville, aged 72 yr 7 mo 25 days; native of Spottsylvania County, Virginia; late of Jefferson City, MO; bur. Weaverville Cem. (TJ June 13, 1863 p 2).

GORDON, LAURA E. Died Eureka, Humboldt County Sun. May 15, 1873, age 30 yr 6 mo 11 days; formerly of Rockland, Maine; wife of David E. Gordon of the West Coast Signal; resident of Weaverville with husband many years. (TJ May 31 and June 7, 1873). [1861 note in TRINITY JOURNAL: Married in Weaverville Sept. 1, 1861 by Judge E. J. Curtis, David E. Gordon and Miss Laura E. Webb, late of Portland, Maine].

GORDON, LISSA A. Died Eureka, Humboldt County, Sept. 16, 1895; native of California, aged 34 yr 1 mo 4 day; widow of the late Charles E. Gordon (son of David E. Gordon); bur. Rohnerville, Humboldt Co. beside late husband. (TJ Sat. Sept 28, 1895 p 1 col 3).

GORDON, SARAH C. Died at Cranesville, Paulding County, Ohio Dec. 14, 1858, aged 17 yr 9 mo 28 days; wife of Lewis S. Gordon. (TJ Sat. Feb. 12, 1859 p 2).

GOSS, ABEL BUTLER. Died Santa Cruz, CA Jan 31, 1894; native of Vermont; abt 72 years; came to Weaverville early 1850s; partner with I. N. Canfield & Luke F. Wells on Point Bar; farmed in Hay Fork; married late; moved to Santa Cruz one year ago. (TJ Feb 17, 1894, pp 2 & 3).

GOULD, WINFIELD. Died Santa Cruz Oct 13, 1897; b. in Trinity County, son of Mr. and Mrs. Alton Gould. (*Gilroy Gazette*). (TJ Nov 6, 1897 p 3 col 4).

GOW, JAMES A. Died May 28, 1859 Weaverville, in 33rd year of age; bur. June 1, 1859 Weaverville cemetery; native of England; migrated with his father to Louisiana 1845; 7th Regiment Louisiana Volunteers under Col. Deruro. (TJ June 4, 1859 p 2). Probate filed July 27, 1859; Probate Book B page 124.

GRANT, MANUEL. Died Aug. 8, 1869 Weaverville, aged 4 yr; son of Manuel Grant. (TJ Aug. 13, 1869).

GRANT, MARY. Died Indian Creek (nr Douglas City) Jan 16, 1897; wife of Manuel Grant; native of Azores Islands, aged abt 50 yr. (TJ Jan 23, 1897).

GRATTON,----- (female). Died one day last week (abt March 1880) near Minersville, of diphtheria; age 12 or 13; sister-in-law of Patrick Larkin. (TJ Mar. 27, 1880 p 3).

GRAUMAR, CHARLES. Died Paulsen's Ranch near Lewiston Oct. 9, 1888; native of Hamburg, aged about 72 years; came Trinity County 1850s. (TJ Sat. Oct. 13, 1888).

GRAVES, COOLEDGE. Died Mar. 22, 1867 Sacramento, CA; native of Brunswick, Maine, aged 57 years; formerly of Weaverville. (TJ Sat. March 30, 1867 p 2).

GRAVES, DAVID RICE. Born 9 Jan 1827; died 29 Dec. 1881; buried at Red Bluff. (source not given). [Widow, Annie Christine Graves, born Sept. 8, 1833 Tennessee, in Trinity County, CA 1900 Census: Trinity Center, page 64, June 8, 1900].

GRAY, OSCAR MINERT. Died Weaverville Feb 19, 1899; b. New York 1835, aged abt 64 yr; came to Trinity County 1850s; never married; leaves a sister Mrs. Dell J. Cline of Clay Center, Neb. (TJ Feb 25, 1899 p 2 & p 3 col 2).

GREEN, CHARLES. Died Sept 29-Oct. 2, 1906 Ruth; age 75. [Index to Deaths 1890-1908].

GREENHOOD, EDWIN D. Died July 23, 1861 Weaverville, aged 1 yr 6 mo; son of Herman and Louisa Greenhood; buried Masonic Cemetery, Weaverville. "St. Louis, MO papers please copy." (TJ July 27, 1861).

GREENHOOD, H. Died Aug. 16, 1867 San Francisco; formerly of Greenhood & Newbauer, Weaverville; no age given. (TJ Aug. 24, 1867 p 2). (Note: 1860 census: "Herman Greenhood, age 38, banker, born Austria.")

GREENHOOD, WILLIAM W. Died in San Francisco Jan 9, 1894; born 1820, aged 73 yr; came to Calif. 1852; had store in Weaverville for sale of cigars, tobacco, fruit, & notions; sold to former clerk Max Lang; opened bank with brother Herman and Joseph Neubauer, known as Greenhood, Neubauer & Co. Mr. Greenhood lived mostly in San Francisco; Herman died earlier; partner Joseph Neubauer services and served as pall bearer. (TJ Jan 20, 1894 pp 2 & 3).

GREENLEAF, A. M. Died March 18, 1890 Springfield, Mass; native of New York, age about 65 years; married Miss Charlotte Stanford in Illinois abt 1856; lived Douglas City 1865-1868. (TJ Apr. 12, 1890).

GREENLEAF, CHARLOTTE E., Mrs. Died Feb/Mar 1895 Chicago, Ill. aged about 65 yr; m.n. Stanford; old resident of Douglas City 1863-1868; Mr. Greenleaf d. "abt 2 years ago". Legend about Mr. Greenleaf p. 3. (TJ Sat. Mar 9, 1895 p 3 col 2).

GREGORY, ELIZABETH H. Died June 3, 1858 Trinity Center, aged 17 years; wife of Leroy Gregory. (TJ Sat. June 12, 1858 p 2).

GRIBBLE, _____. Died at Junction City Feb 18, 1894, only child of Mary and Geo. Gribble; native of Calif, aged 1 yr 10 mo 24 dy. (name and sex not given). (TJ Feb 24, 1894). [dau. b. Mar 26, 1892.] [see also Segalia].

GRIBBEL (sic), JOHN. (Gribble?) "Killed by a cave in a mining claim near Junction City July 23, 1879; native of Wisconsin, aged 31 years." (TJ Sat. July 16, 1879).

GRIBBLE, RICHARD. Died near Junction City Jan. 31, 1887; native of England, aged 66 yr; leaves wife and several children; bur. Weaverville Cemetery. (TJ Sat. Feb. 5, 1887). [1880 Census: Gribble, Richard, Junction City, p7, 6-4-1880, age 60; married, miner, b. England; Jane, 51, b. England; George, 19, single, miner, b. England; Ann, 17, b. Calif; William, 16, b. Calif; Miranda, 14, b. Calif; James, 11, b. Calif; Richard, 8, b. Calif.]

GRIEVES, BOB. Died Aug. 2, 1878 Covelo, Mendocino County; no age given. (TJ Aug. 10, 17, and 24, 1878).

GRIFFIN, CHARLES. Died at home of mother, Mrs. M. W. Murry in Oakland, Alameda Co; bur. Mountain View Cem, Oakland; (young, but no age given). (TJ Dec 22, 1894 p 3).

GRIFFIN, MORRIS FRANKLIN. Died San Francisco April 9, 1884; of Weaverville; born New Brunswick Feb. 1825; married Miss Sadie E. Wood Dec. 31, 1863; arrived Calif. Aug. 4, 1849; Trinity County 1850; long obit. (TJ Apr. 12 and 19, 1884). [see also Wood].

GRIFFITH, CLARENCE. Died Big Bar Sept. 7, 1893, aged 13 mo 8 days. (born July 30, 1892 to the wife of Patrick Thomas Griffith). (TJ Sat. Sept. 16, 1893 and Aug. 1892).

GRIFFITH, LORA. (written "Griffiths"). Died Cox Bar Dec. 30, 1893, native of Calif; aged 27 yr 3 mo 23 days; wife of P. T. Griffith; dau. of W. A. Pattison; husband and infant son survive her. (TJ Sat. Jan. 6, 1894). (Note: Big Bar & Cox Bar are on opposite sides of the Trinity River; basically the same place.) (son was born Dec. 12, 1893 Big Bar).

GRIFFITH, MILLER, Capt. Died Aug 16, 1896 San Rafael, Marin Co., CA; well known in Trinity Co.; wife died July 4, 1896; 2 sons and 3 dau. survive him, all in San Francisco. (TJ Sat. Aug 22, 1896).

GRIFFITH, PATRICK THOMAS. Died Weaverville Aug 24, 1898; native of Calif. aged abt 29 yr; m. Miss Lora Pattison of Cox Bar; 2 children; wife & children preceded Mr. Griffith in death; leaves mother, Mrs. Michael Griffith of San Jose, 4 sis. and 4 bro. obit. worth copying. (TJ Aug 27, 1898 p 2 & p 3, col 2; see also TJ Sep 3, 1898 p 3 col 1).

GRIFFITH, WILLIAM. Died at Big Bar Mar. 6, 1892; only child of Mr. and Mrs. P. T. Griffith, aged 1 yr 4 mo 18 days.

GRIFFITHS, SAMUEL FERRIS. Died Paso Robles, San Louis Obispo County Nov. 23, 1875; native of Missouri, aged 48 yr; old resident of Trinity County; member Trinity #27, F. & A. M. (TJ Dec. 4, 1875).

GRIFFITS, MATTHEW, Mr. Died Weaverville March 13, 1860, aged about 61 years; formerly of Philadelphia. (TJ Mar. 17, 1860).

GRINNEL, J. J. Died San Francisco Jul 8, 1899; of Red Bluff, Tehama Co.; native of Indiana, aged abt 43 yr; leaves wife & son in Red Bluff. (TJ Jul 15, 1899 p 3 col 2).

GRISWOLD, JAMES, Mrs. Died Sacramento Sept. 12, 1884; no age given; formerly Miss Mollie Dunlap, daughter of Mrs. E. C. Dunlap of Weaverville; sister of Mrs. John E. Gibson of Deadwood. (TJ Sat. Sept. 20, 1884 p 3).

GROSHENS, FREDERICK AUGUST. Died Weaverville ca May 28, 1859; native of Newvillei, France, aged 33 years; recently from LaSalle County, Illinois. (TJ Sat. May 28, 1859).

GROSS, PAULIUS. Murdered on the trail leading from Grass Valley (Lewiston) to Weaverville, near Brown's Creek, Friday August 30, 1861; native of Germany, no age given. (DCG Sept. 4, 1861; TJ Sept. 7, 1861; TJ Dec. 21, 1861). ["Sacred to the memory of Paulus Grosse d. Aug 30, 1861 Aged 39 yr. Requiesat in pace. Erected by his affectionate wife Isabella." Gravestone in Weaverville Cem. standing in 1988.] [see also Noll.]

GROTEFEND, ELSIE. Died San Francisco Aug 9, 1894; dau. of Fred and Libbie Grotefend; bur. Redding, Shasta Co. Aug 11, 1894; no age given. (TJ Aug 18, 1894).

GROVE, DAVID. Died April 1, 1878 on China Flat on Lower Trinity (prob. Humboldt County); no age given. (TJ Apr. 6, 1878 p 3).

GROVER, GEORGE M. Died near Junction City Dec. 8, 1883; native of Maine, aged 55 yr; unmarried; came to Calif. 1851; bur. Weaverville Cemetery; good obit. (TJ Sat. Dec. 15, 1883).

GUILFORD,----, Capt. Died "recently", [abt Dec. 1877,] in Alameda County aged abt 65 years. (more). (TJ Sat. Dec. 11, 1877 p 3).

GUILLAUME, PHILLIP. Died Oct. 5, 1890 (Weaverville?); white, 66, male, single, born Prussia. [Index to Deaths 1890-1908].

GUM, ETHELYN. Died Trinity Center Dec 14, 1894; inf. dau of Burd and Isabel Gum; aged 2 mo 15 dy. (TJ Sat. Dec 22, 1894 p 2).

GUNN, MOSES. Accidentally killed by a boulder near Steiner's Flat (nr Douglas City) April 16, 1867; native of Plymouth, Indiana, aged 36 years; bur. Weaverville Cemetery; lived California 15 years (abt 1852). (TJ Sat. Apr. 20, 1867 p 2).

GUPTIL, A. N. Died San Francisco Oct. 31, 1893; formerly of Weaverville; lately of Humboldt Co. (TJ Sat. Nov. 25, 1893).

GUPTILL, BARTLETT SMITH. Died Indian Creek Aug 23, 1898; b. Sep 9, 1828, Lubeck, Maine, aged 69 yr 11 mo 14 dy; came to Trinity Co. May 1852; m. Sept 1868 Miss Mary Moloney, who survives him; bur. Odd Fellows Cem. Weaverville Aug 25, 1898; long obit p 3 col 3). (TJ Aug 27, 1898 pp 2 & 3).

GUTH, ADAM. Died near North Fork (Helena) Sept. 17, 1892; native of Bavaria, aged about 59 yr. (TJ Sat. Sept. 24, 1892).

GUTH, HORACE. Drowned at North Fork of Trinity River Feb. 16, 1859; body recovered March 1859; buried at North Fork (Helena Cemetery)j;. (TJ Feb. 19 and Apr 2, 1859). Probate filed March 31, 1859, Probate Book B page 106.

GUTHRIE, SUSAN, Mrs. Died San Jose, Santa Clara Co. CA Feb 12, 1899; native of Missouri, aged 49; came to Trinity Co. 1873; m. late William Guthrie in July 1873; nine children, eight survive: Mrs. Joseph W. Williams, of Sacramento; Mrs. R. R. Fowler, of Madera; Misses Flora, Carrie, Ruth & Violet, and John and Albert Guthrie of San Jose; husb. died 1888; lived in Weaverville until 1898 when she went to San Jose; bur. Oak Hill Cem. San Jose, with Eastern Star ceremonies. (TJ Feb 25, 1899 p 3 col 2).

GUTHRIE, WILLIE. Died Canon City Aug. 14, 1878 aged 2 yr 24 days; son of William and Susan Guthrie; bur. Masonic Cemetery Weaverville Aug. 15, 1878. (TJ Sat. Aug. 17, 1878). (marker legible 1987).

GUTHRIE, WILLIAM. Died Weaverville July 20, 1888; native of Kentucky, aged about 57 yr; bur. Masonic Cemetery, Weaverville [next to son Willie; no marker;] Sun. July 22, 1888. long obit. (TJ Sat. July 28, 1888 p 2-3).

GWIN, ELIZABETH J. Died Canon City May 2, 1862; no age; wife of F. S. Gwin. (TJ May 3, 1862 p 3).

GWIN, WILLIAM. Died China Flat, Humboldt County, Oct. 31, 1886; native of Alabama, aged 56 yr 7 mo; moved recently to Humboldt County from New River. (TJ Sat. Nov. 8, 1884).

HAACKE, FREDRICK. Died Weaverville May 25, 1881; born Cincinnati, aged 28 yr. Lived Buckeye Creek near Van Matres Ranch. (TJ May 21, 1881 p 3).

HAAS, HENRY. Died San Francisco Mar 11, 1899; b. Trin.Co, age 18 yr 8 mo; son of Fred and Emily Haas of Junction City. (TJ Mar 18, 1899 p 3 col 4).

HACKETT, GEORGE J. Died Deadwood Jun 14, 1897; b. Wisconsin 1851, aged abt 46 yr; came to Calif. 18 years ago; leaves bro. Dr. Hackett in San Francisco; aged mother in Minnesota; unmarried; (TJ Jun 19, 1897 p 2; obit p 3 col 3).

HAFFEY, F. Died Aug. 9, 1904 North Fork; about 35; buried Helena Cemetery. [Index to Deaths 1890-1908].

HAGLEMAN, FREDERICK CHARLES. Died Weaverville Dec. 14, 1868, aged 5 yr 7 days. Son of John and Mena Hagleman. (TJ Sat. Dec. 19, 1868).

HAGELMAN, JOHN. Died Weaverville Aug. 5, 1887; native Bavaria, Germany, aged 55 years 11 days; wife, 2 children; daughter married to Mr. J. Bradbury of Red Bluff; son Johnnie is learning the blacksmith trade. Came to Calif. 1857; member North Star Lodge & Stella Encampment; bur. Sunday Aug. 7, 1887, prob. Odd Fellows Cem. Weaverville. (TJ Sat. Aug. 13, 1887). [see also Weckert].

HAGELMAN, LIZZIE. Died Weaverville May 11, 1885; born Weaverville, aged 18 yr 1 mo 5 days; daughter of John and Minna Hagelman. Fun. Tues. May 12, 1885; bur. Odd Fellows Cemetery. (TJ Sat. May 6, 1885).

HAHN, GEORGE. Died Deadwood Nov. 1, 1893; native of Germany aged about 68 yr. (TJ Sat. Nov. 4, 1893).

HAILSTONE, J. T. Died June 3, 1908 Hayfork; age 71; born England; bur. Hayfork. [Index to Deaths 1890-1908].

HAINES, PETER. Died May 2, 1903 Weaverville; age 66; buried Weaverville. [Index to Deaths 1890-1908].

HALL, ANNIE. Died Weaverville Mar. 22, 1881; born Mar. 22, 1881. Infant daughter of Albert G. and Annie J. Hall. (TJ Mar. 26, 1881 p 2).

HALL, DAVIS. Died Trinity Center Mar. 6, 1878; native of Missouri aged 55 years; old resident of Trinity Center; proprietor of hotel. (TJ Mar. 16, 1878 p 2).

HALL, GEO. WILLIS. Died May 5, 1907 Trinity Center, age 35; born Calif. informant: Mrs. G. W. Hall. [Index to Deaths 1890-1908].

HALL, HANNAH P. Died June 1, 1907 Weaverville, age 34; born Calif. [Index to Deaths 1890-1908]. [Note: this is Hannah Pauline Paulsen Hall, daughter of Peter Minert Paulsen and Anna Barbara Kruttschnitt; married Daniel James Hall May 17, 1900 in Weaverville.]

HALL, HARRY. Died Santa Cruz Jan. 28, 1890, age 22 yr. Son of W. L. Hall of Trinity Center. (TJ Sat. Feb. 1, 1890).

HALL, HENRY G. Died Weaverville Nov 10, 1897; native of Mass., age abt 42 yr; unmarried; "in county about a month; came from Humboldt County". bur. Weaverville Cem. Nov 11, 1897. (TJ Nov 13, 1897).

HALL, JOHN. Killed by a falling tree on Canon Creek May 29, 1882; native of Brooklyn, New York, aged 44 yr 7 mo; bur. Weav. Wed. May 31, 1882; wife and one child. Mrs. Hall dau. of H. C. Osgood. See TJ June 10, 1882 for brother's death 8 days later. (TJ June 3, 1881 p 2).

HALL, ROBERT. Died Weaverville Oct. 5, 1871; aged 10 mo 21 days; son of John P. and Nettie A. Hall. (TJ Oct. 7, 1871 p 2).

HALL, WILLIAM H. Died Oct. 2, 1905 Weaverville, age 73, born Scotland, baker. [Index to Deaths 1890-1908].

HALL, WILLIAM L. Died Trinity Center Dec 7, 1894; native of Missouri, aged 63 yr 9 mo 23 dy. (TJ Sat. Mar 9, 1895).

HALL, WILLIAM P. Died at Etna Mills, Siskiyou County, Dec. 5, 1886; native of Ohio, aged about 57 years; bur. Trinity Center Tues. Dec. 7, 1886; leaves widow. (TJ Sat. Dec. 11, 1886).

HALLER, PHILLIP. Lost on the steamer "Central America" Sept. 12, 1857; formerly of Weaverville; no age given. (TJ Oct. 31, 1857).

HALLEY, _____. Died Hay Fork Apr 03, 1900; inf. dau. of Mr. and Mrs. Frederick Halley, Jr., aged 12 dy; (TJ Apr 21, 1900).

HALLEY, W. Died Mar. 31, 1889, prob. Weaverville, age 18, single, born Calif. [Index to Deaths 1873-1890]. [not in 1880 Census].

HAMILTON, CASANDA (sic) JANE. Died Paskenta, Tehama County Mar. 5, 1874; aged 6 yr; youngest daughter of D. D. Hamilton. (TJ Mar. 21, 1874).

HAMILTON, HUGH. Wounded and died at Camp Anderson, Humboldt County, abt Sept. 1865, 26 years of age; formerly of Orleans Bar; came to Calif. from New York 1851. (TJ Sat. Oct. 2, 1865).

HAMILTON, JANE. Died Paskenta, Tehama County Jan. 25, 1872; native of Tennessee, aged 45 yr; deceased formerly resided at North Fork in this County and is a sister of Thos. B. Price of Cox's Bar. (TJ Feb. 10, 1872).

HAMILTON, ROBERT. Died Feb. 21, 1906, Deadwood, age 62. (TJ Feb 1906.)

HAMILTON, WILLIAM STEVEN, Col. Died 7 August 1850 Sacramento; born New York City Aug. 7, 1797. Youngest son of Alexander Hamilton; pioneer merchant of Weaverville, summer 1850. Left to open business in Sacramento. long story, cols. 1 & 2 TJ Sat. May 12, 1888.

HAMMOND, FREDERIC CHARLES. Died Weaverville Dec. 18, 1878; native of England, aged 51 years 8 months. Born Berry St. Edmonds, Brook Dam Farm, England 17 April 1827. Came U. S. age 2 (1829?) with parents to Vermont, Ohio, Illinois, where parents died. (more) (TJ Dec. 21, 1878 p 2 & 3).

HAMMOND, GRACE ETHRA. Died Lewiston May 16, 1895; aged 11 mo 5 dy; inf. dau. of F. S. and N. E. Hammond. (TJ Sat. May 25, 1895). [marker 1976. Pioneer Cem., Lewiston: Hammond, Gracie E. b. July 11, 1894; d. May 16, 1895.]

HAMMOND, NANCY E. Died Jul 19, 1900; age 44 yr 9 mo 25 dy. (TJ Jan 1901).

HAMMOND, NANCY E. "Wife of F. S. Hammond. b. Oct 24, 1855; d. July 19, 1900"; grave marker (1976) Lewiston Pioneer Cemetery, Lewiston, CA; with dau. Grace Ethra.

HAMPTON, _____. Died Lewiston Feb 9, 1898, inf. son of Mr. and Mrs. William Hampton, native of Calif. aged 3 mo 8 dy. (TJ Feb 12, 1898 p 2).

HAMPTON, ELIJAH POUND. Died Lewiston Dec. 7, 1892; native of New York, aged about 76 yr. Bur. Lewiston Cem. Dec. 9, 1892. Came Trinity Co. 1861/1862 with wife & dau. from Wisconsin; son Jasper Hampton came 1866; dau. married A. J. Ross; leaves widow, son, grandchild. (TJ Dec. 10, 1892 p 2 & p 3 col 2). (see also Ross.) 1880 Census says wife Lucinda, age 61, b. New York.

HAMPTON, GENIEVE B. Died July 23, 1907 Redding's Creek; age 6; born Calif. Harley Hampton, informant. [Index to Deaths 1890-1908].

HAMPTON, JASPAR S. Died March 5, 1908 Redding, Shasta, Calif; age 70; born New York; buried Lewiston. [Index to Deaths 1890-1908]. (son of Elijah Pound Hampton). [1880 Census says "Jasper", wife Jeanette; children: Everett, Burt, Wiley, Otho, Harley, Charles, Nettie, Esther; Lewiston 6-1-1880 p 2.]

HAMPTON, JONATHAN. Died Athens, Georgia, July 9, 1883 age 63 yr; brother of Mr. J. M. Hampton of South Fork. (TJ Aug. 25, 1883 p 3).

HAMPTON, ROSA ELLEN. Died Lewiston Sept. 22, 1885; native of Calif, aged 19 yr 2 mo 28 days. Wife of Everett P. Hampton. "A few months married". Bur. Public Cem. Weaverville Sept. 24, 1885. Fritz Hartman of Shasta, was in town Thursday attending the funeral of his cousin Mrs. Rosa Hampton. (TJ Sat. Sept. 26, 1885).

HANCOCK, J. W. Died Washington Nov. 1892; "carpenter here (Weaverville) for a number of years." (TJ Sat. Dec. 17, 1892 p 3 col 1). Registered to Vote in Weaverville June 2, 1886, John William Hancock, age 26, born Washington Territory.

HANDLEY, JOHN. Died Weaverville Oct. 25, 1879; native of Virginia, aged 52 yr. (TJ Sat. Nov. 1, 1879 p 2).

HANLON, CATHARINE. Died Weaverville May 30, 1869 aged 3 yr 5 mo 15 days; daughter of John and Catharine Hanlon. (TJ June 5, 1869 p 2).

HANLON, ----- (female). Died Weaverville Nov. 12, 1873 aged 4 days, infant daughter of Mr. and Mrs. John Hanlon. (TJ Nov. 15, 1873). [Index to Deaths 1873-1890; adds Hanlon, Baby, white, single, born Calif.]

HANLON, JOHN. Died Gold Hill, Nevada Jan. 6, 1880; no age. Former resident of Trinity County. (TJ Sat. Jan. 17, 1880 p 3). [1870 Census, Junction City: Hanlon, John, 33, b. Ireland; Kate, 27, b. Ireland; Anna, 7; Lizzie, 6; Eddie, 3; John, 1, all born in Calif.]

HANNA, CHARLES. Died Redding, Shasta, CA Sept. 16, 1887; native of Ireland, aged 64 years; resident Weaverville; bur. Catholic Cem. Weav. Sept. 18, 1887; came Trinity Co June 30, 1860; wife and 4 children, out of 11, one of whom is married. (TJ Sat. Sept. 24, 1887).

HANNA, CHARLES. Died Douglas City Apr. 20, 1868, aged 1 year 8 mo; son of Charles and Mary Hanna. (TJ Sat. Apr. 25, 1868).

HANNA, JOHN WILLIAM. Died near Weaverville Sept. 1, 1870 (no age given); son of Charles and Pauline Hanna. (TJ Sept. 2, 1870 p 2) (Was she Mary Pauline?) (TJ Sept. 2, 1870 p 2).

HANSEN, CHAS. H. Died White Rock, New River area, Trinity County abt Jan. 26, 1886; native of Maine, aged 32 years; bur. near White Rock. Bro. living in Woodland, CA; father and sister in Minnesota. Left mine in a storm to hunt for deer; found Jan. 26, 1886. (TJ Feb. 6, 1886).

HANSEN, EARNEST FRANK. Died Elmhurst, Alameda Co. Apr 05, 1900; old resident of Weaverville; b. Wolgast, Pommern, Germany Jan 22, 1827; m. 1869 Maria Mathews, who died in 1890; bur. Weaverville Cem.; good obit. (TJ Apr 14, 1900 pg 3 col 2).

HANSEN, HENRY. Died Weaverville Sept. 30, 1890; native of Germany, aged 30 yr 7 mo 12 days; nephew of Mr. and Mrs. Detlef Hansen; came to U. S. a year ago last August (abt Aug. 1889); leaves mother, 2 brothers and a sister in Germany. (TJ Sat. Oct. 4, 1890). [Index to Deaths 1890-1908 adds white, single].

HANSEN, MARIAH. Died near Weaverville Apr. 14, 1890; native of Orange County, New York, aged about 90 yr; wife of E. F. Hansen, m. 1864; bur. Weav. Pub. Cem. Apr 16, 1890. Mrs. Mariah Mathews, a widow, came to Trinity County in 1851. She had 16 children by her first husband, 7 living: Mrs. P. H. Brown and Wm. Mathews of Weav., Alonzo Mathews of Trinity Center, son and 3 daughters in Iowa. (TJ Apr. 19, 1890).
[Index to Deaths 1873-1890 says "Hansen, Marian, (sic) died Apr. 14, 1890; age 90, white, female, married, born New York."]

HANSEN, PETER. Died San Francisco Mar. 2, 1873; native of Denmark, aged 39 yr. (TJ Mar. 8, 1873). [Index to Deaths 1873-1890 says: "Hansen, Peter, died March 7, 1873 St. Mary's Hospital, San Jose (Santa Clara Co.), Calif; white; no age given; male; married; born Denmark."]
[1870 Census: Hansen, Peter, age 36, res. Weaverville, miner, born Denmark; wife Dorothy, age 30, born Prussia].

HANSON, I. A. Died May 7, 1904 Hay Fork; age 55; born Sweden; bur. Hay Fork. [Index to Deaths 1890-1908].

HARBER, VICTOR. Died Rattlesnake (New River Area), Trinity County July 22, 1895; native of France, aged about 45 yr; shot by partner Henry Hamilton; story p. 3. (TJ Sat. July 27, 1895 and also TJ Aug 3, 1895 p 3 col 2).

HARDESTY,-----. "Mr. Hardesty who was seriously injured by a falling tree in Hay Fork last winter died at the County hospital (Weaverville) this week (abt June 25, 1859). We have not been able to learn where he resided previous to coming to California." (TJ June 25, 1859 p 3.)

HARRINGTON, JOHN. Died Weaverville Mar. 25, 1860; native of County Dublin, Ireland, aged 33 years. Late a resident of Shasta. (TJ Mar. 31, 1860).

HARRIS, EMMA. Died Weaverville July 15, 1858, aged about 9 months; daughter of Dr. J. S. and Emma C. Harris. (TJ July 17, 1858).

HARRIS, I.N., Dr. Died Gilroy (Santa Clara Co.) "about two weeks ago" (abt April 1873); proprietor of the Independence Hotel, Weaverville 1857/1858. (TJ May 10, 1873 p 3).

HARRISON, JOHN. Died Hawkins Bar, Trinity County Jan. 12, 1886; native of Ohio, aged about 77 yr; came California 1850; known as "General Harrison"; sister in Franklin, Ohio; dau. in state of New York. (TJ Sat. Jan. 16, 1886).

HART, JOHN. Died near Hyampom Mon. Nov 19, 1894; native of Tennessee, aged about 62 yr; gunsmith by trade. Shot at Hay Fork Nov 16, 1894 by a man named Williams. (TJ Sat. Nov 24, 1894 pg 3 col 2; TJ Dec 1, 1894 says "born Missouri", p 2; more details pg 3; TJ Dec 22, 1894 pg 3 col 2).

HART, SAMUEL. Died Weaverville Feb. 24, 1858; native of France, aged about 40 yr. (TJ Sat. Feb. 27, 1858 p 2).

HARTMAN, EDWIN LUCIUS. Died San Francisco Nov. 7, 1889; native of New Hampshire, aged about 59 years. (TJ Sat. Nov. 16, 1889).

HARTMAN, JOSEPH DAVID. Died Weaverville Sun. Feb. 7, 1869, aged 11 mo 10 days; son of Charles and Rose Hartman. (TJ Feb. 13, 1869 p 2).

HARTMAN, JOSIE. Died Weaverville Dec. 12, 1875, aged 2 yr 9 mo; born Weaverville; son (sic) of Charles and Rosa Hartman; scarlet fever, 5 children in community in one week. (TJ Sat. Dec. 18, 1875 p 2).

HARTMAN, NELLIE. Died Weaverville Feb. 20, 1877, aged 8 mo. Daughter of Mrs. Chas. Hartman. (TJ Feb. 24, 1877).

HARTMAN, WILLIAM GEORGE. Died Weaverville Mar. 6, 1870; son of Charles and Rosa Hartman. (TJ Mar. 12, 1870 p 2; see also p 3).

HARTMAN, W. P. Died Shasta, Shasta Co. Feb 19, 1900; b. France, age abt 56; postmaster of Shasta; at one time he conducted a barber shop in Weaverville. (TJ Feb 24, 1900 pg 3 col 2).

HARTZ, ANTHONY. Died at Trinity Center Jan. 29, 1892; native of France, aged about 66 yr; bur. in family cemetery of J. E. Carr at Carrville, where he lived. Naturalized Pittsburgh, PA 1848; came to Carrville Aug. 1875; Justice of the Peace of Trinity Center. (TJ Feb. 6, 1892 & Feb. 13, 1892).

HARVEY, ALFRED. Died North Fork Apr 28, 1893; native of England, aged 47 yr 1 mo 12 days; bur. Masonic Cem. Weaverville Apr 30, 1893; came Trinity Co. 1868; miner; two brothers, one in Australia, one in England. (TJ Sat. May 6, 1893).

HARVEY, CHAS. Died at his home in Penzance, Cromwell, (sic) (Cornwall?) England Oct. 16, 1881; leaves 3 brothers in Weaverville. (TJ Nov. 12, 1881 p 3; long obit with all the details of his death, no family info; TJ Nov. 19, 1881 p 3 col 2).

HARVEY, JAMES. Died Redding, Shasta Co, Mar 25, 1898; former res. of Weaverville; b. Cornwall, England 1835, age 63 yr 1 mo 2 dy; came to Trinity Co. 1860s; went back to England and was married, wife surviving and 3 children: Merick, Alfred, and Mrs. Louis Moore, all of Redding; bro. Harry Harvey of Weaverville; moved to Redding 2 years ago; Past Master Trinity Lodge No 27, Free & Accepted Masons. (TJ Apr 2, 1898, p 3 col 3).

HASKALL, CARRIE. Died San Jose Oct. 29, 1889; bur. Nov. 1, 1889 Redding; dau. of Dan Haskall, express messenger; no age. (TJ Nov. 2, 1889).

HASKINS, ALMA AUGUSTA. Died Trinity Center Mar. 17, 1879, aged 41 yr 7 mo; wife of Albert P. Haskins; bur. Callahan's Ranch, Siskiyou Co. Mar. 20, 1879; sister of Mrs. Albert Denny of Callahans Ranch. (TJ Sat. Mar. 29, 1879 p 2).

HASKINS, H. A. Died Recently (abt Dec. 1879) at Leadville, Colorado; formerly of Trinity County. From *West Coast Signal*. (TJ Jan. 10, 1880 p 3).

HASSMER, TERESA. Died Weaverville July 15, 1861, aged 4 mo 21 days; child of Valentine and Teresa Hassmer. (TJ July 20, 1861 p 2).

HATCH, ANN S. Died Reddings Creek May 21, 1866, aged about 33 years; wife of John Hatch. "Mass. papers copy". (TJ Sat. May 26, 1866 p 2).

HATCH, CATHERINE, Mrs. Died San Jose, Santa Clara Co., CA Dec 3, 1895; native of New York, aged 69 yr 6 mo; aunt of Mrs. A. H. Marshall of Douglas City and a sister of the late Mrs. Hiram Mabie. (TJ Sat. Dec 7, 1895, p 3 col 4).

HAUCH, ALOWIS. Died at his claim on Rattlesnake (New River Area), Trinity Co. June 19, 1870; native of Baldhim, Wistemburg, Germany; no age given. (TJ July 2, 1870 p 3).

HAWK, BERTHA MABEL. Died Weaverville Feb 8, 1896; native of Calif. aged 14 yr 9 mo 28 dy; bur. Weaverville Cem.; youngest dau. of John Hawk. (TJ Sat. Feb 15, 1896).

HAWK, JOHN. Died Trinity Center Feb. 11, 1891; native of Ohio, aged about 60 yr. Bur. Trinity Center Cem. Fri. Feb. 13, 1891; came to Calif. 1852; came to Weaverville with James Carson and his uncle, Jacob Huss; moved to North Fork; m. Miss E. Miller (sic) 1870; lived Junction City, then Trinity Center in 1889. Leaves widow & 6 children; eldest is wife of F. E. Conway; youngest a boy 3 years old. (TJ Sat. Feb. 21, 1891 p 2 & Trinity Center News p 3). [Trinity County Marriages Book H page 221: Married at North Fork July 5, 1870 by Charles Schultz, J.P., John Hawk and Lilly (Elizabeth) Schlomer.]

HAWK, LAVINA M. Died Sept. 12, 1893 Trinity Center, age 19, American. [Index to Deaths 1890-1908].

HAWK, VINA, Miss. Died Trinity Center Sept. 12, 1893 age 19 yr 6 mo; (TJ Sept. 16, 1893 says "Vina Shock"; corrected Sept. 23, 1893 p 3 col 3 "Miss Vina Hawk".)

HAWK, LEWIS JACOB. Died North Fork May 15, 1872, aged 9 mo 15 days; son of John and Lily Hawk. (TJ May 24, 1872). [Index to Deaths 1873 says "died May 15, 1873 (sic) North Fork."]

HAY, ELIZABETH JANE, Mrs. Died Lewiston Jan 7, 1898; b. Indiana Dec 20, 1832, aged 60 yr and 18 dy; m. May 21, 1856 J. H. Hay; came to Trinity Co. 2 years ago. (TJ Jan 15, 1898 pp 2 & 3).

HAYES, _____. "Died in 1850 and was buried in the little cemetery at "Graveyard Point", Douglas City; no age given. (TJ Sept. 14, 1889, page one, "Early Days Along the River", by T. E. Jones.).

HAYES, Mary A. Died Weaverville Sept. 9, 1893; native of San Francisco, CA, aged 15 yr 1 mo 13 days; bur. Cath. Cem. Weaverville Sept. 11, 1893; granddaughter of Mr. & Mrs. John Bergin; mother died about 13 years ago. (TJ Sat. Sept. 16, 1893 p 2 & 3).

HAYES, THOS. F. Died Weaverville June 12, 1875; native of Alabama, aged about 48 years. (TJ June 19, 1875).

HEARN, P. A. Died Red Bluff, Tehama Co. Jan. 4, 1875; native of Ireland, aged 37 yr. (TJ Sat. Jan. 16, 1875).

HEATH, NELLIE. Died Minersville Nov. 18, 1882; native of Calif. aged 24 yr; wife of John W. Heath; dau. of Mr. and Mrs. Jesse H. Tourtellotte. (TJ Nov. 25, 1882).

HECKER, ANTON. Died near Douglas City Sept. 9, 1867; native of Prussia, aged 47 years. Buried near his late residence, Douglas City, Sept. 10, 1867 by "Douglas City Rifles" of which he was a member. (TJ Sept. 14, 1867 p 2).

HECKMAN, JOHN F. Died Eureka, Humboldt Co. Sep 18, 1894, aged 65 yr; born Atlantic Ocean between Hamburg, Germany and New York City; came to Calif. and Trinity Co. 1855/56; good obit pg 3 col 2. (TJ Sept 29, 1894).

HENDERSON, HARRY. Drowned in Trinity River at China Flat Sun. Apr 21, 1895; aged 21 yr; aka "Pat Henderson"; body has not been recovered. (*Arcata Union* notice (Humboldt County) in TJ Sat. May 11, 1895 p 3 col 2).

HENNESSEY, DAVID. Died Douglas City May 12, 1882; native of Ireland, aged about 60 yr; bur. Catholic Cem. Weav. May 13, 1882. (TJ May 13, 1882 p 2).

HENNESSY, ESTHER. Died Burnt Ranch May 26, 1916; born June 6, 1868 Calif. bur. Burnt Ranch May 28, 1916; father: P.O.M. Hennessy, b. Ireland; mother: Maria Keely, b. Ireland. (Trinity County Deaths 1914-1931 p 47).

HENNESSY, MARIA TERESA. Died Burnt Ranch Mar. 24, 1931; born Jan. 26, 1847 Dublin, Ireland. father: John Keely, b. Ireland. mother: Margaret O'Brien; lived Burnt Ranch 61 yr, Calif. 72 yr; bur. Hennessy Ranch (Burnt Ranch) Mar. 26, 1931; inf. Mary A. Hennessy, Burnt Ranch. (Trinity County Deaths 1914-1931 p 271).

HENNESSY, PATRICK O'MARA. Died Burnt Ranch Dec. 25, 1901 age 72; b. Tipperary County, Ireland; came to Calif 1850; moved to Burnt Ranch 1869/1870; m. 1863 Miss Maria Keely; 2 sons: John R. Hennessy of Nevada, R. W. Hennessy, Burnt Ranch; 5 dau. Mrs. C. H. Lowe, Idaho; Mrs. Gray McMurtry of Pennington, CA; Misses Mary, Etta, & Kate of Burnt Ranch; member of Capt. I. G. Messec's Co.; postmaster Burnt Ranch; (prob. bur. Hennessy Ranch). (TJ Sat. Dec. 28, 1901 p 3).

HENNESSY, THOMAS. Died Burnt Ranch Mar. 10, 1873, aged 4 mo 8 days; infant son of P.O.M. and Maria Hennessy. (TJ Mar. 22, 1873). [Index to Deaths 1873-1890 has similar information; adds single, born Calif.]

HENNESSY, TIMOTHY. Died Indian Creek Jan 14, 1897; native of Ireland, aged abt 65 yr. (TJ Jan 16, 1897 p 2).

HENNESSY, WILLIE J. Died Burnt Ranch June 5, 1881, aged 4 yr 5 mo 28 days; son of P.O.M. and Maria Hennessy. (TJ Sat. June 11, 1881 p 2).

HENRY, FREDRIC WILLIAM. "A German, found in Trinity River about a mile below Lowden"s Bridge Wed. July 25, 1855. Missing since Sunday July 22; mule not found; accidental drowning; family near Shasta." [Died near Lewiston abt July 22, 1855]. (TT July 28, 1855).

HERDLE,-----. Died Junction City May 14, 1867, aged 11 mo; infant son of William & Christina Herdle. (TJ Sat. May 18, 1867 p 2).

HERDLE, CHARLEY F. Died Junction City Jan. 18, 1867, aged 5 yr 9 mo; son of William and Christina Herdle. (TJ Sat. Jan. 26, 1867 p 2).

HERDLE, HENRY. Died Red Bluff, Tehama Co, Calif. Jan. 25, 1890; born Santa Cruz, (Santa Cruz Co.) age 21. A son of Henry Herdle, pioneer of Trinity County. (TJ Sat. Feb. 1, 1890 p 3).

HERDLE, WILLIAM. Died Davisville (now Davis, Yolo Co) July 8, 1886, age 56 yr 6 mo; bur. Red Bluff (Tehama Co.) abt July 10, 1886. Came Calif 1852, Trinity County until 1873, Red Bluff 1873-1886; butcher; widow and seven children; 5 sons 2 daughters, one Mrs. Paul Stoll of Red Bluff; one son in Fresno City. (*Red Bluff Cause* July 9, 1886) (TJ Sat. July 27, 1886).

HESSAMER, FERDINAND. Died Weaverville Jan. 6, 1863, aged 5 yr 3 mo 16 days; son of Weldan and Terresha Hessamer. (TJ Sat. Jan. 10, 1863 p 2).

HIBBART, SAMUEL. Died Trinity Center Aug. 27, 1883; no age; late of Garberville, Humboldt Co. (TJ Sept. 1, 1883 p 2).

HIGGINS, R., Major. Killed by a falling timber at Lowden's Bridge July 2, 1878; native of Pawtucket, Rhode Island, aged about 48 years; of Red Bluff; buried Red Bluff, Tehama Co. (TJ Sat. July 6, 1878).

HIGGINS, WILLIAM. "Killed by earthquake at Iquique, Peru several weeks ago. Mrs. Higgins a resident of Weaverville." (TJ Aug. 4, 1877 p 3 col 2).

HILI, HARRY. Died March 14, 1902 Long Ridge, age 17. [Index to Deaths 1890-1908].

HILLIARD, JACOB. Died Junction City Aug 24, 1899; native of Penn., aged abt 64 yr. (TJ Aug 26, 1899 p 2; obit. p 3 col 3).

HIMES, WILLIAM H. Died San Francisco Sep 8, 1899; aged abt 60 yr; former res. of Coffee Creek. (TJ Sep 16, 1899 p 3 col 5).

HINDLEY, _____. Died Upper Mattole, Humboldt Co. Oct. 6, 1892, youngest child of Mr. and Mrs. George Hindley, former res. of Weaverville. (TJ Sat. Oct. 15, 1892 p 3 col 1).

HINDLEY, BETTY, Mrs. Died Weaverville Mar. 7, 1885, native of England, aged 68 yr 7 mo; bur. Sunday Mar 8, 1885 Weaverville Cem; widow of Henry Hindley, lately deceased. (TJ Sat. Mar. 14, 1885).

HINDLEY, CHARLIE. Died Upper Mattole, Humboldt Co. Oct. 27, 1877, aged 8 yr 2 mo; son of Margaret & George Hindley. (TJ Sat. Nov. 17, 1877 p 2). (see also Jessie, same notice; both from diphtheria.)

HINDLEY, HENRY. Died Weaverville Mar. 20, 1884; born in England Aug. 1822, aged 61 yr 7 mo 10 days; came to Trinity County 1853, Canon Creek; wife, son George Hindley (Humboldt Co.), dau. Mrs. Thomas W. McAlpine, Tehama (Tehama Co.); Mrs. Henry T. Harvey, Weaverville; fun. Mar. 22, 1884. (TJ Mar. 22, 1884).

HINDLEY, JESSIE. Died Upper Mattole, Humboldt Co. Oct. 10, 1877, aged 3 yr 2 mo 20 days; dau. of Margaret and George Hindley. (TJ Sat. Nov. 17, 1877 p 2).

HINDS, ANDREW. Died at Santa Cruz (Santa Cruz Co.) Oct. 12, 1888 while visiting relatives; former resident; late of Redmond, Washington Territory. (TJ Sat. Oct. 27, 1888 p 3).

HINDS, DAVID. Died Santa Cruz Dec. 4, 1889, age 75; former resident Weaverville; proprietor of St. Charles Hotel, burned July 5, 1859; rebuilt; burned again 1863; Tax Collector 1863; wife and only daughter died some years ago; 4 sons: Samuel, Peter, Firmin, William. (TJ Dec. 7, 1889 p 3).

HINDS, DAVID, Mrs. Died Santa Cruz (Santa Cruz Co.) Dec. 30, 1884; native of New Jersey, aged about 70 years; formerly of Weaverville (before 1866). (TJ Sat. Jan. 10, 1885 p 3).

"Hinds, Kate". see Reese, Catharine.

HINDS, LIZZIE. Died San Jose (Santa Clara Co.) June 11, 1872; formerly of Weaverville; no age. (TJ June 22, 1872).

HINDS, PETER. Died Santa Cruz (Santa Cruz Co.) Feb 23, 1899; native of New Jersey, 55 yr; son of late David Hinds; res. of Weaverville in early days. Father kept the St. Charles Hotel [Main Street, Weaverville] where J. H. Tourtellotte and fam. now reside. Hotel burned in 1863; Hinds family moved away 1860s.

HINDS, SAMUEL NORMAN. Died Seattle, Wash. Apr. 10, 1891. Nephew of late Wm. S. Norman. Two brothers living: Ferman D. Hinds of Oakland, CA and Peter R. Hinds of Santa Cruz; will be buried in Oakland, (Alameda Co.) CA; former resident of Trinity County. (TJ Sat. Apr 25, 1891 p 3).

HINKLE, ISAAC. Died Missouri August 1862; no age; formerly of Douglas City. (TJ Sat. Feb. 28, 1863 p 2).

HIPELIUS, JOHN. Died Weaverville Sept. 27, 1871; native of Bavaria, aged 58 yr; came to Trinity County 1850, known as "Strouse the Musician". One of original proprietors of Union Hotel. (TJ Sept. 30, 1871 pp 2-3).

HOADLEY, ELIAS A. Died San Francisco May 9, 1936. He was born in Lewiston 1854 "one of the first white children born in Trinity County". "He was a familiar figure at the Trinity-Shasta reunion held at Mosswood Park in Oakland each year. His wife Belinda and six children survive him." [son of James F. Hoadley]. (TJ Thurs. May 14, 1936).

HOADLEY, JAMES F. Died Cloverdale, Sonoma Co. Aug. 17, 1891 aged 60 yr. Supervisor Lewiston District 1867-1869, and also in 1850s. (TJ Aug. 29, 1891 p 3 col 4). [Note: Hoadley Peaks were named for this man.] [Moved to Cloverdale abt Aug. 1872. (TJ Sep 7, 1872).]

HOAGLAN, LAURA BELL. Died Long Ridge May 24, 1899; native of Calif. aged 5 mo 6 dy. (TJ Jun 3, 1899 p 2; no further info.)

HOBART, DeFORREST AMOS. Died Weaverville Dec 16, 1899; b. Homer, Courtland Co., New York Sep 22, 1831, age 68 yr 2 mo 24 dy, a son of Amos & Jane Hobart; pioneer res., came to Calif 1851, Trinity Co. 1854; m. Miss Julia Seabury in 1859 in New York; she survives, with 3 children; bur. Weaverville Cem. under auspices of Old Settlers Assn. (TJ Dec 23, 1899 p 3 col 3).

HOBART, HATTIE. Died Taylor's Flat, Trinity River Dec. 27, 1862; aged 1 yr; youngest child of DeForest A. and Julia Hobart. (TJ Sat. Jan. 17, 1863 p 2).

HOBART, SEYMOUR D. Drowned in Trinity River June 19, 1860 by the capsizing of a boat; formerly of Homer, Cortland Co. New York, aged about 23 years; brother at Taylor's Flat. (TJ Sat. June 23, 1860 p 2 col 1 "Distressing Accident"; see also Aug. 4, 1860 p 2 col 1). "Disinterred - the body of Seymour D. Hobart, drowned some six weeks since at Big Bar, in this county, was recently disinterred and buried at Taylor's Flat, Trinity River."

HOBERT, FRED B. Died Weaverville Sunday Dec. 12, 1869, age 9 yr 11 mo 9 days; eldest son of DeForest and Julia Hobert. (TJ Dec. 18, 1869 p 2). (Note: this name is also spelled Hobart.)

HOCKER, CHRISTINA. Died Weaverville Apr. 24, 1875; native of Monterey, Mexico aged 34 years and 9 months; wife of Henry Hocker; mother is Mrs. R. Clifford; bur. Catholic Cem. Monday April 26, 1875. (TJ Sat. May 1, 1875). [see also Clifford.]

HOCKER, CLARA. Died Weaverville Dec. 14, 1875; born Weaverville, aged 1 yr 10 days; dau. of Henry Hocker. (TJ Dec. 18, 1875 p 2).

HOCKER, HERMAN HENRY. Died San Francisco June 30, 1882; native of Hanover, Germany; aged 55 yr 10 mo 7 days; bur. Catholic Cem. Weaverville Thurs July 6, 1882. (TJ July 8, 1882 p 2).

HOCKER, JOHN. Died Red Hill, near Junction City;, Dec. 24, 1881; native of Germany, aged about 50 yr. Brother of Henry Hocker of Weaverville; bur. Catholic Cem. Monday Dec. 26, 1881. (TJ Dec. 311, 1881 p 2 & 3).

HOCKER, ROBERT M. Died Tacoma, WA Dec 10, 1894; born Weaverville Dec 20, 1870; age 24; unmarried; drowned. Sister Miss Lily Hocker of Weaverville. (TJ Dec 16, 1894 p 3; Dec 22, 1894 pg 3 col 3). "Body of Robert M. Hocker interred in Catholic Cemetery, Weaverville April 29, 1895; drowned at Tacoma, Washington Dec 10, 1895; native of Weaverville, aged about 24 yr." obit. worth copying. (TJ Sat. May 4, 1895 p 3 col 5).

HOCKING, JOHN. Died England abt Oct. 1881. no particulars; not in census for 1852, 1860, 1870. (TJ Nov. 12, 1881, p 3).

HOCKING, THOS. H. Died Sep 18, 1900; age 55 yr; b. Cornwall. (TJ Jan 1901).

HOCKINGS, JAMES, Capt. Died San Francisco Nov. 1, 1880; native of Praze, Camborn, Cornwall, England, aged about 48 yr. (TJ Nov. 13, 1880 p 3).

HOEHM, HENRY. Died Weaverville Sept. 2, 1865; native of Germany, aged about 60 years. (TJ Sat. Sept. 9, 1865 p 2).

HOFFMAN, A. J. Dr. Died last week [abt Aug. 15, 1876] at North San Juan, Nevada County, Calif.; no age; formerly of Weaverville. (TJ Aug. 26, 1876).

HOLDEN, EDGAR. Died Trinity Centre March 1, 1858, aged 27 years; formerly of Canada East. (TJ Sat. Mar. 6, 1858 p 2).

HOLLEY, W. Died Hay Fork Mar. 31, 1889; native of Calif, aged about 18 yr. (TJ Sat. Apr. 6, 1889).

HOLMAN, ELGIE F., Mrs. Died San Francisco July 9, 1889; native of Indiana, 42 years. Came to Trinity County 1882; taught school at Hettenshaw; sister of Miss Ray, formerly a music teacher in Weaverville; brothers in San Francisco and Ukiah. (TJ Sat. July 13, 1889).

HOLMAN, JOSEPH. Died Upper Mattole, Humboldt Co. Mar 1897; native of England, abt 67 yr; uncle of Mrs. George Hindley of Upper Mattole; bro. Nicholas Holman lives at Upper Mattole; both Joseph & Nicholas were pioneer residents of Weaverville, Trinity Co. (see also *Humboldt Times* Mar 20, 1897). (TJ Mar 27, 1897 p 3 col 3; also TJ Apr 10, 1897 p 3 col 5, from *Ferndale Enterprise* Mar 30, 1897).

HOLMES, FRED. Died about Jan. 18, 1908 Hayfork; (murder); age 60; born Calif. farmer; buried Weaverville. [Index to Deaths 1890-1908].

HOOVER, EARNEST FRANKLIN. Died Spencerville (Nevada Co.) [later Spenceville] July 25, 1878, aged 3 yr 2 mo 18 days; only son of D. F. and M. E. Hoover. (Wheatland, Yuba County paper) (TJ Sat. Aug. 10, 1878 p 3).

HOPPE, HENRY. Died Weaverville Oct 29, 1897; native of Germany, aged abt 77 yr; came to Calif. 1852, Trin. Co. 1859. (TJ Nov 27, 1897 p 2).

HOPPELL, _____, Mr. Died Snow Gulch abt Nov 19, 1898; aged abt 72 yr; of Los Gatos; bur. Trinity Center Cem. (TJ Dec 3, 1898; see also TJ Nov 19, 1898 p 3 col 2 "Found Dead").

HOPPING, _____. Sheriff Hopping of Shasta County died Jan. 31, 1892; he lived in Trinity County 1851; Shasta Co. 1852 at French Gulch; no age, no first name given. (TJ Feb. 6, 1892).

HORSLEY, A. J. Died Los Angeles July 24, 1862; native of Petersburg, Boone County, KY, aged about 34 years. Mr. Horsley was well known as an Expressman in this section from 1851-1855 and generally respected and beloved by those who knew him. (TJ Sat. Aug. 30, 1862 p 2).

HORSTMEYER, HENRY. Died Canon City July 14, 1889; native of Prussia, aged about 68 yr; came Trinity County 1850s. (TJ Sat. July 20, 1889). [Similar information Index to Deaths 1873-1890].

HORTON, RICHARD EDWARD. Died Weaverville Mar 10, 1894; native of Missouri, aged abt 40 yr; bur. I.O.O.F. Cem. Weaverville; member Ferndale Lodge; came to Weaverville 1887; had a barber shop; leaves wife and 3 small children. (TJ Mar 17, 1894).

HORTON, WILLIAM B., Dr. Died Weaverville July 4, 1852; buried Old Section, Weaverville Public Cemetery; original wooden markers had become illegible and damaged by 1887; Horton owned the American Hotel. He was in financial trouble, but decided to give a big banquet and make money from all the people in town for the Independence Day festivities. He was shot and killed by the Sheriff. Elza [Eliza] Vanderberg, who acted in the capacity of Horton's wife, was shot and killed by one of the posse; no age given. (TJ Sat. Jan. 29, 1887, p 1, T. E. Jones story.) See also Vanderberg.

HORTON note. The story of the death of William Horton July 4, 1842 is re-told in the *TRINITY JOURNAL* for July 3, 1897 on page one.

HOUGH, JOHN H. Died San Francisco Nov. 17, 1867, native of Philadelphia, aged about 32 years; for several years a resident of Douglas City. (TJ Sat. Nov. 30, 1867 p 2).

HOUGH, WILLIE. Drowned at Douglas City Mar. 13, 1861, aged 2 yr 4 mo; son of John H. and Julia Hough. (TJ Sat. Mar. 16, 1861). [see also Estes.]

HOUGHTON, BESSIE. Died Deadwood (Trinity County) Feb. 23, 1886; native of Greenwood, El Dorado County, Calif. aged 6 yr 7 mo 21 days; only child of T. J. and V. M. Houghton; buried Weaverville Cem. Wed. Feb. 24, 1886; a great favorite with everybody, particularly the miners of Deadwood. (TJ Sat. Feb. 27, 1886).

HOWARD, _____. Died Big Bar Apr 1, 1897 inf. dau. of Mr. and Mrs. W. A. Howard, aged 6 dy. (TJ Sat Apr 10, 1897 p 2).

HOWARD, _____. Died near Big Bar Jun 14, 1899, inf. son of Mr. and Mrs. W. G. Howard. (TJ Jul 1, 1899 p 2).

HOWE, AGNES. Died at Napa Insane Hospital Dec. 9, 1891. She was committed to that institution Sept. 20, 1890. "She had been quite ill for some time before death." (TJ Sat. Dec. 19, 1891). [Note: she was 17 in the 1880 census, a boarder with the Sam Smith family at Ruch's. Her father was James Howe, born Illinois.]

HOWE, EMMELINE J., Mrs. Died Philadelphia June 6, 1872; formerly of Weaverville. Born, raised, married in Huntington, Loraine County, Ohio (ref. Willington, Ohio *Enterprise*); married April 1856 H. J. Howe, Esq. of California; survived by brother, father, mother, husband.

HOWE, HENRY J. Died San Francisco Feb. 24, 1879; native of New York, aged 53 yr 4 mo 20 days; formerly Lawyer in Weaverville; will filed for probate in San Francisco. (TJ Mar. 1 & 8, 1879 p 3). [Father: Phineas Howe, native of New Hampshire; died New York 1845. Henry J. Howe came to Calif. and Weaverville 1852; County Surveyor 1853, District Attorney 1854, editor of Trinity Democrat in 1855; returned East and married Miss Emeline Johnson of Ohio in 1856. Cox's Annals, 1940 edition.]

HOWLAND, DANIEL, Major. Died Weaverville Aug. 18, 1884; native of Brunswick Maine, aged 84 yr 8 mo; born Dec. 1799; bur. Masonic Cem. Weaverville; came to Humboldt Bay early, Trinity County 1854-5; carpenter and builder. (TJ Aug. 23, 1884 p 2).

HOYTT, JONATHAN STUKNEY. Died Hay Fork Nov 3, 1899; b. New York 1831, aged abt 69 yr; came to Calif. 1858, Trin. Co. 1866; m. Katherine Woods at Hay Fork 1875; one child, Mrs. Sadie Shock of Hay Fork; Mrs. Hoytt died in Redding five years ago; bur. Hay Fork Nov 4, 1899. (TJ Nov 4, 1899 p 2 & p 3 col 6). (see also Shock).

HUBBARD,------. Died Douglas City Sept. 15, 1875, a daughter of Mr. and Mrs. A. W. Hubbard, aged about 3 years. (TJ Sept. 18, 1875 p 2).

HUBBARD, B.C., Mrs. Died Sisson [now Mount Shasta], Shasta Co. abt Mar 7, 1899; leaves sister, Mrs. G. K. Osborn of Weaverville and a large family of small children. (TJ Mar 11, 1899 p 3 col 1).

HUBBARD, JOHN AUSTIN. Died Weaverville Sept. 15, 1891. Native of Kanawha Co., West Virginia, aged 70 yr 3 mo 13 days. Born on the Great Kanawha river; age 23 went to Shelby Co. Indiana; married there Francis Catlin 1849; they went to Louisiana, then family returned to Indiana; brought his family to Calif 1852, Placer Co., then Poverty Hill, Sierra Co; 5 children born there; mother & one child died Poverty Hill; other children were taken back to Indiana; son & one dau. survive; came to Trinity Co. 1877. Bur. Weaverville Cem. Thurs. Sept. 17, 1891. (TJ Sat. Sept. 19, 1891 p 2 & 3, entire col. 2; obit. worth copying.)

HUBER, JOSEPH. Died North Fork June 2, 1888; native of Grand Duchy of Baden, aged about 72 years; came US 1848; Calif. 1850; leaves wife, 2 sons & a dau. in either Missouri or Iowa. Long history p 3 col 4. (TJ Sat. June 9, 1888).

HUDSPETH, WILLIAM. Died San Francisco Sat. Apr. 18, 1891; buried San Francisco. Native of Newcastle-on-Tyne, Northumberland, England. Came to U.S. as a young man, settled in Pittsburg, Penn where he has a son and daughter living. His wife preceded him to the grave a few months ago [no name available; not on 1860, 1870, 1880 census]; came to Calif 1856, Lewiston soon after, then Weaverville; known as "The tailor of Weaverville". (TJ Sat. Apr. 25, 1891).

HUGHES, ROBERT EDWARD. Died Douglas City Nov. 5, 1884; native of Nova Scotia, aged 54 yr; bur. Weaverville Cem. Nov. 6, 1884; born Halifax, Nova Scotia of American parents; came coast of Calif 1849, Trinidad 1850; m. Miss Marinda Puterman 1857, survives; 1860-1865 on Weaver Creek, near Douglas City; dau. Mrs. M. M. Bennett, several other children. (TJ Sat. Nov. 8, 1884). [see also Nordyke].

HUGHES, WILLIAM EDWARD. Died Weaverville Oct 12, 1897; born Douglas City 1861, age 35 yr 11 mo 11 dy; son of Robert E. Hughes and Miranda Hughes; father died 1884; m. Miss Katie Senger Dec 25, 1895, dau. of M/M Jacob Senger of Weaverville; one child; also leaves 3 bro and 4 sis. Fun. Oct 15, 1897. (TJ Oct 16, 1897 pp 2 & 3).

HULL, SYLVESTER. Died Redding, Shasta Co. Nov 23, 1899; pioneer of Shasta Co., Register of the Land Office for 2 terms. (TJ Dec 2, 1899 p 3 col 2).

HULME, GEORGE. Died San Francisco Jan. 22, 1870; of Weaverville, aged 51 years 11 months, 28 days. (TJ Jan. 29 and Feb. 5, 1870).

HULME, GEORGE. Died Weaverville Aug. 25, 1868, aged 1 year 2 months, 28 days; son of George and Elizabeth V. Hulme. (TJ Sat. Aug. 29, 1868)

HULME, JOHN. Died Weaverville Feb. 7, 1865; native of Patterson, New Jersey, aged 48 yr.(TJ Feb. 11, 1865 p 2, col 1).

HUNT, JAMES, Rev. Father. Died Grass Valley, Nevada Co. Jul 3, 1912; b. 1848 County Kerry, Ireland; Catholic Pastor at Weaverville 1874-1877. (TJ Jul 20, 1912).

HUNTER, CHAS. Died Fort Crook about 6 weeks ago; late of Point Bar in this county. Died abt 1 Dec. 1872. (TJ Jan. 18, 1873 p 3).

HUOT,-----, Mrs. and Huot,-----, child (son). Drowned in flood of Trinity River Dec. 7, 1861 near Lewiston; wife and child of Mr. Huot; Mr. Huot reached shore, probably saved by dog.(TJ Dec. 14, 1861 p 2). Mr. Huot's little son's body was found buried in a sand bar 2 miles below Mooney's Ferry.(TJ Jan. 4, 1862).

HUOT, EUGENIE. Died near Bolt's Hill, above Lewiston, May 15, 1875, aged 1 year 3 months. Child of Joseph Huot and Catherine Huot.

HUOT, FREDERIC. Died Weaverville May 17, 1875, aged 2 yr 6 mo. Child of Joseph Huot and Catherine Huot. (Both references, Eugenie & Frederic, TJ May 22, 1875 pages 2 & 3).

HUPP, ISABEL. Died Weaverville April 15, 1875; native of Ireland aged 33 years; wife of Wm. I. Hupp; buried Weav. Cem. Apr. 16, 1875. (TJ Sat. Apr. 17, 1875).

HUSON,-----, Mrs. Died Rush Creek May 8, 1877, aged 77 years; mother of C. W. Huson; bur. Odd Fellows Cem., Weaverville, prob. May 9, 1877. (TJ May 12, 1877 p 2). "Came here in poor health 2 years ago."

HUSON, ARTHUR T. Died Rush Creek Sept. 10, 1879, aged 5 yr; youngest son of C. W. and Fannie Huson. (Note: see also "Mrs. T. H. Carr".) (TJ Sat. Sept. 13, 1879 p 2).

HUSON, CORNELIUS W. Accidentally killed at George M. Hughes Planing Mill at Nevada City, Nevada Co., CA Sat. July 9, 1892; native of New York, age 60; bur. July 11, 1892 Nevada City, with Odd Fellows Ceremonies; formerly of Rush Creek; left Trinity County "last fall" (1891); leaves a wife, a married dau. Mrs. T. H. Carr of Nevada City, a son aged 24, Nevada City; sister Mrs. W. B. Haywood, of Berkeley, Alameda Co. (TJ July 16, 1892 p 3 col 6; TJ July 23, 1892 p 3 col 2; Nevada City *Transcript* July 11, 1892 has details of accident.) [see also Carr].

HUSON, HENRY H. Died Grass Valley, Nevada Co. Nov 3, 1898, four year old son of Mr. and Mrs. A. S. Huson; leaves grandmother Mrs. C. W. Huson and uncle Joseph Northey. (from *Grass Valley Transcript* Nov 3, 1898). (TJ Nov 12, 1898 p 3 col 3).

HUSTON, JOHN. Died San Francisco, [San Francisco Co.], CA Nov. 13, 1895, aged 63 yr; b. Ireland about 1832; m. June 30, 1889 Miss Clara Showalter, a niece of M. Bartolett. (TJ Nov 16, 1895 p 3 col 3; funeral TJ Sat. Nov. 23, 1895 p 3 col 6). [see also Showalter].

IHNE, THEODORE. Died Rattlesnake (New River area), Trinity Co, CA July 2, 1896; native of Germany, aged abt 76 yr; obit. p 3. (TJ Sat. July 11, 1896).

"INDIAN BILLY". Died Dec. 2, 1905 Lewiston; age 50; male, Indian, born Calif; wood chopper; burned to death. [Index to Deaths 1890-1905].

INGERSOLL, SAMUEL, Mr. Died Weaverville May 19, 1862, aged about 37 yr. (TJ Sat. May 24, 1862 p 3).

INGHAM, CHARLES. Died Lewiston Nov 24, 1894; native of England, aged about 71 yr. (TJ Dec 1, 1894 p 2).

INGRAM,-----. Died Douglas City Aug. 23, 1888, infant son of Mr. and Mrs. Walker Ingram, aged about 3 weeks. Born Douglas City July 28, 1888. (TJ Sat. Aug. 25, 1888).

INGRAM, AUGUSTUS. Died Douglas City Dec. 1, 1889 at residence of W. W. Ingram, his oldest son; native of Georgia, aged about 66 yr. "San Jose papers please copy." Bur. Public cem. Weaverville Dec. 2, 1889. Long obit. p. 3 'The Death Roll'. (TJ Sat. Dec. 7, 1889). [Index to Deaths 1873-1890 says "Ingram, Augusta (sic); d. Dec. 1, 1889 Douglas City, white, 66, male, born Georgia."]

IRWIN, JOHN GWIN. Died Weaverville Jan. 23, 1880; native of Bucyrus, Ohio, aged 48 yr 1 mo 3 days. Came to Trinity Co. 1856; Justice of Peace of Lewiston Township; admitted practice of law by Ninth District Court Apr. 1872; resides Weaverville; D.A. 1876 for 2 years; Bur. Masonic Cem. Weaverville Jan. 25, 1880. (TJ Sat. Jan. 31, 1880, page 2 and page 3 col 1).

ISAACS, FRANK CURTIS. Died Redding, Shasta Co. Dec 9, 1894; inf. son of James E. and Mary E. Isaacs. (from *Shasta Courier*). (TJ Dec 22, 1894 p 3).

ISAACS, ISAIAH. Died Weaverville Dec. 20, 1858, aged 58 years. "Colored." (TJ Sat. Dec. 25, 1858 p 2).

ISAACKS, FRANCES LITTLE. Died Shasta (Shasta County) Mar. 5, 1866; native of Bristol, Maine, aged 45 yr; wife of Samuel Isaacks. (TJ Sat. Mar. 17, 1866 p 2).

IVERSON, EDWARD. Shot at French Gulch (Shasta County) Dec. 14, 1862 by Chas. Franklin; no age given. (TJ Dec. 27, 1862).

IVERSON, HANNAH. Died Steiners Flat "Oct. 12" (sic); should be Sept. 12, 1888; native of Norway, aged about 37 yr. AND:

IVERSON, OLE. Died Steiners Flat Sept. 12, 1888; native of Norway, aged about 35 years. Murdered wife Hannah; suicide. Bur. one grave Weaverville public cemetery Thurs. Sept. 13, 1888. They leave 7 children, 3 born in Trinity County, from the ages of 10 months to 13 years. Mrs. P. Eliason is a sister of Mrs. Iverson. (TJ Sat. Sept. 15, 1888).

IVERSEN, SIGRID. Died Lowden Ranch May 3, 1889; native of Christiania, Norway, aged 13 yr 6 mo 9 days; buried Weaverville Cemetery Sunday May 5, 1889; came with parents in Sept. 1881. Mrs. Eliassen is her aunt. (TJ Sat. May 11, 1889). [Index to Deaths 1873-1889 says: "Iverson, Siegnid (sic) d. May 3, 1889 Lowden's Ranch; white, 13 yr 6 mo 9 days; female, single, born Norway."]

JACINTO, JOHN. Died Weaverville Dec 1, 1894; native of Portugal, aged abt 46 yr; aka "Johnson". (TJ Sat. Dec 8, 1894 p 2).

JACKSON, EDWARD S. Died Weaverville Sept. 15, 1891; native of Mississippi, aged 39 yr. No relatives here. (TJ Sat. Sept. 19, 1891 pp 2 & 3).

JACKSON, KATE MARIA. Died Junction City June 29, 1864, aged 1 yr 7 mo 10 days; dau. of John and Catharine Jackson. (TJ July 2, 1864 p 2).

JACKSON, MAMIE G., Miss. Died San Francisco May 13, 1899; born Trinity Co., dau. of John and Catherine Jackson; bur. St. Mary's Cem. Oakland [Alameda Co.] beside body of her father; leaves mother, sister Mrs. J. F. Reynolds of Oakland, and bro. Arthur J. Jackson of Modoc Co. (TJ May 20, 1899 p 3 col 6; see also TJ May 13, 1899 p 3 col 4).

JACKSON, WM. L., Dr. Died abt Aug. 13, 1859 Pittsfield, [state unknown]; age 33 years; resident Trinity County 1852-1855; deputy Sheriff. (TJ Sept. 24, 1859 p 2).

JACOBI, JOHN S. Died May 20, 1905 Weaverville; about 72; male, white, retired miner; bur. Public Cemetery, Weaverville. [Index to Deaths 1890-1908].

JACOBS, ANNA. Died at Red Hill, near Junction City, June 28, 1879; native of New Orleans, Louisiana, age 25 yr 6 mo 12 days; bur. Catholic Cem. Weaverville. Wife of Henry Jacobs; came to Trinity Co. with parents 1859. (TJ Jul 1879).

JACOBS, BARTHEL. Died at Red Hill, near Junction City, May 28, 1891; native of Germany, aged 54 yr 7 mo 13 days. (TJ May 30, 1891 p 2).

JAMES, WM. Killed at his claim at Red Hill, Canon Creek, last Saturday by a falling bank. Died Mar. 29, 1862; born Ohio, age 28; came to California from Iowa. "Ohio & Iowa papers please copy". (TJ Apr. 5 and 12, 1862).

JENKS, DANIEL A. Died Central Falls, Rhode Island on the 8th of Feb. 1869, in 42nd year of his age; former resident of Siskiyou County, Calif. (TJ Apr. 3, 1869).

JEPSON, JACOB. Remains found Jan. 1885; disappeared from home in Douglas City August 1884; native of Denmark; no age given; built the first water wheel at Ferry Bar in 1852. (TJ Sat. Jan. 10, 1885).

JOHNSON, _____, Mrs. "Mrs. Johnson died at Big Bar abt Jan. 24, 1891. Particulars next week". [none next week]. (TJ Jan. 24, 1891.) [The 1880 Census has Christian Johnson, age 38, miner, b. Denmark and wife Olive H. Johnson age 48, b. Maine at Cox Bar on June 2, 1880 p 2. Cox Bar is across the Trinity River from Big Bar, so this is the only likely couple, but there is no proof.] [1890 Great Register of Voters lists Christian Julius Johnson at Cox Bar; b. Denmark; naturalized Sept. 26, 1868 at Mauch Chunk, Penn.]

JOHNSON, ALFRED, Rev. Died Oakland, Alameda Co., Calif. Jan. 1, 1892. "Mr. Johnson was well liked here. He buried his wife a few years ago in Africa." no age given. (TJ Sat. Jan. 10, 1892).

JOHNSON, CHARLES. Died Apr. 17, 1903 Trinity Center; age about 45; male, white, foreign; bur. Public Cemetery Trinity Center. [Index to Deaths 1890-1908].

JOHNSON, CHARLES C. Died San Francisco March 9, 1873; native of Maine, aged 44 yr. (TJ Mar. 15, 1873).

JOHNSON, FELIX. Died Feb. 8, 1906 Weaverville; age 63, male, white, American, carpenter. [Index to Deaths 1890-1908].

JOHNSON, HENRY S. Died Weaverville Jan. 26, 1887; native of Vermont, aged 71 yr. (TJ Sat. Jan. 29, 1887).

JOHNSON, MANUEL. Died Weaverville Jan. 15, 1866; of Indian Creek; native of Azores Islands, age 41. (TJ Sat. Jan. 20, 1866 p 2).

JOHNSON, SUSANNA, Mrs. Died Fon du lac, Wisconsin Oct. 7, 1866, aged 77 yr 7 mo; formerly of Weaverville; mother of Mrs. R. A. Fagg. (See also Fagg). (TJ Sat. Nov. 24, 1866 p 2).

JOHNSTON, ADALINE ELIZABETH. Died Sidney Hill [near Weaverville] March 13, 1858, aged 6 yr 6 mo 7 days; eldest daughter of William and Elizabeth Johnston. (TJ Sat. Mar. 27, 1858 p 2). [see also Fox].

JOHNSTON, CHAS. C. Died March 9, 1873 St. Mary's Hospital, San Francisco, Calif. white, 44, male, married, born Maine, lumberman. [Index to Deaths 1873-1890].

JOHNSTON, EMELINE. Died Weaverville Feb. 15, 1858, aged 1 yr 10 mo 13 days; daughter of William and Elizabeth Johnston. (TJ Sat. Feb. 20, 1858).

JOHNSTON, LIZZIE, Miss. Died Eureka, Humboldt County, March 3, 1884; no age; formerly of Weaverville, daughter of Wm. H. Johnston, niece of Mr. and Mrs. Orson Fox. (TJ Sat. Mar. 8, 1884). [see also Fox].

JOHNSTON, WALTER. Died Eureka Nov. 8, 1889, nearly 18 years of age; son of W. H. Johnston. (TJ Sat. Nov. 16, 1889 p 3).

JONES, A. F. Supposedly dead, Apr. 5, 1890; res. North Fork, no trace; prob. drowned Trinity River. (TJ Mar. 29, 1890 p 3 col 3; Apr. 5, 1890 p 3). [Index to Deaths 1873-1890: Jones, A. F. died abt Dec. 31, 1889 near Helena, Calif; age about 51, male, white, American; blacksmith; died of exposure; buried Chico (Butte) Calif.]

JONES, HANNAH CORNELIA. Died Gold Hill, Nevada Feb. 19, 1871; wife of Hon. John P. Jones. no age given. (TJ Feb. 25, 1871 p 2).

JONES, HENRY A. Died Gold Hill, Nevada Jan. 9, 1882, age 50; brother of U. S. Senator John P. Jones; formerly Trinity County Deputy Sheriff and Tax Collector. (TJ Jan. 14, 1882 p 3).

JONES, JAMES A. S. Died at Redding, Shasta County Aug. 12, 1884; native of England, aged about 56 years; late of Weaverville; lived in Trinity County 25 years. Obit. p 3. (TJ Sat. Aug. 16, 1884).

JONES, MARY A. Died San Francisco Mar. 12, 1886; native of Lake county, Illinois aged 47 yr 2 days; bur. Tuesday Mar. 16, 1886 Odd Fellows Cem, Weaverville; wife of Judge T. E. Jones of Trinity County; Judge Jones also raised to manhood in Lake Co., Ill. but they met in Weaverville. (TJ Sat. Mar. 20, 1886). [Note: wife #2; wife #3 survived him.] [see also Appendum].

JONES, SARAH J. Died Sacramento Feb. 6, 1868, aged 19 years 3 months 4 days; daughter born in Sacramento Jan. 23, 1868. Wife of Hon. T. E. Jones, Assemblyman from Trinity County. (TJ Feb. 1, 1868; Feb. 15, 1868 p 2 col 1). [Note: wife #1, mother of only daughter]. [see also Appendum and Mary A. Jones, above]. [see also Puterman & Brannan].

JONES, SETH CLARK. Drowned in his flume on Sidney Gulch, Weaverville Feb. 11, 1861; native of Brooke County, Virginia, aged 37 years. "Steubenville, Ohio and Pittsburg, Penn. papers please copy." (TJ Sat. Feb. 16, 1861).

JONES, THEODORE ELDON. [see Addendum; Brannan, Puterman, Mary A. Jones, and Sarah J. Jones].

JONES, THOMAS. Died Canon City (near Junction City) May 1, 1889; native of Calif. aged 8 years; bur. Weav. cem. May 3, 1889; son of Frank Jones of Canon City; fell into sluice-way on Keenan Claim. (Sat. May 4, 1889). [Index to Deaths 1873-1890: similar information; adds drowned, white, male, single, born Calif.] [Trinity Journal gives birth as Feb. 9, 1881, son of Francis and Nancy Jones.]

JONES, THOMAS D. Died Canon City Feb. 11, 1881; native of New Jersey, aged about 54 yr; bur. Weaverville Cem. Sunday Feb. 13, 1881; cripple since accident in a tunnel on Canon Creek in 1856. (TJ Feb. 19, 1881).

JOSE, EDWARD WILLIAM. Shot and fatally wounded at Lewiston, June 1894; native of Calif, aged 87 yr 1 mo 27 dy; shot by F. G. Eddinger. (TJ Jun 16, 1894 pg 3, col 2 & 3). (see also Eddinger.)

JOSEPH, _____. (no first name; no date, but between 1903-1905); died Minersville; age between 85-90; male, white; foreign birth; bur. "Public Cemetery" no place. [Index to Deaths 1890-1908].

JOSEPH, HENRY. Died Stillwater, Shasta County Dec. 8, 1877; no age given; bur. French Gulch Dec. 10, 1877; leaves young wife and babe. (TJ Sat. Dec. 15, 1877 p 3).

JOSLIN, EDWARD G. Died 2 miles from Weaverville on Yreka Trail Mon. Sept. 1, 1856; bur. Weaverville Sept. 3, 1856; accidentally fell from mule, breaking his neck; long resident; no age given. (TJ Sept. 6, 1856 p 2).

JOYNT, JOSEPH. Died Weaverville Aug. 28, 1861 aged about 5 yr 6 mo; died from injuries received by a rolling log; son of Robert and Catherine Joynt. (TJ Aug. 31, 1861).

JULLIARD, MARY ANNETTE. Died Brighton twp, Sacramento county, July 1, 1865, aged 8 mo 15 days; dau. of C. F. and Sarah A. Julliard. (TJ Sat. July 22, 1865 p 2).

JUMPER,-----. Died Weaverville May 19, 1885, infant daughter of Mr. and Mrs. George B. Jumper. (TJ Sat. May 23, 1885).

JUMPER, ALDEN H., Major. Died Osage Co., Kansas near Melvern Feb. 29, 1888, aged 69 yr; born Feb. 1819 Thomastown, Maine; m. Amanda F. Noyes in Dearborn Co., Indiana; brother of George B. Jumper of Weaverville; more. (TJ Sat. Mar. 31, 1888 p 3 col 5).

JUMPER, GEORGE BOWERS. Died Weaverville July 12, 1888; native of Maine, aged 55 yr; married Miss Maggie Colbert May 30, 1883; son 8 months old. Bur. Odd Fellows Cem. July 14, 1888. (TJ Sat. July 14, 1888).

JUNKANS,-----, Mrs. Died Germany Aug. 15, 1879 age 75 yr; children in Weaverville are Messrs. Henry, Wm. F. and Carl Junkans; Mrs. D. Hansen, Mrs. C. Dannenbrink, Mrs. J. Barnickel, and Mrs. J. H. Bremer. (TJ Sept. 20, 1879 p 3).

JUNKANS, CARL. Died Oct. 20, 1905 Weaverville, age 74, born Prussia, Germany; clerk. Informant: Anna A. Junkans. [Index to Deaths 1890-1908].

JUNKANS, HENRY. Died Weaverville Aug 21, 1899; native of Prussia, aged 70 yr 6 mo 26 dy; came to Calif. 1852, Trinity Co. 1854; m. Mrs. Mary Healy Sep 27, 1868; she survives him; obit. p 3 cols 2 & 3 worth copying. (TJ Aug 26, 1899 pp 2 & 3).

JUNKANS, JOHANNA. Died Napa, Napa Co. CA Mar. 30, 1883, native of Germany, aged 36 yr 3 mo 11 days; bur. Odd Fellows Cem, Weav. Apr. 2, 1883; wife of Wm. F. Junkans. (TJ Apr. 7, 1883 p 2 & 3).

JUNKANS, MARIE L. Died Jul 17, 1900; age 76 yr 1 mo 7 dy; b. Germany. (TJ Jan 1901).

JUNKANS, MATTIE. Died Weaverville Aug. 10, 1875 aged 18 yr 1 mo 4 days; wife of Wm. F. Junkans. (TJ Aug. 14, 1875). "Wm. F. Junkans and Miss Mattie Todd were married in Redding (Shasta County) June 15, 1873 by Rev. R. Graves. They were the first couple married in Redding." (TJ June 21, 1873).

JUNKANS, RUDOLPH HENRY. Died in snow slide between Sawyers Bar and Etna, Siskiyou Co. Tues. Mar 6, 1894; born Waldeck, Prussia Apr 13, 1865; came with parents to Weaverville 1876; bur. Odd Fellows Cem. Weaverville Sat. Mar 10, 1894. (TJ Sat Mar 10, 1894 pg 3, col 3 & col 4).

KAPUSTA, WLAHYSLOF. Died March 1, 1908 Minersville, age 6, male, white, born California. [Index to Deaths 1890-1908].

KARSKY, HANNAH, Mrs. Died San Francisco May 31, 1898; she was 66 years of age; mother of Samuel Karsky of Weaverville; 3 dau.: Mrs. Miriam Silver, Mrs. Theresa Lewin, and Sarah Karsky; wife of I. Karsky, who d. San Francisco in 1867; sister of Isaac Abrahms. (TJ Jun 11, 1898).

KARSKY, VICTOR I. Died San Francisco Thursday Jan. 28, 1886; no age; buried San Francisco. Brother of Samuel Karsky Jr; nephew of I. Abrahm. (TJ Sat. Feb. 6, 1886 p 3). [see also Abrahm].

KEACH, JOHN. Drowned Trinity River Aug. 29, 1877; native of Calif., aged 19 yr 3 mo. (TJ Sept. 8, 1877 p 2. See also p 3 col 3 "Drowned").

KEARNAN, PATRICK. (Spelled Kearnan & Keirnan in same paper.) Killed by a land slide on Lower Trinity Jan. 9, 1880; native of Ireland, aged 59 yr; body not found yet; lived at Big Flat as early as 1853. Story p. 3. See also James Collins. (TJ Jan. 17, 1880 p 2 & 3).

KEEFER, XAVIER. Died North Fork (Helena) July 16, 1894; born Grand Duchy of Baden, Germany; aged abt 74 yr; came U.S. 1847; naturalized in Trinity County 1858. (TJ July 21, 1894).

KEELY, JOHN. Died Big Bar Nov. 11, 1882; native of Green Hills, County Dublin, Ireland, aged 70 yr; bur. Catholic Cem, Weaverville, Nov. 13, 1882; stone in Catholic Cem. legible in 1986; pioneer, lived Trinity County more than 30 yr; wife and 3 daughters: Mrs. P. O. M. Hennessy; Mrs. E. A. Leary; Mrs. James Mullane. obit. p 3. (TJ Nov. 18, 1882 p 2).

KEELY, MARGARET, Mrs. Died Burnt Ranch Jan. 4, 1906; native of Dublin, Ireland, aged 85 yr 1 mo 10 days; died at home of dau. Mrs. Maria Hennessy; other dau. Mrs. Lucy Mullane of Eureka; bur. Burnt Ranch, prob. Hennessy Ranch Cem. Jan. 7, 1906; husband d. Nov. 11, 1882. (TJ Jan. 20, 1906 p 2). [see also Leary].

KEELY, THOMAS. Died at res. of father at Manzanita Flat, Trinity River Dec. 23, 1867; native of Co. Dublin, Ireland, age 17 yr 7 mo; bur. Catholic Cem. Weaverville Dec. 26, 1867; (TJ Dec. 28, 1867). [stone legible in Catholic Cem. 1986]. [1860 Census Cox Bar: Keeley (sic), John 46, Margaret 34, Maria 13, Esther 12, Thomas 10, Lucy 8, all born Ireland].

KEENAN, M., Mrs. Died Mar 08, 1900; age 73 yr; b. Ireland. (TJ Jan 1901).

KELLEN, JANE E. Died Weaverville July 19, 1861; aged about 30 yr; bur. Sun. July 21, 1861 Weaverville Cem. Wife of Rev. Robert Kellen, pastor of ME Church (Methodist-Episcopal), Weaverville. more. (TJ Sat. July 27, 1861 p 2 col 3).

KELLOGG, D. M. Died Gilroy June 14, 1871; a native of Herkimer County, N.Y. aged 41 yr 6 mo 18 days. (TJ June 24, 1871 p 2).

KELLOGG, EARNEST AUSTIN. Died Hay Fork June 25, 1877, aged 2 yr 7 mo 4 days; son of L. J. and Sarah F. Kellogg; prob. bur. Kellogg's Cem. (TJ June 30, 1877). born 21 Nov. 1874.

KELLOGG, JOHN J. Died Jordan Valley, Oregon April 10, 1878; no age; for some time res. of Douglas City. (TJ Apr. 27, 1878 p 3). [1860 census Doug. City: age 34, lumberman, b. Ohio].

KELLOGG, LANGDON JACKSON. Died Hay Fork Mar 20, 1899; native of Mass, aged abt 70 yr; aka "Jack" or "L. J."; bur. Kellogg's Cem. Hay Fork; came to Trinity Co. 1851; older bro. Levi Delos Kellogg mined with him in the early days; left Trinity Co. 1855 for Plumas Co. where a 3rd bro. W. W. Kellogg was mining; m. Miss Sarah F. Large Dec 25, 1866, 2nd dau. of late Benjamin Large, who survives him; 3 children in Hay Fork: Albert L. Kellogg, Mrs. Alice Van Matre, and Mrs. Maude Dobbyn; obit. worth copying. (TJ Mar 25, 1899 p 2; obit. p 3 col 3).

KELLUM, W. C., Dr. Died San Francisco Oct. 28, 1872; several professional visits to this section. (TJ Nov. 2, 1872 p 3).

KELLY,-----. Died Eastman's Diggings on Trinity River July 9, 1855; bank of earth caved in on him July 5th. (TT July 14, 1855).

KELLY, ANN. Died Weaverville June 4, 1868, aged about 52 yr; wife of Simon Kelly. (TJ Sat. June 6, 1868 p 2).

KELLY, JAMES. Died San Jose [Santa Clara Co.] July 5, 1867, aged 35 years; late of the Trinity Mountain House. (TJ Sat. July 13, 1867).

KELLY, JAMES. Died Deadwood, Trinity Co. Feb 17, 1894; native of Ireland, aged abt 50 yr; bur. Feb 19, 1894 Catholic Cem. Weaverville. (TJ Sat. Feb 24, 1894, pg 3 col 6).

KELLY, SIMON. Died Weaverville Nov. 20, 1884; native of Ireland, aged about 69 yr. (TJ Nov. 22, 1884).

KELTON, EDWARD A., Capt. Died Weaverville Aug. 22, 1867; native of Mass., aged 35 yr; bur. F.& A.M. Cem. Weav. Aug. 24, 1867. In Trinity Co. 9 yr; partner in firm of Kelton & Kellogg, Douglas City 4 yr; elected Captain of the "Douglas City Rifles"; wife & 4 children. (TJ Aug. 24, 1867 p 2). Correction TJ Aug. 31, 1867, p 2: "Born Montpelier Vermont Oct. 22, 1831; went to Boston age 16; sailed for Calif. 1852."

KELTON, LLOYD. Died Napa, Napa Co. July 8, 1878; b. Douglas City, Trinity Co. May 28, 1861, son of late Captain Edward A. Kelton. (TJ Sat. July 20, 1878 p 3).

KEMP, JOHN. Died Deadwood, Trin. Co. Sept. 30, 1886; native of Canada aged about 50 yr; bur. Lewiston, prob. Pioneer Cem. (TJ Sat. Oct. 9, 1886 p 3).

KENNEDY, ROBERT. Died Redding, Shasta Co., Jun 30, 1897; native of Ireland, aged 64 yr; well-known in Trinity County. (TJ Jul 10, 1897 p 3 col 4).

KENNY, ARTHUR. Died Sacramento (Sacramento Co.) Jan. 20, 1870; native of Nauvoo, Illinois, aged 19 yr 1 mo 22 days; son of Arthur Kenny of Weaverville. (TJ Jan. 29, 1870 p 2).

KENNEY, ARTHUR. Died Jan. 13, 1875 Reading, Shasta Co. CA; native of Ireland, aged 64; wife and several children. (Note: 1860 & 1870 census say "Kenney".) (TJ Sat. Jan. 23, 1875).

KENNEY, JOHN SCHUYLER. Died Sacramento May 15, 1867, aged 26 yr 6 mo; son of Arthur Kenney of Weaverville. (TJ Sat. May 18, 1867 p 2).

KENNON, NIEP. Drowned in Trinity River at Evans Bar, near Douglas City, Jan. 13, 1862. "The unfortunate man left a family to mourn his loss." (DCG Wed. Jan. 22, 1862; also see Jan. 15, 1862).

KEOKIJAKA, aka "George Washington". Died at Lowden's ranch June 2, 1858; a Kanaka, aged about 55 years. (Probably Hawaiian). (TJ Sat. June 12, 1858 p 2).

KERBY, ELLEN M., Miss. Died Weaverville Dec. 17, 1872; aged 18 yr 7 mo; bur. Catholic Cem. [Weaverville] Dec. 19, 1872. (TJ Dec. 21, 1872).

KERBY, FRANCIS MARION. Died Weaverville Jan 20, 1897; native of North Carolina, aged abt 64 yr. (TJ Jan 23, 1897 p 2).

KERLIN, SAMUEL. Died Hyampom May 21, 1893; native of New York, aged about 69 yr; came to Calif. 1851 from Jackson, Michigan; homesteaded in Hyampom for 20 years or more. (TJ Sat. May 27, 1893).

KERNAN, ROSE, Mrs. Died Albany, New York Feb 11, 1897 aged 79 yr; she was a sister of Mrs. Anna Rule and James Morris of Weaverville; visited relatives in Trinity Co. 3 years ago. (TJ Feb 27, 1897 p 3 col 1). [see also Rule and Morris].

KESSLER, WILLIAM. Died Sacramento Mar. 26, 1889; native of Kentucky, aged 64 yr; bur. Redding, Shasta Co. Pioneer merchant of Shasta Co; came to Calif. 1850; veteran of Mexican War. (TJ Sat. Mar. 30, 1889).

KESTER, ALMIRA, Mrs. Died Weaverville Feb. 5, 1871, aged 53 yr 11 mo 5 days. (TJ Feb. 11, 1871 p 2). [see also Farmer.]

KESTER, JOHN A. Died Hay Fork Valley Jan. 4, 1886; native of Missouri, aged about 47 yr; aka "Pony Kester"; shot by brother Josephus Kester. (TJ Sat. Jan. 9, 1886).

KETCHAM, FRANCIS D. Died San Jose, [Santa Clara Co.] July 23, 1885; b. Huntington, N.Y. Dec. 16, 1813; m. Anna Lefferts 1853 Huntington, NY; wife, dau. Mrs. L. L. Nattings, and little grandson; more. (TJ Sat. Aug. 1, 1885 p 3 col 3).

KETCHAM, LETTY ANNA, Mrs. Died nr. San Jose (Santa Clara Co.) Jul 29, 1898; b. Huntington, Long Island, NY, Oct 21, 1813; widow of late F. D. Ketcham; came with husband to Calif. in 1854; only child, Mrs. L. L. Nattinger, was born at North Fork. (TJ Aug 6, 1898 p 3 col 3).

KETWIG, GERHARD. Died North Fork March 17, 1873, aged 1 yr 4 mo. Possibly son of "U. Ketwig" whose daughter was born Sept. 23, 1873 in North Fork (now Helena). (TJ Mar. 29 and abt Sept. 23, 1873). [No Ketwig in 1870 census.] [Index to Deaths 1873-1890 has similar information].

KEYTIN, FRANK. Killed in a mining claim at Douglas City Nov. 21, 1878; native of Azores, aged about 35 years. (TJ Sat. Nov. 23, 1878 p 2).

KINGSBURY, EDNA. Died in Denver, Colorado, prob. April 1891; age about 6 years; dau. of Mr. and Mrs. W. W. Kingsbury, formerly of Weaverville. She is the second daughter to die. (TJ Sat. May 2, 1891 p 3). [1880 Census lists Warren W. Kingsbury, age 27, b. Indiana; wife Ettie age 20, b. Calif. Married in Weaverville May 18, 1880 Etta C. Goering. Marriages Book H page 375].

KINGSBURY, HENRY DWIGHT. Died Hay Fork July 4, 1889; native of Connecticut, aged about 70 years; came to Trinity Co. 1851. (TJ Sat. July 13, 1889).

KINGSBURY, ORSEN. Died Weaverville Jul 3, 1898; native of Calif. aged abt 40 yr. (TJ Jul 9, 1898 p 2 and p 3 col 2; see also TJ Jul 2, 1898 p 3 col 3, tells about accident).

KITTLE, JOHN G. Died Mar. 4, 1906 Minersville; age 37, male, white, miner, born Calif; buried San Francisco. Index to Deaths 1890-1908.

KLASING, JOHN. Died Sacramento June 18, 1869; no age; (not in 1860 census); formerly of Trinity Co. (TJ Jul 3, 1869 p 2).

KLEISER, JONAS. Drowned in Trinity River at Hoopa Sep 28, 1862; leaves wife and daughter; one of early settlers of Hoopa Valley. (TJ Sat. Oct 4, 1862 p 2).

KILGORE, JAMES CLARENCE. Died near Chico, Butte Co. July 2, 1875, aged 2 yr 5 mo 2 days; only son of F. G. and Maggie Kilgore. (TJ July 17, 1875 p 2).

KINCAID, WILLIAM. Died Weaverville Feb. 12, 1880; native of Virginia, aged about 53 yr; unmarried; bur. Weaverville Cem. Feb. 18, 1880; lived Trinity Co. 30 yr. Bro. Willis Kincaid, VA. (TJ Feb. 21, 1880 p 2 & 3).

KING, EZRA S. Died Junction City Apr. 20, 1884; native of Long Island, N.Y., aged 49 yr 11 mo 8 days; leaves wife and 2 children; her parents live in Anderson, Shasta Co; res. California about 25 years. Bur. Vallejo, Solano Co., with child who died earlier. (TJ Sat. Apr. 26, 1884).

KIRBY, MICHAEL. Died French Gulch, Shasta County, March 8, 1867, aged 6 years; orphan brother of Nellie Kirby of Weaverville. (TJ Sat. March 16, 1867 p 2).

KIRKPATRICK, JOHN. Died San Francisco June 11, 1869, aged 44 yr; of Weaverville. (TJ June 19, 1869 p 2).

KISE, CHARLES DOW. Drowned at Lewiston Aug. 17, 1868, aged 18 months; son of Bloomfield and Adaline (sic) Kise. (TJ Sat. Aug. 22, 1863 p 2).

KISE, FLORENCE. Died Lewiston May 16, 1868, aged 4 yr 8 mo; dau. of J. B. and Angeline Kise. (TJ Sat. May 30, 1868 p 2). [1870 Census says Kise, Joseph Bloomfield, wife Angeline, Annie E. & Albert.]

KITCHEN, FRANK. Died on Clear Creek, Shasta County Dec. 20, 1885; buried in Redding. Brother of Mrs. J. M. Carter of Rush Creek; former resident Lewiston and "here" (Weaverville). (TJ Sat. Jan. 2, 1886). [Note: 1880 census: Lewiston 6-19-1880: Kitchen, Eliza age 30, housekeeper, b. Kentucky, parents born Kentucky, head of household; Frank Kitchen, 17 born Kentucky].

KITTO, ORLANDO. Died Altoona Mine, Trinity Co. Nov 30, 1894; native of Cornwall, England, aged about 56 yr; bur. Oakland, Alameda Co. with I.O.O.F. Ceremonies. (TJ Dec 8, 1894 pg 3; Dec 16, 1894, pg 3).

KLAUE, CHRISTIAN. Died Helena, Montana Oct. 1877; resident of Weaverville a number of years ago; bro. in law. of V. C. Lautenschlager of North Fork. (TJ Sat. Nov. 17, 1877 p 3).

KLEEBERGER, GEORGE. Died Weaverville Apr. 15, 1880; infant son of Mr. and Mrs. Geo. R. Kleeberger. (TJ Apr. 17, 1880 p 2).

KLEIN, EMILY. Burned to death on Deadwood June 18, 1886, aged 5 years. Daughter of Mr. and Mrs. George Klein. "She was only missed for 15 minutes." (TJ Sat. June 26, 1886).

KLEIN, IDA, Miss. Died Alameda, Alameda Co., CA Dec 31, 1920; born in Deadwood about 34 years ago; dau. of Mr. and Mrs. George Klein; moved from Weaverville about 20 years ago; survived by her mother and an aunt, Mrs. John Shedd. Her father died at Tower House about fifteen years ago and is buried at Redding. Bur. Catholic cem. Redding. (TJ Jan 8, 1921).

KLINK, JACOB. Died Weaverville Dec. 1, 1886, native of Germany, aged about 60 years. Pioneer resident of Trinity County; sexton of public cemetery. Bur. Dec. 2, 1886 Weaverville Cemetery. Leaves 2 brothers and a sister living at Vincennes, Knox County, Indiana. (TJ Dec 4, 1886).

KNIGHT, SILAS DEXTER, "Deck". Died Virginia City, Nevada "recently" (abt Sep 1877); lived Douglas City many years; 1868 left for East with family (New York), later farm in Missouri, then Utah. (TJ Sep 8, 1877 p 3 col 1).

KNISELY, JACOB. Died Weaverville Feb 20, 1896; native of Ohio; aged abt 70 yr. (TJ Sat. Feb 22, 1896).

KNOWLES, ARCHIE WARREN. Died Hay Fork Aug 7, 1898; native of Calif. aged 18 yr. (TJ Aug 20, 1898 p 2). b. Hay Fork Jun 22, 1880; bur. there Aug 22, 1898; leaves father, 3 bro. 3 sis. (TJ Aug 27, 1898 p 3 col 2)

KNOWLES, ELIZA POTTER. Died Hay Fork Sept. 18, 1884; native of Pennsylvania, aged about 50 yr; bur. Hay Fork Cem. Lived Hay Fork 25 years; leaves husband and 7 children 4 boys and 3 girls. (TJ Sept. 20, 1884). (TJ Sept. 27, 1884): Charlotte Eliza Knowles; native of Bradford County, Penn. Came to Calif. across the plains in 1861. Married Henry Knowles in Weaverville Spring 1862. Children are ages 21 to 4 years. [see also Vaughn].

KNOWLES, PRESTON TULY. Died Cinnabar, Trinity Co. May 23, 1897; native of Indiana, aged abt 62 yr; buried in the private cem. at Stoddard's Ranch, Trinity Center; single man. (TJ May 29, 1897).

KNOWLTON, MARCUS L. Died Napa, Napa County Dec. 31, 1882. Old resident of Canon Creek. (TJ Jan. 6, 1883 p 3).

KNOWLTON, PURLIN. Died Deadwood, Trinity County Sept. 21, 1885; native of Mass. aged about 47 years. Bur. French Gulch, Shasta County Sep 23, 1885. (TJ Sat. Sep 26, 1885 p 2 & 3).

KNUTZE,-----,Mr. Drowned Forks of New River ca May 27, 1871; German. Resident of New River for past 14 years. (TJ June 10, 1871). [1870 Census: Charles Knutz, North Fork, age 50, miner, b.Switzerland].

KOELLE, JOHN. Died near Lewiston Feb. 4, 1884; native of Germany, aged about 36 yrs. (TJ Feb. 9, 1884). [Buried Weaverville Cemetery. Grave- stone fell from mounting 1986].

KOENIG, RICHARD. Died Sacramento Feb 23, 1897; left 3 sons and 2 daughters; former res. Trinity Co.; ran blacksmith shop at Evan's Bar in 1860s. (TJ Feb 27, 1897). [see Koening, below; the name is probably Koenig.]

KOENING, FRITZ. Died Sacramento June 17, 1869, age 38 yr 1 mo 8 days; formerly of Trinity County. (TJ July 3, 1869 p 2).

KOENING, EMILIA. Died Sacramento March 12, 1873; aged 24 yr 4 mo 25 days; wife of Richard Koening. He formerly lived at Evans Bar; blacksmith; left here several years ago; went to Sacramento and there married Emilia Keseberg, the first white girl born in Sacramento and whose death is recorded above. (TJ Mar. 22, 1873 p 3).

KOHLMANN, JOHN. Died Weaverville April 8, 1862; native of Bremen, Germany. (TJ Sat. Apr. 12, 1862 p 2). [no age given; not in 1860 census].

KOLHEPPE, GEO. Drowned Rattlesnake Creek, Trinity County, abt April 1, 1859; missing 2 weeks before body found; native of Hesse Cassel, Germany and recently of St. Charles Co. Missouri. (TJ Apr. 23, 1859).

KOUNTZ, JOSEPH. Died San Francisco March 3, 1879; brother of Frank Kountz. (TJ Mar. 8, 1879 p 3).

KRAFT, HERBERT. Died Red Bluff, Tehama Co. Nov 24, 1895; b. Mar. 15, 1831 Wurtemberg; good obit. (TJ Nov 30, 1895 p 3 col 2).

KRAMOLOFSKY, JOS. Died May 24, 1907 Weaverville; age 52, male, white, miner, born Austria. [Index to Deaths 1890-1908].

KRAUSS, E. Died [prob. Weaverville] Apr. 1, 1879; native of Bavaria, aged 35 yr. (TJ Sat. Apr. 5, 1879 p 3 col 2).

KRUTTSCHNITT, A.M., Mrs. Died near Hunter's Station, Truckee River July 30, 1867; wife of former Treasurer of Trinity County, now Assessor of Storey County, Nevada. Travelling from San Francisco with mother Mrs. Zeiler and 3 children. (TJ Sat. Aug. 10, 1867 p 2 col 2). [1860 census says: Antonie C. Kruttschnitt].

KRUTTSCHNITT, ELIZABETH, Mrs. Died Weaverville Nov. 13, 1889; native of Wurtenberg, Germany, aged 76 yr 2 mo; bur. Masonic Cem. Weaverville Nov 14, 1889. Mrs. P. M. Paulsen only living child. (TJ Nov 16, 1889). [Index to Deaths 1873-1890 adds: white, female, single (widow)].

KUPER, BERNARD T. Died San Francisco June 13, 1874; native of Oldenburg, Germany aged 45 years. (TJ June 20, 1874).

KUPER, CHARLIE. Died Junction City Oct. 22, 1875, aged 1 mo 4 days; son of Charles and Augusta Kuper. (TJ Oct. 30, 1875). [Born Junction City Sept. 18, 1875].

KUPER, WALTER. Died Red Bluff, Tehama Co., abt May 26, 1883; bur. Red Bluff May 28, 1883; youngest child of Mrs. Chas. Kuper. (TJ June 2, 1883). [probably the son born Aug. 21, 1881].

KUPER, CHAS. H. F. Died Weaverville Sept. 3, 1882; native of Vegesack, Bremen, Germany, aged 46 yr 2 mo 23 days; came to Trinity Co. 1854. Bur. Odd Fellows Cem. Weav. Sept. 4, 1882; leaves widow and 3 children, eldest about 5. (TJ Sept. 9, 1882).

LaBAREE,_____, Mrs. Died Oct 7, 1896 in Crockett, Contra Costa Co., mother of Dr. W. H. LaBaree. [no further info.] (TJ Oct 17, 1896).

LACHMAN, ABRAHAM. Died at his residence, 125 Palm Avenue, San Francisco, abt Dec. 22, 1915. He was born in Germany in 1844 and came to California in the 1850s, direct to Trinity Co. where he was employed by his elder brother, Samuel Lachman of Weaverville. (TJ Jan. 1, 1916).

LACHMAN, SAMUEL. Died at residence 603 Sutter St., San Francisco Mar. 24, 1872; born Giesen, Germany 67 years ago. Came to Calif. early 1850s, general merchandise business in Weaverville; went to San Francisco 1864, a partner of Adolph Eberhardt; leaves widow, 2 sons and married dau. Bur. Mar. 27, 1892 Home of Peace Cemetery. San Francisco *Chronicle* Mar. 26, 1892. (TJ Apr 2, 1892 p 3 col 5; Apr 23, 1892 p 3 col 2 tells about Will). Trinity Journal adds: Mr. Lachman came to Trinity Co. 1854; name spelled "Loffman" on Naturalization papers.

LACHENMACHER, BERTHA DOROTHEA. Died Weaverville Dec. 19, 1875; aged 6 yr 9 mo 2 days; daughter of Frederick and Dorothea Lachenmacher; scarlet fever. (TJ Dec. 25, 1875).[See also Dralle]. [Born Mar. 17, 1869 Weaverville; TJ Births].

LACKENMACHER, EMMA AUGUSTA. Died Weaverville Jan. 5, 1876, aged 8 yr 3 mo 9 days; daughter of Frederick and Dorothea Lackenmacher. (TJ Jan. 8, 1876 p 2). [Born Sept. 27, 1867 Weaverville; TJ Births].

LACKENMACHER, WILLIAM HENRY HARRISON. Died Weaverville Dec. 25, 1875; aged 2 yr 6 mo 16 days; son of Frederick and Dorothy Lackenmacher. (TJ Jan. 1, 1876 p 2). [Born June 9, 1873 Weaverville; TJ Births]. [See also Stierlen].

LA CROZE, JNO. Died Carr's Ranch, Trinity Valley "last Friday or Saturday [Oct. 30 or 31, 1880]; of Coffee Creek; no particulars. (TJ Nov. 6, 1880 p 3).

LADD, A. P. Died Shasta Nov. 7, 1869; formerly of Trinity County; recently elected Assessor of Shasta County. (TJ Nov. 13, 1869 p 2).

LaGRANGE, EARNEST de, Baron. Died France Aug 30, 1899; born in France abt 45 years ago; m. 17 years ago; dau. 15 yr, son 13 yr; father Baron Alexis de La Grange. (TJ Sep 2, 1899, p 3 col 4). [see also Rouse].

LAINGER, GEORGE B. Died Feb. 8, 1906 Weaverville; age 24, male, white, American, electrician; informant: John T. Lainger. [Index to Deaths 1890-1908].

LAIRD,_____. Died Jan 12, 1896 Junction City, inf. dau. of Mr. and Mrs. Robert Laird, age 2 dy. (TJ Sat. Jan 18, 1896).

LAMBETH, MILTON. Died San Francisco May 5, 1899; news from C. W. Craig of Redlands. (TJ May 27, 1899 p 3 col 4).

LAMBERT, JOSEPH. Died Taylor's Flat, Trinity County Nov. 7, 1868; native of Connecticut, aged 43 yr. (TJ Nov. 14, 1868 p 2).

LANDERS, WARREN. Died near Weaverville Dec. 8, 1864; native of Milltown, Maine, aged about 45 yr; came to Calif. from Wisconsin; supposed to leave a wife and family in neighborhood of Milwaukee. (TJ Dec. 24, 1864 p 2).

LANEHART, STEPHEN. Died mouth of Rush Creek, nr. Lewiston, June 10, 1877; native of Albany, New York, aged 56 yr; aka Steve Lane; came to Trinity Co. 1851; 1852 had trading post at Arkansas Dam; nephew William Lanehart returned to East abt 1859. (TJ June 16, 1877 p 2-3).

LANGE, CARL FREDERICK WILLIAM. Died San Francisco June 3, 1872; native of Germany aged about 51 years. (TJ June 13, 1872).

LANGE, EMILIA. Died Evans Bar, Trinity River, May 31, 1869; age 2 yr 1 mo 15 days; dau. of William and Louisa Lange. (TJ June 5, 1869).

LANGE, LOUISA, Mrs. Died Weaverville Sept. 7, 1872; native of Germany aged about 36 yr. (TJ Sept. 14, 1872).

LANGE, WILLIAM. Died Yankee Hill, Butte Co. July 20, 1888; German, aged about 45 yr; brother of Mrs. K. Morris of Indian Creek; will be buried in Trinity Co. (TJ July 28, 1888 p 3).

LANSDALE, ISAAC R. Shot and killed at Balls Ferry, Shasta Co. Jan. 1896, by George M. Wright; Wright was arrested. (TJ Feb 1, 1896 p 3 col 3).

LAPPEAS, JAMES, Mr. Died Douglas City Apr. 26, 1861; late of Shasta; buried in Weaverville by I.O.O.F. "It appears that he has a mother residing at Cleveland, Ohio, from which place he probably came." (DCG May 6, 1861). (Trinity Journal May 4, 1861): native of Renssellaer Co. New York, aged about 30 years; bur. Apr. 28, 1861 I.O.O.F. Cem. Weav. "Mother lived Cleveland, Ohio 28 Aug. 1860."

LAPPIN, WILLIAM. Died San Francisco, CA Dec 20, 1895, aged about 70 yr; native of Ireland; old resident of Trinity Co. (TJ Sat. Dec 21, 1895); bur. Catholic Cem., Weaverville abt Dec. 28, 1895; sisters and brothers live in the Parish of Drumbene, County of Donegal, Ireland. (TJ Sat Dec 28, 1895 col 2; Will col 4). [marker in St. Patrick's Church Cemetery; carving on west side of the stone; nearly illegible 1976].

"LAPPIN HEIRS FOUND". (see William). One brother, James Lappin still living, and 4 children of another brother; live in Ireland; letter from Balliutra, County Donegal, Ireland. (TJ Mar 14, 1896).

LARCINE, PETER O. Died Nov. 30, 1907 Denny, Trinity Co. California; age 74, male, white, miner; born Florida; buried Denny. [Index to Deaths 1890-1908].

LARGE, _____. Died at Vinta, Indian Territory Aug 16, 1893; born Douglas City July 23, 1892; daughter of O. Q. Large; mother died Jul 23, 1893. (TJ Sat. Aug 26, 1893 p 3 col 4). [Trinity Co. Marriages: Osceola Q. Large m 1) Miss Agnes E. Hughes, dau. of Robert Hughes Dec. 25, 1890 Douglas City. Book I page 143; m 2) Miss Alice L. Kuffel Sept. 20, 1895 Douglas City. Book I page 227].

LARGE, AGNES E. Died July 23, 1893, prob. Vinta, Indian Territory. (TJ Aug. 26, 1893).

LARGE, BENJAMIN. Died at the residence of J. A. Stafford, his son-in-law, in Hayfork; born Lancaster, Penn; aged 76 yr 10 mo 7 days; came to Calif. 1857; resided Hay Fork since 1884; leaves 8 children, among whom are Mrs. J. A. Stafford, Mrs. L. J. Kellogg, Robert Large of Hay Fork, and Ocea Large of Douglas City. (TJ Sat. Apr 16, 1892 pp 2 & 3). (see also Kellogg).

LARKIN,-----. Died Trinity Center Apr. 12, 1880, aged about 7 months; son of Patrick Larkin. (TJ Apr. 1880).

LARKIN, JERRY. Died LaGrange Ditch at Stuarts Fork July 29, 1897; native of Ireland; aged about ___ years. (TJ Jul 31, 1897 p 3 col 2; TJ Aug 7, 1897).

LARKIN, PATRICK. Died nr Redding, Shasta Co. Jan 29, 1898; native of Ireland about 66 yr; bur. Shasta Cem. Jan 31, 1898. (TJ Feb 5, 1898 pg 3 col 1).

LARKIN, SARAH. Died Minersville Mar. 8, 1880; aged about 18 years; wife of Patrick Larkin; (TJ Mar. 13, 1880 p 2). [Dau. of James L. Grattan; m. Trinity Center Sept. 29, 1877; Patrick age 41, native of Ireland; Sarah age 18, native of Nevada. Trinity County Marriages].

LARSEN, A. Died Coffee Creek abt Jan. 1890; native of Sweden, aged about 55 yr. (TJ Sat. Aug. 9, 1890; p 3 "Coroner"). [Died in an earth cave-in].

LARSEN, IVER. Died Lewiston May 16, 1887; native of Norway, aged about 57 years; single man. (TJ May 21, 1887). [Buried Lewiston pioneer cemetery; stone].

LARSON, JOHN, Mrs. Died Nov 08, 1900; age 48 Yr; b. Calif. (TJ Jan 1901).

LASSETER, JOHN. Body, probably of John Lasseter, who left Cinnabar in June 1877, was found on trail from Trinity Center to Cow Creek; remains taken to Trinity Center for coroner. (TJ May 31, 1879). [no further information].

LAUNCE, A. J. Mr. Died Weaverville May 9, 1859; native of Missouri; aged about 30 years. (TJ May 14, 1859 p 2).

LAUTIER, EDMUND TITUS LOUIS. Died Junction City May 28, 1899; native of Italy, age abt 69 yr; unmarried; no known relatives. (TJ Jun 3, 1899 pp 2 & 3).

LAWLOR, JAMES. Killed on Reading Creek Mar. 16, 1880; native of Ireland aged about 77 yr; coroner's jury says "84 years". (TJ Sat. Mar. 20, 1880 p 2). [not in 1860 or 1870 census].

LAWRENCE,-----, Mrs. Died Indian Creek "this week"; "a Portuguese woman", aged about 60 years; bur. Catholic Cem. Weaverville. (TJ Feb. 17, 1883 p 3).

LAWRENCE, A. C. Died San Bernardino Sept. 19, 1879; native of Virginia, age 43 years; bur. Sept. 19, 1879 San Bernardino; Asst. Editor Trinity Journal 1862; resided Trinity Co. 4 years; wife died Weaverville; leaves daughter. (TJ Sept. 27, 1879).

LAWRENCE, AUSTIN. Died Trinity Center July 2, 1889; native of Vermont aged about 66 years. (TJ July 6, 1889). [Index to Deaths 1873-1890 adds white, male].

LAWS, ANNA LENA. Died near Junction City Jan. 20, 1890; native of Sweden, aged 60 yr 4 mo 1 day; b. Anna Lena Samuels; came to US 1847 age 18 yr; m. George M. Laws 1854, Horsetown, Shasta Co.; came to Trinity Co. 1855. (TJ Jan. 25, 1890). "The funeral of the late Mrs. Anna L. Laws of Junction City will take place in the public cemetery Weaverville Sun. May 25, 1890 at 11 am." (TJ May 17, 1890).
"Body removed-- funeral last Sunday on occasion of removal of remains of late Mrs. George Laws from Junction City to public cemetery, Weaverville. Largest funeral for several months." (TJ May 31, 1890).

LAWS, GEORGE M. Died near Junction City Nov. 27, 1887; native of Lynn, England, aged 57 yr 5 mo 28 days; came to San Francisco 1849; Trinity County 1854 with wife and 3 grown children; bur. Weaverville public cemetery Nov. 29, 1887. (TJ Sat. Dec. 3, 1887).

LAWS, HENRY. Drowned at Sturdevant's ranch while attempting to cross Trinity river in a small boat last Friday Dec. 13, 1861 (the Trinity river was in flood); lately a resident of Weaverville; brother of George Laws. (TJ Dec. 21, 1861 p 2). [not in 1860 census)].

LAWS, JAMES G. Died Sep 1900; no further information. (TJ Jan 1901).

LAWTON, ARTHUR. Died abt April 1886 Mexico; brother of Pat. Lawton of Trinity County. "One of the party of prospectors recently killed by Apaches in Mexico." (TJ May 1, 1886 p 3 col 2).

LEACH,-----. Died Ridgeville Nov. 28, 1857, aged 6 mo 10 days; youngest son of Henry and Mary Jane Leach. (TJ Dec. 5, 1857 p 2).

LEACH,-----. Died near Weaverville July 23, 1863; infant son of F. Leach, Esq. (TJ Aug. 1, 1863 p 2).

LEACH,-----,"Old Mr." Died Cottonwood, Shasta Co. Nov. 27, 1861, age 65; resident of upper portion of Trinity County; father of Fred. Leach, Esq. and Albert Leach; also leaves widow and other children. (TJ Nov. 30, 1861).

LEACH, ALBERT. Died near Hay Fork Mar 05, 1898; b. nr Lansing Mich. Jan 12, 1842, age abt 56 yr; came to Calif. 1852; m. Rohnerville, Humboldt Co. Nov 13, 1877 to Miss Emma A. Hillis; 7 children: 6 boys, 1 girl; wife, 5 sons, dau. survive, and one bro., Sherman Leach, of San Jose; 2 sis. Mrs. Lehman of Portland, Ore. and Mrs. Shanks of Idaho; *Humboldt and San Jose papers please copy.* (TJ Sat. Mar 26, 1898 pp 2 & 3).

LEACH, ALBERT, Mrs. Died Hay Fork Jun 23, 1898; no particulars. (TJ Jun 25, 1898). Emma A. Hillis, b. Knoxville, Iowa Aug 12, "41 years ago"; came to Calif. Oct 1876; m. Albert Leach at Rohnerville, Humboldt Co. Nov 13, 1877; came to Hay Fork last fall; Mr. Leach is deceased; leaves one sis., Mrs. E. Stone of Rohnerville and 6 children, 5 sons, 1 dau. (TJ Jul 2, 1898, p 3 col 2). [not in 1900 Census for Trinity County, California; 1910 census has two likely children: Leach, Newell N., b. June 1880 Calif; fa. b. Mich; mo. b. Iowa; Hayfork p. 11, Apr 22, 1910. **Leach, Warren H.,** b. Aug 30, 1878 Rohnerville, Calif. (I.O.O.F. records); fa. b. Mich; mo. b. Iowa; married 2 yr. to Mary E., age 34, b. Calif;, fa. Ky, mo. Missouri. Hayfork pg 11, Apr 22, 1910. [See also 1900 Census for Rohnerville, Humboldt Co. CA; Humboldt County Library, Eureka, CA, may be a good source].

LEACH, FRED. Died at home of son-in-law A. D. Smith, near Fortuna, Humboldt Co. Sat. Aug 20, 1892; bur. Rohnerville, Humboldt Co. Aug. 21, 1892; crossed plains 1858; came to Trinity Co. as a blacksmith & miner; later lived in Rohnerville; no age given. (TJ Sat. Sep 3, 1892 pg 3 col 2; see Fortuna *Advance* Aug. 25, 1892).

LEACH, SYLVESTER. Died "Rich Gulch" near Minersville Dec 13, 1895; native of Michigan, aged about 64 yr; bur. near Minersville. (TJ Dec 21, 1895 p 3 col 2). [note: those buried at Minersville were removed and re-buried in the Trinity Center-Coffee Creek Cemetery in 1959, before the filling of Trinity Lake; legible marker 1976: "Leach, Sylvester d. 1895"].

LEACH, WILLIAM COLEMAN. Marker in Trinity Center-Coffee Creek Cemetery 1976: "d. 1893; formerly buried at old Minersville".

LEACH, WM. S. Died Oregon Gulch April 22, 1865; native of Ipswich, Mass, aged about 56 yr. (TJ Apr. 29, 1865).

LEARY, ELIZABETH. Died Weaverville Mar. 27, 1893; native of Calif., aged 25 yr 6 mo 6 days; bur. Catholic Cem. Weaverville Mar. 29, 1893; dau. of Edward & Essie Leary; gr.dau. of Mrs. M. Keeley; most of her life spent at Cox Bar. (TJ Apr 1, 1893 p 2 & 3). [see also Keely].

LEARY, THOS. K. Died at Cox Bar June 21, 1892; b. North Fork, (Helena) Calif. aged 22 yr 10 mo 25 days; bur. Catholic Cem. Weaverville June 22, 1892; only son of Edward and Essie Leary, both deceased; leaves sister Miss Lizzie Leary and grandmother Mrs. M. Keely. (TJ Sat. June 25, 1892). [Note: after Thomas died, Mrs. (John) Keely sold her property at Big Bar (TJ July 16, 1892) and she and Elizabeth moved to Weaverville].

LEAS, AMY LORAINE. Died Apr. 25, 1907 Lowden's Ranch, Trinity Co., Calif; age 11 months; female, white, born Calif. Bur. Lewiston Cemetery. [Index to Deaths 1890-1908].

LEAS, EMILY. Died Buck Horn Station Dec. 7, 1887; native of Fayette Co., Ohio, aged 52 yr 6 mo 8 days; wife of Geo. W. Leas; bur. Dec. 9, 1887 Masonic Cem. Weaverville; long obit. (TJ Dec. 10, 1887).

LEAVITT, OLIVE. Died Weaverville Aug. 21, 1887, aged 1 week; b. Weaverville Aug. 14, 1887; dau. of Mr. and Mrs. Wm. J. Leavitt. (TJ Aug. 20 and 27, 1887).

LEE, BILLY. Died Shasta, Shasta Co. Apr 11, 1895; "ran barbershop in Weaverville until 1892"; no age given. (TJ Apr 13, 1895 p 3 col 3). [not in 1880 census].

LEE, BRUCE B. Died Oct. 30, 1890, Red Bluff, Tehama Co; native of Iowa, in 51st year; reared in Sacramento; wife, and married daughter in San Francisco; bur. Red Bluff Sat. Nov. 1, 1890, F & A M. (TJ Nov. 8, 1890).

LEE, JESSE B. Died Weaverville Nov. 20, 1883; native of Ohio, aged 86 yr 2 mo 18 days; b. Miami Valley, Ohio; father built first log house in Cincinnati; soldier in Black Hawk War. (TJ Dec. 1, 1883 p 2 & 3).

LEEDS, J. C. Died Uniontown, Humboldt County, Nevada Territory Nov. 18, 1863, aged 38 yr; formerly of Orange county, New York. (TJ Dec. 12, 1863 p 2).

LEIBENGUTH, GEORGE. Fell over a precipice above Canon City Sun. June 9, 1861; native of Wellesweiler or Ottweiler, Prov. of Rhine, Prussia; late of Worcester, Ohio; age 36 yr. (TJ June 15, 1861 p 2 col 1).

LEIBRANDT, CHRISTINA, Mrs. Died Santa Cruz, Santa Cruz County, May 4, 1878; no age given; mother of Jacob Leibrandt of Junction City and Mrs. Henry Lorenz of Weaverville. (TJ May 18, 1878 p 3). [wife of Jacob Leibbrandt, Sr.; see note below].

LEIBRANDT, FLORINA. Died Red Hill (near Junction City) Aug. 20, 1879; age 17 months; daughter of Jacob and Clara Leibrandt. (TJ Aug. 23, 1879 p 2).

LEIBRANDT, FREDDIE. Died Red Hill (near Junction City) March 6, 1886; aged 9 yr 7 mo 9 days; son of Jacob and Clara Leibrandt; bur. Odd Fellows Cem. Weaverville Sun. Mar. 7, 1886. (TJ Sat. Mar. 13, 1886).

LEIBRANDT, JACOB, Sr. Died Santa Cruz, CA Jan. 8, 1895; native of Bavaria, aged 80 yr; deceased wife was a descendant of Martha Washington; father of Mrs. Henry Lorenz of Junction City and Jacob Leibrandt, former resident, now living in Santa Cruz. [name spelled Leibbrandt in obit]. (TJ Sat. Jan 12, 1895 p 3 col 5).

LEITER, JULIUS. Died at Union Hotel, Weaverville Apr. 21, 1882; of San Francisco; native of Germany, aged about 28 years; relative of Mr. Joseph Weil; body shipped to San Francisco; Masons helped; funeral San Francisco Apr. 24, 1882. (TJ Apr. 29, 1882 p 2 & 3).

LEHAN, _____. Died Oregon Gulch on the 30th ult. (Sept. 30, 1859), wife of John Lehan, aged about 24 years. (TJ Sat. Oct. 8, 1859 p 2).

LENTZ, CONSTANTINE. Died Shasta, Shasta County Dec. 16, 1891; native of Germany, aged 68; bur. Shasta Dec. 17, 1891; came to Calif. 1850; Shasta 1852; musician; organized bands in Weaverville, Yreka, Jacksonville, OR, Millville, and others. *Shasta Courier* Dec. 19, 1891. (TJ Sat. Dec. 26, 1891).

LEON, PHILIP. Died Lewiston June 4, 1885; native of Switzerland, aged about 50 yr. (TJ Sat. June 13, 1885).

LEONARD, SADIE E. Died Douglas City Sept. 18, 1875, aged 25 yr 6 mo; wife of Henry W. Leonard; daughter of Mr. and Mrs. M. Ruch of Hay Fork; came to Calif. 1852, aged 2; bur. Masonic Cem. Weaverville Sept. 19, 1875. (TJ Sept. 25, 1875 p 2 & 3). [see also Ruch].

LEONARD, NELSON. Died Eureka, CA July 9, 1884 of injuries received in an engagement 20 years ago; pioneer of Trinity County; soldier in all the early expeditions against Indians. (TJ Sat. July 26, 1884 p 3).

LEWIS, E. J., Hon. Died Red Bluff Apr. 20, 1881; no age given; Superior Judge, Tehama County. (TJ Apr. 23, 1881 p 3).

LEWIS, JOHN. Died New River Jan. 10, 1890, crushed by snow; no age given. (TJ Sat. Feb. 22, 1890). [not in 1880 census].

LEWIS, WILLIAM SHELBURN. Died May 28, 1896 Canon City; native of Missouri, aged abt 50 yr; aka "Shep" Lewis; bur. May 30, 1896 I.O.O.F. Cem. Weaverville. (TJ Sat. May 30, 1896, & Jun 6, 1896 p 3 col 3).

LEWIS, WM. W. Died Weaverville July 1, 1860, aged about 34 years; formerly of Camden, Loraine County, Ohio. (TJ Sat. July 7, 1860 p 2).

LICHTBLAU, MARTHA. Died Junction City Mar. 31, 1882, aged 6 yr 6 mo 17 days; dau. of Gottleib and Lizzie Lichtblau. (TJ Apr. 8, 1882).

LIGHTNER, FRED. Died Jan. 30, 1879, Chico [Butte County]; born Homberg, Hesse Darmstadt 1819; fun. Jan. 31, 1879; came to Calif. 1848; lived Weaverville; went to Chico when "it was quite small". Leaves sisters. (TJ Sat. Feb. 8, 1879 p 3).

LINCOLN, ABRAHAM, President. Black-bordered columns, Trinity Journal Saturday April 22, 1865 p 1. "President Abraham Lincoln Assassinated April 14, 1865 in Washington; received by telegraph on the 15th."

LINE, "Commodore". Died Shasta [Shasta Co.] abt Feb. 11/12, 1870, about 39 years of age; former res. of Weaverville. (TJ Feb. 19, 1870 p 3).

LIPPEN, PATRICK. Died Oregon Gulch Wed. Oct. 2, 1861, after falling from a bank; native of Ireland, aged about 32 years. (TJ Oct. 5, 1861).

LITSCH, CHAS. Of Shasta; died May 28, 1884; no age given. (TJ Sat. May 31, 1884 p 3).

LITTLE, FANNY. Died at Charlestown, South Carolina Oct. 31, 1866; aged 2 yr 3 mo; youngest daughter of Wm. Little, late of Weaverville; left about 2 months ago. (TJ Sat. Dec. 15, 1866 p 2).

LITTLE, IRENE MAY. Died Weaverville Aug. 7, 1866, aged 2 mo 25 days; infant daughter of William Little. (TJ Sat. Aug. 11, 1866 p 2).

LITTLE, LYDIA L. "In Memory of Lydia L., wife of Wm. Little, died Jun 9, 1866 aged 32 yr 7 mo 24 dy, Also Irene May their daughter, b. May 13, 1861, d. Aug 7, 1866". [Gravestone lying flat on ground, Weaverville Cem. 1988].

LITTLE, JOHN. Died at Searles Ranch on Reddings Creek March 25, 1859, age 59 years; old resident of this county. (TJ Apr. 2, 1859).

LITTLEFIELD, A. D. Died on Red Mountain (near Minersville) Sept. 27, 1895; native of Calif., aged about 30 yr. (TJ Oct 12, 1895 p 2; story p 3 col 3 & col 5; see also TJ Oct 26, 1895 p 3 col 4; Dec 14, 1895 p 3 col 4; Dec 21, 1895 p 3 col 3).

LOAG, JAMES. Died Shasta [Shasta Co.] Jan. 18, 1866, aged 39 yr 6 mo. (TJ Jan 27, 1866 p 2).

LOCKE, ANDREW. Died at the New York house near Trinity Center Nov. 29, 1870; native of New York, aged 28 years. (TJ Dec. 10, 1870 p 2).

LOCKHARD, JOHN. Drowned in Trinity River at French Bar Apr. 6, 1856; native of Niagara, N.Y., abt 25 years of age. (TJ Apr 12, 1856).

LOCKHART, EDWARD. Died Lewiston Jan. 31, 1865; of Rockport, Maine, aged 26 yr 4 mo 8 days; Masonic tribute p 3. (TJ Feb. 4, 1865).

LOCKHART, ROBERT C. Died Mill Creek, Tehama Co. Aug. 14, 1872; native of Parsboro, Nova Scotia, aged 58 yr. (TJ Aug. 17, 1872).

LOCKHART, ELIZABETH ANN, Mrs. Died Weaverville Aug. 8, 1885; born Nova Scotia Feb. 2, 1816, aged 69 yr 6 mo 6 days; husband Robert C. Lockhart died near Tehama, CA 13 years ago; mother of Mrs. C. W. Craig; buried next to son Edward Lockhart in Masonic Cem. Weaverville Aug. 9, 1885. (TJ Sat. Aug. 15, 1885). [see also Craig].

LOEWE, ANTON. Died Weaverville Apr. 7, 1868; native of Bavaria, aged about 65 years. (TJ Apr. 11, 1868 p 2).

LONG, ANN, Mrs. Died Apr 5, 1896 Weaverville; native of County Cavarn, Ireland, aged 75 yr 3 mo 14 dy; b. Dec 21, 1820; m.n. Martin. Came to America 1846; m. Mr. Enright; he died 3 mo after marriage; one child, Mary Enright Montague, dec'd; came to Sacramento, CA 1852; Trinity Co. 1854; m. Jeremiah Long in Trinity Co. (died a number of years ago); bur. Catholic Cem. Weaverville Apr 7, 1896. (TJ Apr 11, 1896 pp 2-3). [see also Montague].

LONG, JEREMIAH. Died Mar. 19, 1886 Waldo, Wisconsin at home of his brother; native of Ireland, aged about 63 yr; left Weaverville in January; arrived Wisconsin Mar 19th, died ten days later. (TJ Apr. 3, 1886 p 3).

LOOMIS, ADONIRAM JUDSON ("A.J."). Died Red Bluff July 24, 1885 ; b. Madison Co., N.Y. 8 May 1826; came to Calif. 1849; Weaverville 1851; County Clerk 1863-1867; moved to Red Bluff 1868; widow and 3 grown sons Jud., Charley & Harry. (see also *Red Bluff Cause* abt July 24, 1885). (TJ Sat. Aug. 1, 1885 p 3 col 2).

LOOMIS, JUD. Died San Diego, CA Dec 2, 1894; native of Trinity County. (TJ Sat. Dec 15, 1894 pg 3 col 1).

LOOMIS, MINNIE. Died Red Bluff Dec. 2, 1877; aged 13 yr 8 mo 2 days; born Weaverville; daughter of A. J. and Minerva Loomis; other daughter Clara died about 2 years ago. (TJ Dec. 15, 1877 p 2 & 3).

LOOTS, JACOB. Died Weaverville Jul 20, 1869; aged 53 yr; bur. July 21, 1869 by Good Templars; I.O.O.F. tribute. (TJ Jul 24, 1869 pp 2 & 3).

LOOTS, LIZZIE C. Died Weaverville Jul 26, 1873; aged 17 yr 8 mo 28 days; bur. Weaverville Cem. Jul 27, 1873. (TJ Aug 2, 1873). [Index to Deaths 1873-1890 adds "female, single, born Calif."]

LORENZ, _____. Died Junction City Mar 17, 1897, inf. son of Mr. and Mrs. Henry Lorenz, aged 1 mo 28 dy. (TJ Mar 20, 1897 p 2).

LORENZ, ADAM. Died Red Hill near Junction City, July 12, 1866; native of Prussia aged about 36 years. (TJ July 14, 1866 p 2).

LORENZ, CHARLIE. Died Weaverville Feb. 5, 1888, aged 1 yr 3 mo 13 days; youngest child of Mr. and Mrs. Henry Lorenz. (TJ Feb. 11, 1888).

LORENZ, FRANK. Died West Bend, Wisconsin Apr. 17, 1876, aged 48 yrs. Deceased was a bro. of Henry Lorenz of Weaverville. (TJ May 6, 1876).

LORENZ, HENRY. Died San Francisco, CA Thurs. Oct 31, 1895; b. Rhenish, Prussia Mar 26, 1829; came to U.S. as a young man; settled first in Wisconsin; arrived San Francisco July 1, 1853; m. Miss Susan Leibbrandt Apr 14, 1861; long obit, worth copying. (TJ Sat. Nov 2, 1895 p 3 col 3; Nov 9, 1895 p 3 col 2; TJ Nov 30, 1895 p 3 col 5 "Will of Henry Lorenz" is a wealth of family information). [gravemarker in I.O.O.F Cem., Weaverville, well preserved in 1977; one of largest in cemetery; lists George J. Mar 3, 1878-Aug 7, 1912; Clara W. Smith, Nov 25, 1886-Oct 8, 1892; Charley Oct 21, 1886-Feb 4, 1888; Mary Anne Feb 5, 1868-Mar 21, 1868; Henry Mar 26, 1825 - Oct 30, 1895 "Father"; Franz Joseph "Joe" 1862-1937; Susan "Mother", July 8, 1844-Apr 3, 1925].

LORENZ, MARY ANN. Died Weaverville Mar 21, 1868, aged 6 weeks 3 days; dau. of Henry and Susan Lorenz. (TJ Sat. Mar 28, 1868 p 2). [born Feb 5, 1868].

LOTT, WILLIAM A. Drowned in East Fork [of Trinity River] May 7, 1890; native of England; no age given. (TJ Sat. May 10, 1890). [Index to Deaths 1873-1890: "Lot, Wm. A. died May 7, 1890; white, born England."]

LOVE, ALEXANDER NUTT. Died Weaverville Sept. 11, 1888; native of Penn; aged about 73 yr; bur. Sept. 13, 1888 Pub. Cem. Weaverville; lived Weaverville for 36 yr; (TJ Sat. Sept. 15, 1888). [see also: Stephen Kempton Turner].

LOVE, GEORGE J. Died Austin, Nevada Mar. 3, 1877. Old resident of Trinity County; Deputy Sheriff under John B. May. (TJ Mar 17, 1877 p 2). [1860 Census: res. Weaverville, age 34, clerk, born Virginia].

LOVEJOY, CELIA ANN, Mrs. Died Weaverville July 11, 1870; native of Salisbury, Vermont aged 56 yr 11 mo; mother of Edward P. Lovejoy, publisher of the TRINITY JOURNAL. (TJ July 16, 1870 p 2).

LOVEJOY, EDWARD PAYSON. Died Waubuska, Nevada Aug. 26, 1891; born St. Louis, Mo. "a little over 55 years old"; m. Miss Julia Holland, a niece of the Dacey brothers. long obit. (TJ Sat. Sept 5, 1891, p 3 col 2). [Note: Edward P. Lovejoy's TRINITY JOURNAL, printed in the 1870s, is still in excellent condition, with fine white paper, in 1998].

LOVERIDGE, ANITA. Drowned in Magdalina river in Colombia; child of Merwin Loveridge. One of twins; brother Albert was saved. (TJ Feb 24, 1894).

LOVERIDGE, "BABY". Drowned in Magdalina river in Colombia; daughter of Merwin Loveridge, aged 4 months. (TJ Feb 24, 1894; Mar 3, 1894 p 3 col 2).

LOVERIDGE, HEPSAY. Died Oregon Mountain Feb. 27, 1886; b. England Aug. 13, 1829, aged 56 yr 6 mo 14 days; bur. Weav Cem. Feb. 28, 1886; wife of O. M. Loveridge; good obit. p 3. (TJ Sat. Mar. 6, 1886).

LOVERIDGE, O. M. Died Nov 23, 1900; age 72 yr 4 mo 29 dy; b. New York. (TJ Jan 1901). [see also Selfridge, Fox, Johnston].

LOWDEN, _____. Died Weaverville Apr. 11, 1875, aged 13 days [born Mar. 29, 1875]; infant daughter of Wm. S. and Helen Lowden. (TJ Apr. 17, 1875).

LOWDEN, ALICE. Died Weaverville June 17, 1875, aged 2 yr 1 mo; bur. June 19, 1875 Weaverville Cem.; dau. of Wm. H. and Mary C. Lowden. (TJ June 19, 1875).

LOWDEN, GEORGE A. Died Weaverville June 12, 1875 aged 4 yr 4 mo; bur. Weav. Cem. June 15, 1875; son of Wm. H. and Mary C. Lowden. [mother of Mrs. Lowden: Mrs. Geo. H. Atkins]. (TJ June 19, 1875).

LOWDEN, LUCY. Died Weaverville June 27, 1875, age 3 yr ___ mo; dau. of Wm. H. and Mary C. Lowden. (TJ July 3, 1875).

LOWDEN, MARSHALL HORACE HOWLAND. Died Weaverville Aug. 31, 1887; native of Mass., born 22 Oct 1834; aged 52 yr 10 mo 9 days; bur. Masonic Cem. Weav. Sept. 1, 1887; came to Trinity Co. 1852; obit. (TJ Sept. 3 & 10, 1887).

LOWDEN, MEHITABLE WHITE BATES. Died Fresno, (Fresno Co.) Dec 26, 1895; age 84 yr 8 mo 8 dy; born Mass. Apr 11, 1811; m. Spencer Lowden 1829 in Mass; moved to Illinois, until 1856, came to Trinity Co. 1856; husband died 1870; 8 children, 4 survive: Wm. S. and Eugene O. Lowden, Trinity Co, Frank Lowden of Walla Walla, Wash. and Mrs. W. J. Tinnin of Fresno. (TJ Sat. Dec 28, 1893). (TJ Sat. Jan 4, 1896 p 3 col 2 "Funeral of Mrs. M. W. Lowden"). [legible gravemarker Old Public Cemetery, Weaverville 1976: "----, inf.dau of W. S. & H.E. Lowden d. 11 Apr 1875, aged 14 dy; Mehitable White 18 Apr 1811-26 Dec 1895 84 yr 8 mo 8 dy; native of Plymouth, Massachusetts; Spencer 20 July 1800-22 Jan 1870 aged 69 yr 6 mo 2 dy, a native of Cummington, Massachusetts"; [note: Mrs. Lowden was a Mayflower descendant]. [Other members of the Lowden family are buried in the Masonic Cemetery, Weaverville].

LOWDEN, SPENSER. Died Grass Valley, Trinity County, Jan. 22, 1870, aged 69 yr 6 mo. (TJ Jan. 29, 1870). [usually spelled Spencer]. [see also Condon, and Lowden records 1900-1950.]

"**LOWDEN**", Old Kit. Died at Lowden Ranch (near Lewiston) Feb. 18, 1892, aged 40 years. "This, the property of O. E. Lowden, was the oldest horse in Trinity County, and carried the children from the time they were large enough to sit on her back." (TJ Sat. Feb. 27, 1892).

LOWE, WALTER. Died Junction City June 22, 1871, aged about 10 years; son of J. T. and Eliza Lowe.(no further info.) (TJ June 24, 1871).

LOWE, WILLIAM M. Died El Dorado Springs, Missouri "latter part of Nov. 1894"; Pioneer Sheriff of Trinity County. (TJ Sat. Dec 22, 1894, p 3). [Not in 1860 Census; 1852 Census, taken 7-18-1852, p. 205: "age 28, hunter, born Kentucky, last from Texas."] [Note: there is no indication as to which of these men named William M. Lowe was the Pioneer Sheriff].

LOWE, WM. M. Killed at Lone Jack, Arkansas, Nov. 1862; rebel army; once Sheriff of Trinity County. [1852 census: age 28, hunter, born Kentucky, last res. Texas]. (TJ Jan. 17, 1863 p 2).

LOWERY, ENOCH. Died Redding, Shasta Co. Jan. 5, 1873, aged 65 yr; native of Carrol County, KY; father of George and Noah Lowery, of Redding, both old res. of Trinity Co. Bur. Shasta [Shasta Co.] Jan. 7, 1873 in I.O.O.F Cem. (TJ Jan. 11, 1873).

LUCKIE, JOHN. Died Mar 3, 1896 Weaverville; native of Calif, aged abt 23 yr. (TJ Sat Mar 7, 1896).

LUCKIE, MARGARET. Died Feb 08, 1900; age 23 yr 10 mo 4 dy; b. Calif. (TJ Jan 1901).

LUDDINGTON, ELIZA A. Died San Francisco July 2, 1866, aged 29 yr; wife of Chas. R. Luddington. (TJ Sat. July 14, 1866 p 2).

LUDWIG, LOUIS W. Died Weaverville Oct. 22, 1872; native of Germany, aged abt 41 yr; one of pioneers of Trinity Co.; came to Calif. 1849 with M. F. Griffin, Ned Fogarty, Henry Conroy, and Calhoun Benham; arr. Lewiston Aug. 1849. (TJ Oct. 26, 1872).

LULO, WILLIAM. Died at Trinity Center Apr. 22, 1892; native of Germany, aged about 57 years. (TJ Sat. Apr. 30, 1892).

LURNAN (or Lurman), GEORGE D. Died Jan. 16, 1907 Weaverville; age 69, male, white, American, miner. [Index to Deaths 1890-1908].

LUTMAN, MARIA. Died Rush Creek (Trinity County) June 17, 1873, aged 39 years; wife of John Lutman. (TJ June 21, 1873). [Index to Deaths 1873-1890: "Lutman, Marie. Died June 17, 1873 Lewiston, white, 39, female; wife of John Lutman; birthplace 'not known'."]

LYNCH, TOBIAS. Died Weaverville Nov. 22, 1877; native of Georgia (colored) aged 67 years; leaves dau. in Cherokee Nation. (TJ Nov. 24, 1877 p 2).

LYON, CHARLES R. Died June 12, 1907 Weaverville; age 42, male, white, miner; born New York. [Index to Deaths 1890-1908].

LYONS, ANDREW. Died Weaverville July 4, 1879; native of Ireland, aged 72 yr; bur. Catholic Cem. Weav. July 5, 1879. (TJ July 23, 1879 p 2 & 3).

LYONS, JAMES. Died Weaverville June 13, 1862; native of Brooke Co, VA, aged 27 yr; bur. Weaverville Cem June 14, 1862. (TJ Sat. June 14, 1862).

LYONS, PATRICK. Died Weaverville Dec 9, 1899; b. County Cork, Ireland, aged abt 65 yr; came to US 1849, Louisiana; to Calif. 1856; never married; bur. Catholic Cem. Weaverville. (TJ Dec 16, 1899 p 2 & p 3 col 3).

MABIE, ELIZABETH. Died Junction City May 12, 1891; wife of Hiram Mabie; native of Waynesburg, New York, aged about 69 years; born Nov. 1822; bur. Public Cem. Weaverville May 13, 1891. Died at res. of dau. Mrs. A. H. Marshall; born Elizabeth Passage; m. Hiram Mabie Jan. 1840; moved to McHenry Co., Ill; came to Calif 1852: Shasta, Humboldt, then Trinity Co. Two children, Frank Mabie of Deadwood and Mrs. Emma Marshall of Junction City; Humboldt and San Jose papers please copy. (TJ Sat. May 16, 1891). [see also Hatch, Catherine].

MABIE, HIRAM. Died Douglas City Sept. 23, 1893 at home of dau. Mrs. A. H. Marshall; native of New York, aged nearly 74 yr; bur. Weaverville Cem. Sept. 25, 1893 beside wife, who died abt 2 years ago; came to Calif. 1852, Trinity Co. winter of 1854-55; obit p 3 col 2 worth copying. (TJ Sat. Sept. 30, 1893 p 2 & 3).

Mc - names beginning with this prefix are alphabetized as if spelled MAC.

McCAIN, JAMES SEWARD. Died Alameda [Alameda Co.] Mar. 18, 1890; native of New York, age about 67 yr; wife died 4 years ago; remarried; widow Ella McCain. Came to Trinity Co. 1852; to San Francisco abt 1865/6. (TJ Mar. 29 & Apr 5, 1890).

McCAMMON, JOHN. Died Albany, New York Sept. 20, 1887; res. of Trin. Co. many years ago; at one time he was Trinity's Assessor. (TJ Oct. 15, 1887). [1860 census: age 42, b. N.Y.]

McCAMPBELL, J. H. Died Guaymas, Mexico Apr. 30, 1866, aged about 35 yr; came to Calif. 1853 from Kingston, Tennessee; father lives in Goliad, Texas; res. Trinity Co. 10 years ago. (TJ May 26, 1866 p 2). [McCampbell, James. born Know County, Tenn. July 16, 1832; came to Trinity Co. 1853. Cox's Annals, 1940 edition.]

McCARTY, GILDIS D. Died Weaverville Mar 25, 1896; native of Johnstown, Penn, aged abt 71 yr; came to Weaverville 1853; lived at Canon Creek until 1894. (TJ Apr 4, 1896).

McCARTHY, GEORGE. Died Roseburg, Oregon Oct. 27, 1877; bur. there Oct. 28, 1877; former res. of Trinity Co. (TJ Sat. Nov. 10, 1877 p 3).

McCLAIN, MARCUS MARION. Died Hay Fork Aug. 10, 1876 aged 4 yr 7 days; son of J. W. and Margaret A. McClain. (TJ Sat. Sept. 9, 1876).

McCLARY, ELSIE. Died Trinity Center Dec. 1, 1891; dau. of Mr. and Mrs. D. R. McClary; native of Calif. aged about 7 years; bur. Thurs. Dec. 3, 1891, Trinity Center Cem. (TJ Sat. Dec. 12, 1891).

McCOLLUM, WILLIAM. Died Weaverville Apr. 4, 1882; native of Illinois aged 57 yr. (TJ Apr. 8, 1882 p 2).

McCLURE, JAMES. Born Oct. 27, 1829 Springfield, Mass. Came to California 1849 with the Hartford Mining and Trading Company, on the ship Henry Lee around Camp Horn to San Francisco; worked at Clear Creek, Shasta Co. 1851-August 1852, came to Weaverville, building by contract; "partner with James McCain". [Cox's Annals, 1940 edition.] [Death date unknown]. [Note: according to Trinity County Deeds, the partner of James Seward McCain was Pennel M. McClure, who was 30 on the 1860 Census, born Connecticut].

McCLURE, _____. Died Weaverville Aug. 25, 1865, infant daughter of P. and Hannah McClure. (TJ Sat. Sept. 2, 1865 p 2). [Note: "Married in Philadelphia Oct. 4, 1860, P. McClure, Esq. of the firm of Jas. S. McCain & Co., Weaverville, California to Miss Hannah Whartenby of Philadelphia." They arrived in San Francisco Nov. 15, 1860, and returned to Weaverville soon after. (TJ Nov. 17, 1860)].

McCOY, WILLIAM. Drowned Trinity River near Hawkins Bar Aug. 11, 1882; native of West Chester, Chester County, Penn., age 20; body recovered Aug. 13; buried on Hawkins Bar. (TJ Aug. 26, 1882 p 2 & 3).

McCULLY, LAWRENCE, Judge. Died Honolulu, Hawaii, April 10, 1892, aged 61 years. Native of New York City; graduate of Yale College; went to Sandwich Islands age 23; First Associate Justice of the Supreme Court of the Hawaiian Kingdom; m. 1866 Miss Eliza Harvey, sister of Mrs. S. I. Thayer, of Douglas City, who survives him. (TJ Sat. May 21, 1892). [see also Harvey and Thayer].

McDANIEL, ANDREW J. Died Deadwood May 12, 1890; native of Coopertown, Penn., aged about 64 yr; brother F. McDaniel of Coopertown, Penn. Bur. Lewiston (Pioneer) Cem. Wed. May 13, 1890. (TJ May 17, 1890). [Index to Deaths 1873-1890 adds white, "married".]

McDANIEL, ANNIE LYDIA. Died Trinity Center Nov. 17, 1861, aged 5 mo 13 days; dau. of W. R. and -----McDaniel. (TJ Dec. 21, 1861 p 2). [no further information; not in 1860 or 1870 census].

McDANIEL, PERCY BURNETT. Died Trinity Center Feb. 15, 1864 aged 1 yr 4 mo; only child of W. R. and -----McDaniel. (TJ Feb. 20, 1864). [see note, above].

McDERMITT, JAMES. Died Stockton, [San Joaquin, Calif.] Aug. 28, 1872. (TJ Aug. 31, 1872 p 3).

McDONALD, _____. "Little daughter of Mr. and Mrs. Thomas McDonald of Deadwood died last week (May 1889) in San Francisco where she was visiting with her mother." (TJ June 1, 1889).

McDonald: see Masterson.

McDUFF, GEORGE H. Died Douglas City Oct. 28, 1862, aged about 9 years. (TJ Nov. 1, 1862). [1860 census: McDuffee, D. B. Indian Creek, age 24, miner, b. Tenn. Martha A. McDuffee, age 9, b. Iowa. George H. McDuffee, age 7, b. Iowa].

McELVANY, H. Died San Francisco Nov. 15, 1870, aged 47 yr. (TJ Nov. 26, 1870 p 2).

McELVANEY, WILLIAM. Died Weaverville May 28, 1879; native of Ireland, aged 59 yr; (TJ May 31, 1879). [probate filed TJ June 21, 1879].

McELVENNY, WILLIAM (sic). "Born in the Co. of Londonderry Ireland Dec 1819 Died May 28, 1879". Gravestone in Weaverville Cem. in good condition 1988.

McFARLAND, ALEXANDER. Died Hettenshaw Aug. 12, 1883; native of Scotland, aged about 51 yr; sheepherder. (TJ Sat. Sept. 1, 1883).

McGINNIS, MICHAEL. Died Weaverville Sept. 30, 1867, aged about 80 years. (TJ Sat. Oct. 5, 1867).

McGOWAN, CORNELIUS, Capt. Died San Francisco Mar. 21, 1891; buried by Calif. Lodge No. 1, I.O.O.F. In 1860s, McGowan worked a claim on East Weaver with his brother James. He was Captain of Halleck Rifles, Weaverville. James McGowan returned home to New York, died more than 20 years ago. Capt. McGowan left Weaverville before 1870 and has resided in San Francisco; married, but no further info. (TJ Sat. Mar. 28, 1891 p 3).

McGOWAN, JAMES. Died Norwich, N.Y. (at res. of sister) Oct. 5, 1866; aged 32 years, late of Weaverville. More. (TJ Nov. 24, 1866 p 2).

McGREGOR, ALEXANDER. Died Oregon Mountain Mar. 2, 1886; native of Canada, aged about 65 yr; Bur. Weaverville Cem. Mar. 3, 1886. Leaves wife, and children in Martintown, Canada. (TJ Mar. 6, 1886).

McINTOSH, DONALD W. Died Weaverville Feb 10, 1900; native of Canada, aged abt 47 yr. (TJ Feb 17, 1900 pg 3 col 2).

McINTYRE, ARCHIBALD. Died Browns Creek (nr Douglas City) Sep 12, 1898; native of Scotland, aged abt 70 yr; reared in Canada; served through the Mexican War in US Army; came to Trinity Co. 1854/1855; ranching & mining; bur. at the top of a knoll near the house where he had lived so long. (TJ Sep 17, 1898 pp 2 & 3). (TJ Sep 24, 1898 notice of Proving Will, p 2 col 2, and p 3 col 1).

McINTYRE, HUGH. Died Canon City Nov 17, 1872; native of Ireland aged 40 yr. (TJ Nov. 30, 1872).

McKAY, FINLEY. Died Apr 10, 1906 Weaverville; age 80, male, white, miner, born Nova Scotia. [Index to Deaths 1890-1908].

McKAY, NETTIE. Died Feb 10, 1906 Junction City, CA; age 11, female, 1/2-Indian; born Calif; school girl; (gunshot wound); bur. Junction City. [Index to Deaths 1890-1906].

McKAY; ZACHARIAH. Died Hyampom Aug 6, 1895; native of Indiana, aged 72 yr 4 mo 11 dy; b. Mar 26, 1823; came to Calif. 1850, Trinity Co. 1850; bur. Hyampom Aug 8, 1895; obit. p 3 col 5. (TJ Aug 17, 1895).

McKEENY, _____. "An aged man by the name of McKeeny died in Red Bluff, Tehama Co., Oct 9, 1896. He came from Mooney Gulch, Trinity Co. 3 months ago; aged 69 yr; bur Catholic Cem." (Red Bluff *Cause* Oct 10, 1896, in TJ Oct 17, 1896 p 3 col 1). [1880 census has McKenney, Michael, age 52, single, miner at Minersville, b. Ireland]. [1892 & 1894 Great Register of Voters has McKenna, Michael, age 63, born Ireland; occupation Miner, Lewiston precinct; 5'10-1/2"; light complexion, blue eyes, brown hair; naturalized Oct. 18, 1856 in Shasta County]. [Mooney Gulch was in the area of Lewiston.]

McKENNA, HUGH. Murdered in Crystal City, Idaho Sept. 1881. (TJ Oct. 1, 1881 p 3). [1860 census: McKenna, Hugh M., North Fork, miner; age 28, b. Penn].

McKENZIE, DAVID. Died Sept 4, 1895 at Hendrick Ranch, Shasta County; former res. of Douglas City; b. Niagara Falls, Canada; abt 60 yr; leaves widow and 2 children, girl 15, boy 7, who live at Buckeye, Shasta Co.; Son-in-law of George Vitzthum of Douglas City. (TJ Sat. Sept 28, 1895).

McKENZIE, NELLIE. Died Douglas City Oct. 29, 1886, aged 3 yr 3 mo 16 days; dau. of Davie and Emma McKenzie. (TJ Nov. 6, 1886).

McKEON, THOMAS. Died Weaverville Jul 28, 1899, aged abt 36 yr. (TJ Jul 29, 1899 p 2.)

McKIERNAN, JOHN. Died Indian Creek, Trinity Co. Sept. 20, 1866; native of Ireland, aged about 35 yr; res. Indian Creek 10 yr; formerly of Hudson Co. New Jersey; father and brother live there. Bur. Catholic Cem. Weaverville. (TJ Sept. 29, 1866 p 2).

McKINLEY, THOMAS. Died July 13, 1907 Coffee Creek, Calif; about 40, male, white, miner; buried Coffee Creek; nativity unknown. [Index to Deaths 1890-1908].

McKNIGHT, CARRIE. Died Weaverville Feb. 9, 1869, aged 2 yr 11 mo; dau. of George and Sarah McKnight. (TJ Feb. 13, 1869 p 2).

McKNIGHT, GEORGE. Died near Jacksonville, Oregon Mar. 2, 1880; native of County Aramagh, Ireland, aged 45 yr; late of Weaverville; bur. Mar. 4, 1880 Jacksonville I.O.O.F. Cem.; came to US 1853; lived Weaverville 17 yr; member Presbyterian Church; leaves wife and one child. (TJ Mar. 13 and Mar. 20, 1880).

McLAUGHLIN, CON. Died Apr. 25, 1903, snow slide, Rush Creek; age 45, male, white, foreign born; remains shipped to San Francisco. [Index to Deaths 1890-1908].

McLEAN,_____, Mrs. Died Jan 19, 1896 at Gore Bay, Ontario, aged 62 yr. Mother of A. W. and John McLean. (TJ Sat. Feb 15, 1896 p 3 col 2).

McLEAN, ALEX. Died Benicia [Solano Co.] "last week" (May 1888); shot by Jas. Trimbath at Deadwood Nov. 25, 1887. (TJ Sat. June 2, 1888).

McLEAN, JOHN. Disappeared in Kootney Valley, British Columbia, abt Jan 23, 1897; may have drowned; bro. of A. W. McLean of Weaverville. (TJ Feb 6, 1897 p 3 col 2).

McLEAN, PETER. Died San Francisco bef. Aug. 29, 1891; Tuesday Will filed for Probate, mentions daughter Anna and grandchildren the Overmohle boys. (TJ Sep 1891). [see also Overmohle].

McLEASH, HENRY. Died near Lewiston in flood of Trinity River Dec. 7, 1861; "old man lived Lewiston several years". (TJ Dec. 14, 1861 p 2).

McMAHON, ANNE. Died Sacramento Jan. 7, 1864; native of County Meath, Ireland, aged 27 yr 9 mo; wife of Joseph McMahon. (TJ Jan. 16, 1864).

McMurry, John, Hon. [see Parberry].

McNAIR, DAVID. Died Trinity Center abt May 1, 1885; native of Penn, aged abt 66 yr. (prob. bur. Trinity Center Cem.). (TJ June 13, 1885).

McNAIRY, MICHAEL. Died Weaverville Nov 6, 1896; native of Ireland, aged abt 84 yr; fun. Nov 7, 1896. (TJ Sat Nov 7, 1896).

McNAMARA, ROY ALTON. Died in Weaverville July 22, 1891; son of Mr. and Mrs. T. J. McNamara; aged 5 mo 21 days; bur. Weaverville Cem. Thurs. Jan. 23, 1891. Six young ladies dressed in white and carrying white wreaths were pall bearers. (TJ Sat. July 25, 1891 pp 2 & 3).

McNEIL, ANGUS. Died at res. of Parents in New Orleans (n.d.); left Trinity Co. last summer. (TJ Mar. 23, 1861).

McNEILL, GODWIN. Died Stoddard's Ranch, Trinity County, Oct. 13, 1884; born Sacramento; buried there; son of John McNeill of Sacramento. (TJ Sat. Oct. 18, 1884 p 3).

McNIEL, LYMAN. Died Weaverville May 29, 1872; native of Connecticut, aged 73 years. (TJ June 1, 1872).

McPHERSON,_____. Died Hyampom Jul 25, 1896; native of US; [male]; aged abt 65 yr; coroner's report p 3 col 5 (probable death by heart trouble). (TJ Sat. Aug 8, 1896).

McWHORTER; A. L. Died Jul 09, 1900; aged 76 yr; b. New York. (TJ Jan 1901). [1870 Census says "Adam L. McWhorter" and wife Barbara, North Fork pg 12.] [may be brother of Miss Lucy].

McWHORTER, LUCY, Miss. Died "while on a visit to relatives in the East" abt Jan 12, 1898; former res. of Weaverville; was a professional nurse; left here about 20 years ago and lived in Oakland; went East 2 years ago. (TJ Mar 5, 1898 p 3 col 3). [1870 Census, Weaverville, Trinity County, California, pg 8, Jun 15, 1870: McWhorter, Lucy, age 50, nurse, b. New York].

MADDEN, JAMES. Died "A few months ago" in 1889, prob. French Gulch, Shasta Co. brother of John Madden; cousins in Weaverville: Wm & John Condon. (TJ Sat. Nov. 23, 1889 p 3).

MADDEN, JOHN. Died Nov. 18, 1889 French Gulch, Shasta Co. Bur. Nov. 22, 1889; no age given; eldest son. (TJ Nov. 23, 1889 p 3).

MADDEN, MAT. Died Dec. 25, 1889 French Gulch, age 22 yr; bur. French Gulch, Shasta Co. Dec. 28, 1889. (TJ Sat. Dec. 28, 1889).

MADDEN, TIMOTHY. Died French Gulch, Shasta Co, Feb 15, 1896; native of Calif, aged 31 yr 5 mo 29 dy; bur French Gulch Cem.; leaves father; 2 sisters, Mrs. G. Reinhaus, of French Gulch, and Miss Annie Madden; cousin of Mrs. T. F. Bergin, Misses Nellie and Annie Condon, and Wm. Condon of Weaverville, and John J. Condon of Redding. (TJ Sat Feb 22, 1896 p 3 col 2). [see also Condon].

MADISON, JOHN HENRY. Died May 10, 1907 Weaverville; age 76, male, black, barber; born Washington, D.C. [Index to Deaths 1890-1908].

MAGAN, JOHN. Died Weaverville Jan. 26, 1872; native of New York, aged about 45 yr; former resident of Klamath. (TJ Feb. 3, 1872 p 2).

MAGNENAT, GEORGE. Died Coffee Creek Aug 6, 1897; native of Switzerland, aged about 67 yr; unmarried; no known relatives. (TJ Aug 14, 1897 pg 3 col 2).

MAGNER, ARTHUR JOSEPH. Died Indian Creek Feb. 4, 1887; aged abt 55 years; bur. Weaverville Cem; came to Trinity Co. 1853; miner; from Woodstock, McHenry Co., Illinois. (TJ Feb. 12 & 19, 1887).

MAGUIRE, LAURENCE. Shot at Deadwood Creek [nr Lewiston] last Sat., Feb. 25, 1865; native of Ireland, about 35 yr. (TJ Sat. Mar. 4, 1865 p 2 col 1).

MAHONEY, DENNIS. Died Mariposa (Mariposa Co.) Mar. 9, 1860; see Mariposa *Gazette* for more information. (TJ Mar. 24, 1860 p 2).

MAJOR, JOHN N. Died Redding, Shasta Co. Nov 20, 1896; bur. Nov. 21, 1896; (no age given). Leaves widow and 2 grown sons; former resident of Weaverville; carried mail from Shasta to Weaverville 20 years ago.

MALONE, ELLA. Died Nov 1, 1907 Weaverville; age 20 days; female, white, born Calif; buried Weaverville. Informant: Mrs. Rosa Malone. [Index to Deaths 1890-1908].

MALONE, MARY. Died San Francisco Aug. 31, 1872; born Weaverville; aged 15 yr 5 mo 4 days; dau. of Michael and Margaret Malone of Weaverville; bur. Catholic Cem. Weaverville Sept. 5, 1872. (TJ Sept. 7, 1872).

MALONE, MORRIS. Drowned Trinity River "one day last week", Sept. 1878; of New River; buried Hoopa Valley. (TJ Sept. 28 and Oct. 5, 1878).

MALONE, PATRICK. Died Weaverville Aug 14, 1887; native of Ireland, aged abt 59 yr; came to Calif. 1856; bur. Catholic Cem. Weaverville. (TJ Sat. Aug. 20, 1887).

MALONE, RICHARD. Died Weaverville Aug. 27, 1881; born Weaverville Feb. 1861, aged 20 yr 7 mo; bur. Catholic Cem., Weaverville Aug. 29, 1881. (TJ Sat. Sept. 3, 1881 p 2).

MALONEY, THOMAS. Died at residence of brother Wm. Maloney, Esq. in San Francisco Dec. 19, 1878; native of Ireland, aged about 55 years; late of Lewiston. (TJ Dec. 28, 1878 p 3).

MANLY, CHARLES. Died June 20, 1907 Weaverville; age 66, male, white, born Maine. Informant: Mark Manly. [also spelled Manley]. [Index to Deaths 1890-1908].

MARBLE, F. D. died May 20, 1900; aged 87 yr; b. Michigan. (TJ Jan 1901).

MARIE, LOUIS. Died Redding "about two weeks ago", Dec. 1875; late of Weaverville; photographer. (TJ Sat. Dec. 25, 1875 p 3).

MARINGER, FRANCE. Died Hay Fork Aug. 2, 1895; native of Austria, aged about 53 yr; buried in Hay Fork. (TJ Aug 10, 1895).

MARKLEY, CYRUS. Died Arizona Jan. 26, 1880; former res. of Weaverville. (TJ Mar. 6, 1880 p 2). [1877 Great Register of Voters: reg. May 19, 1877; Weav. age 30, born Ohio; miner].

MARKLEY, JOSEPH. Died Weaverville Jul 6, 1898; native of New York, aged abt 65 yr. (TJ Jul 9, 1898 p 2; report of accident pg 3 col 4).

MARSH, CHRISTINA, Mrs. Died "last Friday" (prob. Apr. 1891), in Lewiston, Maine; husband Noah Marsh died later same day. He was born Skowhegan, ME 1810; Mrs. Marsh was about 75. Buried Newport, Maine. Mrs. Marsh was the mother of Nathan Wheeler, who died at Trinity Center about 3 years ago. (TJ Sat. Apr. 25, 1891). [see also Wheeler].

MARSH, WM. S. Died in service of our country, abt 1865; member Douglas City Rifles. [not in 1852 or 1860 census]. (TJ June 3, 1865).

MARTIN, _____ . Died Lower Trinity abt Jan 11, 1879, age 9; dau. of R. B. Martin; bur. Jan. 13, 1879. (TJ Sat. Jan. 18, 1879 p 2).

MARTIN, ANTOINETTE WAYLAND YOUNG. Died Weaverville Jul 4, 1897; b. Weaverville Jan 24, 1866, aged 31 yr 5 mo 10 dy; dau. of Francis W. and Mary E. Young; m. George A. Martin Oct 25, 1892; leaves husband, mo. Mrs. Mary E. Young, 2 sis. Stella W. Vanderhoff of Hay Fork, Lucy M. Young, and 3 bro. W. W. Young, Van B. Young, and Henry J. Young; bur. Weaverville Cem. Jul 5, 1897; known as "Nettie". (TJ Jul 10, 1897 pp 2 & 3). [see also Young].

MARTIN, CAROLINE E., Miss. Died at res. of bro. in law Jno. E. Church, Esq., Weaverville; "Carrie"; formerly of Mineral Point, Wisconsin, aged 20 yr 4 mo; bur. [old section], Weaverville Cem. Apr. 29, 1860. (TJ May 5, 1860).

MARTIN, CARRIE. Died Douglas City Feb. 25, 1865, aged 1 yr 8 mo 8 days; dau. of Augustus and Mary Martin. (TJ Sat. Mar. 4, 1865).

MARTIN, ELIZABETH B. Died Eureka, Humboldt Co. Feb. 3, 1868, aged 47 years; wife of Capt. Wm. C. Martin. (TJ Feb. 22, 1868 p 2).

MARTIN, EMMA. Died Weaverville June 19, 1869; age 12 yr 8 mo; dau. of Wm. H. and Jane Martin. (TJ June 26, 1869 p 2).

MARTIN, FRANK. Died Burnt Ranch Jan 25, 1899, native of Portugal, aged abt 65 yr; drowned; left a wife and nine children. (TJ Feb 4, 1899 pp 2 & 3).

MARTIN, GUS. (probably Augustus). Died Garberville Feb. 17, 1879; native of Onondaga Co., New York, aged 46 yr; bur. Rohnerville Feb. 20, 1879; moved to Humboldt Co. from Trin Co. 1869. (TJ Mar. 1, 1879).

MARTIN, HENRY. Died San Francisco Feb. 27, 1893; born Eastport Maine abt. 53 years ago; brother of John Martin; came to Weaverville 1870; m. Apr. 14, 1890, Mrs. May E. More, the widow of Samuel More. obit. p 3 col 2, entire column. (TJ Sat. Mar. 4, 1893; Mar. 11, 1893 p 3 col 2 & col 4; see also references to John Martin.)

MARTIN, HENRY S. Died Alturas, Modoc Co. "last week", May 1884; of Trinity County. (TJ June 7, 1884 p 3).

MARTIN, JAMES. Died Weaverville Oct. 15, 1886; b. Weav. Nov. 16, 1853, aged 32 yr 11 mo; bur. Oct. 17, 1886. [prob. Weav. Cem.] (TJ Sat. Oct. 16, 1886).

MARTIN, JENEFER, Mrs. Died Weaverville Sep 22, 1899; b. Cambonne, England Aug 3, 1827, aged 72 yr 1 mo 18 dy; the dau. of Richard and Jenefer Cox; m. Henry Martin 1852 at Mineral Point, Wisc.; came to Calif. same year; came to Weaverville 1862; 9 children, two survive: Minnie M. and Elizabeth Martin; fun. Sept 23, 1899 under auspices of Order of Eastern Star. (TJ Sep 23, 1899 pp 2 & 3).

MARTIN, JOHN. Died Weaverville July 30, 1892; native of Eastport Maine, aged about 65 yrs; bur. Public Cem. Weaverville July 31, 1892; "Trinity's Foremost Citizen", lived Weaverville 42 years; came to Calif. 1849, ocean route, Trinity Co. March 1850. 4 years ago in San Francisco m. Mrs. Belle Hoffman, who with infant son survives him; also bro. Henry Martin, Deadwood and 1 sister. obit. p 3, entire col 3. (TJ Sat. Aug. 6, 1892; see also TJ Aug. 13, 1892, death of Henry Martin, TJ July 8, 1893, TJ July 15, 22, 1893; body of John Martin exhumed TJ Aug. 5, 1893 p 3 col 3, TJ Aug. 26, 1893 "The Butcher's Daughter; TJ Sept. 9, 1893 "Coroner's jury finds that John Martin did not die from natural causes.", and more reports 1893-1894, 1898.)

MARTIN, LILLY. Died Weaverville Dec. 13, 1875, aged 6 yr 2 mo; dau. of Henry and Jane Martin. (TJ Dec. 18, 1875 p 2).

MARTIN, P. P. Died San Diego, CA Nov 30, 1895, aged 67 yr; wife and one son survived; lived Trinity County at Douglas City and Weaverville; aka "Doc" Martin; good musician. (TJ Sat. Dec 14, 1895 p 3 col 3).

MARTIN, RICHARD. Died Weaverville Dec. 16, 1875, aged 13 years; son of Henry and Jane Martin. (TJ Dec. 18, 1875 p 2).

MARTIN, SAMUEL. Died Port Kenyon [no state given; Maine?] May 1893; native of Maine, aged 74 yr. m. 1845 Miss Matilda Whitmore, sister of John Whitmore of Trinity County, who survives him. Mr. Martin resided in Trinity Co. at one time. (TJ Sat. June 3, 1893 p 3 col 4).

MARTIN, WILLIAM HENRY. Died Stuart's Fork (Minersville area) Oct 29, 1896; native of Weaverville, Calif., aged 33 yr 1 mo 2 dy; bur. Oct 31, 1896 I.O.O.F. Cem. Weaverville; aka "Pike" Martin; son of Mr. and Mrs. Henry Martin; leaves parents, 2 sisters, Misses Minnie & Lizzie Martin of Weaverville. (TJ Sat. Oct 31, 1896 pp 2-3; also TJ Nov 7, 1896 p 3 col 4).

MASON, AVILLA A. Died San Francisco Jan. 5, 1873; aged 27 yr; wife of J. C. Mason of Douglas City, Trinity County. (TJ Jan. 11, 1873).

MASON, JOHN. Died Weaverville Jul 17, 1866; native of Truro, county Cornwall, England, aged about 64 yr; bur. Jul 18, 1866 Weaverville Cem. (TJ Sat. July 21, 1866).

MASTERSON, ELIZA, Mrs. Died French Gulch (Shasta Co.), last Sunday (Jan 3, 1892) and was bur. Tuesday (Jan 5, 1892). Deceased had been a resident of French Gulch for 37 years, and was well known in Trinity County. She was a native of Ireland, age 65. Daughters are Mrs. Luke McDonald of French Gulch and Mrs. Meade Everhart of Woodland. (TJ Sat. Jan. 9, 1892).

MATHEWS, JAMES L. Died Weaverville Aug 26, 1887; born County Cork, Ireland 1810. (TJ Sat. Sept. 3, 1887).

MATHEWS, LETTY ANNA. Died Weaverville Jan 7, 1890; native of New Hampshire, aged 31 yr 1 mo 27 days. (TJ Sat. Jan. 11, 1890). [Index to Deaths 1873-1890 adds white, female, married.]

MATHEWS, THOMAS. "Killed by a caving bank in his claim at Cox's Bar, Trinity County Apr. 13, 1860." 41 years old; leaves wife and 6 children in Cornwall--planned to visit them in autumn. (more) (TJ Sat. April 21, 1860).

MATHEWS, VALENTINE. Killed 17 Oct. 1862 by falling from the trail opposite Fakes' Bar, a distance of 150 feet; about 45 years of age; resident Canon Creek 7 years; bur. Oct. 18, 1862. (TJ Sat. Oct. 25, 1862 p 2). [place not given; prob. Canon Creek, near Junction City].

MATTHEWS, J. A., Mrs. Died Feb 24, 1896 in San Francisco; of Trinity Center; b. Hayfork 1859, m.n. Julia A. Duncan; m. Dec. 3, 1876 to J. A. Mathews; leaves husband and 4 children; 2 bro. A. B. and R. L. Duncan, and sister Mrs. Louisa Shock, of Hayfork, sister Mrs. Emma Bragdon of Trinity Center, and one sister in Idaho. (TJ Sat. Feb 29, 1896). [see also Duncan, Shock, Bragdon.]

MATTHEWSON, JOHN. Died June 22, 1908 Weaverville; age 79, male, white; bur. Weaverville; born Canada. [Index to Deaths 1890-1908].

MATZEN, JOHN D. CHRISTIAN. "Killed in a mining claim at Douglas City Jan. 10, 1872." Native of Schleswig, Germany, aged about 47 years; old resident of Douglas City; member of the Turner Bar Company as early as 1855; wife and 5 young children in Weaverville. (TJ Jan. 13, 1872). [see also Paulsen].

MAY, JOHN B. Drowned in Trinity River near Big Bar March 30, 1884; native of Georgia, aged about 62 yr; came to Trinity County 1851/2; Sheriff 1857-1859; mining at Big Bar; (TJ Sat. Apr. 5, 1884) body not found (TJ Apr. 12, 1884).

MAY, WILLIAM H. Died Junction City Sept. 1, 1866; native of Georgia, aged 47 yr; bur. Weav. Masonic Cem. Sept. 2, 1866; leaves wife and children. "Pittsburg, Penn, St.Louis, Mo, and Van Buren, Arkansas papers please copy." (TJ Sat. Sept. 8, 1866 p 2).

MAYNARD, CHARLES. Died Dec 09, 1900; aged 72 yr 4 mo 29 dy; b. New York. (TJ Jan 1901).

MAYNARD, MARY. Died Hay Fork July 16, 1895; native of Calif., aged abt 54 yr; wife of Chas. Maynard. (TJ July 20, 1895).

MAYOR, OSCAR JOHNSON. Died at Bowerman's Ranch near Minersville May 15, 1891; native of Vermont, aged about 50 years. "Vermont papers please copy." (TJ Sat. May 23, 1891 p 2).

MEAD, ELLEN. Died San Francisco Sept. 7, 1871, age 27 yr; wife of Daniel Mead. (TJ Sept. 16, 1871 p 2).

MEAGHER, DENNIS. Died Grass Valley, Nevada Co. Dec. 1893; native of Ireland; brother of Mrs. Richard Ryan, Sr. of Oregon Gulch and an uncle of Mrs. John Minear of Deadwood; obit. worth copying. (TJ Sat. Dec. 16, 1893 p 3 col 1).

MEAGHER, PATRICK. Died Weaverville Dec 5, 1894; native of Ireland, aged abt 62 yr. (TJ Sat Dec 8, 1894 p 2).

MEARS, CLARA. Died near Weaverville Dec. 15, 1873; aged 24 yr; bur. Weaverville Cem. Dec. 16, 1873; wife of Parker H. Mears. "Less than 3 months ago she came from the East a young and happy bride." (TJ Dec. 20, 1873 p 3). [Index to Deaths 1873-1890 adds white, female, married, born Maine].

MEARS, PARKER A. Died Washington, Knox Co., Maine Sept. 15, 1883; native of Maine, aged 59 years; father of Preston A. Mears; Mr. Mears was well known in this county having lived here a number of years at different times. (TJ Sat. Oct. 6, 1883 p 3).

MECKEL, CHAS. Died Jul 19, 1900; age 25 yr 7 mo 1 dy; b. California. (TJ Jan 1901).

MECKEL, HENRY W. Drowned in North Fork (of Trinity River) May 6, 1890; native of North Fork, CA (now Helena); b. Feb. 20, 1864; aged 26 yr 2 mo 10 days; unmarried; 3rd son of late John Meckel; (TJ Sat. May 10, 1890). body found below Cox Bar Aug. 29, 1890; bur. Weaverville Cem. Sept. 2, 1890. (TJ Sat. Sept. 6, 1890 p 2). [Index to Deaths 1873-1890 adds male, single, born Calif. brewer.]

MECKEL, JOHN. Died Weaverville Mar. 3, 1889; born Oberndorf, Rhenish Bavaria Jan. 7, 1826; aged 63 yr 1 mo 23 days; came U.S. 1841, St. Louis, MO; Calif. 1850; m. 1857 at North Fork, Trinity Co. Mrs. Charlotta Weinheimer, sister of Henry Weinheimer of Weaverville and Mrs. H. Schlomer of North Fork; 6 children: Louisa, Christian, Henry, John, Albert, and Charles, all living; (TJ Mar. 9, 1889). [Index to Deaths 1873-1890 adds: male, married, brewer.]

MEISINGER, GEO. Died June 11, 1903 Nash Mine on Coffee Creek; age 48; male, white, American; buried near mine. [Index to Deaths 1890-1908.]

MEISENHEIMER, RITCHIE M. Died Weaverville Jan. 15, 1875; native of Illinois, aged 48 yr; bur. Masonic Cem, Weaverville Jan. 17, 1875; leaves brother and sister in Jackson County, Illinois. (TJ Sat. Jan. 16, 1875 pp 2 & 3).

MELTON, AMON. Died Placerville May 12, 1887; (no age given); partner of Martin & Watt in the Brown Bear mine of Deadwood; brother John Melton Adm. of estate. (TJ May 21 and June 4, 1887).

MELVIN, MAUD. Died Junction City Apr 7, 1899; native of Calif. aged abt 28 yr; known as "Fay Darrell". (see Darrell). (TJ Apr 8, 1899 and Apr 15, 1899 p 3 col 3).

MENDOZA, INNOCENCIA JOSEPH. Died near Douglas City Dec. 30, 1891; native of Portugal, aged about 62 years. (TJ Jan. 2, 1892).

MERIDETH, DAVID L. Died March 26, 1908 Weaverville; age 49, male, white, rancher; buried Weaverville; born Wales. [Index to Deaths 1890-1908].

MERRICK, ALONZO. Killed by Indians July 23, 1863 at mouth of New River. (TJ Sat. Aug. 1, 1863 p 3). ("and Madame Weaver").

MERRITT, H. P., Dr. Died at his home, Merritt's Station, near Woodland, Yolo Co. Mar. 18, 1893; one of California's pioneers; well known in Weaverville; large land owner Trinity Co. (TJ Sat. Mar. 25, 1893).

MEYER, HENRY. Died Weaverville Sept. 2, 1858; native of Germany, aged 41 years. (TJ Sat. Sept. 4, 1858 p 2).

MEYER, OSCAR. Died San Francisco Sept. 30, 1894; (no age given); left home age 18 yr; settled in State of Mississippi early 1840s; came to Calif. 1851, arriving San Francisco June 21, 1851; returned to San Francisco 1863; leaves wife, six sons, 3 daughters; I.O.O.F. funeral. ["Mr. Meyer was the father-in-law of Mrs. B. F. Meyer, a sister of Morris Abrahm of the firm of Abrahm & Karsky of Weaverville. Ed."] (TJ Oct. 6, 1894 p 3).

MEYERS, MARSHALL E. Died Aug. 5, 1907 Hayfork; age 71, male, white, American, farmer; buried Weaverville Cemetery. [Index to Deaths 1890-1908].

MICHELET, JOHN. aka MITCHELL, JOHN. Died Weaverville Feb. 5, 1877; native of Canada, aged 50 years; French Canadian; lived Weaverville 26 years; bur. Feb. 6, 1877 Weaverville Cem. (TJ Sat. Feb. 10, 1877 p 2 & 3).

MIDDLETON, SAMUEL. Died Weaverville Jan 10, 1894; born Mass. 1801; abt 93 yr; came to Calif 1849, Trinity Co. 1850; 1852 moved to Readings Creek; returned to Weaverville "a few years ago"; carpenter. (TJ Jan 13, 1894).

MILLER, ABRAHAM, Captain. Died Trinidad "Monday last" (either May 29 or May 23) 1881; native of Ohio aged 55. (From Arcata *Leader*, prob. May 1881). (TJ Sat. June 4, 1881 p 3).

MILLER, ALFRED. Drowned in Trinity River at Lowden's Ranch Dec. 5, 1889; native of Denmark, aged about 25 yr. (TJ Dec. 7, 1889, Dec. 14, 1889; Feb. 15, 1890: thanks from parents, F. C. Miller and wife of Horsens, Denmark). "Died Dec. 5, 1889 Trinity River, at Lowden Ranch (drowned); white, 25, male, single, born Denmark." [Index to Deaths 1873-1890].

MILLER, CONRAD. Died San Francisco, CA Mar 2, 1894; native of Hesse Darmstadt, German Empire, born 1821; came to Calif. & Trinity Co. "early"; was mining on Canadian Bar 1853 or 1854; never married. (TJ Mar 17, 1894 p 3).

MILLER, E. J. Died Helmwood, Jewell Co., Kansas at saw and grist mill Aug. 9, 1873; res. Weaverville for several years; left here for his former home in fall of 1869. (TJ Aug. 23, 1873 p 3). [see also Richard Watson].

MILLER, HENRY H. Died Oct. 16, 1890 Weaverville; white, 46, male, single; born Pennsylvania. [Index to Deaths 1890-1908].

MILLER, HENRY HARRISON. Died Weaverville Oct. 16, 1890, native of Pennsylvania, aged abt 46 year; unmarried; bur. Weaverville Cem. Oct. 18, 1890. (TJ Sat. Oct. 18, 1890).

MILLER, JENNY. Died Weaverville abt Oct. 19, 1861. "Alias Ellen Egan". See Egan.

MILLER, PETER. Died Weaverville Oct 8, 1899, native of Schleswig-Holstein, Germany, aged abt 82 yr; pioneer of Trinity County; came abt 1850; 6 yr. ranched in Hyampom in partnership with Jacob Waldorff; bur. Weaverville Cem. with Old Settlers ceremonies. (TJ Oct 14, 1899 p 2 & p 3 col 4). (see also Waldorff).

Miller, Richard T. Born March 1829 St. Louis, MO; 7th child of Major William Miller. Came to Calif. 1850 across the plains; worked at Cold Springs, El Dorado Co. until Jan 1851, came to Weaverville, mined; butcher shop 1854; County Judge of Trinity County, 1854. No date of death. Cox's Annals, 1940 edition.

MILLER, R. T., "Dick". Died Silver City, Owyhee county, Idaho Apr. 11, 1873; no age; leaves wife and two children; at one time County Judge of Trinity County. (TJ Apr. 26, 1873 p 3).

MILLER, THOMAS LOVE. Died Minersville Sep 11, 1898; native of Penn., aged abt 76 yr; never married; bur. Masonic Cem. Weaverville (TJ Sep 17, 1898).

MILES, D. D. Died at sea aboard steamship *St. Louis* May 1, 1864, 60 miles south of Acapulco, buried at sea; late res. of Weaverville, of Ohio; no age given. (TJ June 25, 1864 p 2).

MILLS, MARY, Mrs. Died San Francisco Sat. Mar. 16, 1889; bur. Carson, Nevada (her home). 3 children: 2 sons and Mrs. J. R. Flagg of Weaverville. (TJ Mar. 23, 1889 p 3).

MILTON, JOHN. Died Placerville, (El Dorado Co.), Oct 1, 1899; native of Indiana; no age given. One of the owners of the Brown Bear Mine in Deadwood, Trinity County. (TJ Sat. Oct 7, 1899 p 3 col 3).

MINER, JORDAN ELIAS. Died on Oregon Gulch Mountain near Weaverville Mar 24, 1899; b. Dent Co., Missouri, May 28, 1871, aged 27 yr 9 mo 26 dy; m. Mrs. Cora Sprague Jan 11, 1899; she survives; bur. Foresters Cem. Junction City. (TJ Apr 1, 1899 p 3 col 2; see also TJ Mar 11, 1899 & Mar 25, 1899).

MIRES, GEORGE F., Captain. Died "a few days ago" (Nov. 1888) near Edgewood, Siskiyou County; Assessor Trinity County 1862-3; wife died a few months ago; mined Browns Creek and Rush Creek. (Shasta *Courier*). (TJ Sat. Dec. 1, 1888).

MITCHELL, ANNIE JANE. Died Weaverville Aug. 9, 1859, aged 2 months; infant daughter of Archibald and Elizabeth Mitchell. (TJ Sat. Aug. 13, 1859 p 2).

MITCHELL, ARCHIBALD. Died abt Feb. 20, 1863, Weaverville; Elizabeth Mitchell, of Weaverville, Administratrix. (TJ Feb. 28, 1863 p 2). [1860 census: Mitchell, Archibald, Weaverville, age 30, liquor dealer, born Ireland; Elizabeth age 20, born Ireland; Emmet John, age 2 born California.]

MITCHELL, EMMET. Died Weaverville May 4, 1863 (scarlet fever), aged 5 yr; son of Elizabeth Mitchell. (TJ May 9, 1863 p 2).

MITCHELL, GEORGE WASHINGTON. Died Weaverville Oct. 24, 1866, aged 5 mo 15 days; son of John and Nellie Mitchell. "New York & Philadelphia papers copy". (TJ Oct. 27, 1866 p 2).

MITCHELL, FRED. Died Trinity Center Apr 2, 1896; native of Illinois, aged abt 30 yr. (TJ Apr 11, 1896).

MITCHELL, JOHN. Killed in his claim near Minersville last Sat. Sept. 22, 1860; Englishman; late from Mineral Point, Wisconsin where he has a wife living. (TJ Sept. 29, 1860, page 2 col 1).

MITCHELL, JOHN. Died San Francisco Aug. 9, 1878; native of County Autrim, Ireland, aged 46 yr; merchant at Steiners Flat prior to 1863; lived Weaverville several years, left 8-9 years ago. (TJ Aug. 17, 1878).

MITCHELL, MARY. Died Junction City July 27, 1869, aged 17 days. Daughter of W. W. and Mary A. Mitchell. (TJ July 31, 1869 p 2).

MITCHELL, MAY. Died at Deadwood Aug. 3, 1892, aged 27 yr. (TJ Aug. 6, 1892 p 2).

MITCHELL, W. W. Died Junction City Dec. 11, 1872; native of Pennsylvania, aged 42 yr. (TJ Dec. 14, 1872).

MOFFIT, JOSH. Died Yreka July 31, 1873 aged 45 years; former resident [of Weaverville]. (TJ Aug. 9, 1873 p 3).

MOLONEY, THOMAS. Killed by a falling tree on Indian Creek Aug. 19, 1885; native of Ireland, aged about 39 years. m. Miss Fannie Caswell of Shasta Co. 6 July 1885 (6 weeks ago); sister Mrs. Dan L. Smith d. 10 Oct. 1884 at Eagle Creek, Shasta Co. sister Mrs. B. S. Guptil and Mr. P. and T. Slattery of Oregon Gulch only relatives in this county. Bur. Catholic Cem, Weaverville Aug. 21, 1885. (TJ Sat. Aug. 22, 1885).

MONAHAN, DANIEL. Died Douglas City Dec 28, 1894; born County Monahan, Ireland 1832; m. in Bloomfield, New Jersey (n.d.); came to Calif. 1852; wife came in 1858, lives in Smartsville, Yuba County; came to Trinity County 1860s; lived with Mr. Amos Marshall at Douglas City last 12 years. Bur. Weaverville Cem. Dec 30, 1894. (TJ Sat. Jan 5, 1895 p 3 col 4).

MONTAGUE, CHARLES EDWARD. Died Weaverville Jan. 9, 1874, aged 20 days; infant son of Dr. J. C. and Mary E. Montague. (TJ Jan. 17, 1874). [Index to Deaths 1873-1890: Montague, C. E.; died Jan. 9, 1874 Weaverville; white, 20 days, male, single, born Calif.] [born Dec. 21, 1873; bur. Catholic Cem. Weaverville.]

MONTAGUE, J. A. Died Weaverville Aug 8, 1899; native of Calif., aged 24 yr 4 mo 28 dy. (TJ Sat. Aug 12, 1899 p 2).

MONTAGUE, JOSEPH CRUDUP, Dr. Died Weaverville June 13, 1896; b. North Carolina Dec 1820; came to Calif. 1850; m. Miss Mary Enright 1870; Mrs. Montague d. Dec. 1883; eight children; 2 died in infancy; Mrs. R. W. Stiller; Joseph A; Edwin L.; Charles A.; Dollie E.; and John A. Montague. obit. entire col 3 and col 4 on page 3. (TJ Sat. June 20, 1896).

MONTAGUE, MARY E. Died Weaverville Dec. 29, 1883; native of New York City, aged 32 yr 7 mo 25 days; wife of Dr. J. C. Montague. good obit. p 3. (TJ Sat. Jan. 5, 1884). [see also Long, Ann, Mrs.]

MONTGOMERY, _____. Inf. son of Mr. & Mrs. S. Died Mar 09, 1900; age 9 days; b. California. (TJ Jan 1901).

MONTGOMERY, A. B. "BUCK". Died Middle Creek, Shasta Co. May 16, 1892; stage robbery; John Boyce, driver. Montgomery, the messenger, was mortally wounded; news item; no age given. (TJ Sat. May 21, 1892). [See also TRINITY 1966 pp 4-10 for the story; left wife and 2 small children.]

MOONEY, DENNIS B. Died Weaverville Oct. 11, 1889; native of Tennessee, aged 72 yr; never married. Came to Calif. 1849, Trinity Co. 1854; owned and operated a ferry boat on Trinity river at the mouth of Mooney Gulch above Lewiston. (TJ Sat. Oct. 12, 1889). [Index to Deaths 1873-1890 adds white, male].

MOONEY, PETER PAUL. Died Weaverville May 18, 1897; native of Ireland, aged abt 72 yr; unmarried; bur. Catholic Cem. Weaverville May 20, 1897. (TJ May 22, 1897).

MOORE, AMANDA. Died East Fork, Trinity Co. July 24, 1894; native of Ohio, aged 73 yr 9 mo 23 dy; leaves son James Moore. (TJ Sat. July 28, 1894 pg 2 & 3).

MOORE, IRVIN. Died Hyampom May 3, 1889; native of Ohio, aged about 47 yr. (TJ Sat. May 11, 1889). (TJ Sat. May 18, 1889 p 3: 9 in family: George Moore and Mrs. Jacob Fox of Rawson, Ohio are two;).

MOORE, IRWIN. Died May 3, 1889 San Francisco; white, age 47, male, single, born Ohio. [Index to Deaths 1873-1890]. (prob. Irvin Moore, above).

MOORE, ISAAC. Died Weaverville Jan. 11, 1870; native of Canal Winchester, Ohio, aged 35 years. (TJ Sat. Jan. 15, 1870 p 2).

MOORE, MILTON. Died Oakland [Alameda Co.] Sept. 26, 1880; native of San Francisco, aged 6 yr 10 mo 18 days. Son of F. P. Dann, Esq. of San Francisco; grandson of Captain J. M. Moore of Oakland. (TJ Oct. 2, 1880 p 2).

MORE, SAMUEL. Died Douglas City March 25, 1864; native of County Down, Ireland, aged 23 years. (TJ Sat. Mar. 26, 1864 p 2).

MOREY, ALVILA. Died San Francisco Aug. 1, 1868 (scarlet fever); aged 4 yr 10 mo; daughter of S. B. and M. J. Morey. (TJ Aug. 8, 1868 p 2).

MOREY, S. B. Died at Fruitvale [nr. Oakland, Alameda Co.] May 11, 1885; res. Weaverville 25 years ago; m. Miss Maggie Ruch, who, with several children, survives him. (TJ May 23, 1885 page 3 col 4). [see also Ruch].

MORIE, Madam. Also known as "Madam Marie". Died Weaverville Feb. 9, 1891; native of France, aged about 65 years. (TJ Sat. Feb. 14, 1891; also Feb. 7, 1891 for her illness).

MORGAN, MARY. Died Dec. 17, 1906 Weaverville, age 53, female, white, American. [Index to Deaths 1890-1908].

MOROHAN, H. W., Mrs. Died near Lewiston Oct. 24, 1894 at Blakemore's Ranch; native of Kentucky, aged 20 yr 9 mo 11 dy; bur. Lewiston Oct 27, 1896; of Portland, OR; leaves husband and 3 yr old dau; parents Mr. and Mrs. R. T. Miller and 3 bro. reside in Portland; sister of Mrs. William Blakemore. (TJ Oct 27, 1894 p 3; Nov 3, 1894 p 2 & 3).

MORRIS, JAMES. Died Indian Creek May 17, 1874, native of Ireland, aged 46 years. One of oldest settlers; wife and 5 children; bur. at Indian Creek May 17, 1874. (TJ May 23, 1874). [Married at Indian Creek Aug. 10, 1863 by C. M. Stratton, J.P., James J. Morris and Miss Catherine Lang. Trinity County Marriages Book H page 96]. [1870 Census, Trinity County, California, Indian Creek page 6, 6-27-1870: Morris, James, 47, miner, b. Ireland; Catherine, 39, b. Prussia; Elizabeth, 6, b. Calif; Mary C., 5, b. Calif; William L., 4, b. Calif; John J., 2, b. Calif. Henry A., 8 mo, b. Calif.]

MORRIS, JAMES. Died Dec. 17, 1907 Weaverville; age 73, male, white, born Ireland, hotel keeper; buried Weaverville [Catholic Cemetery]; informant: Mrs. James Morris. [Index to Deaths 1890-1908]. [Married in Weaverville May 22, 1866 by Rev. Father McNulty, James Morris (of New York Hotel) and Miss Mary A. Colbert. Trinity County Marriages Book H page 163.] [note: no children.] [see also Kernan & Rule].

MORRIS, JAMES STAFFORD. Died Hay Fork Jun 8, 1896; inf. son of Mr. and Mrs. John Morris. (TJ Sat. June 13, 1896).

MORRIS, KATE, Mrs. Died Indian Creek June 28, 1889; native of Germany, aged about 40 yr; widow (of James J. Morris); 5 children; bur. Indian Creek June 30, 1889. (TJ July 6, 1889.) [Index to Deaths 1873-1890: Morris, Kate, died June 28, 1889 Indian Creek; white, 50, female, single, born Germany. [note: she was "40" in the 1880 census.]

MORRIS, THOMAS. Died Minersville, Trinity County at res. of father Mar. 15, 1864; native of Missouri aged 31 yr 5 mo 13 days; resided Suisun City, Solano Co., 3 years past; Odd Fellows of Suisun; bur. Minersville. (TJ Mar. 19, 1864 p 2).

MORRISON JOHN. Died at Van Matres Ranch (Minersville) July 17, 1886; native of Wisconsin, aged about 64 years. (TJ Sat. July 24, 1886).

MORRISON, WILLIAM. Died Taylor's flat, Trinity River, Aug. 30, 1857, aged about 35 years. "Mr. Morrison was one of the members of the Fremont expedition which arrived in California in 1846." (TJ Sept. 5, 1857 p 2).

MORTIMER, GEORGE. Killed by mining accident in Weaverville Mar. 25, 1882; native of County Antrim, Ireland, aged about 37 years; came to US with parents at an early age; from Penn. to Calif; owned a farm in Kansas; leaves two sisters in Philadelphia. Bur. F & AM Cem. Weaverville Mar. 26, 1882. (TJ Apr. 1, 1882 pp 2-3).

MORTLAND, JOHN. Died Weaverville Mar. 13, 1868; native of Slippery Rock, near Harrisville, Butler County, Penn. aged about 41 years. (TJ Mar. 21, 1868 p 2).

MORTON, OMAR, *Mrs.* Died Nov. 24, 1859 at the house of P. T. Tuthill, near Weaverville; native of New York, age 33; resided here 4 years, came from Humboldt. Bur. Weav. Cem. Nov. 27, 1859. (TJ Nov. 26 and Dec. 3, 1859).
MOSIER, JOHN. Died Weaverville June 26, 1871, aged about 40 years. (TJ July 1, 1871 p 2).
MOSS, AMOS SEYMOUR. Died Jumpers Mill near Weaverville July 26, 1886; native of Conn. aged 55 years. Came to Trinity Co. 1853; leaves wife and infant child; bur. Odd Fellows Cem, Weaverville July 28, 1886. (TJ July 24 and 31, 1886).
MOTHERWELL, THOMAS. Killed on his mining claim on Oregon Gulch Apr. 19, 1860; leaves widow and orphan children; bur. Apr. 21, 1860 Weaverville Cem. (TJ Apr. 21, 1860). ["Sacred to the Memory of Thomas Motherwell, Born in Ballymota, Co. Sligo, Ireland; Died in Weaverville Apr 19, 1860 in the 34th year of his age." Gravestone in Weaverville Cem., standing in 1988.]
MOXHAM, CHARLES. Died Shasta abt Feb. 10, 1877; former jeweler at Lewiston; see Shasta *Courier*. (TJ Feb. 17, 1877).
MOXLEY, ____. Died Etna, Siskiyou Co. May 1893; son of L. A. Moxley. (TJ Sat. May 27, 1893),
MOXLEY, ____. Died Etna, Siskiyou Co. June 1893, aged 2 yr 3 mo; youngest son of L. A. Moxley, of Etna, who had two sons die within 19 days of each other. (TJ Sat. June 10, 1893 p 3 col 1).
MOXTON, WM. Died abt Aug. 13, 1892 at Hopkins Hollow, near the Tehama/Trinity line in Southeastern Trinity County; native of Michigan, aged 35; prospector; coroner's inquest held; cause unknown. (TJ Aug. 13, 1892 p 3 col 2 & TJ Aug. 20, 1892 p 3 col 1).
MUFFLER, FREDERICK. Killed in mining claim near Weaverville Feb. 10, 1875; native of Baden, Germany, aged 52 years; came to Trinity Co. abt 1874 from Yuba County. Bur. Feb. 11, 1875 I.O.O.F. Cem. [Weaverville]. (TJ Feb. 13, 1875).
MULLANE, EDDIE L. Died Mullane's Ranch, Lower Trinity, July 30, 1880; aged 9 mo 23 days; son of James and Lucy Mullane. "Newport R.I. *Mercury* please copy." (TJ Aug. 7, 1880 p 2).
MULLEN, LARRY. Died at Vina, Tehama County, Jan. 3, 1895; buried at Redding; old settler of Shasta. "It is said he drove the first stage into the town of Shasta, following an old blind trail." (TJ Jan 12, 1895 p 3 col 1).
MULLIGAN, ELLEN. Died Nov. 8, 1907 Weaverville; age 62, female, white, b. Ireland. [Index to Deaths 1890-1908].
MULLIGAN, JAMES. Died Sucker Flat, Yuba County, Aug. 30, 1875, James Mulligan (father of Michael Mulligan of Weaverville) aged 73 years. (TJ Sept. 11, 1875 p 2).
MULTAGH, MICHAEL. Drowned near North Fork Feb. 2, 1890; aged about 45 yr; worked at North Star mine; no trace. (TJ Feb. 15, 1890). [Index to Deaths 1873-1890: Multagh, Michael, died Feb. 2, 1890; white, age 45, male, single].
MUNSON, W. A. Died near Minersville Apr 8, 1895; native of Connecticut, aged about 56 years; wife is dead; daughter lives in Chicago. (TJ Sat. Apr 20, 1895 pp 2 & 3).
MUNSTER, EMMA, *Miss.* Died near Junction City Apr. 10, 1890, aged 28 yr; eldest dau. of John Munster; bur. Weaverville Cem. Apr. 13, 1890. (TJ Apr. 19, 1890). [Index to Deaths 1873-1890 says "married", white, born Calif.]
MUNSTER, JOHN F. Died near Junction City Mar. 16, 1891; native of Calif, aged about 26 yr; also known as "Myers"; father John P. Munster; shot by Geo. Nichols, who said Munster came at him with a knife; Nichols absolved - self defense. (TJ Mar. 21, 1891 pp 2 & 3; Mar. 28, 1891 p 3).
MURPHY, ARCHIBALD. Died near French Gulch, Shasta Co. Jul 5, 1896; old resident of Trinity & Shasta Counties. (TJ Sat. July 18, 1896 p 3 col 1).
MURPHY, CATHARINE, *Mrs.* Died at Tyramadan, County Monaghan, Ireland Feb. 11, 1865 in the 72d year of her age. Deceased was the mother of Hon. John Murphy, Patrick Murphy, and Bernard Murphy of Trinity County. (TJ Sat. May 6, 1865 p 2).
MURPHY, CHARLES. Died Weaverville Dec 31, 1898; native of Canada, aged abt 65 yr; came to Calif. 1854, Trinity Co. 1856 with Roger Dockery; resided at Canon Creek and Deadwood; never married; leaves cousin John Murphy in Trinity County, 2 bro. & 2 sis. in Michigan. (TJ Jan 7, 1899 p 2 & p 3 col 2).

MURPHY, DAVID. Died South Fork Township Jul 15, 1899; native of Ohio, aged about 74 yr; old resident of Blocksburg, Humboldt Co., where he leaves a family. (TJ July 29, 1899 p 2 & 3).

MURPHY, EDWARD. Died Weaverville Mar 18, 1900; native of Ireland, aged abt 76 yr; long obit. (TJ Mar 24, 1900, pg 3 col 2).

MURPHY, JOHN. Died at Kanaka Bar [now Douglas City] July 27, 1859, aged about 50 years. (TJ July 30, 1859 p 2).

MURPHY, JOHN. Died Gilroy [Santa Clara Co.] "a few days ago" (Oct. 1884), an ex-county judge of Trinity County. (TJ Oct. 25, 1884). [Born Tyramedan, Ireland July 10, 1835; came to California 1853, Trinity County Sept. 1854. Cox's Annals, 1940 edition.]

MURPHY, JOHN. Died Dec. 9, 1905 Weaverville; age 80, male, white, miner, b. Canada. [Index to Deaths 1890-1905].

MURPHY, JOHN, Mrs. Died Gilroy "a few days ago" (Apr. 1881); wife of ex-county Judge of Trinity County. (TJ Apr. 30, 1881 p 3).

MURPHY, JOHN WILLIAM. Died Weaverville Nov. 17, 1868; aged 1 year 8 mo; son of Patrick and Mary A. Murphy. (TJ Nov. 21, 1868 p 2).

MURPHY, PATRICK. Died Tyramadan, County Monaghan, Ireland Feb. 1, 1866, aged about 85 yr. Dec. was father of Patrick, Bernard, Peter, and Hon. John Murphy of Trinity County. (TJ June 9, 1866 p 2).

MURPHY, WILLIAM. Died Weaverville Feb. 19, 1886, aged about 50 years; of Trinity Center. (TJ Feb. 27, 1886).

MURRAY, DENNIS. Shot on Main Street, Weaverville Apr. 7, 1856 by partner, John Fehley. (TJ Sat. Apr. 12, 1856 p 2).

MURRAY, E. Died Hayfork June 8, 1894; aged abt 55 yr; of Red Bluff; (TJ Sat. June 16, 1894 pg 3 col 4).

MURRAY, GEORGE. Killed by caving in of the earth on Red Gulch, near Stewart's Fork of Trinity River March 28, 1855; native of Ireland, aged about 30 years of age. (TT Mar. 31, 1855).

MURRAY, KATY. Died Junction City Aug. 3, 1865, aged about 1 yr 4 mo; dau. of Patrick and Mary Murray. (TJ Sat. Aug. 5, 1865 p 2).

MURRAY, PATRICK. Died Junction City June 26, 1866, aged about 38 yr. (TJ Sat. June 30, 1866 p 2). [Trinity County Marriages Book H page 30: "Married in Weaverville Jan. 27, 1858 by Rev. Father Thomas Cody, Patrick Murry and Mary Cunningham."]

MUSSER, JOHN. Died Weaverville Jan. 7, 1888; native of Penn, aged about 82 yr; died in fire at res. of Joseph Arguello on Church street; came to Trinity County 1850; Charter Member of Trinity #27, F & AM; bur. Masonic Cem. [Weaverville] Sun. Jan. 8, 1888; see p 3 col 3, last paragraph for short story. (TJ Sat. Jan. 14, 1888).

MUZZY, MYRA. Died Collinsville, Solano County, Feb. 13, 1871; formerly of Douglas City. (TJ Mar. 4, 1871 p 2).

MYERS, HOSEA. Died Hyampom Jul 3, 1894; aged abt 60 yr. (TJ Sat. July 14, 1894 pg 2 & 3).

MYERS, JACOB. Died Butteville Sept. 7, 1874; res. Trinity County in the early days; bro. John Myers, worked many years in Weaver Basin. (TJ Sept. 13, 1874 p 3). [note: this might be Butte City, Glenn Co.]

NEAFUS, JAS. Died Padlock valley, Washington County, Idaho, January 1897; former resident of Trinity Co. (TJ Mar 13, 1897 p 3).

NEBLETT, EDWARD. Born Virginia 1818; married Miss McCleary of New Albany, Indiana 1842; came to Calif. 1849; Constable Trinity County 1852 & 1853; Sheriff 1854-1857; Legislature 1857. [Cox's Annals, 1940 edition.] Death date unknown.

NEBLETT, EDWARD, Mrs. Died June 6, 1898; resided Weaverville 1855; husband was Sheriff. A kind tribute by David E. Gordon of Eureka, Humboldt Co. (TJ Jun 25, 1898 p 3 col 6).

NEFF, DANIEL. Died July 5, 1907 Weaverville, age 77, male, white, miner, born Canada. [Index to Deaths 1890-1908].

NEIMAN, BERTHA. Died Weaverville Nov. 30, 1868, aged 5 yr 5 mo; dau. of William and Charlotte Neiman; b. July 9, 1863 Weaverville. (TJ Dec. 5, 1868 p 2).

NEIMAN, CONRAD WILLIAM. Died Weaverville Oct 20, 1898; native of Bremen, Germany, aged 68 yr 5 mo 15 dy. "A monument was being erected over the grave of his late wife and he was assisting in the work. When near the cemetery fence, he fell and quickly expired." Came to Calif. 1850, Trinity Co. 1852; in 1860, returned to Germany and m. Miss Charlotte Schroder. Five children, one survived: Mrs. B. A. Crowl of Seattle. fun. Oct 21, 1898. (TJ Oct 22, 1898 p 2 & 3; see also TJ Oct 29, 1898 p 3 col 2, thanks from Mrs. Emilie Crowl).

NEIMAN, C. W., Mrs. Died Tacoma, Wash. Dec 13, 1897; b. Bremen, Germany (no age given); m. at Bremen to C. W. Nieman of Weaverville. She arrived Weaverville 1860, lived Weaverville until 1892 when she moved to Tacoma where dau. Mrs. Emily Crowl lives; husband was in Weaverville when she died. (TJ Dec 18, 1897 p 3 col 2). [1880 census has: Neiman, William age 50, gardener; Charlotte age 40; Emily age 18; Weaverville p 12, Jun 7, 1880].

Neiman, C. W., Mrs. note: "Remains of Mrs. C. W. Neiman were brought to Weaverville Tuesday from Tacoma and were interred in the [Weaverville] cemetery at one o'clock, being followed to their last resting place by many friends. The funeral service was performed by Rev. H. Hammond Cole." (TJ Sat Apr 23, 1898 p 3).

NEIMAN, ELEANOR. Died Weaverville Dec. 12, 1866, aged about 7 months; dau. of William and Charlotte Neiman. b. May 16, 1866 Weaverville. (TJ Dec. 15, 1866 p 2).

NEIMAN, JOHN C. Died near Douglas City Jan. 20, 1892; native of Hanover, aged about 57 yr. (TJ Sat. Jan. 23, 1892).

NEIMAN, GUSTAVUS WILLIAM. Died Weaverville May 25, 1868; infant son of William and Charlotte Neiman. b. Apr. 25, 1868 Weaverville. (TJ Sat. May 30, 1868).

NEIMANN, MARIE. Died Weaverville June 9, 1865, aged 4 mo 18 days; dau. of C. W. and Charlotte Neimann. [prob. b. Jan. 22, 1865]. (TJ Sat June 17, 1865) [Note: 1870 Census lists: Neiman, William age 40, b. Hanover; Charlotte, age 30, b. Bremen; Emily, age 8, b. California; not in 1860 Census. Births from Trinity Journal about the date given].

NELSON, CLARA MATILDA, Mrs. Died New River (nr Denny) Apr 22, 1899; native of Sweden, age 45 yr 11 mo 22 dy. (TJ Sat. May 6, 1899 p 2).

NEWLAND, JAMES B. Died June 2, 1907 Deadwood, CA; age 50, male, white, American, contractor; buried Weaverville. [Index to Deaths 1890-1908].

NEWMAN, JAMES. Died Oregon Gulch Nov. 12, 1867, aged 2 mo 8 days; son of John and Mary Newman. (TJ Sat. Nov. 16, 1867 p 2).

NEWMAN, JOHN. Drowned Oregon Gulch July 29, 1865, aged 10 years; oldest son of John and Mary Newman. (TJ Sat. Aug. 5, 1865 p 2).

NEWMAN, LOUIS. Died Weaverville Oct 18, 1894; inf. son of Mr. and Mrs. L. H. F. Newman, aged 2 mo 24 dy. (TJ Sat. Oct 20, 1894 p 2).

NICHOLS, WM. H. Died Weaverville May 24, 1873; native of Mass., aged 30 years; formerly of Junction City; fun. May 25, 1873; bur Weaverville Cem. (TJ May 31, 1873 p 2). [Index to Deaths 1873-1890 adds married, miner].

NICHOLSON, THADIUS C. Died May 1, 1906 Deadwood; age 24, male, white, miner; (fracture of skull); born Calif. buried French Gulch, Shasta, Calif. [Index to Deaths 1890-1908].

NIELSON, CAROLINE F. Died San Francisco Aug. 27, 1879; native of Mecklenberg, Germany; age 46 yr 7 mo 20 days; wife of Chris. Nielson; former res. of Trinity Co. (TJ Sept. 6, 1879 p 3).

NIELSON, EMMA FRANCISCO. Died San Francisco Mar. 31, 1870, aged 15 mo 29 days; only dau. of Christian and Carolina Francisco Nielson, formerly of Trinity County. (TJ Apr. 9, 1870 p 2).

NIELSON, PAULINE. Died San Francisco Apr. 18, 1868, aged 7 years; only child of Chris. and Caroline Nielson, formerly of Douglas City. (TJ Sat. May 9, 1868 p 2).

NOCK, VINCENT. Drowned Trinity River, near Hocker's ranch, Mon. Apr. 13, 1857; native of Haslach, Baden, Germany; body found Apr. 18, 1857; age about 40. (TJ Apr. 18, 1857 p 2 and Apr. 25, 1857 p 2).

NOLL, THOMAS. Hanged 19 Sept. 1862 in Weaverville; convicted of murdering Paulius Grosse on Aug. 31, 1861. (TJ Dec. 28, 1861; Sept. 13, 1862; Sept. 20, 1862). [See also Gross.]

NOLTON, LULU. Died May 22, 1907 near Hayfork; about 25, female, "red", b. Calif. buried Hayfork. [Index to Deaths 1890-1908].

NOLTON, ROBERT. Died May 13, 1907 near Hayfork, CA; age about 23, male, "red", born Calif; miner; buried Hayfork. [Index to Deaths 1890-1908].

NOONAN, FRANCES. Died Pictou, Nova Scotia, Feb. 14, 1868, aged 75 years; widow of late John H. Noonan, Collector of H. M. Customs of that Port; mother of Geo. E. Noonan of Weaverville. (TJ Sat. Apr. 4, 1868 p 2).

NOONAN, GEO. E. Died June 13, 1902 Weaverville; no age given; male, white, chemist; buried Weaverville cemetery. [Index to Deaths 1890-1908]. George Edmund Noonan, born Halifax, Nova Scotia April 8, 1832. (TJ June 21, 1902). [He was a druggist. Worked at A. Barnickel Drug Store (Weaverville Drug Store) for many years. For a biography, see Hicks, Patricia J., WEAVERVILLE A JEWEL OF A TOWN.]

NOONAN, GEORGE EDMUND. Died Weaverville Jan. 30, 1886; native of Weaverville aged 6 yr 3 mo 2 days; bur. Sun. Jan. 31, 1886 Weav. Cem. son of George E. and Lizzie C. Noonan. (TJ Sat. Feb. 6, 1886).

NOONAN, J. R. Died Pictou (Nova Scotia) Feb 15, 1896; born in Halifax; leaves one son, Wm. H. Noonan of the firm of Noonan & Davis, and one dau. [and brother Geo. E. Noonan of Weaverville, Calif.] (TJ Sat. March 7, 1896).

NORCROSS, BENNY P. Died Weaverville June 10, 1858, age 1 yr 2 mo; son of O.H.P. and Ellen P. Norcross. (TJ Sat. June 12, 1858 p 2).

NORCROSS, OLIVER H. P. Died Weaverville Apr. 19, 1871; native of Maine, aged 46 yr 9 mo; bur. Apr. 21, 1871 F & AM Cem. Weaverville. (TJ Apr. 22, 1871 pp & 3). [note: he was a very early photographer in Weaverville.]

NORDYKE, ROBERT. Died Leesville, Colusa Co., Feb. 22, 1891; infant son of B. J. and May Nordyke, aged 26 days. The mother of Mrs. Nordyke is Mrs. M. Hughes of Douglas City. (TJ Sat. Feb. 28, 1891). [see also Hughes].

NORMAN, WILLIAM S. Died Weaverville Apr. 4, 1889; b. Milton, New Jersey about 1816; aged about 73 yr; unmarried; blacksmith, of Big Flat; bur. Apr. 5, 1889 Weav. Cem. (TJ Apr. 6, 1889). [Index to Deaths 1873-1890 adds white, 73, male]. [See also Hinds.]

NORRIS, JOHN, Mrs. Died at home of Mr. E. G. Crowl on Yager Creek, Humboldt Co, June 23, 1886; of Bridgeville; bur. Odd Fellows Cem. nr Rohnerville. (see Rohnerville *Herald* June 30, 1886). (TJ July 10, 1886 p 3).

NORTON and ??? "Bodies Found. On Feb. 1, 1859 two mining partners, one named NORTON, left Trinity Centre for their cabin on Coffee Creek during a snow storm; bodies found 1-1/2 miles from cabin 3 weeks later; remains buried by Coffee Creek miners." (TJ May 7, 1859 p 2). (Note: check Trinity Co. Misc. Records and Deeds for Norton before Feb. 1859). **NORWOOD, MARY EMMA, Mrs.** Died Nov. 24, 1895 at San Bernardino, [San Bernardino Co.] CA; native of Pittsburg, PA, b. Oct 22, 1856; came to Calif. 1859 w/parents; lived in Trinity Co. until 1873; eldest dau. of Joseph Craig; m. 1879; leaves 2 sons, Edward P. Norwood age 15, and Joseph C. aged 9. (TJ Sat. Dec 7, 1895 p 3 col 3). [see also Craig].

NOYES, L. A. Died Nov. 2, 1906 Weaverville; age 93, male, white, farmer, American. Informant: Thomas Thomas. [Index to Deaths 1890-1908].

NUNNALY, W. A. Died Pioneer City, Idaho June 22, 1872 age 53 yr; native of Huntsville, Alabama; came to Calif. 1849; former res. of Lewiston. U. S. Census Marshal for Trinity County in 1860. F & AM funeral. (TJ July 13, 1872 p 3).

OBERDEENER, MOSES. Died Santa Clara, [Santa Clara Co.] CA, last week of July 1885; leaves widow and 4 grown sons; proprietor of the Weaverville Drug & Book Store abt 1860-1870. (TJ Sat. Aug. 1, 1885 p 3 col 1). [1870 census, Weaverville: Oberdeener, Moses; age 45; bookseller; b. Poland; Elizabeth, age 45; b. Poland; Samuel, age 10, b. Calif.; Charles, age 8, b. Calif.; George, age 6, b. Calif.].

O'CONNELL, CHARLES. Died Reddings Creek, near Douglas City, Apr. 30, 1887; native of Ireland, aged about 71 years; bur. Catholic Cem. Weav. May 2, 1887; never married; came to U.S. 1849; bro. David O'Connell. (TJ Sat. May 7, 1887).

O'CONNELL, DAVID J. Died Reddings Creek, near Douglas City, Mar. 10, 1888; native of Ireland, aged 85 years; bur. Mar. 12, 1888 Catholic Cem. Weaverville; came to Trinity Co. 1861. (TJ Mar. 17, 1888).

O'CONNELL, JANE MALCAHY, Mrs. Died Hay Fork Aug. 25, 1885; native of Ireland, aged about 66 yr; bur. Catholic Cem. Weaverville Aug. 28, 1885; mother of Mrs. D.

Rourke, Mrs. M. Mulligan, and Miss Janie O'Connell; sister-in-law of David and Charles O'Connell of Indian Creek. (TJ Aug. 19, 1885).

O'CONNOR, JAMES. Died Weaverville Jan. 10, 1875; native of Ireland, aged 63 yr. His only living relative is a daughter, Mrs. Chas. Sloan of Humboldt County. (TJ Jan. 16, 1875).

O'CONNOR, JOHN. Died San Francisco Jan. 2, 1869; age 26; native of Prince Edward's Island; at one time a res. of Weaverville. (TJ Jan. 9, 1869).

O'CONNOR, MARY. Died Weaverville Dec. 31, 1858, aged 42 years; wife of James O'Connor. (TJ Jan. 8, 1859 p 2).

O'DONNELL, RICHARD. Died Weaverville Nov. 28, 1872; native of Ireland aged 61 years. (TJ Nov. 29, 1873). [Index to Deaths 1873-1890 adds white, male, married, laborer].

OEST, HERMANN. Died at Brown's Creek Dec. 23, 1862; native of Hamburg, Germany, about 40 years; a miner of the East Fork of the North Fork of Trinity River; bur. Weaverville Cem. (TJ Dec. 27, 1862 p 2).

OHLES, ANDREW. Died Lewiston Feb. 24, 1884; native of Germany, aged about 54 yr. lived at Bolts Hill, above Lewiston. (TJ Sat. Mar. 1, 1884). [prob. bur. Lewiston Pioneer Cem.; no marker].

O'KEEFE, CATHERINE, Mrs. Died Oakland, [Alameda Co.], Jan 2, 1900; husband died abt 10 years ago; family lived in Weaverville in the early 1850s. The two girls, Anne & Mary O'Keefe, live in Oakland. (TJ Jan 6, 1900 pg 3 col 2).

O'KEEFE, JOHN. Died Oakland [Alameda Co.] Nov. 27, 1891; a native of County Cork, Ireland, aged 73 years. Res. of Douglas City in the early days. In 1857 he moved to Smith's Flat; later built a house at the end of the Douglas City bridge, the "Weaverville House", which was washed away by the flood of 1861; built another house on the other side of the river. In 1868 he moved to Alameda County; wife and two daughters, Miss Anne O'Keefe and Mrs. Mary Walsh, survive him. (TJ Sat. Dec. 5, 1891 p 3 col 2).

OLIVER, BENJAMIN. Died Redding, Shasta County Dec. 1890 (n.d.); age 57 yr; leaves wife and 8 children. (TJ Sat. Dec. 20, 1890 p 3).

OLESEN, GUS. Died Hoopa (Humboldt Co.) Oct 7, 1899; native of Sweden; no age given. (Blue Lake *Advocate* Oct 14, 1899). (TJ Oct 28, 1899 p 3 col 4).

OLSEN, JAMES PETER. Died Hyampom July 29, 1893; born Denmark Oct. 13, 1832; aged 60 yr 7 mo 16 days; came to Calif. 1853; Hyampom 1871; leaves wife and 8 children. (TJ Aug. 12, 1893 p 2 & p 3 col 4). [see Addendum for family information].

OLSEN, LOUIS. Died Trinity Center May 13, 1883; native of Norway, aged about 57 yr; old resident of the county; leaves wife and 5 children. (TJ Sat. May 19, 1883 p 2). [Grandson Edward Shuford gave his b.d. as Nov 19, 1827.] [see also Shuford and Addendum].

OLSEN, MARY L., Miss. Died Hyampom Mar 14, 1899; native of Calif., aged 23 yr 1 mo 2 dy; no further info. (TJ Sat. Mar 25, 1899 p 2).

OLSEN, TOBIAS. Died near Lewiston Aug. 10, 1882; native of Norway, aged about 65 years; leaves wife Bridget, but no children. (TJ Aug. 12, 1882 p 2).

O'NEIL, ANNIE, Mrs. Died Weaverville Jul 24, 1899; b. Golden, County of Tipperary, Ireland, Jul 5, 1836, aged 63 yr 18 dy; one of the Pioneer women of Trinity Co; dau. of James and Margaret Griffith; came with parents to New Orleans 1850; m. 1852 at New Orleans Timothy O'Neil, who d. May 24, 1881; ten children, 7 living; Mrs. O'Neil came to Calif. 1854, Trinity Co. Oct 1855; bur. Catholic Cem. Weaverville; obit. worth copying. (TJ Jul 29, 1899 p 2 & p 3 col 2).

O'NEIL, JAMES CORNELIUS. Died Weaverville Dec 2, 1923; b. Weaverville Apr 19, 1865; son of Timothy & Annie Griffith O'Neil; never married; stockraiser; made a home for sister Mary O'Neil. (Rita Hanover's card file of Trinity County Pioneers.) [see also Deaths 1900-1950].

O'NEIL, TIMOTHY. Died near Junction City May 24, 1881; native of Ireland aged 48 yr; expressman Weaverville-Canon City route; obit. p 3. (TJ Sat. May 28, 1881 p 2). [see also Benn]. [There is a very large granite cross with O'NEIL and "In memory of our loved ones eternal rest grant to them, oh Lord" with "Father Timothy" and "Mother Anne" and a few other names without dates in St. Patrick's Catholic Cem. Weaverville.]

O'NEIL, JOHN TIMOTHY. Died Weaverville Dec. 4, 1882; native of Weaverville, aged 11 yr 2 mo 6 days; youngest son of Mrs. Annie O'Neil. (TJ Sat. Dec. 9, 1882, p 2).

O'NEIL, JOSEPH VALENTINE. Died Weaverville Nov. 27, 1879; aged 5 yr 9 mo 13 days; bur. Nov. 29, 1879; son of Timothy and Annie O'Neil. (TJ Sat. Nov. 19, 1879).

OPIE, THOMAS. Drowned in Trinity River half a mile below Steiner's Flat (Douglas City) Feb. 5, 1858. "He was crossing in a boat which capsized." (TJ Sat. Feb. 6, 1858 p 2). "The body of Thomas Opie, drowned in the Trinity two months since, was found last Wednesday at Evans' Bar - three miles from where the accident befell him." (TJ Sat. Apr 3, 1858).

OPIE, WILLIAM. Died Weaverville May 21, 1865; native of Cheswater, Cornwall, England, aged about 60 yrs. (TJ Sat. May 27, 1865 p 2).

O'REILEY, JAMES. Killed by a bank cave at Junction City Dec. 6, 1867; native of County Mayo, Ireland, aged 43 yrs; res. of Trinity Co. since 1854; bur. Catholic Cem. Weaverville Dec. 7, 1867. (TJ Dec. 7 & 14, 1867).

OSBORNE, HENRY. Died Weaverville April 2, 1888; native of England, aged 74 yr. (TJ Sat. Apr. 7, 1888).

OSGOOD, CHARLES W. Killed by a mining accident near Trinity Center June 6, 1882; native of Weaverville, aged 26 years; bur. Weav. Cem. June 8, 1882; second son of Mr. and Mrs. H. C. Osgood; his sister, Mrs. John Hall, was widowed 8 days before. (TJ June 10, 1882 p 2). [see also Hall].

OSGOOD, EMMA, Mrs. Died Weaverville Feb. 26, 1869; age 17 yr 1 mo; wife of Mr. D. F. Osgood. (TJ Mar. 6, 1869). (Trinity County Marriages Book H page 195: married in Weaverville July 15, 1868 by A. J. Felter, County Judge, Daniel Fuller Osgood and Miss Emma Brown, both of Weaverville.) See Mary R. Osgood.

OSGOOD, MARY R. Died Weaverville Feb. 12, 1868; native of New London, New Hampshire, aged 32 yr 8 mo; wife of Daniel F. Osgood; bur. Feb. 13, 1868 I.O.O.F. Cem. Weav. leaves "little Ella, the only child". (TJ Feb. 15, 1868 p 2).

O'SHEA, MICHAEL. Died Weaverville Nov. 30, 1870; native of County Cork, Ireland, aged 48 yr. (TJ Dec. 3, 1870 p 2).

OSTHOFF, J. H. Died San Francisco Dec. 1887 (n.d.); native of Prussia, nearly 60 years of age; res. Junction City for a number of years; blacksmith; m. Miss Elizabeth Schneider 1866, who survives him, and 2 sons. (TJ Sat. Dec. 31, 1887 p 3 col 1). [see also Raab].

OSTHOFF, LIZZIE. Died Junction City Jan. 21, 1874, aged 3 mo 16 days; infant dau. of Henry and Lizzie Osthoff. (TJ Jan. 24, 1874). [Index to Deaths 1873-1890 says 3 yr (sic) 16 days, white, female, single, born Calif.] [Trinity Journal (Oct. 1873) says: Born at Junction City, to the wife of Johann Henry Osthoff, a daughter, Oct. 5, **1873.**]

OSTHOFF, LOUIS. Died Junction City May 3, 1874, aged 3 yr 6 mo; son of J. H. and Elizabeth Osthoff. (TJ May 9, 1874).

OSWALD, FRANK. Died Faggtown in Weaverville Aug. 16, 1872, aged 43 yr; of Canon Creek. (TJ Aug. 17, 1872 p 3).

OVERMOHLE, _____. "Henry Overmohle and wife have had the misfortune to lose their youngest child, a little girl, aged 3 yr 10 months." (TJ Sat. Dec. 29, 1877).

OVERMOHLE, ANNA CATHERINE. Died San Francisco Nov. 10, 1870, aged 1 yr 2 mo 16 days; dau. of Henry and Anna Overmohle, formerly of Weaverville. (TJ Nov. 19, 1870 p 2). [Henry Overmohle and Anna J. McLean, dau. of Peter McLean, m. Weaverville Aug. 24, 1865; Trinity County Marriages Book H page 151.] [see also McLean].

OVERMOHLE, HENRY. Died San Francisco Jan. 9, 1878; native of Hanover, aged 49 years, 11 mo 21 days. (TJ Jan 19, 1878). Born in San Francisco Jan. 15, 1878, to Mrs. Henry Overmohle, a son. (Jan. 26, 1878). [see Overmohle, above, and Births 1850-1900].

OVERMOHLE, WILLIAM JOSEPH. Died San Francisco Feb. 6, 1877; age 10 mo 13 days; son of Henry and Annie J. Overmohle. (TJ Feb. 10, 1877 p 2).

OWEN, MARTIN. Died Apr. 24, 1903 Chloride Mine, Dedrick; age 40, male, white, American; bur. Dedrick cemetery. [Index to Deaths 1890-1903].

OWENS, JOHN. Died Fort Gibson, Arkansas Aug. 12, 1867, aged 69 years. Father of John W. Owens of Weaverville. (TJ Sat. Oct. 12, 1867 p 2).

OWENS, JOHN W. Died Weaverville Dec. 20, 1867; native of Springfield, Sangamon Co., Illinois, aged 36 yr; of firm of Tinnin & Owens; came to Trinity Co. 1851; 2 bro. in Waco, Texas; bro. & sis. in California, Missouri; bur. Dec. 21, 1867 Weaverville Cemetery, near "tombs" of Capt. Gordon & son, friends of his youth. (TJ Dec. 21 & 28, 1867). Remains removed week of Sept. 16, 1871, sent to California, Missouri for interment. (TJ Sat. Sept. 16, 1871 p 3).

OWENS, SAMUEL H. Died St. Louis, Missouri Feb. 22, 1882. (no age given). Brother of late John W. Owens of Weaverville. (TJ Mar. 4, 1882 p 3).

PACHECO, FRANK I. Killed at Washington Mine, French Gulch, Shasta Co., July 19, 1895; tunnel caved in; bur. French Gulch Cem.; m. Miss Annie Caton of Weaverville; 2 young sons. (TJ July 27, 1895 p 3 col 5). [Trinity County Marriages Book I p 168: m. near Weaverville Oct. 9, 1892; Frank age 35, native of Portugal, res. French Gulch; Annie, age 21, native of Calif; parents natives of Portugal; res. of Weaverville].

PACKWARD, AUGUSTUS. Killed in Southern Trinity April 6, 1877; bur. Apr. 7, 1877. aka "Packman" and "Packard", in Mendocino *Dispatch*. (See TJ Apr. 21, 1877 p 3; Aug. 28, 1877 p 3; May 5, 1877 p 3). [no further information; not in 1860 or 1870 Census].

PAGE, GUSTAVUS O. Died Weaverville Jan. 28, 1860, aged about 21 years; formerly of Springwater, Livingston County, N.Y.; bro. in Weav. (TJ Sat. Feb. 4 & 25, 1860).

PALMER, ELIEL. Died Reddings Creek, near Douglas City Aug. 20, 1856; age 27 yr; formerly of Athens, Sommerset Co, Maine; leaves father and mother "at home", brothers near him. (TJ Aug. 23, 1856).

PALMER, JOSHUA, Mr. Died Indian Creek (near Douglas City) June 22, 1863 from injuries received by being thrown from a horse; native of Athens, Maine, aged 34 yr 8 mo. (TJ Sat. June 27, 1863 p 2).

PALMER, THOMAS. Died before Jan. 20, 1855. Estate of Thomas Palmer, dec'd; sale 5 Feb. 1855 at the Lewis Bridge House on Trinity River; an undivided one-half of Lewis Bridge Estate: 160 acres of land, tavern stand, bridge and buildings, also hogs, potatoes, one cow, household furniture. Wm. D. Olendorf, Executor of Estate. TRINITY TIMES Jan. 20, 1855. (See Tom Palmer, below.)

PALMER, TOM. Died 1853 near Trinity Center. (TJ Sat. Dec. 19, 1891 p 1: Old Settlers Paper #2 by W. S. Lowden.) Lowden said that in 1850, Tom Palmer was 45. He was an old Rocky Mountain trapper who came to California in 1849 and to Trinity County in September of that year, working at Point Bar. He established a ferry at Lewiston in Spring of 1851, which he named for his adopted son, Frank Lewis, for whom Lewiston was named. [See also TRINITY 1982, page 25, the Lowden Story. TRINITY is the yearbook of Trinity County Historical Society].

PALMER, TURNER. Date of death unknown (between 1906-1908); Hayfork, about 35, male, white; buried Weaverville. [Index to Deaths 1890-1908].

PARBERRY, NANCY, Mrs. Died Feb. 11, 1896 at Sulphur Springs, KY, aged 64 yr 9 dy; sister of Hon. John McMurry, who visited here recently. (TJ Sat. Feb 22, 1896).

PARKER, LINUS. Died Weaverville Sept. 23, 1871; native of N.Y. aged 55 yr; bur. Sept. 24, 1871 Weav. Cem.; of Canon City. Has a married daughter living at Flint, Gennessee Co., Mich. and a son somewhere in Penn. Member Canyon City Lodge No. 392, Good Templars. (TJ Sept. 30, 1871 pp 2 & 3).

PARKER, PATRICK. Died Weaverville Feb. 14, 1859; of Roscommon, Ireland. prob. bur. Catholic Cem. Weaverville. (TJ Sat. Feb. 19, 1859 p 3).

PARKER, SAMUEL, Mr. Killed instantly by a bank cave in his claim at the head of Digger Creek May 21, 1860; native of Reading, PA, about 50 years of age. (TJ Sat. May 26, 1860 p 2).

PARROTT, JOHN E. Died March 18, 1908 Ruth, Trinity, CA, age 78; male, white; stockman; born West Virginia. Buried Ruth Calif.; informant A. H. Jeans. [Index to Deaths 1890-1908].

PARRY, HARRY. Died Trinity Center Nov. 29, 1889, aged 18 yr 6 mo; son of Mr. and Mrs. H. Parry. (TJ Sat. Nov. 30, 1889). [Index to Deaths 1873-1890 adds "born Calif."] [Note: this is Henry N. Parry, b. June 4, 1871 Trinity Center; parents Henry & Almira Parry. (1880 census and Trinity Journal June 1871).]

PARRY, HENRY. Died Trinity Center Feb. 23, 1894; native of Ohio, aged about 60 yr; story p 3, col 5 "Trinity Center News". (TJ Sat. Mar 3, 1894 p 2).

PATTERSON, JOHN. Died Trinity Center Feb. 16, 1864, aged 32 yr; formerly of Fulton House, Lancaster County, Penn; leaves a wife to whom he was married little more than a year ago. (TJ Feb. 20, 1864 p 2).

PATTERSON, MARY, Miss. Died April 22, 1890; 1/2-breed Indian, age 24 yr, female, single, native of Trinity County, CA. [Index to Deaths 1873-1890]. [note: probably Pattison; see Mary, below.]

PATTISON, _____. Daughter of Mr. Pattison at Cox's Bar d. July 29, 1879, age 4; diphtheria; (TJ Aug. 2, 1879 p 3). [see also Addendum].

PATTISON, CHARLES. Died Dec. 29, 1890; white, 11 yr, male, single, b. Calif. [Index to Deaths 1890-1908]. (TJ Sat. Jan. 3, 1891 has similar info.) [1880 Census: son of William Alanson Pattison & Sally McCollum.]

PATTISON, MARY. Died Cox's Bar May 1, 1890; native of California, aged about 26 years. (TJ May 3, 1890). [Index to Deaths 1873-1890 adds "female, single."]

PATTON, ARTHUR. Died Hay Fork Dec. 10, 1894; aged abt 22 yr; obit. p 3. (TJ Sat. Dec 16, 1894 p 2).

PAULSEN, BERTHA SOPHIA. Died Lewiston Oct 15, 1898; native of Calif. age 23 yr 3 mo 29 dy; only dau. of late Jacob Paulsen and Mrs. Louisa Paulsen. Bur. Masonic Cem. Weaverville with Order of Eastern Star ceremonies. (TJ Oct 22, 1898 pp 2 & 3).

PAULSEN, CHARLES FREDERICK. Died Turners Bar, Trinity River, 28 April 1858; native of Schleswig, 35 years old; brother of Peter Minert Paulsen and Jacob Paulsen. (TJ Sat. May 1, 1858). body found at State Bar 2 months later; bur. Weaverville Cem. abt May 27, 1858. (TJ June 5, 1858). [see also Sohrt & Christianson.]

PAULSEN, HARRY E. Died Sept. __ 1903, Weaverville; age 23, male, white, American; buried Masonic Cem., Weaverville. (another records indicates Sept. 28, 1903.)

PAULSEN, JACOB. Died Weaverville July 17, 1874, aged 1 yr 4 mo; bur. Weaverville Cem. July 17, 1874; son of Jacob and Louisa Paulsen. (TJ July 18, 1874).

PAULSEN, JACOB. Died Lewiston Sun. Nov. 11, 1894; b. May 9, 1829 on the island of Foehr, a part of the province of Schleswig-Holstein, then Denmark, now Germany; came to Calif. 1849; Trinity County 1850; returned to Germany; 1853 returned with brother P. M. Paulsen, making the trip around the Horn in a sailing vessel; m. at Hollister, San Benito Co. in 1870, Miss Louisa Goetze, a sister of William Goetze and Mrs. Charles Hippler of Lewiston, who survives him. Six children: Charles, Bertha, Henry, Eddie and Freddie, now living, and Jacob now dead; two brothers, P. M. Paulsen of Weaverville, John Paulsen of San Francisco; two sisters, Mrs. Hannah Braren of San Francisco and Mrs. Pauline Thompson of Germany are still living. fun. Nov. 13, 1894, F. & A. M.; bur. Masonic Cem. Weaverville. (TJ Nov. 17, 1894 p 2 & long obit. p 3, col 3 & 4). (see also Rath).

PAULSEN, PETER M. Died Weaverville Feb. 6, 1875, aged 4 yr 5 mo 23 days; son of P. M. and A. B. Paulsen. (TJ Sat. Feb. 13, 1875). (for a sister, see Shurtleff). Paulsen, Peter Mienert, see Deaths 1900-1950; has a long obit. in the TRINITY JOURNAL shortly after his death. See also Addendum.

PAUPAW, JOHN. Died Crescent City, Del Norte Co. Oct. 1893; native of Virginia, aged 67. A Volunteer in Mexican War under Capt. Sidney Johnston; Came to Calif. in 1845 with John Chapman; bur. next to Chapman in Masonic Cem. Crescent City; spent a few years in Weaverville; went to Crescent City 1859. (TJ Sat. Oct. 28, 1893 p 3).

PEARCE, MARGARET. Died Douglas City Nov. 29, 1862; native of Caldwell, Essex Co., New Jersey, aged 43; wife of Reuben Pearce, Esq. bur. Weaverville Cem. (TJ Sat. Dec. 6, 1862).

PELLETREAU, ELLEN. Died Taylor's Flat Aug. 21, 1891; wife of Alexander Pelletreau; native of Brighton, England, aged 56 yr 6 mo. (TJ Sat. Aug. 29, 1891 p 2).

PENDER, MARY. Died Chico, Butte Co. Jan. 6, 1879; wife of John Pender, formerly of Douglas City, Trinity County. no age given. (TJ Jan. 18, 1879 p 3).

PERSONETTE, ABRAM, Mr. Died Caldwell, Essex, New Jersey abt May 1881; born Jan. 30, 1790, over 91 years old, "never left his native town". Father of M. W. Personette of Trinity County. (TJ May 28, 1881 p 3). [Mrs. Margaret Pearce was also born in Caldwell.]

PESTNER, ERNEST. Died San Francisco Dec. 12, 1877; native of Hamburg, Germany, aged 43 yr 6 mo 25 days. (TJ Sat. Dec. 22, 1877 p 2).

PETERSEN, CARL HEINRICH. Died Weaverville July 31, 1880; b. Jan. 31, 1815 Schleswig, Germany, aged 65 yr 6 mo; bur. Weaverville Cem. Aug. 1, 1880; came to Calif 1849; Weaverville 1852. (TJ Aug. 7, 1880 pp 2 & 3).

PETERSON, ELIZABETH, Mrs. Died Santa Rosa [Sonoma Co.] Nov. 28, 1890, age 72; bur. San Jose [Santa Clara Co.] near the grave of her husband; mother of N. H. Peterson, Court Reporter; dau. Miss Jennie Peterson. (TJ Sat. Dec. 6, 1890 p 3).

PETERSON, GEORGE. Died Big Bar Aug. 21, 1885; native of Trinity County, aged 22 yr. (TJ Sat. Aug. 29, 1885).

PETERSON, JOHANNES JULIUS. Died Deadwood, Trinity Co, Jun 13, 1896; aged 26 yr 6 mo dy; born 1869 at Wyk, Fohr Island, Germany, native town of P. M. Paulsen; came to US 1885; worked for Jacob Paulsen; leaves bro. P. F. Peterson of Lewiston; mother & 2 sisters at home. Bur. I.O.O.F. Cem. Weaverville. (TJ Sat. June 20, 1896 pp 2-3).

PFAFF, JOHN NICHOLAS. Died Weaverville Feb. 7, 1866; native of Langgericht, Lichtenfeld, Bavaria, aged 64 yr 26 days; bur. Weaverville Cem. by German Hospital Society. (TJ Feb. 10, 1866).

PFIFFER, CHARLES. Died Indian Creek near Douglas City Sept. 14, 1872; native of Germany, aged about 43 yr; sister in Stockton, CA. (TJ Sept. 21, 1872).

PFINGSEN, HENRY. Died Weaverville Apr 12, 1859; native of Hamburg, Germany, aged 31 years 4 days; res. here about 1 year; leader of German Band. (TJ Sat. Apr. 16, 1859 p 2).

PFOSH, ADAM. Died Weaverville Aug. 19, 1883; native of Bavaria, Germany, aged abt 74 years; bur. Aug. 20, 1883 Weaverville Cem.; resident since 1855. (TJ Sat. Aug. 25, 1883).

PHELPS, WILLIE HOMER. Died Weaverville May 27, 1863, aged 5 mo 11 days; son of Ambrose and Joanna Phelps. (TJ Sat. June 6, 1863 p 2).

PHILBROOK, FRANK. Died Weaverville June 9, 1868, aged 2 mo; son of John W. and Kate S. Philbrook. (TJ June 13, 1868 p 2).

PHILBROOK, JOHN J., Capt. Died Ipswich, Mass. July 5, 1894; age over 80 yr; Capt. Philbrook came to Trinity Co. in early days, had store at Junction City; old sea captain; leaves son, John W. Philbrook, Esq. of Weaverville. (TJ Sat. Jul 21, 1894 p 3 col 2).

PHILBROOK, MARY ANN, Mrs. Died Sat. Oct. 22, 1887 Ipswich Mass; born July 22, 1813; wife of Capt. John J. Philbrook; golden wedding Aug. 1885; 4 children dead, 4 living, including J. W. Philbrook of Weaverville. See also Ipswich, Mass. *Chronicle* Oct. 29, 1887. (TJ Nov. 12, 1887). [see also Deaths 1900-1950].

PHILBROOK, SQUIRE. Died near Weaverville at the residence of Dr. Ware, Sun. Aug. 23, 1868; native of South Ware, Hillsborough County, New Hampshire, aged about 38 years; mother at South Ware; only sister at Winona, Minnesota. (TJ Sat. Aug. 29, 1868).

PHILLIPS, ANNIE. Died Weaverville July 6, 1869 aged 29 yr 4 mo; wife of Olney Phillips of Lewiston. (TJ July 10, 1869 p 2). [Annie Spaulding; m. July 4, 1858 Weaverville. TJ record].

PHILLIPS, JANE, Mrs. Died at mouth of Canon Creek (Junction City) Nov. 8, 1859, aged about 36 years. (TJ Nov. 12, 1859 p 2).

PHILLIPS, JANE ORMSBEE (Ormsby?). Died Lewiston Dec. 6, 1884; native of New Boston, Conn, aged 58 yr 10 mo 1 day; bur. Weaverville Cem. Dec. 8, 1884; [2nd] wife of Olney Phillips. (TJ Dec. 13, 1884).

PHILLIPS, JOHN W., Mrs. Died Oakland Dec. 11, 1892; [no age given]; bur. Dec. 13, 1892; in the early days, Mr. and Mrs. J. W. Phillips lived in North Fork; cattle business; moved to Red Bluff 1860s; dau. Mamie born in Red Bluff. (TJ Sat. Dec. 17, 1892 p 3 col 2).

PHILLIPS, LLOYD FRANCIS. Died Feb. 20, 1906 Lewiston, age 7 days; male, white, born Calif; buried Lewiston. [Index to Deaths 1890-1908].

PHILLIPS, OLNEY. Died Lewiston Aug. 30, 1888; native of Rhode Island aged about 68 yr; bur. Weaverville Cem. Aug. 31, 1888. "Married twice, outlived both wives". [See Annie (Spaulding) Phillips and Jane (Ormsby) Phillips.] sons: Benj. Olney Phillips and James Phillips; dau. Lucy and Abbie. (TJ Sat. Sep 1, 1888).
PICKETT, JAMES. Died Weaverville Mar. 17, 1888; native of Kentucky, aged about 63 yr; came to Calif. 1852, Trinity County 1861. (TJ Mar. 24, 1888).
PICKETT, MARIA. Died San Francisco Sept. 23, 1869, aged 26 yr. Wife of James Pickett of Junction City. (TJ Oct. 2, 1869 p 2).
PIERCE, JOHN F. Died Weaverville Apr 11, 1896; native of England, aged about 52 yr; came to Calif from Illinois in 1854, to Trinity County in 1880; never married; bur. Weaverville Cem. Sun. Apr 12, 1896. (TJ Sat Apr 18, 1896).
PILCHY, FREDERICK. Died Weaverville Dec. 3, 1884; native of Maine, aged 74 yr. (TJ Dec. 6, 1884).
PINCUS, _____. Died Weaverville June 26, 1878, infant son of Mr. and Mrs. I. Pincus. (TJ June 29, 1878 p 2).
PINCUS, ISAAC. Died Weaverville June 18, 1888; native of Wreschen, Germany, aged 56 yr; came Weaverville 1854; m. Miss Kazinsky 1864/5; 8 children; 5 girls 2 boys survive. Bur. San Francisco. Executrix Augusta Pincus. long obit. p 3. (TJ Sat. June 23, 1888 and July 21, 1888 p 2 col 2).
PITTS, ROBERT B. Died Weaverville May 29, 1860, aged about 32 years; late of Northampton County, Virginia. (TJ June 2, 1860 p 2).
PITZER, JESSE S. Hon. Died Pioche (Nev.) Feb. 1, 1877, age nearly 60 years. b. Ohio 1818; admitted to bar 1845; came across plains to Calif. 1849, Weaverville 1851; District Judge 1855; settled in Nevada abt 1863. (TJ Feb. 10, 1877 p 3). [Born Licking County, Ohio 1818. Cox's Annals, 1940 edition.]
PLOWMAN, ANDY. Died Salem, Oregon Apr. 8, 1864, aged 3 yr 8 mo. Son of K. P. Plowman. (TJ Sat. June 11, 1864 p 2).
PLOWMAN, K. P. Mrs. Died Salem, Oregon July 29, 1862, age 33; formerly of Weaverville. (TJ Sept. 20, 1862 p 2).
PLOWMAN, SARAH EMMA. Died Weaverville 23 Jan 1861 aged 2 yr 10 mo; dau of K. P. Plowman, late of Salem, Oregon. (TJ Sat. Jan. 26, 1861).
PLUMB, T. Dr. Died at his home in French Gulch [Shasta Co.] May 30, 1886; no age given; a pioneer citizen of Northern California. (TJ Sat. June 5, 1886 p 3).
PLUMMER, JAMES. Died Junction City Sep 3, 1898; native of England aged abt 47 yr; m. in Australia abt 17 years ago and leaves a wife; bur. Foresters Cem., Junction City. (TJ Sep 10, 1898 pp 2 & 3).
(POTELLO, PORTELLO, PORTILLO, probably all "Potillo"). [see also Deaths 1900-1950].
POTELLO, MARCIAL. Died Weaverville July 28, 1883; native of Calif, 18 yr 11 mo 20 days; bur. Catholic Cem. Weaverville July 29, 1883. (TJ Aug. 4, 1883).
PORTELLO, ANGELINA M. Died Weaverville July 27, 1886; native of Trinity County aged 27 yr 5 mo; bur. Catholic Cem. Weaverville Jul 29, 1886; dau. of Mr. and Mrs. Frank Portello. (TJ Sat. July 31, 1886).
PORTILLO, FLORA. Died Weaverville July 7, 1888; b. Weav. aged 22 yr 2 mo 27 days; dau. of Mr. and Mrs. Frank Portillo. (TJ Sat. July 14, 1888).
POST, JOHN CALEB. Died near Junction City Nov. 8, 1884; native of Illinois, aged about 62 yr; Came to Calif. 1849, Trinity Co. 1851, Junction City 1869; five children, all sons. (TJ Sat. Nov. 15, 1884).
POTTER, H. L. Died Virginia City, Nev. abt May 1877; "Hank" formerly lived in Junction City and Canon City. (TJ May 12, 1877 p 3).
POTTER, TRUMAN. Died near Kendall's Mill, Winnesheik County, Iowa Apr. 9, 1871, aged 35 yr; brother of Henry Potter of Canon City. (TJ Apr. 29, 1871 p 2).
POWERS, GUS. Died Harrison Gulch (nr Hayfork) Sep 7, 1899 age 20. (TJ Sep 16, 1899 p 3 col 3).
POWERS, JOHN H. Died Weaverville Sept. 11, 1892; native of Ireland, aged abt 72 yr; remains shipped to San Francisco to be buried next to his wife who died suddenly in San Francisco a few years ago; came to US 1848, first Connecticut, then Calif; French Gulch, Shasta Co. 1851; had a store at Big Bar with D. B. Murphy; m. Miss Murphy, partner's sister; moved to Oakland 3 yrs ago, back to Weaverville Feb 1891. (TJ Sat. Sept. 17, 1892). [TJ Oct. 1858 "married at Big

Flat Oct. 11, 1858 by Rev. Father Patrick O'Neill, John H. Powers and Miss Margaret Murphy, both of Big Flat.]
POWERS, MARGARET. Died San Francisco bef. 1892. (TJ Sept. 17, 1892).
PRATER, WILLIAM H. Died Weaverville Jun 1, 1899; native of England, age about 64 yr. (TJ Jun 3, 1899 p 2).
PREHN, FREDERICK. Pioneer citizen of Shasta Co., died Shasta Sat. Sept 26, 1896; native of Germany, aged about 76 yr; bur. Masonic Cem., Shasta; leaves 6 grown children: Mrs. L. M. Dennis; Mrs. W. P. Hartman; Mrs. F. P. Satterlee, Mrs. Lorenz Garrecht, and Louis and Carl Prehn. (TJ Sat. Oct 3, 1896 p 3).
PRICE, ARCHIBALD GRAHAM, Major. Died Canon Creek Oct. 10, 1885; born North Carolina 1811; aged 74 yr; bur. Masonic Cem. Weaverville Oct. 12, 1885; long obit. (TJ Sat. Oct. 17, 1885).
PRINGLE, GEO. Died at Buckeye (Shasta Co.) abt Mar. 19, 1887; native of South Carolina, aged 70 years. (Shasta *Courier*, n.d.) (TJ Sat. Apr. 2, 1887 p 3).
PRITCHETT, JAS. Died Weaverville Nov. 20, 1880; native of Virginia, aged about 75 years. (TJ Nov. 27, 1880).
PRUETT, CAROLINE. Died Weaverville Mar. 17, 1875 aged 14 yr; bur. Mar. 18, 1875 Weaverville Cem.; living with family of Mr. Henry Hindley for 10 years; mother dead; father res. Humboldt Co. (TJ Mar. 20, 1875).
PRYOR, EDNA ALICE. Died Red Bluff June 13, 1883, aged 1 yr 7 mo 8 days; daughter and only child of J. H. & Flora Pryor.
QUICK, JOHN. Died Alton, Ill. abt Aug. 1882; left here 20 years ago; lived at Eastman's Diggings. (TJ Aug. 19, 1882 p 3). [1860 Census: Quick, John W., Lewiston 6-12-1860; age 34; miner; b. Illinois.]
QUIMBY, CYRUS W. Died Hoopa Valley, Humboldt Co., Dec. 5, 1879; native of Maine, aged 53 years; of New River. (TJ Sat. Dec. 20, 1879).
QUIMBY, FRANKLIN. Died Lower Trinity Apr. 17, 1884, aged 15 yr 8 mo; (TJ June 28, 1884). [no further info; son of Cyrus W. Quimby on 1870 census].
QUIMBY, JOHNSON. Died Lower Trinity Jun 6, 1884, aged 20 yr 5 mo; (TJ June 28, 1884). [no further info; son of Cyrus W. Quimby on 1870 census].
QUINE, THOMAS M. Died Red Bluff, Tehama Co. June 26, 1874; native of Missouri, aged 41 years. (TJ July 4, 1874).
QUINN, ESSIE. Died Eureka, Humboldt Co. Apr. 1, 1878; native of Ireland; dau. of John Keeley of Manzanita Flat, Trinity County. (TJ Apr. 13, 1878 p 3). [1860 Census: Esther, age 12, Cox Bar, with John & Margaret Keeley and others.]
RAAB, -----, Mrs. Died Hesse Darmstadt, Germany Sept. 26, 1872, aged 76 yr 1 mo; mother of Mr. Louis F. Raab and Mrs. J. H. Osthoff of Junction City. (TJ Nov. 9, 1872 p 3)
RAAB, J. H. Died Hesse Darmstadt, Germany abt May 1872); brother of Louis F. Raab of Junction City. (TJ July 6, 1872).
RAAB, WILLIAM HENRY. Died Junction City Aug. 2, 1865, aged 5 yr 2 mo 22 days; only son of Louis and Margaret Raab. (TJ Sat. Aug. 5, 1865). (see also Ruppel).
RABBITT, _____. Died near Douglas City Dec. 1873; child of Manuel Rabbitt. (TJ Dec. 27, 1873 p 2).
RABBITT, ANTONE. Died Stockton, San Joaquin Co. Nov. 1881; native of Portugal; bur. Stockton. (TJ Apr. 7, 1883 p 3). [1860 Census: A. Rabbitt, Douglas City, age 28, miner, b. Portugal].
RABBITT, POLCENA. Died near Douglas City Dec. 21, 1873, aged 5 mo; dau. of Mr. and Mrs. Manuel Rabbitt. "Manuel Rabbitt, a Portuguese living near Douglas City lost two of his children from whooping cough." (TJ Dec. 27, 1873 p 2). [1870 Census: Rabbitt, Manuel, Indian Creek, age 39, farmer, b. Portugal; Rosie, age 29, b. Portugal; Mary age 2, b. California; Rosie age 1, b. California]. [Index to Deaths 1873-1890 says: Rabbit, Porcena; died Dec. 21, 1873 Indian Creek; white, 5 months, female, single, born Calif.]
RADDLE, EDWARD HENRY ALEXANDER. Died Weaverville Dec. 14, 1893; native of Prussia, aged abt 69 yr; pioneer of Trinity County; came to US 1851, Calif. 1853, Trinity Co. 1853; miner. obit. p 3 col 2. (TJ Sat. Dec. 16, 1893).
RADLER, GEORGE. Died Shasta, Shasta Co. "last Sat." (Mar. 12, 1892); bur. Shasta Cem. Mar. 13, 1892; native of Germany; (no age given). "He was the discoverer of the Tellurium mine on Salt Creek." Redding *Democrat*. (TJ Sat. Mar. 19, 1892 p 3 col 4). <u>Trinity Journal</u> adds: "Radler was better known here as `Peg-Leg'. About

20 years ago, he had his leg injured in the Salmon country and had it amputated. On arriving in Weaverville, the boys took up a collection for him with which to purchase a wooden leg, and he afterward went to Shasta County."

RAEGNER, CARL. Died Weaverville Nov. 15, 1868; native of Germany, aged about 43 years. (TJ Sat. Nov. 21, 1868 p 2).

RAINER, MARY. Died Weaverville Dec. 27, 1892; native of Calif, aged 16 yr 7 mo; bur. Catholic Cem. Weaverville Dec. 28, 1892; lived with the family of Wm. Todd. (TJ Sat. Dec. 31, 1892).

RAINER, WILLIAM S. Died Weaverville Oct. 13, 1877; native of England, aged 50 yr; no known relatives; Constable of Weaverville 1873. (TJ Oct. 20, 1877).

RAIRICK, JOHN P. Died Canon City May 10, 1855; resident for 1-1/2 years; leaves a widow and three children; formerly a resident of Ohio. (TT May 19, 1855).

RAGNER, EMELIA. Died Weaverville Aug 31, 1894; native of Germany, aged 87 yr 8 mo 6 dy; bur. Weaverville Cem. Sep 1, 1894. (TJ Sat. Sept 1, 1894 p 2).

RALPH, GERTRUDE HORTENSE, Miss. Died Deadwood Jan 17, 1898; b. Lewiston Jan 1, 1880, aged 18 yr 17 dy. (TJ Jan 22, 1898 p 2).

RALPH, JOHN. Died Redding [Shasta Co.] Dec. 26, 1894; abt 52 years of age; leaves wife and 4 children; lived Lewiston several years. (TJ Sat. Jan. 6, 1894 p 3 col 1). [1880 Census: Lewiston p 2 6-1-1880: John, age 38, miner, b. Ireland; Ella, 25, b. New York; Cora (b. Lewiston May 1874); Lewis, age 4, b. Calif.; Rachel (b. Lewiston Jan. 22, 1878); Gertrude (b. Lewiston Dec. 30, 1879). John & Ella m. Lewiston abt July 6, 1872 (TJ July 6, 1872).]

RAMSEY, JAMES. Died July 26, 1906 Weaverville; age 79, male, white, miner; American; buried Weaverville. [Index to Deaths 1890-1908].

RANTZAU, CHAS. E. Died in fire in Sacramento Oct. 15, 1867; formerly of Trinity Co. (TJ Sat. Oct. 19, 1867 p 2). [1860 census: Lewiston, age 21, trader, b. Hanover].

RATH, CHRISTIAN FREDERICK. Died Weaverville Jul 23, 1899; native of Kill, Provence of Holstein, Germany, aged abt 70 yr; came to Trinity Co. in 1855 with the late Jacob Paulsen; res. of Lewiston; never married; bur. Weaverville Cem. with Old Settlers Assn. service. (TJ Jul 29, 1899 pp 2 & 3). [see also Paulsen].

RATIGAN, THOMAS. Died San Francisco Sept. 25, 1872, aged 40 yr. (TJ Oct. 5, 1872).

REAS, LYDIA ANN, Mrs. Died Pacific Township, Humboldt Co. Aug. 31, 1861, aged 41 yr; formerly of Zanesville, Athens Co., Ohio. (TJ Sat. Sept. 28, 1861 p 2).

REAVES, -----, Mr. Found dead at toll-gate at Shasta end of Weaver-Shasta Wagon Road Tues. July 27, 1875. (TJ July 31, 1875 p 3).

REAY, JOHN K. Died Greymouth, New Zealand abt May 22, 1877; son of Robt. Reay, formerly of Junction City. (TJ July 7, 1877 p 3 col 3 and Sept. 29, 1877 p 3).

REDDING, TIMOTHY. Died Indian Creek [nr Douglas City] Feb. 21, 1885; native of Ireland, aged about 60 years. (TJ Sat. Feb. 28, 1885).

REDSON, JOHN. Died Burnt Ranch Nov. 17, 1871; native of Steuben Co., N.Y., aged about 53 yr; lived in Michigan before Calif. (TJ Nov. 25, 1871 pp 2 & 3).

REED, EDGAR L. Died Sept. 20, 1906 Weaverville; age 52, male, white, merchant, American. [Index to Deaths 1890-1908]. [see also Whitmore].

REED, FRANK. Killed in a bank cave in claims of Reed & Leary, Red Hill, Trinity River [nr Junction City] Apr. 1, 1863; native of New York City, aged 34 yr; bur. Weaverville Cem. Apr. 2, 1863. (TJ Sat. Apr. 4, 1863 p 2). [see also Leonard Rogers].

REED, HELEN. Died Junction City June 30, 1893; native of Calif. aged 5 yr 8 mo 23 days; bur. Weaverville Cem. July 1, 1893; thrown from a buggy; (TJ Sat. July 8, 1893). [b. Junction City Oct. 7, 1887; dau. of Edgar L. Reed and "Tillie M. Whitmore", m. Nov. 11, 1880].

REED, WILLIAM C. Drowned in Trinity River at Whetstone Bar July 26, 1876; native of Amherst, N.H., aged 27 yr; bur. Weaverville Cem. July 27, 1876. (TJ July 29, 1876 p 2).

REESE, CATHARINE. Died Weaverville Oct. 4, 1865; native of Ireland, aged about 35 years. aka "Kate Hinds". (TJ Sat. Oct. 9, 1865).

REID, BABY. Died Weaverville Sept. 1, 1893, aged 17 days; infant son of Mr. and Mrs. D. G. Reid. (TJ Sept. 2, 1893). [m. at Douglas City May 19, 1887, Daniel Garrard Reid and Miss Lizzie Mary Allen. Trin. Co. Marriages Book I page 73].

REID, MARVIN GIBSON. Died July 14, 1906 Weaverville, age 1, male, white, born Calif; buried Weaverville. [Index to Deaths 1890-1908].

REIS, _____. Died Indian Creek May 13, 1898; native of Calif., aged 7 mo; dau. of Mr. and Mrs. Manuel Reis. (TJ Sat May 21, 1898 p 2).

REIS, ROSA de. Died Apr 6, 1908 Weaverville; age 37, female, white, b. Calif. [Index to Deaths 1890-1908]. [Trinity County Marriages Book I pg 131: Married in Weaverville May 20, 1890 by Rev. Father Austin Bohn, Manuel Cavalho DeReis and Miss Rosa Mintell. Manuel, age 23, native of Portugal, res. Deadwood. Rosa, age 19, native of Calif., res. Douglas City.]

RENNIE, WILLIAM NAPIER. Died Hay Fork Nov 25, 1899; native of Scotland, aged abt 50 yr. (TJ Dec 23, 1899 p 2).

REYNOLDS, _____. Died Weaverville Dec. 19, 1876; native of Old Town, Maine, aged about 40 yr. (TJ Dec. 23, 1876 p 2).

REYNOLDS, E. A., Mrs. Died Weaverville July 5, 1860; aged abt 34 years; bur. Weaverville Cem. July 7, 1860. (TJ Sat. July 7, 1860).

RHODEHAMEL, ROYAL HENRY. Died Shasta, Shasta Co. Oct. 2, 1865, aged 6 mo 11 days; son of W. H. and Anna M. Rhodehamel. (TJ Oct. 14, 1865).

RHODEHAMEL, ROLLIN. Died Marysville, Yuba Co. Dec. 3, 1867, at the Western House, aged 1 yr 3 mo; son of W. H. and Annie Rhodehamel. (TJ Dec. 14, 1867 p 2).

RHODES, THOS. Died Los Angeles Sept. 11, 1893; no age given. (TJ Sat. Sept. 16, 1893 p 3 col 2).

RICHARDS, HENRY. Drowned in reservoir of Baillett & Richard May 17, 1864; native of Breage Parish, County Cornwall, England, aged 34 years; leaves 2 brothers residing in Weaverville. (TJ May 21, 1864 p 3).

RICHARDS, HARRY R. Died Apr. 12, 1907 Lewiston; age 1, male, white, born Calif. (whooping cough); buried Lewiston; informant Wm. Richards. [Index to Deaths 1890-1908].

RICHARDS, LUCILLE. Died Apr. 18, 1907 Lewiston, age 7 months, female, white, born Calif. (whooping cough); buried Lewiston; inf. Wm. Richards. [Index to Deaths 1890-1908].

RICHARDS, STEPHEN. Died Carrville Aug 2, 1896; native of Wales, aged abt 76 yr. (TJ Sat Aug 8, 1896 pp 2-3).

RICHARDS, WILLIAM. Died Deadwood Nov. 19, 1899; b. Hellebone, England Aug 9, 1837, aged 62 yr 3 mo 10 dy; m. 1859 in Cornwall, England, to Miss Mary Ann Tyeke, who survives him; 4 children, 3 living; came to US 1861; bur. Weaverville Cem. (TJ Nov 25, 1899 pp 2 & 3).

RILEY, ELIZABETH. Died Lewiston May 9, 1874, aged 70 yr; bur. Weaverville Cem. May 10, 1874 "next to daughter Caroline who died many years ago, dau. Mrs. Church with 2 of her children, and a brother from Red Bluff."; wife of Richard Riley; b. England. (TJ May 16, 1874).

RILEY, RICHARD. Died Weaverville Aug. 17, 1891; native of Leeds, England; aged about 82 yr. Bur. Weaverville Cem. in Martin lot by the side of his wife, who died 17 yr. ago. Came from England with wife and 2 children; 1st wife d. abt 1847; m 2) Mrs. Martin, mother of Mrs. J. E. Church of San Francisco, Richard Martin, Esq., of Tehama Co., W. H. Martin, Esq.; came to Calif. 1852; mined, saved nice sum of gold dust; in 1854, in company with N. P. Wheeler, A. G. Cone, and John Gelabert (Spanish Jack), he bought the Eastman property of the late C. B. Eastman; Wheeler & Cone put up no money; Eastman took back the property. Family came to Trinity Co. in June 1855; son died in cave on claim. Family moved to Lewiston, where Mrs. Riley d. in 1874; leaves daughter, married & settled at Mineral Point, Wis. and step-children. (TJ Sat. Aug. 22, 1891, p 2 & p 3, col 3).

RIPLEY, RICHARD. Died Shasta County Sept. 26, 1891; no age given. He was well known by residents of Trinity County. He was treasurer of Shasta County for 1883-4. (TJ Sat. Oct 3, 1891 p 3 col 1).

RITTER, CHARLES MATHEW. Died Deadwood, Trinity Co. Oct. 24, 1885; native of Virginia, aged about 53 yr; bur. Weaverville Cem. Oct. 26, 1885. (TJ Oct. 31, 1885).

RITTERBUSH, WILLIAM. Died Musser Hill, near Weaverville June 17, 1880; native of New Hampshire, aged about 55 yr; resident of Trinity County 30 years; expert penman. (TJ June 19, 1880 p 2).

RIVERS, JOE. Drowned in Trinity River near Lowden Ranch (Lewiston) June 8, 1896; native of Calif; aged abt 17 yr; of French extraction; came from San Francisco; parents there. (TJ Sat. June 13, 1896 pp 2-3). Body found, brought to Weaverville Sunday; funeral Mon. July 13, 1896; bur. Weaverville Cem. (TJ Sat. July 18, 1896 p 3).

ROAN, JOHN. Died Weaverville May 2, 1875; native of Ireland, aged about 48 yr. (TJ Sat. May 8, 1875).

ROBBINS, JERRY I. Died Bangor, Butte Co. Sept. 17, 1865; native of Ohio, aged abt 32 years; formerly in the employ of the California Stage Company. (TJ Sat. Sept. 30, 1865).

ROBINSON, _____. Died Browns Creek near Douglas City, infant daughter of Mr. and Mrs. David S. Robinson. b. Apr. 23, 1883; d. Apr. 25, 1883. (TJ Sat. Apr. 28, 1883 p 2).

ROBINSON, DAVID SMITH. Died Weaverville Apr 2, 1891; native of New Brunswick, aged 35 yr 9 mo 22 days; came to Calif. in 1877. He was married to Miss Phoebe Allen July 20, 1879; 4 children, 3 living: 2 boys aged 4 and 9 and girl 4. Cousin of R. K. and S. M. Gibson of Weaverville and John Gibson of Trinity Center; mother and brother Edward reside at Bayside, Humboldt Co.; bur. I.O.O.F. Cem. Weaverville Sat. Apr 4, 1891. (TJ Sat. Apr 4, 1891).

ROBINSON, ELIZA JANE. Died Princeton, Colusa Co. Dec. 15, 1871; native of Augusta County, Virginia, aged 42 yr; wife of S. A. Robinson; res. Weaverville nearly 10 yr. (TJ Dec.30, 1871).

ROBINSON, GEORGE. Died Weaverville June 2, 1868; native of Bath, Lower Avon, England, aged 48 yr. (TJ Sat. June 6, 1868 p 2).

ROBINSON, GEORGE W. Died Weaverville May 18, 1872; native of Tennessee, aged 69 yr. (TJ June 1, 1872.

ROBINSON, WILLIAM A. Died Mar. 31, 1907 Douglas City; age 26, male, white, born Calif; buried Weaverville. [Index to Deaths 1890-1908].

ROBINSON, W. E. Died Jan 13, 1900; age 18 yr 4 mo 16 dy; b. California. (TJ Jan 1901).

RODGERS, _____. Died Indian Creek, near Douglas City, infant son of Frank Rodgers, aged 11 mo 13 days. (TJ Sat. June 2, 1888).

ROGERS, AUGUSTUS. Died Weaverville Aug. 27, 1871; native of Portugal aged 32 yr; (TJ Sept. 2, 1871). [may be Rodrigues].

ROGERS, LEONARD. Died Red Hill, Trinity River, nr Junction City Apr 1, 1863; native of Maine, age 32 yr; bur. Weaverville Cem. Apr 2, 1863. (TJ Sat. Apr. 4, 1863 p 2). [See also Frank Reed.]

ROHRER, CALVIN. Died Santa Rosa, Sonoma Co. abt Mar 4, 1896, aged 78 yr; born Hagerstown, Maryland; came to Calif 1849; one of oldest settlers. (TJ Sat Mar 14, 1896 p 3 col 2).

ROSE, GEORGE. Died Weaverville Feb. 1, 1890; native of England, aged about 68 yr; came to U.S. & Calif. 1851; Trinity Co. 1855; miner. (TJ Sat. Feb. 8, 1890).

ROSE, GEORGE. Died Feb. 1, 1891 (sic), white, 68, male, single, born England. [Index to Deaths 1890-1908]. (The date in the Trinity Journal is probably correct: **1890**; see above.)

ROSE, JOHN. Died Smith's Flat [nr Douglas City] July 26, 1869, age 6 months; son of John Rose. (TJ July 31, 1869 p 2).

ROSE, JOHN, Mrs. Died Douglas City Oct. 8, 1878; native of Azores, aged abt 50 years. (TJ Oct. 12, 1878 p 2).

ROSS, S. __. Died Weaverville Aug. 23, 1866; formerly of St. Louis, MO, aged about 44 yr. (blot on second initial). (TJ Sat. Aug. 25, 1866 p 2).

ROSS, EUGENIE. Died Lewiston Dec. 30, 1873, aged about 30 years; bur. Lewiston; [Pioneer Cem. Marker 1984]. Wife of A. J. Ross. (TJ Jan. 3, 1874). [Index to Deaths 1873-1890 says "Eugenia"; adds white, female, married, born U.S.] [see also Hampton.]

ROSS, DELBERT. Died Redding, Shasta Co. Sept. 24, 1885; bur. Lewiston, his old home, by the side of his mother. (TJ Oct. 3, 1885 p 3). (TJ Dec. 10, 1892 says "Delbert H. Henterleiten, son of Mrs. A. J. Ross"). [see also Hampton.]

ROTHE, WILLIAM. Died Weaverville Dec. 19, 1894; native of Prussia, aged about 64 yr; also known as "Hardscrabble Bill"; came to Calif. & Trinity Co. 1850; miner. (TJ Sat. Dec. 22, 1894 p 2 & 3).

ROURKE, DENIS. Died Dec 21, 1900; age 69 yr; b. Ireland. (TJ Jan 1901).

ROUSE, W. P., Col. Died Medford, Oregon Mar 6, 1898, aged 65 yr; his company constructed the big La Grange (mining) ditch in Trinity County. (TJ Mar 19, 1898 p 3 col 3).

ROWE, EDWIN ALBERT, Capt. Died Fresno, [Fresno Co.] Nov. 16, 1884; native of Portsmouth, N.H. aged 58 yr 9 days (more, p. 3) (TJ Sat. Dec. 6, 1884).

ROWE, W. F. Died Fresno May 16, 1896; native of New York, aged 64 yr; well known by all Old Settlers; with brothers Capt. Ed. A. Rowe and Charles Rowe, all in express business in Weaverville 1852-1856; leaves five children and an unmarried sister in Fresno. (TJ Sat. May 23, 1896 p 3 col 3).

ROWE, WILLIAM. Killed by a cave near Junction City Apr. 2, 1888; native of England, aged 55 yr; bur. Weaverville Cem. Apr. 3, 1888. Mother and 4 brothers in Butte County; nephew of Mrs. Gribble. (TJ Apr. 7, 1888).

ROWLES, JAMES. Died April 3, 1907 Minersville; age 71, male, white, miner; buried Weaverville. [Index to Deaths 1890-1908].

RUCH, ELIZABETH G. Died Hay Fork July 25, 1879, aged 2 yr 9 mo; dau. of William H. and Lavina A. Ruch. (TJ Sat. Aug. 9, 1879 p 2).

RUCH, ELIZA, Mrs. Died Oakland, Alameda Co. Dec. 28, 1882, at res. of dau. Mrs. Simon B. Morey; husband Mr. Michael Ruch died a few months ago. (TJ Jan. 20, 1883 p 2). [see also Morey].

RUCH, MICHAEL, Mr. Died Sonoma County abt Sept. 15, 1882; a few weeks ago he and wife were here on a visit to their son Wm. H. Ruch of Hay Fork and dau. Mrs. H. W. Leonard of Douglas City. (TJ Sept. 16, 1882).

RUGGLES, CHARLES. Hanged near railroad tracks in Redding, Shasta Co. for the killing of Messenger Montgomery (May 16, 1892). (TJ Sat. July 30, 1892 p 3 col 2 & 3). [see also TRINITY 1966 pp 4-10 for the story].

RUGGLES, JOHN. Hanged near railroad tracks in Redding, Shasta Co. for the killing of Messenger Montgomery (May 16, 1892). (TJ Sat. July 30, 1892 p 3 col 2 & 3). [see also TRINITY 1966 pp 4-10 for the story].

RULE, BENJAMIN BENNETT. Died Dec. 3, 1905 Weaverville; age 76, male, white, miner, born England. [Index to Deaths 1890-1908]. [brother of Silas]. [see also Barkla in Deaths 1900-1950].

RULE, SILAS. Died at his res. in Faggtown, Weaverville Apr. 30, 1892; native of England, aged 59 yr 6 mo 9 days; bur. May 1, 1892 I.O.O.F. Cem; came to US at very early age; family settled in Wisconsin; came to Calif. age 18: 2 years in Tuolumne and Nevada Co., to Trinity Co. 1854; m. Mrs. Anna Brady 1874; no children, but he was an indulgent father to Mrs. Rule's children; survivors: widow; B. B. Rule, and wife; W. J. Rule and fam., James Barkla and fam., and Isaac Barkla, the last two being half-brothers of the deceased, and step-children: M. A. Brady, Mrs. H. L. Lowden, and Mrs. J. W. Bartlett; a fourth, Mrs. Johnson Field, now lives in the State of Michigan. (TJ Sat. May 7, 1892, p 2 & p 3, col 2). [see also Kernan, Morris, Brady, Freitas]. [Mrs. Anna Morris Brady was the widow of Bernard Brady, who d. Dec 19, 1867; sister of James Morris.]

RULE, WILLIAM JOHN. Died March 6, 1900 Weaverville; age 65, male, white, miner, born England; buried I.O.O.F. Cemetery, Weaverville. [Index to Deaths 1890-1908]. [brother of Silas.]

RULE, William John. (see above). Died Weaverville Mar 06, 1900; b. Cornwall, England Feb 6, 1835; son of Benjamin and Emma Rule. Came with parents to U.S. 1835; married in Dodgeville, Wisconsin Dec. 5, 1874, Miss Sarah J. Bartle; long obit, with fam. inf. (TJ Mar 10, 1900 pg 3 col 3).

RUMFELT, MARY, Mrs. Died near Jackson, Missouri Feb. 2, 1868, aged 64 yr; mother of Augustus Rumfelt of Trinity Center. (TJ March 28, 1868).

RUNK, HONORA, Mrs. Died San Francisco June 20, 1886 age 54 yr; deceased was a sister of Mrs. John Sheridan of Junction City. (TJ June 26, 1886 p 3).

RUPPEL, CONRAD. Died Wisconsin recently [Mar 1898]; b. Hesse Darmstadt abt 69 years ago; leaves 2 sons in Wisconsin and sister Mrs. Louis F. Raab in Junction City; former Pioneer of Trinity Co. (TJ Mar 19, 1898 p 3 col 2).

RUSS, _____. Died Long Ridge [Southern Trinity] Mar 2, 1899; inf. son of Mr. and Mrs. Augustus Russ, aged 4 dy. (TJ Apr 15, 1899 p 2).

RUSSELL, PETER, Mrs. Died Camptonville, Yuba Co. Feb 17, 1899; mother of Mrs. W. F. Arnold, former res. of Weaverville; native of Bangor, North Wales, age 60 yr 1 mo 24 dy; "A Pioneer of 1854". (TJ Feb 25, 1899 p 3 col 3; obt. of "Mrs. Ellen Russell" TJ Mar 4, 1899 p 3 col 3).

RUTLEDGE, _____. Died on Van Duzen river near Hettenshaw Sept. 17, 1895, inf. dau. of Mr. and Mrs. Arthur Rutledge, native of Calif. age 15 days. (TJ Oct 12, 1895 p 2; see also TJ Sept. 28, 1895).

RUTLEDGE, ARTHUR, Mrs. Died at Hettenshaw Sept. 18, 1895, **Maggie**, wife of Arthur Rutledge; native of Calif. aged 22 yr 3 mo 10 dy. (TJ Oct 12, 1895 p 2.) "Mrs. Arthur Rutledge of Hettenshaw and child died at that place last week and were buried on Friday Sept 20, 1895. They were stopping at L. P. Duncans." (TJ Sept. 28, 1895 p 3). [Arthur Rutledge and Miss Maggie A. Davis m. at Long Ridge Nov 26, 1893 by James Howe, J.P. Trinity Co. Marriages Book I p 196].

RYAN, _____. Died Oregon Gulch Aug. 11, 1874 aged 5 days; infant dau. of Richard and Mary Ryan. (TJ Aug. 15, 1874).

RYAN, _____. Died at Whitmore's Mill (Oregon Mtn) Nov. 27, 1895, inf. son of Mr. and Mrs. P. J. Ryan, aged 1 yr 2 mo. (TJ Sat. Nov 3, 1895).

RYAN, CORNELIUS RICHARD. Died Deadwood Oct. 12, 1893; born Junction City, CA, Dec. 24, 1868, aged 26 yr 9 mo 18 days; bur. Catholic Cem, Weaverville Oct. 13, 1893; leaves parents, 2 bro., 3 sisters. (TJ Sat. Oct. 14, 1893 p 2 & p 3 col 2.) [1880 Census: Ryan, Richard R., b. Ireland; Catherine b. Ireland; Margaret, b. CA; Sarah, b. CA; Cornelius, b. CA; Thomas, b. CA; Mary, b. CA; William, CA.]

RYAN, EDWIN. Died Weaverville Sep 7, 1896; inf. son of Mr. and Mrs. P. J. Ryan; native of Calif, aged 2 mo 14 dy; bur. Weaverville Cem. (TJ Sat Sep 12, 1896 p 2).

RYAN, ELLEN. Died Weaverville June 27, 1860, aged abt 6 months; dau. of R. Ryan. (TJ June 30, 1860 p 2).

RYAN, MARY. Died Weaverville July 9, 1858, aged abt 10 months; dau. of Richard Ryan. (TJ Sat. July 17, 1858 p 2).

RYAN, SARAH. Died Weaverville Apr. 13, 1863, aged 4 yr 6 mo 3 days; dau. of Richard and Catherine Ryan. (Scarlet fever). (TJ Apr. 18, 1863 p 2).

RYAN, JAMES. Killed by Indians in Hyampom May 14, 1864; bur. May 15, 1864 (TJ May 21, 1864 p 3). [probably bur. Hyampom].

RYAN, PATRICK. Died Douglas City June 7, 1866 by a caving bank. Native of Ireland, aged 40 yr; bur. Cath. Cem. Weaverville June 8, 1866. (TJ June 9, 1866 p 2).

RYAN, SMITH. Reported killed after he left this county; is still alive. (TJ Jan. 23, 1892 p 3 col 1).

RYAN, VINCENT A., Mrs. Drowned in Vallejo, (Solano Co.) Oct 1898; Mr. Ryan conducted the Trinity _Press_ here in 1870-71. (TJ Oct 29, 1898 p 3). [not in 1870 census].

RYAN, WILLIAM. Died June 30, 1899; b. 1877 Trinity Co. CA. [Rita M. Hanover note: 1880 census: son of Richard R. and Catherine Ryan]. [see below] [first source not given].

RYAN, WILLIAM J. Died Deadwood Jun 30, 1899; b. Junction City, aged abt 22 yr; bur. Catholic Cem. Weaverville. (TJ July 8, 1899 pp 2 & 3).

SAELTZER, R. M., Mrs. Died San Francisco abt Feb. 1894; of Redding, Shasta Co.; dau. of A. R. Andrews, pioneer of Shasta Co., and a sister of the wife of Judge Edward Sweeny; no age given. (TJ Sat. Feb. 17, 1894 p 3 col 6).

SAGAS, JOSE GONCASE. Died Red Bluff, Tehama Co. May 10, 1881; native of Portugal, aged 68 yrs; he was mining near Lewiston, Trin. Co. for several years past; bur. Oak Hill Cem. Red Bluff May 11, 1881. (TJ May 14, 1881 p 3).

SALADIN, MARGUERIGE (sic), Mrs. Died Junction City Jul 7, 1898; native of Breuilly, Cher. France, age 31 yr 4 mo 8 dy; [in same column on page 2: "born at Junction City Jul 6, 1898, to the wife of E. Saladin, a daughter."] Fun. Jul 9, 1898. "Body will be embalmed and taken to France for burial." (TJ Jul 9, 1898 pp 2 & 3; Jul 23, 1898 p 3 col 1). [see also Addendum].

SALADIN, MARGUERITE CAMILLE ESTELLE JAEHLE KOEHLER. Died Junction City, Calif., Jul 7, 1898; age 31, female, white, b. foreign (France); wife; d. childbirth. [Index to Deaths 1889-1908].

SALMON, WM. C. Died Rush Creek Apr 5, 1896; native of Michigan, aged abt 71 yr. Bur. I.O.O.F. Cem, Weaverville Apr 6, 1896; leaves brother John Salmon and a wife in Australia; came with brother from Oregon 6 weeks ago. (TJ Apr 11, 1896 pp 2-3).

SALTERBACH, _____. Killed by the caving of a bank at Canon Creek, July 18, 1857; no age. Partner with Wright in Wright & Co. mine. (TJ July 18, 1857).

SAMUELS, STEPHEN A. Died Hayfork Sept. 15, 1866; no age; (TJ Sept. 22, 1866 p 2 col 1). [not in 1860 census].

SANDERSON, ELLA, Miss. Died San Jose, Santa Clara Co., Apr. 5, 1892. She was the guest of the Wallace family of Junction City last summer, and her friends will be pained to learn of her death. Her parents reside at Seattle, Wash. (TJ Sat. Apr 16, 1892).

SANDS, FLORA, Mrs. Died Vance's Bar, Trinity County Mar. 24, 1882, aged about 28 yr. (TJ Apr. 1, 1882 p 2).

SANTA CRUZ, JOSE. Drowned in Trinity River near Junction City May 20, 1881; native of Calif. aged about 37 years. (TJ May 28, 1881 p 2). Remains found on a bar near North Fork June 10, 1881; in the river 2 weeks, found 6 miles below where he went in. (TJ June 18, 1881 p 3).

SARVIS, GEO. C. Died May 1895 Eureka, Humboldt Co.; native of England, aged 64 yr; came to Calif. 1873, Trinity Co. for a few years; leaves wife and 5 children. (TJ Sat. June 1, 1895 p 3 col 4).

SAUNDERS, HENRY, Mr. Died Douglas City Apr. 26, 1862; native of Mass. aged about 42 yr. (TJ Sat. May 3, 1862 p 3).

SAWYER, HUMPHRY W. Died Weaverville Mar. 21, 1888; born Burn, Worcester Co., Mass 1822; aged 66 yr; came Calif. 1849; lived in Nevada, served in Nevada Volunteers. (TJ Mar. 24, 1888).

SAX, PAUL. Died Hay Fork Sep 19, 1896; native of Germany, aged about 14 yr. (TJ Sat Sept 26, 1896).

SAXE, JOHN. Died May 25, 1907 Hayfork; age 81, male, white, born Austria; farmer; buried Hayfork. [Index to Deaths 1890-1908].

SAYRE, HALSEY JEHIEL. Died Weaverville Jul 16, 1898; native of New York, aged abt 76 yr. (TJ Sat. Jul 23, 1898 p 2).

SCAMMON, AUGUSTUS. Died Shasta [Shasta Co.] Aug. 31, 1865; native of Enfield, Maine, aged about 28 yr. (TJ Sept. 2, 1865 p 2).

SCANLAN, THOMAS. Died Weaverville Nov. 20, 1872; native of Maryland aged 66 years. (TJ Nov. 23, 1872).

SCHACHT, T.M., Mrs. Died Hay Fork May 26, 1881, aged about 37 years. (TJ June 4, 1881).

SCHADE, CHAS. Died Douglas City abt Oct. 16/17, 1867. (TJ Sat. Oct. 19, 1867 and Oct. 26, 1867). Body found in Trinity river near mouth of Browns Creek Nov. 3, 1867. Bur. Weaverville Cem. Nov. 5, 1867 by the Trinity Rifles; leaves sister. (TJ Sat. Nov. 9, 1867).

SCHAFFER, _____, Mr. Died St. Helena, Napa County Aug. 24, 1886; native of Germany, aged about 60 years; bur. St. Helena Aug. 25, 1886; resident there 7 years; formerly a resident of Trinity County. See St. Helena *Star* Aug. 27, 1886. (TJ Sat. Sept. 11, 1886).

SCHAFFER, AUGUST, Mrs. Died Weaverville Oct 16, 1899; native of Germany, aged 48 yr 4 mo 10 dy. (TJ Oct 21, 1899 p 2).

SCHALL, JOHN LEWIS. Died Nov. 22, 1906 Weaverville, age 79, male, white, shoemaker; born Germany; informant: Louis Schall. [Index to Deaths 1890-1908].

SCHAMOR, EMILE. Died Weaverville Sat. Sept. 1, 1855 age 19. (TT Sept. 8, 1855). [no further information].

SCHLEIGH, J. S. Died Anderson, Shasta Co. Apr. 4, 1886; native of Penn. aged 56 yr; bur. by Anderson Lodge No. 254, I.O.O.F., of which he was a Charter Member; pioneer res. of Trinity Co; left abt 1866. (TJ Sat. April 17, 1886 p 3 col 2).

SCHLICKERMAN, FRITZ. Died Weaverville May 14, 1882; native of Germany aged about 34 years; came from Missouri less than a year ago; leaves wife and one child;

wife has buried 7 children, the last one on the journey to Calif; will return to Missouri. (TJ May 20, 1882 p 2).

SCHLOMER, CHARLES. Died Helena [formerly North Fork] Apr 02, 1916; b. Helena Oct 1861; leaves mother, Miss Louisa Schlomer and Grant Schlomer of Helena, Mrs. Barbara Hinters of Arizona, and Chris. Schlomer of Ukiah. Bur. Helena Cem. (TJ Apr 8, 1916, p 1 col 1).

SCHLOMER, CHRISTIAN H. Died Ukiah, Mendocino, CA Jan 20, 1921; born North Fork (Helena) Jul 16, 1873; bur. Helena Cem Jan 24, 1921. (TJ Jan 29, 1921 p 1 col 5).

SCHLOMER, HARMON KARL. Died Helena Mar 12, 1898; b. Hanover, Germany Jul 21, 1825 (sic); came to U.S. 1852, worked as blacksmith at St. Louis and New Orleans; crossed the plains to Calif. in 1854; returned to Germany 1860 and upon return, m. Miss Louisa Weinheimer in Pekin, Illinois; she is the sister of Henry Weinheimer and Mrs. Charlotte Meckel of Weaverville; nine children were born of this union; five survive: Mrs. Adolph Hinters, of Los Angeles, Charles, Henry (Grant), Christian H. and Lulu Schlomer of North Fork. (TJ Sat. Mar 19, 1898 p 3).

SCHLOMER, HERMAN. Died North Fork, Trinity County, CA, aged 18 months; bur. Helena Cem. son of Herman [Harmon] and Louisa Schlomer. (TJ May 15, 1869 p 2).

SCHLOMER, HENRY GRANT. Died North Fork Nov 21, 1956, age 91 yr; b. May 23, 1865 North Fork; never married. (Trinity Co. Birth and Deaths Jan 1, 1956 - June 1960 page 37). (TJ Nov 22, 1856 pg 1 col 2)

SCHLOMER, LOUISA, Mrs. Died July 14, 1925 Helena (formerly North Fork); b. Miss Louisa Weinheimer Feb 14, 1841 Pekin, Illinois, dau. of Christian Weinheimer and Barbara Bransel. m. Harmon Karl Schlomer in Pekin in 1860; lived Helena CA for 65 yr. (Trinity Co. Deaths 1914-1931 pg 192).

SCHLOMER, LOUISA, Miss. Died Huntington Park (Los Angeles County) Mar 14, 1957; formerly of North Fork (Helena); b. Mar 30, 1871 at North Fork; bur. North Fork Cemetery Mar 19, 1957; survived by her sister Mrs. Barbara Hinters, niece Lou Stevens, and nephew [William Jennings] Bryan Hinters, all of Los Angeles. (TJ Mar 21, 1957 pg 1 col 7).

SCHNABEL, EARNEST. Died San Jose, Santa Clara Co. Jan. 25, 1889; native of Saxony, Germany, b. 1829; arrived Sacramento Sept. 9, 1850; went to Germany 1860; married Mrs. Clara Bretschnieder in Philadelphia; lived in Trinity County, San Francisco, then San Jose in 1872. Much information. (TJ Sat. Feb. 2, 1889 p 3; Feb. 9, 1889 p 3).

SCHNABEL, LOUIS. Died Weaverville June 12, 1862; native of Penig, Saxony, aged 36 yr 7 mo; born 1826; came to Calif. 1850 from Philadelphia; has a brother living there. (TJ June 14, 1862 p 2).

SCHNEIDER, HENRY CONRAD. Died Junction City Dec 19, 1896; born Trais-Holoff, Hesse Darmstadt, Germany, aged 59 yr 10 mo 28 dy; came to Trinity Co. Feb 15, 1864; leaves wife and 3 children, Mrs. J. Q. Adams; Henry D. and Charles Schneider. Bur. Masonic Cem. Weaverville Dec 20, 1896. (TJ Sat Dec 26, 1896 p 3 col 2).

SCHNEIDER, MICHEL. Died Weaverville June 26, 1875; native of Freshweiler, Alsace, aged 60 yr. (TJ July 3, 1875).

SCHNELLBACHER, MAIRYE. Died near Lowden Ranch Jan 31, 1899; b. Indianola, Iowa, aged 18 yr 5 mo 10 dy; came to Trinity County 6 months ago to join her father. (name not given). (TJ Feb 4, 1899 pp 2 & 3).

SCHROEDER, JOHN D. Died Sept. 1, 1907 Hayfork, age 71, male, white, miner, born Germany; buried Hayfork. [Index to Deaths 1890-1908].

SCHWING, JOSEPH. Died Reading (Shasta Co) Feb. 5, 1879; known as "Cooper Joe"; worked at Pacific Brewery several years ago. (TJ Sat. Feb. 15, 1879). (not in 1870 census).

SCOTT, JAMES. "Died Sep 9, 1867, aged 32 yr. Dearest husband thou has left us/ and thy loss we deeply feel/ It is God that has bereft us/ He can all our sorrows heal/ Erected by his beloved Wife Margaret Scott". Gravestone in St. Patrick's Catholic Cem., Weaverville, in excellent condition Apr 1990.

SCOTT, JAMES MADISON. Died Weaverville Feb 12, 1897; native of Alabama aged abt 76 yr; served in the Mexican War; came to Calif. at an early day; during the Civil War, he served in the Humboldt regiment; lived near the South Fork of the

Trinity where he ranched and raised cattle; came to Weaverville recently; fun. Feb 14, 1897; (TJ Feb 20, 1897 p 2 & p 3 col 3).
SEABRING, BILL. "Frozen to death this week on the Modoc line". (TJ Sat. Dec. 28, 1889 p 3); no further information.
SELFRIDGE, J. M., Mrs. Died at her home in Oakland [Alameda Co.] last Monday Nov 14, 1898. She was related to O. M. Loveridge of this place, and at one time was quite largely interested in the Ward mine before it was sold to the LaGrange company. (TJ Nov 19, 1898 p 3 col 2). (see also Loveridge).
SEAMAN, LULU. Died Bethlehem, Penn Oct. 11, 1865; dau. of H. J. and Maria Seaman. (TJ Sat. Dec. 23, 1865).
SEAMAN, HENRY J. Died in Bethlehem, Penn "a few years since"; son of Capt. Benson Seaman and Mrs. Eliza Seaman of N.Y. (TJ Sat. Mar. 26, 1881 p 3). (Rita Hanover has date of death as Sep 11, 1874.) (see also Addendum).
SEAMAN, ELIZA, Mrs. Died at res. of son-in-law John A. Watson, Eureka, Humboldt Co. Mar. 11, 1881, age 85 yr; widow of the late Capt. Benson Seaman of New York. (more information) (TJ Sat. Mar. 26, 1881 p 3). [see also Watson].
SEARS, WILLIAM, Judge. Died in San Francisco Feb. 27, 1891. He was in Weaverville about 2 years ago and spent some time at East Fork in figuring on mining property. In 1863 he was elected Speaker of the Assembly and in 1884 was appt. by Pres. Arthur Collector of the Port of San Francisco. For several years prior to his death he served as Internal Revenue Collector. (TJ Sat. Mar. 7, 1891).
SEDENBURG, JOHN. Drowned in Trinity River at Evans bar, near Junction City, June 7, 1861; resided here several years. (TJ Sat. June 15, 1861 p 2 col 1).
SEELYE, HENRY, Col. Died at mouth of Canon Creek [Junction City] Sep 12, 1857, aged about 65 yr; formerly of St. George, New Brunswick, B.N.A. (TJ Sat. Sept. 19, 1857 p 2).
SEGALIA, ALEXANDER. Died Red Hill, near Junction City Apr. 16, 1889; native of Calif, aged about 28 yr; only son of Antone Segalia of Junction City; bur. Weaverville Cem. Apr. 18, 1889. (TJ Apr. 20, 1889). [Index to Deaths 1873-1890 adds white, male, single, born Calif].
SEGALIA, ANTONE. Died Weaverville Feb. 29, 1892; native of Greece, aged about 72 yr. Pioneer citizen; came to Calif. from Greece in 1848; landed San Francisco Mar. 1849; Feb. 1850 came up Trinity River to this county; miner; only one dau. Mrs. Mary Gribble is living; bur. Tues. Mar. 1, 1892 Weaverville Cem. (TJ Sat. Mar 5, 1892). [see also Woods].
SEGALIA, JANE. Died Red Hill Sept. 6, 1879, aged about 45 yr; wife of Antone Segalia. (TJ Sept. 13, 1879 p 2).
SEIFFER, FRED. Died North Fork [Helena] June 23, 1865; native of Germany aged about 40 yr; came from San Francisco to this county. (TJ July 1, 1865 p 2).
SENGER, JACOB ADAM. Died Weaverville Oct. 17, 1893; born Weaverville 1865, aged 28 yr 2 mo; second son of Mr. and Mrs. Jacob Senger; killed by a cave in the Woodbury mine; bur. Odd Fellows Cem. Weav. (TJ Sat. Oct. 21, 1893). [see also Hughes].
SERVICE, JOHN. Died Jan. 10, 1890, white. no further information given. [Index to Deaths 1873-1890].
SEVEDGE, FRANK. Died Dec. 26, 1903 near Carrville, Trinity County, Calif; age 35, male, white, American; buried French Gulch Cemetery, Shasta County, Calif. [Index to Deaths 1890-1908].
SEWALL, STEPHEN B., Dr. Died Weaverville Dec. 23, 1864; native of Lynn, Mass, age 48 yr. (TJ Dec. 31, 1864).
SHAFER, H. C. Drowned crossing Browns Creek in flood Dec. 7, 1861; native of Penn. age 34; married last spring; leaves a sorrowing wife. (TJ Dec. 14, 1861 p 2). [not married in Trinity County; not in 1860 census.]
SHAFTER, MEINRAD. Died Shasta, Shasta Co. abt July 1, 1892, aged about 70 yr.; a former owner of the Tower House, near Shasta. (TJ Sat. July 9, 1892 p 3 col 1).
SHANE, EDWARD. Killed in Garden Gulch, Weaverville Feb. 14, 1859; aged 26 years; from Lewiston, Niagara Co, New York where parents reside. Bur. Catholic Cem. Weaverville Feb. 15, 1859. (TJ Feb. 19, 1859 p 3).
SHANNON, ISAAC T. Died Battle Creek Meadows, Tehama Co. Oct. 2, 1883; worked at Jumper's Mill on Browns Creek summer 1880. (TJ Nov. 17, 1883 p 3).

SHATTUCK, ELIZABETH KIMBALL. Died Weaverville Oct. 28, 1892; native of Rhode Island, aged 26 yr 9 days; dau. of C. C. Shattuck. (TJ Sat. Nov. 5, 1892).

SHEA, JOHN. "A native of Cork, Ireland, died Aug 6, 1860, aged 32 years." Gravemarker St. Patrick's Catholic Cem., Weaverville standing Apr 1990.

SHEEHY, ISABELL THERESA. Died Eastman Gulch Aug. 2, 1888; native of Table Bluff, Humboldt Co. Cal, aged 1 yr 10 mo 22 days; youngest child of Mr. and Mrs. John Sheehy. (TJ Aug. 11, 1888).

SHEFFIELD, ELIAZER E. Died New River Aug. 15, 1888; native of Ohio, aged 62 yr. (TJ Aug. 25, 1888).

SHEPARD, ALBERT. Died San Francisco Mar. 13, 1882; native of New York, aged 57 yr; wife and 2 daughters. Fun. Mar. 15, 1882; bur I.O.O.F. Cem. San Francisco; old-time resident of Trinity County. (TJ Mar. 25, 1882 p 3). [In 1860 census: Weaverville, laborer, age 35, b. New York].

SHERIDAN, JOHN. Died Feb. 22, 1903 Junction City, CA; drowned; age 72, male, white, foreign born; bur. Catholic Cemetery, Weaverville. [Index to Deaths 1890-1908]. (see Phillip Sheridan for names of parents.)

SHERIDAN, MARY, Mrs. Died Junction City Mar 21, 1900; wife of John Sheridan, who survives her; b. County Tipperary, Ireland, aged 72 yr 2 mo 20 dy; good obit. (TJ Mar 24, 1900 pg 3 col 2). [see also Runk].

SHERIDAN, PHILLIP. Died Weaverville Dec 5, 1899; b. County Cavan, Ireland 1823, aged abt 76 yr; son of Philip and Mary Sheridan; Mrs. Sheridan d. before 1826 when father emigrated with family to America. Came with brother John Sheridan to Trinity County; bur. Catholic Cem. Weaverville. (TJ Dec 9, 1899 p 2 & p 3 col 2).

SHERIDAN, THOMAS. Died San Francisco Aug. 9, 1876; native of Ireland aged 54 yr. (TJ Aug. 19, 1876 p 2).

SHERWOOD, STEPHEN. Died [Coeur], New River, Trinity Co. June 24, 1894; native of Penn, aged about 83 yr; discovered New River Mining Dist. in 1882; found the Sherwood and Uncle Sam mines. (TJ Sat. July 14, 1894 p 2; TJ May 21, 1898). [1880 Census, New River area, Jun 9, 1880: Sherwood, Stephen, age 68, miner, widower, b. Penn; father b. N.Y., mother b. Germany.] [see also Addendum].

SHERWOOD, WILLIS. Died New River July 7, 1893; native of Illinois, aged about 24 yr; "fatal Fourth of July accident". (TJ Sat. July 15, 1893 p 2 & 3, col 2; see also TJ July 22, 1893 p 3 col 2). See Hicks, <u>WEAVERVILLE TRINITY COUNTY, CALIFORNIA</u> for an account of Mr. Sherwood's purchases in 1893 before his death. [youngest son of Stephen Sherwood]. [O. P. Sherwood half-brother of Willis Sherwood; (Minutes of Probate No. 5, 1892-1897, Superior Court of Trinity County, Calif. p 233)]

SHINE, WILLIAM H. Died Deadwood Dec. 30, 1891; native of Ireland, aged about 65 yr. (TJ Jan. 2, 1892).

SHIPLER, R. R. Died Lewiston Aug. 24, 1882; native of Brownsville, Penn. aged 39 yr 9 mo; bur. Odd Fellows Cem. Weaverville. Leaves father, mother and sister in Brownsville; brother in Utah or Colorado. (TJ Aug. 26, 1882 p 2&3).

SHOCK, ALBERT. Died Weaverville May 27, 1896; aged abt 21 yr; of Hay Fork; buried Hayfork. (TJ Sat. May 30, 1896).

SHOCK, LOUISE R. Died March 11, 1906 Hayfork; age 37, female, white, born Calif; buried Hayfork. [Index to Deaths 1890-1908].

SHOCK, SADIE, Mrs. note: father Jonathan Stukney Hoytt; mother Katherine Woods. [see Hoytt entry].

SHOCK, THOMAS MILTON. Died Hay Fork July 30, 1895; native of Missouri, aged abt 54 yr. (TJ Sat. July 6, 1895 p 2).

"SHOCK", VINA. see Hawk. (TJ Sept. 16, 1893 says "Vina Shock"; corrected Sept. 23, 1893 to "Miss Vina Hawk".

SHOCK, WILLIAM RILEY. Died Hay Fork Oct. 9, 1894; native of Missouri, aged 63 yr 4 mo 2 dy; came to Calif. 1850, stayed 4 years; married Isabell P. James in Missouri; returned to Calif.; 5 sons. (TJ Sat. Oct. 20, 1894 p 3).

SHOEMAKER, HENRY. Killed near Ridgeville by caving of a bank Sat. June 7, 1856; from Athensville, Green Co, Illinois; buried by Sons of Temperance; "young man"; no age given. (TJ Sat. June 14, 1856 p 2). [prob. bur. Ridgeville Cem.]

SHORT, ELLEN. Died Junction City Apr. 27, 1879, aged 20 yr 2 mo 5 days; wife of F. M. Short. (TJ May 3, 1879 p 2).

SHOWALTER, ISABEL. Died at Port Providence, Penn. Dec. 11, 1891, aged 76 yr 7 months and 17 days; beloved mother of Clara Huston and sister of M. Bartolett of Weaverville. "Blessed are they that die in the Lord." (TJ Sat. Dec. 26, 1891).

SHUFORD, AMANDA, Mrs. Died Weaverville Feb. 23, 1869. (TJ Feb. 27, 1869). [She had smallpox, and was buried in a lone grave at the top of what is Amanda Avenue in 1998; marker legible in 1989.]

SHUFORD, DAVID M., Mr. Died Weaverville Aug. 28, 1856, aged 30 years; formerly of Perryville, Perry Co. Missouri. (TJ Sat. Aug. 30, 1856).

SHURTLEFF, CALEB. Died Weaverville Apr 16, 1892; native of Vermont, aged about 73 yr. (TJ Sat. Apr 23, 1892).

SHURTLEFF, NATHANIEL BENJAMIN. Died Weaverville Feb 12, 1897; b. Shasta, Shasta Co. Jul 6, 1858, son of Harrison J. Shurtleff and Adeline Shurtleff; came to Weaverville 1860; father d. Seattle Wash. 1865; m. Nov 12, 1887 to Minnie S. Paulsen, dau. of P. M. Paulsen; one son, Meinert Jerome Shurtleff; purchased interest in TRINITY JOURNAL 1895; one of best newspaper men in Northern California; bur. Odd Fellows Cem. Feb 14, 1897; obit. worth copying. (TJ Sat. Feb 20, 1897 p 2 & p 3, col. 2 & 3; notices of respect TJ Feb 27, 1897 and also TJ Mar 13, 1897 p 3 col 4). (see also Paulsen).

SIEBERT, GOTTLIEB ALEXANDER. Died Weaverville Feb. 7, 1883; native of Germany, aged 56 yr; painter; old resident of Trinity County. (TJ Feb. 10, 1883 p 2).

SIEGFRIED, JOHN BOYER. Died Indian Creek Nov 5, 1897; native of Penn., aged abt 74 yr; unmarried; has relatives in the East; bur. Weaverville Cem Nov 6, 1897. (TJ Sat Nov 6, 1897 pp 2 & 3).

SIGNER, MORGAN. Died near Weaverville May 23, 1860 of injuries received from a bank cave; formerly of Galena, Illinois; aged 26 years; bur. Weaverville Cem. May 23, 1860, with Episcopal burial services by H. J. Seaman, Esq. (TJ Sat. May 26, 1860 p 2).

SILANDER, DAVID S. Died Weaverville Apr. 22, 1877; native of Sweden, aged about 50 years; bur. Weaverville Cem. Apr. 23, 1877; single man; mined Douglas City last 15-16 years; came to U.S. many years ago. (TJ Apr. 28, 1877 p 2-3).

SILCOX, RICHARD. Died at res. of George Vitzthum near Douglas City Mar. 10, 1891; native of Penn., aged about 69 yr; bur. Public Cem. Weaverville Mar 12, 1891. Pioneer of California 1849; came to Trinity Co. 1856; wife deceased; dau. Mrs. Conway of Pittsburg, Penn only child. (TJ Sat. Mar. 14, 1891).

SILVA, FRANK. Died Douglas City Aug. 26, 1885; native of Trinity County; aged 14 yr. (TJ Aug. 29, 1885). [He may be the son of Frank & Mary Silva, born Dec. 4, 1871; 1880 census and Trinity Journal Births Dec. 1871].

SILVA, MARY. Died Douglas City Oct. 21, 1885; native of Portugal, aged about 40 years; wife of Frank Silva. (TJ Oct. 24, 1885).

SILVA, MARY. Died Douglas City Feb. 3, 1886, aged about 9 years; daughter of Frank and Mary Silva. (TJ Feb. 6, 1886).

SIMCOE, JOSEPH. Died Weaverville Nov. 15, 1864; native of Virginia, aged about 55 years; late of New Albany, Indiana. (TJ Nov. 19, 1864).

SIMONDS, FRED B. Died Redding, Shasta Co. Mar 23, 1897; native of Vermont, aged abt 70 yr; Pioneer resident of Trinity Co., lived at Trinity Center. (TJ Sat. Apr 3, 1897 p 3 col 2.)

SIMMONS, CHAS. S. Died July 31, 1855 at Chadbourne's Ranch; native of Illinois, about 23 years old; in county over 2 years. ("Accidental firing of a colt's revolver mortally wounded the young man.") (TT, Aug. 4, 1855).

SIMMONS, ORVILLE. Died Cedar Flat Apr. 8, 1880; native of Michigan, aged 53 years; leaves 3 children, all grown. (TJ Apr. 17, 1880).

SIMMONS, MARY, Miss. Died near Arcata, Humboldt County, Sept. 13, 1887; well known in Trinity County. (Arcata *Union*). (TJ Oct. 1, 1887).

SIMPSON, HENRY H. Died Weaverville Feb. 21, 1892; native of Ohio, aged about 73 yr; came to Calif 1850, Trinity Co. 1854; Mexican War Veteran who drew a pension. (TJ Sat. Feb. 27, 1892 pp 2 & 3).

SIMPSON, MOSES W. Died Elk Mills, Missouri July 22, 1877, aged about 53 years; left Trinity County 1876 for former home. (TJ Sept. 8, 1877, p.3, col 3 "Dead").

SKEWIS, EDWARD. Died Weaverville Oct 16, 1899; native of England, aged 79 yr 2 mo 13 dy. (TJ Sat. Oct 21, 1899 p 2). [see also Coleman].

SKILLEN, JAMES E. Died Weaverville Apr 5, 1900; native of Missouri, aged 30 yr 6 mo 8 dy. (TJ Apr 7, 1900).

SLACK, _____, Mrs. Died West Lebanon, N.H., Sep 2, 1891; aged 77 yr 18 mo 16 days; bur. Sep 3, 1891 beside her husb. at Hartford. Mother of O. L. Slack, who wrote the news Sep 3, 1891. (TJ Sat. Sept. 12, 1891).

SLATTERY, _____, Mrs. Died at Oregon Gulch May 7, 1862; wife of John Slattery. (TJ May 10, 1862 p.3). [Not in 1860 census].

SLATTERY, ANN. Died Oregon Gulch Jan. 6, 1871, aged 56 yr; wife of Edward Slattery. (TJ Jan 14, 1871). [1870 census: age 54, born Ireland; family source gave maiden name as Murray].

SLATTERY, ANNE. Died Oregon Gulch June 5, 1893; native of Ireland, aged about 60 yr; bur. Catholic Cem. Weaverville June 6, 1893; wife of Patrick Slattery; maiden name Anne Hogan; came to US from Ireland 1849; m. Patrick Slattery in New York; came to Trinity Co. 1860. (TJ Sat. June 10, 1893).

SLATTERY, JOHN. Died Gold Hill, Nevada Oct. 9, 1873; left Trinity Co. abt June 1873; brother of Thomas and Patrick Slattery of Oregon Gulch. (TJ Oct. 18, 1873; see also Oct. 11, 1873.)

SLATTERY, MARY, Mrs. Died San Francisco Jan. 22, 1884; native of Ireland, aged 57 years; wife of late John Slattery; daughter of Dennis and Mary Murray, formerly of Junction City. (TJ Feb 2, 1884).

SLATTERY, EDWARD. Died Junction City Aug. 8, 1884; native of Ireland, aged 64 years. Bur. Catholic Cem., Weaverville Aug. 9, 1884. (TJ Aug. 9, 1884). [See also Moloney, Thomas, d. Aug. 19, 1885]. [See also Smith, Maggie Maloney, d. Oct. 10, 1884].

SLAUGHTER, JOHN. Died Scott Mountain Jan. 26, 1887; native of Kent, England; aged 24. Brothers John Slaughter, of Etna, and Geo. Slaughter. (TJ Jan. 29, 1887 and Feb. 5, 1887).

SLEEPER, GEO. W. Died Adin, Modoc County, abt Nov. 17, 1885 [no age given]; went to Adin 4 years ago from Shasta County; elected Justice of Peace; (Shasta Co. *Democrat*). (TJ Dec. 5, 1885).

SLEETH, CHARLES A. Died Red Bluff, Tehama, CA Sept. 27, 1881; buried Red Bluff; mined in Trinity County 1853-1857; later ran a pack train from Red Bluff to Weaverville. (TJ Oct. 1, 1881).

SLOAN, CHARLES. Died Long Ridge township Mar. 27, 1884; native of Mt. Vernon, Ohio, aged 58 years; came to Weaverville 1850s; married & had a family; moved to Humboldt County, then to Southern Trinity. (TJ Apr 5, 1884).

SLOAN, CHARLES WILSON. Died Eureka, Humboldt Co. Sept 5, 1895; b. Weaverville Sept 3, 1860; moved to Humboldt Co. with parents 1868; lived at Garberville; unmarried; leaves mother, sister Mrs. Burgess, both of Blocksburg, younger brother residing at Siskiyou Co.; from Eureka *Times* Sept 5, 1895. (TJ Sat. Sept 14, 1895 p 3 col 2).

SLOAN, JOHN. Died Weaverville May 30, 1861, aged 3 mo 16 days; infant son of Charles and Ellen Sloan. (TJ June 8, 1861). [born Weaverville Feb. 4, 1861; TJ births].

SLOAN, JAMES. "James Sloan had neck broken from fall from horse on way from Idaho to Virginia, Nevada, recently; formerly lived on Canon Creek, Trinity County." (TJ Dec. 15, 1866). [1860 census: age 28, miner, born Missouri; James A. Sloan].

SLONEKER, MARK. Fell in Battle of South Mountain Gap with the Union Army; left Sardine Bar for eastern home 18 months ago. (TJ Dec. 1, 1862). [not on 1860 census].

SMALL, THOMAS. Died Lewiston, Idaho Territory, Aug. 1, 1878; aged 60; left here nearly 20 years ago. (TJ Aug. 17, 1878 and Oct. 19, 1878 p 3 col 1).

SMILEY, JOHN WESLEY. Died Weaverville Nov. 12, 1881; native of Penn; aged 43 yr; Sheriff of Trinity County. Bur. Nov. 14, 1881 Masonic Cem. Weaverville; came to Trinity Co abt 1861 from Yreka, Siskiyou Co. (TJ Nov. 19, 1881).

SMITH, _____. Died Cox's Bar Jan. 19, 1860, infant daughter of John and _____ Smith. (TJ Jan. 28, 1860). [1860 Census, Aug 10, 1860: Smith, John B., age 29, rancher; b. N.Hampshire; Cox Bar; Smith, Rebecca W., age 33, b. N.Hampshire. Smith, Abner A. age 4, b. N.Hampshire].

SMITH, _____. Died Hay Fork Oct. 13, 1888, infant son of Mr. and Mrs. Joseph Smith. (TJ Nov. 3, 1888). [Not in 1880 census].

SMITH, ASA. Drowned in creek near Chas. Fenton's place about March 5, 1890; body recovered. (TJ Apr. 5, 1890). [Not on 1880 census].

SMITH, CLARA. Accidentally killed near Junction City Oct. 8, 1892, native of Trinity Co. CA, aged 5 yr 10 mo 13 days; bur. Odd Fellows Cem. Weaverville Oct. 9, 1892; only child of Mr. and Mrs. J. W. Smith; thrown from a buckboard. (TJ Sat. Oct. 15, 1892). [Trin. Co. Mar. Book I page 54 - Married in Weaverville Dec. 29, 1885, Joseph William Smith and Miss Christina Lorenz]. [see also Lorenz].

SMITH, CHRIS R. Died at Readings Creek (near Douglas City) Sept 18, 1895; native of Calif. aged 14 yr; son of Abial W. and Alma Smith. (TJ Sat. Sept 28, 1895 p 2).

SMITH, DAVID D. Died Douglas City Nov. 19, 1885; native of Maine, aged 26 yr; nephew of John W. Smith, Esq. of Douglas City; bur. Weaverville Cem. Nov. 20, 1885. (TJ Nov. 21, 1885) (See also TJ Nov. 19, 1892). ["Sacred to the Memory of David D. Smith born Aug 19, 1859; departed this life Nov 19, 1885. In God We Trust." Gravestone in Weaverville Cem. standing in 1988.]

SMITH, E. Drowned in Wilson Creek, Long Ridge, 2 miles east of the Horse ranch, Apr. 15, 1890. (TJ May 10, 1890). [Index to Deaths 1873-1890 adds white, female, married]. No further information.

SMITH, FRANK. Died at Harrison Gulch "last week"; of Hay Fork; aged 31 yr. (TJ Apr 14, 1900 pg 3 col 5).

SMITH, HATTIE. Died Junction City Dec. 8, 1884; native of Trinity County, aged about 16 years; dau. of John F. Smith. (TJ Dec. 13, 1884).

SMITH, HEZEKIAH. Died East Fork, Trinity Co. Oct. 16, 1894; native of Ohio, aged about 68 yr. (TJ Oct 20, 1894, pg 2 & pg 3 col 3; Oct 27, 1894 p 3).

SMITH, JAMES G. Died Weaverville Dec. 7, 1873; native of Anson, Maine, aged about 44 years; came Weaverville 1852. Bur. Dec. 8, 1873 Weaverville Cem. by Beacon Lodge #300, Good Templars. (TJ Dec. 13, 1873). [Index to Deaths 1873-1890 adds white, male, single].

SMITH, JOEL D. Died Red Bluff, Tehama Co. Mar. 25, 1873, native of Maine, aged 36 yr. (TJ Mar. 29, 1873).

SMITH, JOHN WENTWORTH. Died Hay Fork at the res. of Wm. Farmer, Dec. 29, 1891; native of Cornville, Somerset Co., Maine; aged 66 yr 11 mo; never married; came to Trinity Co. 1854 with brother Nathaniel; survived by brothers Clark, Nat, Sam, and Josiah; all but Josiah res. of Trinity Co. at one time. (TJ Jan. 2, 1892 p2 & obit p 3; obit. entire col 2; worth copying.) TJ Nov. 19, 1892 p 3 col 1: "The remains of John W. Smith were brought in from Hay Fork Nov. 17, 1892 and interred by the side of his nephew, David Smith, in the Public Cem. Weaverville; temporarily buried at the Farmer ranch last winter. A tomb stone will be erected to mark the last resting place of deceased, a pioneer of Trinity County." [marker still legible 1980; marker adds "b. 29 Jan 1825"].

SMITH, JONATHAN. Died Indian Creek, Trinity Co. Nov 25, 1894; native of Penn., aged abt 66 yr; bur. Weaverville Cem.; came to Calif. from Johnstown, PA in early 1850s; at one time partner in mining of Sheriff James Bowie. (TJ Sat. Dec. 1, 1894). [see also Bowie].

SMITH, LUCIUS B. Uncle of C. W. Smith; died age 82, leaving sister Sophronia H., 87, E. Vernon 84, Edwin N. 80; Julia M. 73, Albert M. 71. No place given. (TJ Sat. Feb. 13, 1892 p 3 col 2).

SMITH, MAGGIE MALONEY. Died Eagle Creek, Shasta Co., Oct. 10, 1884; native of County Tipperary, Ireland, aged 25 yr. Wife of Daniel L. Smith. Bur. Catholic Cem. Weaverville Oct. 11, 1884. Uncle: Patrick Slattery; sister Mrs. B. S. Guptill. (TJ Oct. 18, 1884).

SMITH, MARGARET. Died Aug. 25, 1906 Weaverville; age 72, female, white, born Ireland; informant Henry Smith. [Index to Deaths 1890-1908].

SMITH, MICHAEL. Died Weaverville Mar 9, 1897; native of Ireland, aged abt 72 yr; came from Ireland to New York, to Trinity Co. 1857; miner; leaves bro. in Penn.; bur. Catholic Cem. Mar 10, 1897. (TJ Mar 13, 1897 p 2 & p 3 col 3).

SMITH, ROLLIN. Born Dec. 1816 New York. Died after June 5, 1900 (1900 census). Buried in Ca_on City Cem.; no marker. (Map of Ca_on City Cemetery 1989). [Prob. Smith, Roland (sic), d.Mar 26, 1911, age 96 yr; TJ Jan 1912].

SMITH, ROLLIN H. Died Carbondale, Penn. Jan. 19, 1888; buried with Masonic honors. Father: Rollin Smith, Esq. of Canon Creek, Trinity Co., Cal. (TJ Feb. 18, 1888 p 3)

SMITH, SIDNEY. Died Stockton, San Joaquin Co., Nov. 22, 1873; native of England, aged about 37 yr. (TJ Nov. 29, 1873). [Index to Deaths 1873-1890 adds: white, male, married].

SMITH, THOMAS DAVID. Died Hay Fork Nov. 3, 1890; native of Scotland, aged about 64 yr. (TJ Nov. 15, 1890). [Index to Deaths 1890-1908 adds: white, male, married].

SNIDER, HENRY. Died Weaverville June 26, 1882; native of New Brunswick, aged 55 yr. Bur. Weav. Cem. June 27, 1882. One child, 13, residing with her uncle C. W. Long at Eureka, Humboldt Bay. (TJ July 1, 1882).

SNOW, JAMES O. Died Lewiston Aug. 29, 1875; native of New York, aged 48 yr. (TJ Sept. 4, 1875). [Prob. bur. Lewiston Pioneer Cem.]

SNYDER, _____. Died Junction City Feb. 6, 1866, infant son of Henry R. and Catherine Snyder. (TJ Feb. 17, 1866 p 2).

SOHM, J. G., Mrs. Died Sohm's ranch near Trinity Center abt Nov. 1877. (TJ Dec. 1, 1877). [1870 census: Sohm, John G. age 36, b. Austria. Sohm, Margaret, age 39, born France].

SOHRT, HERMAN. Died Germany abt Nov. 1886. "Old Trinitarians will remember Mr. Sohrt as a member of the old-time Turner Bar Company." (TJ Dec. 4, 1886). [see also Paulsen].

SOTO, PEDRO. Died near Weaverville May 8, 1868; native of Mexico, aged about 35 years. (TJ May 16, 1868 p 2).

SOULE, CHARLES N. Died San Francisco May 20, 1885, aged 58 yr. In 1850s, prosperous trader and rancher at Texas Bar. Returned to Wisconsin 1863; married; came to S.F. with family 2 years ago. Brother E. Soule in wagon-making business in San Francisco. (TJ May 30, 1885).

SOULE, E. G. Died Westport, Point., Mass. Jan. 2, 1869; one time res. of Steiner's Flat, Trinity County. (TJ Feb. 13, 1869 p.3).

SOUTHERN, CORNELIUS. Died Bolt's Hill, Trinity County, Feb. 11, 1874; native of Virginia, aged about 49 years. (TJ Feb. 21, 1874). [Index to Deaths 1873-1890 adds: Bolt's Hill [near Lewiston], stockraiser, white, male].

SOWDEN, JAMES. Died in landslide on Oregon Mtn. near Weaverville Mar. 7, 1890; native of England, aged 33 yr; unmarried; bur. Mar. 9, 1890 Odd Fellows Cem. Weaverville. (brother of John). (TJ Mar. 15, 1890, story p.3 col 2-3; Memorium p. 3). [Index to Deaths 1873-1890 adds male, single].

SOWDEN, JOHN. Died in landslide on Oregon Mtn. near Weaverville Mar. 7, 1890; native of England, aged 48 yr; leaves wife in England; bur. Mar. 9, 1890 Odd Fellows Cem. Weaverville. (brother of James). (TJ Mar. 15, 1890; see above for other details.) [Index to Deaths 1873-1890 adds white, male, married].

SPAHR, WILLIAM L. Died Booneville, Missouri May 17, 1896; married with 3 children; was a tinner for Max Lang of Weaverville about 18 years ago. (TJ Jun 6, 1896 p 3).

SPENCER, -----, Lt. Died at Hoopa Valley May 23, 1876 "from wounds inflicted by the robber, Bosqui, now in jail in Eureka." (TJ June 3, 1876 p 2).

SPENCER, M. Dr. Died Tucson, Arizona bef. Oct 16, 1896; came to Weaverville in 1850s or early 1860s, later res. Hydesville, Humboldt Co; age 70; leaves wife, daughter, and sons. (TJ Oct 24, 1896 p 3 col 5).

SPENCER, S. Died French Gulch, Shasta Co. Jun 1897; age abt 62 yr; carpenter; of Sacramento; was prospecting at Trinity Center with John Wilson and Brown Rawles. (TJ Jun 26, 1897 p 3).

SPIEGELBERG, HENRY. Died Stockton, San Joaquin Co, Mar. 13, 1877; native of Mecklenberg, Schwerin, Germany, aged 60 yr. (TJ Mar. 17, 1877 and Apr. 7, 1877).

SPRAGUE, MARSHALL C. Died near Junction City Jun 16, 1898; b. Hillsdale, Michigan, age 45 yr 6 mo 29 dy; came to Trinity Co. abt 10 years ago; leaves a wife and one dau. Lilian. Bur. Weaverville Cem. Jun 18, 1898. (TJ Sat Jun 18, 1898 p 2 & p 3 col 2).

SPRAGUE, MARY E., Mrs. Died at Whitmore's Saw Mill (on Oregon Mountain), Jul 22, 1897; native of New York aged abt 61 yr; m. M. C. Sprague 1872; bur. Weaverville Cem. Jul 23, 1897. (TJ Jul 24, 1897).

SPRATT, CHARLES CLIFTON. Died Douglas City Sep 30, 1894; native of Calif. aged 3 mo 7 days; inf. son of Dr. and Mrs. C. W. Spratt. (TJ Oct 6, 1894 p 2).

SPRATT, EARLE CRAWFORD. Died Douglas City Feb 12, 1894; native of Calif. aged 1 yr 3 mo 8 dy; son of Dr. and Mrs. Charles W. Spratt. (TJ Sat. Feb. 17, 1894).

SPRATT, WILLIAM C. Died Bangor, Maine Jan 19, 1899; b. in China, Missouri Dec 24, 1826; in 1853 m. Christiana Crawford; 4 sons & 2 dau; father of C. W. Spratt of Douglas City, Trinity Co. Calif. (from the Bangor, Maine *Weekly Commercial*). (TJ Sat Feb 11, 1899 p 3 col 3).

SPRINGSTED, HARVEY. Died near Lewiston Apr 1, 1897; native of Onandago Co., NY, aged abt 77 yr. (TJ Apr 10, 1897 p 2).

STACKPOLE, FINNIS MARY. Died March 2, 1907 Weaverville, age 1 month, female, white, American; buried Weaverville. [Index to Deaths 1890-1908].

STADTLANDER, CORNELIUS. Died near Junction City Jan. 21, 1885; native of Holland, aged about 67 yr. (TJ Jan. 31, 1885).

STAFFORD, ALBERT. Died San Francisco Oct. 31, 1893; born Winston, Forsythe Co. North Carolina 1850; bur. Laurel Hill Cem., San Francisco; nephew of J. A. Stafford of Hay fork and H. F. Stafford of Deadwood; came to Calif. 1875. (TJ Sat. Nov. 18, 1893 p 3 col 5).

STAFFORD, A., Mrs. Died Sep 20, 1900; aged 55 yr; b. Indian Territory. (TJ Jan 1901).

STAFFORD, HENRY FRANKLIN. Died Hay Fork Dec 20, 1899; native of North Carolina, aged abt 69 yr; leaves bro. J. A. Stafford, of Hay Fork. (TJ Dec 23, 1899 p 2 & p 3 col 6).

"Stage Robber, Unknown". Shot and Killed Oct. 24, 1876; first robbery. Shasta County Coroner held inquest at Tower House. (TJ Oct. 28, 1876).

STANMORE, JAMES. Died at Ruch's Ranch, Hay Fork Feb. 9, 1858; native of England, age 39. (TJ Feb. 20, 1858).

STARKE, HENRY. Died Brown's Creek June 5, 1880; native of Germany, aged about 60 years. "One of survivors of Stevenson Regiment; arrived San Francisco Mar. 7, 1847. Private in Captain Seymour G. Steele's Company." (TJ June 12, 1880).

STARR, AUGUSTUS. Died Polk Street, San Francisco Oct 12, 1891; no age given; no known relatives. He was teaming near Weaverville 1860s; went to San Francisco in 1867; G.A.R. (TJ Sat. Apr 28, 1894 p 3 col 3, long article; "died 3-1/2 years ago"). [1860 census says age 24, native of Maryland, operates a livery stable].

STEDMAN, ROBERT. Died abt April 1875 San Rafael, [Marin Co.]; left here abt 1858. Old Settler of Indian Creek, opposite mouth of Spring Gulch; leaves son Stephen. (TJ May 1, 1875 p 3).

STEELE, S.G., Capt. Died San Diego, [San Diego Co.] Feb. 5, 1887; age 70 years of age. "Came to Calif. in command of a company of Col. Stevenson's Regiment. Came to Trinity Co. 25 years ago [abt 1862], left soon after, finally settling in San Diego; m. 1870 Miss Mary A. Harvey (sister of Mrs. S. I. Thayer) who survives him." (TJ Feb. 19, 1887 p 3). [see also Starke, above]. [see also Harvey, Thayer, McCully].

STEEN, MOSES. Died Mineral Park, Mohave Co., Arizona Mar. 30, 1884. Adobe house collapsed, killed Steen, Mrs. Steen, and dau. Nellie Trask Steen. Dau. Mabel, age 3 and son Henry, age 8, survived. (TJ Apr. 12, 1884, p. 3).

STEEN, MOSES, Mrs. Died Mineral Park, Mohave Co., Arizona Mar 30, 1884; native of Trinity Co., Cal., step-daughter of Thomas Baker of Lewiston. (See Steen, Moses.) (TJ Apr. 12, 1884). [not in 1860, 1870, 1880 census; no further information].

STEEN, NELLIE TRASK. Died Mineral Park, Mohave Co., Arizona Mar. 30, 1884; born Trinity Co., Calif. (See Steen, Moses). (TJ Apr. 12, 1884).

STEPHENS, THOMAS. Died Deadwood Nov 18, 1899; native of England, age abt 69 yr; buried at Deadwood. (TJ Nov 25, 1899 p 2 & p 3 col 3).

STEPHENSON, NELSON. Died Weaverville May 29, 1883; native of Ohio, aged 61 yr. (TJ June 2, 1883).

STERLING, JOHN, Mr. Instantly killed in his mining claim on Smith's Flat, Trinity River [nr.Douglas City], June 1, 1861; native of Schuyler, Herkimer Co.,

New York. Buried Weaverville Cem. June 2, 1861. (TJ June 8, 1861). [1860 census: age 40]. [see partners Young & T.E. Jones].

STERLING, FRANK, Mr. Drowned in Sacramento River at Red Bluff, Tehama Co. July 1861. Candidate of the American party of Trinity County for the Assembly in 1858. (TJ July 20, 1861 p 2 col 2; DCG July 24, 1861; Red Bluff (CA) *Beacon*, abt July 14, 1861).

STEVENSON, JOHN A. Died San Francisco [San Francisco Co.], Apr 5, 1866; native of Vermont, aged about 48 yr; late of Canon Creek, Trinity Co. (TJ Apr 14, 1866 p 2).

STEWART, JAMES, Mr. Killed in mining claim on Oregon Gulch, prob. before Mar. 29, 1861 when body was found; native of Belfast, Ireland, age between 35-40 years. Bur. Weaverville Cem. Mar. 30, 1861. (TJ Apr 6, 1861). [Not on 1860 census].

STEWART, JOSEPH A. Died Arkansas Hot Springs [no state given] abt Apr. 1889; age about 63 yr; married. (TJ June 1, 1889 p 3).

STEWART, WILLIAM. Died Weaverville Apr. 13, 1857, aged about 55 years. Res. Trinity Co. past 2-3 years. Came to Calif. in 1850 from Bethany, Brooks County, Virginia. (TJ Apr. 18, 1857 p 2).

STIERLEN, JOHN FREDERICK. Died Weaverville Jan. 23, 1867; native of Wurtemburg, Germany, aged about 42 years. (TJ Jan. 26, 1867 p 2).

STIERLEN, SUSANNAH. Died Weaverville Mar. 16, 1865; aged 8 mo 15 days; daughter of Fred. and Madora Stierlen. (TJ Mar. 18, 1865). [Born Weaverville July 1, 1864; TJ Births]. [Note: Mrs. Stierlen was also known as Dorothea S., Dorothy, and Dora. As Mrs. Dorothy Graffelman, form. of New York, she married (2) Stierlen in Weaverville Mar. 31, 1863; she married (3) Fred L. Lachenmacher in Weaverville Mar. 16, 1867. According to the 1870 census, she was age 33, born Hanover. She and Fred Lachenmacher had 2 children: Emma C., age 2, and Bertha D., age 1. Not in 1880 census.] [See also Lackenmacher and Dralle].

STILLER, ALBERT J. Died Weaverville Dec. 19, 1871, aged 3 mo 9 day. Inf. son of Alexander and Louisa Stiller. (TJ Dec. 23, 1871 p 2). [Born Sept. 10, 1871 Weaverville. TJ Births]. [Name from grave marker in Odd Fellows Cem. Weaverville].

STILLER, ALEXANDER ANDREW. Died Weaverville Oct. 30, 1890; native of Dantzic, Prussia; aged about 61 year. Came to U.S. - Philadelphia - 1847, California 1849, Shasta 1851, Trinity County, at Evans Bar 1858. Bur. Odd Fellows Cem. Weav. Nov. 1, 1890. long obit. (TJ Nov. 1, 1890). [Index to Deaths 1890-1908: Stiller, A.A., adds white, male, married].

STILLER, ALEXANDER FREDERICK. Died at Evans Bar (on the Trinity River between Douglas City and Junction City) Aug. 15, 1861, aged 1 year 10 months 5 days. Oldest son of Alex. and Louisa Stiller. Shasta *Courier* please copy. (DCG Aug. 21, 1861). (Also incomplete listing TJ Aug. 17, 1861 p 2). [Born Oct. 11, 1859, Evans Bar. TJ Births]. [Marker in I.O.O.F. Cemetery, Weaverville].

STILLER, AUGUSTA L. Died Dec. 10, 1899. Born Weaverville Aug. 4, 1857. [Rita Hanover's Trinity County Births]. [Marker in I.O.O.F. Cemetery, Weaverville.] (see below for more details).

STILLER, AUGUSTA LOUISA. Died Weaverville Dec 10, 1899; native of Calif. aged 42 yr 4 mo 6 dy; dau. of late A. A. and Louisa J. Stiller; long obit, worth copying; as "Miss Gussie Stiller", she was a member of the "JOURNAL force", an important member of the staff of the TRINITY JOURNAL. (TJ Dec 16, 1899 p 2 & p 3 col 3).

STILLER, FREDERICK ANDREW. Died Evans Bar May 13, 1865, aged 3 mo 28 days. Son of Alex. and Louisa Stiller. (TJ May 20, 1865). [see note above; born Evans Bar Jan. 15, 1865. TJ Births]. [Marker in I.O.O.F. Cem. Weaverville.]

STILLER, JOHN. Born May 1856 Prussia (Germany). Died after June 11, 1900. Miner at Trinity Center in 1900 Census. Also on 1860 Census with parents Alexander and Louisa Stiller. May be in grave in Odd Fellows Cemetery, Weaverville with a mosaic marker, but no name. [see Deaths 1900-1950].

STILLER, LOUISA. (Mother). Born 1827 Wurtemburg, Germany; died Dec 29, 1901; may be in unmarked grave between the markers of Frederick and Matilda in Odd Fellows Cemetery, Weaverville. [see Deaths 1900-1950]. [see also Montague].

STILLER, MARY. Marker in I.O.O.F. Cemetery, Weaverville: "Age 22 years". Daughter of Richard W. Stiller and Mary F. Montague, b. Weaverville Nov. 30, 1889. [TJ Births and 1900 census]. [prob. died in 1911].

STILLER, MATILDA "TILLIE" P., Miss. Died Red Bluff, Tehama Co., CA June 9, 1884; born Weaverville Sept. 4, 1858, aged 25 yr 9 mo 4 days. Daughter of Alexander A. and Louisa Stiller. Bur. Odd Fellows Cem. Weaverville, "next to 5 children of same parents". Leaves father and mother, sister Gussie L. Stiller, brothers Richard W. Stiller and Chas. E. Stiller. long obit. p 3. (TJ June 14, 1884). (Marker in I.O.O.F. Cemetery, Weaverville.)

STILLER, RAYMOND W. Born Dec. 13, 1898. Died Oct. 23, 1904. [Son of Richard W. Stiller and Mary F. Montague. Information from marker in Odd Fellows Cem., Weaverville.] [see Deaths 1900-1950].

STILLER, RICHARD W. Born July 16, 1862; Died June 5, 1903. Information from marker in Odd Fellows Cem., Weaverville. [1900 census: Treasurer, Trinity County, California].

STILLER, THEODORE. Died Junction City Apr. 29, 1869, age 9 years. Son of Alexander Stiller. (TJ May 1, 1869 p 2). [Born Evans Bar Dec. 28, 1860. TJ Births]. [Marker in I.O.O.F Cemetery, Weaverville].

STILLER, WILLIAM DAVID. Died Evans Bar Aug. 1, 1866, aged 3 mo 21 days. Son of Alex. and Louisa Stiller. (TJ Aug. 4, 1866 p 2). [Born Apr. 10, 1866 at Evans Bar. TJ Births. Marker in I.O.O.F. Cem. Weaverville].

STILWELL, WILLIAM M. Died Aug 10, 1903 Douglas City; age 77, male, white, American; bur. Public Cem., Weaverville. [Index to Deaths 1890-1908].

STITTS, JACKSON. Died Greenhorn Gulch near Minersville Apr 12, 1892; native of Ireland, aged about 70 yr. (TJ Sat. Apr 23, 1892 p 3 col 2).

STODDARD, MARY ROSALIE. Died at New York House, Trinity County, north of Trinity Center Aug. 4, 1885, aged 5 yr 5 mo 28 days. Born Jan. 6, 1880. Daughter of John R. and Inez Stoddard. (TJ Aug. 8 and Aug. 15, 1885).

STONE, CLARA. Died Petrolia, Humboldt Co. Dec. 29, 1875; age 16 years; dau. of Mr. and Mrs. R. M. Stone. (TJ Jan. 15, 1876 p 2).

STONE, JOHN. Died Weaverville Dec 3, 1894; native of Germany, aged abt 77 yr. (TJ Sat. Dec 8, 1894 p 2).

STOREY, GRACE ALICE. Died May 7, 1908 Trinity Center, age 22, female, white, born Calif. (buried Trinity Center Cem.). [Index to Deaths 1890-1908].

STOTTS, BOBBIE. Died Williams, Colusa Co., abt Jun 1, 1881, aged about 8 years. "The horse he was riding fell upon him; visited Weaverville about 2 years ago." (TJ June 11, 1881 p 3).

STRASEN, MARTIN. Killed in a mining claim at Junction City Feb. 10, 1871; native of Prussia, aged 31 yr. Bur. Weaverville Cem. by German Hospital Society. (TJ Feb. 18, 1871 pp 2 & 3).

STRODE, JAMES McGOWAN. Died Weaverville Aug 5, 1894; native of Kentucky, aged abt 70 yr. (TJ Sat. Aug 11, 1894 p 2).

STROUP, MARY J., Mrs. Died at the Oak Lawn House, Cottonwood, Tehama Co., Aug. 15, 1860; form. of Trinity County. (TJ Sept. 1, 1860).

STOUT, JOSEPH. Died Lewiston Feb. 17, 1898; native of Illinois, aged 42 yr 4 mo 27 dy. (TJ Sat. Feb 26, 1898 p 2).

STOUT, JOSEPH, Mrs. Died Lewiston Jun 3, 1898; native of Ohio, aged abt 39 yr. (TJ Jun 4, 1898).

STUART, ROBERT GIFFEN. Died Olympia, Wash. Jun 16, 1891; came to Trin. Co. Sept. 1850; worked in father's store [Matthew Stuart - built the first building in Weaverville], on the site of the market now kept by J. C. O'Neil. Born Mar. 12, 1825, Knox Co. Ohio. *Olympian* June 17, 1891; (TJ Sat. July 11, 1891.) [See Hicks, Patricia, Some Called It `Weaver' for the story of Matthew Stuart and his son Robert.]

STUDDIN, JOHN. Died Weaverville Dec. 8, 1872; native of England, aged 51 yr. (TJ Dec. 14, 1872).

STURDIVANT, JOSEPH ALLEN. Died near Junction City Jan 26, 1895; native of Georgia, aged abt. 81 yr; b. 1813; bur. Masonic Cem. Weaverville, Jan 28, 1895; known as "Uncle Joe" Sturdivant; owned Sturdivant Ranch, now owned by W. C. Given; came to Trinity Co. 1850/51. long obit. p 3. (TJ Sat. Feb 2, 1895).

SULLIVAN, D. Died East Fork Aug 23, 1899; native of Ireland, aged abt 59 yr. (TJ Aug 26, 1899 p 2).

SULLIVAN, DANIEL W. Died "recently" in Texas; former res. of Junction City. (TJ Feb. 22, 1873 p 3).

SUMMERS, GEORGE. Died Lewiston Mar 6, 1896; native of Indiana, aged abt 65 yr. (TJ Sat Mar 7, 1896).

SUSAND, NATHANIEL C. Died San Francisco (San Francisco Co.), Feb. 9, 1888; came to Weaverville 1884; Palace Barber Shop. Leaves mother Elizabeth Susand of Bay City, Michigan. (TJ Feb. 11 and 18, 1888).

SUTTON, NEWTON. Died Weaverville Mar 17, 1896; native of Indiana, aged abt 66 yr; one of the pioneers of Trinity Co; resident of Lewiston for many years. (TJ Sat Mar 21, 1896).

SWEENY, M. J. Died Red Bluff, Tehama Co., Feb. 11, 1890, age 27 years. Brother of Edward Sweeny, attorney, of Redding, Shasta Co. (TJ Feb. 22, 1890).

SWIFT, EDWARD D. Died Jan. 29, 1907 Weaverville; age 76, male, white, American; buried Weaverville. [Index to Deaths 1890-1908].

TAYLOR, ASA. Died July 1, 1878 in San Francisco; native of New York City; aged 51; pioneer Californian, resident of Trinity County upwards of 20 years; late County Clerk. Buried in The City (San Francisco) Cemetery. Leaves married sister in Pamrapo, New Jersey. (TJ July 6 & 13, 1878, p. 3).

TAYLOR, JAMES. Died April 1865, Trinity County, California. (TJ Apr. 22, 1865, note on page 2.) [no age given].

TEBBE, HENRY H. Drowned in Canyon Creek Mar. 9, 1877; native of Germany, aged 53 years. (TJ Mar. 17, 1877).

TEBO, C. F. Died Lewiston Jan 17, 1899, aged abt 45 yr; newcomer to Trinity County; came to Lewiston from Oregon abt 10 months ago; leaves a wife in Portland, Ore. (TJ Jan 21, 1899 p 2 & p 3 col 3).

TEMPLE, A. J. Died July 9, 1904 Weaverville; about 40, male, white, birthplace unknown; buried Public Cemetery, Weaverville. [Index to Deaths 1890-1904].

TEMPLETON, _____, Mrs. Died Hay Fork May 13, 1860; aged about 35 years; wife of Benj. Templeton. (TJ May 19, 1860) [1860 census, taken in July 1860, lists Benj. S. Templeton, age 30, farmer, born Ohio].

TERRY, WM. S. "Killed by Indians about 2 weeks ago at Taylor's Flat" (died abt Sept. 5, 1863). Buried near Cox's Bar; brother in Hayfork. (TJ Sept 19, 1863 p 2, col 1.).

TESTY, EDDIE. Killed by a caving bank in a mining claim near Weaverville Feb. 22, 1873, aged 9 yr 9 mo 6 days; born Weaverville May 17, 1863; son of Mr. and Mrs. Jos. Testy; buried Weaverville Cem. Feb. 23, 1873. (TJ Mar. 1, 1873 p 2). [Index to Deaths 1873-1890 adds "crushed by a caving bank; male, single, born Calif."]

TESTY, JOSEPH EDWARD. Died Weaverville Dec. 12, 1875; aged 14 yr 7 days; son of Joseph and Sarah Testy; born Weaverville Dec. 5, 1861. (TJ Dec. 18, 1875).

TESTY, JOSEPH T. Died near Weaverville Oct. 14, 1892; native of New York, aged about 68 yr; miner; leaves widow & 3 children. (TJ Sat. Oct. 8, 1892).

THACKER, WILLIAM. Died Red Bluff, Tehama, CA Nov. 24, 1876; native of Texas, aged 27 yr 10 mo 14 days; son of Mrs. Harriet Browder of Weaverville. (TJ Dec. 2, 1876 p 2). [see also Browder].

THAYER, GEO. F. "Died in the service of our country; member of the Douglas City Rifles." (TJ June 3, 1865). [1860 Census: res. Ferry Bar (on Trinity River, near Douglas City); age 23, miner, born Mass.]

THEDE, GUSTAVE. Died abt Sept. 18, 1890 Bishop, Inyo Co.; native of Germany, aged abt 65 years; left here 1871/2 for Virginia City, Nev. (TJ Oct. 4, 1890 p 3 col 4). [Trinity County Marriages Book H page 87: Gustave Thede and Miss Catherine Weckman m. Canon City Mar. 28, 1863].

THOMAS, _____. Died New River (area of Denny) Aug. 15, 1879, aged 5 years; daughter of R. L. Thomas. (TJ Aug. 23, 1879).

THOMAS, _____. Died New River Aug. 16, 1879, aged 9 yr 6 mo; daughter of R. L. Thomas. (TJ Aug. 23, 1879). [Note: this was probably Martha, who was 5 months old on the 1870 Census, Aug. 12, 1870. Parents were Robert L. Thomas and his wife Betsy Baker; see Trinity Co. Marriages Book H p 185. They lived at North Fork in 1870; there were several children].

THOMAS, _____, Mrs. Died suddenly at Lodi, San Joaquin Co. Aug. 12, 1880; wife of Nathan H. Thomas. (TJ Aug. 21, 1880, p 3). [See also Phillip Thomas]. [1870 Census: Nathan H. Thomas, age 49, miner, b. Penn. Cornelia Thomas, age 35, b. N.Y. Not in Trinity Co. Marriages].

THOMAS, CHARLES. Died Weaverville Feb 11, 1897; b. Crown Point, NY Mar 2, 1809, aged 87 yr 11 mo 9 dy; fam. moved to Vermont 1812, then to Calhoun Co, Mich., then Hartford, Conn, then to Hawkins Ferry, Vir.; left there for Calif, arriving in San Francisco Feb 28, 1852; architect and master builder; arr. Trinity Co. Apr 20, 1855; built the Catholic Church destroyed by fire last Aug., the McCain & McClure bldg., the old Tinnin & Owen store, the drug store and the Davidson dwelling house; (Thomas') Theater 1859; Todd's hall; in 1880 the Sunday School building which was burned in 1889; m. Apr 16, 1867 at Windsor, Conn., Miss Harriet Parker; two sons, both deceased; bur. Weaverville Cem. Feb 12, 1897 under auspices of Old Settlers Assn. (TJ Feb 12, 1897 p 2 & p 3 col 2).

THOMAS, DAVID CROCKETT. Died Junction City Dec. 16, 1886; native of Ohio, aged about 61 years; bur. Weav. Cem. Dec. 17, 1886; early resident of Trinity County. (TJ Dec. 18, 1886).

THOMAS, JOHN. Died Weaverville Dec. 27, 1882; native of Sweden, aged about 55 yr. (TJ Jan. 6, 1883 p 2).

THOMAS, PHILLIP. Died Douglas City Jun 1, 1871; native of Wales, aged about 84 years; father of N. H. and D. C. Thomas. (TJ June 3, 1871 p 2). [gravestone in Old Section, Weaverville Cemetery; photographed 1986; stone says "80 years"].

THOMAS, RICHARD A., Dr. Died Weaverville June 28, 1867; native of Cambridge, Guernsey County, Ohio, aged 41 yr 7 mo 14 days; graduated Penn. Medical University 1850; lived Athens, MO 1851-55; Weav. 1856-1867; leaves widow and orphan. (TJ July 6, 1867 p 2 col 3). [not in Trinity County Marriages; widow not apparent in 1870 census].

THOMPSON, CHARLES FREDERICK. Died Weaverville Dec. 6, 1893; native of Prussia, aged abt 85 yr. (TJ Sat. Dec. 16, 1893).

THOMPSON, CHAUNCEY. Died Weaverville Jan. 21, 1884; native of New York; aged 57 years. (TJ Jan. 26, 1884).

THOMPSON INFANT. Stillborn; born, died, Feb. 16, 1908 Weaverville; female, white. [Index to Deaths 1890-1908].

THOMPSON, JOHN. Died Lewiston Feb. 18, 1885; native of New York; aged about 54 years. (TJ Feb. 28, 1885).

THOMPSON, JOSEPH SPROUL. Died at Big Flat, on the South Fork of the Salmon River July 30, 1868; aged 63 years. (TJ Aug. 22, 1868 p 2).

THOMPSON, SOPHIE, Mrs. Died near Junction City Jan 9, 1898; native of Calif, aged abt 32 yr; dau. of late Peter Verstegen, one of first residents of Junction City; left six children in a destitute condition; Mrs. D. C. Dedrick has taken charge of one of the children; the other five are temporarily at the County Hospital. (TJ Jan 15, 1898 pp 2 & 3). [see Addendum for more info.] [m. Thomas S. Thompson Mar 17, 1881.] [see also Verstegen].

THOMPSON, R. J. "Died Napa, Napa County, California some time ago; went there 20 months ago; former resident of Trinity County." (TJ Aug. 31, 1878 p 3).

THORN, EDWARD. Died Deadwood, Trinity Co., Sep 30, 1897; native of England, aged abt 38 yr. (TJ Oct 9, 1897 p 3 col 2; correction of "Samuel" Thorn; see below).

THORNE, SAMUEL (sic); actually Edward Thorn. Died Deadwood Sep 30, 1897; native of England, aged abt 36 yr (sic); leaves wife and four children; bur. Lewiston Cem. Oct 2, 1897. (TJ Oct 2, 1897 pp 2 & 3: correction TJ Oct 9, 1897 p 3 col 2).

THORP, L. B. Died Memphis, Tennessee "some months ago"; wife survives him; former resident of Weaverville (TJ June 9 1866 p 2 col 1). [Note: TJ Aug. 19, 1865 p 2 says "L. B. Thorp left Weaverville 4-5 years ago. He has been in Selma, GA for 2 years. In June 1861 he entered the Confederate service as a Captain of Infantry."]

THURSTON, ALBERT. Died Weaverville Nov. 30, 1891; native of Illinois, aged 53 yr. (TJ Sat. Dec. 5, 1891).

THURSTON, JOHN M. Died Weaverville Apr. 12, 1885; native of New York, aged about 70 years. Bur. Weaverville Cem. Apr. 13, 1885. (TJ Apr. 18, 1885).

TICE, JEROME EDWARD. Died Hay Fork Valley July 6, 1867; native of New York, aged 28 years. (TJ July 13, 1867).

TIMMERMAN, ANNA CATHARINA MARIA. "12 Apr 1801 - 9 Nov 1874 aged 73 yr 6 mo 27 days"; double gravestone in Old Section, Weaverville Cem. "erected by their children; peace to their ashes". Standing in good condition 1988.

TIMMERMAN, CARL W. Died Weaverville Nov. 30, 1871; native of Germany, aged about 77 yr. (TJ Dec. 2, 1871 p 2). [Note: buried Old Section, Weaverville Cem. grave marker 1988 "Carl Wilhelm Timmerman 20 Jul 1794 - 28 Nov 1871 aged 77 yr 4 mo 8 dy"]

Tinnen, W. J. Born Jackson, Mississippi 7 Oct 1829; left for Calif. Feb 1850; arrived San Francisco May 20, 1850, Trinity Co. 1851, mining at mouth of Weaver Creek and at Turner's Bar, also at French Gulch; became a partner with brother W. W. Tinnin who opened a hardware store in May 1852; not married in 1858. Cox's Annals, [1940].

TINNEY, JOHN J. Died Shasta, Shasta Co., CA "several days ago" (abt Feb. 1879); former resident of Trinity Co. (TJ Mar. 1, 1879 p 3).

TINSLEY, CHARLIE ALBERT. Died Cox's Bar Sept. 19, 1879; aged 2 yr 9 mo 22 days; son of James and Mary J. Tinsley. (TJ Sep 1879).

TINSLEY, E. S. Died May 01, 1900; age 30 yr 11 mo 17 dy; b. California. (TJ Jan 1901).

TINSLEY, WILLIAM. Drowned in Trinity River near North Fork Oct. 26, 1889; native of Trinity County, aged 29 yr 10 mo; oldest son of Mr. and Mrs. J. A. Tinsley of Cox Bar; unmarried. (TJ Nov. 2 & 9, 1889). [Index to Deaths 1873-1908 adds: male, single, born Calif.].

TINSLEY, W. LLOYD. Died Indian Creek Oct 23, 1899; native of Calif. aged 9 mo 12 dy; son of Mr. and Mrs. J. T. Tinsley. (TJ Oct 28, 1899 p 2).

TISSERANT, FRANK. Died Weaverville Oct. 17, 1876; native of France, aged abt 45 years. (TJ Oct. 21, 1876).

TODD, ALEXANDER. Died Weaverville June 16, 1869; aged 17 years; son of William and Eliza Todd; bur. Weaverville Cem. June 17, 1869. (TJ June 19, 1869 p 2 & 3). [1860 Census says "age 9 born Calif."] [See also William Todd. One note says: "His mother carried him over the mountain from Shasta to Weaverville in July 1851."]
TJ Feb. 3, 1877: "Body of Alexander Todd moved from village cemetery to Catholic grounds; died 8 years ago." Buried next to brother William.

TODD, ELIZA. Died Weaverville Sept 16, 1895; native of Ireland, aged about 67 yr; native of Rush, County of Dublin, Ireland, b. abt 1828; m.n. Eliza **Archbold**; m. William Todd Nov 1849 in New Orleans, LA; 12 children; long obit. worth copying p 3. (TJ Sat. Sept 21, 1895).

TODD, MARY A. Died Jan. 7, 1907 Weaverville, age 51, female, white, American; informant: Louis O. Todd. [Index to Deaths 1890-1908].

TODD, WILLIAM. Died Weaverville Jan. 28, 1877; born Weaverville 1854; age 21 yr 11 mo 11 days; son of William and Eliza Todd. Bur. Catholic Cem., Weaverville. "A large grave was prepared in the Catholic grounds and the two brothers laid side by side." The body of Alexander Todd, died 8 years ago, was moved from the village cemetery to the Catholic grounds. (TJ Feb. 3, 1877 p 2 & 3.) [See also Alexander Todd.]

TODD, WILLIAM. Died Weaverville Apr 8, 1896; aged 82 yr 11 mo 24 dy. b. Houston, County Renfrewshire, Scotland Apr 14, 1813; came to Trinity Co July 1852; m. Eliza Hartford (sic)in New Orleans Nov. 1849; wife died Sep 18, 1895; twelve children: William, Martha, John, Eliza now dead; 2 unnamed infants; and John A. Todd, Mrs. Chas. Creamer, L. O. Todd, E. N. Todd, and Mrs. Earnest Greenwell, all of Weaverville. bur. Catholic Cem, Weaverville Apr 10, 1896. (TJ Sat. Apr 11, 1896).

TODD, GEORGE WASHINGTON. Died Junction City, Trinity County, Calif. Sept. 15, 1878; native of Indiana, aged 47 yr 7 mo; bur. Old Pub. Cem., Weaverville Sept. 16, 1878. (TJ Sept. 21, 1878 p 2). [Not the family of Alexander and William Todd, above; connected with the Day family.]

TODION, LOUIS. Drowned crossing Trinity River at Sailor Bar Mar. 27, 1861; with his partner, both Frenchmen; bodies not found. (TJ Mar. 30, 1861). [Note: 1860 Census says "Tordian, Louis B., Cox Bar, Aug. 10, 1860; age 35, trader, b. Switzerland".]

TOLLEY, JAMES. Died Trinity Valley (near Trinity Center, 1989) Aug. 13, 1868; native of Missouri, aged 61 years; late of Mineral Point, Wisconsin. (TJ Aug. 22, 1868 p 2).

TOLLEY, WM. H. Died Nevada City, Montana Territory Aug. 13, 1867; aged 36 yr 6 mo 6 days; late of Trinity County, Cal. (TJ Sept. 7, 1867 p 2). [1860 Census: Minersville June 15, 1860; age 28; miner; b. Kentucky].

TOMER, HENRY L. Died Weaverville Nov. 27, 1884; native of Virginia, aged about 43 years; res. of Trinity Co. more than 20 years. (TJ Nov. 29, 1884).

TOMPKINS, WINONEY. Died nr Junction City Sep 29, 1896; native of California aged 40 yr 8 mo 28 dy; b. Shasta Co; wife of John M. Tompkins; bur "Foresters" Cem., Junction City; leaves husband and 3 dau: Mrs. D. L. Smith, Mabel and Grace. (TJ Sat Oct 3, 1896; obit p 3 col 6).

TOMS, WILLIAM, Major. Died at China Flat Dec 21, 1897; leaves a wife and 3 sons. (TJ Jan 1, 1898 p 2).

TOOMBS, ALEXANDER. Died Weaverville Jan. 31, 1887; native of Scotland; aged 60 yr; came to Trinity County in 1853. (TJ Feb. 5, 1887).

TOURTELOTTE, FANNIE E. Died Jan. 27, 1908 Weaverville; age 76, female, white, born Connecticut; buried Weaverville; informant: J. F. Tourtelotte. [Index to Deaths 1890-1908]. [see also Bowerman].

TOURTELLOTTE, JOHN B. Died Tower House, Shasta County Oct. 12, 1868; of Minersville, Trinity County; native of Connecticut, aged 33 yr 4 mo 9 days. (TJ Oct. 17, 1868).

TOWER, CHARLES F. Died Nov 30, 1900; age 6 yr 2 mo 28 dy; b. Calif. (TJ Jan 1901).

TOWER, LEVI H. Died San Francisco Nov. 14, 1865; native of Mass; aged 45 years; left Boston Dec. 1848 on ship Edward Everett; became owner of Tower House property, Shasta County 1850; resided there 15 years. (TJ Nov. 14, 1865 p 2).

TRACY, EDWARD W. Died Portland, Oregon July 14, 1866; native of New York; aged about 39 years; brother of Felix Tracy, Esq. Former res. of Shasta County. (TJ July 28, 1866).

TRASK, EDWARD, Dr. Died at sea between San Francisco and Australia on Pacific Mail steamship City of New York before Oct. 24, 1883 (last voyage; buried at sea). He was a resident and practicing physician in Weaverville from 1851 to about 1865; went to Red Bluff, then on Australian line of steamers. Wife Caroline E. and three daughters. (TJ Oct. 27, 1883). [1860 Census says born 1824 Mississippi. Obit. in TJ says native of Mass.] "Valuable Acquisition - The wife and daughter of Dr. Trask, of Weaverville, arrived on the last steamer. Also Harry Seaman, formerly clerk of Trinity County, together with his newly acquired wife, and his mother and sister. We envy Weaverville such acquisitions." *Shasta Courier*; (TJ May 22, 1858).

TRASK, BENJAMIN FRANKLIN. Died Weaverville Aug. 29, 1885; native of State of Maine; age about 52 years. Blacksmith. Bur. Weaverville Cem. Aug. 30, 1885. (TJ Sept. 5, 1885 p 3). [see also Frost.]

TRASK, JAMES. Died Douglas City Mar. 4, 1869; aged 3 yr 6 mo; son of B. F. and L. Trask. (TJ Mar. 6, 1869). Buried in the little cemetery on top of "Graveyard Point", Douglas City, Trinity, California, with his mother Sarah Lena Hood Trask. [Graveyard Point is above the Douglas City Campground, 1998].

TRASK, SARAH LENA (HOOD), "LENA". Died Douglas City March 22, 1869; aged 23 years; (Daughter of Mrs. Elizabeth Hood). (TJ Mar. 27, 1869 p 2; Sept. 5, 1885). Buried in the little cemetery on top of "Graveyard Point", Douglas City, Trinity County, California with her son James. Both died of smallpox. The daughter Minerva and son George Nelson survived their father, B. F. "Frank" Trask. [See also Hays, d. 1851; also buried at Graveyard Point].

TRASK, RUFUS. Died Kennet, Shasta County, CA Oct. 5, 1890; lived San Bernardino for many years; brother of Mrs. W. S. Lowden, of Weaverville. (TJ Oct. 11, 1890 p 3). [see also Lowden].

TREAT, ORRIN. Died Hyampom Dec. 22, 1893; native of New York aged about 57 yr; obit. p 3 col 2. (TJ Sat. Dec. 30, 1893).

TRELOAR, CHARLES. Died Weaverville Mar. 7, 1868; aged 14 months; son of Thomas and Selina Treloar. (TJ Mar. 14, 1868, page 2, column 4, bottom).

TRELOAR, WILLIAM HENRY. Died Weaverville May 31, 1868; aged 5 yr 6 mo; son of Thomas and Selena Treloar. (TJ June 6, 1868 p 2). [b. Weaverville Nov. 18, 1862]. [Note: the 1860 Census spells the name Salina. She and Thomas were born in England. In 1860 he was 28; she was 21].

TRIMBLE, GRANGER. Died nr. Cox Bar Jun 25, 1897; native of Calif. aged abt 17 yr; son of Pierce Trimble. (TJ Jul 10, 1897 p 2 & p 3 col 5).

TRIMBLE, GROVER CLEVELAND. Died Big Flat Aug. 16, 1892, aged 8 yr 1 mo 10 days. p 3 col 5 "A Chapter of Accidents. The little eight year old son of Pierce Trimble at Big Flat was fooling with a pistol last Tuesday, and while looking down the muzzle, pulled the trigger. The boy was killed almost instantly." (TJ Sat. Aug. 20, 1892).

TROMBACH, William, note. "William Trombach, reported killed in a mine explosion in Colorado two years ago, was seen in San Francisco last week." (TJ Feb 13, 1897 p 3).

TRUE, THOMAS. Died Canyon City, Oregon Jan. 3, 1868; formerly of Trinity Center. (TJ Mar. 28, 1868 p 2). [Not in 1860 census].

TRUFANT, DAVID H., Capt. Died Bath, Maine Jul 18, 1897, aged 73 yr 6 mo; came to Weaverville in 1852, carpenter with late S. K. Turner; became a partner with F. A. Buck in the wood business; left Weaverville 1866, Montana for 3 years, then returned to old home in Bath; he left no family. (TJ Aug 28, 1897 p 3 col 6). [see also Buck & Turner].

TRUMBACK, PAUL. Died Deadwood, Butte County, CA Jan. 5, 1885; native of Trieste, Austria, aged about 65 years; pioneer of Trinity County; son William in Weaverville; married daughter in Humboldt County. (TJ Jan. 10, 1885). [1870 Census: Trumbach, Paul, Douglas City (with son William); age 50; miner; born Austria. See Mrs. Tydd for married daughter.]

TURNER, STEPHEN KEMPTON. Died Weaverville May 10, 1892; b. 23 Apr 1815, Fair Haven, Mass.; aged 77 yr 17 days; bur. May 11, 1892 at the side of his old associate, A. N. Love in Weaverville Cem. Became a sea faring man in whaling fleet, later in steamers; spent some time in Charleston, S.C.; Mexican war veteran - employed on a vessel in Government service; no pension; came to Calif 1850, Trin. Co. 1852, working at Rattlesnake (New River Area); engaged in saloon business; never married. (TJ Sat. May 14, 1892). [see also Love and Trufant].

TWAMBLEY, CARRIE. Died Vina, Tehama County, Feb. 17, 1885; born Trinity County; aged 17 yr 1 mo 13 dy. (TJ Feb. 28, 1885 p 3). [Born Readings Creek, Trinity County, CA Jan. 5, 1868].

TWAMBLEY, "JOSIE". Died Vina, Tehama County, Mar. 8, 1885; aged 9 yr 8 days; youngest SON of Chas. W. and Hattie Twambley; sister Carrie was oldest daughter. (TJ Mar. 14, 1885). [Note: this may be JOHN in 1880 census; born Weaverville March 5, 1876].

TWAMBLY, LYMAN. Died Vina, Tehama County, May 27, 1883; aged 9 mo 14 days; son of Chas. W. and Hattie Twambly. (TJ June 2, 1883 p 2).

TYDD, _____, Mrs. Drowned in Eel River, Humboldt County April 1, 1886 with son Fred; sister and nephew of Wm. Trombach of Rohnerville, Humboldt County; adopted daughter of late David Gibson of Hydesville. (TJ Apr. 17, 1886, from Rohnerville, Humboldt County, Herald.) [see also "Trumback"].

TYDD, FRED. Drowned in Eel River, Humboldt County, with mother; aged 5. (TJ Apr. 17, 1866). [See also Mrs. Tydd, Paul Trumbach, and David Gibson].

TYE, _____. Died Evans Bar, Dec. 1, 1862; infant son of Wm. and _____ Tye. (TJ Dec. 6, 1862). [Born Evans Bar Nov. 26, 1862]. [1860 Census: Tye, William, Evans Bar July 18, 1860, age 28, miner, b. England. Eliza J., age 28, b. Canada; John F., age 4, b. Canada; Delilah, age 2, born Canada. Also in TJ: daughter born Feb. 14, 1864 Evans Bar. Not in 1870 census.]

TYE, HOWARD. Died July 21, 1908 near Lewiston; drowned; age 6, male, "red", born California; buried Lewiston. [Index to Deaths 1890-1908].

UNDERWOOD, NORMAN. Died at Mr. H. Willburn's home at Hettenchow Aug. 26, 1892; native of Illinois, aged about 60 years; of Hyampom; returning from Eel River when he became ill; never married; mother and brother in Humboldt County. (TJ Sat. Sept. 3, 1892).

UNKNOWN. Drowned crossing Trinity River at Sailor Bar Mar. 27, 1861; Frenchman; partner of Louis Todion (or Tordian) who also drowned. (TJ Mar 30, 1861).

UNKNOWN. Died 1905 (suicide by hanging), about 45, male, white, Mt. Yolo Bally; buried Mt. Yolo Bally. [Index to Deaths 1890-1908].

UNKNOWN. Died (1905-1908) near Trinity Center, about 35, male, white; buried near Trinity Center. [Index to Deaths 1890-1908].

VALENCIA, PAUL. Died Weaverville Apr 10, 1892; native of Mexico, aged about 49 yr; bur. Catholic Cem. Weaverville Apr 11, 1892; partner of Frank Portillo in mine on West Weaver. Came to Weaverville from Scott Valley, Siskiyou Co., about 17 years ago. (TJ Sat. Apr 15, 1892, pp 2 & 3). [see also Potillo, all spellings].

VAN AERMAN,_____ Mr. Killed by Indians "earlier this month" (Sept. 1863), five miles below Taylor's Flat. (TJ Sept. 19, 1863). [Not in 1860 Census].

VAN AMMIN, LOWERY. Died Trinity Center Oct. 7, 1890; native of Kentucky, aged about 69 yr. (TJ Oct. 11, 1890). [Index to Deaths 1890-1908 adds white, male, single]. [Buried Trinity Center-Coffee Creek Cemetery; legible grave marker "d. 1890" (1980).]

VAN CLEAVE, MATILDA JANE, Mrs. Died Redding, Shasta Co., Calif. Jan. 5, 1920. Born Ohio; aged 80 years; came to Calif. 1870; lived Trinity Co.; she moved to Redding 2 years ago; bur. Lewiston Jan. 7, next to husband, who died in 1914. Children: Arthur M. Van Cleave, Loyalton; H. B. Van Cleave, Roseville; Charles Van Cleave, San Francisco; C. H. Van Cleave, Redding; Mrs. Dolores Moore, Seattle. (TJ Jan. 10, 1920, p 1).

VAN CLEAVE, ROY CHETWIND. Died near Lowden's Ranch Jul 24, 1897; native of Dall Co. Iowa, aged 24 yr 3 mo 6 dy; leaves father, mother, 2 bro. Carl & Charles & sis. Dovie at Lowden Ranch; Joseph at Lewiston; Arthur at Sierra Valley; Bart at Truckee; Frank at Honey Lake, and Ward at Yolaton; sister Mrs. Nancy Hammond of Lewiston; bur. Lewiston Cem Jul 25, 1897. (TJ Sat Jul 31, 1897 pp 2 & 3). [see also Hammond].

VAN CLEAVE, WM. C. Died Apr. 14, 1908 Lowden's Ranch (near Lewiston), Trinity County, Calif; age 11 days, male, white, born Calif.; buried Lewiston. [Index to Deaths 1890-1908].

VANDERBERG, ELZA. "Shot while defending her rights, July 4, 1852". Buried next to Dr. William B. Horton in the Old Section, Weaverville Cemetery. "Original wooden marker undecipherable in 1887"; no longer extant. Elza acted in the capacity of Horton's wife. (TJ Sat. Jan. 29, 1887, page 1, in a story by T. E. Jones). [see Horton.] [Note: the American Hotel was on the site next to the Weaverville Drug Store on the East Side of Main Street. Both the Edgecombe Bldg. and the Magnolia Bldg. deeds mention the American Hotel property.]

VANDENBURG, ELIZA. (same as Elza Vanderberg above). The story of the death of Eliza Vandenburg on July 4, 1852 is repeated. (TJ Jul 3, 1897 p 1).

VANDERFORD, J. W. Died Sept. 16, 1903 Junction City, age 19, male, white, American; buried cemetery at Dedrick [Canon Creek]. [Index to Deaths 1890-1908].

VANDERHOFF, CLARENCE. Died August 7, 1908 Weaverville; age 4, male, white, born California. [Index to Deaths 1890-1908]. [see also Young & Martin].

VAN HORN, G. W. Died Weaverville Nov. 26, 1862; native of Virginia, aged about 56 years; formerly of Newark, Ohio. (TJ Nov. 29, 1862).

VAN MATRE, BERT. Died Lewiston Jan. 6, 1890; native of Calif, aged 15 yr 9 mo 4 days; born Apr. 3, 1874 Minersville; youngest son of Mr. and Mrs. Mart Van Matre. (TJ Sat. Jan. 11, 1890). [Index to Deaths 1873-1890 adds: white, male, single]. [Note: buried in Lewiston Pioneer Cemetery; grave marker "B.B.Van Matre" 1980.]

VAN MATRE, FORDYCE. Died at Bates' ranch, Trinity County (near Minersville) Sept. 6, 1857, aged about 3 years; son of Peter and Almira Van Matre. (TJ Sep 1857). [see also Addendum].

VAN MATRE, HORACE. Died Mineral Point, Wisconsin abt Mar. 3, 1894; abt 23 yr; bur. Yellowstone Cem. (Mineral Point); youngest son of Joseph and Jane Martin Van Matre of Fayette, Wisc. (TJ Sat. Mar 24, 1894 p 3 col 6).

VAN MATRE, PETER. Died near Minersville Aug. 9, 1884; b. Feb. 25, 1825 Clinton County, Ohio; aged 59 yr 5 mo 15 days; came to Calif. 1849, Trinity County 1850; wife and 10 children, 5 sons and 5 daughters. Bur. Masonic Cem. Weaverville Aug. 10, 1884. (TJ Aug. 16, 1884).

VAN METER, GEORGE W. Died Sacramento Nov. 6, 1888; probably drowned; leaves wife and brother, Dr. M. E. Van Meter, of Red Bluff. (TJ Nov 1888).

VAN NESS, HENRY B. Died North Fork Aug. __ 1876; native of New Jersey aged 46 yr. (TJ Sept. 2, 1876 p 2).

VAN SCHAACK,_____ Mr. Died San Francisco "last week" (Oct. 1883); one of the earliest settlers of Trinity County; did most of the building at Big Flat in its palmy days. (TJ Nov. 3, 1883 p 3). [1860 Census: John H. Van Schaack; Big Flat; b. 1831 New York; not in 1870 Census.]

VAN WIE, A. W. Died Shasta, Shasta County "last week" (May 1874). Proprietor of the Oak Bottom House on the road from Weaverville to Shasta. (TJ May 16, 1874).

VAUGHN, WILLIAM DAVID. Died Hay Fork Nov 30, 1899; native of Calif, aged abt 36 yr; m. Miss Emma Knowles Dec 17, 1885, dau. of Henry Knowles; leaves widow and several small children to mourn his loss, and bro. Willis H. Vaughn and sis. Mrs. Henry Friend in Hay Fork and parents and several bro. & sis. in Oregon. (TJ Nov 4, 1899 pp 2 & 3). [see also Knowles].

VAUGHAN, WM. F., Esq. Drowned in Klamath River May 2, 1862; formerly an attorney at law in Weaverville; native of Virginia. (TJ May 31, 1862).

VENAAS, WILLIAM. Died _____1905 Hayfork; age 27, male, white, miner, bur. Weaverville. [Index to Deaths 1890-1908]. [not in Deaths 1900-1950; no further information.]

VENNER, LOUIS. Died Weaverville Mar. 15, 1879; Canadian Frenchman residing on Indian Creek. (TJ Mar. 22, 1879 p 3). [Not on 1870 Census.]

VERNAMAN, GEORGE. Died at Trinity Center Aug. 3, 1891; native of Calif., aged 16 years. (TJ Sat. Aug. 29, 1891).

VERSTEGEN, PETER. Died Junction City Apr. 7, 1885; native of Prussia, aged 61 yr; came Trinity Co. 1852; daughter Mrs. T. S. Thompson of Junction City. (TJ Apr. 11, 1885). [see also Thompson].

VINCENT, JAMES. Died Weaverville Dec. 10, 1865; son in law of Henry Doxie; bur. Dec. 12, 1865 Weaverville Cem; leaves wife and child. (TJ Dec. 16, 1865). [Note: James Vincent m 1) Miss Martha A. Doxie May 4, 1862 (in TJ); m2) Louisa C. Doxie Nov. 23, 1864 (Marriages Book H page 121)]. [1860 Census: res. East Weaver; miner; native of England, b. 1832.] [see also Doxey].

VINCENT, MARTHA M., Mrs. Died Weaverville May 30, 1863; born Roscoe, Winnebago County, Illinois; aged 24 yr; came Calif. 1861; wife of James Vincent. (TJ June 6, 1863 p 2). [see also Doxey].

VIZENO, SAM'L. Killed on Reading's Creek, near Douglas City, by the caving of a bank; native of France, aged about 45 years. (DCG June 19, 1861).

VOELKER, PHILIP. Drowned Trinity River at Independence Bar May 25, 1865; native of Hesse Darmstadt, Germany, aged about 38 yr. Formerly resided near Frankfort-on-the Main; brother living at Illinoistown, Missouri. Fun. May 26, 1865. (TJ May 27, 1865 p 2).

VOGEL, ERNST. Died Virginia City, Nevada "recently". Former proprietor of Union Hotel. (TJ Mar 20, 1880 p 3). [1860 Census: born 1828 Baden]. [Marriages Book H page 41: m. Miss Therese Dettinger in Weaverville June 28, 1860].

VOLLMERS, ALFRED. Died Weaverville Aug. 17, 1880; b. Weaverville Nov. 12, 1862; aged 17 yr 9 mo 5 days; second son of Otto Vollmers of Union Hotel. (TJ Aug. 21, 1880 p 2).

VOLLMERS, C., Mrs. Died Jan 05, 1900; age 65 yr 8 mo 2 dy; b. Germany. (TJ Jan 1901).

VOLLMERS, MICHAEL, Mr. Died Virginia City, Nevada Apr. 30, 1881; native of Hamburg, aged abt 52 years; former res. of Weaverville; brother of Otto Vollmers of Weaverville, and Mr. Wm. Vollmers. (TJ May 7, 1881 p 3). [1860 Census: Weaverville; not in 1870 Census]. [see also Allison].

VOLLMERS, OTTO. Died Weaverville Dec. 26, 1863; b. Weaverville Nov. 18, 1860; aged 3 yr 1 mo 10 days; son of Otto and Chatrine (sic) Vollmers. (TJ Jan. 2, 1864 p 2). [Note: 1870 Census says Catherine].

VOLLMERS, OTTO. Died Weaverville Nov. 23, 1883; native of Hamburg; aged 60 years. Came to Trinity Co. 1852. Bur. Masonic Cem. Weaverville Nov. 25, 1883. (TJ Nov. 24 and Dec. 1, 1883).

VORRAINE, JEAN. Died Weaverville April 13, 1880; native of France, aged about 55 years.

VOSZ, WILLIAM. Murdered at Harrison Gulch, Trinity County Apr 5, 1897; the supposed murderer is Albert Weingartner. (TJ Apr 10, 1897 p 3).

WALDER, NIELS. Died San Francisco Apr. 9, 1889; native of Norway, aged about 57 yr; res. Trinity County 6 years; of Canon City. (TJ Apr. 13, 1889 p 3).

WALDORFF, E. A., Mrs. Died Cox Bar Nov. 29, 1890; native of California, aged 22 yr 9 mo 2 days; dau. of W. A. Pattison; leaves husband and infant daughter [Elsie Waldorff Tye]. (TJ Dec. 6, 1890). [Index to Deaths 1890-1908 adds white, female, married, born Calif.] [Josephine Pattison m. Earnest Anderson Waldorff Jul 3, 1889; he d. Jun 8, 1921.] [see Addendum].

WALDORFF, JACOB THEODORE. Died Weaverville Mar 17, 1902, aged 79 yr (TJ Mar 22, 1902). [b. Germany Dec 1823; came to US 1846, Trinity early 1850s (on 1852 Tax Roll); Naturalized in Trin. Co. May 6, 1866; moved to Hyampom 1876; sold ranch early 1890s; lived on French Creek with sons. m. Maria Louisa Eicke in Germany. bur. Weaverville Cem., nr marked grave of daughter; no grave marker. Records of Patricia J. Hicks and Rita M. Hanover]. [see also Peter Miller, Pattison, Trimble].

WALDORFF, MATILDA. Died near Weaverville Feb. 7, 1863; aged 5 yr 4 mo 27 days; dau. of Jacob and Maria Waldorff. (TJ Feb. 14, 1863 p 2). [Bur. Old Section, Weaverville Cem.; marker legible 1980]. [see also Addendum].

WALDORFF, MARY LOUISA. Drowned Hyampom Valley May 5, 1878; native of Hanover, Germany, aged 57. Wife of Jacob Waldorff; body not found. See also Mary Matilda Waldorff. (TJ May 11, 1878 p 2).

WALDORFF, MARY MATILDA. Drowned Hyampom Valley May 5, 1878; native of Weaverville, aged 12; dau. of Jacob Waldorff; body not found. See also her mother, Mary Louisa. (TJ May 11, 1878 p 2).

WALDRON, FRANK. "The remains of little Frank Waldron lost near Centerville in Humboldt County several weeks since have been discovered. He was evidently devoured by a bear." (TJ Sept. 27, 1862 p 2).

WALKER, FLORENCE. Died at Napa, [Napa Co.] recently [prob. Jan. 1891] from diphtheria; youngest daughter of J. Mc. Walker, at one time Superintendent of the Taylor Flat mining company; mother is sick with same disease, but is improving. (TJ Sat. Feb. 7, 1891). [see J. M. C. Walker, below].

WALKER, ELIZABETH, Mrs. Died New River Mar. 18, 1891; aged 31 yr 10 mo 18 days; "Vallejo papers please copy." (TJ Apr. 11, 1891). [Trinity Co. Marriages, Book H pg 335: Married at Big Bar May 27, 1878 by E. B. Barnum, J.P., George W. Walker and Miss Elizabeth Thomas. George, age 27, native of Ill., res. of South Fork; Elizabeth, age 19, native of Calif. res. of Martinville; neither previously married.]

WALKER, J. M. C. Died Napa City, Napa Co. Jan 25, 1895; lived Napa 12 years; leaves widow & 2 daughters; a brother & sister reside at Vacaville. Superintendent of the Taylor's Flat property on Lower Trinity 1880 & 1881; left county 1882. (TJ Feb 2, 1897 p 3 col 2).

WALKER, MINERVA PHOEBE, Mrs. Died Yreka, Siskiyou Co., CA Sept. 17, 1891, aged 45 years; wife of Mr. W. B. Walker; came to Siskiyou County 1856; mother of Mrs. John Colbert, of Weaverville. (TJ Sat. Sept. 26, 1891). [see also Colbert].

WALL, ALBERT G. Died Weaverville Feb. 7, 1855; aged 20 years; formerly of Lewisburgh, Union County, Penn. (TT Feb. 10, 1855).

WALLACE, CHARLES. Died Weaverville Nov. 24, 1862; aged one year and eight months; son of Epenetus and Susan Wallace. (TJ Nov. 29, 1862 p 2). [gravestone Weaverville Cem. "Charlie E. Wallace, Born 1860, Died 1862" standing in 1988; similar stone for Willie Wallace.]

WALLACE, DAVID. Died Brown's Creek near Douglas City Dec. 25, 1871; aged about 2 yr 10 mo; son of James and Letitia Wallace. (TJ Dec. 30, 1871 p 2). [see also Mary Ida Wallace].

WALLACE, MARY IDA. Died Brown's Creek May 12, 1869, age 4 yr 8 mo; dau. of James C. and Letitia Jane Wallace; Pittsburg papers please copy. (TJ May 15, 1869 p 2). [see also David Wallace].

WALLACE, THOMAS. Died Indian Creek Nov. 21, 1882; native of Ireland, aged 53 yr. (TJ Nov. 25, 1882).

WALLACE, WILLIE. "Born 1863; Died 1864". Gravestone standing in Weaverville Cemetery 1988, next to that of Charlie E. Wallace, above.

WALTER, VICTOR EMANUEL. Died in Weaverville Aug. 24, 1860; aged 8 mo 16 days; only child of Frederick and Mary Ann Walter. (TJ Sept. 1, 1860 p 2). [Note:

bur. in Catholic Cem., Weaverville. In 1976, his gravestone was standing, one of the oldest extant in the cemetery. This stone rose off the base, turned around and smashed in the earthquake of Nov. 8, 1980. It was found broken the next day by the author, who had photographed the standing stone in 1976. The pieces of stone were set in cement at a later date.] [note: father, Fred Walter, lived in Mansfield, Ohio in 1899; "lived in Trinity Co. for 16 years". (TJ Jan 28, 1899 p 3 col 4)].

WALTERS, CHARLES A. Died near Canon City Jan. 13, 1892; native of Stockholm, Sweden, aged 54 yr. (TJ Jan. 23, 1892).

WALTERS, WILLIAM. Died Anderson, Shasta Co., Nov. 11, 1888. "Worked in Trinity County lately". (TJ Nov. 17, 1888). [no age given].

WALTERMEYER, MARY C. Died Douglas City Sept. 25, 1860; aged about 3 years; daughter of Henry and Mary Ann Waltermeyer. (TJ Sept. 29, 1860 and 1860 Census).

WALTON, DAN. Died May 23, 1906 Hayfork; age 4, male, "red", born Calif; bur. Hayfork. [Index to Deaths 1890-1908].

WARD, GEORGE WASHINGTON. Died at the Douglas City Hotel Jan. 13, 1891; native of Ohio, aged about 65 yr; bur. I.O.O.F. Cem. Weaverville Jan. 15, 1891; came to Shasta County 1850; last Charter Member of Stella Encampment No. 12, I.O.O.F. (TJ Sat. Jan. 17, 1891).

WARD, HARRY. Died abt Jan. 10, 1900 Browns Creek, Trinity Co.; age about 88, male, white, born Sweden; buried Browns Creek, Trinity Co. [Index to Deaths 1890-1908]. "Died Jan 06, 1900"; age 88 yr; b. Sweden. (TJ Jan 1901).

WARD, JAMES. Died near Weaverville Aug 17, 1896; aged 81 yr 3 mo 5 dy; b. May 12, 1815 England; came to Trinity Co 1852, from Fall River, Mass; bur. Weaverville Cem; (TJ Sat Aug 22, 1896; obit p 3 col 6).

WARD, JOHN. Died Weaverville Dec. 17, 1865; native of Cork, Ireland, aged about 45 years. (TJ Dec. 23, 1865 p 2).

WARD, JOHN. Murdered in Shasta County Feb 20, 1896; age 26; home in Red Bluff; buried there; killed by John H. Ryan. (TJ Sat Feb 22, 1896).

WARE, HENRY. Died New River May 1, 1877; native of England, aged 40-45 years; unmarried man. (TJ May 12, 1877 p 3).

WARE, WILLIAM, Dr. Died Alameda, [Alameda Co.], Calif. Dec. 10, 1883; native of New Jersey, aged 80 years; late of Trinity Co.; came to Trinity County July 1850; long obit. p. 3. (TJ Sat. Dec. 15, 1883, pgs 2-3). [Cox's Annals, 1940 says: "Born Jan. 4, 1804 Rockhill, Somerset Co., New Jersey; left for California Jun 23, 1849; arrived San Francisco Aug 18, 1849."]

WARREN, FRANK WRIGHT. Died at mouth of Oregon Gulch (nr Junction City) Feb. 23, 1858; aged four months. (TJ Feb. 27, 1858 p 2).

WARREN, ELIZA JANE. Died Weaverville May 14, 1878; native of Newland West, County Cornwall, England, aged 29 years; wife of Archlos Warren; bur. Weaverville Cem. May 16, 1878. (TJ May 18, 1878 p 2).

WARREN, HARKEY. Killed by a mining accident in Colorado, abt Dec. 1885; former res. of Trinity County. (TJ Jan. 2, 1886). [no further information].

WARREN, A. T., Mrs. Died San Francisco Mar. 14, 1887; "Mrs. Warren passed her early childhood at Canon City, Trinity County". (TJ Mar. 19, 1887, p 3). [prob. born 1854] [1860 Census: Hodges, James, Mary, John H., and Mary, age 6); dau. of James Hodges].

WASHINGTON, ORIN. Died Eureka, Humboldt Co Apr 17, 1896; native of Virginia aged abt 67 yr; member of Capt. Messic's Trinity Company in the Mountaineer Battalion. (TJ May 2, 1896 p 3).

WASKEY, TILFORD B. Died Junction City Feb. 2, 1884; native of Virginia; aged about 57 years; came to Trinity Co. 1854; no known relatives. (TJ Feb 9, 1884).

WASMER, F. Died San Francisco June 25, 1877; native of Baden, Germany, age 48 years; former partner of B. Baumgartner of Canon City. (TJ July 14, 1877 p 3). [see also Baumgartner].

WATERMAN, CHARLES. Drowned near China Flat, Trinity River July 18, 1886; no age given. "Deceased was a member of the Republican Central Committee of Humboldt County." (TJ July 31, 1886 p 3).

WATSON, JOHN A. Died Eureka, Humboldt Co. Nov. 9, 1883; arrived Calif. 1851; settled in Humboldt County 1863. (TJ Nov. 17, 1883 p 3). [see also Seaman].

WATSON, RICHARD. Killed by a bank cave at Junction City Dec. 6, 1867; native of Cleveland, Hancock Co., Indiana; parents there; age 36; bur. I.O.O.F. cemetery, Weaverville. Came to Calif. from Iowa 1860 with E. J. Miller of Weaverville and James Noble of Junction City. (TJ Dec. 7 & 14, 1867). [see also Miller].

WATSON, WILLIAM. Died French Gulch, Shasta Co. abt Sept. 22, 1877; aged 48 yr; bur. Shasta Cem. by Masonic Order; leaves wife and 2-3 children. (TJ Sept. 22, 1877 p 3 col 1).

WATT, C. H. Died San Francisco, Jan 10, 1899; one of the owners of the Brown Bear Mine at Deadwood; leaves a widow; remains were interred in Sacramento Jan 12, 1899. "Out of respect to his memory, the Brown Bear mine and mill was closed down on the day of his funeral." (TJ Jan 14, 1899 p 3). [TJ Jan 28, 1899 p 3 col 2 - Watt's Will Filed; his name was Charles H. Watt; his widow was Hattie P. Watt].

WAUGH, RODERICK G. Died Weaverville June 29, 1864; native of Virginia, age 38 yr; came to Trinity Co. 1851; bur. Masonic Cem., Weaverville June 30, 1864. "Glasgow, Mo. papers please copy". (TJ July 2, 1864 p 2).

WEAVER, "Madame". Killed at mouth of New River July 23, 1863. Also Alonzo Merrick. (TJ Aug. 1, 1863 p 3). [1860 Census: Merrick, Alonzo, age 40, b. New York; miner; Weaver, Catherine, age 46, b. Germany; South Fork 8-7-1860].

WEBSTER, THOMAS. Died Wildwood, Trinity Co. Apr 27, 1895; native of Canada, aged 70 yr. (TJ Sat. May 4, 1895).

WECKERT, JACOB, Mrs. Died at Bannock City [San Bernardino Co.] abt Dec. 1864; formerly of Weaverville; sister-in-law of John Hagelman of Weaverville. (TJ Jan. 28, 1865). [Not in 1860 Census]. [see also Hagelman].

WEED, DAVID BENNETT. Died Weaverville Jan. 19, 1895; native of New York, aged abt 68 yr; bur. Jan 20, 1895 Weaverville Cem.; came to Trinity Co. early 1850s; partner with Craven Lee in store at Bagdad (near North Fork); operated hotel with George Yohe at North Fork (later Helena). (TJ Sat Jan 26, 1895). [see also Yohe].

WEEDEN, JOHN D. Died Weaverville Dec. 20, 1894; native of Scotland, aged abt 73 yr; came to Trinity Co. 1850s; mined at Minersville. (TJ Sat. Dec. 22, 1894 p 2 & 3).

WEINHEIMER, JOHNNIE. Died Weaverville Dec. 19, 1875; aged 1 yr 11 mo 13 days; son of Henry and Catherine Weinheimer. (TJ Dec. 25, 1875). [see also Dockery]. [see also 1900-1950 references].

WEISS, MARTIN. Died Burnt Ranch Sept. 9, 1866; native of Switzerland; aged about 40. (TJ Sept. 15, 1866 p 2).

WEITFELDT, FREDERICK. Died Red Bluff, Tehama Co. Mar 6, 1897; formerly lived near Lowden Ranch, Trinity County. (TJ Mar 13, 1897 p 3 col 5). [see also Wietfeldt.]

WELLENDORF, ADALINE M. Died Shasta, Shasta, Calif. June 6, 1873; native of Millford, Maine, aged 39 yr 11 mo; wife of L. Wellendorff. (sic) (TJ June 14, 1873). [dau. b. Shasta May 31, 1873; (TJ Jun 7, 1873)]. [son b. Shasta Mar 23, 1867, Boggs, p. 483]
Wellendorf, Louis. "Shasta Postmaster" (TJ Jan 19, 1878). [Former owner of the Weaverville Drug Store, 1860s; bought drug store in Shasta; later became a dentist.] [m2] Mrs. Mildred Bacon Bartlett in San Francisco Jul 19, 1874; in June 1879 lived in San Pablo, Contra Costa Co.] [Boggs, MY PLAYHOUSE WAS A CONCORD COACH, has a portrait and biography of Louis Wellendorf; limited edition, copy in Trinity County Library.]

WELLENDORF, OSCAR. Died Shasta, Shasta, Calif. Nov. 25, 1869; no age given; formerly of Weaverville. (TJ Dec. 4, 1869 p 3).

WELLENDORFF, PAUL. Died near Trinity Center Jun 6, 1896; (explosion); native of Calif, aged abt 25 yr; bur Shasta, Shasta Co. (TJ June 13, 1896; story p 3 col 2). [might be a son of Louis & Adaline; check Shasta Co. census and official records].

WELLS, HENRY H. Died Grand Ronde Valley, Oregon about Dec. 1863; formerly of Weaverville and Douglas City; teaching school; native of State of New York. (TJ Jan. 2, 1864; correction Jan. 16, 1864 p 3, included.)

WELLS, JOHN R. Died Humboldt County Oct. 6, 1877; aged 16 yr 6 mo; born Douglas City Spring 1861; son of J. W. and Elizabeth A. Wells; nephew of R. B. Wells, Esq. of Hay Fork. (TJ Nov. 17, 1877 p 3).

WELLS, L. F. [Luke Ford]. "The Miners Poet". Died Aug 25, 1896 at Comet, Montana; bur. Sandy, Utah; former res. of Trin. To, leaving here in 1873. (TJ Oct 10, 1896 p 3 col 4 & TJ Oct 24, 1896 p 3 col 5) [note: Wells' poem The Forty Niners, from the *Trinity Times*, Dec. 16, 1854, is reprinted in the TRINITY JOURNAL Feb. 25, 1899 p 3 col 4]. [see also Goss.]

WELLS, MEDORA ANN, Mrs. Died Sandy City, Utah Feb 13, 1895, aged 60 yr 3 mo; wife of L. F. Wells; mother of Horace Childers and Mrs. Wm. Drinkwater of Hay Fork; sister of Mrs. Wm. Farmer of Hay Fork and Mrs. Nelson Hosmer of Rock Point, Oregon; husband was known as "The Miners Poet" in Trinity County; lived Sandy, Utah for 22 yr; born 1834; m. L. F. Wells in Trinity County in 1868. (TJ Sat. Mar 2, 1895 p 3 col 5).

WELLS, ROBERT. Died Weaverville Jan 29, 1899; native of Virginia, aged abt 68 yr. (TJ Feb 4, 1899 p 2 & p 3 col 6).

WELSH, HUGH. Died Canon Creek, Mar. 25, 1894; native of Ireland, aged about 46 yr; bur. near Canon City; miner; came to Trinity Co. 1879. (TJ Sat. Mar 31, 1894).

WEST, HENRY. Died Deadwood Jan. 7, 1893; native of Wisconsin, aged about 48 yr; obit. p 3 col 1. (TJ Jan. 14, 1893).

WEYAND, ZACHARY TAYLOR. Died March 23, 1907 Weaverville; age 56, male, white, laborer; buried Weaverville; inf. J. F. Whitchurch. [Index to Deaths 1890-1908].

WHALEN, JAMES. "Lost on the steamer Central America Sept. 12, 1857; formerly of Illinois and Weaverville." (TJ Oct. 31, 1857).

WHALEY, JOHN A. Died Arcata, Humboldt Co. July 24, 1888; native of New York, 72 years of age; pioneer of Humboldt Co. Internal Revenue Collector for nearly 25 years. (TJ Aug. 4, 1888 p 3).

WHALEY, JOHN A., Jr. Died Arcata, Humboldt Co. Nov. 24, 1868; age 4 yr 5 mo. (TJ Dec. 5, 1868 p 2).

WHEELAN, EDWARD. Died Summit Creek, Hay Fork Valley Oct. 4, 1881; native of New York, aged 49 yr. (TJ Oct. 8, 1881 p 2).

WHEELER, DORA F. Died near Minersville June 12, 1880; aged 9 yr 2 mo 15 days; dau. of Nathan and Lizzie A. Wheeler. (TJ June 19, 1880 p 2).

WHEELER, FRANK, "Red". Died San Francisco abt Feb. 7, 1879; buried by Masonic Fraternity Feb. 9, 1879. Private Secty for several years to John P. Jones. (TJ Feb. 15, 1879 p 3).

WHEELER, NATHAN. Died Trinity Center Nov. 1, 1888; born Hartland, Maine 1840; m. Elizabeth Jewett in Hartland, Maine; leaves wife & 3 children. Odd Fellows funeral; bur. French Gulch, Shasta County, Nov. 2, 1888. (TJ Nov. 3, 1888). [See also Dora F. Wheeler, and Christina Marsh].

WHEELRIGHT, GEORGE, Mr. Killed at Big Bar, Trinity River Aug. 8, 1861; aged about 40 years; formerly from Swanton Falls, VT. (TJ Aug. 10, 1861 p 2 col 1 & col 4).

WHEITE, FRANK. Died [prob. Weaverville] Jan. 27, 1859; native of Ireland, aged about 33 years. (TJ Jan. 29, 1859 p 3).

WHELAN, MICHAEL. Died Mayfield, San Mateo Co., Calif. Feb. 23, 1870; aged 44 years; formerly of Big Flat, Trinity River. (TJ Mar. 5, 1870).

WHITCHURCH, EMMA GRACE. Died Aug. 7, 1906 Weaverville; age 15, female, white, born Calif; buried Weaverville; inf. J. F. Whitchurch. [Index to Deaths 1890-1908].

WHITCHURCH, GEORGE W. Died June 13, 1906 Weaverville; age 18, male, white, born Calif.; inf. J. W. Whitchurch. [Index to Deaths 1890-1908].

WHITE, CHARLES. Died Weaverville Apr 10, 1899, native of Germany, aged abt 64 yr. (TJ Sat. Apr 15, 1899 p 2).

WHITE, HANNAH BERGIN. Died Weaverville abt Sept. 27, 1885; daughter of John and Margaret Bergin. "Her little sister, Helena Bergin, d. Sept. 25, 1885". (TJ Oct. 3, 1885; see p 3 col 1 also.) [See also Bergin, Helena.] [1880 Census: White, Charles W. age 28, Census Taker, b. Ohio. Hannah, age 32, b. Mass. Charles' parents: father b. North Carolina, m. b. Ohio; Hannah: parents b. Ireland. (m. Weaverville Apr. 11, 1880). See also Nellie May White.]

WHITE, JOHN. Died Shasta, Shasta Co. Nov. 17, 1872; native of Ireland, aged 49 years. (TJ Nov. 30, 1872).

WHITE, NELLIE MAY. Died Weaverville Sept. 27, 1885; native of Trinity Co; age 1 yr 6 mo 11 days; Tues. Sept. 29, 1885 Masonic Cem. Weaverville; dau. of Charles W. and Hannah White. (TJ Oct. 3, 1885).

WHITEBREAD, ADOLPH. Died Weaverville Dec 8, 1896; native of Switzerland, aged abt 63 yr; brought to U.S. at one year of age; bur. Masonic Cem, Weaverville Wed Dec 9, 1896; leaves wife, Mrs. Ann Whitebread, and 2 daughters. (TJ Sat. Dec 12, 1896) [m. Mrs. Ann Roach Sep 25, 1887.] [marker in Masonic Cem., Weaverville: "Apr 15, 1833 - Dec 8, 1896 erected by Mrs. Annie W. Whitebread"].

WHITEBREAD, ANNA. Died Clipper Mills, near Oroville, [Butte Co.] Feb. 18, 1879; aged 31 yr 11 mo 11 days; wife of Adolph Whitebread. "Probably the same Whitebread who resided here for awhile, a tinner in the employ of Mr. H. Junkans." (TJ Mar. 15, 1879 p 3). [Mr. A. Whitebread returned to Weaverville Apr 1883, as tinner with M. Lang. (TJ Apr 28, 1883)].

WHITEBREAD, ANNIE W., Mrs. Died San Francisco Aug 9, 1912 at home of dau. Mrs. Margaret O'Keefe; b. Queens Co. Ireland 84 years ago; mar. twice; leaves children: Mrs. Margaret O'Keefe, Mrs. Julia Cunco, and William Roache (sic), all of San Francisco; bur. Holy Cross Cem., San Francisco Aug 12, 1912. (TJ Aug 17, 1912 p 3). [1900 Census, Trinity Co., Calif: b. Aug 1833 Ireland; par. b. Ireland; came US 1844; Weaverville Jun 9, 1900; similar info. 1910 census].

WHITEBREAD, CHARLEY. Died Rock Island, Illinois Aug 21, 1895; native of Calif., aged 21. "Father A. Whitebread of Weaverville". (TJ Sat. Aug 31, 1895 p 3 col 4).

WHITMORE, CHRISTIANA J. Died Weaverville July 18, 1884; native of Maine, aged 57 years 10 mo 27 days; married John Whitmore 1852 in Maine; came to Calif. Dec. 1860, to Junction City. leaves husband and one dau. Mrs. Edgar L. Reed of Junction City. (TJ July 19, 1884).

WHITMORE, FRANKIE ELLEN. Died at Sturdivant's Ranch, Trinity River, Jan. 10, 1863; aged 2 yr 5 mo 17 days; dau. of John and Christiana Whitmore. (TJ Jan. 17, 1863 p 2).

WHITMORE, JEREMIAH. Died Rhonerville, Humboldt Co. Jan. 20, 1868; aged 42 years; formerly of Trinity Co. "brother of John Whitmore, Esq." (TJ Feb. 15, 1868 p 2; see also `Lowden' col 1 for note about John Whitmore.)

WHITMORE, MARY. Died at Sturdivant's Ranch, Trinity County, May 30, 1859; aged about 19 years; wife of Mr. Jeremiah Whitmore; bur. "Weaverville burying place" Tues. May 31, 1859. (TJ June 4, 1859 p 2).

WHITNEY, ALVIN A. Died April 8, 1907 Minersville, CA; age 65, male, white, miner; buried Weaverville. [Index to Deaths 1890-1908].

WICKS, WILEY. Murdered in Lewiston Oct. 26, 1862; native of Tennessee, aged 36. (TJ Nov. 1, 1862 p 2).

WIEFELDT, DORA. Died Weaverville July 9, 1870; aged 33 years; of Lewiston, wife of Fred. "Wittfeld". (TJ July 16, 1870 p 2). [Note: "Dora, wife of Fred. Wiefeldt" is buried in the old section of Weaverville Cem. A broken gravestone was legible in 1988]. [see Weifeldt, Frederick.]

WILBUR, PERRY. Died Weaverville Sept. 10, 1861; native of Mass., aged 33 years. (DCG Sept. 14, 1861). (Similar information TJ Sept. 14, 1861).

WILLBURN, _____. Died Long Ridge Mar. 11, 1893, aged 9 days; infant daughter of Mr. and Mrs. Sidney Willburn. (TJ Sat. Apr. 16, 1893).

WILLBURN, EDWARD. Died Hettenshaw Valley Dec. 28, 1885; native of Kentucky, aged about 82 yr; burned to death; house in ashes; lived 3/4 mile from son H. D. Willburn; known as "Grandpa Willburn"; bur. Hettenshaw Valley Cem. Dec. 31, 1885. (TJ Jan. 9, 1886).

WILLBURN, NANCY, Mrs. Died Hettenshaw July 22, 1889; b. Apr. 25, 1811, Camel County, East Tennessee; aged 78 yr 2 mo 26 days; bur. next to husband's body in burial ground at Hettenshaw. 8 children, 50 grandchildren and 10 great-grandchildren. (Some children listed p. 3 col 2). (TJ July 27, 1889.) [Index to Deaths 1873-1890 says died Kettenchow; white, female, single].

Willburn note: this family is large. Some information is available in FAMILIES, Round Valley Public Library, Covelo, Mendocino Co., CA 1990. Check Mendocino Co. (Ukiah) and Humboldt Co. (Eureka) for additional records.

WILLEY, HIRAM E. Died San Francisco Feb. 11, 1884; native of Vermont, age 52 yr; leaves wife and one child; long time resident of Deadwood, and Trinity and Shasta Counties. (TJ Feb. 16, 1884 p 3).

WILLEY, JEROME. Died Deadwood, Trinity Co. Sep 5, 1894; born French Gulch, Shasta Co. Aug 1, 1879; aged 15 yr; bur. French Gulch Cem; mother Mrs. M. Falan, of Deadwood. (TJ Sat. Sep 8, 1894 p 2, & Oct 6, 1894 p 3).

WILLIAMS, EMMA., Mrs. Died Trinity Center May 28, 1883; aged 57 yr; widow of late Geo. Williams. (TJ June 2, 1883 p 2).

WILLIAMS, GEO. W. Died Whiskeytown, Shasta Co. abt Sept. 5, 1887; former res. of Weaverville; m. "a few months ago" Mrs. Geo. W. Laingor, a former resident. (TJ Sept. 10, 1887). [Note: Trinity Co. Marriages Book I page 40 says: George W. Laingor and Miss Minnie M. Allen, both of Weaverville, were married near Weaverville Oct. 12, 1884 by Judge T. E. Jones. George, age 24, native of Illinois; Minnie age 20, native of Calif. Rita Hanover note: "divorced Apr. 1887; immediately after Minnie m. George W. Williams who died in Sept. the same year.] [Not Mrs. Emma Williams, above].

WILLIAMS, HANK. Died Redding, Shasta Co. abt Oct. 21, 1883, age 45 years; old resident; kept the Trinity Mountain House on the Scott Valley Road, now owned by Richard Feeney; in saloon business in Redding; leaves a devoted wife and 3 children, the eldest 13 years of age. (TJ Nov. 3, 1883, p 3, from Shasta County *Democrat*).

WILLIAMS, JOHN. Died Weaverville May 16, 1863; native of Wales, aged about 35 years. (TJ May 23, 1863 p 2).

WILLIAMS, L. S. Died San Francisco Oct. 16, 1860; Senator from Trinity & Klamath Counties 1853; County Clerk of Trinity Co. afterwards; left Weaverville 1856; res. San Francisco 2 years. (TJ Oct. 27, 1860).

WILLIAMS, M. Died San Francisco Dec. 16, 1871; native of Prussia, aged 38 yr. (TJ Dec. 23, 1871 p 2).

WILLIAMS, MARY. Died Smith's Flat (nr Douglas City) July 29, 1869 aged 4 years; dau. of Manuel Williams. (TJ July 31, 1869 p 2).

WILLIAMS, MANUEL. Died Smith's Flat (nr Douglas City) Aug. 1, 1869, aged 5 yr; son of Manuel Williams. (TJ Aug. 7, 1869 p 2).

WILLIAMS, SARAH. Died Indian Creek Dec. 5, 1893, aged about 21 yr; wife of Antone Williams. (TJ Sat. Dec. 9, 1893).

WILSHIRE, WILLIAM. Died Big Bar Jan. 4, 1891; native of Ohio; born 1825, aged about 66 yr; came to Northern Calif. 1857. (TJ Sat. Jan. 10, 1891).

WILSON, BEATRICE BLANCHE. Died Oregon Gulch Nov. 29, 1873; age 12 weeks 6 days; dau. of V. V. and Eliza Wilson; bur. Odd Fellows Cem., Weav. (TJ Dec. 6, 1873). [Index to Deaths 1873-1890 adds female, single, born Calif].

WILSON, ELIZA. Died Weaverville Feb. 17, 1881; native of Barnsley, Yorkshire, Eng. aged 49 yr 5 mo 3 days; bur. Odd Fellows Cem., Weav. Feb. 19, 1881; formerly Mrs. Motherwell; (TJ Feb. 19, 1881 pp 2 & 3). [see also Motherwell].

WILSON, ELMER. Died Deadwood Dec. 27, 1891; native of Calif. aged 6 mo and 5 days; infant son of James and Hattie Wilson. (TJ Jan. 2, 1892).

WILSON, HOMER. Died Deadwood Sept. 24, 1890; aged 2 mo 18 days; infant son of James and Hattie Wilson. (TJ Oct. 4, 1890). [Index to Deaths 1890-1908 adds male, single, b. Calif.]

WILSON, J. J. Died Mount Sterling, Illinois Jun 7, 1897, aged 69 yr; Pioneer of California 1849; returned to Illinois after a few years; father of Ed Wilson of Lowden Ranch. (TJ Jun 19, 1897 p 3 col 2).

WILSON, JEFFRIES. Killed on Canon Creek by a caving bank Mar. 2, 1866; b. Delaware, Maryland, age 44 years; went to Philadelphia at an early age; arrived Calif. 1849. "Richmond, Indiana and Philadelphia papers please copy." (TJ Mar. 10, 1866 p 2 & Mar. 24, 1866 p 2 col 1).

WILSON, J. M. "Resident of New River, found this week; dead some time; buried where found; last seen 6 weeks ago." (TJ Aug. 31, 1889 p 3). [died abt July/Aug. 1889].

WILSON, VITRUVIUS VIVIAN. Died Weaverville Dec. 16, 1884; native of Madison, Indiana, aged 57 years; came to Calif. 1849; bur. Odd Fellow Cem., Weaverville Dec. 18, 1884; (TJ Dec. 20, 1884; obit. p 3 col 2). [see Eliza Wilson, and Beatrice Wilson].

WILT, GEORGE. Died Kittanning, Penn. Mar. 2, 1871; aged 80 years; father of H. C. Wilt of Canon City. (TJ Mar. 18, 1871 p 2).
WILT, JOHN C. Died Portland, Oregon Nov. 1st or 2d 1881; leaves a wife. (TJ Nov. 12, 1881 p 3).
WINDRICK, ANNA J. Died Jun 05, 1900; age 25 yr 2 mo 5 dy; b. Calif. (TJ Jan 1901).
WINES, _____. Died Hay Fork July 20, 1876; infant son of Mr. and Mrs. N. C. Wines. (TJ July 29, 1876 p 2).
WINKELREID, LOUIS. Died Nov. 10, 1904 Hayfork (murder); age 38, male, white, born Switzerland; buried Hayfork. [Index to Deaths 1890-1908].
WINSTON, B. W. Died Jefferson City, Missouri Aug. 27, 1873; old pioneer of Trinity County. (TJ Sept. 20, 1873 p 3).
WISE, JOHN. Sentenced to be hung on July 10, 1856 for murder; stay of sentence abt July 4, 1856. (TJ June 7, 1856 and July 4, 1856).
WOLFF, GEORGE. Died Canon City Nov. 9, 1881; native of Germany, aged 64 yr. (TJ Nov. 12, 1881 p 2).
WOLFF, _____ Mrs. Died Canon City Mar. 19, 1882; native of Germany, aged 81 years; (TJ Mar. 25, 1882). [prob. mother of Nicholas Wolff, of Canon City, 1880 census].
WOOD, CEPHAS, Mr. Died Gilroy, Santa Clara County July 30, 1881; [age about 71 yrs]; formerly of Lewiston, Trinity Co; father of Mrs. M. F. Griffin and Mrs. Mollie E. Kellogg. (TJ Aug. 6, 1881 p 3). [1860 Census: age 50, b. Vermont, farmer, res. Lewiston].
WOOD, JAMES E. Died Weaverville Dec 23, 1894; native of Calif., aged 24 yr; bur. Weaverville Cem. Dec. 24, 1894; parents live in Coquille City, Oregon. (TJ Sat. Dec 29, 1894 p 2 & 3).
WOOD, JOEL CHILTON. Died Weaverville Dec. 14, 1885; native of Tenn., aged about 63 yr; came to Trinity Co. 1850/51; bur. Dec. 16, 1885 Masonic Cem. Weav. Services by Trinity #27, F & AM and St. John's 14, OES. good obit. (TJ Dec. 19, 1885).
WOODBURN, ROBERT. Died Oct 07, 1900; aged 76 yr; b. Ireland. (TJ Jan 1901).
WOODBURY, DAVID L. Died Weaverville Nov. 13, 1885; native of Maine, aged about 60 years; brother of Isaac Woodbury; came to Trinity County 1865; served in Union Army. (TJ Nov. 21, 1885).
WOODBURY, ELIZABETH DORSEY, Mrs. Died Weaverville Nov 7, 1898; b. San Francisco 1854, aged 43 yr 10 mo 26 dy; moved with parents to Weaverville; m. David Woodbury 1871; seven children, six living: Flora, Fred, Raymond, Clye, Leroy & Earl; also leaves mother, Mrs. Neatherly; 2 sis. Hannah Dorsey and Mrs. Ida Mathews, of Ferndale (Humboldt Co.) and a sis. Mrs. M. L. Woodbury, of Weaverville. Bur. Weav. Cem. (TJ Nov 12, 1898 pp 2 & 3).
WOODBURY, ISAAC. Died Weav. Feb. 29, 1869 (TJ says "March"); aged 18 yr; late of Hartland, Maine, nephew of Mr. Isaac Woodbury. (TJ Mar. 6, 1869 p 2). [Bur. Old Section Weaverville Cem.; gravemarker readable 1988].
WOODBURY, ISAAC. Died Weaverville May 20, 1891; native of Hartland, Maine, born Apr 3, 1830, aged 61 yr 1 mo 17 days. Bur. May 22, 1891 Weaverville Cem. "San Francisco papers please copy." Came to Calif. spring 1852 to Placer Co., Shasta Co., and Trinity Co. 1853; mined on Garden Gulch; youngest of a family of 2 brothers and 2 sisters living in Maine; m. Louisa Dorsey 1865; 5 children. (TJ Sat. May 23, 1891, pp 2 & 3). [see also Dorsey].
WOODBURY, WILLIE. Drowned at Hay Fork Nov. 26, 1876; aged 2 yr 3 mo; son of David and Lizzie Woodbury; bur. Weaverville Cem. Nov. 28, 1876. (TJ Dec. 2, 1876). [legible gravestone 1980].
WOODS, GEO. W. Died Weaverville Aug. 27, 1873; native of Indiana, aged 40 yr 6 mo; of Rush Creek; pioneer of Trinity Co. (TJ Aug. 30, 1873).
WOODS, HORACE. Died Ca_on Creek Nov 7, 1898; b. Eureka North, Sierra Co. Calif Dec 8, 1858, aged 39 yr 10 mo 29 dy; description of accident p 3 col 3; bur. Weaverville I.O.O.F. Cem. "Sierra County papers please copy." (TJ Nov 12, 1898 pp 2 & 3).
WOODSIDES, JOHN. Died Lewiston Sept. 18, 1860 "of injuries received in his mining claim"; native of Ireland, late of Philadelphia, aged about 28 years. Bur. Weav. Cem. Sept. 19, 1860. (TJ Sept. 22, 1860 p 2, col 4 & col 1).

WOODS, L. B., Mrs. Died Fall River City, Shasta Co., Mar. 30, 1889; formerly of Junction City, nee Segalia; left Weaverville abt 1888; fun. Mar. 31, 1889 Fall River, Shasta Co., CA. (TJ Apr. 6, 1889 p 3 & Apr. 13, 1889 p 3). [Trinity Co. Marriages Book I page 77: Married at Junction City June 29, 1887 by J. C. Clark, J. P., Lewis Baldwin Woods and Miss Martha Jane Segalia, both of Junction City; Lewis age 32, native of New Hampshire; parents American; Martha, age 19, native of Calif; father Greek; mother Irish; neither previously married]. [see also Segalia].

WOTTRING, JOSEPH. Died Weaverville Oct 13, 1894; native of Penn., aged about 68 yr. (TJ Sat. Oct 20, 1894 p 2).

WYKOFF, GEORGE. Died Virgin Creek, New River area, Trinity Co. July 10, 1894; native of Penn, aged about 56 yr. (TJ Sat. July 21, 1894).

YALE, M. H. Died Weaverville August 1897; native of Conn., aged abt 81 yr; located at Canon Creek in 1853. (TJ Sep 11, 1897 p 2).

YANCEY, WILLIAM K. Died Weaverville Sept. 22, 1863; aged 31 years. Formerly of Lick Creek, Ralls County, Missouri. (TJ Sept. 26, 1863).

YOHE, GEORGE. Died Weaverville abt Jan. 21, 1893; native of Penn, aged about 69 yr; one of earliest residents of Trinity County; kept a hotel at North Fork (Helena); lived there until a little over a year ago. (TJ Sat. Jan. 21, 1893). [see also Weed].

YOUNG, DOLLY. Died Hay Fork Nov. 9, 1873; aged 2 months. Daughter of F. W. and Mary E. Young. (TJ Nov. 15, 1873). [Index to Deaths 1873-1890 adds white, female, single, born Calif.] [Legible grave marker in I.O.O.F. section of the Weaverville Cemetery 1976].

YOUNG, FRANK WAYLAND. Died Weaverville Apr 1, 1882; born Fiskville, nr. Pawtucket, Rhode Island 20 June 1827; aged 54 yr 9 mo 12 days; left home Mar. 5, 1849; came to Trinity County 1852/3 via Trinity River from Humboldt Bay; m. Nov. 21, 1861, Miss Mary E. Bayles, of Hay Fork; leaves brother in California; mother, brother & sister in Cambridgeport, Mass. (TJ Apr. 8, 1882 p. 2 & 3). [One brother: John T. Young, conducted Bank Exchange Saloon with Frank W. Young; left Weaverville 1865; went to Humboldt Co.; Deputy Sheriff of Humboldt Co. Aug. 1892. (TJ Sat. Aug 6, 1892 p 3 col 2)]. [see also Vanderhoff & Martin].

YOUNG, FRANK WHEELER. Died Weaverville July 8, 1875; aged 6 yr 8 mo 6 days; son of Frank W. and Mary E. Young. Bur. Weaverville Cem. [Odd Fellows' section] July 9, 1875. (TJ July 10, 1875).

YOUNG, GEORGE W. Died Hyampom Nov 29, 1899; native of Calif., aged 42 yr 2 mo 23 dy. (TJ Dec 9, 1899 p 2).

YOUNG, NATHAN AUGUSTUS. Died Weaverville June 5, 1878; born 23 April 1835 in Pawtucket, R.I.; aged 43 yrs 1 mo 13 days. Came to Calif. Mar. 1852, Weaverville June 1852; unmarried; Sgt. in Union Army; brother of Frank W. Young, Weaverville; John T. Young in Humboldt County; mother, sister & brother in Eastern States. Bur. in family plot of Frank W. Young in Odd Fellows Cem., Weaverville Thurs. June 6, 1878. (TJ June 8, 1878 p. 2 & 3).

YOUNG, SAMUEL. Died Eureka, Humboldt County, March 26, 1870; aged 4 mo 26 days; only child of John T. and Elizabeth Young. (TJ Apr. 16, 1870 p 2).

YOUNG, THOMAS, Mr. Died at residence of J. F. Hoadley, Trinity County, May 28, 1859; born at Stark, Herkimer Co, New York; aged about 43 years; formerly of Sandy Creek, Orleans County, New York; lived in the Ferry Bar area of Douglas City; miners' tribute. (TJ June 4, 1859 p 2).

YOUNG, THOMAS. Shot at Lewiston in May 1859; native of the town of Schuyler, Herkimer County, New York. Buried in Weaverville Cem. nr. the grave of his lifelong friend John Sterling, who died June 1, 1861 in Douglas City. Both were former partners of T. E. Jones, publisher of the Douglas City Gazette. (DCG June 5, 1861). (see Sterling & Jones.)

YULE, ELIZABETH. Died San Francisco June 14, 1890; age 45; widow of John Yule, who disappeared mysteriously two years ago. (TJ June 21, 1890).

ZEIGLER, DAVID ISAIAH (written Zigler). Died Willow Creek, Humboldt Co. Oct. 20, 1877; aged 8 mo 8 days; son of I. Zeigler. (TJ Oct. 27, 1877 p 2). [at North Fork, Trinity Co., 1860 census].

ZIMMERMAN, EDWARD E. Died August 5, 1907 Hayfork, abt 32, male, white, miner; buried Weaverville. [Index to Deaths 1890-1908].

ZWISSIG, JOHN. Died Aug. 17, 1905 near Wildwood, Trinity County, CA; age 50, male, white, born Germany; teamster. Buried by Knights of Pythias in Harrison Gulch, Shasta County, Calif. [Index to Deaths 1890-1908].

END TRINITY COUNTY DEATHS 1850 - 1950

PIONEER RECORDS OF TRINITY COUNTY, CALIFORNIA
TRINITY COUNTY, CALIFORNIA INDEX TO DEATHS
1900 - 1950

See the LEGEND for the sources for this Index.

[Note: many residents of Trinity County have died in Redding, Shasta, California, and some in Eureka, Humboldt, California. If a name is not in this list, check the other counties.]

NAME	DATE OF DEATH	AGE	BIRTHPLACE
ABANDO, ESTIBON	Aug 09, 1930	19 yr	
ABBOTT, JOHN F.	Aug 14, 1939	83 yr 2 mo	California
ABSHIER, RAYMOND VIRGIL	Jun 21, 1949	21 yr	California
ACKERMAN, CHARLES L.	Sep 27, 1947	87 yr 4 mo 4 dy	Idaho
ACKERMAN, J. C.	Feb 19, 1905	abt 48 yr	New York
ADAMS, C. F. Mrs.	Feb 15, 1901	65 yr	
ADAMS, HARRY A.	Nov 01, 1946	47 yr	
ADAMS, HAZEL M.	Jan 10, 1908	abt 4 yr	California
ADAMS, JOHN QUINCY	Jul 14, 1925	64 yr 11 mo 25 dy	
ADLER, GEORGE M.	May 14, 1925	65 yr 11 dy	
AH BOW	Jun 18, 1912	78 yr	
AH CHIN	Jan 19, 1911	70 yr	
AH DIN	Jul 15, 1912	70 yr	
AH DOCK	Apr 27, 1912	65 yr	
AH FIE	Feb 01, 1913	86 yr	
AH GONG	Apr 27, 1923	abt 80 yr	
AH GOW	Sep 28, 1924	66 yr	
AH MOY	Jan 31, 1913	77 yr	
AH OCK	Mar 28, 1912	64 yr	
AH OCK	May 27, 1933	84 yr	China
AH SENG	Feb 22, 1932	84 yr	China
AH SHUCK	May 03, 1921	abt 83 yr	
AH SING	Sep 09, 1926	80 yr	
AH SON	Sep 22, 1910	86 yr	
AH YOU	Dec 17, 1911	70 yr	
ALBIEZ, KARL	Dec 07, 1936	82 yr 6 mo 22 dy	Germany
ALDRICH, ELERY FRANCIS	Feb 15, 1949	70 yr 1 mo 4 dy	Oregon
ALDRICH, JAMES E.	Oct 29, 1906	abt 25 yr	Kansas
ALEXANDER, JAMES	Feb 07, 1903	85 yr	Louisiana
ALEXANDER, ROBERT	Sep 27, 1931	65 yr	
ALLEN, B. W.	Oct 09, 1908	abt 48 yr	Illinois
ALVERSON, CHESTAIN	May 19, 1900	50 yr	Kentucky
AMES, C. H.	Oct 21, 1909	abt 43 yr	Minnesota
AMMON, MARY	Jan 28, 1946	76 yr 5 mo 23 dy	California
ANDERLINI, JOHN JOSEPH	Aug 17, 1915	65 yr 15 dy	
ANDERSON, BABY (female)	Dec 31, 1939	stillborn	California
ANDERSON, EDWARD EMANUEL	Sep 30, 1938	50 yr 8 mo 9 dy	Iowa
ANDERSON, JAMES TEMPLE	Dec 20, 1907	abt 73 yr	Tennessee
ANDERSON, JOSEPH	May 13, 1907	abt 23 yr	Utah
ANDERSON, LUDWIG MITTIANCE	Mar 03, 1940	49 yr	Minnesota
ANDERSON, SAMUEL	Dec 14, 1908	abt 47 yr	Michigan
ANDISON, BABY (unnamed female)	Jan 26, 1947	5 hr	California
ARBUCKLE, AMANDA MELVINA	Jan 04, 1927	87 yr 1 mo 12 dy	
ARGUELLO, FRANK	Jan 24, 1907	23 yr 9 mo 23 dy	California
ARGUELLO, MARGARET JEANETTE, Mrs.	Feb 12, 1927	69 yr 5 mo 11 dy	
ARKINS, JAMES	Sep 15, 1908	abt 85 yr	Rhode Is.
ARMENTROUT, HARRIET ELIZA	May 29, 1917	69 yr 1 mo 15 dy	
ARMENTROUT, JOHN W.	May 10, 1929	48 yr 5 dy	

Name	Date	Age	Birthplace
ARMENTROUT, JOHN WILLIAM	Dec 15, 1916	82 yr 9 mo 15 dy	
ARMENTROUT, LOAG	Dec 17, 1950	73 yr	California
ARMSTRONG, HAZEL	Nov 22, 1904	10 yr 10 mo 11dy	California
ARNOLD, CHARLES HENRY	Aug 21, 1937	64 yr 5 mo 24 dy	Louisiana
ASMUSSEN, ANDREW	Jun 28, 1902	abt 81 yr	Germany
ATHERTON, CHARLES LA VERNE	Feb 23, 1934	43 yr 7 mo 2 dy	Michigan
ATKESON, WM E.	Nov 10, 1900	63 yr 8 mo 25dy	Ohio
ATKINS, FRANK MERCULESS	Aug 13, 1935	71 yr 5 mo 25 dy	New York
ATKINS, HELEN CATHERINE	Oct 03, 1936	46 yr	California
AUGHINBAUGH, JAMES CLAYTON	Nov 30, 1916	42 yr	
AULT, PAUL L.	Oct 22, 1933	31 yr	Indiana
BACH, PETER	May 28, 1944	72 yr 1 mo 11 dy	Wisconsin
BACHER, J. M.	Aug 04, 1901	63 yr	Germany
BACHMAN, EDGAR	Oct 01, 1918	50 yr	
BAILEY, CHESTER WYATT	Sep 15, 1949	62 yr	Texas
BAILEY, FRANK LESLIE	Jun 12, 1950	75 yr	Oregon
BAILEY, Inf.dau. M/M G. L.	Jul 14, 1901	b.d.	California
BAILEY, Inf.dau. M/M GEO. L.	Apr 04, 1903	b.d.	California
BAKER, JACKSON EDWARD	Apr 12, 1940	47 yr	Indiana
BAKER, LOTTIE MIRANDA	Dec 28, 1930	80 yr 4 mo 24 dy	
BAKER, LUCINDA, Mrs.	May 18, 1903	84 yr 11 mo 23dy	Canada
BALCERA, JEAN	Mar 09, 1944	80 yr 5 mo 7 dy	France
BALCH, HENRY RIPLEY	Dec 17, 1944	72 yr 8 mo 5 dy	California
BALCH, ISABELLE McDONALD	Mar 03, 1943	68 yr 1 mo 14 dy	New York
BANDEL, ELLA	Sep 15, 1940	61 yr	California
BANKEY, JOSEPH C.	Oct 22, 1932	49 yr 10 mo 18dy	Georgia
BANNON, JAMES HOLIDAY	Nov 11, 1935	78 yr 10 mo 6 dy	Penn.
BARBER, HARRY S.	Dec 09, 1907	21 yr 9 mo 26 dy	California
BARBER, HENRY DWIGHT	Sep 14, 1934	89 yr 8 mo 10 dy	Mass.
BARBER, RUTH ANN	Nov 27, 1932	84 yr 8 mo 19 dy	Rhode Is.
BARGER, JOHN PATTERSON	Apr 27, 1946	52 yr 8 mo 21 dy	Tennessee
BARKER, GEORGE	Nov 09, 1916	50 yr 6 mo	
BARKER, H. M., Dr.	May 14, 1905	abt 59 yr	Michigan
BARKER, inf.dau M/M D.	Dec 03, 1900	b.d.	California
BARKLA, ANNIE ELIZABETH	Nov 17, 1946	90 yr 2 mo 26 dy	Missouri
BARKLA, JAMES	Dec 09, 1910	77 yr	
BARKLA, ISAAC	Mar 04, 1921	78 yr 8 mo 22 dy	
BARNES, GEO. W.	Jul 05, 1900	71 yr 5 mo 18dy	New York
BARNHART, CLELL HIRAM	Feb 25, 1939	47 yr 1 mo 23 dy	Kansas
BARNICKEL, BERNHARD	Oct 27, 1921	45 yr 1 mo 23 dy	
BARRETT, CHARLES LEWIS (Elsie)	Apr 10, 1947	39 yr 6 mo 3 dy	California
BARRINGER, EDWIN LOREN	Sep 12, 1939	54 yr 11 mo 26dy	Wyoming
BARRY, EDW. R.	Jan 05, 1900	51 yr	New York
BARSTOW, CORWIN E.	Oct 24, 1934	69 yr	New York
BARSTOW, MAJOR	Oct 24, 1934	30 yr	Illinois
BARTLETT, DELIA NETTIELLEN	Aug 09, 1941	1 yr 6 mo 17 dy	California
BARTLETT, JAMES WILLIAM	Mar 15, 1936	73 yr 10 mo	
BARTLETT, LAVINA ROSE, Mrs.	Feb 04, 1927	66 yr 7 mo 14 dy	
BARTOLET, MONASSES	Jul 09, 1904	85 yr 9 mo 6 dy	Penn.
BASSHAM, ELBERT H.	May 03, 1923	50 yr 6 mo 7 dy	
BATES, ROBERT LEE	May 23, 1938	not given	Missouri
BATES, WALTER	Sep 15, 1917	46 yr	
BAUER, FREDERICK	Jan 19, 1902	55 yr	England
BEAN, ALMA C.	Oct 18, 1931	57 yr 6 mo 1 dy	
BEAN, LEONARD CROCKER	Sep 09, 1940	71 yr	California
BEARD, WILLIAM	Oct 24, 1917	84 yr	
BEAVERS, SAMUEL	Jul 09, 1901	60 yr	Ohio
BEBEAU, JOSEPH	Jan 18, 1908	abt 71 yr	Canada
BECK, ROY O.	Sep 25, 1946	39 yr	
BEERBOWER, NELSON HORATIO	Feb 27, 1949	83 yr	California
BEERBOWER, CARLIN URIAH	Jul 29, 1949	71 yr	California
BEHRING, ANTONE	Feb 15, 1940	78 yr	Germany
BELL, EDWARD STANLEY	Dec 12, 1940	55 yr	California

DEATHS 1900 - 1950

Name	Date	Age	Birthplace
BELL, FRANK A.	Apr 14, 1909	abt 85 yr	
BELL, MATHIAS	Dec 01, 1926	69 yr 2 mo 21 dy	
BELLI, ELVY	Jul 23, 1903	15 yr 7 mo 4 dy	Nevada
BENDER, HENRY	Nov 01, 1900	60 yr	Germany
BENDER, ORE	Sep 09, 1932	62 yr	Illinois
BENNETT, BENJAMIN McP.	Mar __, 1901	24 yr	California
BENNETT, CARRIE ELIDA	May 06, 1932	78 yr 7 mo	Norway
BENNETT, FLORA EMMELINE	Feb 22, 1950	90 yr	California
BENNETT, FRANCIS, Mrs.	Mar 10, 1904	abt 60 yr	
BENNETT, HARVEY SQUIRES	Mar 09, 1938	42 yr 8 mo 12 dy	New York
BENNETT, LOUIS	Mar 04, 1949	72 yr	California
BENNETT, LULA MAY	May 08, 1909	17 yr 4 dy	California
BENNETT, MARCUS MORTON	Dec 11, 1921	80 yr 4 mo 6 dy	
BENNETT, WILLIAM TECUMSEH	Dec 18, 1911	44 yr	
BENSON, CARL JOHN	Jun 19, 1914	64 yr 15 dy	
BENSON, JOHN	May 15, 1939	84 yr 1 mo	Ireland
BERBER, WILLIAM HENRY	Jul 26, 1919	82 yr 8 mo 22 dy	
BERG, GUSTAVE	Jul 16, 1926	22 yr 3 mo	
BERGIN, ALAFAIRE	Feb 20, 1940	55 yr	California
BERGIN, CHAS. E.	Mar 22, 1900	32 yr 10 mo 28 dy	California
BERGIN, MARGARET HANNAH	Aug 21, 1914	73 yr 5 mo 26 dy	
BERGSTROM, WILLIAM JOHN	Dec 18, 1940	57 yr	California
BESTON, THOMAS J.	Dec 21, 1945	70 yr 2 mo 28 dy	California
BESTTON, THOMAS J.	May 30, 1946	70 yr	
BETTENCOURT, MARIA A., Mrs.	Nov 10, 1906	81 yr 7 mo 26 dy	Azores Is.
BETZER, inf.ch. M/M R.R.	Aug 16, 1912	4 dy	
BICKETT, ARTHUR JOSEPH	Jun 30, 1938	48 yr 2 mo 13 dy	California
BIGELOW, HARVEY LOWELL	Feb 19, 1946	54 yr 1 mo 23 dy	California
BIGELOW, JAMES ALLEN	Jan 03, 1941	6 yr 10 mo 6 dy	California
BIGELOW, LOWELL CLEMENT	Sep 05, 1925	b.d.	
BIGELOW, MAUD AVILLA	Apr 22, 1944	76 yr 2 mo 14 dy	California
BIGELOW, WILLIAM R., Sr	Jun 05, 1934	71 yr 6 dy	Australia
BIGGERSTAFF, ARDEN CROSBY	Feb 12, 1937	63 yr 2 mo 2 dy	Arkansas
BIRMINGHAM, MICHAEL	Oct 31, 1908	abt 93 yr	Ireland
BISHOP, J. W.	Jul 13, 1928	43 yr 2 mo	
BISSETT, HATTIE A., Mrs.	Nov 30, 1950	73 yr	Missouri
BLACKWELL, GEO. WASHINGTON	Nov 10, 1905	abt 55 yr	Ohio
BLAGRAVE, GEORGE H.	Jun 22, 1918	47 yr 6 dy	
BLAIR, BENJAMIN M.	Aug 17, 1937	76 yr 8 mo 23 dy	California
BLAIR, JAMES GIBSON	Mar 25, 1913	6 mo 11 dy	
BLAIR, JOHN	Aug 02, 1910	73 yr 8 mo 8 dy	
BLAIR, ROBERT	Jan 15, 1916	86 yr	
BLAKE, DORA, Mrs.	Aug 05, 1902	23 yr 10 mo 15dy	Oregon
BLAKE, MORRIS JACK	Jun 09, 1947	54 yr 10 mo 7 dy	Kansas
BLAKE, SELDEN M.	Oct 11, 1904	17 yr 8 mo 13 dy	California
BLAKEMORE, J. A.	Oct 03, 1900	76 yr	Virginia
BLAKEMORE, URSULA, Mrs.	Aug 17, 1906	56 yr 3 mo 25 dy	Germany
BLANEY, HONORA, Mrs.	Jan 18, 1910	67 yr 5 mo 16 dy	
BLANEY, HUGH	Dec 20, 1928	76 yr	
BLANKENSHIP, FRANCES EMMA	Oct 09, 1937	37 yr	Illinois
BLANKENSHIP, GEORGE DANIEL	Jan 24, 1941	41 yr 11 mo 0 dy	Rhode Is.
BLARE, HENRY	Jun 11, 1922	65 yr	
BLUE, LINDA IRENE	Sep 23, 1941	3 mo 24 dy	California
BLUFORD, ADDISON	Dec 20, 1907	abt 78 yr	
BOB, MARY	Mar 23, 1910	80 yr	
BOGLE, MICHAEL	Nov 09, 1911	79 yr	
BOIDES, JOHN	Oct 24, 1907	abt 81 yr	France
BOLES, B. F.	Sep 07, 1904	abt 64 yr	
BOLES, JOHN	Aug 06, 1911	81 yr	
BOLTZ, JOHN	Mar 15, 1915	90 yr	
BOND, SYLVESTER	Jan 21, 1921	66 yr 7 mo 17 dy	
BOPE, JOHN FRANCIS	Apr 26, 1935	74 yr 4 mo 9 dy	California
BORGES, JAUQUIN A.	Nov 20, 1929	44 yr 3 mo 19 dy	

Name	Date	Age	Birthplace
BOSWORTH, M., Mrs.	Dec 27, 1900	27 yr 1 mo 1 dy	California
BOUERY, inf.son M/M PIERRE	Jan 30, 1913	b.d.	
BOURGOIS, RAYMOND LEE	Jun 05, 1950	28 yr	California.
BOWEN, LAWRENCE HENDERSON	Jul 28, 1946	53 yr 11 mo 24dy	Minnesota
BOWER, MARTIN BAX	Sep 01, 1931	69 yr 4 dy	
BOWERMAN, FRANK LESLIE	May 15, 1920	45 yr 8 mo 19 dy	
BOWERMAN, JACOB	Oct 11, 1917	83 yr 11 mo 17dy	
BOWERS, ELIZABETH HELEN	Apr 01, 1936	60 yr 4 mo 29 dy	Indiana
BOWERY, T. E.	Jun 25, 1902	65 yr	
BOWIE, JAMES	Oct 20, 1901	57 yr 11 mo 10 dy	Penn.
BOWLES, SARAH JANE	Apr 23, 1938	88 yr 8 mo 29 dy	Missouri
BOX, BERTHA LENORA	Feb 26, 1915	15 dy	California
BOYCE, CHARLES O.	Dec 26, 1936	46 yr 8 mo 15 dy	California
BOYCE, HELEN MARGARET, Mrs.	Jan 08, 1948	84 yr 11 mo 20dy	California
BOYCE, JOHN HENRY	Aug 12, 1941	77 yr 8 mo 3 dy	California
BOYD, ALEXANDER	Jan 13, 1918	81 yr	
BOYLE, HUGH	Oct 28, 1912	59 yr	
BRADBURY, JOSEPHUS	Jan 31, 1904	78 yr 10 mo 27 dy	England
BRADLEY, JOHN PAUL	Jun 18, 1945	84 yr 11 mo 27dy	S.Carolina
BRADLEY, W.	Apr 06, 1933	24 yr	
BRAGDON, EDWIN H.	Oct 05, 1909	abt 52 yr	Maine
BRAMLET, JOSEPH EDWARD	Aug 03, 1941	44 yr 6 mo 28 dy	California
BRANEN, AUGUST	Oct 05, 1908	abt 40 yr	Sweden
BRANNAN, JAMES	Mar 04, 1907	82 yr 1 mo 25 dy	Ireland
BRANNUM, EDWARD WILLIAM	Jun 09, 1933	64 yr 7 mo 3 dy	Germany
BREMER, ELONIA LOUISE	Jan 09, 1915	1 DAY	California
BREMER, CARL WILLIAM	Dec 21, 1950	81 yr	Germany
BREMER, J. H.	Jan 19, 1928	86 yr 3 mo 19 dy	
BREMER, LOUISA	Jul 24, 1912	69 yr 27 dy	
BREWER, ANTHONY	Jul 27, 1930	39 yr	
BRINK, NESS NEILING	Feb 05, 1933	66 yr 7 mo 16 dy	Denmark
BRINKMAN, SUSIE	Aug 14, 1920	22 yr	
BRODERICK, ALONZO G.	Jul 17, 1927	77 yr 7 mo 16 dy	
BRODT, GEORGE	Mar 18, 1912	53 yr	
BROOKS, SMITH B.	Jul 25, 1907	abt 74 yr	Ohio
BROWDER, HARRIETT, Mrs.	Jun 02, 1901	68 yr	Tennessee
BROWDER, NELSON I.	Aug 31, 1912	48 yr	
BROWN, ARTHUR	Jul 01, 1948	67 yr 8 mo 2 dy	Iowa
BROWN, BOYER RITTER	Mar 19, 1938	62 yr 5 mo 14 dy	Nevada
BROWN, CAROLINE	May 13, 1900	70 yr	N.Scotia
BROWN, CHAS. L.	Jan 25, 1900	71 yr	Austria
BROWN, DOLPH G.	Aug 28, 1935	39 yr 2 mo 15 dy	California
BROWN, HERBERT U.	Aug 25, 1935	44 yr 6 mo 10 dy	Illinois
BROWN, JULIA ANN, Mrs.	Apr 08, 1908	85 yr 9 mo 1 dy	New York
BROWN, JULIA ANN WELDEN, Mrs.	May 24, 1926	54 yr 16 mo 28 dy	
BROWN, MARION	Sep 29, 1910	3 yr 8 dy	California
BROWN, RICHARD	Dec 06, 1913	77 yr	
BROWN, RICHARD C.	Oct 04, 1931	46 yr 2 mo 1 dy	
BROWN, T. J.	Mar 31, 1928	87 yr 10 mo 8 dy	
BROWN, THEODORE M.	Jul 21, 1932	30 yr	
BROWN, WESLEY JAMES	Dec 13, 1924	1 yr 8 mo 15 dy	
BROWN, WILLIS G.	Feb 09, 1933	65 yr	Illinois
BROWNE, HORACE GUSTAVUS	Jan 12, 1912	75 yr 2 mo 1 dy	
BROWNE, PHILLIP SAMUEL	Nov 29, 1912	78 yr 5 mo 13 dy	
BROWNING, WILLIAM OLIVER	Oct 16, 1947	83 yr 7 mo 25 dy	Illinois
BUCHTEL, WILLIAM WAUGH	Mar 02, 1949	40 yr	Colorado
BUCKLEY, JOHN A.	Sep 27, 1941	60 yr 11 mo	Minnesota
BUDRICK, RUBY OPAL	Nov 02, 1936	42 yr 11 mo 12dy	Illinois
BURGER, JOHN	Apr 10, 1949	61 yr	California
BURGER, MAY ELIZABETH	Sep 05, 1947	71 yr 1 mo 9 dy	Missouri
BURGESS, CLARA EMMA	Feb 22, 1940	79 yr	Maine
BURGESS, EDWARD FRANCIS	Sep 10, 1931	76 yr 2 mo 10 dy	
BURGESS, GEORGE HOWARD	Aug 22, 1912	1 yr 7 dy	

Name	Date	Age	Origin
BURGESS, IRENE E.	Jul 17, 1944	47 yr 3 mo 2 dy	California
BURGESS, ZERA EDWARD	Nov 08, 1911	30 yr 9 mo 26 dy	
BURGETT, HENRY	Aug 21, 1930	63 yr 6 mo	
BURGOYNE, Mrs.	Jan 16, 1904	81 yr	Wisconsin
BURKE, WILLIAM CURTIS	Jul 23, 1948	76 yr 6 mo 1 dy	California
BURMAN, CLARA L.	Jul 15, 1942	64 yr 8 mo 20 dy	Texas
BURNS, ALEXANDER	Jun 18, 1924	4 dy	
BURNS, SALLIE	Jul 11, 1927	47 yr	
BURNSIDE, WALTER	MAY 08, 1942	23 yr 8 mo 23 dy	Oklahoma
BUSH, ABRAHAM LINCOLN	Jan 21, 1934	70 yr 7 mo 4 dy	California
BUSH, JAMES A.	Jan 28, 1903	52 yr	Missouri
BUSH, MARY JANE	Nov 10, 1931	75 yr 3 mo 10 dy	
BUSS, HARRY FREDERICK, Jr.	Aug 19, 1950	1 dy	California.
BUTCHER, CLARK	Jun 04, 1912	80 yr	
BUTLER, ALLEN	Jul 26, 1900	81 yr 9 mo 26 dy	England
BUTLER, FREDERIC PIERCE	Sep 16, 1941	66 yr 1 mo 27 dy	California
BUTLER, inf.dau.M/M JESSE R.	Oct 24, 1911	b.d.	
BUTLER, L. F. R.	May 19, 1928	65 yr 9 mo 14 dy	
BUTTERFIELD, PAUL FRANCIS	Apr 24, 1937	27 yr 5 mo 19 dy	Nevada
BUTTS, JOSHUA	Sep 25, 1910	81 yr	
BUXTON, WILLIAM	Aug 22, 1933	23 yr 2 mo 22 dy	California
BYRUM, WILLIAM P.	Mar 12, 1915	86 yr	
CADEMARTORI, FRANK	Oct 01, 1926	82 yr 7 mo 14 dy	
CADEMARTORI, MADELENE FEDORA	Apr 28, 1905	22 yr 2 mo 8 dy	California
CADERMARTORI, MARY A.	Nov 23, 1922	68 yr 3 mo 23 dy	
CADWELL, DADDRIDGE RUSSELL	Mar 15, 1931	77 yr	
CAINE, ERVIN JOSEPH	Jul 03, 1937	32 yr 8 mo	
CAMERON, CONSTANT FIELDS	Jun 07, 1934	65 yr 6 mo 1 dy	Illinois
CAMERON, MINNIE ANN	Feb 15, 1946	80 yr 2 mo 0 dy	Kansas
CAMPBELL, CYREL HENRY	Nov 23, 1908	2 mo 22 dy	California
CAMPBELL, DONALD NIEL	Mar 07, 1944	67 yr 2 mo 16 dy	Michigan
CAMPBELL, ELMER THOMAS	Sep 09, 1907	4 mo 7 dy	California
CAMPBELL, inf.son M/M THOMAS	Sep 08, 1907	b.d.	California
CAMPBELL, inf.dau M/M W.	Jan 10, 1901	b.d.	
CAMPBELL, NICHOLAS H.	Jun 25, 1905	27 yr	California
CAMPBELL, THOMAS, Mrs.	Jan 27, 1902	abt 60 yr	
CAMPBELL, VIRGINIA MAY	May 01, 1925	16 yr 11 mo 19 dy	
CAMPBELL, WILLIAM, Mrs.	Mar 27, 1908	abt 29 yr	
CANCIENCE, WILLIAM J.	Feb 13, 1926	44 yr	
CANE, JOHN C.	Nov 07, 1921	71 yr 10 mo	
CANFIELD, ELIZABETH FRANCIS	Feb 18, 1902	68 yr 1 mo	Ohio
CANWELL, JOHN P.	Jan 08, 1908	abt 46 yr	New York
CARISCH, CHRIS	May 27, 1906	abt 45 yr	
CARLSEN, ANDREW EVERETT	May 19, 1934	67 yr 8 mo 6 dy	Kentucky
CARPENTER, CHARLES H.	Feb 05, 1916	76 yr 10 mo 8 dy	
CARPENTER, C. W.	Jul 13, 1928	39 yr 11 mo 29 dy	
CARPENTER, HARNEY HERMAN	Nov 05, 1923	2 mo 19 dy	
CARPENTER, SARAH JANE	Aug 11, 1902	5 mo 22 dy	California
CARR, ALEXANDER CONSTANTINE	Dec 22, 1941	89 yr 2 mo 5 dy	Indiana
CARR, ALICE MAY	Nov 30, 1902	18 yr 8 mo 27 dy	California
CARR, CHARLES A.	Sep 28, 1946	71 yr 10 mo 8 dy	Iowa
CARR, FREDERICK ELMER	Feb 21, 1918	31 yr 2 mo 5 dy	
CARR, GEO. L.	May 12, 1910	45 yr	
CARR, JULIA	Dec 18, 1936	47 yr 2 mo 21 dy	New York
CARR, MARY EMILY	Feb 16, 1917	85 yr 8 mo 22 dy	
CARR, SARAH JANE, Mrs.	Nov 02, 1902	64 yr 8 mo 3 dy	Ireland
CARR, WILLIAM DOUGLAS	Apr 20, 1935	85 yr	Indiana
CARSON, JAMES	Nov 10, 1906	84 yr 7 mo	Ireland
CARTER, JAMES A.	Apr 28, 1926	61 yr 8 mo 18 dy	
CARTER, JOHN W.	Mar 11, 1907	80 yr 10 mo 1 dy	Tennessee
CARTER, inf.son M/M J.A.	Feb 05, 1903	1 mo 3 dy	California
CARTER, MILLARD F.	Aug 21, 1914	56 yr 8 mo 11 dy	
CARTER, R.J. MRS	Apr 27, 1900	61 yr 3 mo 21 dy	Ind.Terr.

Name	Date	Age	Birthplace
CARTER, ROBERT M.	Dec 27, 1945	unknown	
CASS, CHARLES LUCIEN	Jan 08, 1911	76 yr 5 mo 19 dy	
CHAMBERLAIN, J. J.	Nov 24, 1908	abt 66 yr	Wisconsin
CHAMBERLAIN, JOSEPH C.	Feb 03, 1907	60 yr	U.S.A.
CHANCE, CORA, Miss	Apr 16, 1900	20 yr	Ohio
CHANEY, IRA J.	Jun 23, 1944	65 yr 2 mo 28 dy	Ohio
CHANEY, WM. OLIVER	Jan 01, 1944	46 yr 9 mo 3 dy	Oregon
CHANNER, W. B.	Jun 07, 1928	29 yr	
CHAPDELAINE, ROBERT FRANCIS	Oct 14, 1945	32 yr 3 mo 12 dy	California
CHAPMAN, GEORGE FRANCIS	Mar 04, 1911	5 mo 1 dy	
CHAPMAN, GEO. P.	Oct 08, 1901	72 yr 8 mo 23 dy	New York
CHAPMAN, LENA MARIE	Nov 26, 1936	30 yr 11 mo 22dy	Colorado
CHAPMAN, STELLA BELLE	Jan 22, 1915	24 yr 3 mo 25 dy	
CHAPPELL, GLENN ALFRED	Nov 21, 1941	27 yr 10 mo 9 dy	California
CHAPPELL, LYLE JACK	Jan 14, 1950	23 yr	California
CHEN TOY	Apr 01, 1919	98 yr	
CHESBRO, inf.dau M/M JAMES	Aug 06, 1916	6 mo 5 dy	
CHESBRO, MILTON J.	Sep 15, 1931	21 yr	
CHESEBRO, inf.ch. M/M JAS.	Mar 10, 1913	4 mo	
CHESTER, inf.son M/M W. M.	Apr 27, 1918	10 mo	
CHEW GEE	Jul 20, 1915	75 yr	
CHEW YOUNG	Sep 27, 1915	75 yr	
CHILDERS, FREDERICK NEWTON	Nov 08, 1939	57 yr 7 mo 19 dy	California
CHIN, LIM	Nov 05, 1946	unknown	
CHIN QUONG PAN	Oct 19, 1923	80 yr	
CHING, JIM	Aug 08, 1910	68 yr	
CHRISTINE, LYELL HOWARD	May 10, 1947	30 yr 9 mo 28 dy	Kansas
CHRONBSALL, EDWARD HENRY	Jan 15, 1913	40 yr	
CHUE CHIN	Jun 25, 1925	48 yr 3 mo 10 dy	
CLARK, ARTHUR C.	Nov 06, 1914	43 yr	
CLARK, ARTHUR ROBIN	Aug 16, 1933	55 yr 4 mo 24 dy	Arizona
CLARK, FRANK	Aug 07, 1949	81 yr	Penn.
CLARK, JAMES C.	Sep 27, 1901	68 yr	New York
CLARK, MARTHA ELIZABETH	Mar 03, 1918	22 yr 21 dy	
CLARK, SAMUEL	Jul 12, 1910	48 yr	
CLARKE, inf.son M/M ARTHUR	Nov 21, 1905	5 mo 17 dy	California
CLARKE, LAWRENCE PAUL	Sep 17, 1947	82 yr 2 mo 11 dy	Penn.
CLARKE, THOMAS	May 20, 1911	63 yr	
CLAVICH, JOHN	Mar 17, 1915	33 yr 9 mo 16 dy	
CLAY, THOMAS C.	Apr 14, 1904	abt 62 yr	Missouri
CLAYTON, GEORGE HIGGINS	Jul 20, 1914	82 yr 17 dy	
CLAYTON, HARVEY S.	Jan 27, 1947	67 yr 11 mo 27dy	California
CLEAVES, BABY (male)	Dec 21, 1948	9 hr 30 min	California
CLEAVES, CHARLES DeFOREST	May 13, 1941	51 yr 10 mo 3 dy	California
CLEAVES, CHARLES SAMUEL	Feb 10, 1918	58 yr 9 mo 21 dy	
CLEAVES, MYRTIE J.	Mar 15, 1940	70 yr	California
CLEMENT, CHARLES EDWIN	May 22, 1936	71 yr 7 mo 12 dy	California
CLEMENT, WILLIAM H.	Aug 13, 1923	60 yr 11 mo 20dy	
CLEMENTS, OLIVER C.	May 18, 1902	61 yr	Iowa
CLIFFORD, ELLEN	Sep 15, 1927	77 yr	
COBB, IRVIN T., Jr.	Apr 26, 1944	unknown	Alabama
COBRAGES, M.	Jul 07, 1913	unknown	
COCHRAN, HENRY	Feb 07, 1923	35 or 36 yr	
COCHRAN, WILLIAM	Apr 19, 1947	57 yr 0 mo 6 dy	Nebraska
COCKEYE JIM	Jan 10, 1917	85 yr	
COHEN, EDWARD H.	Mar 24, 1923	48 yr	
COLBERT, JOHN	Aug 04, 1925	73 yr 3 mo	
COLEMAN, JOHN	Apr 12, 1941	38 yr 3 mo 27 dy	
COLLAR, EVA MAY	Aug 05, 1921	28 yr 4 mo 13 dy	
COLLINS, IRA C.	Jul 21, 1915	80 yr	
COLLINS, RICHARD	Apr 10, 1903	76 yr	Ireland
COLLINS, THOMAS	Oct 13, 1935	88 yr 5 mo 27 dy	Ireland
COLLOPY, JOHN	Nov 12, 1915	82 yr	

DEATHS 1900 - 1950

Name	Date	Age	Place
COMPTON, JOHN B.	Sep 18, 1910	58 yr	
CONDON, CARRIE IRENE	Jul 06, 1944	84 yr 11 mo 29dy	California
CONDON, JOHN JOSEPH	Nov 26, 1924	59 yr 6 mo 14 dy	
CONDON, WILLIAM	Jun 03, 1912	48 yr 9 mo 21 dy	
CONDON, WM S	Feb 04, 1900	3 mo 27 dy	California
CONLIN, ANDREW S.	Jul 01, 1916	45 yr	
CONNELL, JOHN	Jun 21, 1905	abt 82 yr	Ireland
CONNELL, LAWRENCE E.	May 25, 1942	54 yr 7 mo 19 dy	New York
CONNELLY, MICHAEL	Feb 03, 1939	66 yr 4 mo 22 dy	Minnesota
CONNER, inf.son M/M J. B.	Oct 31, 1910	28 dy	California
CONNER, JOHN BOONE	Sep 03, 1925	62 yr 5 mo 17 dy	
CONNOLLY, ELIZABETH BURGOYNE	Dec 10, 1937	83 yr 4 mo 20 dy	Wisconsin
CONNOR, JOHN	Jan 06, 1913	55 yr	
CONOVER, DANIEL SHELDON	Oct 30, 1939	64 yr 1 mo 13 dy	New York
CONWAY, ELLEN NORA	Jan 27, 1938	67 yr 7 dy	California
CONWAY, ELMER ELSEWORTH	Oct 08, 1949	61 yr	Kansas
COOK, J. W.	Jun 24, 1916	62 yr	
COOKSEY, HOWARD LEE ROY	Feb 23, 1939	31 yr 1 mo 6 dy	Missouri
COOPER, A. A.	Aug 19, 1928	52 yr	
COPELAND, CHARLES HOSEA	Oct 09, 1943	75 yr 9 mo 18 dy	N.Carolina
CORDES, GEORGE W.	Sep 01, 1943	60 yr	California
CORDOZA, inf.son M/M FRANK (twin #1), Mar 3, 1908, b. Mar 3, 1908			California
CORDOZA, inf.son M/M FRANK (twin #2), Mar 5, 1908, b. Mar 3, 1908			California
CORNELL, ELONZO	Jul 17, 1904	75 yr 6 mo 9 dy	Ohio
COSTA, inf.son OF M/M JESSE	Aug 09, 1902	4 mo	California
COSTA, JESSE	Feb 07, 1932	70 yr 10 mo 20 dy	Azores Is.
COSTELLO, THOMAS	Nov 24, 1901	70 yr	Ireland
COUMBS, CHARLOTTE E.	Dec 03, 1901	4 yr 8 mo 10 dy	California
COUMBS, DAISY M.	Jun 05, 1942	73 yr 4 mo 6 dy	Vermont
COUMBS, JOHN	Sep 24, 1902	74 yr	England
COUMBS, JOYCE MAITLAND	Jul 01, 1949	38 yr	California.
COUMBS, MARY ELIZABETH	Jul 03, 1903	28 yr	California
COUMBS, THOMAS	Mar 16, 1912	69 yr 10 mo 13 dy	
COUMBS, T. W.	Jul 04, 1928	28 yr 8 mo 23 dy	
COUMBS, WALTER SCOTT	Oct 21, 1921	86 yr 11 mo 16dy	
COURSEY, LeROY	Jan 11, 1950	57 yr	Kansas
COWAN, DAVID A.	Aug 23, 1922	57 yr	
COWENS, GERTRUDE, Mrs.	Nov 19, 1908	abt 64 yr	Iowa
COX, inf.son M/M SOL	Nov 30, 1903	b.d.	California
COX, JAMES H.	Apr 25, 1925	60 yr 10 mo 25dy	
COYLE, MARION C.	Feb 26, 1942	68 yr 9 mo 10 dy	Texas
CRANE, J. A.	Sep 02, 1907	abt 44 yr	Michigan
CRANK, JOHN R.	Oct 09, 1915	31 yr	
CRAWFORD, B. T.	Jun 03, 1900	28 yr 6 mo 3 dy	California
CRAWFORD, JAMES C.	Apr 01, 1913	30 yr	
CRAWFORD, JULIA GOOLA MARY	Oct 20, 1950	65 yr	Wisconsin
CREATH, GRACE GERTRUDE	May 09, 1939	50 yr 8 mo 22 dy	Ohio
CRESON, VERNON LEONARD	Aug 14, 1931	33 yr 10 mo 11dy	
CREWS, ANNIE MAY	Jul 21, 1947	79 yr 11 mo 27dy	California
CREWS, ROBERT H.	Oct 27, 1929	66 yr 1 mo 22 dy	
CRINE, RODERICK	Jul 15, 1918	18 yr 24 dy	
CROSS, WM. C.	Oct 06, 1913	87 yr	
CROSSON, IRA	Jun 26, 1918	54 yr	
CROWE, CHARLES WILLIAM	May 22, 1931	74 yr 1 mo 20 dy	
CROWE, JOHN MADISON	Feb 28, 1913	88 yr 11 mo	
CRUTHIS, JESSE D.	Sep 13, 1913	80 yr 6 mo 2 dy	
CUFF, RICHARD WILLIAM	May 04, 1934	73 yr 4 mo 28 dy	Ireland
CULBERTSON, CAROLINE PIERCE	Oct 27, 1945	65 yr 7 mo 5 dy	Mass.
CULBERTSON, WM. JOHN	Apr 15, 1946	71 yr 2 mo 13 dy	Canada
CUMMINGS, CLARA	Apr 01, 1937	68 yr 6 mo 1 dy	Wisconsin
CUMMINGS, FEDORA	Aug 06, 1905	46 yr 11 mo 18 dy	California
CUMMINGS, JAMES	Sep 03, 1908	abt 79 yr	England
CUMMINGS, JOHN F.	Mar 24, 1933	80 yr	Mass.

Name	Date	Age	Birthplace
CUMMINGS, JOHN HENDERSON	Jan 07, 1944	78 yr 7 mo 20 dy	California
CUMMINGS, JOHN SCOTT	Mar 23, 1904	abt 80 yr	England
CUMMINGS, THOMAS ALEXANDER	Nov 20, 1919	89 yr 11 mo 20 dy	
CURINGTON, TOM J.	Nov 05, 1948	69 yr	Texas
CURLESS, GEORGE S.	Jul 25, 1931	51 yr 2 mo 23 dy	
CURLY, EDWARD	Mar 17, 1900	51 yr	New York
CURTIS, LILY MAY	Feb 19, 1912	44 yr 6 mo 9 dy	
CURTZ, NETTIE MARGARET	Dec 09, 1943	71 yr 11 mo 24 dy	California
CURTZ, ZELL	Sep 21, 1942	37 yr 11 mo 15 dy	Idaho
CUSTER, WALTER HARRISON	Dec 06, 1935	27 yr	Indiana
DAGGETT, JOHN	Sep 02, 1912	23 yr	
DAHL, NILS	Apr 23, 1903	38 yr	Sweden
DAHLGREN, BERNHARD	Feb 25, 1939	48 yr 11 mo 10 dy	Sweden
DAILEY, CONRAD WILLIAM	Jul 05, 1938	2 yr 7 mo 10 dy	California
DAILEY, H. J.	Jul 27, 1911	7 yr 5 mo 24 dy	
DAILEY, MARY JANE	Aug 12, 1939	30 yr 6 mo 2 dy	California
DALE, MARTHA JANE	Oct 05, 1936	44 yr 8 mo 5 dy	California
DALLAIRE, NEVA MARGARET	Oct 10, 1949	26 yr	Oregon
DANIEL, JAMES	Jul 07, 1901	67 yr	Penn.
DANIELL, JOHN J.	Mar 22, 1910	70 yr	
DANIELS, CHARLES	Dec 27, 1941	`old Indian'	California
DANIELS, FRED	Oct 09, 1929	50 yr	
DANNENBRINK, HENRY F.	May 08, 1938	73 yr 8 mo 21 dy	California
DANNENBRINK, WILLIAM F.	Nov 10, 1922	52 yr 6 mo 23 dy	
DARR, BONNIE JEWELL	Jul 14, 1949	62 yr	Alabama
DAVENPORT, KEITH STEPHEN	Jan 22, 1950	2 dy	California
DAVENPORT, SARAH JANE	Mar 11, 1932	71 yr 5 mo 29 dy	Texas
DAVIES, THOMAS D.	Jan 30, 1925	72 yr	
DAVIS, CATHERINE	May 05, 1923	abt 80 yr	
DAVIS, CLARENCE LESLIE	Jun 18, 1946	73 yr 1 mo 16 dy	California
DAVIS, DUDLEY LOUIS	May 15, 1914	65 yr 3 mo 4 dy	
DAVIS, EDWARD	Sep 08, 1948	64 yr 11 mo 21dy	Colorado
DAVIS, EUGENE A.	Mar 15, 1936	76 yr 6 mo 9 dy	California
DAVIS, GRIFFITH T.	Nov 04, 1936	66 yr 8 mo 27 dy	New York
DAVIS, JAMES N.	Nov __, 1901	25 yr	California
DAVIS, MINNIE, Mrs.	Oct 05, 1905	abt 45 yr	California
DAVIS, THOMAS GRIFFITH	Jun 22, 1915	6 yr 1 mo	
DAVIS, WILLIAM D., Sr.	Jun 26, 1919	88 yr 9 mo 27 dy	
DAVIS, WILLIAM McPHEE	Apr 05, 1940	64 yr	Colorado
DAWSON, ANNA B.	Aug 05, 1911	3 mo 15 dy	
DAWSON, CHARLES T.	May 25, 1927	60 yr	
DAWSON, HETTY	Mar 05, 1947	73 yr 11 mo 26dy	California
DAY, AGNES RUTH	Aug 20, 1921	5 yr 8 mo 18 dy	
DAY, JOHN	Jul 18, 1935	74 yr 4 mo 1 dy	Illinois
DAY, JOHN RAYMOND	Nov 09, 1934	1 yr 4 mo 28 dy	California
DAY, ULYSSES GRANT	Nov 05, 1924	58 yr 1 mo 9 dy	
DAY, WALTER ANDREW	Jan 19, 1935	58 yr 3 mo 19 dy	California
DEAM, W. J.	Jul 05, 1917	49 yr	
DeBUS, JACK CHAS.	Jun 28, 1941	49 yr 3 mo 8 dy	Penn.
DEDRICK, ANTONIO	Feb 22, 1913	66 yr 2 mo 6 dy	
DEDRICK, CHAS. G.	Jan 22, 1937	67 yr	b.Rio De Janeiro
DEDRICK, DANIEL CHARLES	Apr 25, 1938	90 yr 3 mo	Ohio
DEGEN, LEWIS ABRAHAM	Dec 17, 1948	69 yr 7 mo 16 dy	Idaho
DeLEON, AUBREY M.	Aug 04, 1932	54 yr	
DeLONG, GEORGE S.	Jan 11, 1907	abt 78 yr	England
DEMPF, JOSEPH	May 06, 1930	72 yr 4 mo	
DEMPSEY, THOMAS MICHAEL	Aug 04, 1946	26 yr	
DENNIS, JOHN M.	Sep 02, 1947	76 yr 6 mo 29 dy	Wisconsin
DETRO, MARY PAMELIA	Oct 31, 1944	66 yr 9 mo 2 dy	Kansas
DETWILER, LEWIS FRANKLIN	Nov 07, 1933	83 yr 2 mo 12 dy	Penn.
DeWAR, ORRIN ALEX	May 07, 1946	48 yr 3 mo 28 dy	California
DEXTER, JOHN WESLEY	Jan 08, 1914	83 yr 8 mo	

DEATHS 1900 - 1950

DICKERSON, LEWIS ARTHUR	Jan 08, 1921	61 yr	
DICKERSON, MAHLON E.	Jan 29, 1939	42 yr 2 mo 23 dy	W. Virginia
DICKEY, J. C.	Nov 30, 1910	79 yr 7 mo 9 dy	
DICKEY, JOHN E.	May 14, 1936	67 yr 4 mo 16 dy	Iowa
DICKSON, J. E.	Apr 25, 1924	74 yr	
DILLER, CLIFF W.	May 11, 1908	21 yr 7 mo	
DILLER, JOHN WESLEY	Jun 02, 1927	74 yr 9 mo 25 dy	
DIMI, FILIDE, Mrs. (Diqi?)	Jul 25, 1906	abt 44 yr	Italy
DINKEL, FRANCES, Mrs.	Mar 12, 1908	46 yr 9 mo 23 dy	Iowa
DISHMAN, JAMES WYLEY	Sep 12, 1940	61 yr	Texas
DOBBIN, MELVIN	Dec 01, 1933	72 yr 4 mo 3 dy	New York
DOCK, ELMER	Apr __, 1908	5 yr	California
DOCK, LIDIA	Mar 03, 1909	30 yr	
DOCKERY, CECELIA C.	Nov 12, 1901	14 yr 23 dy	California
DOCKERY, GRACE COLE	Sep 20, 1934	68 yr 3 mo 13 dy	Canada
DODGE, MARY	Apr 11, 1917	78 yr 5 mo 10 dy	
DODGE, WILBUR SILAS	Mar 27, 1912	85 yr	
DOIG, JOHN	Jan 21, 1904	abt 53 yr	Scotland
DOLLIFFE, JOHN FRANKLIN	Mar 15, 1902	abt 76 yr	Maine
DOMENICI, GEORGE DAVE	Dec 27, 1931	40 yr 2 mo	
DOMMES, WILLIAM	Jan 13, 1915	48 yr 11 mo 22 dy	
DONAHUE, JOHN WILLIAM	Jul 09, 1932	71 yr 5 mo 22 dy	Michigan
DONNALLY, THOMAS C.	Apr 15, 1931	54 yr	
DONOVAN, CORNELIUS	Oct 23, 1912	26 yr	
DONOVAN, JAMES	Jan 25, 1916	65 yr	
DOOM, A. G.	Sep 17, 1920	64 yr 11 mo	
DOUGLAS, FRANK	Dec 29, 1902	21 yr 3 mo 22 dy	California
DOWLING, GUY ELLIS	Feb 15, 1938	46 yr 5 mo	Michigan
DOYLE, JOHN F.	Jul 13, 1909	abt 48 yr	
DRAKE, ASA	Jun 16, 1934	74 yr 5 mo 10 dy	Missouri
DRENNAN, JAMES C.	Nov 27, 1908	66 yr	Missouri
DRINKWATER, W. C.	Feb 28, 1909	79 yr	Missouri
DU CAN, TOM	Jun 11, 1913	78 yr	
DUARTE, MARY R., Mrs.	Aug 03, 1909	54 yr 4 mo 18 dy	Azores Is.
DUFFY, HAROLD RAY	Aug 22, 1936	41 yr 14 dy	New York
DUGGER, ROBERT E.	Nov 01, 1942	64 yr 8 mo 19 dy	Kansas
DUNAIERE, PHILLIP W.	Mar 24, 1950	67 yr	New York
DUNCAN, DANIEL GORDON	May 01, 1924	7 yr 1 mo 5 dy	
DUNCAN, HENRY CLAY	Sep 11, 1906	abt 28 yr	California
DUNCAN, L. P.	Aug 28, 1916	73 yr 8 mo 7 dy	
DUNCAN, LILLIAN	May 09, 1920	29 yr 10 mo 21 dy	
DUNCAN, MARY F., Mrs.	Apr 14, 1909	55 yr 2 mo 2 dy	
DUNCAN, R. L.	May 16, 1910	44 yr 19 dy	
DUNCAN, ROBERT FLEMING	Oct 07, 1943	53 yr 9 mo 18 dy	California
DUNCAN, STEPHEN	Apr 13, 1927	31 yr 2 mo 20 dy	
DUNCAN, THOMAS W.	Mar 06, 1907	71 yr 6 mo 10 dy	Arkansas
DUNCAN, THOMAS W.	Jun 03, 1917	25 yr 5 mo 3 dy	
DUNLAP, ELECTA CLARINDA	Mar 05, 1925	89 yr 10 mo 25 dy	
DUNPHY, JOHN R.	Aug 14, 1934	64 yr 9 mo 4 dy	Wisconsin
DUTRO, DAVID	Mar 27, 1937	79 yr 6 mo 27 dy	Illinois
DWEYER, JOHN	Feb 20, 1920	66 yr	
DYER, GEORGE	Apr 06, 1946	78 yr 4 mo 22 dy	New York
DYSERT, LEONARD	Jul 17, 1926	16 yr 7 mo 2 dy	
EALY, WILLIAM C.	Oct 15, 1918	42 yr 9 mo 8 dy	
EASTMAN, MINNIE MAY	Aug 19, 1926	53 yr	
EBENDORF, HENRY THEODORE	Jul 10, 1931	78 yr 10 mo 12dy	
EDDY, WILLIAM	Oct 24, 1901	68 yr	England
EDGAR, LOUIS	Mar 15, 1904	abt 31 yr	California
EDGMON, WELDON WADE	May 07, 1946	51 yr 10 mo 28dy	California
EDMONDS, THOMAS	Nov 12, 1937	76 yr 2 mo 14 dy	Missouri
EDWARDS, MELVIN I.	Dec 18, 1933	67 yr 3 mo 22 dy	Iowa
EFAU, EVA EVELYN	Jan 24, 1943	45 yr 2 mo 22 dy	California
EHRENDRIECH, HENRIETTA AUGUSTA,	Nov 15, 1921	84 yr 10 mo 23 dy	

Name	Date	Age	Birthplace
EHRMANN, GEORGE HENRY	Mar 30, 1908	abt 75 yr	Germany
EHRMANN, GEORGE HENRY	Jun 23, 1937	66 yr 2 mo 4 dy	California
EHRMANN, WM. F.	Jul __, 1946	72 yr	
EKSTROM, FRED	Nov 11, 1943	60 yr 30 dy	Finland
ELIGH, JAMES	Oct 12, 1900	89 yr	Canada
ELKINS, JOHN STEPHEN	Sep 12, 1927	50 yr 1 mo 12 dy	
ELLERBROOK, JOSEPH	Jun 17, 1903	79 yr 5 mo 6 dy	Germany
ELLIOTT, GEORGE WASHINGTON	Feb 05, 1912	69 yr	
ELLISTON, inf.son M/M WM.	Apr 23, 1908	3 dy	California
ELLISTON, J. N.	Nov 29, 1910	54 yr 8 mo 25 dy	
ELLSWORTH, ALLEN	May 18, 1914	48 yr	
ENGBLOM, CHARLES	Dec 27, 1913	age unknown	
ENGLISH, GEORGE WILLIAM	Apr 04, 1948	70 yr 7 mo 21 dy	Iowa
ENOS, JOHN BARGUS	Sep 22, 1937	64 yr 5 mo 19 dy	California
ENOS, JOSEPH	Feb 14, 1909	abt 72 yr	Azores Is.
ENOS, JOSEPH	Jan 29, 1924	58 yr 5 mo 3 dy	
ENOS, MARY J., Mrs.	Apr 20, 1903	68 yr	Azores Is.
ERICKSON, JOHN	Sep 19, 1918	67 yr	
ERICKSON, JOHN MARTIN	Jul 03, 1937	56 yr 7 mo 16 dy	Sweden
ERVIN, JESSE ROBERT	Feb 01, 1949	74 yr	Texas
ESCARREGA, RAYMOND	Jul 24, 1942	24 yr 27 dy	Mexico
ESTES, EARL LEN	May 31, 1947	29 yr 4 mo 17 dy	Oklahoma
EVANS, IRWIN	Apr 15, 1912	3 yr 11 mo 9 dy	
EVANS, NELLIE MAUD	Nov 22, 1932	50 yr 2 mo 10 dy	California
EVANS, SUSIE BELLE	Oct 07, 1933	60 yr 1 mo 9 dy	Oregon
EVANS, WAYNE THOMAS	Jul 11, 1938	10 mo 12 dy	California
EVANS, WILLIAM	Jul 18, 1938	70 yr 10 mo 11dy	Wisconsin
EVEREST, HARRY	Aug 30, 1934	60 yr 1 dy	England
EVERHART, ADELINE W.	Mar 08, 1903	76 yr 7 mo 14 dy	Mass.
EVERHART, WM. D.	Aug 28, 1901	73 yr 21 dy	Ohio
FADER, DELLA	Sep 04, 1924	25 yr 10 mo 24 dy	
FADER, JIM	Dec 15, 1935	100 yr	California
FAIRBANKS, O. A.	Jul 04, 1926	78 yr	
FARMER, CHARLES H.	Nov 20, 1948	84 yr 10 mo 5 dy	California
FARMER, CYRIL DAVIDSON	Jul 19, 1932	32 yr 9 mo 9 dy	California
FARMER, GEORGE H.	May 09, 1942	76 yr 2 mo 16 dy	California
FARMER, JUNE ELICE	Nov 05, 1921	19 dy	
FARMER, NANCY N.	Jul 10, 1945	70 yr 2 mo 7 dy	California
FARNHAM, N. T.	Jan __, 1909	abt 72 yr	
FARR, JOHN, Jr.	May 08, 1942	27 yr 1 mo 20 dy	Illinois
FARRAR, M. V.	May 20, 1916	35 yr	
FELIX, ANTONE	Jun 10, 1900	35 yr	Portugal
FENLEY, THEODORE WILLIAM	Jun 05, 1950	64 yr	Oregon
FENTON, MICHAEL	Dec 28, 1909	abt 78 yr	Ireland
FEOUR, JAMES CHARLES	Oct 05, 1915	64 yr	
FERGUSON, DAVID OSCAR	Mar 07, 1943	78 yr 10 mo 3 dy	Penn.
FERGUSON, JANETTE EDORA	Aug 10, 1947	91 yr 4 mo 10 dy	California
FERGUSON, JOHN	Jan 24, 1941	70 yr 6 mo 6 dy	Kentucky
FERGUSON, THOMAS JEFFERSON	May 31, 1916	66 yr 5 mo	
FEUVRAIS, PETER	Jun 26, 1939	37 yr 18 dy	France
FIELDS, J. N.	Oct 18, 1900	85 yr 9 mo 6 dy	Michigan
FINEGAN, JOHN P.	Jun 19, 1935	59 yr 7 mo 13 dy	Wisconsin
FINGAL, JOHN G.	Jun 14, 1947	abt 76 yr	
FISHER, C.F.W.	Dec 04, 1902	61 yr	Switzerland
FISHER, JOHN STUART	Mar 20, 1906	abt 85 yr	Penn.
FISK, HAZEL ELLEN	Jul 10, 1928	34 yr 6 mo 10 dy	
FISK, J. E.	Jul 09, 1928	8 yr 6 mo 14 dy	
FITZGERALD, TIMOTHY	Oct 10, 1918	85 yr	
FLAGG, AMASA ARTEMUS	Apr 22, 1932	83 yr 9 mo 15 dy	Maine
FLAGG, EBEN S.	May 15, 1936	83 yr 3 mo 18 dy	Maine
FLAGG, FIDELIA, Mrs.	Jan 20, 1901	52 yr 4 mo 20 dy	Maine
FLAGG, GEORGIANA	May 06, 1941	87 yr 1 mo 2 dy	Maine
FLAGG, G. F.	Nov 07, 1910	42 yr 2 mo 25 dy	

Name	Date	Age	Birthplace
FLAGG, JACOB REDDING	Oct 30, 1919	81 yr 9 mo 2 dy	
FLAGG, JAMES JUDSON	Mar 24, 1935	55 yr 8 mo 10 dy	California
FLAGG, JENNIE	Mar 29, 1944	94 yr 7 dy	England
FLAGG, WILLIAM C.	Dec 30, 1903	18 yr	California
FLEMING, LYNN	Mar 11, 1943	59 yr 6 mo 3 dy	Minnesota
FLORAINE, JOHN A.	Sep 11, 1902	83 yr	N. Scotia
FLORES, GEORGE THOMAS	Jun 03, 1947	54 yr 8 mo 16 dy	California
FLOWERS, inf.son M/M WM.	Dec 21, 1900	1 mo 7 dy	California
FLOWERS, ROSA	Jan 01, 1949	70 yr 2 mo 0 dy	California.
FLOWERS, WILLIAM F.	Jul 11, 1947	72 yr 10 mo 8 dy	California
FOLEY, THOMAS	Feb 10, 1908	abt 85 yr	Ireland
FONG THIN	Dec 03, 1921	95 yr	
FORBES, JAMES	Dec 03, 1901	78 yr	Scotland
FORD, BARTHOLOMEW	Apr 30, 1910	75 yr	
FORD, CLARA MAY	Nov 06, 1906	6 wks 3 dy	California
FORGARTY, PETER D.	Sep 29, 1933	80 yr	Ireland
FORST, ALBERT	Jan 07, 1921	abt 71 yr	
FORT, JAMES E.	Jul 07, 1938	70 yr 4 mo 27 dy	Wisconsin
FOX, EARL	May 16, 1923	38 yr	
FOX, ELIZABETH, Mrs.	Mar 28, 1908	75 yr 2 mo 13 dy	Ireland
FOX, SOLOMON	Aug 04, 1907	abt 74 yr	Ohio
FRASER, CLARA ETTA	Jan 08, 1941	70 yr 1 mo 1 dy	Indiana
FRASER, DONALD C.	Aug 14, 1905	29 yr 6 mo 2 dy	N. Scotia
FRATUS, ANTONE GRANT	Feb 26, 1925	34 yr 3 mo 9 dy	
FRATUS, MARY (Freitus?)	Jul 13, 1910	26 yr	
FREE, CARL	Apr 01, 1942	72 yr 7 mo 27 dy	Germany
FREETHY, WILLIAM ELLIS	Jun 26, 1906	56 yr 1 mo 12 dy	England
FREITAS, MARY, Mrs.	May 01, 1907	abt 41 yr	California
FRENCH, SALLY	Feb 11, 1931	90 yr	
FRENZEL, JOE	Mar 08, 1939	76 yr 8 mo	Indiana
FREY, FREDERICK	Feb 22, 1908	83 yr 1 mo 10 dy	Germany
FRICK, CHRISTIAN	Apr 30, 1900	77 yr	New York
FRICKINGER, GEORGE	Jul 14, 1918	55 yr 11 mo 20 dy	
FRIEND, ASHBY	Mar 17, 1904	abt 20 yr	California
FRIEND, inf.dau M/M THOS.	Nov 27, 1911	2 mo 10 dy	
FRIEND, MARY S., Mrs.	Mar 04, 1903	48 yr	Arkansas
FRIEND, THOMAS F.	Feb 03, 1914	40 yr	
FRIEND, WILLIAM HENRY	Sep 06, 1907	abt 86 yr (??)	Missouri
Great Register of Voters 1892 says "age 51" [b. 1841]			
FRITZ, ALBERT	May 30, 1930	69 yr 2 mo 28 dy	
FRIZISE, PHILLIP	Nov 25, 1912	64 yr	
FROELICH, CHARLES W.	Nov 17, 1938	70 yr 9 mo 8 dy	New York
FROST, ARTHUR C.	Jan 01, 1948	70 yr 4 mo 9 dy	California
FRUIT, JOHN ALLEN	Aug 08, 1919	63 yr	
FRYE, LOUIS	Oct 11, 1916	84 yr 9 mo 28 dy	
FULLER, ROY THOMAS	Jan 26, 1949	63 yr 2 mo 21 dy	Illinois
GALLAGHER, EDWARD R.	Feb 13, 1950	90 yr	Maine
GALLAGHER, FRANK	Feb 11, 1930	78 yr	
GALLAHER, J. H.	May 28, 1918	86 yr	
GAMALIELSON, J.	Sep 10, 1928	77 yr 11 mo 10 dy	
GARCIA, ALFONSO SANCHEZ	Jul 14, 1943	21 yr	Mexico
GARCIA, AMADO FLORES	Aug 12, 1944	23 yr	Mexico
GARRISON, CALVIN	Mar 22, 1938	89 yr 5 mo 19 dy	New York
GARRITY, M.	Dec 30, 1928	71 yr 6 mo 25 dy	
GARTLER, JOHN A.	Feb 09, 1929	76 yr	
GARVIN, LELA H.	Jul 17, 1944	36 yr 2 mo 3 dy	California
GATES, ALFRED RUSSELL	Nov 19, 1949	85 yr	New York
GATES, BIRDIE EVADNA	Sep 12, 1902	15 yr 4 mo 24 dy	California
GATES, JACOB F.	Sep 09, 1943	76 yr 5 mo 7 dy	Penn.
GATES, MERCER HORACE	Aug 22, 1941	46 yr 7 mo 23 dy	Missouri
GAUNCE, DAVID LESLIE	Jan 07, 1949	63 yr 1 mo 29 dy	California
GEESE, ELMER ELLSWORTH	Aug 24, 1948	79 yr 5 mo 4 dy	Ohio
GEHM, CORA W., Mrs.	Aug 08, 1902	31 yr 8 mo 17 dy	California

Name	Date	Age	Birthplace
GEHM, GEORGE FREDERICK	Dec 28, 1926	58 yr	New York
GEMMELL, ALEXANDER	Jan 21, 1904	abt 36 yr	Scotland
GENTRY, HENRY	Mar 12, 1903	36 yr	Indiana
GEORGE, ALEX. CUMMINGS	Apr 13, 1912	86 yr	
GEORGE, WILLIAM	Jun 12, 1937	unknown	California
GERKEY, FREDA LUCILE	Jul 29, 1912	9 yr 1 mo 23 dy	
GIBBONS, CORNELIUS WALLACE	Aug 09, 1939	53 yr 7 mo 9 dy	California
GIBBS, inf.dau. M/M J. B.	Dec 28, 1905	2 dy	California
GIBSON, CHARLOTTE T.	Oct 24, 1946	78 yr	
GIBSON, MARY ANN	Mar 01, 1927	69 yr 1 mo 1 dy	
GIBSON, ROBERT KING	Apr 03, 1941	89 yr 2 dy	b. New Brunswick
GIBSON, WILLIAM STEWART	Mar 24, 1939	57 yr 3 mo 10 dy	California
GIDDINGS, GEORGE W.	Feb 21, 1933	58 yr 7 mo 26 dy	Vermont
GIDDINGS, VARD WILSON	Oct 15, 1934	44 yr 9 mo 15 dy	California
GILBERT, RICHARD LEE	Jun 30, 1934	68 yr 1 mo 14 dy	Montana
GILFILLEN, FORREST	Oct 02, 1935	48 yr 24 dy	California
GILL, MARSHALL BOOKER	Jul 02, 1935	62 yr 7 mo 29 dy	California
GILL, RICHARD	Aug 23, 1929	60 yr	
GILLELAND, JACOB S.	Sep __, 1905	abt 62 yr	Missouri
GILMAN, HERBERT MARION	Mar 29, 1939	66 yr 28 dy	California
GILZEAN, ALEXANDER	Mar 08, 1915	56 yr 11 mo 24 dy	
GILZEAN, ALEXANDER	Aug 03, 1946	52 yr	California
GILZEAN, CHARLES E.	Aug 08, 1901	5 yr 5 mo 10 dy	California
GILZEAN, CHRISTINE CLEMENTINE,	Nov 17, 1945	85 yr 3 mo 14 dy	California
GILZEAN, EDNA FRANCES	Feb 10, 1905	6 mo 24 dy	California
GILZEAN, HARRIETT WINIFRED	Jan 25, 1905	32 yr 7 mo 19 dy	California
GILZEAN, inf.son M/M C. E.	Aug 24, 1904	2 mo 6 dy	California
GILZEAN, JAMES HENRY	Apr 28, 1902	45 yr 6 mo 1 dy	California
GILZEAN, MARGARET, Mrs.	Oct 29, 1905	77 yr 2 mo 14 dy	Ireland
GILZEAN, MARION	Dec 30, 1946	66 yr 9 mo 25 dy	California
GILZEAN, MARY AGNES	Oct 06, 1902	11 mo 20 dy	California
GILZEAN, VIVIAN LAURETTA	Jul 05, 1902	2 yr 4 mo 3 dy	California
GIVEN, GEORGE CHAPMAN	Apr 25, 1923	51 yr 2 mo 13 dy	
GIVEN, JAMES E.	Feb 01, 1931	74 yr 11 mo	
GIVEN, MINNIE MAY	Jan 12, 1934	64 yr 11 mo 3 dy	Virginia
GLASSON, JAMES	Aug 01, 1908	abt 71 yr	England
GLEN, SAMUEL	Jul 11, 1907	abt 39 yr	N. Scotia
GLOWEN, JOHN	Feb 18, 1932	48 yr	U.S.A.
GODFREY, CHARLES WILLARD	Jan 28, 1918	72 yr 3 mo 12 dy	
GODFREY, CLARA H.	Nov 13, 1926	72 yr 2 mo 2 dy	
GOETZE, HENRY WILLIAM	Feb 07, 1937	83 yr 2 mo 4 dy	Germany
GOETZE, LOUISA FREDERICA	Feb 20, 1923	63 yr 5 mo 1 dy	
GOLDEN, JIM	Jun 18, 1922	70 yr	
GOODRICH, JAMES	Oct 06, 1917	67 yr 3 mo 2 dy	
GOODWIN, HIRAM LAFAYETTE	Dec 22, 1937	77 yr 9 mo 17 dy	California
GOODWIN, JOHN	Dec 27, 1929	72 yr 2 mo 12 dy	
GOODWIN, MARY J., Mrs.	Feb 17, 1910	47 yr 7 mo 13 dy	
GOODWIN, WILLIAM T.	Aug 22, 1940	73 yr	California
GOODYEAR, CHARLES EUGENE	Sep 30, 1922	66 yr	
GOODYEAR, ELIZABETH SABINA	Mar 17, 1935	71 yr 2 mo 21 dy	California
GOODYEAR, EUGENE MERRITT	Mar 26, 1940	53 yr	California
GOON, DANIEL	Jul 19, 1915	78 yr 6 mo	
GORDAN, GEORGE L.	Jun 16, 1932	69 yr	
GORE, JOSEPH W.	Apr 10, 1942	85 yr 5 mo 10 dy	Kentucky
GORE, MARY JANE	Mar 10, 1925	84 yr 7 mo 28 dy	
GOULD, ELBA	Aug 07, 1912	15 yr 10 mo 16 dy	
GOULD, KATIE	Aug 07, 1912	14 yr 2 mo 29 dy	
GOW, Mrs.	Jun 29, 1922	45 yr	
GRACE, MARION (M.Beauclaire)	Jun 14, 1941	63 yr 6 mo 11 dy	Germany
GRACEY, HATTERAS S.	Apr 12, 1920	68 yr 7 mo	
GRAHAM, CHARLES VARY	Jul 20, 1943	83 yr 7 mo 3 dy	California
GRAHAM, HENRY HARRISON	Jun 10, 1927	80 yr 11 mo 10 dy	

Name	Date	Age	Birthplace
GRAHAM, JAMES	Feb 20, 1934	84 yr	New York
GRAHAM, JOHN	Apr 21, 1938	69 yr 4 mo 15 dy	New York
GRANER, ADOLPH T.	Apr 04, 1929	65 yr 8 mo 16 dy	
GRANT, JOHN HENRY	Jul 09, 1911	65 yr 7 mo 5 dy	
GRANT, THOMAS HARRISON	Nov 20, 1946	84 yr 7 mo 6 dy	California
GRATTAN, JAS.	Apr 17, 1915	58 yr 1 dy	
GRAVES, ANNA C.	Oct 20, 1904	17 yr 10 mo 27dy	California
GRAVES, ANNA CHRISTINE, Mrs.	Jun 11, 1920	86 yr 9 mo 4 dy	
GRAVES, JOHN B.	Jun 01, 1925	57 yr 7 mo 28 dy	
GRAVES, RICHARD BENJAMIN	Sep 17, 1918	61 yr 3 dy	
GRAY, BRUCE H.	Jul 26, 1946	75 yr	
GRAY, DAVID BASKINS	Jul 20, 1902	70 yr	Penn.
GRAY, JESSIE S.	Jun 24, 1911	11 yr 8 mo 7 dy	
GRAY, MINNIE AMANDA	Oct 09, 1919	76 yr 9 mo 30 dy	
GREELEY, ARTHUR HOWARD	Mar 03, 1940	43 yr	Penn.
GREEN, CARRIE	Jun 21, 1948	64 yr 4 mo 14 dy	Illinois
GREEN, FRANK MORRIS	Mar 12, 1946	69 yr 2 mo 13 dy	Colorado
GREEN, JOHN C.	Jul 10, 1918	77 yr	
GREENLEAF, GEORGE PARSON	Dec 02, 1914	83 yr	
GREENWELL, ERNEST A.	Nov 08, 1901	33 yr 1 mo 13 dy	California
GREENWELL, WILLIAM ERNEST	Jun 01, 1920	26 yr 5 mo 9 dy	
GREGG, GEORGE	Jan 28, 1911	1 yr 4 mo 11 dy	
GRIFFIN, BARNEY	Jan 10, 1901	55 yr	Ireland
GRIFFITH, FORESTUS LAWSON	Feb 13, 1948	68 yr 3 mo 6 dy	Illinois
GRIFFITH, JOHN MORRIS	Jul 11, 1949	78 yr	California
GRIFFITH, LINZAY	Feb 28, 1912	85 yr	
GRIGSBY, PLESANT	Jan 24, 1941	63 yr 5 mo 22 dy	California
GRIGSBY, ROSE NELL	Oct 12, 1949	68 yr	Colorado
GROGER, HERMAN	Aug 20, 1945	59 yr 1 mo 9 dy	Germany
GRUSS, THEODORE	Nov 02, 1910	54 yr	
GUERRERO, ANDRES MONTOYA	Aug 12, 1944	22 yr	Mexico
GUILL, WILLIAM, Mrs.	Aug 23, 1907	abt -- yr	California
GUINASSO, LOUIS	Jul 11, 1935	38 yr 11 mo 30dy	California
GULICK, JAMES H.	Feb 15, 1903	59 yr	New Jersey
GUNDERSON, MARTHA ELIZABETH	Jul 16, 1938	71 yr 10 mo 16dy	Wisconsin
GUPTILL, MARY, Mrs.	Apr 14, 1901	56 yr	Ireland
GURR, ELLEN MARIE	Jan 12, 1939	4 dy	California
GUTSCHE, ADOLPH	Aug 22, 1937	51 yr 4 mo	Poland
GUTZEN, GUSTAF	Mar 15, 1917	79 yr	
HAAS, FREDERICK GOTTLIEB	Dec 02, 1912	73 yr 11 mo 11 dy	
HABER, PHILLIP	Dec 06, 1932	88 yr 7 mo 9 dy	France
HAFLEY, FRANK	Aug 08, 1904	abt 35 yr	Wisconsin
HAGELMAN, JOHN	Sep 30, 1922	55 yr	
HAGEMAN, JOHN N.	Dec 09, 1948	70 yr 5 mo 15 dy	
HAGELMAN, MINNIE	Oct 31, 1918	78 yr 1 mo 25 dy	Sweden
HAGINS, ELLLIS FRANK	Apr 3-5, 1940	25 yr	Colorado
HAILSTONE, ALLAN FRANCIS	Jan 26, 1920	1 dy	
HAILSTONE, JOHN THOMPSON	Jun 03, 1908	abt 70 yr	England
HAILSTONE, PINDER FRANKLIN	Apr 29, 1947	75 yr 0 mo 10 dy	California
HAINES, MARY ELIZABETH	Jun 14, 1923	87 yr 5 mo 12 dy	
HAINES, PETER	May 02, 1903	66 yr	Penn.
HALE, MARCELLUS L.	May 06, 1934	68 yr 11 mo 18dy	California
HALES, WILLIAM JOHN	Sep 26, 1923	64 yr 11 mo 7 dy	
HALL, GEORGE WILLIS	May 05, 1907	abt 34 yr	California
HALL, HANNAH PAULINE, Mrs.	Jun 01, 1907	24 yr 6 mo 18 dy	California
HALL, LOUIS A.	Oct 15, 1933	66 yr 11 mo 4 dy	Indiana
HALL, WESLEY JOHN	Nov 20, 1950	60 yr	Kansas
HALL, WILLIAM H.	Oct 28, 1905	abt 74 yr	Scotland
HALLEY, FREDERICK	Dec 19, 1908	3 yr	California
HALLEY, FREDERICK F.	Jun 07, 1905	72 yr 3 mo 3 dy	Kentucky
HALLEY, inf.dau. M/M F.	Apr 05, 1900	11 dy	California
HALLEY, inf.dau M/M F.	Apr 07, 1910	8 dy	California
HAMES, ERNEST V.	Aug 10, 1944	38 yr 10 mo 22 dy	California

HAMILTON, CHARLES B.	Aug 29, 1948	85 yr 9 mo 9 dy	California
HAMILTON, GUSTUS	Jul 19, 1902	46 yr	Maine
HAMILTON, ROBERT	Feb 23, 1906	63 yr 11 dy	Virginia
HAMILTON, ROBERT W.	May 12, 1948	76 yr 6 mo 9 dy	California
HAMMERSLEY, LYDIA ELLEN	Aug 29, 1949	67 yr	Oregon
HAMMERSLEY, OREN ALONZ	Mar 30, 1943	69 yr 7 mo 29 dy	Oregon
HAMMOND, FRANCIS C.	Apr 19, 1903	26 yr	California
HAMMOND, NANCY E.	Jul 19, 1900	44 yr 9 mo 25 dy	
HAMPTON, GENEVIEVE BEATRICE	Jul 23, 1907	6 yr 3 dy	California
HAMPTON, inf.dau M/M HARLEY	Nov 27, 1908	[prob.b. Nov.27]	California
HAMPTON, J. M.	Nov 13, 1917	82 yr 11 mo 13 dy	
HANNA, JOSEPH	Sep 25, 1934	49 yr 7 mo 7 dy	Bohemia
HANNA, MARY	Dec 13, 1917	75 yr 5 mo 25 dy	
HANOVER, FRANK SMITH	Nov 04, 1931	68 yr 3 mo 16 dy	
HANSEN, DETLEF	May 11, 1914	79 yr 9 mo 2 dy	
HANSEN, DOROTHEA JUNKANS	Jun 24, 1916	76 yr 4 mo 24 dy	
HANSEN, I. A.	May 06, 1904	abt 55 yr	Sweden
HANSEN, NELSE P.	Aug 09, 1932	68 yr	Denmark
HANSON, inf.dau. M/M W. J.	Oct 18, 1901	b.d.	California
HANSON, JOHN	Sep 23, 1948	80 yr 9 mo 25 dy	Germany
HARDIN, DAVID	Oct 15, 1902	74 yr 10 mo	Ohio
HARDIN, GEORGE W.	Nov 09, 1934	77 yr 9 mo 4 dy	Missouri
HARDIN, JOHN T.	Jul 25, 1921	67 yr	
HARDING, SARAH E.	Jun 02, 1929	76 yr	
HARDY, WILLIAM A.	Aug 27, 1946	80 yr 7 mo 10 dy	Penn.
HARMAN, SOLOMAN	Apr 03, 1929	88 yr	
HARMON, REBECCA (HARMAN?)	Apr __, 1903	87 yr	Kentucky
HARMON, THOMAS F.	Jun 13, 1940	81 yr	Tennessee
HARRIFF, ROBERT M.	Jun 14, 1950	70 yr	Penn.
HARRIGAN, EDWARD E.	Sep 06, 1926	65 yr 4 mo 20 dy	
HARRINGTON, P.	Sep 27, 1901	40 yr	
HARRIS, TALBERT N.	May 23, 1933	52 yr	Texas
HARRISON, RALPH CLINTON	Jan 23, 1939	28 yr 22 dy	California
HART, EMMA N., Mrs.	Aug 13, 1911	34 yr 4 mo	
HART, LESLIE C.	Dec 04, 1915	32 yr 10 mo 8 dy	
HARTIGAN, JOHN	Sep 12, 1910	84 yr	
HARVEY, HENRY THOMAS	Apr 05, 1901	64 yr 27 dy	England
HARVEY, SILVA MARION	Apr 12, 1934	67 yr 5 mo 13 dy	California
HASKINS, BEVERLY P.	Aug 03, 1942	61 yr 10 mo 15dy	Kentucky
HAUN, THOMAS J.	Jun 26, 1934	71 yr 8 mo 14 dy	California
HAWK, ENID MERLE	Aug 28, 1941	46 yr 1 mo 28 dy	California
HAWK, HILTON ALEXANDER	Aug 20, 1946	33 yr 8 mo 7 dy	California
HAWKEY, LUCY	Dec 25, 1914	3 mo 17 dy	
HAWKEY, OTTO	Jun 22, 1938	66 yr 6 mo 3 dy	England
HAYDEN, FRANCIS E.	Sep 24, 1909	8 mo 22 dy	California
HAYES, GEORGE SAMUEL	Nov 11, 1944	82 yr 19 dy	Utah
HAYES, MARY FRANCES	Mar 31, 1924	67 yr 4 mo 21 dy	
HAYS, OSCAR O.	Jun 07, 1926	67 yr	
HAYWARD, CALVIN STEWART	Sep 15, 1926	2 hr	
HAYWARD, JOHN DAVIS	Nov 12, 1916	69 yr	
HAYWARD, OSCAR H.	Jun 15, 1942	60 yr 5 mo 23 dy	California
HEATH, CHARLES JESSE	Nov 30, 1948	66 yr 4 mo 9 dy	California
HEAVEY, MICHAEL	Aug 13, 1907	abt 69 yr	Ireland
HEDSTROM, CHAS. L.	Dec 03, 1944	78 yr 8 mo 18 dy	Sweden
HEIDEWALD, CHARLES MAX	Jun 14, 1941	73 yr 3 mo 12 dy	Germany
HEIMBURGER, LOUIS	May 17, 1927	78 yr 8 mo 8 dy	
HEINES, HENRY	Apr 02, 1925	71 yr 11 dy	
HEIST, CHRISTOPHER	Aug 20, 1920	75 yr	
HELLER, SAMUEL WAYWARD	Jan 23, 1932	75 yr	Illinois
HEMBREE, HUSTON	Feb 27, 1928	89 yr 5 mo 7 dy	
HENDERSON, HENRY	Jun 03, 1910	60 yr 5 mo 16 dy	
HENDERSON, HERBERT L.	Aug 02, 1926	32 yr	
HENDERSON, ROSE MARY	Apr 04, 1936	3 dy	California

Name	Date	Age	Origin
HENDERSON, WILLIAM VALENTINE	Jan 01, 1931	37 yr 10 mo 18 dy	
HENNESSY, ELLEN	Nov 30, 1932	84 yr 2 mo 9 dy	Ireland
HENNESSY, ESTHER	May 26, 1916	48 yr	
HENNESSY, MARIA TERESA	Mar 24, 1931	84 yr 1 mo 28 dy	
HENNESSY, MARY AGNES	Apr 12, 1948	84 yr 0 mo 8 dy	California
HENNESSY, NELLIE M.	May 11, 1928	40 yr 8 mo 28 dy	
HENNESSEY, P. O. M.	Dec 25, 1901	72 yr	Ireland
HENNESSY, RICHARD W.	Jul 27, 1912	37 yr 2 mo 15 dy	
HENRIQUES, EPIPHANIA AUGUSTA	Feb 11, 1943	86 yr 1 mo 5 dy	Azores Is.
HENRY, JOHN A.	Feb 22, 1909	abt 25 yr	
HENSLEY, SAMUEL JACKSON	Mar 06, 1919	71 yr 7 mo 1 dy	
HERMANSEN, C. O.	Sep 30, 1922	43 yr	
HEROUX, PETER MOSES	Aug 19, 1905	abt 64 yr	Canada
HERRICK, LAUREN ELLIS	Sep 27, 1933	14 yr 10 mo 27 dy	Washington
HERRICK, LAURIN ANGIER	Aug 04, 1935	51 yr 9 mo 11 dy	California
HERRING, JAMES D.	Aug 21, 1914	15 yr	
HERTZER, CHARLES	May 17, 1929	not given	
HETHINGTON, J. D.	Nov 17, 1910	64 yr	
HEURTEVANT, FRANCIS	May 25, 1905	abt 56 yr	France
HICKEY, CORNELIUS	Jul 14, 1903	68 yr	New York
HIGGINS, BERT	Apr 06, 1945	79 yr 3 mo 3 dy	California
HILDRETH, JEFFREY	Jul 21, 1922	70 yr	
HILDRETH, RUBY ELLEN	Aug 02, 1905	16 yr 8 mo 19 dy	California
HILDRETH, WILMARTH ALDRICH	Dec 01, 1936	70 yr 24 dy	California
HILL, JAMES HENRY	Sep 28, 1930	54 yr 9 mo 23 dy	
HILLSTEAD, ADOLF LEANDER	Dec 11, 1940	50 yr	Sweden
HINIKER, WILLIAM G.	Aug 22, 1945	73 yr 3 mo 28 dy	Minnesota
HINTON, OSCAR FITZ ALLEN	Jan 11, 1904	79 yr 2 mo 4 dy	Ohio
HIPPLER, OTTO	May 21, 1946	unknown	California
HITCHCOCK, SILAS MARION	Mar 28, 1920	89 yr 5 mo 12 dy	
HITE, HARRY	Mar 14, 1902	abt 17 yr	
HIXON, OTIS C.	May 28, 1949	63 yr	California
HOARD, CHESLEY	Nov 09, 1942	39 yr	
HOBART, JULIA SEABURY	Jan 28, 1913	78 yr 10 mo 25 dy	
HOCKING, THOS H	Sep 18, 1900	55 yr	Cornwall
HODGDON, ALVAH PERCY	Dec 23, 1916	58 yr	
HOFFMAN, A. J.	Nov 09, 1928	63 yr 9 mo 10 dy	
HOFFMAN, MAX	Sep 27, 1916	42 yr	
HOLMES, FRED	Jan 18, 1908	abt 60 yr	Canada
HOLTOFF, OTTO	Apr 09, 1921	37 yr 3 mo 13 dy	
HOLTORF, MARIE, Mrs.	Oct 15, 1905	abt 59 yr	Holstein
HONG SO	Dec 30, 1911	64 yr	
HOOPENGARNER, MAX	Dec 26, 1938	62 yr 8 mo 20 dy	Oregon
HOOVER, THOMAS	JUL 11, 1934	47 yr	U.S.A.
HOPEN, ROY ARNOLD	Nov 14, 1945	23 yr 4 mo 10 dy	New Jersey
HOPPER, CHRISTINE ELIZABETH	Aug 27, 1920	52 yr 1 mo 19 dy	
HOSEMDOLLY, ELLEN	May 10, 1918	90 yr	
HOUCK, ERNEST G.	Nov 09, 1938	52 yr 9 mo 11 dy	Michigan
HOWARD, JAMES DONALD	Jun 25, 1945	20 yr 4 mo 29 dy	Texas
HOWARD, ROBERT M.	Dec 19, 1908	abt 46 yr	Missouri
HOWE, JAMES	Feb 29, 1912	91 yr	
HOWE, WILLIAM T.	Dec 21, 1945	75 yr 5 mo 14 dy	New York
HOWELL, WILLIAM	Jun 26, 1921	75 yr	
HOWERTON, RALPH A.	Dec 01, 1941	65 yr 3 mo 24 dy	N.Carolina
HOWSON, CHRISTOPHER	Feb 07, 1937	63 yr 4 mo 23 dy	Canada
HUDSON, ANNA M.	Oct 23, 1945	65 yr 10 mo 24dy	Indiana
HUESTIS, GEORGE WASHINGTON	Nov 11, 1923	86 yr 6 mo 5 dy	
HUESTIS, HARRY HOWARD	Feb 27, 1931	29 yr 2 mo 11 dy	
HUFFMAN, CLARA	Feb 27, 1934	48 yr 2 mo	Minnesota
HUFFMAN, FRED	Sep 27, 1916	45 yr	
HUGGARD, THOMAS JOHN	Feb 09, 1945	73 yr 1 mo 18 dy	Ireland
HUGHES, DORA BELLE	Jun 30, 1941	41 yr 5 mo 17 dy	Tennessee
HUGHES, GEORGE LINCOLN	Apr 13, 1940	79 yr	Illinois

Name	Date	Age	Birthplace
HULSE, JOSEPH JACOB	Dec 09, 1945	64 yr 8 mo 0 dy	Illinois
HUNT, EBENEZER TAYLOR	Jan 10, 1916	69 yr 2 mo 17 dy	
HUTCHENS, JOHN	Sep 14, 1916	86 yr 8 mo 10 dy	
HUTCHENS, JOSEPH	Nov 26, 1917	61 yr 10 mo 28 dy	
HUTCHINS, HENRY	Feb 16, 1910	53 yr 7 mo 1 dy	
HUTCHINSON, WILLIAM	Nov 05, 1935	70 yr	Ireland
INDIAN DOC	Apr 09, 1912	70 yr	
INDIAN FANNY	May 24, 1911	80 TO 90 yr	
INDIAN SALLY	Oct 27, 1915	95 yr	
IRONS, FRANCIS A.	Oct 15, 1929	55 yr 10 mo 15 dy	
IRVING, CATHERINE A.	Nov 06, 1942	79 yr 10 mo 6 dy	Ireland
IRVING, FRANK	Jan 18, 1910	15 yr	
IRVING, GEO. J.	Jul 08, 1908	53 yr 6 mo 18 dy	N.Brunswick
IRVING, HELLEN	Aug 10, 1904	14 dy	California
IRVING, IDA MAY	Dec 25, 1946	63 yr 2 mo 9 dy	N. Scotia
ISEBELL, JOHN HUTTEY	Apr 26, 1912	66 yr	
IVEY, JULIA	Dec 12, 1941	75 yr 9 mo 9 dy	California
IVEY, RUBY ANN (b.May 22,1949)	Jun 10, 1949	20 dy	California.
JACK, ANDREW RENNIE	Apr 01, 1917	86 yr 11 mo 4 dy	
JACKMAN, ARTHUR WARREN	Apr 09, 1924	infant	
JACKMAN, EARL G.	May 22, 1948	58 yr 4 mo 18 dy	Washington
JACKS, RICHARD M.	Aug 30, 1922	44 yr 9 mo 19 dy	
JACKSON, HARRY M.	May 28, 1946	59 yr 10 mo 20dy	California
JACKSON, HOWARD JAMES	Feb 27, 1936	1 dy	California
JACKSON, JOANNE VELMA	Jan 07, 1949	12 yr 1 mo 12 dy	California.
JACKSON, JOHN	Jul 30, 1902	65 yr	
JACKSON, LEMUEL	May 05, 1933	72 yr 8 mo 5 dy	Oregon
JACKSON, NANCY E.	Mar 31, 1938	87 yr 6 mo 20 dy	Missouri
JACKSON, RUDOLPH ALTON	Jan 09, 1927	7 yr 4 mo 23 dy	
JACKSON, SAMUEL THEODORE	Jun 10, 1948	70 yr 4 mo 2 dy	Oregon
JACKSON, WILBERT LESLIE	Nov 05, 1941	84 yr 2 mo 3 dy	Iowa
JACKSON, WILBUR OSCAR	Dec 23, 1912	27 yr 7 mo 13 dy	
JACKSON, WILLARD LESLIE	Nov 27, 1915	4 yr 2 mo 27 dy	
JACOB, HENRY	Jun 02, 1917	75 yr 2 mo 27 dy	
JACOB, JOHN	Aug 16, 1918	66 yr	
JACOBI, JOHN S.	May 20, 1905	abt 73 yr	England
JACOBS, ELIZA	Mar 04, 1913	81 yr 11 mo 1 dy	
JACOBS, MAX W.	Dec 01, 1938	62 yr 9 mo 2 dy	Germany
JACOBSON, ANDREW	Feb 05, 1941	76 yr 1 mo 25 dy	Finland
JACOBSON, JACOB	Nov 09, 1921	abt 52 yr	
JAMES, EDWIN R.	Jul 11, 1929	20 yr 8 mo 29 dy	
JAMES, SARAH W., Mrs.	Feb 04, 1904	84 yr 4 mo 4 dy	Ohio
JAMES, THOMAS SIDNEY	Jan 13, 1912	55 yr 3 mo 2 dy	
JAMES, WALTER WARDER	Jan 27, 1904	abt 84 yr	Kentucky
JANES, CHARLES	May 15, 1937	65 yr 5 mo 25 dy	Bohemia
JEFFERSON, JAKE PRICE	Apr 06, 1945	85 yr 3 mo 9 dy	California
JENSEN, MINNIE GRIBBLE	Jul 20, 1949	82 yr	California
JENSEN, PETER H.	Feb 22, 1942	77 yr 11 mo 22dy	California
JOHANSON, CARLOS	May 26, 1936	73 yr 1 mo 5 dy	Denmark
JOHNSON, ALFRED G.	Jan 09, 1934	41 yr 8 mo 26 dy	Sweden
JOHNSON, ANITA	Mar 17, 1923	20 yr 20 dy	
JOHNSON, ARTHUR GUSTAF	Jan __, 1946	62 yr	
JOHNSON, AUGUST THEODORE	May 15, 1940	62 yr	Sweden
JOHNSON, CATHERINE WADDELL	Nov 02, 1949	65 yr	Iowa
JOHNSON, CHARLES	Apr 16, 1903	45 yr	Denmark
JOHNSON, FELIX	Feb 08, 1906	61 yr 8 mo 16 dy	Indiana
JOHNSON, FRANK	Jun 09, 1911	"middle aged"	
JOHNSON, FREDERICK ALONZO	Jan 08, 1932	58 yr 10 mo 12dy	Nebraska
JOHNSON, HANDRE C.	Mar 19, 1938	44 yr 10 mo 13dy	Sweden
JOHNSON, JAMES	Nov 21, 1920	93 yr 8 mo 17 dy	
JOHNSON, JOHN B.	Mar 19, 1938	73 yr 10 mo 19dy	Illinois
JOHNSON, LLOYD ALEXANDER	Aug 01, 1944	56 yr 10 mo 16dy	California
JOHNSON, MARY LUELLA	Jul 12, 1908	abt 32 yr	California

Name	Date	Age	Birthplace
JOHNSON, NELLIE	Feb 25, 1947	73 yr 11 mo 20dy	California
JOHNSON, ROBERT	Mar 22, 1916	84 yr	
JOHNSTON, JAMES LEWIS	Aug 18, 1931	83 yr 20 dy	
JOHNSTON, NATHANIEL EDWIN	Jan 16, 1938	63 yr 7 mo 27 dy	Missouri
JONES, ASIL	Apr 12, 1934	21 yr 1 mo 21 dy	Idaho
JONES, CLARENCE REECE	Apr 24, 1933	35 yr	Tennessee
JONES, CLEO	Jul 24, 1912	4 yr	
JONES, GEORGE B.	Dec 04, 1934	73 yr	England
JONES, IDA BELL	Aug 05, 1923	66 yr 10 mo 1 dy	
JONES, MONROE	Jan 26, 1939	93 yr 8 mo 19 dy	Illinois
JONINON, GEORGE EDWARD	Oct 20, 1940	72 yr	California
JORDAN, inf.son M/M M.C.	Aug 22, 1902	b.d.	California
JORDAN, JESSIE ELONIA	May 16, 1941	69 yr 3 mo 22 dy	California
JORDAN, KENNETH	Jul 17, 1928	26 yr 8 mo 23 dy	
JORDAN, MARY ELENOR	Jan 26, 1935	10 yr 6 mo 3 dy	California
JOSEPH, JOAQUINA SANTOS	Oct 25, 1914	60 yr 11 mo 23 dy	
JOSEPH, MANUEL	Dec 12, 1903	80 yr	Azores Is.
JOSEPH, MICHAEL	Jan 03, 1919	82 yr 6 mo 14 dy	
JUHL, MARTIN	Jun 09, 1938	61 yr 3 mo 15 dy	Denmark
JUHL, MATT CHRISTIAN	Aug 03, 1915	62 yr	
JULIOT, WALLACE B.	Apr 26, 1944	age unknown	Wisconsin
JUNKANS, CARL	Oct 20, 1905	74 yr 8 mo 14 dy	Prussia
JUNKANS, JULIE	Jun 07, 1921	78 yr	
JUNKANS, KARL H.	Jul 28, 1922	52 yr 25 dy	
JUNKANS, LOUIS K.	Dec 06, 1929	66 yr 11 mo 23 dy	
JUNKANS, MARIE L.	Jul 17, 1900	76 yr 1 mo 7 dy	Germany
JUNKANS, RUDOLPH C.	Feb 24, 1916	17 yr 5 mo 12 dy	
JUNKANS, RUDOLPH HENRY	Nov 14, 1947	68 yr 3 mo 14 dy	California
JUNKANS, WILLIAM FREDERICK	Apr 05, 1918	72 yr 2 mo 16 dy	
KAHLKE, JACOB	Oct 04, 1932	80 yr 7 mo 6 dy	Denmark
KAPUSTA, KLABYSLOF	Mar 01, 1908	5 yr 3 mo 17 dy	California
KAY, inf.dau M/M C.B.	Aug 20, 1910	16 dy	California
KEATCH, JASPER W.	Jun 18, 1939	72 yr 3 mo 2 dy	California
KEATING, THOMAS	Jun 13, 1915	65 yr	
KEATING, WILLIAM E.	Oct 12, 1933	45 yr 1 mo 16 dy	California
KECK, LESTER LESLIE	Oct 17, 1940	19 yr	N.Dakota
KEELY, MARGARET, Mrs.	Jan 04, 1906	85 yr 1 mo 10 dy	Ireland
KEENAN, M., Mrs.	Mar 08, 1900	73 yr	Ireland
KEENHOLTS, JAMES ERNEST	Nov 20, 1950	32 yr	Montana
KELL, ROBERT FITZSIMMONS	Sep 26, 1949	49 yr	California
KELLEY, JACOB HEPLER	Mar 26, 1924	83 yr 6 mo 4 dy	
KELLOGG, ALBERT LANGDON	May 03, 1940	71 yr	California
KELLY, GERTRUDE	May 22, 1938	42 yr 2 mo 18 dy	Mass.
KELLY, JOHN FRANCIS	Feb 23, 1911	24 yr	
KELSEY, NORMAN	Mar 07, 1934	79 yr 9 mo 27 dy	New York
KELSO, CLARICE OPAL	Sep 14, 1945	37 yr 11 mo 7 dy	Texas
KELSO, JOHN BERNARD	Aug 15, 1949	50 yr	Kansas
KENNEDY, GERALD	Jul 16, 1910	20 yr 21 dy	
KENNEDY, WILLIAM	Aug 11, 1948	89 yr 1 mo 4 dy	Kentucky
KERR, JOHN HENRY	Oct 03, 1939	79 yr 1 mo 3 dy	Mississippi
KIDD, MAGGIE S.	Jan 05, 1946	94 yr	
KIEARNAN, OLIVER C.	Jul 25, 1934	66 yr	California
KILLINS, RICHARD	Feb 03, 1901	50 yr	Canada
KIM DOEY	Sep 26, 1934	95 yr	China
KIMSEY, VERNARD LESTER	Oct 15, 1936	23 yr 5 mo 10 dy	California
KINDERMAN, CHARLES ARNOLD	Sep 22, 1912	51 yr	
KINDRED, E. A.	Mar 13, 1909	abt 15 yr	California
KING, ELSEN FRAYNE, Mrs.	Jan 26, 1926	28 yr	
KING, GLENNETTE	Apr 21, 1937	55 yr	Minnesota
KING, JAMES	Oct 24, 1936	74 yr 10 mo 1 dy	Missouri
KING, JOSEPH	Jun 28, 1914	62 yr	
KING, ROBERT J.	Nov 30, 1943	88 yr 2 mo 26 dy	Canada
KINGSBURY, CHARLES BARNES	Dec 09, 1944	74 yr 6 mo 24 dy	California

Name	Date	Age	Birthplace
KINGSLEY, JACKSON C.	May 08, 1948	71 yr 1 mo 3 dy	Wisconsin
KIRACK, ALEXZANDER	Nov 04, 1948	61 yr 11 mo 7 dy	Michigan
KIRKPATRICK, AARON RUTHERFORD,	Jul 28, 1913	6 mo 16 dy	
KISTLER, G. W.	Mar 06, 1928	54 yr	
KITTLE, JOHN G.	Mar 04, 1906	abt 35 yr	California
KNAPP, ARTHUR MANLEY	Aug 24, 1943	65 yr 4 mo 21 dy	Illinois
KNIGHT, ANNA	Jan 03, 1942	51 yr 25 dy	Sweden
KNIGHT, WILLIAM K.	Sep 14, 1911	52 yr	
KNIGHT, W. L.	Sep 25, 1910	62 yr	
KNISS, EMELINE	Dec 06, 1937	77 yr 4 mo 22 dy	Indiana
KNISS, LESTER RALPH	Jun 05, 1920	11 dy	
KNISS, MYRTLE, Miss	Jul 14, 1903	19 yr 3 mo	
KNOWLES, CHARLES HORACE	Jan 25, 1934	70 yr 8 mo 8 dy	California
KNOWLES, GEORGE, Mrs.	Jan 29, 1903	25 yr	California
KNOWLES, HENRY	Apr 25, 1911	78 yr 5 mo 29 dy	
KNOWLES, HENRY LINCOLN	Nov 04, 1944	78 yr 10 mo 28dy	California
KNOWLES, LILLY A.	Aug 21, 1939	60 yr 11 mo 10dy	California
KNUDSEN, CONRAD	Mar 06, 1926	74 yr	
KOCH, C.	Jul __, 1928	64 yr	
KOLL, JOHN, Sr.	Jan 09, 1912	84 yr 24 dy	
KOLL, WINNIE	Jul 03, 1917	84 yr 5 mo 26 dy	
KOON, CORA, Mrs.	Mar 29, 1916	54 yr	
KOON, JOHN ALEXANDER	Mar 08, 1932	87 yr 9 mo 1 dy	New York
KOONS, ARTHUR	Nov 07, 1908	abt 20 yr	California
KOTTMEIER, CHARLES A.	Nov 08, 1948	77 yr 4 mo 7 dy	Oregon
KRAMOLOWSKY, JOSEPH	May 24, 1907	abt 52 yr	Austria
KRIEGBAUM, FRITZ ADAM	Feb 25, 1939	28 yr 2 mo 3 dy	Illinois
LADD, ELLEN ELIZABETH	Feb 10, 1922	61 yr 1 mo 28 dy	
LADD, FRANK JAMES	Feb 17, 1932	80 yr 1 mo 16 dy	Maine
LADEWIG, KARL M.	Jun 25, 1936	51 yr 11 mo 2 dy	Illinois
LAFEVER, FRED E.	Jun 21, 1939	50 yr 6 mo 13 dy	Indiana
LAFFRANCHINI, CHARLES	Nov 18, 1934	71 yr 7 mo 23 dy	Switzerland
LAFFRANCHINI, DELPHINE JULIA	May 11, 1946	74 yr	
LAINGOR, GEORGE B.	Feb 08, 1906	24 yr 4 mo 28 dy	California
LAINGOR, JOHN JASPER	Oct 09, 1912	69 yr 11 mo 26 dy	
LAIRD, ROBERT ROY	Jun 09, 1902	10 mo 25 dy	California
LAKE, GEORGE	Dec 28, 1942	90 yr 4 mo 10 dy	Ireland
LAKEY, WILLIAM EDWARD	Jul 09, 1946	24 yr 4 mo 13 dy	Arkansas
[Lambert, Charles, see TUNG MAO MA]			
LAMBERT, HUGH WESTEN	Sep 02, 1938	62 yr 5 mo 21 dy	California
LAMPLEY, FRANK	May 31, 1944	84 yr 4 mo 14 dy	California
LAMPLEY, OLIVE SARAH	Dec 05, 1931	67 yr 3 mo 5 dy	
LANDIS, EDGAR	Feb 12, 1914	62 yr	
LANE, DOCTOR THOMAS	Feb 20, 1950	78 yr	California
LANGE, THEODORE	Aug 16, 1940	70 yr	California
LANIGAN, BERNICE GERALDINE	Jun 16, 1946	52 yr 8 mo 25 dy	Ohio
LARCINE, MARY B., Miss	Feb 03, 1901	17 yr 5 mo 15 dy	California
LARCINE, PETER OLANDER	Nov 30, 1907	74 yr 9 mo 2 dy	Florida
LARGE, ROBERT	Aug 13, 1926	79 yr 8 mo 10 dy	
LARISON, PERRY	Jan 30, 1901	50 yr	Illinois
LARSON, JOHN	Aug 07, 1916	66 yr	
LARSON, JOHN, Mrs.	Nov 08, 1900	48 yr	California
LARSON, KATHLEEN ELINOR	Jul 21, 1902	18 yr 6 mo	California
LASH, FREDERICK A.	Aug 22, 1932	70 yr	Mass.
LATHAM, RAYMOND H.	Mar 06, 1948	58 yr 7 mo 20 dy	Nebraska
LAUTENSCHLAGER, VALENTINE	Nov 05, 1923	87 yr 6 mo 18 dy	
LAWS, JAMES G.	Sep __, 1900	unknown	
LAYMAN, J. B.	Mar 11, 1911	63 yr 8 mo 29 dy	
LAYMAN, MARY CATHERINE	Nov 18, 1934	80 yr 6 mo 27 dy	Iowa
LAYTON, MARY	Mar 27, 1935	50 yr	Oregon
LEACH, GEORGIA ANN	May 17, 1929	68 yr 11 mo	
LEACH, MARY ELLEN	Dec 29, 1940	69 yr 9 mo 8 dy	California
LEACOCK, FOREST PENN	Jul 01, 1914	21 yr 2 mo 24 dy	

LEAN, WALTER J.	Jul 02, 1933	57 yr 10 mo 13dy	Nevada
LEAS, AMY LORRAINE	Apr 25, 1907	11 mo 13 dy	California
LEAS, BETTY DIANE	Feb 10, 1935	3 dy	California
LEAS, ELIZABETH, Mrs.	Jul 05, 1910	43 yr 5 mo 12 dy	
LEAS, GEORGE W.	Dec 29, 1903	76 yr 5 mo 25 dy	Indiana
LEAS, THOMAS C.	Dec 06, 1930	72 yr 2 mo 2 dy	
LEAS, WM. JOHN	May 14, 1914	23 yr 18 dy	
LEAVITT, JANE D.	Mar 04, 1939	74 yr 3 mo 8 dy	Wisconsin
LEAVITT, SCOTT	Jul 17, 1946	7 yr	
LeBLANC, GEORGE	Nov 11, 1918	66 yr	
LEDGERWOOD, THOMAS C.	Apr 26, 1913	57 yr	
LEE HOW	Jul 04, 1941	abt 90 yr	China
LEE, Inf.Ch of SAM LEE	Jan 19, 1913	3 dy	
LEE, SAM (father of Moon)	Jan 20, 1947	84 yr 9 mo 9 dy	China
LEE, SAM, Mrs.	Jan 19, 1913	36 yr	
[Lee, see also Addendum]			
LEE SAM (not fa. of Moon)	Dec 04, 1924	96 yr	
LEHNHOFF, CHARLES	May 07, 1942	81 yr 4 mo 4 dy	Germany
LEHNHOFF, WM. J. T.	Jan 31, 1942	54 yr 4 mo 18 dy	New York
LEMON, NEWTON J.	Jan 04, 1931	80 yr 1 mo 21 dy	
LENKER, EDWARD S.	Apr 26, 1944	unknown	Penn.
LEONARD, HENRY WILLIAM	May 08, 1919	83 yr 28 dy	
LEONARD, LUCINA M.	Jul 27, 1910	38 yr 11 dy	
LeROY, BICKMORE	Feb 14, 1932	59 yr	U.S.A.
LEUTERITZ, KURT	Oct 08, 1924	36 yr	
LEVEQUE, HENRY	Jan 19, 1922	63 yr	
LEW DOW CHUEN	Dec 21, 1914	78 yr	
LEW TONG	Jan 05, 1917	82 yr	
LEWIS, ALBERT R.	Aug 01, 1942	69 yr 6 mo 25 dy	New York
LEWIS, CLARA ROSE	Apr 01, 1921	42 yr 4 mo 9 dy	
LEWMAN, GEORGE FRANKLIN	Jun 21, 1949	85 yr	Oregon
LIGHTHALL, O. W.	May 18, 1934	50 yr	
LIM AH MOY	Apr 26, 1935	95 yr	China
LIM, JACK	Aug 23, 1940	49 yr	California
LIM, MARY	Aug 16, 1914	72 yr	
LIM SING	Nov 09, 1915	45 yr 3 mo	
LINCK, ANTHONY	Apr 17, 1938	66 yr 9 mo 7 dy	
LINDER, FRED	Apr 23, 1903	45 yr	Germany
LINTON, JOHN GORDON	Dec 19, 1943	71 yr 8 mo 20 dy	Kansas
LISTON, DICK	Jan 13, 1902	45 yr	
LLOYD, CECIL ELIAS	Mar 03, 1940	36 yr	Nebraska
LLOYD, VAUGHAN LANDEN	Jun 01, 1938	54 yr 7 mo 13 dy	Washington
LOBDELL, CHARLES	Mar 16, 1904	abt 78 yr	New York
LOBDELL, ORRIN	Jul 23, 1909	abt 78 yr	New York
LONG, CHARLES	May 07, 1947	60 yr 9 mo 15 dy	Kansas
LONG, JAMES ALBERT	Jul 07, 1939	58 yr 8 mo 28 dy	Oregon
LONG, JAMES B.	Jun 21, 1929	50 yr	
LOOMIS, ALBERT GIFFORD	Feb 03, 1920	4 dy	
LOOMIS, BERNICE LORAINE	Nov 03, 1914	9 yr 11 mo 3 dy	
LORD, ANDREW PALM	Mar 24, 1940	71 yr	Michigan
LORENZ, GEORGE J.	Aug 07, 1912	33 yr 8 mo 6 dy	
LORENZ, MARY ANN	Nov 28, 1950	39 yr	Azores Is.
LORENZEN, THOMAS	Jan 03, 1903	73 yr	Germany
LOSCH, WALTER E.	Aug 07, 1938	38 yr	
LOTT, EVA LORRAINE	Aug 20, 1949	81 yr	Penn.
LOUIE CHONG	Jul 23, 1921	63 yr	
LOVEJOY, SUMNER GATES	Mar 22, 1937	72 yr	Iowa
LOVERIDGE, O. M.	Nov 23, 1900	72 yr 4 mo 29 dy	New York
LOWDEN, AMANDA MORRIS	May 28, 1936	77 yr 9 mo 20 dy	California
LOWDEN, FRANK WILLIAM	Mar 19, 1932	73 yr 1 mo 18 dy	California
LOWDEN, G. S.	Aug 04, 1922	26 yr 7 mo 18 dy	
LOWDEN, HELEN EMILY TRASK,Mrs.,	Mar 20, 1904	71 yr 11 mo 14 dy	Penn.
LOWDEN, HENRY LARKIN	Nov 26, 1935	78 yr 1 mo 14 dy	California

Name	Date	Age	Birthplace
LOWDEN, LUCY L., Mrs.	May 12, 1901	55 yr 15 dy	England
LOWDEN, MARY TRASK	May 08, 1936	75 yr 3 mo 1 dy	California
LOWDEN, OWEN EUGENE	Feb 27, 1904	66 yr 3 mo	Illinois
LOWDEN, WM. SPENCER	Jan 10, 1912	81 yr 6 mo	
LOWE, MARGARET, Mrs.	Mar 19, 1946	80 yr 8 mo 25 dy	California
LOWRY, BLANCHE ADELE	Jul 19, 1946	22 yr 2 mo 23 dy	California
LOWRY, PHILIP BURTON	Aug 16, 1946	21 yr 0 mo 8 dy	California
LUCKIE, JAMES	Jan 01, 1916	86 yr 4 dy	
LUCKIE, MARGARET	Feb 08, 1900	23 yr 10 mo 4 dy	California
LUCKY, KATE	Feb 25, 1937	94 yr	California
LUMAN, HENRY DAVID	Jan 16, 1907	69 yr	Illinois
LUNDBERG, ALFRED	Oct 07, 1927	72 yr 6 mo 17 dy	
LUNDY, GRANDVILLE	Aug 15, 1938	59 yr 7 mo 12 dy	Missouri
LUNNING, JOE	Nov 14, 1944	52 yr	California
LUTMAN, DAVID C.	Aug 24, 1918	86 yr 6 mo 15 dy	
LUX, CARRIE HAYWARD	Mar 23, 1939	72 yr	California
LYBARGER, EDWARD CARL	Apr 02, 1938	64 yr 1 mo 10 dy	Illinois
LYONS, BOBBY WILLIAM	Jul 11, 1934	15 yr 1 mo 14 dy	Arizona
LYONS, CHARLES R.	Jun 18, 1907	abt 48 yr	New York
MABIE, FRANK	Aug 12, 1936	87 yr 9 mo 12 dy	Illinois
MABIE, LELAND	May 10, 1909	31 yr 5 mo 7 dy	California

Mc - names beginning with this prefix are alphabetized as if spelled MAC.

Name	Date	Age	Birthplace
McADAMS, MARGARET LOUISE	Jul 27, 1937	34 yr 6 mo 3 dy	Washington
McCAMPBELL, DELBERT	Jan 28, 1905	17 yr 9 mo 12 dy	California
McCANDLESS, MATTIE, Mrs.	Sep 11, 1905	abt 43 yr	Ohio
McCASLIN, ARTHUR HENRY	Oct 19, 1947	81 yr 11 mo 28 dy	California
McCLAREN, WM. J.	May 25, 1948	77 yr 5 mo 12 dy	Canada
McCLEES, JAS. LEWIS	Jan 19, 1914	61 yr 2 mo 7 dy	
McCLOUD, PETER	Jun 08, 1934	86 yr 4 mo 14 dy	Wisconsin
McCOY, JAMES H.	Oct 22, 1932	31 yr 7 mo 22 dy	Arkansas
McCRACKEN, HUGH FOSTER	Oct 06, 1924	39 yr 13 dy	
McCUE, FLORENCE BELLE	Jan 21, 1905	unknown	California
McCUSH, JOHN	Nov 24, 1901	52 yr	N. Scotia
McDEVITT, GOLDIE ALBERTA	Jul 29, 1933	26 yr 2 mo 17 dy	Oregon
McDONALD, CLARA B.	Oct 30, 1901	1 mo 15 dy	California
McDONALD, JOHN D.	Oct 21, 1942	91 yr 10 mo 5 dy	California
McDONALD, MARY FRANCES	Nov 21, 1935	62 yr 11 mo 19 dy	California
McDONALD, RICHARD	Sep 06, 1941	55 yr 7 mo 27 dy	Montana
McDONALD, THERESA M., Mrs.	Apr 20, 1926	63 yr 9 mo 15 dy	
McDONALD, WILLIAM	Dec 23, 1916	73 yr	
McDONOUGH, JOHN H.	Jul 28, 1936	77 yr 6 mo 24 dy	Wisconsin
McDREW, DEAN L.	Jul 16, 1933	28 yr 11 mo 14 dy	Missouri
McFARLAND, LEWIS ERNEST	May 31, 1948	68 yr 1 mo 1 dy	California
McGOVERN, DELMER JAMES	Mar 22, 1920	2 mo 3 dy	
McGOVERN, JOSEPH WALTER	Jul 14, 1922	b.d.	
McGOWAN, LYLE S.	Apr 20, 1923	44 yr	
McGRAW, SAMUEL	Mar 13, 1903	40 yr	
McHENRY, BETTE VALENTINE	Sep 24, 1938	8 yr 7 mo 10 dy	California
MacILWAINE, ANNIE MARIE	Sep 24, 1935	69 yr 4 mo 8 dy	California
MacILWAINE, MATHEW HARRIS	Nov 19, 1947	87 yr 8 mo 27 dy	Ireland
McINTYRE, VERNON GLENN	Sep 21, 1946	41 yr 7 mo 6 dy	N. Dakota
McKAY, ANNA	Mar 17, 1934	96 yr	California
McKAY, DIANA W.	May 13, 1903	34 yr	California
McKAY, FINLEY	Apr 10, 1906	abt 80 yr	N. Scotia
McKAY, JOHN	Jan 29, 1948	84 yr 9 mo 27 dy	California
McKAY, NETTIE	Feb 10, 1906	11 yr 10 mo 8 dy	California
McKAY, RICHARD WARREN	Nov 16, 1946	21 yr 7 mo 3 dy	Oregon
McKAY, WILLIAM	Feb __, 1903	42 yr	California
McKEE, THOMAS	Mar 03, 1909	36 yr 8 mo	Missouri
McKENZIE, EMMA, Mrs.	Sep 23, 1901	30 yr 4 mo 4 dy	California
McKIBBIN, GLADYS LAURENA	Feb 16, 1931	4 dy	
McKINLEY, THOMAS	Jul 13, 1907	abt 60 yr	
McLAUGHLIN, CON.	Mar 11, 1903	43 yr	Ireland

Name	Date	Age	Place
McLEAN, A. WALLACE	Dec 01, 1931	45 yr 7 mo 21 dy	
McMANUS, HENRY	AUG 20, 1912	66 yr	
McMORROW, MART	Sep 13, 1936	56 yr	U.S.A.
McMURCHY, DANIEL WEBSTER	Jun 23, 1934	57 yr 15 dy	Wisconsin
McNAMARA, ALICE	Aug 04, 1921	59 yr 2 mo 20 dy	
McNAMARA, ELLSWORTH	Apr 20, 1944	60 yr 11 mo 17 dy	California
McNAMARA, THOMAS JAMES	Aug 17, 1916	66 yr 5 mo 2 dy	
McNULTY, JOHN A.	Apr 28, 1935	52 yr	Maine
McNUTT, GEORGE ELMER	Jul 01, 1943	63 yr 1 mo 14 dy	Illinois
McNUTT, SADIE J.	Oct 30, 1942	65 yr 4 mo 26 dy	California
McPHERSON, LAWRENCE C.	May 05, 1937	57 yr 9 mo 18 dy	California
McPHERSON, ROBERT	Mar 18, 1940	67 yr	N.Carolina
McVAY, REBECCA	Mar 28, 1929	not given	
McWHORTER, A.L.	Jul 09, 1900	76 yr	New York
McWHORTER, BARBARA	Mar 10, 1916	86 yr 5 mo 23 dy	
McWILLIAMS, JOHN	Jun 12, 1903	76 yr	Ireland
MACHADO, JOHN FRATUS	Oct 25, 1933	80 yr 2 mo	Portugal
MADDEN, FRED J.	Dec 16, 1933	65 yr	U.S.A.
MADDUX, FRANCIS	Sep 24, 1931	66 yr 11 mo 10 dy	
MADISON, JOHN HENRY	May 09, 1907	abt 82 yr	Wash.D.C.
MAHON, JAMES C.	Apr 04, 1930	68 yr	
MAHONEY, FRANK	Dec 16, 1940	69 yr	Illinois
MAKER, AMY CAROLINE	Apr 26, 1940	16 yr	California
MAKER, VINCENT	Apr 17, 1915	25 dy	
MALA, DICK	Jun 24, 1914	80 yr	
MALLOY, ISABELLE	Feb 05, 1915	33 yr 9 mo 18 dy	
MALONEY, WM.	Mar 21, 1914	46 yr	
MANN, RONALD GLENN	May 12, 1937	11 mo 28 dy	California
MANSFIELD, inf.dau. M/M ABE	Jan 31, 1907	4 mo 14 dy	California
MAR SING	Mar 11, 1911	76 yr	
MARAVIOV, BABY (male)	Sep 04, 1948	1 Hr 15 Min	California
MARBLE, F. D.	May 20, 1900	87 yr	Michigan
MARCUS, inf.son M/M JAMES	Nov 18, 1902	b.d.	California
MARKER, DELBERT EARL	Apr 23, 1946	59 yr 8 mo 16 dy	Iowa
MARLETT, GEORGE HENRY	Jul 05, 1927	72 yr 1 mo 24 dy	
MARLETT, SUSAN	Apr 05, 1945	77 yr 6 mo 21 dy	Oregon
MARSH, FRANKLIN	Jun 20, 1905	abt 81 yr	Mass.
MARSHALL, AMOS HUFFMAN	Apr 03, 1919	89 yr 18 dy	
MARSHALL, EMMA ROSELLA	Sep 01, 1917	71 yr 2 mo 10 dy	
MARSHALL, ISABELLE MAUD FLORENCE,	Apr 16, 1923,	44 yr 9 mo 23 dy	
MARSHALL, REID CLARK	Jun 24, 1912	3 yr 2 mo 17 dy	
MARTIN, ELIZABETH	May 22, 1937	69 yr 1 mo 26 dy	California
MARTIN, HARRY FRANK	Apr 21, 1934	55 yr 11 mo 12dy	California
MARTIN, JAMES	Oct 19, 1936	83 yr 4 mo 27 dy	California
MARTIN, LILLIAN JULIA	Sep 26, 1935	3-1/2 dy	California
MARTIN, MARICE (Maurice?)	Mar 11, 1911	68 yr	
MARTIN, MARION	Mar 28, 1903	10 yr	California
MARTIN, MINNIE, Miss	Jul 17, 1927	59 yr 8 mo 6 dy	
MARTIN, WILLIAM HENRY	Mar 08, 1912	83 yr 9 mo 23 dy	
MASON, JOEL PIEREZ	Jan 31, 1916	83 yr 15 dy	
MASON, JOHN CLIFTON	Jul 04, 1921	91 yr 7 mo 23 dy	
MASON, LOUIE S.	Jun 09, 1941	48 yr 6 mo 5 dy	Missouri
MASTERSON, MARCELLUS	May 12, 1948	73 yr 9 mo 0 dy	Oregon
MATHESON, BELLE	Apr 06, 1938	70 yr 5 mo 21 dy	California
MATHEWS, FRANK E.	Mar 12, 1904	abt 21 yr	California
MATHEWS, JAMES ALONZO	Dec 07, 1915	82 yr 2 mo 24 dy	
MATHEWS, SARAH HARDY	Jul 03, 1948	60 yr 7 mo 12 dy	California
MATHEWS, WILLIAM	Sep 23, 1913	70 yr	
MATHEWSON, JUNE	Jun __, 1908	abt 79 yr	
MATSON, MATT	Jul 04, 1940	66 yr	Sweden
MAXWELL, WILLIAM	Feb 21, 1901	60 yr	Scotland
MAYNARD, CHAS	Dec 09, 1900	72 yr 4 mo 29dy	New York
MAYNARD, JOHN GRANGER	Aug 19, 1902	59 yr	Michigan

MEAD, CORYDON J.	Jan 08, 1942	64 yr 9 mo	California
MEAD, CORYDON MILLARD	Aug 19, 1912	84 yr 4 mo 11 dy	
MEAD, C. V., Mrs.	Apr 26, 1901	45 yr	Maine
MEADOR, JAMES W.	Aug 17, 1935	40 yr 5 mo 17 dy	California
MECKEL, CHAS.	Jul 19, 1900	25 yr 7 mo 1 dy	California
MECKEL, CHARLOTTE, Mrs.	Jan 18, 1919	82 yr 6 mo 14 dy	
MECKEL, CHRISTIAN	MAY 13, 1904	75 yr 21 dy	Bavaria
MECKEL, EDNA MAY (Fred. C.)	Sep 01, 1946	63 yr 2 mo 12 dy	Kansas
MECKEL, EDWARD	Feb 09, 1942	63 yr 11 mo 12dy	California
MECKEL, JOHN WEINHEIMER	Sep 03, 1945	87 yr 5 mo 3 dy	California
MECKEL, LILY JOSEPHINE	Jul 12, 1921	14 yr 7 mo 7 dy	
MECKEL, LOUISA	Jul 19, 1932	72 yr 8 mo 21 dy	California
MECKEL, MARY TERESA	Sep 10, 1916	43 yr 5 mo 27 dy	
MEIER, CHARLES HERMON	Feb 11, 1932	69 yr 3 mo 25 dy	Germany
MEISINGER, GEORGE	Jun 19, 1903	48 yr	Penn.
MELEH, ROBERT J.	Apr 26, 1944	unknown	New Jersey
MELENDY, RICHMOND WARNER	Jun 19, 1943	50 yr 5 mo 18 dy	California
MERCIER, LOUISE	Jun 18, 1911	55 yr	
MEREDITH, DAVID LLOYD	Mar 26, 1908	abt 49 yr	England
MEREDITH, OLIVER H.	Mar 07, 1919	69 yr	
MERRICK, JOHN DAVID (b.d.)	Jul 10, 1950	12 hr 5 min	California
MEYER, FRANCES ADELINE	Feb 18, 1937	70 yr 4 mo 11 dy	California
MEYER, LEONA	Jun 27, 1917	52 yr	
MEYER, VALENTINE	Jul 25, 1917	78 yr	
MEYERS, JOHN	Sep 01, 1911	16 yr 4 mo	
MICHAELSON, WILLIAM	Feb 11, 1941	72 yr 4 mo 3 dy	Wisconsin
MILLER, CLARENCE R.	Feb 05, 1930	25 yr 5 mo 10 dy	
MILLER, EMMA AGNES	Apr 06, 1938	69 yr 8 mo 12 dy	California
MILLER, FRANK M.	Oct 02, 1934	58 yr 7 mo 3 dy	Illinois
MILLER, FRED E.	Apr 25, 1943	87 yr 5 mo 6 dy	Tennessee
MILLER, HENRY	Jun 07, 1912	86 yr	
MILLER, HENRY ADOR	Nov 15, 1925	infant	
MILLER, HENRY D.	Jul 04, 1940	59 yr	California
MILLER, IRMA GOODYEAR	Jan 22, 1930	40 yr 8 mo 15 dy	
MILLER, JOHN	Feb 27, 1930	70 yr	
MILLER, L. S.	May 16, 1925	82 yr	
MILLER, OLGA S.	Dec 29, 1948	42 yr 7 mo 6 dy	Illinois
MILLER, SAMUEL CALVIN	Jun 05, 1927	56 yr 7 mo 19 dy	
MILLER, STANLEY	Mar 14, 1939	54 yr 10 mo 6 dy	Conn.
MILLS, M. L.	Nov 26, 1928	71 yr	
MILLS, SARAH A.	Sep 30, 1903	77 yr 6 mo 6 dy	
MILLS, WILLIAM	Mar 03, 1903	83 yr	Penn.
MIRANDA, JOHN	Apr 11, 1933	26 yr	California
MITCHELL, CASSIE K.	Jul 10, 1942	66 yr 5 mo 21 dy	England
MITCHELL, FRANK	Mar 28, 1911	83 yr	
MITCHELL, HELEN MacILWAINE	Jan 12, 1946	46 yr	
MOCK FAWN	Sep 10, 1933	78 yr	China
MOCK, JOSEPH	Jun 09, 1944	77 yr 4 mo 1 dy	Switzerland
MODIN, AUGUST	Oct 21, 1922	74 yr	
MOLITOR, ERED	Jun 06, 1927	65 yr 1 mo 16 dy	
MONTAGUE, ELLA	Sep 20, 1946	unknown; d.Redding	
MONTGOMERY, ESAU N.	Feb 08, 1950	70 yr	California
MONTGOMERY, inf.son M/M S.	Mar 09, 1900	9 dy	California
MONTGOMERY, M. A., Mrs.	Jun 22, 1901	33 yr 4 mo 28 dy	California
MONTGOMERY, MAGGIE	Feb 08, 1950	73 yr	California.
MONTGOMERY, RAYMOND JOE	Oct 14, 1948	18 yr 9 mo 13 dy	Colorado
MOORE, FRANK L.	Jan 31, 1922	54 yr	
MOORE, RAYMOND E.	Dec 27, 1942	41 yr 2 mo 23 dy	Washington
MOORE, ROCKEY SIBLEY	Jan 05, 1950	74 yr	Colorado
MOORE, WILLIAM ARTHUR	Aug 22, 1932	45 yr 6 mo 25 dy	Illinois
MORGAN, MARY, Mrs.	Dec 16, 1906	53 yr 4 mo 28 dy	N.Hampshire
MORI, JOHN	Oct 31, 1919	28 yr	
MORRIS, GEORGE	Jul 10, 1912	71 yr	

MORRIS, HENRY A.	Jan 01, 1944	74 yr 2 mo 22 dy	California
MORRIS, JAMES	Dec 17, 1907	73 yr 8 mo	Ireland
MORRIS, JOHN JAMES	Apr 27, 1944	76 yr 3 mo 30 dy	California
MORRIS, JOSEPH WILLIAM	May 28, 1919	59 yr 9 mo 17 dy	
MORRIS, VICTORIA STAFFORD	Jan 11, 1938	68 yr 9 mo	California
MORRISON, ALONZO	Feb __, 1917	65 yr	
MORRISON, JAMES L.	Apr 04, 1936	77 yr 4 mo	
MORRISSEY, ELLA SHELTON	Jan 20, 1916	50 yr 6 mo 14 dy	
MORTENSON, NILA	Sep 24, 1912	19 yr	
MORTIMER, JOHANNA	Apr 17, 1943	69 yr 8 mo 4 dy	California
MORTIMER, WASHINGTON	Feb 21, 1922	72 yr	
MORTON, PHILLIP	Dec 01, 1931	93 yr 11 mo 6 dy	
MOSER, BERTHA LIZABETH	May 26, 1946	65 yr 6 mo 19 dy	California
MOSER, CHARLES FREDRICK	Apr 08, 1914	11 yr 3 mo 19 dy	
MOSER, CHAS. ROBERT	Feb 13, 1944	79 yr	Switzerland
MOTHERWELL, MARY ELLEN	Oct 16, 1921	81 yr	
MOTHERWELL, THOMAS V.	Nov 18, 1932	76 yr 4 mo 20 dy	California
MOUNTFORT, EDMUND	Jun 18, 1901	70 yr	Maine
MULLANE, JAMES	Nov 29, 1922	81 yr	
MULLIGAN, ELLEN, Mrs.	Nov 08, 1907	abt 63 yr	Ireland
MULLIGAN, MICHAEL	Nov 06, 1909	abt 71 yr	Ireland
MULLINS, BILLIE NEAL	Oct 28, 1934	5 mo 7 dy	Oregon
MUNROE, GLEN ALEXANDER	Feb __, 1935	21 yr 10 mo	Idaho
MUNSELL, MARY M.	Oct 27, 1940	41 yr	California
MUNSTER, JOHN DEDRICK	Jan 21, 1915	93 yr	
MUNZBURG, RICHARD	May 06, 1934	58 yr 2 mo 24 dy	Germany
MURPHY, ALLIE (f.)	May 21, 1949	93 yr	Illinois
MURPHY, ALVIN	Oct 02, 1917	29 yr 7 mo 10 dy	
MURPHY, BENJAMIN	Sep 20, 1931	69 yr 4 mo 16 dy	
MURPHY, EDWARD	Mar 18, 1900	76 yr	Ireland
MURPHY, FRANCIS J.	Jan 24, 1910	27 dy	California
MURPHY, FRANK	Dec 10, 1913	44 yr	
MURPHY, JOHN	Dec 09, 1905	80 yr 5 mo 15 dy	Canada
MURPHY, JOHN G.	May 08, 1909	2 yr 10 mo	California
MUZZY, JAMES SAMUEL	Jan 31, 1950	69 yr	Wisconsin
MYERS, JOHN	Jul 19, 1903	74 yr	Penn.
MYERS, MARSHALL E.	Aug 05, 1907	abt 71 yr	Virginia
NECKER, OTTO FRITZ	Apr 28, 1947	57 yr 2 mo 3 dy	Germany
NEFF, DANIEL	Jul 04, 1907	abt 77 yr	Canada
NELSON, CHARLES	Aug 06, 1932	68 yr	Sweden
NELSON, IVER	Sep 24, 1938	46 yr 11 mo 21dy	Sweden
NELSON, J. A. T.	Jul 31, 1922	45 yr 8 mo 5 dy	
NELSON, NELS	_____, 1937	83 yr 6 mo	Sweden
NESBIT, JAMES K.	Aug 08, 1903	29 yr	California
NEUSSE, KARL	Apr 06, 1925	79 yr 7 mo 5 dy	
NEUSSE, SOPHIA	Feb 28, 1913	69 yr 9 mo 27 dy	
NEWELL, inf.son M/M C.B.	Nov 10, 1903	b.d.	California
NEWLAND, JAMES BEAN	Jun 03, 1907	86 yr 6 mo 4 dy	Tennessee
NEWLAND, ROBERT DIXON	Apr 09, 1901	30 yr 3 mo 5 dy	California
NEWMAN, EDWARD L.	Feb 24, 1925	67 yr 25 dy	
NICHOLS, H. W.	Jan 15, 1910	67 yr	
NICHOLS, inf.son M/M W.J.	Sep 07, 1902	1 mo 14 dy	California
NICHOLSON, JAMES T.	Aug 26, 1946	58 yr	
NICHOLSON, THADDEUS C.	May 01, 1906	abt 24 yr	California
NOBLE, ROSE CLARICE	Mar 26, 1940	61 yr	California
NOBLE, SADIE, Mrs.	Jan 23, 1922	75 yr	
NOBLE, STEPHEN	Feb 24, 1915	82 yr 6 mo 4 dy	
NOBLE, STEPHEN	Mar 31, 1920	20 yr 11 mo 21 dy	
NOLAN, ROBERT	May 13, 1907	abt 28 yr	California
NOLING, CHARLES R.	Apr 13, 1912	44 yr	
NOLTON, ALBERT	Feb 24, 1914	33 yr	
NOLTON, JIM	Oct 04, 1918	66 yr	
NOLTON, LULU	May 22, 1907	abt 25 yr	California

Name	Date	Age	Birthplace
NOLTON, MARGIE	Jun 13, 1921	13 yr 4 mo 1 dy	
NONNEMAKER, HARRY S.	Dec 05, 1941	71 yr 9 mo 8 dy	Maryland
NOONAN, GEORGE EDMUND	Jun 13, 1902	71 yr 2 mo 5 dy	N. Scotia
NORGAAR, CHRIS	Aug 30, 1923	65 yr 7 mo	
NORGAAR, EVELYN	Nov 08, 1922	2 yr 21 dy	
NORGAAR, MORRIS	Dec 21, 1910	21 yr	
NORGARD, STOSEL	Nov 01, 1905	1 yr 10 mo	California
NORTON, JAMES	Dec __, 1902	77 yr	New York
NOUKELY, VICTOR FREDERICK WARSAW	Jan 19, 1916	76 yr	
NOYES, L. A.	Nov 03, 1906	abt 92 yr	Vermont
O'NEIL, JAMES CORNELIUS	Dec 02, 1923	58 yr 7 mo 13 dy	
O'NEIL, MARY	Jun 18, 1941	84 yr 9 mo 4 dy	California
O'SHAY, JOANNA, Mrs.	Feb 02, 1902	-- yr	Ireland
O'SHEA, DANIEL J.	Feb 11, 1948	88 yr 2 mo 21 dy	Ireland
OAKLEY, MABLE CLAIRE	Mar 25, 1939	49 yr 9 mo 12 dy	Tennessee
OGBURN, RALPH	Jun 07, 1946	44 yr	
OLHAUSEN, ALEX C.	Oct 23, 1916	55 yr 1 mo 11 dy	
OLSEN, CHARLES	Jun 28, 1910	56 yr	
OLSEN, ELLEN A., Mrs.	Dec 22, 1926	83 yr 10 mo 15 dy	
OLSEN, J. J., Mrs.	Sep 22, 1903	23 yr 4 mo	California
OLSEN, JOHN JAMES	Apr 17, 1948	74 yr 10 mo 15 dy	California
OLSEN, MARION J.	Jul 28, 1943	52 yr 1 mo	California
OLSON, NELS P.	Jan 31, 1932	74 yr 8 mo 7 dy	Sweden
OLSEN, NORMAN TRIMBLE	Sep 11, 1949	37 yr	California
OLSEN, ROBERT HARDY	Aug 25, 1925	24 yr 10 mo 25 dy	
OLSEN, WILBERT	Oct 24, 1918	19 yr	
ON LEE	Nov 03, 1911	65 yr	
OSGOOD, CAMILLA IRENE	Oct 05, 1914	3 yr 1 mo 13 dy	
OSGOOD, HEZEKIAH COLBEY	Aug 21, 1913	87 yr 7 mo 4 dy	
OSGOOD, MARY JANE, Mrs.	Oct 11, 1904	72 yr 9 mo 25 dy	Mass.
OURTH, FRED NICOLAS	Oct 04, 1936	81 yr 6 mo 9 dy	Luxembourg
OWEN, JOHN	Jun 04, 1943	64 yr 3 mo 10 dy	California
OWEN, MARTIN	Apr 23, 1903	40 yr	Texas
OWINGS, J. M.	Jan 12, 1911	85 yr 1 mo 16 dy	
PACHECO, FRANK	Apr 19, 1903	10 yr	California
PAGE, PAULINE MARY	Sep 18, 1948	81 yr 7 mo 6 dy	Ohio
PAGET, FREDERICK HETTON	Sep 16, 1949	51 yr	N. Scotia
PALMER, PETER	Dec 05, 1914	70 yr	
PAOLI, INNOCENCE	Aug 17, 1926	58 yr 6 mo 11 dy	
PARLIN, MALCOLM B.	Sep 28, 1920	86 yr 9 mo 12 dy	
PARMENTER, LE ROY J.	Nov 04, 1934	78 yr 6 mo 17 dy	Penn.
PARROTT, JOHN EDWARD	Mar 18, 1908	abt 76 yr	W. Virginia
PARRY, SARAH R.	Jul 08, 1928	63 yr 9 mo 19 dy	
PATRICK, LOUISE A.	Jul 24, 1942	66 yr 2 mo 2 dy	California
PATTERSON, CHRISTOPHER COLUMBUS	Apr 10, 1905	abt 72 yr	New York
PATTISON, FENNER WARD	Mar 17, 1905	21 yr 11 mo 6 dy	California
PATTISON, THOMAS COX	Sep 27, 1916	45 yr 8 mo 24 dy	
PATTISON, W. A., Sr., Mrs.	Feb 19, 1910	67 yr	
PATTISON, WILLIAM ALANSON, Sr	Mar 12, 1923	90 yr 3 mo 1 dy	
PATTISON, WM. ALANSON, Jr.	Aug 12, 1939	65 yr 11 mo 13 dy	California
PATTON, BETTY LOU	Jun 19, 1948	3 yr 7 mo 20 dy	California
PATTON, HOWARD L.	Sep 15, 1925	Infant	
PATTON, T. W.	Nov 01, 1928	18 yr 1 mo 12 dy	
PATTON, WM.	Aug 28, 1911	76 yr	
PAULSEN, ANNIE IRVING	Aug 11, 1931	63 yr 6 mo 15 dy	
PAULSEN, HENRY W.	Jul 19, 1943	66 yr 1 mo 17 dy	California
PAULSEN, PETER MINERT	Oct 18, 1913	79 yr 3 mo 21 dy	
PEACOCK, HENRY F.	Jan 24, 1948	64 yr 3 mo 25 dy	N. Carolina
PEARCE, EMILY PEARL	Oct 08, 1941	51 yr 4 mo 10 dy	Kansas
PEASE, WILLIAM S.	Aug 26, 1931	62 yr 11 mo 9 dy	
PEEPLES, PRISCILLA DARLENE	Mar 20, 1940	6 mo	California
PELLETREAU, ALEXANDER	May 06, 1926	63 yr 6 mo 17 dy	
PELSTER, JOHN	Dec 28, 1921	56 yr	

Name	Date	Age	Origin
PENTREATH, ARTHUR	Sep 03, 1909	abt 44 yr	Minnesota
PENWELL, BENJAMIN	Nov 13, 1918	53 yr	
PERHAM, HARRIET	Oct 15, 1915	78 yr 4 mo 28 dy	
PERKINS, EDWARD D.	Nov 05, 1942	69 yr 1 mo 14 dy	New York
PERKINS, SAMUEL EDWARD	Nov 10, 1944	83 yr 4 mo 22 dy	Arkansas
PERKINS, THOMAS	Aug 18, 1915	80 yr	
PERRY, JOHN W.	Aug 13, 1926	67 yr 3 mo 17 dy	
PETERSON, LAWRENCE ELLSWORTH	May 01, 1946	68 yr	
PETTIGREW, MILDRED D.	Jul 12, 1936	18 yr 8 mo 16 dy	Illinois
PHILBROOK, JOHN WILLIAM	Sep 05, 1904	67 yr 10 mo 6 dy	Mass.
PHILLIPS, BARNET A.	Sep 08, 1946	74 yr 1 mo 4 dy	California
PHILLIPS, JAMES WHIPPLE	Jul 26, 1915	82 yr 6 mo 25 dy	
PHILLIPS, LLOYD FRANCIS	Feb 20, 1906	7 dy	California
[Phillips, Lloyd Francis	son of M/M J.W. Phillips]		
PICKENS, ARTHUR E.	Jul 17, 1910	20 yr 5 mo 15 dy	
PICOTTE, JOSEPH	Sep 25, 1921	79 yr 1 mo	
PIERCE, ARTHUR B.	Nov 16, 1947	63 yr 4 mo 23 dy	
PIERCE, JAMES E.	Dec 11, 1942	59 yr 2 mo 4 dy	Kentucky
PINKHAM, GEORGE BYRON	Feb 25, 1921	68 yr	
PLEFF, SIMON	Apr 30, 1934	64 yr 2 mo 4 dy	Switzerland
PLUMMER, MARIAN HENRIETTA	Apr 18, 1950	56 yr	California
PLUMBER, PETER	Aug 10, 1917	95 yr	
POAGE, LEVI PRICE	Apr 04, 1950	67 yr	California
POE, ELLEN IDA	Nov 17, 1923	28 yr 9 mo 9 dy	
POHLEY, BENJAMIN C.	Jul 31, 1950	80 yr	California.
POKRIOTS, ELI DANIEL	Sep 14, 1946	60 yr 8 mo 8 dy	Serbia
POLLARD, WILLIAM C.	Oct 22, 1929	70 yr 6 mo	
PORTER, LAWRENCE FRANCIS	Aug 08, 1947	45 yr 9 mo 14 dy	Canada
PORTER, THOMAS MANSFIELD	Feb 21, 1945	67 yr 1 mo 6 dy	Georgia
POST, ALEXANDER J.	Sep 14, 1908	abt 29 yr	California
POST, JAMES J.	May 22, 1924	63 yr 11 mo 21 dy	
POST, PHILLIP S.	May 23, 1909	3 yr 4 mo 18 dy	California
POST, THOMAS CARLISLE	Dec 15, 1911	56 yr	
POTILLO, ESTHER	Oct 08, 1935	73 yr 7 mo 9 dy	California
POTILLO, FRANK	Oct 28, 1915	82 yr 3 mo 22 dy	
POTILLO, LUCY	May 14, 1931	70 yr 4 mo 19 dy	
POTILLO, MONICA, Mrs.	Jan 20, 1919	83 yr 8 mo 4 dy	
POTILLO, NICHOLAS	Aug 11, 1905	34 yr 7 mo 27 dy	California
POTILLO, PAUL	Feb 23, 1931	62 yr 3 mo 5 dy	
POTTER, ANNA SHARP	Jan 04, 1942	77 yr 8 mo 8 dy	New York
POWELL, HARRY LAWRENCE	Jan 22, 1947	89 yr 4 mo 12 dy	Ohio
POWERS, EDWARD F.	Oct 02, 1950	65 yr	Ohio
PRATT, ROBERT	May 24, 1931	70 yr	
PRAY, ROBERT LEONARD	Sep 13, 1943	39 yr 4 mo 17 dy	Illinois
PRESCOTT, HOWARD M.	Dec 03, 1942	49 yr 7 mo 12 dy	Minnesota
PRICE, JAMES ROBERT	Oct 12, 1947	25 yr 2 mo 9 dy	W. Virginia
PRICE, THOMAS BOLES	Oct 16, 1911	87 yr 7 mo 1 dy	
PROCTOR, WILFRED E.	Oct 10, 1914	48 yr 1 mo	
PRUE, GEORGE	May 13, 1926	25 yr 4 mo 12 dy	
PULLMAN, LEROY L.	Jun 04, 1944	58 yr 3 mo 16 dy	Illinois
PURDON, JOHN	Apr 20, 1950	69 yr	Texas
PURTILL, JOHN R., Rev.	Dec 28, 1945	unknown	
QUINN, MERILYN JOSEPHINE	Aug 08, 1939	stillborn	California
RAAB, LOUIS FREDRICK	Jul 26, 1902	79 yr 10 mo 21 dy	Germany
RAAB, MARGARET, Mrs.	Feb 14, 1901	67 yr	Germany
RAGLIN, THOMAS	Jun 04, 1922	89 yr	
RAINE, CHARLES ELLIS	May 23, 1949	63 yr	Kansas
RAIS, AGNES LORAINE	Feb 03, 1931	1 mo 12 dy	
RAIS, ANNIE PAVA, Mrs.	Nov 10, 1928	61 yr 6 mo 11 dy	
RAIS, FRANK E.	Apr 07, 1926	30 yr 9 mo 5 dy	
RAIS, MANUEL, Sr.	Sep 12, 1947	79 yr 8 mo 11 dy	Azores Is.
RAIS, MARJORIE IRENE	Aug 18, 1933	1 mo 6 dy	California
RAIS, WILLIAM WILFORD	Aug 14, 1927	36 yr 5 mo 27 dy	

Name	Date	Age	Birthplace
RALFS, JOHN	Dec 27, 1917	90 yr 9 mo 3 dy	
RALLENS, JAMES	Sep 09, 1902	45 yr	Cornwall
RALPH, ANNIE DORA	Jul 04, 1917	41 yr 3 mo 14 dy	
RALPH, LEWIS DAVID	Nov 20, 1950	74 yr	California.
RAMM, MIKE	Jan 07, 1909	71 yr	
RANDOLPH, LYMAN	Mar 01, 1922	34 yr	
RANN, FREDERICK	Sep 24, 1931	71 yr 7 mo 19 dy	
RAU, JOHN	May 15, 1944	89 yr 2 mo 7 dy	Germany
RAY, DAVID	Jul 17, 1950	83 yr	Missouri
RAY, FRANK PIERPONT	May 22, 1927	59 yr	
RAYBURN, SAMUEL B.	Mar 03, 1935	58 yr 1 mo 10 dy	Mississippi
READ, GAIL GILBERT	Oct 02, 1949	73 yr	Conn.
REED, ANDREW JACKSON	Oct 10, 1914	78 yr 1 mo 15 dy	
REED, EDGAR LIVINGSTON	Sep 20, 1906	52 yr 5 mo 4 dy	N.Hampshire
REED, FRED	Sep 18, 1923	47 yr	
REED, FRED KIRK	Mar 30, 1932	59 yr 1 mo 8 dy	California
REED, JOHN WILDER	Nov 20, 1901	61 yr	N.Hampshire
REGNECK, BESSIE	Dec 24, 1913	14 yr	
REGNIER, PAUL	Aug 09, 1920	24 yr	
REICHEL, ALEX	Aug 08, 1924	38 yr 5 mo 5 dy	
REICHERT, JOHN F.	Nov 08, 1949	76 yr	Penn.
REID, MARVIN GIBSON	Jul 14, 1906	1 yr 2 dy	California
REID, ROSA ANNE	Jul 08, 1915	23 yr 7 mo 29 dy	
REIS, ROSE DEL	Apr 06, 1908	abt 37 yr	California
REITER, FRANK	Feb 23, 1948	68 yr 3 mo 8 dy	Germany
RENFREW, GRANT	Apr 19, 1911	45 yr	
RENNER, CHAS. H.	Jan 21, 1944	69 yr 4 mo 27 dy	California
REX, THEODORE HARRY	Sep 29, 1919	59 yr 2 mo 21 dy	
RICHARDS, E. A.	Sep 01, 1925	68 yr	
RICHARDS, HARRY RAYMOND	Apr 12, 1907	1 yr 10 mo 17 dy	California
RICHARDS, LUCILLE	Apr 18, 1907	7 mo 11 dy	California
RICHARDS, WILLIAM	Jul 16, 1950	76 yr	California
RICHARDSON, ALBERT LEONARD	Apr 11, 1930	79 yr 9 mo 11 dy	
RICHARDSON, ELVA CAROLYN	Feb 05, 1940	49 yr	Oregon
RICHARDSON, HERMAN DAVID	Mar 31, 1946	48 yr 3 mo 29 dy	Nevada
RICHARDSON, JAMES W.	Oct 22, 1946	27 yr 8 mo 5 dy	Arkansas
RICHARDSON, THOMAS	Nov 02, 1939	51 yr 8 mo 7 dy	Idaho
RICHEY, ERVILLE LEE	Jun 07, 1935	5 yr 1 mo 18 dy	Missouri
RIGBY, HUGH L.	Sep 17, 1928	16 yr 7 mo 17 dy	
RIGDON, CLARENCE MARTIN	Sep 12, 1940	29 yr	N. Mexico
RILEY, CHARLES S.	Feb 06, 1943	22 yr 7 mo	Georgia
RILEY, WILLIAM J.	Feb 07, 1926	72 yr	
RINGSTORE, JOHN F.	Apr 29, 1946	60 yr	
RISING, KAP H.	Oct 14, 1947	26 yr 0 mo 7 dy	Idaho
RITCHIE, M.	Mar 03, 1904	74 yr	Missouri
RIVERS, JOHN S.	Nov 02, 1933	75 yr 5 mo 21 dy	Georgia
ROBERTS, HELENE	Aug 27, 1915	68 yr 3 mo 6 dy	
ROBERTS, PETER	Feb 02, 1912	65 yr	
ROBERTS, THOMAS BENTON	Sep 09, 1922	72 yr 10 mo 12 dy	
ROBERTSON, CAROLINE	Sep 07, 1933	80 yr	Alabama
ROBERTSON, WADE H.	Feb 20, 1927	83 yr	Kentucky

(TJ says "Roberts"; Robertson:Trinity Co. Deaths 1913-1931, p. 218.)

Name	Date	Age	Birthplace
ROBINSON, ALFRED	Jul 19, 1939	66 yr 3 mo 15 dy	Minnesota
ROBINSON, W. E.	Jan 13, 1900	18 yr 4 mo 16 dy	California
ROBINSON, WILLIAM ALLEN	Mar 31, 1907	abt 27 yr	California
ROBLES, MARY ADDIE	Jun 17, 1938	73 yr 2 mo 3 dy	Indiana
ROCHFORD, THOMAS JEFFERSON	Oct 12, 1917	52 yr	
ROCKER, TOM	Mar 01, 1913	110 yr (sic)	
RODGERS, MARY	Jun 19, 1914	51 yr 6 mo 14 dy	
ROGERS, GEORGE WASHINGTON	Jan 14, 1905	abt 29 yr	California
ROOKE, JAMES E.	Dec 17, 1929	66 yr 9 mo 14 dy	
RORIE, RUEBEN	May 19, 1948	18 yr 10 mo 15dy	Arkansas
ROSA, HENRY	Jan 31, 1939	66 yr 10 mo	Illinois

DEATHS 1900 - 1950

Name	Date	Age	Origin
ROSE, FRANK W.	Oct 18, 1938	53 yr 3 mo 9 dy	California
ROSE, M. P.	Jul 21, 1922	76 yr	
ROSE, WILSON SHANNON	Jan 19, 1922	63 yr	
ROSENBERGER, JOHN	Dec 25, 1946	90 yr 5 mo 0 dy	Germany
ROSS, MARY ELLEN	Jan 29, 1946	86 yr 3 mo 8 dy	California
ROSS, WILLIAM BRUCE	Nov 22, 1939	1 mo 14 dy	California
ROSS, WILLIAM CLARK	Oct 31, 1915	51 yr	
ROSSEN, R. P.	Feb 04, 1914	50 yr	
ROUNDTREE, FRANK MARTIN	Aug 26, 1937	67 yr 5 mo 12 dy	Washington
ROURKE, DENIS	Dec 21, 1900	69 yr	Ireland
ROURKE, DENNIS	Apr 29, 1946	61 yr 10 mo 20 dy	California
ROURKE, IDELL BARBARA	Aug 26, 1948	57 yr 9 mo 19 dy	California
ROWE, ELLEN	Jan 20, 1938	90 yr 18 dy	England
ROWE, GEORGE	Jan 08, 1901	83 yr	England
ROWLAND, FRANCIS A.	Mar 05, 1942	57 yr 12 dy	California
ROWLAND, WILLIAM T.	Aug 19, 1948	67 yr 0 mo 6 dy	Tennessee
ROWLES, JAMES	Apr 03, 1907	72 yr	Missouri
ROYLE, JOHN WILLIAM	Jun 17, 1947	72 yr 9 mo 8 dy	Illinois
RUCH, JESSE	Sep 08, 1922	63 yr	
RUCKER, LEE MADISON	Nov 02, 1913	56 yr 6 mo 6 dy	
RUCKERT, HENRY	Dec 11, 1931	67 yr 1 mo 16 dy	
RUCKMAN, WILLIAM L.	Jan 31, 1937	42 yr 5 mo 27 dy	Missouri
RUEGG, LEONARD DAVID	Sep 04, 1945	54 yr 9 mo 29 dy	Penn.
RUHSER, FREDERICK WILLIAM	Jan 07, 1932	55 yr 6 mo 7 dy	California
RULE, ANNA M.	Feb 23, 1913	78 yr 10 mo 6 dy	
RULE, BENJAMIN BENNETT	Dec 03, 1905	abt 76 yr	England
RULE, KATHARINE, Mrs.	Dec 15, 1908	78 yr 4 mo 2 dy	England
RULE, WM J.	Mar 06, 1900	65 yr 1 mo	England
RUSSELL, ALBERT JOHNSTON	Jan 21, 1945	74 yr 11 mo 18 dy	Tennessee
RUSSELL, ALMA LEVI	Sep 27, 1931	57 yr 5 mo 25 dy	
RUSSELL, GEORGE W.	Apr 16, 1934	80 yr 2 mo 2 dy	California
RUSSELL, JAMES	Sep __, 1910	45 yr	
RUSSELL, LUCIE ELLEN	Feb 03, 1914	56 yr 10 mo 13 dy	
RUSSELL, MARY JOSEPHINE	Sep 21, 1913		
RUSSELL, O. F.	Apr 14, 1909	49 yr 6 mo 2 dy	
RUSSELL, W. A.	Sep 05, 1937	51 yr 11 mo 4 dy	Iowa
RYAN, JEANETTE	Oct 31, 1903	14 mo	California
RYAN, PATRICK JOSEPH	Jun 26, 1930	62 yr 10 mo 18 dy	
RYAN, RICHARD	Jul 07, 1904	4 mo 2 dy	California
[Ryan, Richard, son of M/M P. J. Ryan]			
RYS, JOSEPH	Jun 13, 1941	78 yr 3 mo 20 dy	Czech.
SACCHI, FRED P.	Oct 12, 1941	41 yr 1 mo 24 dy	California
SAFFELL, VERNET S.	Oct 25, 1903	1 yr 7 mo 15 dy	California
SALAZAR, FRANCIS	Feb 20, 1917	2 yr 4 mo 21 dy	
SANBURN, FLORENCE EVELYN CARTER,	Apr 19, 1916	50 yr 1 dy	
SANBURN, JOHN GOULD	May 08, 1916	87 yr 4 mo 23 dy	
SANSOME, FRANK A.	Apr 18, 1934	40 yr	California
SASS, PETER	Jun 17, 1911	65 yr	
SAWYER, HAROLD F.	Feb 19, 1926	25 yr	
SAXE, JOHN	May 26, 1907	abt 81 yr	Austria
SCHAFFER, AUGUST	Mar 03, 1910	73 yr 6 mo 14 dy	
SCHAFFER, FREDERICK A.	Nov 29, 1949	69 yr	California
SCHAFFER, IDA May	Mar 13, 1946	68 yr 1 mo 1 dy	Illinois
SCHALL, J. L.	Nov 22, 1906	79 yr 2 mo 28 dy	Germany
SCHALL, MAGDALENA, Mrs.	Sep 04, 1902	65 yr 11 mo 21 dy	Germany
SCHERER, G. H.	Jun 13, 1928	62 yr 11 mo 24 dy	
SCHLOMER, CHARLES	Apr 02, 1916	54 yr 5 mo 20 dy	
SCHLOMER, LOUISA	Jul 14, 1925	84 yr 5 mo	
SCHMIDT, LOUIS	Jun 02, 1909	76 yr 4 mo 2 dy	
SCHNEIDER, ANNA HERUSHA	Oct 02, 1943	77 yr 3 mo 28 dy	Iowa
SCHNEIDER, CHARLES	Mar 23, 1947	74 yr 3 mo 15 dy	California
SCHNEIDER, HENRY O.	Mar 25, 1912	39 yr 8 mo 2 dy	
SCHNEIDER, KATHERINE	Jan 06, 1920	87 yr 1 mo 26 dy	

Name	Date	Age	Birthplace
SCHNEIDER, WILLIAM F.	Jul 08, 1949	80 yr	Penn.
SCHOLFIELD, ALICE	Mar 06, 1937	45 yr 11 mo 4 dy	Canada
SCHOOLING, HELEN A.	May 30, 1946	85 yr	
SCHOPPE, CHARLES A.	Dec 24, 1903	70 yr	Germany
SCHROEDER, JOHN D.	Sep 01, 1907	abt 71 yr	Germany
SCHROTER, ARTHUR ALVIN	Mar 08, 1932	70 yr 3 mo 12 dy	California
SCHUENEMANN, ALBERT	Jun 07, 1935	71 yr 5 mo 21 dy	Germany
SCOTT, ANNA K.	Feb 07, 1935	79 yr 1 mo 10 dy	Illinois
SCOTT, BOB	Feb 10, 1918	64 yr	
SCOTT, JOHN W.	Jun 26, 1935	72 yr 6 mo 3 dy	Kansas
SCOTT, LUCY D.	May 01, 1911	70 yr	
SCOTT, SILVESTER DAVID	Jan 15, 1904	74 yr 8 mo 2 dy	Ohio
SCOTT, W. J.	Jan 21, 1911	76 yr	
SEARLE, J. A.	Dec 16, 1910	77 yr	
SEARLES, FRANK E.	Aug 27, 1938	74 yr 5 mo 23 dy	California
SEASTROM, HERMAN OTTO	Apr 09, 1936	44 yr	Sweden
SEBRING, PHILANDER ALVIN	Jun 08, 1940	73 yr	Michigan
SEEK, AUGUST	Mar 08, 1932	88 yr	
SEEMANN, GEORGE WILHELM	Mar 20, 1943	67 yr 22 dy	Germany
SELER, CHARLES AUGUSTUS	Mar 18, 1902	32 yr	Penn.
SENGER, JACOB, Mrs.	Nov 26, 1902	64 yr 3 mo 4 dy	Germany
SENTENEY, ROBERT	Apr 28, 1933	54 yr 6 mo 15 dy	California
SETAK, WILLIAM	May 04, 1932	61 yr	Germany
SEVEDGE, EDGAR F.	Dec 26, 1903	35 yr	California
SEVEDGE, N. E., Mrs.	Oct 26, 1911	76 yr 4 mo 12 dy	
SHARROCKS, CHARLES	Jan 30, 1917	79 yr	
SHATUNO, BRUNO	Jan 11, 1938	52 yr 11 mo 21 dy	Illinois
SHEPARDSON, MILTON D.	Nov 17, 1915	86 yr	
SHERIDAN, JOHN	Dec 24, 1902	abt 71 yr	Ireland
SHERIDAN, JOHN JOSEPH	Jan 30, 1933	48 yr	Ireland
SHERIDAN, M., Mrs.	Mar 21, 1900	72 Y 2 mo 20 dy	Ireland
SHERMAN, ROXELANA LOVINA	Jun 03, 1946	76 yr 10 mo 7 dy	California
SHERWOOD, OREN PARKER	Jan 03, 1905	abt 64 yr	Illinois
SHIELDS, NINA	Jul 03, 1937	76 yr 11 mo 20 dy	California
SHOCK, CHARLES HECTOR	Aug 31, 1913	32 yr 9 mo 15 dy	
SHOCK, DAVID EDWARD	Mar 11, 1917	51 yr 6 mo 29 dy	
SHOCK, HAROLD L.	Mar 27, 1910	13 yr	
SHOCK, ISABEL, Mrs.	Nov 14, 1919	84 yr 9 mo 12 dy	
SHOCK, J. P.	Oct 11, 1909	39 yr 6 mo 10 dy	
SHOCK, LOUIS R., Mrs.	Mar 11, 1906	37 yr 9 mo 10 dy	California
SHOCK, WALTER	Oct 14, 1922	31 yr	
SHOCK, ZINA L.	Jul 29, 1909	49 yr 11 mo 15 dy	Missouri
SHOEMAKER, ARTHUR	Oct 15, 1939	45 yr 7 mo 24 dy	California
SHOEMAKER, MILTON	Apr 25, 1918	88 yr	
SHORE, MERTON EDWARD	Jan 10, 1935	73 yr 9 mo 22 dy	Indiana
SHORES, RINCK	Feb 26, 1913	40 yr	
SHOVE, ALICE BARBER	Feb 20, 1912	43 yr 7 mo 15 dy	
SHREVE, GEORGE	Dec 01, 1946	91 yr 11 mo 15dy	Indiana
SHUFORD, JOHN WILLIAM	Jun 13, 1935	79 yr 3 mo 19 dy	California
SHULES, WILLIAM	May 08, 1940	88 yr	Illinois
SIHLIS, CARL	Jan 25, 1943	64 yr 3 mo 24 dy	Latvia
SILIGO, LOUIS	Oct 16, 1933	59 yr 7 mo 7 dy	Italy
SILVA, BENTON LeROY	Mar 22, 1901	9 mo 3 dy	California
SILVA, FRANK	Dec 01, 1910	70 yr	
SILVA, JOHN B.	Apr 08, 1942	60 yr 1 mo 8 dy	California
SILVA, JOSEPH B.	May 07, 1947	74 yr 3 mo 11 dy	California
SIMIMON, JOSEPHINE	Jan 18, 1910	15 yr 10 mo 15 dy	
SIMMONS, EUGENE	Mar 13, 1945	77 yr 11 mo 2 dy	Oregon
SIMONDS, DANIEL AZRO	Feb 24, 1901	79 yr	N.Hampshire
SIMONS, A. J.	Feb 24, 1912	82 yr	
SIMPSON, GEORGE M.	Jun 25, 1915	71 yr 6 mo 3 dy	
SIMPSON, THOMAS	Dec 16, 1941	3 dy	California
SIMPSON, WARREN HAROLD	Feb 06, 1912	5 yr 5 mo 13 dy	

DEATHS 1900 - 1950

Name	Date	Age	Birthplace
SINCLAIR, THOMAS	Jun 23, 1950	34 yr	California
SISCHO, RUBIN D.	Aug 13, 1941	72 yr 6 mo 20 dy	Wisconsin
SKEWIS, JOHN	Dec 27, 1939	85 yr 4 mo 5 dy	Wisconsin
SKILLEN, JAS E	Apr 05, 1900	30 yr 6 mo 8 dy	Missouri
SLATER, N. K.	Mar 25, 1903	74 yr	Missouri
SLY, LAURA ELMIRA	Jan 29, 1931	73 yr 7 mo 7 dy	
SMITH, A. W.	Jan 04, 1905	abt 76 yr	New York
SMITH, BUD L.	Jul 25, 1934	55 yr	California
SMITH, CHARLES SYDNEY	Jan 09, 1950	57 yr	Texas
SMITH, HARRY LEWIS	Jul 27, 1950	59 yr	Illinois
SMITH, HELEN MARY (CONDON)	May 11, 1946	47 yr 4 mo 22 dy	California
SMITH, JAMES WALTER	Jan 12, 1947	81 yr 1 mo 2 dy	Texas
SMITH, JERE	Apr 04, 1921	abt 75 yr	
SMITH, JOHN	May 02, 1903	74 yr	Missouri
SMITH, JOHN	Jul 26, 1913	72 yr 8 mo 22 dy	
SMITH, JOHN	Apr 22, 1928	86 yr	
SMITH, JOSEPH	Oct 27, 1911	44 yr	
SMITH, JOSEPH G.	Jan 18, 1942	70 yr 3 mo 20 dy	Tennessee
SMITH, JOSEPH LEO	Oct 27, 1939	52 yr 6 mo 1 dy	California
SMITH, JULIA ENOS	Nov __, 1946	74 yr	
SMITH, MARGARET, Mrs.	Aug 25, 1906	abt 72 yr	Ireland
SMITH, MARGARET HARRIET	Dec 05, 1949	40 yr	Colorado
SMITH, MARY	Oct 27, 1932	58 yr 2 mo 8 dy	California
SMITH, MYRA ELLEN	Apr 20, 1915	22 yr 6 dy	
SMITH, NEWTON	Mar 03, 1938	62 yr 10 mo 24 dy	New York
SMITH, ORTIGAL ROSS	Jun 14, 1902	72 yr	Mass.
SMITH, RILEY D.	Jul 30, 1949	65 yr	Indiana
SMITH, ROLAND	Mar 26, 1911	96 yr	
SMITH, RUTH VIRGINIA	Dec 08, 1934	40 yr 6 mo 11 dy	W. Virginia
SMITH, VIRGIL J. LEE	Oct 06, 1945	39 yr 9 mo 7 dy	Colorado
SNELL, CHARLES ALEXANDER	Jun 21, 1948	75 yr 4 mo 23 dy	California
SNOW, CHARLES	Jul 03, 1912	46 yr	
SORENSEN, HANS-AKELS GEORGE	Mar 30, 1949	54 yr	Denmark
SPARKS, HARRY B.	Nov 04, 1920	62 yr	
SPARKS, ROY	Nov 29, 1946	39 yr	
SPARKS, ROY E.	Jul 24, 1942	54 yr 5 mo 18 dy	California
SPATZ, LENA RUTH	Sep 01, 1926	7 hours	
SPENCER, JOHN ALONZO	Mar 05, 1941	89 yr 6 mo 20 dy	Indiana
SPENCER, THOMAS	Jun 15, 1918	90 yr 1 mo	
SPRAGUE, L. Z.	Jun 28, 1932	53 yr 10 mo 6 dy	Michigan
SPRATT, ADA CAROLYN	Oct 12, 1920	28 yr 26 dy	
SPRATT, CARL WILLIAM	Feb 03, 1902	1 yr 1 mo 28 dy	California
SPRATT, LAURA CAROLYN	Apr 15, 1948	0 yr 1 mo 7 dy	California
SPURR, JAMES MILTON	Jan 01, 1901	70 yr	Kentucky
STACKPOLE, inf.dau.M/M FRANK	Mar 02, 1907	1 mo	California
STAFFORD, A., MRS	Sep 20, 1900	55 yr	Ind.Territory
STAFFORD, JAMES A.	Jul 21, 1905	abt 79 yr	N.Carolina
STANLEY, ROBERT PERRY	Aug 09, 1938	72 yr 8 mo 28 dy	Missouri
STANSFIELD, FLOYD L.	Jan 24, 1942	39 yr 29 dy	Colorado
STARR, RAYMOND CHARLES	Feb 14, 1950	51 yr	Iowa
STEE, BYRON HENRY	Dec 30, 1941	3 mo 8 dy	California
STEININGER, ARTHUR WILLIAM	May 18, 1940	47 yr	California
STEINKELLER, THOMAS J.	May 19, 1930	51 yr 7 mo 26 dy	
STEPHENS, CHARLES H.	Mar 28, 1950	88 yr	Indiana
STERLING, BENJAMIN	Mar 18, 1947	81 yr 3 mo 18 dy	California
STEVENS, GEO. W.	Oct 27, 1926	68 yr 1 mo 11 dy	
STEWART, OLLIVER	Jun 07, 1903	73 yr	
STIDGER, JOHN PERRY	Oct 19, 1914	59 yr 1 mo 25 dy	
STILLER, CHARLES	Oct 17, 1922	54 yr	
STILLER, LOUISA J.	Dec 29, 1901	72 yr 5 mo 20 dy	Germany
STILLER, JOHN ALEXANDER	Apr 28, 1932	75 yr 11 mo 16dy	Germany
STILLER, RAYMOND WILLIAM	Oct 23, 1904	5 yr 8 mo 10 dy	California

Name	Date	Age	Birthplace
STILLWELL, WILLIAM L.	Aug 10, 1903	77 yr	Mass.
[Stillwell, William may be William Marvel, not William L.]			
STODDARD, ROSALIE E.	Mar 22, 1910	23 yr	
STOFER, RAYMOND LESLIE	Sep 10, 1911	2 yr 8 mo 23 dy	
STOFER, WILMA	Jul 25, 1910	3 yr 1 mo 21 dy	California
STOLL, GEORGE JOHN	Jun 25, 1923	65 yr 4 mo 15 dy	
STONE, ALBERT	Apr 14, 1905	abt 81 yr	Canada
STONE, S. L.	Jul 31, 1901	44 yr	Kentucky
STOOKEY, LYMAN B., Dr.	Feb 13, 1940	60 yr	Illinois
STOREY, GRACE ALICE	May 07, 1908	23 yr 8 mo 13 dy	California
STOWERS, WILLIAM ALEXANDER	Aug 08, 1918	71 yr	
STRIBLING, PAUL T.	Aug 14, 1913	45 yr 2 mo 8 dy	
STRINGER, LAURA	Oct 10, 1946	68 yr 4 mo 24 dy	Colorado
STROBRIDGE, JAMES HARVEY	Aug 19, 1950	67 yr	California
STRONG, ALLEN DEARING	Sep 29, 1935	Stillborn	California
STRIKER, CHARLES FREMONT	Aug 13, 1933	76 yr 5 mo 16 dy	Wisconsin
STURGESS, ALONZO	Feb 09, 1911	58 yr	
STURGILL, ELIZABETH O.	Mar 30, 1934	82 yr 2 mo 6 dy	Kentucky
SULLIVAN, EDWIN LEE	Jul 05, 1948	30 yr 2 mo 6 dy	Idaho
SUNDERLIN, JULIA ANN	Jan 16, 1930	84 yr 11 mo 6 dy	
SUTTON, DANIEL LEROY	Nov 26, 1947	2 dy	California
SWANSON, C. AUGUST	Jan 22, 1914	38 yr	
SWANSON, NELS	Mar 24, 1942	85 yr 2 mo 6 dy	Norway
SWEATT, ARTHUR GILBERT	Oct 15, 1933	51 yr 2 mo 2 dy	N.Hampshire
SWEENEY, FRANK	Sep 03, 1948	79 yr 3 mo 27 dy	Penn.
SWIFT, EDWARD DEXTER	Jan 28, 1907	76 yr 1 mo 6 dy	New York
SWIM, ISAAC T.	Mar 06, 1901	71 yr	Kentucky
SWIRTSEN, CHRIS.	May 06, 1947	85 yr 6 mo 6 dy	Norway
TABOR, TOM	Jul 08, 1946	88 yr	
TANATA, CHRIST	Jan 20, 1945	73 yr 8 mo 23 dy	Germany
TARPLEY, inf.son M/M E.L.	Mar 20, 1903	b.d.	California
TAYLOR, DAVID	Aug 04, 1902	74 yr 3 mo 18 dy	New York
TAYLOR, JAMES EDWARD	Aug 03, 1931	58 yr 11 mo 19dy	
TAYLOR, JESSE J.	Sep 15, 1937	60 yr 6 mo 21 dy	Kansas
TAYLOR, H. R.	May 03, 1901	70 yr	Tennessee
TAYLOR, LYLE WALTER	Nov 01, 1945	4 yr 3 mo	California
TAYLOR, VIOLET AUDREY TINSLEY,	Oct 02, 1935	26 yr 10 mo 3 dy	California
TAYLOR, WILLIAM H.	Mar 22, 1924	70 yr	
TELLESFEN, JOHNNIE	Jul __, 1946	4 yr	
TEMPLE, A. J.	Jul 05, 1904	abt 40 yr	
TENNY, FRANK	Feb 13, 1937	54 yr 8 mo 18 dy	California
TESTY, CHARLES JEROME	Nov 06, 1947	73 yr 9 mo 6 dy	California
TESTY, JOSEPH J., Mrs.	Aug 31, 1909	80 yr 6 mo 16 dy	Wales
TEWIS, BOB DARLING	Jan 04, 1923	abt 90 yr	
THAYER, SARAH ELONIA, Mrs.	Jun 29, 1904	63 yr 4 mo 21 dy	Maine
THAYER, STEPHEN IRVING	Dec 15, 1933	98 yr 11 mo 16dy	Mass.
THOMAS, BARBARA JOSEPHINE	Aug 17, 1938	38 yr 9 mo 25 dy	California
THOMAS, FRED R.	Jun 20, 1930	60 yr 5 mo	
THOMAS, NELEY	Dec 02, 1948	94 yr 0 mo 12 dy	California
THOMAS, THOMAS	Dec 02, 1914	68 yr 4 mo 1 dy	
THOMASON, BLUFORD WINFIELD	Aug 17, 1950	59 yr	Washington
THOMPSON, ALBERT POWELL	Apr 14, 1931	53 yr 4 mo 29 dy	
THOMPSON, WILLIAM	Sep 18, 1919	74 yr	
THOMPSON, WILLIAM E.	Jun 23, 1929	51 yr 6 mo 9 dy	
THOMSEN, THOMAS SORENSEN	Jan 20, 1918	67 yr 5 mo 2 dy	
THORN, MOSES	Mar 02, 1936	69 yr	
THORNE, GEORGE	Mar 23, 1949	92 yr	England
THORNTON, JOHN H.	Mar 17, 1940	83 yr	Missouri
THRESHIE, JOHN WELDON	Jul 17, 1921	abt 58 yr	
THURMAN, FLORENCE ELIZABETH	Jun 19, 1950	32 yr	Missouri
TIFFANY, JESSE ALMOND	Apr 24, 1940	55 yr	Nebraska
TINSLEY, E.S.	May 01, 1900	30 yr 11 mo 17 dy	California
TINSLEY, GEORGE W.	Feb 23, 1934	67 yr 3 mo 6 dy	

DEATHS 1900 - 1950

Name	Date	Age	Birthplace
TIPTON, JANET L.	Jul 20, 1931	42 yr 2 mo 8 dy	
TODD, BRYAN	Jul 27, 1904	1 yr 9 mo 1 dy	California
TODD, MARY AMANDA, Mrs.	Jan 06, 1907	53 yr 7 mo 17 dy	Missouri
TOMMY, FANNY	Nov 12, 1921	abt 90 yr	
TOOLE, ALFRED HEATH	Jul 03, 1949	45 yr	Wyoming
TOOLE, ERNEST H.	Feb 28, 1942	44 yr 5 mo 15 dy	Idaho
TOURTELLOTTE, FANNIE E, Mrs.	Jan 27, 1908	76 yr 10 mo 25 dy	Conn.
TOURTELLOTTE, JESSE H.	Dec 21, 1903	77 yr 3 mo 8 dy	Conn.
TOWER, CHAS F.	Nov 30, 1900	6 yr 2 mo 28 dy	California
TOY SING	Mar 30, 1922	68 yr	
TRASK, AVERY L.	Oct 07, 1948	51 yr 6 mo 7 dy	N. Dakota
TRASK, GEORGE N.	Oct 05, 1937	69 yr 8 mo 13 dy	California
TREADWELL, EDWARD C.	Jan 14, 1913	37 yr	
TRELOAR, THOMAS, Sr.	Dec 25, 1919	88 yr 1 mo 12 dy	
TRELOAR, THOMAS	Apr 04, 1942	82 yr 2 mo 6 dy	California
TREMPER, THEODORE POCHLER	Jun 22, 1931	44 yr 8 mo 1 dy	
TRIMBLE, LEROY ANTHONY	Nov 18, 1918	1 mo 16 dy	
TRIMBLE, PIERCE	Jul 04, 1910	80 yr	
TRIMBLE, RAE ALEXANDER	Mar 03, 1940	43 yr	California
TRIMBLE, REBECCA ELLEN	Jan 02, 1914	54 yr 1 mo 28 dy	
TRIMBLE, SARAH ELLEN	Feb 16, 1914	2 mo 22 dy	
TRISDALE, MARY ANN	Apr 02, 1948	85 yr 0 mo 28dy	Canada
TRUBEY, WILLIAM J.	Jul 15, 1948	72 yr 4 mo 8 dy	Kansas
TRUBSCHENCK, W. H. A.	Jul 18, 1912	56 yr 7 mo	
TUNG MAO MA (CHARLES LAMBERT),	Dec 04, 1939	88 yr 4 mo 17 dy	California
TUTTLE, GEORGE	Feb 08, 1935	69 yr 8 mo	Illinois
TUTTLE, GERTRUDE JOUGHLIN	Oct 12, 1936	44 yr 1 mo 29 dy	California
TWINE, CHARLES	May 13, 1937	76 yr 10 mo 27dy	California
TYE, EDNA F.	Sep 05, 1909	14 yr 1 mo 23 dy	California
TYE, FRANK	Apr 10, 1910	10 yr	California
TYE, FRIEDA	Jul 17, 1910	1 yr 7 mo	California
TYE, LLOYD	May 30, 1910	6 yr 20 dy	California
UMDENSTOCK, JOHN	Jan 08, 1910	71 yr 10 mo 29 dy	
UPHAM, FRANK LESLIE	Dec 02, 1950	74 yr	Kansas
UPHAM, HARRY, inf.dau.	Apr 22, 1946	b.d.	California
UPHAM, SARAH ELIZABETH	Jul 01, 1950	70 yr	Kansas
URSHUR, JAMES	Jan 07, 1918	80 yr	
VAN AMMON, WILLIAM	Aug 23, 1913	52 yr 5 mo 16 dy	
VAN CLEAVE, JOSEPH ALBERT	Dec 19, 1911	51 yr	
VAN CLEAVE, inf.son M/M CHAS.	Apr 14, 1908	10 dy	California
VAN MATRE, ADRIAN JUDSON	Jul 24, 1945	89 yr 8 mo 14 dy	California
VAN MATRE, ALBERT J.	Aug 20, 1909	16 yr 20 dy	California
VAN MATRE, inf.dau. M/M J.C.	May 17, 1902	18 dy	California
VAN MATRE, JOHN CHANDLER	Aug 19, 1921	62 yr 2 mo 24 dy	
VAN MATRE, MARY	Feb 09, 1933	78 yr 7 mo 13 dy	Maine
VAN MATRE, MORRIS	Nov 21, 1941	94 yr 11 mo 26dy	Wisconsin
VAN NESS, E. F.	Sep 07, 1902	45 yr	
VAN ZILE, JOSEPH W.	Jul 03, 1942	81 yr 3 mo 22 dy	New York
VANCE, JAMES V.	Jun 08, 1942	58 yr 10 mo 6 dy	California
VANCE, NELDA DOROTHEA	Jul 24, 1913	1 dy	
VANDERFORD, JOHN W.	Sep 16, 1903	19 yr	Illinois
VANDERHOFF, CLARENCE	Aug 07, 1908	abt 5 yr	California
VANDERHOFF, JOHN HENRY	Nov 16, 1913	79 yr 2 mo 15 dy	
VANDERHOFF, STELLA MAE	Dec 20, 1914	20 yr 7 mo 15 dy	
VANN, THOMAS A.	May 12, 1904	abt 79 yr	Tennessee
VAUGHN, DeFOREST	Oct 27, 1940	44 yr	California
VAUGHN, HARRY	Oct 02, 1946	58 yr	
VAUGHN, MARIAH	Sep 27, 1921	66 yr 6 mo 22 dy	
VAUTHIER, JOSEPH	Jan 11, 1901	72 yr 8 mo 11 dy	France
VAUTHIER, MARY	Jun 04, 1939	81 yr 5 mo 10 dy	California
VAWTER, RUBY IOLA	Aug 25, 1938	19 yr 6 mo 6 dy	Idaho
VENNAMON, ANDREW	Apr 20, 1935	61 yr	California
VENNAMON, JENNIE	Feb 19, 1918	70 yr	

Name	Date	Age	Birthplace
VILAS, EDWARD PLATT	SEP 18, 1927	61 yr 3 mo 9 dy	
VILLATA, PHILLIP MARTIN	Jul 21, 1950	2 mo 1 dy	California.
VINCENT, JACKIE WM. (male)	Oct 26, 1948	prem. birth	California
VINE, FLORENCE V.	Jan 15, 1950	57 yr	New York
VIRDEN, MARK NELSON	Nov 07, 1948	74 yr 11 mo 2 dy	Colorado
VITZTHUM, GEORGE	Sep 20, 1911	90 yr 11 mo 5 dy	
VITZTHUM, WILLIAM PRESIDENT	Oct 21, 1940	66 yr	California
VOGEL, GEORGE	Apr 26, 1944	unknown	Mass.
VOLLMERS, C., Mrs.	Jan 05, 1900	65 yr 8 mo 2 dy	Germany
WADE, HARRY	Aug 01, 1948	58 yr 0 mo 28 dy	Michigan
WAGGETT, CHARLES	Oct 31, 1907	abt 63 yr	
WAGNER, CAROLINE HASSWELL	Sep 11, 1934	54 yr 5 mo 14 dy	Nevada
WAGNER, MARY JUNE	Apr 07, 1931	74 yr	
WAGNER, MYRA MYRTLE	Apr 11, 1941	40 yr 7 mo 11 dy	California
WAGNON, JOSEPH S.	May 13, 1934	48 yr 9 mo 18 dy	Oregon
WAH DOY	Nov 28, 1937	85 yr	China
WALDORFF, ERNEST ANDERSON	Jun 08, 1920	59 yr	
WALDORFF, JACOB	Mar 17, 1902	79 yr	Germany
WALDORF(f), JOHN	Apr 04, 1926	65 yr	
WALDRON, JOHN A.	Mar 29, 1929	76 yr 1 mo 23 dy	
WALKER, JOSEPH R.	Oct 27, 1937	68 yr 9 mo 10 dy	Missouri
WALLACE, DAVID	Apr 15, 1946	67 yr	
WALLACE, inf.son M/M J.A.	May 21, 1904	b.d.	California
WALLACE, JAMES CUBBAGE	Jan 28, 1913	75 yr 4 mo	
WALLACE, LETITIA JANE	Aug 28, 1917	82 yr 3 mo 18 dy	
WALLACE, WILLIAM	Feb 07, 1934	71 yr 2 mo	Ireland
WALTER, FRANK	Jun 21, 1915	55 yr 1 mo	
WALTER, FRANK M.	Jul 21, 1936	70 yr 3 mo 28 dy	Illinois
WALTERS, ALVIN G.	Feb 07, 1932	50 yr 3 mo 11 dy	Penn.
WALTERS, HENRY	May 18, 1910	74 yr	
WARD, ELLA ZINE	Oct 13, 1939	77 yr 7 mo 13 dy	Missouri
WARD, HARRY	Jan 06, 1900	88 yr	Sweden
WARD, JOHN MARSHALL	Apr 03, 1947	38 yr 2 mo 4 dy	Utah
WARD, WILLARD STANLEY	Jun 15, 1932	3 dy	California
WARDE, CHESTER FREDERICK	Feb 23, 1938	36 yr 7 mo 2 dy	Michigan
WARE, RICHARD NORMAN	Feb 11, 1948	1 dy	California
WARNER, CHARLES, Dr.	Sep 04, 1902	26 yr	California
WARREN, HENRY SHERMAN	Mar 12, 1948	55 yr 6 mo 12 dy	Nebraska
WARRINGTON, W. H.	Jun __, 1901	45 yr	England
WATROUS, JOSEPH B.	Jul 30, 1905	abt 78 yr	Conn.
WATSON, GEORGE	Jul 07, 1913	60 yr	
WATSON, JOHN HENRY	Oct 27, 1949	73 yr	Texas
WEAVER, ABE D.	Jul 13, 1946	72 yr 1 mo 12 dy	Missouri
WEAVER, ELLEN (Indian)	Jul 14, 1925	Between 95-105 yr	
WEAVER, LAURA (Mrs. Abe)	Sep 01, 1946	74 yr	
WEAVER, WILLIAM	Oct 06, 1914	90 yr	
WEBSTER, AUDREY CLARICE	Oct 18, 1933	20 yr 6 mo 3 dy	California
WEINHEIMER, CATHERINE CECILIA,	Mar 16, 1936	86 yr 29 dy	New Jersey
WEINHEIMER, HENRY	Jan 21, 1930	84 yr 10 mo 12 dy	
WELCH, HOBSON GARFIELD	May 29, 1947	48 yr 10 mo 28 dy	Montana
WELLS, RICHARD B.	Jul 23, 1901	75 yr	Missouri
WEST, CHARLES ERNEST	Jul 23, 1919	72 yr	
WEST, WILLIAM W.	Aug 10, 1912	52 yr	
WEYAND, ZACHARY TAYLOR	Mar 23, 1907	abt 59 yr	Kansas
WHEELER, LOREN	Oct 10, 1940	66 yr	Wisconsin
WHEELER, WILLIAM EDWIN	Oct 16, 1945	23 yr 8 mo 10 dy	Montana
WHIPPLE, W. V.	Sep 14, 1910	32 yr 8 mo	
WHITCHURCH, EMMA GRACE	Aug 07, 1906	15 yr 8 mo 23 dy	California
WHITCHURCH, GEORGE WESLEY	Jun 13, 1906	18 yr 2 mo 14 dy	California
WHITCHURCH, RUSSELL F.	Apr 15, 1909	26 yr 2 mo 16 dy	California
WHITE, ADA, Mrs.	Mar 13, 1946	59 yr	
WHITE, CLINTON S.	Nov 14, 1929	57 yr	
WHITE, HORACE RAYMOND	Jun 07, 1926	27 yr 5 mo 5 dy	

Name	Date	Age	Place
WHITE, SAMUEL HUGH	Oct 15, 1949	81 yr	Oregon
WHITE, WILLIAM PITT	Jul 16, 1924	87 yr 11 mo 1 dy	
WHITEMAN, GEORGE H.	Oct 03, 1931	69 yr 3 mo 8 dy	
WHITNEY, ALVIN AUGUSTUS	Apr 07, 1907	abt 67 yr	Maryland
WHITNEY, FRANK J.	Jul 26, 1939	70 yr 6 mo 29 dy	New York
WHITTLESEY, F. D.	Mar 19, 1911	60 yr	
WIBLEY, ELI SARGENT	Sep 29, 1913	78 yr	
WILLBURN, HIRAM	Apr 21, 1924	57 yr	
WILLBURN, HYRAM DAVID	May 30, 1943	91 yr 13 dy	Texas
WILLBURN, JAMES ST. CLAIR	Aug 29, 1904	abt 75 yr	Texas
WILLBURN, MARTHA ELIZABETH	Sep 12, 1946	87 yr 5 mo 28 dy	California
WILLBURN, RICHARD (colored)	Jul 18, 1925	abt 58 yr	
WILLIAMS, ANNIE P.	Nov 30, 1915	44 yr 6 mo 18 dy	
WILLIAMS, ARABELLA, Mrs.	Feb 12, 1926	93 yr 12 dy	
WILLIAMS, CHARLES EDWIN	Aug 21, 1905	77 yr	Virginia
WILLIAMS, DAVID FRANKLIN	Jan 14, 1913	42 yr	
WILLIAMS, FRANK	Apr 26, 1912	86 yr	
WILLIAMS, GEORGE	Jul 20, 1922	24 yr	
WILLIAMS, GRANT LOGAN	May 14, 1934	11 yr 11 mo 13dy	Oregon
WILLIAMS, JAMES LOGAN	Aug 22, 1931	84 yr 10 mo 6 dy	
WILLIAMS, MANUEL	Nov 30, 1919	89 yr 10 mo 1 dy	
WILLIAMS, MANUEL	Oct 15, 1932	62 yr 5 mo 21 dy	California
WILLIAMS, MARY PIMENTAL	Mar 08, 1926	88 yr 5 mo 4 dy	
WILLIAMSON, FRANK	Feb 25, 1912	54 yr	
WILLIS, DAVE	Aug 31, 1950	60 yr	California
WILLITTS, JAMES	Jun 10, 1930	55 yr	
WILSON, CHARLES	Oct 23, 1906	abt 75 yr	Sweden
WILSON, CHARLES SAMUEL	Oct 17, 1912	35 yr 2 mo 3 dy	
WILSON, DON EMERY	Jun 15, 1935	14 yr 4 mo	California
WILSON, FRIEND WARREN	Oct 07, 1902	68 yr 7 mo 15 dy	New York
WILSON, HATTIE C.	Oct 22, 1935	75 yr 6 mo	Oregon
WILSON, HAZEL MARTIN	Mar 08, 1923	25 yr 6 mo 8 dy	
WILSON, INEZ MARIE	Apr 02, 1947	71 yr 11 mo 14dy	California
WILSON, JAMES	Sep 24, 1933	80 yr 5 mo 14 dy	Scotland
WILSON, JOAN MAXINE	Jan 10, 1937	4 yr 6 mo 21 dy	California
WILSON, LLOYD VANOTE	Mar 23, 1947	49 yr 11 mo 20dy	New Jersey
WILSON, MILDRED	Sep 13, 1934	8 yr 4 mo 26 dy	California
WILSON, RICHARD	Jun 10, 1911	"middle aged"	
WILSON, RUFUS COLLINS	Feb 20, 1911	66 yr	
WILSON, WILLIAM B.	Jul 30, 1941	68 yr 11 mo 16dy	California
WILSON, WILLIAM McKINLEY	Sep 10, 1939	40 yr 5 mo 16 dy	Arkansas
WILSON, W. W.	Mar 08, 1922	51 yr	
WINDRICK, ANNA J.	Jun 05, 1900	25 yr 2 mo 5 dy	California
WINEFELD, FRITZ KARL	Nov 20, 1934	44 yr 3 dy	Germany
WINKELRIED, LOUIS	Nov 09, 1904	abt 38 yr	Switzerland
WISE, ANDREW JACKSON	Aug 02, 1914	87 yr	
WISE, EBENEZER JESSE	Nov 18, 1917	59 yr 7 mo 28 dy	
WISE, JESSE	Apr 08, 1910	21 yr	
WITT, GEORGE F.	Aug 27, 1918	82 yr	
WOFFORD, BOB F.	May 11, 1940	49 yr	Mississippi
WOLF, CLARENCE VICTOR	Aug 29, 1950	67 yr	Ohio
WOLF, GEORGE C.	Mar 26, 1936	64 yr 2 mo 21 dy	California
WOLFE, ALFRED HERMAN	Jan 22, 1933	80 yr 26 dy	Penn.
WOLFF, CHRISTINA	Jul 11, 1930	36 yr (grave marker:1845-1930)	
WOLFF, WILLIAM FREDERICK	Apr 23, 1923	43 yr 2 mo 26 dy	
WOLFF, NICHOLAS	May 23, 1903	76 yr	Germany
WOMACK, GEORGE	Sep 07, 1911	45 yr	
WON JON	May 24, 1926	83 yr	
WONG BACK YOU	Mar 26, 1913	51 yr	
WONG DOO YUEN	Aug 04, 1919	74 yr	
WONG LEE	May 08, 1934	81 yr	China
WONG LIN	Mar 25, 1922	82 yr	
WOOD, NADINE S.	Sep 30, 1945	56 yr 0 mo 17 dy	Germany

WOODBURN, ROBERT	Oct 07, 1900	76 yr	Ireland
WOODBURY, FRANK ISAAC	Dec 21, 1950	76 yr	California.
WOODFILL, EMILY P.	Feb 15, 1948	66 yr 6 mo 6 dy	California
WOODFILL, JAY	Feb 15, 1948	75 yr 5 mo 0 dy	Illinois
WOODS, LEMUEL (black)	Jul 01, 1947	55 yr 10 mo 1 dy	Kentucky
WOODWARD, GEORGE	Nov 10, 1908	abt 67 yr	
WORTHINGTON, FREDERICK	Mar 31, 1921	65 yr	
WORTHINGTON, RUTH ELAINE	Mar 24, 1936	2 mo 12 dy	California
WRIGHT, CLARA E.	Jul 08, 1946	83 yr 7 mo 7 dy	California
WRIGHT, ERNEST ROY	May 02, 1932	26 yr 5 mo 21 dy	Oregon
WRIGHT, W. A., Mrs.	Dec 18, 1911	62 yr 5 dy	
WYANT, EVERETT	Apr 27, 1940	61 yr	W. Virginia
WYCKOFF, FILLMORE CURTIS	Sep 04, 1915	58 yr 11 mo 20 dy	
YATES, HENRY, Dr.	Jul 18, 1946	79 yr	
YATES, MARY E.	Jan 05, 1943	59 yr 7 mo 28 dy	
YOHE, CHARLES N.	Apr 14, 1950	76 yr	Missouri
YOUNG, HENRY JUNKANS	Nov 04, 1949	69 yr	California
YOUNG, MARY ELIZA VIRGINIA	Feb 03, 1926	85 yr 4 mo 6 dy	
YOUNG, MATT	Aug 09, 1901	56 yr	Kentucky
YOUNG, WILLIAM WARE	May 28, 1921	57 yr 7 mo 15 dy	
YOUNT, GEORGE WALTER	Aug 01, 1917	74 yr 2 mo 28 dy	
YTCAINA, LEON	Aug 05, 1950	25 yr	California
YU HONG	Jul 17, 1922	87 yr	
ZACHARY, WANDA CLEO	Mar 25, 1929	9 mo 21 dy	
ZARLI, FRED	Jan 29, 1915	80 yr	
ZEIGLAR, ISAH	May 17, 1924	80 yr 6 mo 7 dy	
ZERGA, JOHN	Jun 30, 1910	50 yr	
ZIMMERMAN, EDWARD	Aug 05, 1907	abt 25 yr	Illinois
ZOOK, SAMUEL	Apr 24, 1911	93 yr	
ZUELLA, PETE	Jan 17, 1944	89 yr 8 mo 30 dy	Austria
ZWISSIG, JOHN	Aug 17, 1905	abt 50 yr	Germany

END TRINITY COUNTY DEATHS 1900-1950

INDEX TO TRINITY COUNTY, CALIFORNIA, MARRIAGES 1850-1900
From an unpublished manuscript by RITA M. HANOVER
in Trinity County Library, Weaverville, California
Used with permission.

HUSBAND, WIFE, and MARRIAGE DATE:

ABBOTT, BENJAMIN F. & Kester, Nancy Y., Miss m. Jan21, 1861
ABBOTT, BENJAMIN F. & -----, Mary Jane, Indian m. Mar11, 1865
ABBOTT, JOHN FRANKLIN & Franck, Julia, Miss m. Jun03, 1885
ABRAMS, FRED SHAW & Crawford, Bessie, Miss m. Nov15, 1890
ADAMS, JOHN Q. & Schneider, Kate m. Jul17, 1890
ADAMS, WILLIAM JESSE & Vaughn, Carrie E., Miss m. Dec10, 1900
ALEXANDER, JOHN J. & Connell, Louisa m. Jul04, 1864
ALLEN, GEORGE B. & Underwood, Marian, Mrs. m. Dec03, 1878
ALLEN, HENRY CLAY & Yumcheera, Julia m. Nov30, 1862
ALLEN, RALPH & Mabie, Emma, Miss m. Apr20, 1865
ANDERLINI, FERDINAND FRANCISCO & Walpolt, Babette, Miss m. Jun14, 1888
ANDERLINI, JOHN JOSEPH & Ehrmann, Mary Louisa, Miss m. Nov10, 1885
ANDERLINI, JOSEPH ANTONE & Dickey, Sarah M., Miss m. May19, 1892
ANDREWS, JULIUS & Cochell, Adaline W. m. Dec04, 1871
ARGUELLO, JOSE & Bowler, Maggie M., Mrs. m. Nov23, 1877
ARMSTRONG, WILLIAM H. & Arguello, Lillie, Miss m. Sep13, 1893
ARONHALT, JESSE W. & Gates, Flora H., Miss m. Oct27, 1897
ASHWORTH, WILLIAM D. & Readington, Anne m. Nov04, 1855
BACHELDER, WILLIAM H. & Kelton, Julia A., Mrs. m. Oct15, 1871
BACON, EDGAR W. & Morris, Mary K., Miss m. Apr11, 1883
BAKER, THOMAS & Carrett (or Spangle), Miss m. Sep16, 1857
BAKER, WALTER J. & Fetzer, Magdalena, Miss m. Oct30, 1884
BAKER, WILLIS EUGENE & Bearden, Hattie (Harriet) V., Mrs. m. May27, 1888
BALCH, JAMES R. & Robb, Margaret, Miss m. Oct03, 1867
BALLEAU(Belleau), LOUIS FRANK & Hartman, Rosalie, Mrs. m. Jan06, 1878
BARKER, DAVID E. V. & -----, Jane (Indian) m. Apr20, 1865
BARKLA, JAMES & Hensley, Ann Elizabeth m. Nov01, 1874
BARNES, JOHN & McQuiety, Mary A., Mrs. m. Oct10, 1876
BARNICKEL, JACOB & Junkans, Anna, Miss m. Feb25, 1872
BARTHOLOMEW, MITCHELL O. & Morris, Lucy J. m. Sep09, 1866
BARTLETT, CHARLES & Kennedy, Bridget, Miss m. May27, 1861
BARTLETT, JAMES W. & Brady, Vina, Miss m. Jan08, 1890
BATES, JOHN G. & Bates, Mary Jane, Miss m. Feb14, 1861
BEAN, HIRAM P. & Bayer, Mary Ann m. Feb07, 1853
BEAN, LEONARD C. & Rice, Catherine Alma m. Jun01, 1898
BEARDEN, JAMES P. & Newman, Hattie V., Miss m. Dec27, 1880
BECKETT, HENRY & Myers, Elizabeth, Mrs. m. Nov18, 1863
BEGEL, THEODORE & Weiman, Eugenie L. (Handbine), Mrs. m. Jul03, 1895
BEHM, NICHOLAS & Holleran, Margaret, Miss m. Jun30, 1859
BELCHER, GALITZIN & Edwards, Elizabeth B., Mrs. m. Aug12, 1860
BENNETT, MARCUS M. & Hughes, Flora E., Miss m. Jun09, 1878
BERGER, ROBERT & Junkans, Anna M. Miss m. Aug27, 1882
BERGIN, JOHN WILLIAM & Laws, Lena Alice, Miss m. Oct13, 1887
BERGIN, THOMAS FRANCIS & Condon, Mary Ellen, Miss m. Oct30, 1889
BERKHAM, JOHN & Burns, Margaret m. Jul02, 1861
BERKLEY, RICHARD L. & Gribble, Mary A., Miss m. Jan01, 1870
BETICURA, MANUEL & Rabbitt, Anna m. Nov12, 1870
BIGELOW, WILLIAM RALPH & Thayer, Maud A., Miss m. Oct24, 1888
BIGGS, J. J. & Maupen, Angeline P., Mrs. m. Nov16, 1862
BINGAMAN, JOHN & Winchell, Fanny, Mrs. m. Nov02, 1864
BIXBY, GEORGE & Strong, Lydia Ann m. Jul08, 1865
BLAGRAVE, BANNISTER & Kelly, Milla J., Miss m. Apr10, 1864
BLAGRAVE, JAMES H. & Leonard, Gertrude Elizabeth, Miss m. Oct11, 1899
BLAGRAVE, WALTER LEE & Todd, Annie Laura, Miss m. Oct16, 1893
BLAGRAVE, WILLIAM A. & Kelly, Elizabeth, Miss m. May12, 1865

BLAIR, BENJAMIN MOOR & Wilson, Maud m. Mar22, 1895
BLAIR, HUGH NEWELL & Clancie, Eva m. Nov25, 1897
BLAKE, SELDON L.,MD & Norcross, Ensie May, Miss m. Apr03, 1886
BLAKEMORE, ALBERT J. M. & Blagrave, Vetura V., Miss m. Apr02, 1885
BLANEY, HUGH & Cochran, Ann, Mrs. m. Dec12, 1878
BOORD, L. L. & Johnston, Mary m. May18, 1860
BOWERMAN, FRANK L. & Bolton, Nellie May m. Jul07, 1895
BOWERMAN, JACOB & Hall, Anne F. m. Dec11, 1872
BOWIE, JAMES & Jumper, Maggie (Colbert), Mrs. m. Nov01, 1897
BOWMAN, CHARLES GUSS & Garvin, Edrin, Miss m. Sep04, 1894
BOYNTON, ALFRED W. & Morrison, Mary E., Miss m. Jul02, 1865
BRADBURY, JOSEPHUS & Hagelman, Theresa, Miss m. Jun30, 1880
BRADY, MORRIS A. & Dannenbrink, Louisa H. m. Aug24, 1889
BRAGDON, EDWIN H. & Duncan, Emily J., Miss m. Nov01, 1891
BRANCH, ROBERT HILL & Buttman, Margarette m. Jul23, 1895
BRANNAN, HENRY W. & Vitzthum, Lizzie, Miss m. Oct02, 1892
BREMER, AUGUST F. & Offutt, Maud M., Miss m. Jun24, 1896
BREWSTER, LEWIS & Sprowl, Orvila, Miss m. Dec29, 1876
BRITTON, JOSEPH & Dockery, Julia, Miss m. Aug24, 1897
BROWDER, ALFRED & Thatcher, Anna Maria Harriet,Mrs. m. Apr09, 1856
BROWN, BOYER RITTER & Benton, Mary I., Miss m. Apr06, 1899
BROWN, DANIEL & Garcia, Elizabeth, Mrs. m. Nov15, 1896
BROWN, FLEMING E. & Domenici, Louisa m. Oct20, 1897
BROWN, JAMES HENRY & Trimble, Harriet L., Miss m. Nov12, 1896
BROWN, JEREMIAH M. & Mabie, Irene Estelle, Miss m. Oct21, 1896
BROWN, PHILLIP S. & Mathews, Julia A., Miss m. Sep21, 1865
BROWN, RICHARD B. & Shehan, Catherine, Miss m. Nov25, 1878
BROWN, THOMAS J. & Jones, Nettie, Mrs. m. Aug30, 1899
BRUMM, PETER & Watermeyer, Elizabeth m. May03, 1857
BUCKLEY, JOHN F. & Rule, Carrie W., Miss m. Jul02, 1900
BURGER, JOHN A. & Smith, Mary Anne, Mrs. m. Nov26, 1874
BURKE, HARRY & Atkinson, Margaret, Miss m. Jul19, 1861
BURNETT,JAMES ALEXANDER & Willard, Harriet, Miss m. Jun14, 1890
BUSCH, JULIUS & Matzen, Anne M., Mrs. m. Jul28, 1875
BUSH, HENRY TARTON & Paulsen, Annie Barbara, Miss m. May08, 1887
BUSSELL, PINDOR F. & Clark, Hattie, Miss m. Dec22, 1864
BUTTS, JOSHUA & -----, Julia (Indian) m. Jan03, 1865
CADEMARTORI, FRANK & Cummings, Mary A., Miss m. Mar30, 1882
CAHALAN, MICHAEL & Colbert, Margaret, Mrs. m. Oct22, 1865
CAHNBLY, PETER & Junkans, Dorothea, Miss m. Sep30, 1860
CAMPBELL, THOMAS G. & Lindsay, Mary m. Jun28, 1875
CAMPBELL, WILLIAM & Walker, Mary m. Dec24, 1896
CARDOZA, FRANK & Duarte, Flora Rodgers, Miss m. May27, 1900
CARLSON, CHARLES ALFRED & Bremer, Dora J., Miss m. Jul08, 1893
CARNES (KARNES), DANIEL & Conlin, Catherine m. Jun27, 1860
CARPENTER, CHARLES H. & Kimsey, Sarah J. m. Apr09, 1898
CARR, ALEXANDER & Gribble, Annie, Miss m. Feb23, 1881
CARR, ALEXANDER C. & Jones, Hattie M., Mrs. m. Aug16, 1899
CARR, GEORGE LEE & Ursher, May m. Jun01, 1890
CARR, THOMAS H. & Huson, Ella A. m. May28, 1874
CARTER, CLEMENT A. & Drinkwater, Dora E., Miss m. Nov29, 1899
CARTER, JAMES A. & Nichols, Margaret D. m. May15, 1895
CARTER, JAMES M. & Kitchen, Eliza, Miss m. Nov26, 1880
CARTER, JOHN W. & Duncan, Rebecca, Miss m. May14, 1857
CARTER, ROBERT L. & Marshall, Cassie D., Miss m. Jun15, 1893
CASTNER, LOUIS PRESTON & Willard, Huldah, Miss m. Sep07, 1886
CATON, ANTONE & Williams, Louisa m. Aug08, 1900
CATON, JOHN & Atkins, Lulu L., Miss m. Sep04, 1900
CHILDERS,JAMES HORACE & Shook, Clara May, Miss m. Jan08, 1883
CHINN, W. J. & Maxwell, Jane, Miss m. Jul12, 1856
CHRISTIANSEN, FRED & Dawson, Mary J., Miss m. Sep26, 1880
CHURCH, JOHN E. & Martin, Elizabeth A., Miss m. Nov28, 1856
CLAYTON, GEORGE H. & Sinclair, Mary J., Mrs. m. Sep28, 1876

MARRIAGES 1850 - 1900

CLEAVES, CHARLES SAMUEL & Hobart, Myrtle Jane, Miss m. Nov06, 1887
CLEMENS, HENRY E. & Swazy, Catherine, Miss m. Dec22, 1864
CLEMENT, ALBERT CURTIS & Coumbs, Jessie, Miss m. Feb28, 1893
CLEMENT, CHARLES E. & Barkla, Virginia Belle m. Dec09, 1896
CLEMENT, WILLIAM HENRY & Carr, Florena A., Miss m. Jan18, 1888
COBB, JOHN RUFUS & Crabtree, Mary Ellen, Miss m. May03, 1889
COCHRAN, JAMES & O'Connell, Ann m. Jul11, 1861
COLBY, JOHN HENRY & Robly, Maggie M., Mrs. m. Nov27, 1887
COLE, CHARLES C. & Owings, Marguerite, Miss m. May11, 1897
COMSTOCK, JAMES J. & Bennett, Lavina m. Sep04, 1860
CONDON, MORRIS & O'Keefe, Ellen m. Feb02, 1864
CONDON, WILLIAM & Desmond, Mary, Miss m. Nov04, 1862
CONDON, WILLIAM & Lowden, Carrie Irene m. Apr16, 1896
CONWAY, FREDERICK EDMUND & Hawk, Ellen Nora, Miss m. Apr15, 1886
COUMBS, JOHN H. & Wallace, Mary E., Miss m. Jun28, 1893
COX, THOMAS C. & Beals, Elizabeth, Miss m. Dec22, 1864
COX, WILLIAM H. & Kindred, Phoebe A. m. Sep22, 1872
CRAIG, CHRISTIAN WOLFF & Lockhart, Elizabeth E. m. May03, 1870
CRAIN, JUDSON & Schaffer, Anna Hortense, Miss m. Aug29, 1898
CRAWFORD, MONROE T. & Treloar, Salina, Mrs. m. Jan03, 1869
CREAMER, CHARLES N. & Todd, Minnie J., Miss m. Nov08, 1882
CRITCHLOW, JOHN & Ripley, Sarah M., Miss m. May23, 1877
CROCKER, CHARLES & Hollister, Hattie, Miss m. Jul09, 1865
CROWL, BRADFORD A. & Nieman, Emily, Miss m. Feb23, 1892
CULLEN, PATRICK & Ryan, Ellen m. Jul10, 1860
CULY, GEORGE C. & Vaughn, Parmelia m. Jul13, 1879
CUMMINGS, JOHN H. & Hocking, Clara L. m. Sep23, 1891
CUNNINGHAM, BENJAMIN & Fuller, Sarah B., Mrs. m. Nov19, 1866
CUNNINGHAM, MORRIS & Flagg, Lucinda, Miss m. May04, 1887
CURRIE, ALGERNON S. & McIlvane, Rebecca, Miss m. Oct04, 1860
CURT, FRANCISCO SILVA BRETAU & Riquas, Maria m. Feb06, 1871
DACK, ELISHA R. & Baker, Isabella E., Miss m. Sep06, 1874
DAMSELL, JOSEPHUS & Stafford, Stella A., Miss m. Jun19, 1895
DANNENBRINK, CONRAD & Junkans, Augusta, Miss m. Jul11, 1863
DART, DIXON & Campbell, Jessie m. Dec30, 1896
DAVIS, ALLEN & Akers, Nancy Jane m. Sep03, 1860
DAVIS, DAVID PERRY & Junkans, Ida F., Miss m. Oct26, 1889
DAWSON, THOMAS F. & Sturdivant, Lucy, Miss m. Dec13, 1864
DAWSON, THOMAS R. & Hailstone, Hettie m. Dec07, 1896
DAY, J. T. & Herrick, Harriet Elizabeth, Miss m. May27, 1861
DAY, JOHN D. C. & Todd, Maybella A., Miss m. Sep02, 1880
DAY, ULYSSES GRANT & Dickey, Minerva Jane, Miss m. Dec24, 1891
DAYTON, HIRAM B. & Coman, Marian, Miss m. Sep24, 1865
DAYTON, WILLIAM H. & Mathews, Martha J., Miss m. Oct03, 1869
DeREIS(RAIS), MANUEL CAVALHO & Mintell, Rosa, Miss m. May20, 1890
DEAN, HARVEY GEORGE & Fetzer, Louisa, Miss m. Sep28, 1893
DELWISCH, GERHARD HENRY & Richard, Adelaide, Miss m. Nov05, 1895
DeMELLO, AUGUST SMITH & Louise, Audzaline m. May21, 1871
DENNISON, LEWIS & Koll, Bertha, Miss m. Jul02, 1881
DESTY, ROBERT & Davison, Mary, Miss m. May09, 1860
DeVALLE, JOSEPH REQUARDO & De Cousence, Mary Joseph m. Feb09, 1870
DIAS, FRANK V. & Enos, Flora, Miss m. Jan07, 1888
DICKEY, JOHN E. & Cruthis, Ella Rose m. Oct31, 1894
DIDDY, JOHN & Ripley, May M., Miss m. Nov14, 1899
DIMOCK, FRANK LESLIE & Olsen, Flora Ida, Miss m. May14, 1892
DIX, HENRY & Brannan, Mary, Miss m. Oct17, 1880
DOBBYN, JOHN P. & Kellogg, Maude, Miss m. Oct05, 1898
DOCKERY, JAMES EDWARD & Murray, Margaret Frances m. Apr19, 1898
DOCKERY, JOHN WM. & Coumbs, Mary, Miss m. Nov27, 1895
DOCKERY, MICHAEL WM. & Coumbs, Grace, Miss m. Dec23, 1886
DODGE, JOHN C. & Gardiner, Diana Prudence, Miss m. Dec11, 1861
DORR, JAMES C. & Reynolds, Ellen, Miss m. Jul22, 1860
DOUGHERTY, JAMES & Dorsey, Catherine, Mrs. m. Nov26, 1863

DOUGLASS, GEORGE F. & Slattery, Mary Ann m. Jan03, 1876
DOWNHOUR, JOHN J. & Sloper, Phoebe, Mrs. m. Jul10, 1858
DRAKE, JUDSON L. & Wentworth, A. E., Miss m. Apr01, 1857
DRIVER, JOHN R. & Gilzean, Mary E., Miss m. Dec11, 1872
DUARTE, FRANCISCO & Enos, Maria J. m. May06, 1878
DUNCAN, LEONIDAS P. & Fleming, Mary, Miss m. Sep29, 1874
DUNHAM, WARREN & Livingston, Elizabeth, Miss m. Jun24, 1865
DUTTON, GEORGE W. & Trask, Minerva, Miss m. Jun10, 1883
DYER, S. TRUE & Philbrick, Laura N. m. Dec01, 1860
EASTMAN, ELBRIDGE G. & Blakemore, Goldie V., Miss m. Nov21, 1881
EASTMAN, JAMES & Crittenden, Betsy, Mrs. m. May31, 1856
EDGAR, SIDNEY & Diggins, Ellen, Miss m. Jul14, 1890
EDGMON, WILLIAM A. & Friend, DeEtt E. m. Oct23, 1893
EHRMANN, HENRY & Bellig, Kathrina, Miss m. Jun27, 1863
EINFALT, JOHN MICHAEL & Smith, E. J., Miss m. Jan11, 1866
ELIGH, JAMES R. & Downing, Lillie, Miss m. May26, 1882
ELLIS, ELI & Horton, Lillie E., Mrs. m. Nov26, 1896
ELLIS, FRANKLIN & Gardner, Elizabeth J., Miss m. Sep19, 1867
ELLIS, HENRY H. M. & Van Matre, Louisa, Miss m. Jul25, 1885
ELLSWORTH, GEORGE W. & Nixon, Drucilla m. Jan01, 1853
ENOS, MANUEL & Joseph, Annie m. Nov16, 1868
ESTES, JOHN M. & Turot (Tourot), Elsie m. May28, 1856
ESTES, WILLIAM C. & Breen, Harriet, Mrs. m. Jul18, 1859
ESTES, WILLIAM C. & Cowen, Hannah, Mrs. m. Oct27, 1867
EUSTICE, RICHARD & Keefe, Amelia m. Jan23, 1853
EVEREST, HARVEY W. & Allen, Phoebe B., Miss m. Jun20, 1861
EVERHART, WILLIAM D. & Ward, Ada, Miss m. Jun12, 1862
FALAN, JOSEPH & Smith, Lillian M., Miss m. Dec28, 1878
FALAN, JOSEPH & Willey, Mary, Mrs. m. Feb07, 1886
FARMER, CHARLES H. & Halley, Laura m. Feb01, 1897
FARMER, WILLIAM GRANT & Davidson, Daisy A. M., Miss m. Jan27, 1897
FARRELL, MICHAEL & Carrigan, Delia, Miss m. Nov10, 1857
FEENEY, RICHARD HENRY & Doole, Sarah Jane, Miss m. Aug24, 1875
FEOUR, JAMES C. & Dack, Macie J., Miss m. Jun11, 1879
FERRIS, CLIFF & Roff, Carrie, Miss m. abt NOV, 1893
FIELD, JOHNSON N. & Brady, Elvira, Miss m. Sep11, 1889
FITZGERALD, WILLIAM & Robb, Esther m. Jun26, 1862
FLANDERS, THOMAS & Whittier, Ann J., Mrs. m. Oct14, 1866
FLOURAUD, MATHIEU & Negre, Maria, Miss m. Aug02, 1896
FLOWERS, WILLIAM F. & Silva, Rose, Miss m. Apr10, 1900
FLOWERS, WILLIAM FRANKLIN & Given, Carrie Etta, Miss m. Dec24, 1896
FLOYD, WILLIAM D. & Morehouse, Minnie m. Oct31, 1886
FOGG, CALVIN P. & Hood, Elizabeth C., Miss m. Jul03, 1861
FOOTE, ANDREW N. & Moore, Venus, Mrs. m. Aug04, 1868
FOSTER, PHILLIP S. & Kise, Anna Eliza, Miss m. Jan25, 1872
FOX, ORSON & Johnston, Elizabeth m. Aug15, 1861
FRANCIS, JOHN & Hessig, Rosa, Mrs. m. Mar17, 1863
FRATERS, MANUEL & Silva, Mary, Miss m. Jul10, 1864
FRATES, JOHN & Louise, Anne m. Nov27, 1871
FREETHY, RICHARD E. & Bassham, Annie, Miss m. Dec17, 1883
FREITAS, MATHEW J. & Rule, Laura May m. Oct06, 1897
FRENCH, GREENLEAF C. & Burgess, Orinda F., Mrs. m. Sep01, 1880
FRY, JAMES S. & Barkla, Luella, Miss m. Sep08, 1900
GAFFNEY, MILES & Heinlan, Catherine m. Oct28, 1860
GAGE, J. R. (RALPH) & Campbell, Josephine, Miss m. Jul30, 1890
GAGE, LEWIS C. & Brannan, Carrie, Miss m. Nov17, 1878
GARFIELD, PLUNKET & Rafferty, Mary m. Jun04, 1863
GATES, ALEX & Kester, Alvira, Mrs. m. Sep04, 1860
GATES, OSCAR J., Dr. & Karnes, Charlotte H., Mrs. m. Dec18, 1857
GENTRY, STEVE & Rogers, Rebecca, Miss m. Jul13, 1889
GIBBS, JOHN BERNIE & Leas, Mary Louise, Miss m. Sep12, 1895
GIBSON, JOHN E. & Dunlap, Milly M., Miss m. Aug27, 1882
GIBSON, ROBERT K. & Allen, Mary Ann, Miss m. Nov28, 1878

MARRIAGES 1850 - 1900

GIBSON, STEWART M. & Coumbs, Charlotte T., Miss m. Oct27, 1886
GILBERT, PETER & Nicholson, Mary, Mrs. m. Jan16, 1864
GILZEAN, ALEXANDER & Gates, Harriet W., Miss m. Nov02, 1893
GILZEAN, CHARLES E. & Ursher, Rose A., Miss m. Feb24, 1889
GILZEAN, CHARLES E. & Harvey, Rebecca, Miss m. Feb13, 1894
GILZEAN, CHARLES ERIC & Jacobs, Mollie A. m. Jan01, 1885
GILZEAN, JAMES H. & Laws, Clementina, Miss m. Mar23, 1878
GIRARD, LOUIS & King, Annie, Miss m. Aug27, 1883
GIVAN, JAMES C. & Ralph, Cora, Miss m. Dec25, 1889
GIVEN, HORACE ROBERT & Blakemore, May M., Miss m. Apr24, 1897
GIVEN, JAMES EDGAR & Jones, Dora, Miss m. Feb22, 1886
GIVEN, JAMES EDGAR & Buys, Alice, Miss m. Sep09, 1894
GIVEN, WILLIAM CUSHMAN & Chapman, Caroline A., Miss m. Apr22, 1871
GLASS, WILLIAM & Kester, Sarah, Mrs. m. Nov12, 1889
GODFREY, CHARLES W. & Huston, Clara, Mrs. m. Jun11, 1898
GOETZE, WILLIAM HENRY & Gaum, Louisa, Miss m. Dec25, 1879
GOEWEY, JAMES M. & Bates, Susan, Miss m. Apr09, 1863
GOODWIN, MICHAEL & Campbell, Susan, Mrs. m. May14, 1859
GOODYEAR, CHARLES EUGENE & Paulsen, Elizabeth S., Miss m. Oct30, 1883
GORDON, DAVID E. & Webb, Laura E., Miss m. Sep02, 1861
GORE, ROBERT F. & Caldwell, Gertrude L. m. Apr26, 1897
GORHAM, HENRY H. & Wolff, Mary m. Aug22, 1896
GORMAN, THOMAS & Ryan, Johanna m. Apr24, 1865
GRANT, WILLIAM E. & Flowers, Mary E., Miss m. Oct11, 1888
GRAVES, JOHN BURGESS & Dunlap, Hattie m. Oct13, 1892
GREENWELL, ERNEST ALBERT & Todd, Emma Agnes, Miss m. Sep26, 1888
GREGORY, LEROY & Henry, Amelia, Miss m. Apr19, 1857
GRIBBLE, GEORGE & McCormack, Mollie E., Miss m. Sep26, 1882
GRIBBLE, GEORGE & Segalia, Mary Adeline, Miss m. Sep19, 1891
GRIBBLE, JAMES H. & Lorenz, Susie, Miss m. Dec21, 1892
GRIBBLE, WILLIAM & Lorenz, Tillie, Miss m. Sep10, 1891
GRIFFIN, MORRIS F. & Wood, Sarah E., Miss m. Dec31, 1863
GRIFFITH, MICHAEL & Ryan, Margaret, Miss m. Oct26, 1865
GRIGSBY, ROBERT L. & Nicholson, Mabel, Miss m. Jun01, 1899
GROSS, JOSHUA FREEMAN & Small, E. L. (Lena) m. Dec19, 1869
GUILL, WILLIAM EDWARD & Hawk, Elizabeth, Miss m. Aug09, 1893
GUM, BIRD HICKS & Owens, Isabel, Miss m. Sep25, 1892
GUPTIL, BARTLETT S. & Maloney, Mary, Miss m. Sep24, 1868
GUTHRIE, WILLIAM & Harris, Susan m. Jul31, 1873
GWINN, FRANKLIN SHERMAN & Day, Elizabeth J., Miss m. Nov07, 1857
HAAS, FREDERICK G. & Junkans, Emily, Miss m. Jul25, 1880
HAGAN, JOHN J. & Gillson, Mary R., Mrs. m. Dec21, 1898
HAGELMAN, JOHN & Weckert, Wilhelmina (Maria) m. Apr13, 1861
HAILSTONE, JOHN THOMPSON & Bussell, Nancy A. m. Jan21, 1871
HAILSTONE, PINDOR F. & Godin, Sarah J., Mrs. m. Nov03, 1896
HALL, ALBERT G. & Colbert, Anna J., Miss m. May19, 1880
HALL, DANIEL JAMES & Paulsen, Hannah Pauline, Miss m. May17, 1900
HALL, GEORGE W. & Bassham, Florence L., Miss m. Apr14, 1895
HALL, JOHN P. (JACK) & Osgood, Nettie A., Miss m. Sep04, 1870
HALL, WILLIAM LEWIS & Spencer, Mary E., Miss m. Jun28, 1869
HALL, WILLIAM P. & Myers, Mary Hannah m. Sep04, 1861
HALLEY, FREDERICK F. & Richardson, Mabel M., Miss m. Jun15, 1899
HAM, JOSEPH & Voshay, Fanny, Miss m. May17, 1874
HAMILTON, D. D. & Gilbert, Jane, Mrs. m. Apr12, 1856
HAMMOND, CHARLES & Williams, Minnie, Mrs. m. Sep12, 1900
HAMMOND, FRANK C. & Duarte, Anna V. Rodgers m. Oct21, 1899
HAMPTON, EVERETT P. & Hartman, Rosa E., Miss m. Feb22, 1885
HAMPTON, EVERETT P. & Moss, Alice S., Mrs. m. May14, 1889
HAMPTON, HARLEY & Butts, Louisa Lena, Miss m. Dec24, 1896
HANNA, HUGH R. & Osgood, Viola, Miss m. Jul15, 1897
HANOVER, FRANK S. & Joseph, Adeline, Miss m. Dec19, 1900
HANSEN, DETLEF & Junkans, Dorothea m. Sep27, 1868
HANSEN, ERNEST F. & Mathews, Maria, Mrs. m. May05, 1867

HARDY, ROBERT & Bussell, Sarah Jane m. Jul07, 1880
HARRIS, FREDERICK WILLIAM & Howell, Jessie m. Aug15, 1897
HARVEY, HENRY THOMAS & Hindley, Rebecca, Miss m. Dec25, 1866
HARWOOD, WILLIAM H. & Bolton, Ida D. m. Jun25, 1896
HASKINS, ALBERT P. & Wheeler, Elizabeth A., Mrs. m. Nov19, 1895
HATCH, ISAAC A. & Passage, Catherine, Miss m. Feb07, 1861
HATCH, JOHN M. & Tuley, Ann, Mrs. m. Dec18, 1864
HAWK, JOHN & Schlomer, Lilly (Elizabeth) m. Jul05, 1870
HAYS, HIRAM B. & Dickerson, Alice A., Miss m. Jul04, 1874
HAYWARD, JOHN D. & Martin, Carrie, Miss m. Oct04, 1888
HEALY, ALECK & Einfalt, Maria, Miss m. Jul02, 1860
HEATH, JOHN W. & Warren, Charlotte Ann, Miss m. Dec31, 1894
HEATH, JOHN WESLEY & Tourtelotte, Nellie G., Miss m. Oct09, 1879
HECHTMAN, ALBERT J. & Van Matre, Carrie C., Miss m. Mar22, 1880
HENNESSEY, PATRICK O'MALLEY & Keely, Maria, Miss m. Jun08, 1863
HENNESSEY, TIMOTHY & Wallace, Ellen, Mrs. m. Jan24, 1886
HERRICK, HENRY J. & Harvey, Harriet A., Miss m. Jan13, 1863
HIGGINS, WILLIAM & Holman, Mary Ann, Miss m. Dec19, 1869
HILL, ERNEST C. & Tompkins, Grace V. m. Mar28, 1899
HINDLEY, GEORGE & Holman, Margaret, Miss m. Dec25, 1866
HOAGLIN, ROBERT & Davis, Eva J., Miss m. Apr14, 1890
HOCKER, HENRY & Morgan, Christina, Miss m. Jun03, 1859
HOFFMAN, ELIAS M. & Winters, Sarah V., Miss m. Feb14, 1892
HOLLAND, PATRICK & Coyle, Katherine, Miss m. Feb20, 1882
HOLLINGSWORTH, FRANK O. & Lowden, Nellie S., Miss m. Mar07, 1898
HOLLISTER, HIRAM W. & Brown, Elizabeth Virginia m. Jun06, 1861
HORTON, RICHARD E. & Harvey, Lillie E., Miss m. Sep11, 1887
HOSLINGER, VALENTINE & Cochran, Mary, Miss m. Jan26, 1868
HOWARD, WILLIAM GREEN & Frank, Minnie, Miss m. Dec27, 1894
HOYT, JONATHON S. & Pritchard, Catherine F. m. Mar05, 1874
HUBBARD, THEODORE J. & Clayman, Angelina m. Oct24, 1860
HUESTIS, WILBUR A. & Tinsley, Helen A., Miss m. Oct30, 1898
HUGHES, JOHN E. & Cousins, Alma, Miss m. Feb23, 1899
HUGHES, ROBERT & Putterman, Miranda, Miss m. Dec31, 1856
HUGHES, WILLIAM EDWARD & Senger, Catherine m. Dec25, 1895
HULL, NATHAN & Myers, Elizabeth Jane m. Oct03, 1861
HULME, GEORGE & Hollister, Elizabeth V., Mrs. m. Dec13, 1866
HUNGERFORD, ZACHARIAH & Myers, Etta C., Miss m. Nov05, 1867
HUNTER, CHARLES DECATUR & _____, Martha (Indian) m. Jan03, 1865
HUOT, JOSEPH & Severiano, Kate, Miss m. Apr01, 1872
HUPP, WILLIAM I. & Johnson, Isabella Miss m. Aug10, 1865
HUSCROFT, JOHN J. & Rose, Lucy, Miss m. Dec09, 1862
HUSTON, JOHN & Showalter, Clara, Miss m. Jun30, 1889
HUTCHINS, EDWARD M. & Hawk, Elizabeth, Mrs. m. May28, 1893
HUTCHINS, HENRY E. & Searles, Ida C., Miss m. Jul28, 1890
HYDE, MAURICE & Murphy, Kate, Miss m. Jan14, 1874
INGRAM, WALTER W. & Hoyt, Catherine, Mrs. m. Jan03, 1881
JACKSON, WILBERT L. & Senger, Madeline, Miss m. Dec06, 1883
JACOB, BARTHEL & Kennedy, Eliza, Miss m. Oct12, 1865
JACOBS, HENRY & Waldron, Anne, Miss m. Oct13, 1873
JENSEN, PETER H. & Gribble, Minnie, Miss m. Oct27, 1890
JEWETT, PRESTON A. & Bean, Addie A. m. Jan13, 1884
JOHNSTON, JAMES A. & Casey, Margaret, Mrs. m. May09, 1872
JONES, THEODORE E. & Puterman, SARAH J., Miss m. Mar28, 1867
JONES, THEODORE E. & Barnes, Mary A., Mrs. m. Apr04, 1877
JONES, THEODORE ELDON & Huggins, Clara I., Miss m. Oct17, 1887
JORDAN, ALBERT & Brown, Lillie, Miss m. Sep20, 1889
JORDAN, MELVILLE CRAIG & Thayer, Jessie E., Miss m. Jun20, 1894
JOSE, EDWARD W. & Dockery, Mary, Miss m. Nov29, 1882
JUMPER, GEORGE B. & Colbert, Maggie, Miss m. May30, 1883
JUNKANS, HENRY & Healy, Maria, Mrs. m. Sep27, 1868
JUNKANS, WILLIAM & Senger, Nettie, Miss m. Oct07, 1896
JUNKANS, WILLIAM F. & Hoppe, Johanna, Miss m. May06, 1877

MARRIAGES 1850 - 1900

KELLOGG, DANIEL M. & Wood, Mary E., Miss m. Nov18, 1862
KELLOGG, JOHN J. & Brooks, Martha m. Sep17, 1863
KELLOGG, LANGDON J. & Large, Sarah F., Miss m. Dec25, 1866
KESTER, JOHN A. & Drake, Sarah, Miss m. Oct22, 1885
KIDD, WILLIAM DAVID, Rev. & Spiers, Anna, Miss m. Jul29, 1897
KILGORE, FELIX G. & Conway, Margaret D., Miss m. Mar18, 1872
KIMSEY, JAMES E. & Campbell, Sarah J. m. Jul30, 1890
KING, HUMPHREY E. & Manley, Julia, Miss m. Jun25, 1862
KING, JOHN & Caton, Fannie A., Miss m. Sep12, 1889
KINGSBURY, WARREN W. & Goering, Etta C., Miss m. May18, 1880
KISE, ELISHA S. & Rule, Elizabeth E., Miss m. Aug18, 1897
KNIGHT, SILAS D. & Passage, M. A., Miss m. Jan24, 1866
KNOWLES, HENRY & Potter, Charlotte E., Miss m. May17, 1862
KNOWLTON, GILES H. & Fisher, Sarah E., Mrs. m. May13, 1868
KOLL, JOHN, Jr. & Joseph, Louise, Miss m. Oct30, 1897
KOON, JOHN ALEXANDER & O'Donnell, Cora m. Jul10, 1895
KRAFT, ELMER P. & Hupp, Mary L., Miss m. Oct18, 1893
KRUTTSCHNITT, AUGUST M. & Lippert, Charlotte Antoine, Miss m. May16, 1860
KUPER, CHARLES & Bentz, Eva, Miss m. Oct10, 1865
LaBAREE, WILLIAM H. & Balch, Emily A., Miss m. Jun19, 1889
LACHENMACHER, FRED & Stierlen, Dorothea (Doris S.), Mrs. m. Mar16, 1867
LAINGOR, GEORGE W. & Allen, Minnie M., Miss m. Oct12, 1884
LANDIS, JAMES S. & Loveridge, Bertha C., Miss m. May13, 1875
LANDVOIGT, GEORGE & Simon, Marie Therese, Mlle. m. Oct26, 1857
LARGE, OSCEOLA & Hughes, Agnes E., Miss m. Dec25, 1890
LARGE, OSCEOLA & Kuffel, Alice L. m. Sep20, 1895
LARGE, ROBERT & Shock, Annie L., Miss m. Dec23, 1886
LARKIN, PATRICK & Grattan, Sarah Agnes m. Sep29, 1877
LARSEN, JOHN & Coyle, Maggie A., Miss m. Aug29, 1877
LAWRENCE, DAVID & Passage, Mary, Miss m. Aug26, 1860
LEARY, EDWARD & Keely, Esther m. Nov01, 1866
LEAS, JOHN & Jones, Elizabeth, Mrs. m. Aug13, 1890
LEAVITT, GEORGE WASHINGTON & Driver, Mary E., Mrs. m. Jun07, 1887
LEAVITT, WILLIAM JOSIAH & Dunlap, Nettie, Miss m. Nov15, 1886
LEHMAN, JACOB & Leach, Emma, Miss m. Jul04, 1860
LENNOX, JOHN A. K. & Blakemore, Mabel m. Feb15, 1899
LEONARD, HENRY W. & Ruch, Sadie E. m. Oct11, 1871
LEONARD, HENRY W. & Ruch, Mary, Miss m. Oct18, 1876
LEONARD, NELSON & White, Kitty m. Dec25, 1877
LEWIS, JOHN VALENTINE & Huskins, Mollie, Miss m. Jun11, 1896
LICHTY, WILLARD JUSTICE & Wood, Ellen B., Miss m. Jan27, 1898
LOOMIS, A. J. & Anderson, Minerva, Miss m. Oct08, 1857
LOOMIS, LEANDER V. & Wetsel, Louisa, Miss m. Jul23, 1863
LORD, GEORGE H. & Lockhart, Julia A., Miss m. Dec31, 1863
LORENZ, FRANK & Cotton, Mary m. Aug28, 1870
LORENZ, HENRY & Leibrandt, Susan, Miss m. Apr13, 1861
LORENZ, HENRY, Jr. & Wilson, Ida Belle, Miss m. Nov09, 1892
LORENZ, WILLIAM D. & Fetzer, Josephine W. m. Jun18, 1898
LOVE, FRANCIS MERRIAM & Gates, Agnes Snow m. Jun25, 1900
LOVEJOY, EDWARD PAYSON & Holland, Julia C., Miss m. Oct30, 1869
LOVERIDGE, MERWIN W. & Fox, Flora, Miss m. Jul18, 1883
LOWDEN, FRANK WILLIAM & DeLong, Minnie, Miss m. Oct24, 1887
LOWDEN, HENRY L. & Brady, Amanda M., Miss m. Jan24, 1883
LOWDEN, MARSHALL H. & Glasgow, Matilda Isabelle m. Feb10, 1875
LOWDEN, OWEN EUGENE & Downing, Lucy L., Mrs. m. Jan01, 1867
LOWDEN, WILLIAM JEFFERSON & Ryan, Anna M., Miss m. Jun06, 1887
LOWERY, GEORGE & Trebelcock, Katie, Miss m. Jun07, 1877
LULO, WILLIAM & Miller, Mary m. Dec13, 1864
LYON, WILLIAM L. & Dunlap, Mary, Miss m. Jan22, 1877
MABIE, FRANK & Clement, Emma, Miss m. Sep27, 1874
Mc - names beginning with this prefix are alphabetized as if spelled MAC.
McBROM, JOHN N. & Abrams, Annie A. m. Sep21, 1881
McCAMPBELL, ROBERT & Stafford, Elizabeth B., Miss m. Oct15, 1885

McCLARY, DAVID R. & Parry, Emma J., Miss m. Oct13, 1878
McCULLY, ALBURN C. & Millsap, Georgia, Miss m. Sep07, 1899
McDONALD, BERNARD & Cochran, Mary Ellen, Miss m. Jan06, 1887
McDONALD, JAMES DOUGLAS & McWhorter, Pauline m. Nov16, 1887
McGILLIVRAY, JOSEPH & Pottinger, Barbara, Mrs. m. May30, 1857
McGINNIS, JOHN B. & Carroll, Eliza, Mrs. m. Jul16, 1863
McGOVERN, JOHN J. & Gilzean, Anna E., Miss m. May09, 1900
McGRATH, PHILLIP & Rourke, Katy, Miss m. Jan11, 1863
McKAY, JOHN & Bussell, Diana W., Miss m. Jul08, 1889
McKINNEY, JOSEPH & -----, Mary, Miss (Indian) m. Dec13, 1864
McMAHAN, JOSEPH & Hoxey, Ann, Miss m. Dec01, 1860
McNAMARA, THOMAS J. & Brannan, Alice, Miss m. Jun08, 1879
McWHORTER, ADAM L. & Konzan, Barbara, Miss m. May24, 1868
MAHER, NICHOLAS & Brady, Mary, Miss m. Sep18, 1859
MAHONEY, WARREN A. & Wallace, Orie M., Miss m. Nov19, 1884
MALONEY, THOMAS & Caswell, Fannie E. m. Jul06, 1885
MALONEY, WILLIAM & O'Keefe, Mary Ann, Miss m. Apr25, 1856
MANSFIELD, ABRAHAM & Wolff, Anna C., Miss m. Jul27, 1889
MARINGER, FRANK & Barker, Louisa L. m. Jul01, 1895
MARKWELL, PARIS TRACY & Burger, Marguerite, Miss m. Dec23, 1896
MARSHALL, AMOS H. & Allen, Emma R., Mrs. m. Aug31, 1870
MARSHALL, ROBERT C. & Gilzean, Isabelle Maude, Miss m. Jan06, 1898
MARTIN, CHARLES E. & Iverson, Astha M. m. Sep28, 1897
MARTIN, FRANCIS & Coelha, Flomena m. Jun01, 1868
MARTIN, FRANK & Rabbitt, Margaret, Miss m. Jun01, 1868
MARTIN, GEORGE A. & Young, Antoinette W., Miss m. Oct25, 1892
MARTIN, LORENZO & Thanwald, Annie, Miss m. Sep13, 1892
MARTIN, RICHARD & Tolley, Mary E., Miss m. Nov15, 1865
MARTIN, ROBERT B. & Davis, Walty, (Indian) m. Dec22, 1864
MASON, JOHN C. & Harvey, Avilla A., Miss m. May21, 1871
MATHEWS, JAMES ALONZO & Duncan, Julia Ann, Miss m. Dec03, 1876
MATHEWS, JOHN D. & Kester, Susan, Miss m. Oct21, 1860
MAYNARD, CHARLES & _____, Adeline (Indian) m. Mar30, 1865
MEAD, CORYDON C. & Jewett, Caroline V. m. Oct13, 1874
MENDOCE, MANUEL & Fleece, Mary m. Jun13, 1864
MENDOZA, INNOCENTA JOSE & Jesus, Philomina L. m. Jun29, 1878
MESSNER, HENRY & Stoddard, Fanny Fredrica, Miss m. Aug11, 1900
MEYER, CHARLES AUGUSTUS & Flagg, Gertrude Mary, Miss m. Jun20, 1894
MEYERS, GEORGE & Kelly, Eliza, Miss m. Jan23, 1860
MIDDLETON, THOMAS & Mosier, Almidier, Mrs. m. Nov08, 1868
MILLER, GEORGE & Wood, Mary, (Indian) m. Oct24, 1872
MILLER, WILLIAM D. & Trimble, Jennie, Miss m. Feb13, 1889
MILLS, GEORGE & Millsap, Jessie, Miss m. Apr21, 1898
MINEAR, JOHN & Ryan, Maggie, Miss m. Sep11, 1888
MINER, JORDAN E. & Sprague, Cora, Mrs. m. Jan11, 1899
MONTAGUE, JOSEPH C., Dr. & Enright, Mary E., Miss m. Sep18, 1868
MONTGOMERY, THOMAS J. & Carter, Mary Elizabeth m. Oct26, 1892
MONTGOMERY, WILLIAM T.S. & m. Nichols, Matilda A., Miss m. Nov18, 1899
MOORE, FLORANCE A. & Carter, Edith A., Miss m. Feb16, 1888
MOORE, JOHN EDGAR & Burner, Loda A. m. Nov20, 1900
MOORE, LOUIS & Harvey, Lillian, Miss m. Dec21, 1892
MOREY, SIMON B. & Ruch, Margaret J., Miss m. May13, 1861
MORRIS, JAMES & Colbert, Mary A., Miss m. May22, 1866
MORRIS, JAMES J. & Lang, Catherine, Miss m. Aug10, 1863
MORRIS, JOHN JAMES & Stafford, Victoria S., Miss m. Jun19, 1895
MORTIMER, WASHINGTON & Dannenbrink, Johanna M., Miss m. May27, 1897
MORTON, JOHN & Jones, Nancy Jane, Miss m. Oct11, 1870
MORTON, OMAR & Bronk, Jane E. m. Nov29, 1857
MOSER, HENRY & Edgar, Lissie m. Jan05, 1891
MOSS, AMOS S. & Senger, Alice, Miss m. Dec23, 1879
MOTHERWELL, JOHN VIVIAN & Harvey, Mary E., Mrs. m. Dec21, 1886
MOTHERWELL, THOMAS & Adin, Eliza, Miss m. Aug21, 1856
MULLANE, JAMES & Keely, Lucy, Miss m. Nov08, 1870

MARRIAGES 1850 - 1900

MULLIGAN, MICHAEL & O'Connell, Ellen m. Sep06, 1876
MURCHADO, MANUEL FRATUS & Amelia, Mary m. Aug20, 1874
MURPHY, JOHN J. & Bergin, Elizabeth M., Miss m. Oct30, 1895
MURRAY, JOHN ENSLEY & Carter, Jennie, Miss m. Dec06, 1886
MURRAY, MARTIN W. & Griffin, Sarah E., Mrs. m. Oct20, 1888
MURRY, PATRICK & Cunningham, Mary m. Jan27, 1858
MYERS, HOSEA E. & Hamilton, Martha A. m. Mar25, 1888
MYERS, MILFORD B. & Young, Kate, Miss m. Dec22, 1864
MYERS, MILFORD B. & Gribble, Elizabeth, Miss m. Nov23, 1870
NEATHERY, THEOPHILUS & Rineman, Susan, Mrs. m. Jun21, 1859
NEILSON, JAMES & Thayer, Mary I., Miss m. Jan15, 1894
NEUSSE, CHARLES & Brey, Sophia m. Jun14, 1874
NEWMAN, EDWARD & Morris, Lizzie, Miss m. Feb03, 1887
NEWMAN, LOUIS HENRY FREELAND & Ehrmann, Kate, Miss m. Jul03, 1884
NICHOLS, WILLIAM HENRY & Dawson, Julia, Miss m. Dec13, 1864
NICKELS, HARRY L. & Yule, Adelia Helen m. May31, 1882
NIEVELLES, CHARLES & O'Connell, Ann m. Dec15, 1857
NOBLE, CHARLES TYLER & Mosier, Maria m. Jan18, 1881
NOBLE, STEPHEN & Dyer, Sally, (Indian) m. Aug21, 1871
NOBLE, WILLIAM & Thomas, Annie, Miss m. Oct04, 1885
NOONAN, GEORGE E. & Shurtleff, Elizabeth C., Miss m. May26, 1877
NORDYKE, BENJAMIN JAMES & Hughes, Sarah May, Miss m. Jul03, 1888
NORGAAR, CHRIS & Frank, Annie, Miss m. Mar10, 1892
NORMAN, WARREN & Pelletreau, Josephine, Miss m. Mar20, 1886
NUNNALLY, WILLIAM A. & Mesa, Ramona, Miss m. Dec13, 1861
O'LEARY, RICHARD & Long, Mary D., Miss m. Aug04, 1867
O'SHAY, GERALD & Hall, Mary H., Mrs. m. Jan03, 1889
OLSEN, EMIL M. & Sharer, Anna, Miss m. Apr15, 1900
OLSEN, JAMES PETER & Lee, Rosa, (Indian) m. Dec22, 1864
OLSEN, JAMES PETER & Adams, Mary Jane, Miss m. Sep10, 1874
OLSEN, JOHN J. & Hardy, Mary J. m. Jun14, 1899
OSGOOD, DANIEL FULLER & Brown, Emma, Miss m. Jul15, 1868
OSGOOD, MORRIS F. & Barnes, Lizzie A., Miss m. Dec25, 1887
OSGOOD, ULYSSES GRANT & Warren, Alice, Miss m. Oct13, 1900
OSTHOFF, HENRY & Schneider, Elizabeth, Miss m. Jul09, 1866
OVERMOHLE, HENRY & McLean, Annie J., Miss m. Aug24, 1865
OWINGS, G. W. C. & Allison, Minnie E., Miss m. Dec09, 1880
PACHECO, FRANK I. & Caton, Annie, Miss m. Oct09, 1892
PARTRIDGE, FERD L. & Day, Mary E., Miss m. Jun30, 1892
PATTISON, THOMAS C. & McKay, Mary, Miss m. Oct08, 1900
PATTISON, WILLIAM A. & McCollum, Sally, (Indian) m. Dec22, 1864
PAULIUS, FRANK & Enos, Mary m. Jul18, 1880
PAULSEN, PETER M. & Kruttschnitt, Anna B., Miss m. Feb13, 1863
PEACOCK, JOHN R. & Childers, Medora Ann, Mrs. m. Dec22, 1862
PELLETREAU, ALEX & Chuff, Ellen Louisa, Miss m. Jan04, 1858
PENNEY, RALPH EDWARD & Judd, Nellie May, Miss m. Nov15, 1895
PERHAM, HIRAM M. & Seabury, Harriet A., Mrs. m. Jun16, 1870
PETERSON, ERIC & Murray, Nellie, Miss m. Apr13, 1879
PETTYJOHN, CHRISTOPHER C. & Philbrick, R. D., Miss m. Jul26, 1863
PHILLIPS, JAMES WALTER & Phillips, Ella M. m. Nov21, 1894
PHILLIPS, OLNEY & Spaulding, Annie, Miss m. Jul04, 1858
PHILPOT, MOSES & Maynard, Rosa m. Aug24, 1890
PICKETT, JAMES M. & Lynch, Maria, Miss m. Jun17, 1868
PIEPER, CHARLES H. & Blakemore, Minnie E., Miss m. Jun03, 1891
PORTILLO, FRANK (`Porteal') & Asceleido, Monica m. Jul17, 1871
POST, JOHN S. & Ham, Fannie (Voshay), Mrs. m. Dec09, 1878
POTTER, HENRY L. & Romeras, Monica m. Apr15, 1856
POWERS, JOHN H. & Murphy, Margaret, Miss m. Oct11, 1858
PRESTON, SAMUEL H. & Bumgerten, Eliza m. Aug20, 1858
PRUETT, ALFRED H. & Pruett, Susannah, Miss (Indian) m. Dec13, 1864
QUEEN, HENRY LEWIS & Douglas, Emma Florence, Miss m. Feb28, 1897
QUIMBY, CYRUS W. & Baker, Julia, (Indian) m. Nov21, 1868
RAGLIN, LLOID & Owings, Ella, Miss m. Oct03, 1892

RALPH, JOHN & Dickerson, Luella, Miss m. Jun29, 1872
RAPPERTY, JAMES & Feeny, Caroline m. May09, 1861
REARDON, EUGENE & Mahoney, Margaret, Miss m. Dec03, 1861
REAS, P. W. & Besswick, Ann m. Sep06, 1855
REED, EDGAR L. & Whitmore, Tillie M., Miss m. Nov11, 1880
REID, DANIEL GARRARD & Allen, Lizzie Mary, Miss m. May19, 1887
REID, LATEN P. & Bennett, Ida C., Miss m. Sep05, 1900
ROACH, JOHN A. & Hall, Nettie J., Mrs m. Feb19, 1884
ROBINSON, DAVID S. & Allen, Phoebe E. A., Miss m. Jul20, 1879
ROBINSON, GEORGE W. & Gates, Alvina, Mrs. m. Jul07, 1868
ROBINSON, J. H. & Dallas, Susan, Miss m. Nov22, 1856
ROBINSON, THOMAS EDWARD & Blackwell, Sarah Ann, Miss m. May21, 1885
ROSS, ANDREW J. & Hampton, Eugenia m. Nov21, 1863
ROURKE, DENNIS & O'Connell, Mary, Miss m. Jan16, 1879
RUCH, WILLIAM H. & Vaughn, Lavina, (`Laverna') m. Dec20, 1874
RULE, SILAS & Brady, Anna, Mrs. m. Feb10, 1873
RUMFELT, AUGUSTUS & Rieves, Josephine, Miss m. Aug03, 1873
RUTLEDGE, ARTHUR ELMER & Davis, Maggie A., Miss m. Nov26, 1893
RYAN, D. EDWARD & Weinheimer, Annie L., Miss m. Jan10, 1900
RYAN, PATRICK JOSEPH & Wolff, Katie, Miss m. May21, 1893
RYAN, RICHARD FRANKLIN & Wolff, Mary m. Mar31, 1894
SAFFELL, JOSEPH EDWARD & Campbell, Ida Grazilla m. Dec18, 1900
SAMMONS, JOHN B. & Pouleur, Mary m. Sep20, 1865
SANBURN, JOHN G. & Hupp, Louisa m. Feb20, 1873
SAWYER, HOMER W. & Holden, Rhoda R., Miss m. May19, 1859
SAWYER, JOHN & Senger, Josephine m. Sep19, 1880
SCHALL, LOUIS & Gaum, Madeline, Mrs. m. Jul31, 1870
SCHIAVO, VENANZIO & Stringa, Pia m. Oct15, 1892
SCHNEIDER, HENRICH & Bocher, Catronia, Miss m. Apr21, 1864
SCHNELLBACHER, BRAXTON B. & Hammong, Letha L., Miss m. May18, 1900
SCOFIELD, TRACY & Abbey, Martha E. m. Jan16, 1862
SCOTT, JASPER & Koelle, Annie, Miss m. Nov21, 1881
SENTENEY, J. Y. & Keller, Louise m. Nov16, 1873
SENTER, THOMAS C. & Whiting, Mary E., Mrs. m. Jun28, 1894
SHANKS, JACOB & Leach, A. Delphine m. Jul04, 1861
SHERIDAN, JOHN & Newman, Mary, Mrs. m. Aug09, 1869
SHOCK, GEORGE HENRY & Duncan, Louisa, Miss m. Nov14, 1887
SHOCK, JOHN P. & Hoyt, Sadie, Miss m. Apr30, 1894
SHOCK, WILLIAM THOMAS & Knowles, Hiza May m. Jun30, 1894
SHOCK, ZINA L. & Enos, Julia, Miss m. Jun01, 1893
SHOLES, THEODORE FREDERICK & Garvin, Maggie Z. m. Apr04, 1893
SHORT, FRANCIS M. & Martin, Ellen, Miss m. Nov03, 1878
SHUFORD, JOHN W. & Olsen, Louisa Isabel m. Dec01, 1886
SHURTLEFF, NATHANIEL BENJAMIN & Paulsen, Minnie Sophia, Miss m. Nov12, 1887
SILVA, ANTONE JOSEPH & Bargas, Josephine, Miss m. Nov18, 1883
SILVA, MANUEL JOSEPH & Enos, Maria m. Jul31, 1871
SILVER, MANUEL & DeJesus, Maria, Miss m. Nov08, 1868
SILVERA, FRANK & Louise, Marie m. Dec18, 1870
SILVEY, EDMUND & Drown, Carrie, Miss m. Dec31, 1877
SIMPSON, WILLIAM JOSEPH & Stoddard, Clara Jane m. Oct08, 1896
SINCLAIR, JAMES & Eastman, Mary J. m. May03, 1864
SKINNER, ROBERT ALEXANDER & Olsen, Minnie, Miss m. Jan25, 1891
SLATTERY, JOHN & Murray, Mary, Mrs. m. Jul03, 1870
SLOAN, CHARLES & O'Connor, Ellen, Miss m. Nov03, 1858
SMITH, ABIAL W. & Sears, Alma m. Dec27, 1874
SMITH, BISHOP TILDEN & Smith, Lucelia (Butts) m. Aug23, 1894
SMITH, CHAMPION W. & Norcross, Nellie Z., Miss m. Oct10, 1867
SMITH, DANIEL L. & Maloney, Margaret, Miss m. Aug28, 1881
SMITH, DANIEL L. & Tompkins, Laura Louisa m. Mar25, 1893
SMITH, JOHN F. & -----, Mary, Miss (Indian) m. Dec13, 1864
SMITH, JOHN H. & Eastman, Lucy m. Jul10, 1861
SMITH, JOSEPH & Candia, Maria, Miss m. Sep09, 1866
SMITH, JOSEPH WILLIAM & Lorenz, Christina, Miss m. Dec29, 1885

SMITH, SYDNEY & Roach, Mary Ann, Miss m. Aug01, 1868
SOHM, JOHN G. & Schneider, Josepha m. Jan08, 1883
SPEARS, WILLIAM & Sullivan, Clara, Mrs. m. Feb22, 1900
SPOTTS, SAMUEL C. & O'Connell, Elizabeth m. May13, 1897
SPRATT, CHARLES WILLIAM & Thayer, Sadie Abbie, Miss m. Jun21, 1887
SQUIRES, HECTOR T. & Lowe, Mary Ann, Miss m. Jan19, 1869
STACKPOLE, FRANK LESLIE & Jordan, Lydia Grace m. Feb14, 1893
STAFFORD, JAMES A. & Large, Amanda C., Miss m. Jul12, 1866
STEELE, SEYMOUR G., Capt. & Harvey, Mary A., Miss m. Jul10, 1870
STIERLEN, FRITZ & Graffelman, Dorothy, Mrs. m. Mar31, 1863
STILLER, RICHARD W. & Montague, Mary F., Miss m. Jan09, 1889
STINE, WILLIAM HENRY & Lutman, Alice, Miss m. Nov29, 1869
STODDARD, JOHN R. & Tourtelotte, Inez F., Miss m. Jul03, 1873
STOFFER, FRANKLIN B. & Kelley, Martha E., Miss m. Oct14, 1866
STOFFER, WILLIAM H. & Schmitt, DeSoia Mary m. Aug18, 1859
STRAUSS, E. L. & Wilham, Mary T., Mrs. m. Feb19, 1867
SULLIVAN, PETER J. & Jordan, Ida B., Miss m. Apr26, 1898
SWAIN, FRANK R. & Hupp, Georgia, Miss m. Apr17, 1895
SWEET, DAVID WARREN & Testy, Mary E., Miss m. Jan31, 1886
TAPIE, EUGENE A. & Bassham, Gertrude A., Miss m. May05, 1888
TARPLEY, HARVEY J. & Kell, Mahala A., Miss m. Oct22, 1865
TAYLOR, ARTHUR JOHNSON & Todd, Nettie, Miss m. May05, 1889
TAYLOR, CHARLES W. & Ashworth, Elizabeth, Miss m. Sep02, 1859
TAYLOR, DAVID & Sheehan, Mary H., Miss m. Aug23, 1866
TESTY, JOSEPH & Jenkins, Sarah, Miss m. Feb20, 1861
TESTY, WILLIAM BERNARD & Jackson, Alice, Miss m. Nov06, 1895
THAYER, STEPHEN I. & Harvey, Sarah E., Miss m. Apr22, 1866
THEDE, GUSTAVE & Weckman, Catherine, Miss m. Mar28, 1863
THOMAS, ROBERT L. & Baker, Betsy (Indian) m. Aug24, 1867
THOMAS, ROBERT L., Jr. & Noble, Annie m. Apr14, 1884
THOMPSON, HERMAN & Hanna, Essie, Miss m. Sep30, 1886
THOMPSON, RANKIN & Blake, Mary S., Mrs. m. Sep22, 1861
THOMPSON, THOMAS S. & Verstegen, Sophie, Miss m. Mar17, 1881
THORPE, ABRAHAM (`Tharp') & Allen, Emma E. R., Miss m. Oct26, 1871
TIBBALS, WILLIAM & Dodge, Anna M., Miss m. Sep23, 1879
TIMMERMAN, LOUIS & Goering, Amelia, Miss m. Jun27, 1857
TINNEN, WILEY J. & Lowden, Irene, Miss m. Aug19, 1861
TINSLEY, GEORGE WASHINGTON & Allen, Nellie May, Miss m. May19, 1887
TINSLEY, JOHN T. & Williams, Pauline, Miss m. Oct09, 1898
TITUS, D. M. & McAllison, Elizabeth m. Jun13, 1861
TODD, EDWARD N. & Harvey, Dora J., Miss m. May31, 1893
TODD, LOUIS OWEN & Benton, Mary, Mrs. m. Jul19, 1891
TODD, WILLIAM D. & Tinsley, Mary L., Miss m. May17, 1893
TOEDT, GEORGE & Miles, May, Mrs. m. Nov19, 1896
TOMPKINS, JOHN EDWARD & Ross, Eliza, Mrs. m. Oct14, 1889
TOURTELOTTE, JOHN B. & Lowes, Eliza M., Miss m. Aug27, 1868
TOWER, FRANK B. & Hanna, Ellen, Miss m. Mar01, 1892
TRASK, BENJAMIN F. & Hood, Sarah L., Miss m. Dec17, 1862
TRASK, GEORGE N. & Knowles, Mary E., Miss m. Dec27, 1892
TRASK, MADISON N. & Baker, Minnie V., Miss m. Dec16, 1871
TRELOAR, EDWARD W. & Flagg, Jennie Alice, Miss m. Oct11, 1899
TRIMBLE, BRICE ALEXANDER & Jordan, Mertie C., Miss m. Jan02, 1892
TRIMBLE, PIERCE & Adams, Rebecca E., Miss m. Nov17, 1872
TRIMMER, WILLIAM WILEY & Christopher, Nellie May, Miss m. Feb24, 1889
TRIPP, SAMUEL V. & Ramsey, Rose A., Miss m. Apr02, 1854
TRUBY, WILLIAM J. & Rodgers Duarte, MARY F. m. Jun20, 1898
TRUE, THOMAS & Westfall, Mary Jane m. Feb18, 1862
TRUMBACH, PAUL & -----, Anna (Indian) m. Mar23, 1865
TUDOR, HUMPHREY & Vanderford, Nettie, Miss m. Dec07, 1898
TWAMBLEY, CHARLES W. & Loots, Hattie A., Miss m. May15, 1865
TWINE, ELIAS & Williams, Clara, Miss m. Aug26, 1871
UNKICH, PHILLIP & Klein, Elizabeth, Mrs. m. Apr08, 1862
VALENTINE, WILLIAM S. & Shropshire, Gena m. Apr18, 1898

VAN CLEAVE, JOHN WILLIAM WARD & Ralph, Luella, Mrs. m. Jul02, 1900
VAN CLEAVE, JOSEPH & Blagrave, Laura C. m. Jul04, 1882
VAN MATRE, ADRIEN JUDSON & Kellogg, Alice S., Miss m. Nov16, 1886
VAN MATRE, JOHN C. & Dennison, Bertha, Mrs. m. Feb06, 1891
VANDERHOFF, JOHN H. & Young, Stella W., Miss m. May29, 1883
VAUGHN, WILLIAM DAVID & Knowles, Emmeline L., Miss m. Dec17, 1885
VAUGHN, WILLIS & Greenleaf, Maria m. Jul13, 1879
VINCENT, JAMES & Doxie, Martha A., Miss m. May04, 1862
VINCENT, JAMES & Doxie, Louisa C. m. Nov23, 1864
VITZTHUM, GEORGE & Meier, Theresa, Miss m. Jul27, 1862
VOELKER, PHILIP & Barbra, Anna, Miss m. Jul25, 1858
VOGEL, ERNEST & Dettinger, Therese, Miss m. Jun28, 1860
VOLLMERS, MICHAEL & Rohug, Katherine, Miss m. May19, 1863
VOLLMERS, WILLIAM & Allison, Lucy J., Miss m. Mar27, 1881
WALDORFF, ERNEST A. & Pattison, Josephine, Miss m. Jul03, 1889
WALDORFF, WILLIAM H. & Trimble, Ada Elizabeth, Miss m. Nov13, 1876
WALKER, GEORGE W. & Thomas, Elizabeth, Miss m. May27, 1878
WALLACE, JAMES ADDISON & Woodbury, Nellie Louise, Miss m. Jan01, 1894
WALLACE, ROBERT F., Dr. & Harvey, Ada, Miss m. May26, 1897
WALLACE, THOMAS & O'Connell, Ellen, Miss m. Oct05, 1873
WALTERS, HENRY AUGUSTUS & Smith, Esther, Miss m. Dec31, 1890
WARREN, CHARLES & Benton, Barbara G. m. Oct19, 1898
WATKINS, CHARLES & Meyers, Sarah A. m. May13, 1861
WATSON, JOHN A. & Seaman, Anne E., Miss m. Dec06, 1858
WEAVER, WILLIAM J. & Weaver, Mary, Mrs. (Indian) m. Dec13, 1864
WEBSTER, GEORGE & Richards, Edythe, Miss m. Oct05, 1896
WECKERT, JACOB & Bentz, Eliza, Miss m. Oct25, 1860
WEEKS, EDWARD E. & Dix, Carrie O., Miss m. Aug31, 1898
WEINHEIMER, HENRY & Dockery, Catherine, Miss m. Jan12, 1869
WELLS, JAMES B. & Tolley, Elizabeth H., Miss m. Nov20, 1861
WELLS, LUKE F. & Childers, (`Childres'), Medora A. m. Nov01, 1864
WEYAND, ZACHARY TAYLOR & Senger, Amelia, Miss m. Oct12, 1887
WHEELER, FRANK WILLIAM & Wheeler, Clara Jewett, Miss m. Apr08, 1894
WHITE, CHARLES W. & Bergin, Hannah, Miss m. Apr11, 1880
WHITEBREAD, ADOLPH & Roach, Ann, Mrs. m. Sep25, 1887
WHITMORE, JEREMIAH & Peoples, Mary Ann m. May14, 1857
WHITMORE, JOHN & Ryan, Kate T., Miss m. Jan27, 1888
WILLBURN, HIRAM D. & Pozey, Nancy J. m. Sep18, 1889
WILLBURN, JAMES S. & Wathen, Julia L. m. Jan24, 1881
WILLBURN, SIDNEY & Duncan, Georgia Ann, Miss m. Jun16, 1891
WILLBURN, WILLIAM J. & Shener, Mary A. m. Jul27, 1874
WILLIAMS, CHARLES & Pratt, Clara, Mrs. m. Sep08, 1876
WILLIAMS, GEORGE & Turner, Emma, Mrs. m. Oct21, 1868
WILLIAMS, JOHN & Rodgers, Mamie, Miss m. Sep13, 1899
WILLIAMS, JOSEPH WALTER & Guthrie, Capitola E., Miss m. Mar04, 1895
WILSON, EDGAR EVERETT & Lowden, Macie Irene, Miss m. Nov20, 1895
WILSON, THOMAS MARION & Wilson, Agnes Rogene, Miss m. Sep28, 1899
WILSON, V. V. & Motherwell, Eliza, Mrs. m. Sep01, 1862
WINKEL, AUGUST & Mullen, Bridget, Mrs. m. Aug08, 1864
WINSLETT, JOHN W. & Cunningham, Louisa M. m. Aug16, 1861
WISER, HUBERT A. & Rider, Sarah, Miss m. Apr23, 1865
WOOD, FRANK ALBERT & Haskins, Alena A. m. Dec01, 1895
WOOD, JOHN F. & Prichett, Catherine, Miss (Indian) m. May10, 1869
WOODBURY, DAVID & Dorsey, Elizabeth, Miss m. Oct26, 1871
WOODBURY, ISAAC & Dorsey, Mary Louise, Miss m. Sep23, 1865
WOODS, JERRY D. & Savio, Ada, Miss m. Oct28, 1862
WOODS, LEWIS BALDWIN & Segalia, Martha Jane, Miss m. Jun29, 1887
YOHE, GEORGE & Richards, Elizabeth m. Oct31, 1854
YOUNG, FRANK W. & Bayles, Mary E. m. Nov21, 1861
YOUNG, HENRY D. & Davis, Phoebe, Miss m. Sep30, 1859
YOUNG, WILLIAM WARE & Wallace, Emma C., Miss m. Oct13, 1898
ZAVIER, ROLLIN JOSEPH & Jesus, Pulsana m. Apr13, 1863
ZEIGLER, CYRUS W. & Corning, Mabel R. m. Sep29, 1896

ZEIGLER, ELIJAH & Coman, Cara, Miss m. Jan01, 1870
ZEIGLER, ISIAAH & Kidd, Patty, Miss m. Sep07, 1872
ZEIGLER, ISIAAH & Quimby, Jeanette m. Jun13, 1877

PIONEER RECORDS OF TRINITY COUNTY, CALIFORNIA

INDEX TO HANOVER, RITA M., TRINITY COUNTY MARRIAGES 1850-1900

MARRIAGES OF WOMEN

WIFE, HUSBAND, and MARRIAGE DATE

_____, ADELINE (Indian) & Maynard, Charles m. Mar30, 1865
_____, ANNA (Indian) & Trumbach, Paul m. Mar23, 1865
_____, JANE (Indian) & Barker, David E. V. m. Apr20, 1865
_____, JULIA (Indian) & Butts, Joshua m. Jan03, 1865
_____, MARTHA (Indian) & Hunter, Charles Decatur m. Jan03, 1865
_____, MARY, Miss (Indian) & McKINNEY, JOSEPH m. Dec13, 1864
_____, MARY, Miss (Indian) & SMITH, JOHN F. m. Dec13, 1864
_____, MARY JANE, (Indian) & Abbott, Benjamin F. m. Mar11, 1865
ABBEY, MARTHA E. & Scofield, Tracy m. Jan16, 1862
ABRAMS, ANNIE A. & McBrom, John N. m. Sep21, 1881
ADAMS, MARY JANE, Miss & Olsen, James Peter m. Sep10, 1874
ADAMS, REBECCA E., Miss & Trimble, Pierce m. Nov17, 1872
ADIN, ELIZA, Miss & Motherwell, Thomas m. Aug21, 1856
AKERS, NANCY JANE & Davis, Allen m. Sep03, 1860
ALLEN, EMMA E. R., Miss & Thorpe, Abraham (`Tharp') m. Oct26, 1871
ALLEN, EMMA R., Mrs. & Marshall, Amos H. m. Aug31, 1870
ALLEN, LIZZIE MARY, Miss & Reid, Daniel Garrard m. May19, 1887
ALLEN, MARY ANN, Miss & Gibson, Robert K. m. Nov28, 1878
ALLEN, MINNIE M., Miss & Laingor, George W. m. Oct12, 1884
ALLEN, NELLIE MAY, Miss & Tinsley, George Washington m. May19, 1887
ALLEN, PHOEBE B., Miss & Everest, Harvey W. m. Jun20, 1861
ALLEN, PHOEBE E. A., Miss & Robinson, David S. m. Jul20, 1879
ALLISON, LUCY J., Miss & Vollmers, William m. Mar27, 1881
ALLISON, MINNIE E., Miss & Owomgs, G. W. C. m. Dec09, 1880
AMELIA, MARY & Murchado, Manuel Fratus m. Aug20, 1874
ANDERSON, MINERVA, Miss & Loomis, A. J. m. Oct08, 1857
_____, ANNA (Indian) & Trumbach, Paul m. Mar23, 1865
ARGUELLO, LILLIE, Miss & Armstrong, William H. m. Sep13, 1893
ASCELEIDO, MONICA & Portillo, Frank (`Porteal') m. Jul17, 1871
ASHWORTH, ELIZABETH, Miss & Taylor, Charles W. m. Sep02, 1859
ATKINS, LULU L., Miss & Caton, John m. Sep04, 1900
ATKINSON, MARGARET, Miss & Burke, Harry m. Jul19, 1861
BAKER, BETSY (Indian) & Thomas, Robert L. m. Aug24, 1867
BAKER, ISABELLA E., Miss & Dack, Elisha R. m. Sep06, 1874
BAKER, JULIA, (Indian) & Quimby, Cyrus W. m. Nov21, 1868
BAKER, MINNIE V., Miss & Trask, Madison N. m. Dec16, 1871
BALCH, EMILY A., Miss & LaBaree, William H. m. Jun19, 1889
BARBRA, ANNA, Miss & Voelker, Philip m. Jul25, 1858
BARGAS, JOSEPHINE, Miss & Silva, Antone Joseph m. Nov18, 1883
BARKER, LOUISA L. & Maringer, Frank m. Jul01, 1895
BARKLA, LUELLA, Miss & Fry, James S. m. Sep08, 1900
BARKLA, VIRGINIA BELLE & Clement, Charles E. m. Dec09, 1896
BARNES, LIZZIE A., Miss & Osgood, Morris F. m. Dec25, 1887
BARNES, MARY A., Mrs. & Jones, Theodore E. m. Apr04, 1877
BASSHAM, ANNIE, Miss & Freethy, Richard E. m. Dec17, 1883
BASSHAM, FLORENCE L., Miss & Hall, George W. m. Apr14, 1895
BASSHAM, GERTRUDE A., Miss & Tapie, Eugene A. m. May05, 1888
BATES, MARY JANE, Miss & Bates, John G. m. Feb14, 1861
BATES, SUSAN, Miss & Goewey, James M. m. Apr09, 1863
BAYER, MARY ANN & Bean, Hiram P. m. Feb07, 1853
BAYLES, MARY E. & Young, Frank W. m. Nov21, 1861
BEALS, ELIZABETH, Miss & Cox, Thomas C. m. Dec22, 1864
BEAN, ADDIE A. & Jewett, Preston A. m. Jan13, 1884
BEARDEN, HATTIE(HARRIET) V., Mrs. & Baker, Willis Eugene m. May27, 1888
BELLIG, KATHRINA, Miss & Ehrmann, Henry m. Jun27, 1863
BENNETT, IDA C., Miss & Reid, Laten P. m. Sep05, 1900

MARRIAGES 1850 - 1900

BENNETT, LAVINA & Comstock, James J. m. Sep04, 1860
BENTON, BARBARA G. & Warren, Charles m. Oct19, 1898
BENTON, MARY I., Miss & Brown, Boyer Ritter m. Apr06, 1899
BENTON, MARY, Mrs. & Todd, Louis Owen m. Jul19, 1891
BENTZ, ELIZA, Miss & Weckert, Jacob m. Oct25, 1860
BENTZ, EVA, Miss & Kuper, Charles m. Oct10, 1865
BERGIN, ELIZABETH M., Miss & Murphy, John J. m. Oct30, 1895
BERGIN, HANNAH, Miss & White, Charles W. m. Apr11, 1880
BESSWICK, ANN & Reas, P. W. m. Sep06, 1855
BLACKWELL, SARAH ANN, Miss & Robinson, Thomas Edward m. May21, 1885
BLAGRAVE, LAURA C. & Van Cleave, Joseph m. Jul04, 1882
BLAGRAVE, VETURA V., Miss & Blakemore, Albert J. M. m. Apr02, 1885
BLAKE, MARY S., Mrs. & Thompson, Rankin m. Sep22, 1861
BLAKEMORE, GOLDIE V., Miss & Eastman, Elbridge G. m. Nov21, 1881
BLAKEMORE, MABEL & Lennox, John A. K. m. Feb15, 1899
BLAKEMORE, MAY M., Miss & Given, Horace Robert m. Apr24, 1897
BLAKEMORE, MINNIE E., Miss & Pieper, Charles H. m. Jun03, 1891
BOCHER, CATRONIA, Miss & Schneider, Henrich m. Apr21, 1864
BOLTON, IDA D. & Harwood, William H. m. Jun25, 1896
BOLTON, NELLIE MAY & Bowerman, Frank L. m. Jul07, 1895
BOWLER, MAGGIE M., Mrs. & Arguello, Jose m. Nov23, 1877
BRADY, AMANDA M., Miss & Lowden, Henry L. m. Jan24, 1883
BRADY, ANNA, Mrs. & Rule, Silas m. Feb10, 1873
BRADY, ELVIRA, Miss & Field, Johnson N. m. Sep11, 1889
BRADY, MARY, Miss & Maher, Nicholas m. Sep18, 1859
BRADY, VINA, Miss & Bartlett, James W. m. Jan08, 1890
BRANNAN, ALICE, Miss & McNamara, Thomas J. m. Jun08, 1879
BRANNAN, CARRIE, Miss & Gage, Lewis C. m. Nov17, 1878
BRANNAN, MARY, Miss & Dix, Henry m. Oct17, 1880
BREEN, HARRIET, Mrs. & Estes, William C. m. Jul18, 1859
BREMER, DORA J., Miss & Carlson, Charles Alfred m. Jul08, 1893
BREY, SOPHIA & Neusse, Charles m. Jun14, 1874
BRONK, JANE E. & Morton, Omar m. Nov29, 1857
BROOKS, MARTHA & Kellogg, John J. m. Sep17, 1863
BROWN, ELIZABETH VIRGINIA & Hollister, Hiram W. m. Jun06, 1861
BROWN, EMMA, Miss & Osgood, Daniel Fuller m. Jul15, 1868
BROWN, LILLIE, Miss & Jordan, Albert m. Sep20, 1889
BUMGERTEN, ELIZA & Preston, Samuel H. m. Aug20, 1858
BURGER, MARGUERITE, Miss & Markwell, Paris Tracy m. Dec23, 1896
BURGESS, ORINDA F., Mrs. & French, Greenleaf C. m. Sep01, 1880
BURNER, LODA A. & Moore, John Edgar m. Nov20, 1900
BURNS, MARGARET & Berkham, John m. Jul02, 1861
BUSSELL, DIANA W., Miss & McKay, John m. Jul08, 1889
BUSSELL, NANCY A. & Hailstone, John Thompson m. Jan21, 1871
BUSSELL, SARAH JANE & Hardy, Robert m. Jul07, 1880
BUTTMAN, MARGARETTE & Branch, Robert Hill m. Jul23, 1895
BUTTS, LOUISA LENA, Miss & Hampton, Harley m. Dec24, 1896
BUYS, ALICE, Miss & Given, James Edgar m. Sep09, 1894
CALDWELL, GERTRUDE L. & Gore, Robert F. m. Apr26, 1897
CAMPBELL, IDA GRAZILLA & Saffell, Joseph Edward m. Dec18, 1900
CAMPBELL, JESSIE & Dart, Dixon m. Dec30, 1896
CAMPBELL, JOSEPHINE, Miss & Gage, J. R. (Ralph) m. Jul30, 1890
CAMPBELL, SARAH J. & Kimsey, James E. m. Jul30, 1890
CAMPBELL, SUSAN, Mrs. & Goodwin, Michael m. May14, 1859
CANDIA, MARIA, Miss & Smith, Joseph m. Sep09, 1866
CARR, FLORENA A., Miss & Clement, William Henry m. Jan18, 1888
CARRETT(or Spangle), Miss & Baker, Thomas m. Sep16, 1857
CARRIGAN, DELIA, Miss & Farrell, Michael m. Nov10, 1857
CARROLL, ELIZA, Mrs. & McGinnis, John B. m. Jul16, 1863
CARTER, EDITH A., Miss & Moore, Florance A. m. Feb16, 1888
CARTER, JENNIE, Miss & Murray, John Ensley m. Dec06, 1886
CARTER, MARY ELIZABETH & Montgomery, Thomas J. m. Oct26, 1892
CASEY, MARGARET, Mrs. & Johnston, James A. m. May09, 1872

CASWELL, FANNIE E. & Maloney, Thomas m. Jul06, 1885
CATON, ANNIE, Miss & Pacheco, Frank I. m. Oct09, 1892
CATON, FANNIE A., Miss & King, John m. Sep12, 1889
CHAPMAN, CAROLINE A., Miss & Given, William Cushman m. Apr22, 1871
CHILDERS, MEDORA ANN, Mrs. & Peacock, John R. m. Dec22, 1862
CHILDERS,(`Childres'),MEDORA A. & Wells, Luke F. m. Nov01, 1864
CHRISTOPHER,NELLIE MAY, Miss & Trimmer, William Wiley m. Feb24, 1889
CHUFF, ELLEN LOUISA, Miss & Pelletreau, Alex m. Jan04, 1858
CLANCIE, EVA & Blair, Hugh Newell m. Nov25, 1897
CLARK, HATTIE, Miss & Bussell, Pindor F. m. Dec22, 1864
CLAYMAN, ANGELINA & Hubbard, Theodore J. m. Oct24, 1860
CLEMENT, EMMA, Miss & Mabie, Frank m. Sep27, 1874
COCHELL, ADALINE W. & Andrews, Julius m. Dec04, 1871
COCHRAN, ANN, Mrs. & Blaney, Hugh m. Dec12, 1878
COCHRAN, MARY ELLEN, Miss & McDonald, Bernard m. Jan06, 1887
COCHRAN, MARY, Miss & Hoslinger, Valentine m. Jan26, 1868
COELHA, FLOMENA & Martin, Francis m. Jun01, 1868
COLBERT, ANNA J., Miss & Hall, Albert G. m. May19, 1880
COLBERT, MAGGIE, Miss & Jumper, George B. m. May30, 1883
COLBERT, MARGARET, Mrs. & Cahalan, Michael m. Oct22, 1865
COLBERT, MARY A., Miss & Morris, James m. May22, 1866
COMAN, CARA, Miss & Zeigler, Elijah m. Jan01, 1870
COMAN, MARIAN, Miss & Dayton, Hiram B. m. Sep24, 1865
CONDON, MARY ELLEN, Miss & Bergin, Thomas Francis m. Oct30, 1889
CONLIN, CATHERINE & Carnes (Karnes), Daniel m. Jun27, 1860
CONNELL, LOUISA & Alexander, John J. m. Jul04, 1864
CONWAY, MARGARET D., Miss & Kilgore, Felix G. m. Mar18, 1872
CORNING, MABEL R. & Zeigler, Cyrus W. m. Sep29, 1896
COTTON, MARY & Lorenz, Frank m. Aug28, 1870
COUMBS, CHARLOTTE T., Miss & Gibson, Stewart M. m. Oct27, 1886
COUMBS, GRACE, Miss & Dockery, Michael Wm. m. Dec23, 1886
COUMBS, JESSIE, Miss & Clement, Albert Curtis m. Feb28, 1893
COUMBS, MARY, Miss & Dockery, John Wm. m. Nov27, 1895
COUSINS, ALMA, Miss & Hughes, John E. m. Feb23, 1899
COWEN, HANNAH, Mrs. & Estes, William C. m. Oct27, 1867
COYLE, KATHERINE, Miss & Holland, Patrick m. Feb20, 1882
COYLE, MAGGIE A., Miss & Larsen, John m. Aug29, 1877
CRABTREE, MARY ELLEN, Miss & Cobb, John Rufus m. May03, 1889
CRAWFORD, BESSIE, Miss & Abrams, Fred Shaw m. Nov15, 1890
CRITTENDEN, BETSY, Mrs. & Eastman, James m. May31, 1856
CRUTHIS, ELLA ROSE & Dickey, John E. m. Oct31, 1894
CUMMINGS, MARY A., Miss & Cademartori, Frank m. Mar30, 1882
CUNNINGHAM, LOUISA M. & Winslett, John W. m. Aug16, 1861
CUNNINGHAM, MARY & Murry, Patrick m. Jan27, 1858
DACK, MACIE J., Miss & Feour, James C. m. Jun11, 1879
DALLAS, SUSAN, Miss & Robinson, J. H. m. Nov22, 1856
DANNENBRINK, JOHANNA M., Miss & Mortimer, Washington m. May27, 1897
DANNENBRINK, LOUISA H. & Brady, Morris A. m. Aug24, 1889
DAVIDSON, DAISY A. M., Miss & Farmer, William Grant m. Jan27, 1897
DAVIS, EVA J., Miss & Hoaglin, Robert m. Apr14, 1890
DAVIS, MAGGIE A., Miss & Rutledge, Arthur Elmer m. Nov26, 1893
DAVIS, PHOEBE, Miss & Young, Henry D. m. Sep30, 1859
DAVIS, WALTY, (Indian) & Martin, Robert B. m. Dec22, 1864
DAVISON, MARY, Miss & Desty, Robert m. May09, 1860
DAWSON, JULIA, Miss & Nichols, William Henry m. Dec13, 1864
DAWSON, MARY J., Miss & Christiansen, Fred m. Sep26, 1880
DAY, ELIZABETH J., Miss & Gwinn, Franklin Sherman m. Nov07, 1857
DAY, MARY E., Miss & Partridge, Ferd L. m. Jun30, 1892
De COUSENCE, MARY JOSEPH & DeValle, Joseph Requardo m. Feb09, 1870
DeJESUS, MARIA, Miss & Silver, Manuel m. Nov08, 1868
DeLONG, MINNIE, Miss & Lowden, Frank William m. Oct24, 1887
DENNISON, BERTHA, Mrs. & Van Matre, John C. m. Feb06, 1891
DESMOND, MARY, Miss & Condon, William m. Nov04, 1862

MARRIAGES 1850 - 1900

DETTINGER, THERESE, Miss & Vogel, Erbest m. Jun28, 1860
DICKERSON, ALICE A., Miss & Hays, Hiram B. m. Jul04, 1874
DICKERSON, LUELLA, Miss & Ralph, John m. Jun29, 1872
DICKEY, MINERVA JANE, Miss & Day, Ulysses Grant m. Dec24, 1891
DICKEY, SARAH M., Miss & Anderlini, Joseph Antone m. May19, 1892
DIGGINS, ELLEN, Miss & Edgar, Sidney m. Jul14, 1890
DIX, CARRIE O., Miss & Weeks, Edward E. m. Aug31, 1898
DOCKERY, CATHERINE, Miss & Weinheimer, Henry m. Jan12, 1869
DOCKERY, JULIA, Miss & Britton, Joseph m. Aug24, 1897
DOCKERY, MARY, Miss & Jose, Edward W. m. Nov29, 1882
DODGE, ANNA M., Miss & Tibbals, William m. Sep23, 1879
DOMENICI, LOUISA & Brown, Fleming E. m. Oct20, 1897
DOOLE, SARAH JANE, Miss & Feeney, Richard Henry m. Aug24, 1875
DORSEY, CATHERINE, Mrs. & Dougherty, James m. Nov26, 1863
DORSEY, ELIZABETH, Miss & Woodbury, David m. Oct26, 1871
DORSEY, MARY LOUISE, Miss & Woodbury, Isaac m. Sep23, 1865
DOUGLAS, EMMA FLORENCE, Miss & Queen, Henry Lewis m. Feb28, 1897
DOWNING, LILLIE, Miss & Eligh, James R. m. May26, 1882
DOWNING, LUCY L., Mrs. & Lowden, Owen Eugene m. Jan01, 1867
DOXIE, LOUISA C. & Vincent, James m. Nov23, 1864
DOXIE, MARTHA A., Miss & Vincent, James m. May04, 1862
DRAKE, SARAH, Miss & Kester, John A. m. Oct22, 1885
DRINKWATER, DORA E., Miss & Carter, Clement A. m. Nov29, 1899
DRIVER, MARY E., Mrs. & Leavitt, George Washington m. Jun07, 1887
DROWN, CARRIE, Miss & Silvey, Edmund m. Dec31, 1877
DUARTE, ANNA V. RODGERS & Hammond, Frank C. m. Oct21, 1899
DUARTE, FLORA RODGERS, Miss & Cardoza, Frank m. May27, 1900
DUNCAN, EMILY J., Miss & Bragdon, Edwin H. m. Nov01, 1891
DUNCAN, GEORGIA ANN, Miss & Willburn, Sidney m. Jun16, 1891
DUNCAN, JULIA ANN, Miss & Mathews, James Alonzo m. Dec03, 1876
DUNCAN, LOUISA, Miss & Shock, George Henry m. Nov14, 1887
DUNCAN, REBECCA, Miss & Carter, John W. m. May14, 1857
DUNLAP, HATTIE & Graves, John Burgess m. Oct13, 1892
DUNLAP, MARY, Miss & Lyon, William L. m. Jan22, 1877
DUNLAP, MILLY M., Miss & Gibson, John E. m. Aug27, 1882
DUNLAP, NETTIE, Miss & Leavitt, William Josiah m. Nov15, 1886
DYER, SALLY, (Indian) & Noble, Stephen m. Aug21, 1871
EASTMAN, LUCY & Smith, John H. m. Jul10, 1861
EASTMAN, MARY J. & Sinclair, James m. May03, 1864
EDGAR, LISSIE & Moser, Henry m. Jan05, 1891
EDWARDS, ELIZABETH B., Mrs. & Belcher, Galitzin m. Aug12, 1860
EHRMANN, KATE, Miss & NEWMAN, Louis Henry Freeland m. Jul03, 1884
EHRMANN, MARY LOUISA, Miss & Anderlini, John Joseph m. Nov10, 1885
EINFALT, MARIA, Miss & Healy, Aleck m. Jul02, 1860
ENOS, FLORA, Miss & Dias, Frank V. m. Jan07, 1888
ENOS, JULIA, Miss & Shock, Zina L. m. Jun01, 1893
ENOS, MARIA & Silva, Manuel Joseph m. Jul31, 1871
ENOS, MARIA J. & Duarte, Francisco m. May06, 1878
ENOS, MARY & Paulius, Frank m. Jul18, 1880
ENRIGHT, MARY E., Miss & Montague, Joseph C., Dr. m. Sep18, 1868
FEENY, CAROLINE & Rapperty, James m. May09, 1861
FETZER, JOSEPHINE W. & Lorenz, William D. m. Jun18, 1898
FETZER, LOUISA, Miss & Dean, Harvey George m. Sep28, 1893
FETZER, MAGDALENA, Miss & Baker, Walter J. m. Oct30, 1884
FISHER, SARAH E., Mrs. & Knowlton, Giles H. m. May13, 1868
FLAGG, GERTRUDE MARY, Miss & Meyer, Charles Augustus m. Jun20, 1894
FLAGG, JENNIE ALICE, Miss & Treloar, Edward W. m. Oct11, 1899
FLAGG, LUCINDA, Miss & Cunningham, Morris m. May04, 1887
FLEECE, MARY & Mendoce, Manuel m. Jun13, 1864
FLEMING, MARY, Miss & Duncan, Leonidas P. m. Sep29, 1874
FLOWERS, MARY E., Miss & Grant, William E. m. Oct11, 1888
FOX, FLORA, Miss & Loveridge, Merwin W. m. Jul18, 1883
FRANCK, JULIA, Miss & Abbott, John Franklin m. Jun03, 1885

FRANK, ANNIE, Miss & Norgaar, Chris m. Mar10, 1892
FRANK, MINNIE, Miss & Howard, William Green m. Dec27, 1894
FRIEND, DeETT E. & Edgmon, William A. m. Oct23, 1893
FULLER, SARAH B., Mrs. & Cunningham, Benjamin m. Nov19, 1866
GARCIA, ELIZABETH, Mrs. & Brown, Daniel m. Nov15, 1896
GARDINER, DIANA PRUDENCE, Miss & Dodge, John C. m. Dec11, 1861
GARDNER, ELIZABETH J., Miss & Ellis, Franklin m. Sep19, 1867
GARVIN, EDRIN, Miss & Bowman, Charles Guss m. Sep04, 1894
GARVIN, MAGGIE Z. & Sholes, Theodore Frederick m. Apr04, 1893
GATES, AGNES SNOW & Love, Francis Merriam m. Jun25, 1900
GATES, ALVINA, Mrs. & Robinson, George W. m. Jul07, 1868
GATES, FLORA H., Miss & Aronhalt, Jesse W. m. Oct27, 1897
GATES, HARRIET W., Miss & Gilzean, Alexander m. Nov02, 1893
GAUM, LOUISA, Miss & Goetze, William Henry m. Dec25, 1879
GAUM, MADELINE, Mrs. & Schall, Louis m. Jul31, 1870
GILBERT, JANE, Mrs. & Hamilton, D. D. m. Apr12, 1856
GILLSON, MARY R., Mrs. & Hagan, John J. m. Dec21, 1898
GILZEAN, ANNA E., Miss & McGovern, John J. m. May09, 1900
GILZEAN, ISABELLE MAUDE, Miss & Marshall, Robert C. m. Jan06, 1898
GILZEAN, MARY E., Miss & Driver, John R. m. Dec11, 1872
GIVEN, CARRIE ETTA, Miss & Flowers, William Franklin m. Dec24, 1896
GLASGOW, MATILDA ISABELLE & Lowden, Marshall H. m. Feb10, 1875
GODIN, SARAH J., Mrs. & Hailstone, Pindor F. m. Nov03, 1896
GOERING, AMELIA, Miss & Timmerman, Louis m. Jun27, 1857
GOERING, ETTA C., Miss & Kingsbury, Warren W. m. May18, 1880
GRAFFELMAN, DOROTHY, Mrs. & Stierlen, Fritz m. Mar31, 1863
GRATTAN, SARAH AGNES & Larkin, Patrick m. Sep29, 1877
GREENLEAF, MARIA & Vaughn, Willis m. Jul13, 1879
GRIBBLE, ANNIE, Miss & Carr, Alexander m. Feb23, 1881
GRIBBLE, ELIZABETH, Miss & Myers, Milford B. m. Nov23, 1870
GRIBBLE, MARY A., Miss & Berkley, Richard L. m. Jan01, 1870
GRIBBLE, MINNIE, Miss & Jensen, Peter H. m. Oct27, 1890
GRIFFIN, SARAH E., Mrs. & Murray, Martin W. m. Oct20, 1888
GUTHRIE, CAPITOLA E., Miss & Williams, Joseph Walter m. Mar04, 1895
HAGELMAN, THERESA, Miss & Bradbury, Josephus m. Jun30, 1880
HAILSTONE, HETTIE & Dawson, Thomas R. m. Dec07, 1896
HALL, ANNE F. & Bowerman, Jacob m. Dec11, 1872
HALL, MARY H., Mrs. & O'Shay, Gerald m. Jan03, 1889
HALL, NETTIE J., Mrs & Roach, John A. m. Feb19, 1884
HALLEY, LAURA & Farmer, Charles H. m. Feb01, 1897
HAM, FANNIE (Voshay), Mrs. & Post, John S. m. Dec09, 1878
HAMILTON, MARTHA A. & Myers, Hosea E. m. Mar25, 1888
HAMMOND, LETHA L., Miss & Schnellbacher, Braxton B. m. May18, 1900
HAMPTON, EUGENIA & Ross, Andrew J. m. Nov21, 1863
HANNA, ELLEN, Miss & Tower, Frank B. m. Mar01, 1892
HANNA, ESSIE, Miss & Thompson, Herman m. Sep30, 1886
HARDY, MARY J. & Olsen, John J. m. Jun14, 1899
HARRIS, SUSAN & Guthrie, William m. Jul31, 1873
HARTMAN, ROSA E., Miss & Hampton, Everett P. m. Feb22, 1885
HARTMAN, ROSALIE, Mrs. & Balleau (Belleau), Louis Frank m. Jan06, 1878
HARVEY, ADA, Miss & Wallace, Robert F., Dr. m. May26, 1897
HARVEY, AVILLA A., Miss & Mason, John C. m. May21, 1871
HARVEY, DORA J., Miss & Todd, Edward N. m. May31, 1893
HARVEY, HARRIET A., Miss & Herrick, Henry J. m. Jan13, 1863
HARVEY, LILLIAN, Miss & Moore, Louis m. Dec21, 1892
HARVEY, LILLIE E., Miss & Horton, Richard E. m. Sep11, 1887
HARVEY, MARY A., Miss & Steele, Seymour G., Capt. m. Jul10, 1870
HARVEY, MARY E., Mrs. & Motherwell, John Vivian m. Dec21, 1886
HARVEY, REBECCA, Miss & Gilzean, Charles E. m. Feb13, 1894
HARVEY, SARAH E., Miss & Thayer, Stephen I. m. Apr22, 1866
HASKINS, ALENA A. & Wood, Frank Albert m. Dec01, 1895
HAWK, ELIZABETH, Miss & Guill, William Edward m. Aug09, 1893
HAWK, ELIZABETH, Mrs. & Hutchins, Edward M. m. May28, 1893

MARRIAGES 1850 - 1900

HAWK, ELLEN NORA, Miss & Conway, Frederick Edmund m. Apr15, 1886
HEALY, MARIA, Mrs. & Junkans, Henry m. Sep27, 1868
HEINLAN, CATHERINE & Gaffney, Miles m. Oct28, 1860
HENRY, AMELIA, Miss & Gregory, Leroy m. Apr19, 1857
HENSLEY, ANN ELIZABETH & Barkla, James m. Nov01, 1874
HERRICK, HARRIET ELIZABETH, Miss & Day, J. T. m. May27, 1861
HESSIG, ROSA, Mrs. & Francis, John m. Mar17, 1863
HINDLEY, REBECCA, Miss & Harvey, Henry Thomas m. Dec25, 1866
HOBART, MYRTLE JANE, Miss & Cleaves, Charles Samuel m. Nov06, 1887
HOCKING, CLARA L. & Cummings, John H. m. Sep23, 1891
HOLDEN, RHODA R., Miss & Sawyer, Homer W. m. May19, 1859
HOLLAND, JULIA C., Miss & Lovejoy, Edward Payson m. Oct30, 1869
HOLLERAN, MARGARET, Miss & Behm, Nicholas m. Jun30, 1859
HOLLISTER, ELIZABETH V., Mrs. & Hulme, George m. Dec13, 1866
HOLLISTER, HATTIE, Miss & Crocker, Charles m. Jul09, 1865
HOLMAN, MARGARET, Miss & Hindley, George m. Dec25, 1866
HOLMAN, MARY ANN, Miss & Higgins, William m. Dec19, 1869
HOOD, ELIZABETH C., Miss & Fogg, Calvin P. m. Jul03, 1861
HOOD, SARAH L., Miss & Trask, Benjamin F. m. Dec17, 1862
HOPPE, JOHANNA, Miss & Junkans, William F. m. May06, 1877
HORTON, LILLIE E., Mrs. & Ellis, Eli m. Nov26, 1896
HOWELL, JESSIE & Harris, Frederick William m. Aug15, 1897
HOXEY, ANN, Miss & McMahan, Joseph m. Dec01, 1860
HOYT, CATHERINE, Mrs. & Ingram, Walter W. m. Jan03, 1881
HOYT, SADIE, Miss & Shock, John P. m. Apr30, 1894
HUGGINS, CLARA I., Miss & Jones, Theodore Eldon m. Oct17, 1887
HUGHES, AGNES E., Miss & Large, Osceola m. Dec25, 1890
HUGHES, FLORA E., Miss & Bennett, Marcus M. m. Jun09, 1878
HUGHES, SARAH MAY, Miss & Nordyke, Benjamin James m. Jul03, 1888
HUPP, GEORGIA, Miss & Swain, Frank R. m. Apr17, 1895
HUPP, LOUISA & Sanburn, John G. m. Feb20, 1873
HUPP, MARY L., Miss & Kraft, Elmer P. m. Oct18, 1893
HUSKINS, MOLLIE, Miss & Lewis, John Valentine m. Jun11, 1896
HUSON, ELLA A. & Carr, Thomas H. m. May28, 1874
HUSTON, CLARA, Mrs. & Godfrey, Charles W. m. Jun11, 1898
IVERSON, ASTHA M. & Martin, Charles E. m. Sep28, 1897
JACKSON, ALICE, Miss & Testy, William Bernard m. Nov06, 1895
JACOBS, MOLLIE A. & Gilzean, Charles Eric m. Jan01, 1885
JENKINS, SARAH, Miss & Testy, Joseph m. Feb20, 1861
JESUS, PHILOMINA L. & Mendoza, Innocenta Jose m. Jun29, 1878
JESUS, PULSANA & Zavier, Rollin Joseph m. Apr13, 1863
JEWETT, CAROLINE V. & Mead, Corydon C. m. Oct13, 1874
JOHNSON, ISABELLA Miss & Hupp, William I. m. Aug10, 1865
JOHNSTON, ELIZABETH & Fox, Orson m. Aug15, 1861
JOHNSTON, MARY & Boord, L. L. m. May18, 1860
JONES, DORA, Miss & Given, Janes Edgar m. Feb22, 1886
JONES, ELIZABETH, Mrs. & Leas, John m. Aug13, 1890
JONES, HATTIE M., Mrs. & Carr, Alexander C. m. Aug16, 1899
JONES, NANCY JANE, Miss & Morton, John m. Oct11, 1870
JONES, NETTIE, Mrs. & Brown, Thomas J. m. Aug30, 1899
JORDAN, IDA B., Miss & Sullivan, Peter J. m. Apr26, 1898
JORDAN, LYDIA GRACE & Stackpole, Frank Leslie m. Feb14, 1893
JORDAN, MERTIE C., Miss & Trimble, Brice Alexander m. Jan02, 1892
JOSEPH, ADELINE, Miss & Hanover, Frank S. m. Dec19, 1900
JOSEPH, ANNIE & Enos, Manuel m. Nov16, 1868
JOSEPH, LOUISE, Miss & Koll, John, Jr. m. Oct30, 1897
JUDD, NELLIE MAY, Miss & Penney, Ralph Edward m. Nov15, 1895
JUMPER, MAGGIE (COLBERT), Mrs. & Bowie, James m. Nov01, 1897
JUNKANS, ANNA M. Miss & Berger, Robert m. Aug27, 1882
JUNKANS, ANNA, Miss & Barnickel, Jacob m. Feb25, 1872
JUNKANS, AUGUSTA, Miss & Dannenbrink, Conrad m. Jul11, 1863
JUNKANS, DOROTHEA & Hansen, Detlef m. Sep27, 1868
JUNKANS, DOROTHEA, Miss & Cahnbly, Peter m. Sep30, 1860

JUNKANS, EMILY, Miss & Haas, Frederick G. m. Jul25, 1880
JUNKANS, IDA F., Miss & Davis, David Perry m. Oct26, 1889
KARNES, CHARLOTTE H., Mrs. & Gates, Oscar J., DR. m. Dec18, 1857
KEEFE, AMELIA & Eustice, Richard m. Jan23, 1853
KEELY, ESTHER & Leary, Edward m. Nov01, 1866
KEELY, LUCY, Miss & Mullane, James m. Nov08, 1870
KEELY, MARIA, Miss & Hennessey, Patrick O'Malley m. Jun08, 1863
KELL, MAHALA A., Miss & Tarpley, Harvey J. m. Oct22, 1865
KELLER, LOUISE & Senteney, J. Y. m. Nov16, 1873
KELLEY, MARTHA E., Miss & Stoffer, Franklin B. m. Oct14, 1866
KELLOGG, ALICE S., Miss & Van Matre, Adrien Judson m. Nov16, 1886
KELLOGG, MAUDE, Miss & Dobbyn, John P. m. Oct05, 1898
KELLY, ELIZA, Miss & Meyers, George m. Jan23, 1860
KELLY, ELIZABETH, Miss & Blagrave, William A. m. May12, 1865
KELLY, MILLA J., Miss & Blagrave, Bannister m. Apr10, 1864
KELTON, JULIA A., Mrs. & Bachelder, William H. m. Oct15, 1871
KENNEDY, BRIDGET, Miss & Bartlett, Charles m. May27, 1861
KENNEDY, ELIZA, Miss & Jacob, Barthel m. Oct12, 1865
KESTER, ALVIRA, Mrs. & Gates, Alex m. Sep04, 1860
KESTER, NANCY D., Miss & Abbott, Benjamin F. m. Jan21, 1861
KESTER, SARAH, Mrs. & Glass, William m. Nov12, 1889
KESTER, SUSAN, Miss & Mathews, John D. m. Oct21, 1860
KIDD, PATTY, Miss & Zeigler, Isiaah m. Sep07, 1872
KIMSEY, SARAH J. & Carpenter, Charles H. m. Apr09, 1898
KINDRED, PHOEBE A. & Cox, William H. m. Sep22, 1872
KING, ANNIE, Miss & Girard, Louis m. Aug27, 1883
KISE, ANNA ELIZA, Miss & Foster, Phillip S. m. Jan25, 1872
KITCHEN, ELIZA, Miss & Carter, James M. m. Nov26, 1880
KLEIN, ELIZABETH, Mrs. & Unkich, Phillip m. Apr08, 1862
KNOWLES, EMMELINE L., Miss & Vaughn, William David m. Dec17, 1885
KNOWLES, HIZA MAY & Shock, William Thomas m. Jun30, 1894
KNOWLES, MARY E., Miss & Trask, George N. m. Dec27, 1892
KOELLE, ANNIE, Miss & Scott, Jasper m. Nov21, 1881
KOLL, BERTHA, Miss & Dennison, Lewis m. Jul02, 1881
KONZAN, BARBARA, Miss & McWhorter, Adam L. m. May24, 1868
KRUTTSCHNITT, ANNA B., Miss & Paulsen, Peter M. m. Feb13, 1863
KUFFEL, ALICE L. & Large, Osceola m. Sep20, 1895
LANG, CATHERINE, Miss & Morris, James J. m. Aug10, 1863
LARGE, AMANDA C., Miss & Stafford, James A. m. Jul12, 1866
LARGE, SARAH F., Miss & Kellogg, Langdon J. m. Dec25, 1866
LAWS, CLEMENTINA, Miss & Gilzean, James H. m. Mar23, 1878
LAWS, LENA ALICE, Miss & Bergin, John William m. Oct13, 1887
LEACH, A. DELPHINE & Shanks, Jacob m. Jul04, 1861
LEACH, EMMA, Miss & Lehman, Jacob m. Jul04, 1860
LEAS, MARY LOUISE, Miss & Gibbs, John Bernie m. Sep12, 1895
LEE, ROSA, (Indian) & Olsen, James Peter m. Dec22, 1864
LEIBRANDT, SUSAN, Miss & Lorenz, Henry m. Apr13, 1861
LEONARD, GERTRUDE ELIZABETH, Miss & Blagrave, James H. m. Oct11, 1899
LINDSAY, MARY & Campbell, Thomas G. m. Jun28, 1875
LIPPERT, CHARLOTTE ANTOINE, Miss & Kruttschnitt, August M. m. May16, 1860
LIVINGSTON, ELIZABETH, Miss & Dunham, Warren m. Jun24, 1865
LOCKHART, ELIZABETH E. & CRAIG, Christian Wolff m. May03, 1870
LOCKHART, JULIA A., Miss & LORD, George H. m. Dec31, 1863
LONG, MARY D., Miss & O'Leary, Richard m. Aug04, 1867
LOOTS, HATTIE A., Miss & Twambley, Charles W. m. May15, 1865
LORENZ, CHRISTINA, Miss & Smith, Joseph William m. Dec29, 1885
LORENZ, SUSIE, Miss & Gribble, James H. m. Dec21, 1892
LORENZ, TILLIE, Miss & Gribble, William m. Sep10, 1891
LOUISE, ANNE & Frates, John m. Nov27, 1871
LOUISE, AUDZALINE & DeMello, August Smith m. May21, 1871
LOUISE, MARIE & Silvera, Frank m. Dec18, 1870
LOVERIDGE, BERTHA C., Miss & Landis, James S. m. May13, 1875
LOWDEN, CARRIE IRENE & Condon, William m. Apr16, 1896

LOWDEN, IRENE, Miss & Tinnen, Wiley J. m. Aug19, 1861
LOWDEN, MACIE IRENE, Miss & Wilson, Edgar Everett m. Nov20, 1895
LOWDEN, NELLIE S., Miss & Hollingsworth, Frank O. m. Mar07, 1898
LOWE, MARY ANN, Miss & Squires, Hector T. m. Jan19, 1869
LOWES, ELIZA M., Miss & Tourtelotte, John B. m. Aug27, 1868
LUTMAN, ALICE, Miss & Stine, William Henry m. Nov29, 1869
LYNCH, MARIA, Miss & Pickett, James M. m. Jun17, 1868
MABIE, EMMA, Miss & Allen, Ralph m. Apr20, 1865
MABIE, IRENE ESTELLE, Miss & Brown, Jeremiah M. m. Oct21, 1896
Mc - names beginning with this prefix are alphabetized as if spelled MAC.
McALLISON, ELIZABETH & Titus, D. M. m. Jun13, 1861
McCOLLUM, SALLY, (Indian) & Pattison, William A. m. Dec22, 1864
McCORMACK, MOLLIE E., Miss & Gribble, George m. Sep26, 1882
McILVANE, REBECCA, Miss & Currie, Algernon S. m. Oct04, 1860
McKAY, MARY, Miss & Pattison, Thomas C. m. Oct08, 1900
McLEAN, ANNIE J., Miss & Overmohle, Henry m. Aug24, 1865
McQUIETY, MARY A., Mrs. & Barnes, John m. Oct10, 1876
McWHORTER, PAULINE & McDonald, James Douglas m. Nov16, 1887
MAHONEY, MARGARET, Miss & Reardon, Eugene m. Dec03, 1861
MALONEY, MARGARET, Miss & Smith, Daniel L. m. Aug28, 1881
MALONEY, MARY, Miss & Guptil, Bartlett S. m. Sep24, 1868
MANLEY, JULIA, Miss & King, Humphrey E. m. Jun25, 1862
MARSHALL, CASSIE D., Miss & Carter, Robert L. m. Jun15, 1893
MARTIN, CARRIE, Miss & Hayward, John D. m. Oct04, 1888
MARTIN, ELIZABETH A., Miss & Church, John E. m. Nov28, 1856
MARTIN, ELLEN, Miss & Short, Francis M. m. Nov03, 1878
MATHEWS, JULIA A., Miss & Brown, Phillip S. m. Sep21, 1865
MATHEWS, MARIA, Mrs. & Hansen, Ernest F. m. May05, 1867
MATHEWS, MARTHA J., Miss & Dayton, William H. m. Oct03, 1869
MATZEN, ANNE M., Mrs. & Busch, Julius m. Jul28, 1875
MAUPEN, ANGELINE P., Mrs. & Biggs, J. J. m. Nov16, 1862
MAXWELL, JANE, Miss & Chinn, W. J. m. Jul12, 1856
MAYNARD, ROSA & Philpot, Moses m. Aug24, 1890
MEIER, THERESA, Miss & Vitzthum, George m. Jul27, 1862
MESA, RAMONA, Miss & Nunnally, William A. m. Dec13, 1861
MEYERS, SARAH A. & Watkins, Charles m. May13, 1861
MILES, MAY, Mrs. & Toedt, George m. Nov19, 1896
MILLER, MARY & Lulo, William m. Dec13, 1864
MILLSAP, GEORGIA, Miss & McCully, Alburn C. m. Sep07, 1899
MILLSAP, JESSIE, Miss & Mills, George m. Apr21, 1898
MINTELL, ROSA, Miss & De Reis (Rais), Manuel Cavalho m. May20, 1890
MONTAGUE, MARY F., Miss & Stiller, Richard W. m. Jan09, 1889
MOORE, VENUS, Mrs. & Foote, Andrew N. m. Aug04, 1868
MOREHOUSE, MINNIE & Floyd, William D. m. Oct31, 1886
MORGAN, CHRISTINA, Miss & Hocker, Henry m. Jun03, 1859
MORRIS, LIZZIE, Miss & Newman, Edward m. Feb03, 1887
MORRIS, LUCY J. & Bartholomew, Mitchell O. m. Sep09, 1866
MORRIS, MARY K., Miss & Bacon, Edgar W. m. Apr11, 1883
MORRISON, MARY E., Miss & Boynton, Alfred W. m. Jul02, 1865
MOSIER, ALMIDIER, Mrs. & Middleton, Thomas m. Nov08, 1868
MOSIER, MARIA & Noble, Charles Tyler m. Jan18, 1881
MOSS, ALICE S., Mrs. & Hampton, Everett P. m. May14, 1889
MOTHERWELL, ELIZA, Mrs. & Wilson, V. V. m. Sep01, 1862
MULLEN, BRIDGET, Mrs. & Winkel, August m. Aug08, 1864
MURPHY, KATE, Miss & Hyde, Maurice m. Jan14, 1874
MURPHY, MARGARET, Miss & Powers, John H. m. Oct11, 1858
MURRAY, MARGARET FRANCES & Dockery, James Edward m. Apr19, 1898
MURRAY, MARY, Mrs. & Slattery, John m. Jul03, 1870
MURRAY, NELLIE, Miss & Peterson, Eric m. Apr13, 1879
MYERS, ELIZABETH JANE & Hull, Nathan m. Oct03, 1861
MYERS, ELIZABETH, Mrs. & Beckett, Henry m. Nov18, 1863
MYERS, ETTA C., Miss & Hungerford, Zachariah m. Nov05, 1867
MYERS, MARY HANNAH & Hall, William P. m. Sep04, 1861

NEGRE, MARIA, Miss & Flouraud, Mathieu m. Aug02, 1896
NEWMAN, HATTIE V., Miss & Bearden, James P. m. Dec27, 1880
NEWMAN, MARY, Mrs. & Sheridan, John m. Aug09, 1869
NICHOLS, MARGARET D. & Carter, James A. m. May15, 1895
NICHOLS, MATILDA A., Miss & Montgomery, William T. S. m. Nov18, 1899
NICHOLSON, MABEL, Miss & Grigsby, Robert L. m. Jun01, 1899
NICHOLSON, MARY, Mrs. & Gilbert, Peter m. Jan16, 1864
NIEMAN, EMILY, Miss & Crowl, Bradford A. m. Feb23, 1892
NIXON, DRUCILLA & Ellsworth, George W. m. Jan01, 1853
NOBLE, ANNIE & Thomas, Robert L., Jr. m. Apr14, 1884
NORCROSS, ENSIE MAY, Miss & Blake, Seldon L.,MD m. Apr03, 1886
NORCROSS, NELLIE Z., Miss & Smith, Champion W. m. Oct10, 1867
O'CONNELL, ANN & Cochran, James m. Jul11, 1861
O'CONNELL, ANN & Nievelles, Charles m. Dec15, 1857
O'CONNELL, ELIZABETH & Spotts, Samuel C. m. May13, 1897
O'CONNELL, ELLEN & Mulligan, Michael m. Sep06, 1876
O'CONNELL, ELLEN, Miss & Wallace, Thomas m. Oct05, 1873
O'CONNELL, MARY, Miss & Rourke, Dennis m. Jan16, 1879
O'CONNOR, ELLEN, Miss & Sloan, Charles m. Nov03, 1858
O'DONNELL, CORA & KOON, John Alexander m. Jul10, 1895
O'KEEFE, ELLEN & Condon, Morris m. Feb02, 1864
O'KEEFE, MARY ANN, Miss & Maloney, William m. Apr25, 1856
OFFUTT, MAUD M., Miss & Bremer, August F. m. Jun24, 1896
OLSEN, FLORA IDA, Miss & Dimock, Frank Leslie m. May14, 1892
OLSEN, LOUISA ISABEL & Shuford, John W. m. Dec01, 1886
OLSEN, MINNIE, Miss & Skinner, Robert Alexander m. Jan25, 1891
OSGOOD, NETTIE A., Miss & Hall, John P. (Jack) m. Sep04, 1870
OSGOOD, VIOLA, Miss & Hanna, Hugh R. m. Jul15, 1897
OWENS, ISABEL, Miss & Gum, Bird Hicks m. Sep25, 1892
OWINGS, ELLA, Miss & Raglin, Lloid m. Oct03, 1892
OWINGS, MARGUERITE, Miss & Cole, Charles C. m. May11, 1897
PARRY, EMMA J., Miss & McClary, David R. m. Oct13, 1878
PASSAGE, CATHERINE, Miss & Hatch, Isaac A. m. Feb07, 1861
PASSAGE, M. A., Miss & Knight, Silas D. m. Jan24, 1866
PASSAGE, MARY, Miss & Lawrence, David m. Aug26, 1860
PATTISON, JOSEPHINE, Miss & Waldorff, Ernest A. m. Jul03, 1889
PAULSEN, ANNIE BARBARA, Miss & Bush, Henry Tarton m. May08, 1887
PAULSEN, ELIZABETH S., Miss & Goodyear, Charles Eugene m. Oct30, 1883
PAULSEN, HANNAH PAULINE, Miss & Hall, Daniel James m. May17, 1900
PAULSEN, MINNIE SOPHIA, Miss & Shurtleff, Nathaniel Benjamin m. Nov12, 1887
PELLETREAU, JOSEPHINE, Miss & Norman, Warren m. Mar20, 1886
PEOPLES, MARY ANN & Whitmore, Jeremiah m. May14, 1857
PHILBRICK, LAURA N. & Dyer, S. True m. Dec01, 1860
PHILBRICK, R. D., Miss & Pettyjohn, Christopher C. m. Jul26, 1863
PHILLIPS, ELLA M. & Phillips, James Walter m. Nov21, 1894
POTTER, CHARLOTTE E., Miss & Knowles, Henry m. May17, 1862
POTTINGER, BARBARA, Mrs. & McGillivray, Joseph m. May30, 1857
POULEUR, MARY & Sammons, John B. m. Sep20, 1865
POZEY, NANCY J. & Willburn, Hiram D. m. Sep18, 1889
PRATT, CLARA, Mrs. & Williams, Charles m. Sep08, 1876
PRICHETT, CATHERINE, Miss (Indian) m. Wood, John F. m. May10, 1869
PRITCHARD, CATHERINE F. & Hoyt, Jonathon S. m. Mar05, 1874
PRUETT, SUSANNAH, Miss (Indian) & Pruett, Alfred H. m. Dec13, 1864
PUTERMAN, SARAH J., Miss & Jones, Theodore E. m. Mar28, 1867
PUTTERMAN, MIRANDA, Miss & Hughes, Robert m. Dec31, 1856
QUIMBY, JEANETTE & Zeigler, Isiaah m. Jun13, 1877
RABBITT, ANNA & Beticura, Manuel m. Nov12, 1870
RABBITT, MARGARET, Miss & Martin, Frank m. Jun01, 1868
RAFFERTY, MARY & Garfield, Plunket m. Jun04, 1863
RALPH, CORA, Miss & Givan, James C. m. Dec25, 1889
RALPH, LUELLA, Mrs. & Van Cleave, John William Ward m. Jul02, 1900
RAMSEY, ROSE A., Miss & Tripp, Samuel V. m. Apr02, 1854
READINGTON, ANNE & Ashworth, William D. m. Nov04, 1855

MARRIAGES 1850 - 1900

REYNOLDS, ELLEN, Miss & Dorr, James C. m. Jul22, 1860
RICE, CATHERINE ALMA & Bean, Leonard C. m. Jun01, 1898
RICHARD, ADELAIDE, Miss & Delwisch, Gerhard Henry m. Nov05, 1895
RICHARDS, EDYTHE, Miss & Webster, George m. Oct05, 1896
RICHARDS, ELIZABETH & Yohe, George m. Oct31, 1854
RICHARDSON, MABEL M., Miss & Halley, Frederick F. m. Jun15, 1899
RIDER, SARAH, Miss & Wiser, Hubert A. m. Apr23, 1865
RIEVES, JOSEPHINE, Miss & Rumfelt, Augustus m. Aug03, 1873
RINEMAN, SUSAN, Mrs. & Neathery, Theophilus m. Jun21, 1859
RIPLEY, MAY M., Miss & Diddy, John m. Nov14, 1899
RIPLEY, SARAH M., Miss & Critchlow, John m. May23, 1877
RIQUAS, MARIA & Curt, Francisco Silva Bretau m. Feb06, 1871
ROACH, ANN, Mrs. & Whitebread, Adolph m. Sep25, 1887
ROACH, MARY ANN, Miss & Smith, Sydney m. Aug01, 1868
ROBB, ESTHER & Fitzgerald, William m. Jun26, 1862
ROBB, MARGARET, Miss & Balch, James R. m. Oct03, 1867
ROBLY, MAGGIE M., Mrs. & Colby, John Henry m. Nov27, 1887
RODGERS DUARTE, MARY F. & Truby, William J. m. Jun20, 1898
RODGERS, MAMIE, Miss & Williams, John m. Sep13, 1899
ROFF, CARRIE, Miss & Ferris, Cliff m. abt NOV, 1893
ROGERS, REBECCA, Miss & Gentry, Steve m. Jul13, 1889
ROHUG, KATHERINE, Miss & Vollmers, Michael m. May19, 1863
ROMERAS, MONICA & Potter, Henry L. m. Apr15, 1856
ROSE, LUCY, Miss & Huscroft, John J. m. Dec09, 1862
ROSS, ELIZA, Mrs. & Tompkins, John Edward m. Oct14, 1889
ROURKE, KATY, Miss & McGrath, Phillip m. Jan11, 1863
RUCH, MARGARET J., Miss & Morey, Simon B. m. May13, 1861
RUCH, MARY, Miss & Leonard, Henry W. m. Oct18, 1876
RUCH, SADIE E. & Leonard, Henry W. m. Oct11, 1871
RULE, CARRIE W., Miss & Buckley, John F. m. Jul02, 1900
RULE, ELIZABETH E., Miss & Kise, Elisha S. m. Aug18, 1897
RULE, LAURA MAY & Freitas, Mathew J. m. Oct06, 1897
RYAN, ANNA M., Miss & Lowden, William Jefferson m. Jun06, 1887
RYAN, ELLEN & Cullen, Patrick m. Jul10, 1860
RYAN, JOHANNA & Gorman, Thomas m. Apr24, 1865
RYAN, KATE T., Miss & Whitmore, John m. Jan27, 1888
RYAN, MAGGIE, Miss & Minear, John m. Sep11, 1888
RYAN, MARGARET, Miss & Griffith, Michael m. Oct26, 1865
SAVIO, ADA, Miss & Woods, Jerry D. m. Oct28, 1862
SCHAFFER, ANNA HORTENSE, Miss & Crain, Judson m. Aug29, 1898
SCHLOMER, LILLY (ELIZABETH) & Hawk, John m. Jul05, 1870
SCHMITT, DESOIA MARY & Stoffer, William H. m. Aug18, 1859
SCHNEIDER, ELIZABETH, Miss & Osthoff, Henry m. Jul09, 1866
SCHNEIDER, JOSEPHA & Sohm, John G. m. Jan08, 1883
SCHNEIDER, KATE & Adams, John Q. m. Jul17, 1890
SEABURY, HARRIET A., Mrs. & Perham, Hiram M. m. Jun16, 1870
SEAMAN, ANNE E., Miss & Watson, John A. m. Dec06, 1858
SEARLES, IDA C., Miss & Hutchins, Henry E. m. Jul28, 1890
SEARS, ALMA & Smith, Abial W. m. Dec27, 1874
SEGALIA, MARTHA JANE, Miss & Woods, Lewis Baldwin m. Jun29, 1887
SEGALIA, MARY ADELINE, Miss & Gribble, George m. Sep19, 1891
SENGER, ALICE, Miss & Moss, Amos S. m. Dec23, 1879
SENGER, AMELIA, Miss & Weyand, Zachary Taylor m. Oct12, 1887
SENGER, CATHERINE & Hughes, William Edward m. Dec25, 1895
SENGER, JOSEPHINE & Sawyer, John m. Sep19, 1880
SENGER, MADELINE, Miss & Jackson, Wilbert L. m. Dec06, 1883
SENGER, NETTIE, Miss & Junkans, William m. Oct07, 1896
SEVERIANO, KATE, Miss & Huot, Joseph m. Apr01, 1872
SHARER, ANNA, Miss & Olsen, Emil M. m. Apr15, 1900
SHEEHAN, MARY H., Miss & Taylor, David m. Aug23, 1866
SHEHAN, CATHERINE, Miss & Brown, Richard B. m. Nov25, 1878
SHENER, MARY A. & Willburn, William J. m. Jul27, 1874
SHOCK, ANNIE L., Miss & Large, Robert m. Dec23, 1886

SHOOK, CLARA MAY, Miss & Childers, James Horace m. Jan08, 1883
SHOWALTER, CLARA, Miss & Huston, John m. Jun30, 1889
SHROPSHIRE, GENA & Valentine, William S. m. Apr18, 1898
SHURTLEFF, ELIZABETH C., Miss & Noonan, George E. m. May26, 1877
SILVA, MARY, Miss & Fraters, Manuel m. Jul10, 1864
SILVA, ROSE, Miss & Flowers, William F. m. Apr10, 1900
SIMON, MARIE THERESE, Mlle. & Landvoigt, George m. Oct26, 1857
SINCLAIR, MARY J., Mrs. & Clayton, George H. m. Sep28, 1876
SLATTERY, MARY ANN & Douglass, George F. m. Jan03, 1876
SLOPER, PHOEBE, Mrs. & Downhour, John J. m. Jul10, 1858
SMALL, E. L. (LENA) & Gross, Joshua Freeman m. Dec19, 1869
SMITH, E. J., Miss & Einfalt, John Michael m. Jan11, 1866
SMITH, ESTHER, Miss & Walters, Henry Augustus m. Dec31, 1890
SMITH, LILLIAN M., Miss & Falan, Joseph m. Dec28, 1878
SMITH, LUCELIA (BUTTS) & Smith, Bishop Tilden m. Aug23, 1894
SMITH, MARY ANNE, Mrs. & Burger, John A. m. Nov26, 1874
SPAULDING, ANNIE, Miss & Phillips, Olney m. Jul04, 1858
SPENCER, MARY E., Miss & Hall, William Lewis m. Jun28, 1869
SPIERS, ANNA, Miss & Kidd, William David, Rev. m. Jul29, 1897
SPRAGUE, CORA, Mrs. & Miner, Jordan E. m. Jan11, 1899
SPROWL, ORVILA, Miss & Brewster, Lewis m. Dec29, 1876
STAFFORD, ELIZABETH B., Miss & McCampbell, Robert m. Oct15, 1885
STAFFORD, STELLA A., Miss & Damsell, Josephus m. Jun19, 1895
STAFFORD, VICTORIA S., Miss & Morris, John James m. Jun19, 1895
STIERLEN, DOROTHEA (DORIS S.), Mrs. & Lachenmacher, Fred m. Mar16, 1867
STODDARD, CLARA JANE & Simpson, William Joseph m. Oct08, 1896
STODDARD, FANNY FREDRICA, Miss & Messner, Henry m. Aug11, 1900
STRINGA, PIA & Schiavo, Venanzio m. Oct15, 1892
STRONG, LYDIA ANN & Bixby, George m. Jul08, 1865
STURDIVANT, LUCY, Miss & Dawson, Thomas F. m. Dec13, 1864
SULLIVAN, CLARA, Mrs. & Spears, William m. Feb22, 1900
SWAZY, CATHERINE, Miss & Clemens, Henry E. m. Dec22, 1864
TESTY, MARY E., Miss & Sweet, David Warren m. Jan31, 1886
THANWALD, ANNIE, Miss & Martin, Lorenzo m. Sep13, 1892
THATCHER, ANNA MARIA HARRIET, Mrs. & Browder, Alfred m. Apr09, 1856
THAYER, JESSIE E., Miss & Jordan, Melville Craig m. Jun20, 1894
THAYER, MARY I., Miss & Neilson, James m. Jan15, 1894
THAYER, MAUD A., Miss & Bigelow, William Ralph & m. Oct24, 1888
THAYER, SADIE ABBIE, Miss & Spratt, Charles William m. Jun21, 1887
THOMAS, ANNIE, Miss & Noble, William m. Oct04, 1885
THOMAS, ELIZABETH, Miss & Walker, George W. m. May27, 1878
TINSLEY, HELEN A., Miss & Huestis, Wilbur A. m. Oct30, 1898
TINSLEY, MARY L., Miss & Todd, William D. m. May17, 1893
TODD, ANNIE LAURA, Miss & Blagrave, Walter Lee m. Oct16, 1893
TODD, EMMA AGNES, Miss & Greenwell, Ernest Albert m. Sep26, 1888
TODD, MAYBELLA A., Miss & Day, John D. C. m. Sep02, 1880
TODD, MINNIE J., Miss & Creamer, Charles N. m. Nov08, 1882
TODD, NETTIE, Miss & Taylor, Arthur Johnson m. May05, 1889
TOLLEY, ELIZABETH H., Miss & Wells, James B. m. Nov20, 1861
TOLLEY, MARY E., Miss & Martin, Richard m. Nov15, 1865
TOMPKINS, GRACE V. & Hill, Ernest C. m. Mar28, 1899
TOMPKINS, LAURA LOUISA & Smith, Daniel L. m. Mar25, 1893
TOURTELOTTE, INEZ F., Miss & Stoddard, John R. m. Jul03, 1873
TOURTELOTTE, NELLIE G., Miss & Heath, John Wesley m. Oct09, 1879
TRASK, MINERVA, Miss & Dutton, George W. m. Jun10, 1883
TREBELCOCK, KATIE, Miss & Lowery, George m. Jun07, 1877
TRELOAR, SALINA, Mrs. & Crawford, Monroe T. m. Jan03, 1869
TRIMBLE, ADA ELIZABETH, Miss & Waldorff, William H. m. Nov13, 1876
TRIMBLE, HARRIET L., Miss & Brown, James Henry m. Nov12, 1896
TRIMBLE, JENNIE, Miss & Miller, William D. m. Feb13, 1889
TULEY, ANN, Mrs. & Hatch, John M. m. Dec18, 1864
TURNER, EMMA, Mrs. & Williams, George m. Oct21, 1868
TUROT (TOUROT), ELSIE & Estes, John M. m. May28, 1856

MARRIAGES 1850 - 1900

UNDERWOOD, MARIAN, Mrs. & Allen, George B. m. Dec03, 1878
URSHER, MAY & Carr, George Lee m. Jun01, 1890
URSHER, ROSE A., Miss & Gilzean, Charles E. m. Feb24, 1889
VAN MATRE, CARRIE C., Miss & Hechtman, Albert J. m. Mar22, 1880
VAN MATRE, LOUISA, Miss & Ellis, Henry H. M. m. Jul25, 1885
VANDERFORD, NETTIE, Miss & Tudor, Humphrey m. Dec07, 1898
VAUGHN, CARRIE E., Miss & Adams, William Jesse m. Dec10, 1900
VAUGHN, LAVINA, (`Laverna') & Ruch, William H. m. Dec20, 1874
VAUGHN, PARMELIA & Culy, George C. m. Jul13, 1879
VERSTEGEN, SOPHIE, Miss & Thompson, Thomas S. m. Mar17, 1881
VITZTHUM, LIZZIE, Miss & Brannan, Henry W. m. Oct02, 1892
VOSHAY, FANNY, Miss & Ham, Joseph m. May17, 1874
WALDRON, ANNE, Miss & Jacobs, Henry m. Oct13, 1873
WALKER, MARY & Campbell, William m. Dec24, 1896
WALLACE, ELLEN, Mrs. & Hennessey, Timothy m. Jan24, 1886
WALLACE, EMMA C., Miss & Young, William Ware m. Oct13, 1898
WALLACE, MARY E., Miss & Coumbs, John H. m. Jun28, 1893
WALLACE, ORIE M., Miss & Mahoney, Warren A. m. Nov19, 1884
WALPOLT, BABETTE, Miss & Anderlini, Ferdinand Francisco (Frank) m. Jun14, 1888
WARD, ADA, Miss & Everhart, William D. m. Jun12, 1862
WARREN, ALICE, Miss & Osgood, Ulysses Grant m. Oct13, 1900
WARREN, CHARLOTTE ANN, Miss & Heath, John W. m. Dec31, 1894
WATERMEYER, ELIZABETH & Brumm, Peter m. May03, 1857
WATHEN, JULIA L. & Willburn, James S. m. Jan24, 1881
WEAVER, MARY, Mrs.(Indian) & Weaver, William J. m. Dec13, 1864
WEBB, LAURA E., Miss & Gordon, David E. m. Sep02, 1861
WECKERT, WILHELMINA (MARIA) & Hagelman, John m. Apr13, 1861
WECKMAN, CATHERINE, Miss & Thede, Gustave m. Mar28, 1863
WEIMAN, EUGENIE L.(HANDBINE), Mrs. & Begel, Theodore m. Jul03, 1895
WEINHEIMER, ANNIE L., Miss & Ryan, D. Edward m. Jan10, 1900
WENTWORTH, A. E., Miss & Drake, Judson L. m. Apr01, 1857
WESTFALL, MARY JANE & True, Thomas m. Feb18, 1862
WETSEL, LOUISA, Miss & Loomis, Leander V. m. Jul23, 1863
WHEELER, CLARA JEWETT, Miss & Wheeler, Frank William m. Apr08, 1894
WHEELER, ELIZABETH A., Mrs. & Haskins, Albert P. m. Nov19, 1895
WHITE, KITTY & Leonard, Nelson m. Dec25, 1877
WHITING, MARY E., Mrs. & Senter, Thomas C. m. Jun28, 1894
WHITMORE, TILLIE M., Miss & Reed, Edgar L. m. Nov11, 1880
WHITTIER, ANN J., Mrs. & Flanders, Thomas m. Oct14, 1866
WILHAM, MARY T., Mrs. & Strauss, E. L. m. Feb19, 1867
WILLARD, HARRIET, Miss & Burnett, James Alexander m. Jun14, 1890
WILLARD, HULDAH, Miss & Castner, Louis Preston m. Sep07, 1886
WILLEY, MARY, Mrs. & Falan, Joseph m. Feb07, 1886
WILLIAMS, CLARA, Miss & Twine, Elias m. Aug26, 1871
WILLIAMS, LOUISA & Caton, Antone m. Aug08, 1900
WILLIAMS, MINNIE, Mrs. & Hammond, Charles m. Sep12, 1900
WILLIAMS, PAULINE, Miss & Tinsley, John T. m. Oct09, 1898
WILSON, AGNES ROGENE, Miss & Wilson, Thomas Marion m. Sep28, 1899
WILSON, IDA BELLE, Miss & Lorenz, Henry, Jr. m. Nov09, 1892
WILSON, MAUD & Blair, Benjamin Moor m. Mar22, 1895
WINCHELL, FANNY, Mrs. & Bingaman, John m. Nov02, 1864
WINTERS, SARAH V., Miss & Hoffman, Elias M. m. Feb14, 1892
WOLFF, ANNA C., Miss & Mansfield, Abraham m. Jul27, 1889
WOLFF, KATIE, Miss & Ryan, Patrick Joseph m. May21, 1893
WOLFF, MARY & Gorham, Henry H. m. Aug22, 1896
WOLFF, MARY & Ryan, Richard Franklin m. Mar31, 1894
WOOD, ELLEN B., Miss & Lichty, Willard Justice m. Jan27, 1898
WOOD, MARY E., Miss & Kellogg, Daniel M. m. Nov18, 1862
WOOD, MARY, (Indian) & Miller, George m. Oct24, 1872
WOOD, SARAH E., Miss & Griffin, Morris F. m. Dec31, 1863
WOODBURY, NELLIE LOUISE, Miss & Wallace, James Addison m. Jan01, 1894
YOUNG, ANTOINETTE W., Miss & Martin, George A. m. Oct25, 1892
YOUNG, KATE, Miss & Myers, Milford B. m. Dec22, 1864

YOUNG, STELLA W., Miss & Vanderhoff, John H. m. May29, 1883
YULE, ADELIA HELEN & Nickels, Harry L. m. May31, 1882
YUMCHEERA, JULIA & Allen, Henry Clay m. Nov30, 1862

END

INDEX TO HANOVER, RITA M., TRINITY COUNTY MARRIAGES 1850-1900

Reprinted with permission.

INDEX TO TRINITY COUNTY, CALIFORNIA, MARRIAGES
1900 - 1950
See the LEGEND for sources for 1900-1945.
Marriages 1946 - 1950 are from Official Records.

[Note: If a Marriage did not take place in Trinity County, try Reno, Washoe Co., Nevada, Redding, Shasta Co., California, or Eureka, Humboldt Co., California.]

HUSBAND and WIFE, with MARRIAGE DATE

ABBOTT, JULIUS & Aherin, Patricia Joyce m.Jun25, 1938.
ADAMS, WILLIAM & Vaughn, Carrie m.Dec10, 1900.
ALDRICH, JAMES E. & Ellery, Minnie Myrtle m.Jul05, 1905.
ALGAR, ROBERT CLAIR & Griffith, Mae Ellen m.Jun09, 1935.
ALWARD, LESLIE THORNTON, Jr. & Yancey, Ruth Anna m.Mar14, 1934.
ANDERSON, RICHARD ARTHUR & Gray, Elizabeth Carolyn m.Jun10, 1950.
ANDREWS, ROBERT FRANK & Parsons, Donna Jean m.Dec20, 1947.
ARBUCKLE, HARVEY WOODROW & Clement, Edna Rose m.May18, 1934.
AREY, JOSEPH WILLIAM & Amort, Marilyn Jean m.Sep22, 1948.
ARGUELLO, HAROLD EUGENE & McCampbell, Mabel Rena m.May03, 1919.
AVERA, HARRY LAVELLE & McNeill, Mina Adeline m.Nov19, 1936.
BACK, WILLIAM WALTER & Rush, Matty Lavina, Miss m.Aug18, 1923.
BAILEY, JOHN WESLEY & Green, Violet m.May31, 1938.
BAIRD, CHARLES FRANCIS & Counts, Alice Elizabeth m.Aug13, 1906.
BAKER, LESTER WILLARD & Vitzthum, Wilma Teresa m.Aug12, 1927.
BARNICKEL, BERNHARD & Cottrell, Loyola Genrose m.Jun06, 1904.
BARRETT, JAMES F. & Ryan, Claire m.Apr10, 1947.
BARSE, WALTER E. & Sturdivant, Opal m.May02, 1948.
BARTLETT, THOMAS F. & Ross, Helen Louisa m.Jun21, 1931.
BARTLETT, LANCE TAYLOR & Pierce, Patricia m.Oct07, 1932.
BASSHAM, ALBERT & Peterson, Dora m.Sep28, 1902.
BENNETT, CURTIS MORTON & Anderlini, Ella Teresa, Miss m.Nov25, 1911.
BENNINGTON, RICHARD C. & Doebelin, Fannie, Mrs. m.Apr13, 1906.
BENTON, EMERSON J. & Paulsen, Edna E. m.May07, 1901.
BERGIN, GEO. & Kay, Alafaire Cademartori m.Dec16, 1914.
BERGLUND, TOREY & Thompson, Grace m.Aug06, 1946.
BETTERTON, CHALMER & Lockwood, Geraldine Young m.Feb03, 1947.
BETTERTON, EDWARD LEE & Markham, Rita Marion m.Jun09, 1936.
BIANCALANA, ALESSANDRO J. & Sellars, Bernice F. m.Jan04, 1936.
BIGELOW, SAMUEL JAMES & Allen, Margaret m.Apr15, 1933.
BIGGERSTAFF, TALBERT JAMES & Collins, Geraldine m.Jun28, 1932.
BLAIR, JAMES RUSSELL & Thorne, Ida Ruland, Miss m.Apr12, 1911.
BLAKE, FRANK TILDEN & Sanburn, Delia Martha m.Dec27, 1904.
BLAKEMORE, CHRISTIAN & Yarbrough, Jessie Louisa m.Jan19, 1908.
BLANEY, JOHN J. & Barber, Bessie m.Oct11, 1907.
BLANEY, ROBERT JAMES & Cantrall, Geraldine E. m.Sep04, 1948.
BLANKENSHIP, GEORGE D. & Chetwood, Gladys m.Jul10, 1939.
BLEREWS, ARCHIE & Jones, Rose W. m.Sep25, 1946.
BONNEY, M. PIERCE & Caton, Alice Gertrude m.Nov26, 1921.
BOOTH, EUGENE V. & Smith, Vera m.Mar16, 1947.
BORDEN, WILLIAM RUSSEL & Caton, Margaret Louise m.Aug17, 1946.
BORING, CARTHEL F. & Browne, Edna K. m.Sep30, 1942.
BOTILLER, JOE & Arnandos, Tomasso m.Jan17, 1921.
BOUDREAUX, JULES EDWARD & Bailey, Alice Denice m.Dec20, 1946.
BOUERY, PIERRE & Jayne, Lulu m.Mar23, 1903.
BOWMAN, CHARLES ELMER & Huestis, Mary Helen m.Apr28, 1919.
BOX, REUBEN P. & Anderlini, Anita m.Feb24, 1915.
BOX, ANDREW H. & Van Matre, Irene m.Oct20, 1912.
BOYCE, JESSE & Laingor, Anne m.Oct09, 1906.
BOYD, HAROLD GEORGE & Owen, Edna Marie m.Dec21, 1930.
BRACKETT, ALBERT JAMES & Blery, Sarah Elizabeth m.Nov05, 1907.
BRAZENALL, WM. & Dickerson, Nellie May m.Oct26, 1908.

BREARCLIFFE, ABRAHAM LINCOLN & Brown, Helen Medora m.Dec21, 1921.
BREMER, CARL WILLIAM & Thayer, Edna Coddington m.Jan01, 1908.
BRINKMAN, LESTER & Hutchens, Susie Gladys m.Dec12, 1917.
BROSSARD, WILLIAM J. & Cantwell, Adaline m.Jul28, 1939.
BROWN, ALBERT THOMAS & Young, Della Leona m.Oct05, 1935.
BROWN, BOWYER B. & Reimers, Alida K. m.Aug03, 1913.
BROWN, CHARLES LEROY & Cleaves, Margaret Jane, Miss m.Jul20, 1920.
BROWN, DAVID DUDLEY & Schalsky, Anna m.Jun21, 1926.
BROWN, JERRY M. & Vitzthum, Nellie Allen m.Aug14, 1901.
BROWN, MELVILLE HARRISON & Phillips, Marjorie, Miss m.Jun30, 1920.
BROWN, STANLEY B. & Arbuckle, Genevieve, Miss m.Feb22, 1923.
BRUNKEN, LUDWIG R. & Leavitt, Nettie M., Mrs. m.Dec22, 1903.
BUCKLEY, JOHN F. & Rule, Carrie W. m.Jul02, 1900.
BUHLMAN, RUDOLPH ROBERT & Beckett, Dorothy May m.Dec28, 1938.
BUNCH, PORTER J. & Johansson, Mary S. m.Aug27, 1945.
BUNTAIN, HUBERT EARL & Swain, Irene Marion m.Oct21, 1934.
BURGARD, JAMES J. & Duncan, Louisa m.Jul06, 1905.
BURGESS, ZERA EDWARD & Gassaway, Lillian Beatrice m.May07, 1907.
BURNS, THOMAS & Dact, Esthel m.Jun05, 1929.
BURWELL, GEORGE RAYMOND & Asplund, Clara Belle m.Mar06, 1948.
BUSH, CHAUNCEY CARROLL & Condon, Annie m.Oct09, 1901.
BUTLER, LUCIUS F. R. & Peck, Minnie Anna m.Jan27, 1921.
BUYS, HIRAM EDWARD & Douglas, Irene m.Jan18, 1901.
CAHOONE, WILLIAM MUIR & Gibson, Helen Elizabeth m.Aug23, 1935.
CAMPBELL, HAROLD HARDIN & Danielson, Neva Ida m.Jun16, 1944.
CAMPBELL, THOMAS H. & Friend, Mary Eva m.Aug08, 1905.
CAMPBELL, LINDSAY & Vaughn, Maud m.Dec01, 1903.
CANFIELD, ROSS DOE & Jeans, Alice Marguerite m.Oct07, 1913.
CANTRALL, DONALD DEAN & Scott, Bonnie Jean m.Jul17, 1949.
CARLSON, HERBERT WILLIAM & Moser, Bertha M. m.Nov06, 1939.
CARPENTER, ELMER B. & Chesbro, Emma m.Sep23, 1922.
CARR, HARRIN STANLEY & Ford, Frieda Fay m.Feb17, 1933.
CARR, FRANK WILLIS & Chapman, Bonnie Louise m.Mar07, 1921.
CARR, FRANK WILLIS & Dickey, Catherine Irene m.Mar03, 1931.
CARR, FRANK DEMAUNT & Nicholson, Elizabeth m.Jun26, 1902.
CARR, CHARLES A. & Simmons, Violet, Mrs. m.Oct31, 1925.
CARR, FRED ELMER & Guill, Mildred I. m.Dec01, 1914.
CARR, CLARENCE & Gossett, Mildred m.Oct15, 1930.
CARR, OTIS & Barbour, Madeline E., Miss m.Jul30, 1923.
CATON, JOHN & Atkins, Lulu m.Sep04, 1900.
CATON, ANTONE & Williams, Louisa m.Aug08, 1900.
CESCHI, HECTOR & Alssa, Grayce m.Oct11, 1937.
CHANEY, SIDNEY T. & Ferguson, Mary Ruth m.Jan09, 1929.
CHAPMAN, WILLIAM F. & Tibessart, Ethel, Miss m.Jul12, 1920.
CHECKETTS, LA MOINE & Wilcox, Ida May m.May19, 1934.
CHERRY, OBIE RONALD & Gaines, Maybelle Madeline m.Nov17, 1926.
CHESBRO, JAMES & Saxie, Ellen m.Dec29, 1922.
CHILDERS, FRED NEWTON & Olsen, Mary Jane m.Feb26, 1922.
CLARK, LAWRENCE P. & Weinheimer, Katherine Theresa m.Oct01, 1913.
CLARK, ARTHUR R. & Burger, Julia m.Jun03, 1903.
CLARK, CLAUDE E. & Noonan, Adelyne Frances m.Dec14, 1904.
CLARK, W. W. & Rogers, Katie m.May25, 1915.
CLARKE, LELAND ARTHUR & Wright, Edna Mae m.Jun22, 1931.
CLARKE, WILLIAM NELSON & Morris, Kathleen, Mrs. m.Oct30, 1924.
CLARKE, RUSSELL O. & Calvert, Marie Kathleen m.Nov20, 1941.
CLEAVES, JOSEPH & Angel, Alice V. (Davis?) m.May26, 1947.
CLEAVES, FORREST & Hutchins, Aimee m.Dec22, 1910.
COLLINS, WILLIAM G. & Thorne, Mabel m.Jun05, 1907.
CONDON, J. J. & Hughes, Katherine m.Nov17, 1904.
CORDOZA, FRANK & Rogers, Flora m.May27, 1900.
COSTA, FRANK & Hafley, Maida Hazel m.Dec24, 1939.
COSTA, GEORGE & Thorp, Ethel Louise m.Feb23, 1937.
COUMBS, MERLE & Heaton, Billie Lavonne m.Oct21, 1935.

MARRIAGES 1900 - 1950

COUMBS, WALTER SCOTT & Hailstone, Diana Webster m.Feb28, 1913.
COUMBS, ROLLIN WILLIAM & Hunt, Dorothy Belle m.Aug14, 1938.
COUMBS, WALTER SCOTT & Swayze, Cora Mae m.Apr14, 1935.
COWAN, JACK & Bishop, Veda m.Dec26, 1946.
COX, SOLOMON & Gray, Miss ____ m.Sep25, 1901.
CRABTREE, FRED & Duncan, Jane m.Sep15, 1906.
CRAFT, GEORGE JEWELL & Ryan, Marie Teresa m.Feb06, 1918.
CREEACH, WILLIAM RICHARD & Wellock, Chloe Ione m.Oct05, 1944.
CREWS, WILBERT L. & Maringer, Mary Bernice m.Nov14, 1913.
CREWS, ELMER CLAIR & Vaughn, Alice m.Jan12, 1914.
CROCKER, HARRY & Ellery, Carrie p. m.Sep16, 1906.
CRUSON, EARL LESLIE & Arbuckle, Elizabeth Marvell m.Feb27, 1946.
CUFF, LESTER L. & Cleaves, Harriet Marie m.Mar03, 1932.
CULBERTSON, DAVID E. & Peirce, Caroline m.Feb14, 1939.
CUMMINGS, ROBERT LEE & Wilson, Harriett V. m.Feb24, 1901.
CUNNINGHAM, PAUL JOSEPH & Mann, Bonnie m.Oct31, 1936.
CUSSINS, ADELLBERT E. & Dawson, Ruth m.May01, 1901.
DAILEY, GEORGE J. & McKnight, Mary Jane m.Mar18, 1931.
DANFORTH, RICHARD S. & Danforth, Myra m.Nov09, 1936.
DAVIS, ROBERT W. & Miller, Eva B. m.Jul20, 1936.
DAVIS, GRIFFITH T. & Newell, Carrie m.May27, 1905.
DAWSON, HAROLD EDWARD & Hetrick, Katherine Maggie m.Jun16, 1947.
DAY, WALTER A. & Flagg, Sadie A. m.Sep18, 1905.
de GENERES, HAROLD ERWIN & Crume, Helen Faye m.Aug06, 1940.
de REIS, MANUEL C. & Marara, Anna m.Mar29, 1913.
de REIS, WILLIAM WILFORD & Moreira, Maria Loares m.May31, 1913.
De H'ARCOURT, HARRY J. & Potter, Bertha T. m.Jul31, 1939.
DEAN, SAMUEL T. & Newland, Maud m.Mar04, 1903.
DERRICK, GRANT, Jr. & Friend, Marguerite m.Jun10, 1931.
DESMOND, AMBROSE JACKSON & Griffith, Helen Mary m.Jun03, 1929.
DEWEY, ARTHUR O. & Flynn, Dollie m.Nov02, 1903.
DOCKERY, CHARLES M. & Wieland, Maxine H. m.Sep21, 1945.
DOCKERY, JAMES EDWARD & Laffranchini, Irene Martha m.Oct22, 1921.
DOCKERY, JOHN HENRY & Leavitt, Wilda Mae m.Jun14, 1917.
DOMENICI, DOMENICO & Post, Frances Vothier, Mrs. m.Apr29, 1916.
DUNCAN, JAMES HENRY & Supan, Thelma Marian m.Apr29, 1944.
DUNCAN, WILLIAM C. & Bacon, Matie m.Jan31, 1906.
DUNCAN, BEN H. & Wilburn, Lillian m.May25, 1910.
DUNLAP, GEORGE A. & Clarke, Ina Marie m.Jul13, 1946.
DUNN, SAMUEL ALLEN & Cooley, Blanche, Miss m.Nov16, 1925.
EDWARDS, CHARLES H. & Dannenbrink, Eleanor C. m.Jul07, 1915.
EFAU, JAMES HENRY & Frates, Eva Evelyn m.Dec24, 1915.
EGAN, WILLIAM MARTIN & Rourke, Sophia Agnes m.Apr11, 1948.
ELLERY, ELIAS K. & Larsen, Margaret L. m.Aug23, 1914.
ELLINGWOOD, JOHN E. & Lambert, Loretta Nevada m.Apr14, 1934.
ELLISTON, THOMAS R. & Whitchurch, Lelia Olive m.May13, 1906.
ELLISTON, WILLIAM P. & Vaughn, Birdie E. m.Oct03, 1904.
ENDICOTT, SAMUEL PARTRIDGE & Domenici, Emily Marie m.Apr05, 1912.
ENOS, JOSEPH & Williams, Florence m.Aug11, 1909.
ENOS, THOMAS M. & Atkins, Ethel F. m.Apr09, 1902.
EUGENE, JOSEPH KIMBALL & Vitzthum, Mary Elaine m.Sep01, 1928.
EVEREST, HARRY & Huestis, Ida L. m.Apr19, 1903.
EWELL, RATHBORNE E. & Hale, Idolene H. m.Jun25, 1932.
FARMER, HARVEY ALLEN & Townsend, Mamie Mary m.Dec01, 1928.
FARMER, GEORGE H. & Hailstone, Nancy A. m.Oct23, 1901.
FEHR, JACOB PETER & Carr, Mildred I. m.Dec03, 1918.
FERGUSON, JAMES RALPH & Dawson, Beulah Isabelle m.May10, 1921.
FETHERTON, WILLIAM HENRY & Halley, Thelma Frances m.Sep29, 1927.
FfOULKES, WADE H. & Pearson, Jean A. m.Jun25, 1915.
FfOULKES, THOMAS C. & Ffoulkes, Jean A. m.Jul07, 1926.
FIELD, MILTON WAYNE & Walsh, Alma Pearl, Miss m.Nov04, 1925.
FIELDS, DAVID BLACKSTONE & Blaney, Honora m.Aug07, 1908.
FINNICUM, MAX L. & Olsen, Bertha Frances m.Jun26, 1934.

FISHER, JUAREZ CUIDAD & Lewis, Marjorie m.Jan07, 1946.
FISHER, CARLOS O. & Meyer, Gladys Rae, Miss m.Sep02, 1924.
FISK, GEORGE B. & Bryan, Betty m.Jan29, 1946.
FLANNERY, PATRICK & Remick, Rachel Suzane m.Jan06, 1943.
FLOWERS, W. F. & Silva, Rosa m.Apr10, 1900.
FOOTE, CHARLES ARTHUR & Calhoun, Audrey Beverly m.Oct19, 1946.
FORD, DENIS & Van Cleave, Dolores m.Sep14, 1904.
FORSLUND, DERO BRADFORD & Conner, Myrtle Ruth m.Jan01, 1940.
FOSS, MARTIN W. & Prow, Maude L. m.Oct11, 1950.
FOSTER, JOSEPH MELVIN & Osborn, Evelyn Mildred m.Aug02, 1935.
FRANCK, ANTONIUS NORGARD & Shock, Claudie m.Mar06, 1916.
FRASER, WILLIAM THOMAS & Potter, Vance Rhom m.Jul30, 1933.
FRENCH, RICHARD A. & Dellaire, Mary D. m.Oct22, 1942.
FRIEND, THOMAS & Mathews, Viola B. m.Dec14, 1903.
FROLOFF, ALBERT STEPHEN & Noble, Hazel Bernice m.Aug06, 1939.
FRY, JAMES & Barkla, Ella m.Sep02, 1900.
GATES, DEWEY RALPH & Gilzean, Marvel Louisa m.Feb17, 1921.
GATES, CALVIN ANDREW & Layman, Mary Agnes m.Apr09, 1914.
GEHM, GEORGE F. & Woodbury, Coraline Kate m.Oct30, 1901.
GEHM, G. F. & Fox, Elizabeth H. m.Apr06, 1909.
GILMAN, JAMES HERBERT & Wegg, Grace Aileene m.Aug05, 1948.
GILZEAN, JAMES ALBERT & Dawson, Nancy M. m.Mar29, 1931.
GILZEAN, JAMES ALBERT & Silva, Marian m.Jul01, 1902.
GILZEAN, WARREN MAYHEW & Bigelow, Masie Elonia m.Aug10, 1916.
GOETZE, WILLIAM ADOLPH & Boyce, Clara E. m.Jan26, 1905.
GOODRICH, GUY E. & Bowerman, Elsie Anna m.Jun24, 1915.
GOODYEAR, HAL EUGENE & Rourke, Dorothy Carol m.May17, 1944.
GOODYEAR, EUGENE MERRITT & Shoup, Elsie C., Miss m.Dec20, 1911.
GORE, JOSEPH W. & Tinsley, Mary J., Mrs. m.Mar01, 1917.
GRATTON, FREDERICK CHRISTOPHER & Lindstrom, Marie Wilhelmina m.Aug20, 1914.
GRAY, ALBERT FRAY & Wilburn, Zue, Miss m.Nov09, 1911.
GREEN, STANLEY & Switzer, Pauline m.Jan04, 1947.
GREENWELL, WM. ERNEST & Bowerman, Amy E. m.Feb26, 1914.
GRIBBLE, RICHARD & Dickey, Emily m.Jul06, 1904.
GRIFFITH, JOHN J. & Williams, Mary m.Apr21, 1901.
GRIFFITH, JAMES R. & Rourke, Vera Patricia m.Jun02, 1934.
GRIGSBY, PLEASANT & Carr, Rose m.May07, 1902.
GRIGSBY, CALVIN & Packard, Jessie M. m.Jul25, 1912.
GUESPARI, BRUNO JOHN & Guglielmetti, Esther Virginia m.Jun29, 1937.
GUTHRIE, HUGH DELMAR & Harris, Elizabeth Anne m.Mar04, 1950.
HAACKE, JULIUS & Large, Alice, Mrs. m.Aug07, 1911.
HAFLEY, F. H. & Newell, Myrtle m.Sep27, 1907.
HAILSTONE, ZACHARIAH & McDonald, Ethel W. m.Jul26, 1913.
HAILSTONE, ZACH & Olsen, Sadie m.Feb25, 1903.
HALL, DANIEL J. & Paulsen, Hanna Pauline m.May17, 1900.
HALL, GEO. A. & Macy, Cransolia m.Sep13, 1910.
HAMILTON, IRA C. & Samuels, Dorothy J. m.Sep20, 1912.
HAMMACK, LEE & Gagel, Frankie m.Nov01, 1947.
HAMMERSLY, OWEN KENNETH & Woodworth, Annie Frances m.Jan30, 1932.
HAMMOND, CHARLES & Williams, Minnie m.Sep12, 1900.
HANCOCK, THOMAS DENNIS & Lattari, Anita m.Jul20, 1949.
HANNA, CHARLES & Weinheimer, Marie m.Jun21, 1905.
HANOVER, HARVEY HILTON & Lehman, Frances Violet m.Apr25, 1934.
HANOVER, FRANK & Joseph, Adaline m.Dec19, 1900.
HANOVER, ALTON DALE & Chambers, Juanita Hortense m.Jan01, 1928.
HARRINGTON, JOSEPH J. & Koll, Winnie C. m.Jul09, 1927.
HARRY, ROBERT MERIT & Haberkam, Maude Allen m.Oct19, 1946.
HARVEY, WILTON MILBERRY & Ambler, Thelma Dixie m.Jun02, 1927.
HARVEY, WILLIAM L. & Mabie, Jennie D. m.Aug03, 1908.
HASS, WARREN MAXINE & Zwiebel, Catherine Mary m.Aug15, 1934.
HAWK, HILTON ALEXANDER & Sherman, Gertrude m.Mar16, 1936.
HAWK, HOWARD CLINTON & Carter, Enid Merle m.Jul16, 1912.
HAWKEY, OTHO E. & Leyrer, Nelda m.Aug17, 1914.

MARRIAGES 1900 - 1950

HAWKINS, RUSSELL BUCHANAN & Walker, Alice Winifred m.Jul26, 1940.
HAWKSLEY, H. H. & Carpenter, Mattie T. m.Feb08, 1901.
HAYDEN, FRANK M. & Post, Lubertha E. m.Nov28, 1907.
HAYES, GEORGE S. & Thomas, Isabella, Mrs. m.Jul25, 1924.
HAYWARD, OSCAR HORACE & Martin, Eleanor Albina, Mrs. m.Aug29, 1917.
HAYWARD, LYSANDER WHETMAN & Babcock, Josephine May Mrs. m.Mar10, 1916.
HAYWARD, JOHN D. & Loomis, Elsie Catherine, Miss m.Sep16, 1925.
HEATH, CHARLES JESSE & Bragdon, Ora Gladys m.Jun26, 1918.
HENDERSON, WILLIAM V. & Dawson, Emma Norine m.Jan07, 1920.
HENRY, BENJAMIN HARRISON & Bigelow, Leila Maud, Miss m.Jun19, 1920.
HENRY, WILLIAM JUSTIN & Walter, Esther m.Mar23, 1913.
HERRICK, VERNON & Hays, Opal m.Aug07, 1936.
HIGGINS, FREDERICK ERNEST & Weston, Eva Lillian m.Sep14, 1913.
HITCHCOCK, CHARLES & Bonce, Louisa m.Sep12, 1901.
HOAGLIN, WILLIAM & Myers, Hattie m.Apr31, 1913.
HODGES, LEONARD B. & Adams, Bernice M. m.Sep23, 1933.
HODSON, HENRY & Bennett, Annie May m.Feb18, 1902.
HOELLING, FRANK WILLIAM & Kask, Olga Louise m.Sep10, 1938.
HOLBROOK, JOHN T. & Allen, Gladys m.Oct10, 1931.
HOLLAND, H. H. & Blakemore, Vivian V. m.Oct01, 1910.
HOLMES, ARTHUR LLOYD & Tomlinson, Roberta Lou m.Oct15, 1949.
HOSKINS, ALBERT & Douglas, Eileen m.Jun10, 1930.
HOWARD, E. H. & Harvey, Clara m.Sep28, 1903.
HOWELL, BUD PERCY & McNamara, Eunice L. m.Apr25, 1917.
HUGHES, EVERETT LISLE & Ffoulkes, Ruth Catherine Pearson m.Jun05, 1929.
HUNT, ROWLAND MERRITT & Hale, Beta Isabelle m.Apr11, 1938.
HUNTER, JOSEPH EDGAR & Eldridge, Hazel Alleen m.Sep01, 1918.
HUTCHINS, H. C. & Records, Nannie m.Jun10, 1910.
HUTCHINSON, EDGAR ERNEST & Cornett, Louise m.Sep08, 1945.
HYLTON, KENNETH P. & Crewdson, Daisy m.Sep21, 1934.
HYPE, LAWRENCE P. & Sweatt, Mae E. m.Mar27, 1942.
IRVINE, CLAUDE ROBERT & Barkley, Gladys Marie m.Jun18, 1949.
IRVING, HARRISON L. & Grills, Myrtle Meeker m.Sep16, 1936.
IVERSEN, ADOLPH LEFFREN & Siligo, Anna Elizabeth m.Sep05, 1918.
IVERSON, HORACE G. & Bennett, Mary I. m.Jun26, 1909.
IVY, WILLIAM H. & Abbott, Julia m.Sep13, 1909.
JACKMAN, CHARLES E. & Anderson, Mary E. m.Mar05, 1922.
JACKSON, RAYMOND A. & Unzicker, Elsa Mabel, Miss m.Nov04, 1925.
JACKSON, ALFRED STEWART & Henderson, Jane m.Sep03, 1939.
JACKSON, NATHANIEL J. & Hill, Ethel A. m.Nov28, 1928.
JACKSON, LEMUEL T. & Albiez, Genevieve, Miss m.Dec06, 1924.
JACKSON, EDWIN MERLE & Kopp, Ida m.Dec18, 1932.
JACKSON, SAMUEL BALLAN & Knapp, Billy June m.Sep27, 1931.
JACKSON, MELVIN CLARENCE & Forrester, Marion Katherine m.May06, 1950.
JACKSON, FRANCIS O. & Price, Inez H. m.Mar14, 1942.
JENKINS, L. B. & NEWMAN, MARY K., Miss m.Feb22, 1911.
JENKINS, FALLIS W. & Thompson, Leona m.May08, 1938.
JENNINGS, FRANK & Denning, Irene E. m.Aug01, 1946.
JENSEN, LYLE H. & Ettline, Jean E. m.Jul28, 1947.
JOBE, MAURICE G. & Jeans, Agnes F. m.Jun07, 1918.
JOHNSON, DONALD LEWIS & Lampert, Bertha Mae m.Jul24, 1950.
JOHNSON, FRANK DANIEL & McClintock, Elma Louise m.Dec22, 1924.
JOHNSON, CHARLES ALFORD & Miller, Geraldyne Elouise m.Nov03, 1949.
JOHNSON, EDWARD RUSS & Scott, Adeline m.Jun16, 1939.
JOHNSON, DARREL JAMES & Bennion, Dorothy Douglas m.Dec06, 1936.
JOHNSON, FRED & Dunlap, Nellie m.Mar22, 1902.
JOHNSON, ROBERT LEE & Lemmon, Henrietta m.Oct29, 1926.
JONES, BENJAMIN CLAYTON & Dabbs, Ladessa Elaine m.Aug26, 1938.
JONES, GUY P. & Todd, Zelita, Miss m.Aug01, 1923.
JUMPER, GEO. M. & Yount, Lucia R. m.Sep28, 1910.
JUNKANS, RUDOLPH H. & Weinheimer, Agnes Helena m.Dec07, 1904.
KAROLSKI, HARRY JOSEPH & Brown, Kathryn m.Jul22, 1944.
KEFFER, R. F. & Allen, Dorothea E. m.Oct23, 1910.

KENTEMEYER, HENRY F. & Rousselott, Sarah M. m.May03, 1909.
KERN, HARRY & Burger, Eliza m.Jun27, 1907.
KIBLER, HERBERT LEE & Brown, Maude F. m.Sep03, 1938.
KINYON, JAMES EARLE & Greenwell, Clara Gertrude m.Sep22, 1921.
KISE, COMMODORE C. & Billmeyer, Lucy A., Mrs. m.Jun04, 1925.
KNAGGS, ORVILLE & Hale, Alice m.Mar24, 1938.
KNOWLES, H. L. & Armstrong, Lily, Mrs. m.Dec03, 1902.
KNOWLES, HENRY MERLYN & Allen, Helen Hansen m.Dec10, 1938.
KREISS, CHARLES F. & Van Matre, Clara Eunice m.Jun11, 1929.
LADINE, ROY R. & Briggs, Bessie Irene m.May23, 1937.
LAFFELL, JOSEPH E. & Campbell, Ida Grazilla m.Dec18, 1900.
LAFFRANCHINI, ALLEN CHARLES & Olsen, Laverne Emeline m.Aug20, 1927.
LANGDON, HORACE JOSEPH & Kaufman, Velma May m.Jul25, 1934.
LANGSTROFF, ADOLPH JOSEPH & Fields, Anna Elvira, Mrs. m.Aug06, 1916.
LANGWORTHY, JOHN ROBERT & Bigelow, Elizabeth Pearl m.Jul24, 1945.
LATTIN, FRANKLIN & Nye, Harriet F. m.Sep04, 1934.
LAUGHLIN, JAY LAWRENCE & Prindle, Georgia Marian m.May31, 1941.
LAWTON, JACKSON CHEROKEE & Wiggle, Mary Jane m.Feb01, 1930.
LAYMAN, LOWELL J. & Maloney, Mary Agnes m.Nov22, 1905.
LAYMAN, WALTER LAWRENCE & Selby, Wildeth Jean m.Jun11, 1950.
LE MAR, GEORGE KENT & Wilburn, Sarah Gertrude m.May20, 1915.
LEA, RALPH MALCOLM & Wessa, Barbara Jean m.Jul12, 1947.
LEACH, EARLE N. & Brannan, Edna Teresa m.Jul12, 1914.
LEACH, RUEL PAUL & Hostler, Marjorie m.Jul29, 1946.
LEAROYD, WALTER RUTLEDGE & Terry, Florence m.Sep17, 1933.
LEAS, GEORGE W. & Siligo, Barbetta, Mrs. m.Jun22, 1905.
LEAVITT, HORACE J. & Bennett, Vivian E. m.Jul09, 1933.
LEDERER, LESTER & Ashbaugh, Imogene m.Aug02, 1930.
LEDFORD, MELVIN LEROY & Powell, Frances Louise m.Jul16, 1935.
LEE, B. F.[in San Francisco] & Barnickel, Detta, Miss m.Jan03, 1905.
LEE, THOMAS L. & McKew, Agnes B. m.Jun14, 1926.
LEONARD, HORACE LESTER & Hanover, Juanita Hortense m.Apr05, 1931.
LESSING, EARL PRESTON & Ellis, Miriam Marie m.Aug07, 1926.
LEVY, PHIL MORTON & Barnickel, Johanna m.Jun18, 1902.
LEWMAN, GEORGE F. & Greenlief, Annie m.Sep03, 1906.
LINDLEY, GEORGE WILLIAM & Hayley, Altea Oravella m.Apr08, 1950.
LLOYD, WALTER DELMAR & Wallace, Grace Vineyard m.Dec11, 1948.
LOCKLIN, GEORGE R. & Hagerty, Edith Loreta, Miss m.Jan12, 1920.
LOOMIS, WALTER & Luckie, Jessie m.Oct05, 1915.
LORENZ, JOHN NICHOLAS & Clement, Minnie DeCora m.Aug26, 1915.
LORENZ, FLOYD HOFFMAN & Miller, Naomi Catherine m.Jul10, 1938.
LOUIE, KEE & Lim, Epp Lucile [100 in 1997] m.Dec25, 1918.
LOWDEN, FREDERICK S. & Wilson, Elizabeth A. m.Sep27, 1903.
LOWDEN, EUGENE E. & Ralph, Ray M. m.Mar20, 1902.
LOWDER, EMIL OLIVER & Laughlin, Leona Louise m.Apr15, 1940.
LOWREY, CLARENCE W. & Records, Jenny May m.Aug25, 1906.
LUND, ADOLPH & Walton, Bonita m.Oct03, 1946.
LUNG, ROBERT L. & McKenzie, Lola May m.Nov20, 1937.
LYNCH, FRED & Ham, Maud m.Nov06, 1906.
Mc - names beginning with this prefix are alphabetized as if spelled MAC..
McCANN, EARL JAMES & Brice, Ruth Adelle m.May09, 1918.
McCLEARY, MARRION W. & White, Gladys m.Nov10, 1933.
McCLENDON, JOHN & Morwood, Gertrude Alice m.Oct19, 1935.
McCLINTOCK, GLENN RICHARD & Day, Evelyn June m.Jul10, 1949.
McDANIEL, FRED A. & Giumelli, Josephine m.Oct10, 1931.
McDONALD, JOHN A. & Bradbury, Therisa m.Nov26, 1908.
McDONALD, O. A. & Wilburn, mary W. m.Aug21, 1909.
McDONALD, JOHN DAVID & Russ, Grace W. m.May05, 1921.
McFADDEN, JAMES PATRICK & Brown, Frances Berdeen m.Dec30, 1936.
McGAIN, ROY & Howell, Marjorie Joy m.Oct30, 1941.
McGEE, REX CECIL & Young, Ruth Edith m.Jun21, 1949.
McGOVERN, JOHN JAMES & Kapusta, Agnes Avelina m.Oct04, 1919.
McGOVERN, PERCY TOLLEY & Crotzer, Essie Grace m.May27, 1918.

MARRIAGES 1900 - 1950

McGOVERN, J. J. & Gilzean, Anna E. m.May09, 1900.
McKAY, HORACE & Ringle, Shirley Ruth m.Dec28, 1949.
McKAY, ROBERT & Smith, Nellie m.Oct05, 1915.
McKAY, JOHN & George, Lucy m.Dec17, 1919.
McKEE, MALCOLM D. & Leonard, Virginia L. m.Jun26, 1927.
McKEEVER, LAWRENCE LEE & Hiett, Mabel Sarah m.Aug07, 1936.
McKIBBON, FRANKIE & Nalton, Gracie m.Oct10, 1920.
McKNIGHT, JOSEPH FLAVIUS & Rogers, Fannie C. m.Jul20, 1902.
McKNIGHT, JAS. N. & Crabtree, Jane m.Nov24, 1914.
McLEOD, EDWARD O. & Pattison, Anna May m.Jun20, 1942.
McPHETRES, D. M. & Jordan, Nellie M. m.Jan12, 1910.
MADSEN, LAWRENCE & Bartlett, Doris m.Jun02, 1934.
MAKER, GEORGE I. & McKay, Lucy m.Oct10, 1907.
MALLOY, ROBERT WATSON & Post, Isabelle m.Jul16, 1906.
MANSFIELD, HAROLD H. & Milne, Gertrude m.Dec22, 1915.
MANTAGUE, H. E. I.[Montague?] & Elliston, Ella Lee m.Mar21, 1906.
MARCUS, JAMES E. & Cussins, Olive m.Jul05, 1901.
MARSHALL, EDWARD E. & Conlan, Virginia m.Apr01, 1939.
MARSHALL, ROBERT LAWS & Rourke, Mary Agnes m.Jun01, 1935.
MARTIN, ROBERT B. & Chesebro, Lucy m.Dec29, 1922.
MATHEWS, RALPH BERTRAM & Spratt, Loice Eleanor m.Feb15, 1948.
MATTHEWS, WILLIAM & Day, Mary, Mrs. m.Nov28, 1901.
MAZZETTA, ANGELO JAMES & Bergin, Evelyn Alafaire m.Mar05, 1938.
MEACHAM, JUSTIN A. & Lewis, Marguerite m.Nov21, 1918.
MEAD, CORYDON JEWETT & Martin, Susie Elizabeth m.Dec01, 1912.
MEAD, HARLAND E. & Friend, Viola B. m.May20, 1915.
MESSNER, HENRY & Stoddard, Fanny Fredrica m.Aug11, 1900.
MEYER, JAMES & Foster, Eveline m.Jul19, 1933.
MEYER, PETER J. & Albiez, Frieda m.Nov08, 1906.
MEYER, CHARLES WILLIAM & Biggerstaff, Rose m.Mar30, 1941.
MEYERS, B. F. & Shock, Cora m.Oct31, 1915.
MILLER, FRANCIS MARION & Goodyear, Irma m.Mar18, 1914.
MILLER, SAMUEL CALVIN & Greenwell, Emma Agnes m.Nov21, 1907.
MILLER, ALVIN RICHARD & Costa, Elva m.Jan07, 1934.
MILLS, RAYMOND LEROY & Copeland, Lennie Lea m.Nov28, 1947.
MOLIN, JAMES A. & Domenici, Julia E. m.May10, 1905.
MONROE, CHARLES & Rule, Mattie I. m.Nov14, 1901.
MONTGOMERY, NATHANIEL ESAU & Munster, Augusta m.Apr12, 1915.
MONTGOMERY, EARL H. & Farley, Agnes M. m.May29, 1942.
MONTGOMERY, EARL HOUSTON & Crews, Maud Mary Mabel m.Nov09, 1917.
MOORE, JOHN EDGAR & Burner, Loda m.Nov30, 1900.
MOORE, W. C. & Van Cleave, Dolores m.Oct11, 1909.
MOORE, JOHN WESLEY & Lowden, Artie Lenora m.Jan08, 1905.
MORAN, JOHN GARFIELD & Greenwell, Amy Eleanor m.Nov06, 1921.
MORAN, SAMUEL ALEXANDER & Fetzer, May Elaine m.Jan01, 1928.
MORGAN, A. B. & Quigley, Mary, Mrs. m.Oct13, 1901.
MORTON, CLAUDE D. & Vanderhoff, Iris m.Nov12, 1906.
MUNCY, KENNETH E. & Perkins, Louise Olive m.Jul12, 1948.
MUNSELL, LESTER J. & Brown, Mary Merrissa m.Nov11, 1936.
MURPHY, ALBERT E. & Flowers, Hattie m.Apr07, 1901.
MURRAY, BERNARD & Criss, Bertha m.Oct23, 1937.
NACHAND, RAYMOND ANDREW, Jr. & Bray, Ada Lee m.Jan01, 1946.
NEEDHAM, CARL & Briley, Myrl m.Sep22, 1934.
NEELY, WILLIAM WARREN & Anderson, Cora m.Mar14, 1916.
NEISINGH, ALFRED JEROME & Sevensen, Theodora Otille m.Jul23, 1921.
NIGHTINGALE, MARCUS & Ritchie, Hallie Buelah m.Jun20, 1945.
NILSON, HARRY FERD & Jenkins, Betty Lou m.Aug30, 1950.
NOBLE, JACKSON & Hutchins, Vera m.Apr14, 1919.
NOBLE, JOSEPH F. & Montgomery, Hazel B. m.Feb23, 1929.
NOBLET, F. I. & Brown, Mary Luvene m.Aug01, 1945.
NOONAN, HARRY H. & Heath, Florence J. m.Jul05, 1901.
NORMAN, KENNETH & Cook, Roberta m.Dec22, 1941.
O'KEEFE, THOMAS M. & Iverson, Camilla G. m.Sep18, 1902.

O'NEILL, MICHAEL & Fetzer, Louise m.Apr22, 1903.
OLSEN, JOHN JAMES & Alleman, Marion Elinor m.Apr16, 1934.
OLSEN, WILLIAM V. & Day, Georgia Alice m.Jun18, 1929.
OLSEN, EMIL M. & Sharer, Anna m.Apr15, 1900.
OLSEN, JOHN JAMES & Shock, Sadie E., Mrs. m.Jun11, 1911.
OLSEN, NORMAN TRIMBLE & Hussey, Carol Irene m.Jun17, 1938.
OSGOOD, U. G. & Warren, Alice m.Oct13, 1900.
OSGOOD, FRANK A. & Iversen, Alecia m.Nov05, 1903.
OSWILL, DON C. & Kivett, Elma O. m.Nov03, 1933.
OU, ROBERT RAY & Jessee, Millicent Glow m.Nov06, 1949.
OWNBY, WILLIAM ADOLPH & Mead, Susie Elizabeth m.Aug17, 1944.
PALMER, VICTOR M. & Schenkel, Leona May m.May22, 1939.
PATTISON, THOS. & McKay, Mary m.Oct08, 1997.
PATTON, W. A. & Vaughn, Lottie M. m.Feb04, 1904.
PATTON, JAMES W. & Vaughn, Charlotte m.Feb04, 1904.
PAULSEN, ALBERT L. & Leonard, Sadie Elenore m.Oct16, 1901.
PAULSON, FRANK V. & Giser, Elsie Hedwig m.Mar31, 1936.
PENNING, HENRY FRED & McMurphy, Isabella Loretta m.Jun18, 1937.
PERDUE, HARLEY JENE & Heath, Lois Fern m.Dec30, 1949.
PERENIN, FRANK J. & Schaffer, Zita m.Sep05, 1904.
PETTIS, WILLIAM TURNER & Steele, Virginia Lee m.Jun28, 1933.
PICTOW, LESTER WAYNE & Chanceller, Clara Elizabeth m.Feb15, 1941.
PLATZ, MARTIN J. & Hailstone, Merissa m.Feb07, 1905.
POWELL, HENRY J. & Flickinger, Roxie M. m.Jul09, 1934.
PRATT, ASA & Stevens, Ella m.Dec16, 1930.
PRITCHETT, WARREN S. & Marsen, Ruby m.Nov16, 1932.
PUTNAM, JAMES B. & Collins, Annie Margaret m.Jul14, 1929.
QUIMBY, BYRHL DEAN & DeForest, Alice June m.Aug14, 1947.
QUINN, GEORGE ARTHUR & Johnson, Laura Nell m.Sep27, 1938.
RADCLIFF, ROYAL E. & Philbrook, Susie m.Oct08, 1922.
RAIS, FRED & Long, Jean m.Apr05, 1947.
RAIS, M. & Rais, Maria Soares m.Dec27, 1930.
RALPH, LOUIS F. & McKay, Annie m.Sep30, 1903.
RANDOLPH, BENJAMIN H. & Bramlet, Jessie Lena m.Aug01, 1915.
RANSOM, JOE KURT & Morgan, Lula Belle m.May30, 1946.
RAYMOND, FRACER D. & Shadley, Madeline Grace m.May13, 1939.
READE, CHARLES DWIGHT, Jr. & Wyckoff, Dorothy Edra m.Aug29, 1937.
REED, ROYAL WALLACE & Shock, Ila May Miss m.Mar04, 1920.
REESE, THOMAS E. & Stanfield, Bernice m.Aug19, 1938.
REEVES, BELE B. & Fowler, Mabel Susan m.Nov08, 1943.
REID, GEORGE BRITON McCLELLAN & Coumbs, Elizabeth M. m.Jan15, 1902.
REID, HANS C. & Paul, May, Mrs. m.Jul29, 1925.
REID, LATEN P. & Bennett, Ida C. m.Sep04, 1900.
REYNOLDS, RODNEY F. & Marshall, Verna E. m.Jun22, 1922.
REYNOLDS, JOHN B. & Benton, Edna E. m.Dec01, 1914.
RICE, KEITH & Ebenspecher, Eileen m.Aug27, 1934.
RICHARDS, WILLIAM & Scott, Clara May m.Mar02, 1904.
RILEY, EVERT & Riley, Betty m.Mar20, 1947.
ROBERTS, FRANCIS NIBLO & Averitt, Margarette Pauline m.Feb20, 1934.
ROBERTS, PETER & Frank, Helena, Mrs. m.Nov28, 1903.
ROBERTS, WILLIAM THOMAS & Williams, Adeline Martha m.Nov11, 1912.
ROBINSON, DAVID H. & Shock, Nora Irene, Miss m.Mar09, 1920.
RODGERS, JOHN F. & McMullen, Amelia H. m.Nov20, 1901.
ROSE, JOHN LESTER & Rucker, Ruby m.Feb27, 1932.
ROSS, WILLIAM WAYNE & Buck, Barbara Jane m.Feb14, 1938.
ROURKE, CHARLES JAMES & Dedrick, Agnes Rebecca m.Jul31, 1913.
ROURKE, JOHN DONALD & McDonald, Idell Barbara m.Apr28, 1919.
RUSSELL, BENJAMIN F. & Lock, Eva Lena m.Aug18, 1915.
RUSSELL, CLARENCE ODELL & Crum, Pearl Louise m.Nov13, 1930.
RYAN, RICHARD HENRY & Smith, Mary Katherine m.Nov27, 1937.
RYAN, EDWARD & Weinheimer, Annie L. m.Jan10, 1900.
SALSBURY, DEVILLO A. & McKnight, Amanda Kathryn m.Apr07, 1912.
SAMUELSON, WESLEY & Dix, Emeline Mary m.Jul25, 1936.

SANBURN, CHARLES R. & Carter, Eveline F. m.Dec03, 1903.
SCHAFFER, ARTHUR A. & Hooker, Agnes, Mrs. m.Mar02, 1923.
SCHAFFER, ARTHUR AUGUST & Norwood, Letha m.Jun29, 1940.
SCHLOTTER, JACK WOODWARD & Bigelow, Virginia Maude m.Dec27, 1948.
SCHMITT, FRED WILLIAM & Nightingale, Catherine Josephine m.Oct05, 1943.
SCHNEIDER, WILLIAM & Smith, Atha m.Nov20, 1946.
SCHNELLBACHER, BRAXTON B. & Hammond, Letha L. m.May13, 1900.
SCHOLE, WILLIAM & Rayburn, Jennie C. m.Dec31, 1934.
SCHULTZ, ALEXANDER & Thorne, Alice Burton m.Jun05, 1913.
SCHURRER, JOE & Riley, Evelyn m.Mar09, 1934.
SCOTT, EDWARD RAY & Crockenberg, Joan Marie Harper m.Oct22, 1947.
SCOTT, W. I. & Owings, Nora L. m.Jan31, 1910.
SCRIBNER, RICHARD G. & Greatorex, Dorothy L., Miss m.Jan01, 1923.
SENGER, GEORGE W. & Arguello, Irene I. m.Dec03, 1903.
SENGER, MILAN A. & Goodyear, Vera A. m.Oct30, 1903.
SEWARD, LLOYD SCOTT & Fox, Betty Jean m.Oct28, 1941.
SHAW, JOSEPH J. & Junkans, Elfrieda m.Jun12, 1901.
SHAW, HARRY R. & Colbert, Margarita M. m.Jan22, 1902.
SHEARER, JOSEPH M. & Orewiler, Stella m.Aug28, 1906.
SHIMMIN, HOMER LOUIS & Boehm, Elma Gladys m.Dec22, 1939.
SHOCK, J. S. & Vaughn, Emeline L., Mrs. m.Oct11, 1906.
SHULES, WILLIAM & Gates, Cordelia, Mrs. m.Aug31, 1923.
SILIGO, EDWARD J. & Kapusta, Annie m.Dec24, 1914.
SIMMONS, WILLIAM H. & Lanktree, Eleanor M. m.Oct11, 1937.
SIMPSON, THOMAS J. & Rodgers, Josephine E., Miss m.Nov22, 1911.
SMITH, ROBERT WILLARD & Prindle, Elizabeth Aloha m.Jun01, 1936.
SMITH, LOYAL T. & Spencer, Rubye Eugenia m.Jun29, 1946.
SMITH, BRADLEY I. & Conner, Greta Mae m.Dec16, 1946.
SMITH, FRANK M. & Weinheimer, Caroline E. m.Aug12, 1903.
SMITH, DOUGLAS N. & Bailey, Emma Lou m.Jul03, 1946.
SMITH, HENRY CARROLL & Gribble, Mary, Mrs. m.Jan10, 1911.
SMITH, PETER D. & Paulina, Mary m.Jun12, 1907.
SMITH, MAX F. & Stein, Gladys m.May28, 1936.
SPEARS, WILLIAM & Sullivan, Carrie m.Feb22, 1900.
SPECHT, RICHARD CHARLES & Armentrout, Effie Bell m.Nov08, 1913.
SPEICH, GEORGE M. & Barr, Anna m.Oct19, 1930.
SPINDLER, HAROLD ALBERT & McNeill, Violet Permilla m.Jun18, 1932.
SPINDLER, DAVID & Mayfielld, Neva m.Apr07, 1934.
SPRATT, HOWARD CODDINGTON & Reed, Alice Josephine m.Oct20, 1941.
SPRATT, STEPHEN T. & Hutchins, Ada C. m.Aug20, 1912.
SPRATT, HENRY THAYER & Stenbit, Adele Grace m.May01, 1935.
STEEL, SIDNEY ALLEN & Goodrich, Leota Belle m.May01, 1908.
STEELE, MERTON E. & Neilson, Joy m.Apr09, 1939.
STETTER, VICTOR JOSEPH & Leighter, Ellarena A. m.Jul20, 1937.
STEWART, JAMES P. & Ludden, Helen m.Sep21, 1934.
STOFER, H. C. & Joseph, Annie m.Dec02, 1905.
STORY, STANLEY EDWARD & Duncan, Shirley Evelyn m.Apr17, 1949.
SUTHERLAND, HENRY I. & Woodbury, Ethel Clare m.Jun15, 1904.
SWAIN, ROBERT BRUCE & Sherman, Pauline m.Mar27, 1948.
SWITSER, TRUMAN GRANT & Hailstone, Ethel Pauline m.Mar09, 1935.
TARDIFF, LEONARD & Burns, Dorothy m.Dec09, 1946.
TARPLEY, J. W. & Ellis, Margaret m.Dec24, 1910.
TARPLEY, EDWARD LEE & Vitzthum, Lena m.Jun25, 1902.
TATHAM, WILLIAM FRANCIS & Carter, Ella Jane m.Dec25, 1918.
TAYLOR, EDWARD MILTON & Bartlett, Mary Alice m.Jun06, 1917.
TAYLOR, PAUL CLEMENT & Campbell, Lillian m.Nov25, 1926.
TAYLOR, JESSE J. & Wood, Helen Mar m.Oct30, 1926.
TAYLOR, JAMES ORION & Ryan, Katherine Mary m.Feb22, 1948.
TAYLOR, JOHN H. & Stone, Luberta m.Apr17, 1947.
TAYLOR, LYLE SAMUEL & Day, Mary m.Jan27, 1943.
TERRILL, RAYMOND DILLON & Freeman, Helen Leota m.Jun14, 1949.
TESTY, CHARLES J. & Henderson, Leola Violet m.Mar21, 1906.
TESTY, CHARLES JEROME & Clark, Linnie Alice m.Dec18, 1926.

THOMAS, BRIGHAM & Goodyear, Barbara, Miss m.Feb29, 1924.
THORNE, GEORGE ISAAC & Van Matre, Vivian Helen m.Mar26, 1912.
THOZA, MANUEL SILVA & Joseph, Fanny m.Jun15, 1911.
TINGLEY, WILLIAM LEROY & Grant, Gladys M. m.Jul11, 1950.
TODD, JOHN A. & Henderson, Leona M. m.Jul13, 1901.
TOURTELLOTTE, JESSE FRANCIS & Fox, Isabel Johnson m.Jul23, 1902.
TRAVIS, WILLIAM, Jr. & Wright, Shirley Mardis m.Oct19, 1940.
TRELOAR, E. W. & Gates, Delia m.Apr29, 1915.
TRIMBLE, JOHN W. & Wilson, Sarah m.Jul30, 1903.
TRIMBLE, RAYMOND ALEXANDER & Madsen, Esther m.Nov12, 1919.
TRIMBLE, FRANK L. & Jordan, Sarah A. m.Jul15, 1922.
TRUSTY, ROBERT L. & Clarke, Marie Kathleen m.Oct24, 1950.
TUCK, RAYMOND & Chapman, Evelyn m.Sep13, 1950.
ULLOM, ELLON CHASE & Wilson, Norma Lorem m.Jun06, 1931.
UPTON, J. D. & McNamara, Mattie Belle m.Mar15, 1907.
URBAN, EUGENE & Neusse, Bertha m.Jul28, 1906.
VALENTINE, JAMES & Rovelli, Violette m.Aug11, 1934.
VALENTINE, CHARLES EUGENE & Tallman, Dorothy Jane m.May03, 1949.
VAN CLEAVE, JOHN W. W. & Ralph, Luella Mrs. m.Jul02, 1900.
VAN MATRE, WALTER JOHN PETER & Junkans, Karlyn Helen m.Nov29, 1928.
VAN MATRE, JUDSON C. & McMillan, Martha G. m.Dec02, 1933.
VANCLEAVE, CARL V. & Joseph, Marie m.Jul27, 1901.
VAUGHN, DeFOREST H. & Trimble, Rebecca E. m.Jan19, 1922.
VAUGHN, CHARLES RAYMOND & Blair, Luella m.Mar03, 1917.
VAUGHN, HARRY BENJAMIN & McKay, Edith Delia m.Apr19, 1915.
VAUGHN, DAN & Trimble, Belle m.Apr03, 1915.
VERBURG, EDWARD DONALD & Orrell, Dorothy Louise m.Dec05, 1934.
VICK, WILLIAM BRYAN & Todd, Amy Lucille m.Jul12, 1929.
WAGNER, BUD & Rauzi, Myra, Miss m.Jun09, 1924.
WALKER, JOHN P. H. & Hughes, Naomi Mitten m.May14, 1949.
WALKER, W. N. & Grigsby, Florence I. m.Jun07, 1903.
WALLEN, FRANK & Irving, Annie m.Jun29, 1930.
WALTERS, JOHN ULRICH & Andrews, Gladys m.Apr02, 1938.
WARKENTIN, THEODORE N. & Pennington, Muriel N. m.Jun28, 1932.
WEINHEIMER, NORMAN F. & Goodyear, Janet Elsie m.Dec31, 1939.
WEINHEIMER, HENRY D. & Flagg, Clara May m.Aug10, 1904.
WELLOCK, GEORGE WALTER & Bresler, Stella Pearl m.Dec18, 1937.
WELSH, MICHAEL & Koelle, Marie m.May05, 1905.
WERT, WILLIAM DALE & Driskell, Edythe E. m.Oct17, 1934.
WHEAT, ARTHUR LLOYD & Hackler, Wilma Clarice m.Jun17, 1939.
WHITE, JORDAN HERBERT & Sherman, Lovenia m.Sep30, 1925.
WHITE, EDWARD OTTO & Perry, Clara Buleah m.Sep19, 1906.
WHITE, WILLIAM W. & Black, Annabelle m.Nov22, 1936.
WHITNEY, CHARLES LEO & Dillon, Phyllis Loraine m.Nov11, 1938.
WIGTON, JAMES & Crews, Mattie m.Nov14, 1915.
WILLIAMS, WILLIAM ORANGE & Hammond, Annie V. m.Feb20, 1907.
WILLIAMS, FREDERICK H. & Carter, Elizabeth M. m.Aug23, 1905.
WILSON, WARD THOMAS & Meeks, Louann Eunice m.Oct23, 1950.
WILSON, HAROLD J. & Adrian, Mary Josephine m.Dec12, 1922.
WOLD, HENRY & Eberspecher, Katherine m.Mar15, 1947.
WOLF, FRED & Larson, Hilma O. m.Jan09, 1942.
WONG, FREDERICK S. N. & Lee, Lena Elizabeth m.Jan15, 1921.
WOOD, DONALD THOMAS & Kiefer, Jerrine, Miss m.Aug06, 1920.
WOODS, MARK HERBERT & Loven, Helen Hilda m.Jun01, 1941.
WRIGHT, JEAN MELVIN & Tinsley, Inez Charline m.Jan23, 1937.
YOUNG, VAN BRUNT & Meckel, Anna Marie m.Jun17, 1903.
YOUNG, LAWRENCE GEORGE & Miller, Elva Costa m.Jun29, 1938.
YOUNG, HENRY J. & Robinson, Mary m.Nov25, 1909.
ZACHARY, JOHN LYMAN & Morris, Pansy Elizabeth m.Nov08, 1927.
ZOSEL, EARLE L.& George, Abbie m.Dec09, 1943.

MARRIAGES 1900 - 1950

WIFE and HUSBAND, with MARRIAGE DATE.

ABBOTT, JULIA & IVY, William H. m.Sep13, 1909.
ADAMS, BERNICE M. & Hodges, Leonard B. m.Sep23, 1933.
ADRIAN, MARY JOSEPHINE & Wilson, Harold J. m.Dec12, 1922.
AHERIN, PATRICIA JOYCE & Abbott, Julius m.Jun25, 1938.
ALBIEZ, GENEVIEVE, Miss & Jackson, Lemuel T. m.Dec06, 1924.
ALBIEZ, FRIEDA & Meyer, Peter J. m.Nov08, 1906.
ALLEMAN, MARION ELINOR & Olsen, John James m.Apr16, 1934.
ALLEN, DOROTHEA E. & Keffer, R. F. m.Oct23, 1910.
ALLEN, GLADYS & Holbrook, John T. m.Oct10, 1931.
ALLEN, HELEN HANSEN & Knowles, Henry Merlyn m.Dec10, 1938.
ALLEN, MARGARET & Bigelow, Samuel James m.Apr15, 1933.
ALSSA, GRAYCE & Ceschi, Hector m.Oct11, 1937.
AMBLER, THELMA DIXIE & Harvey, Wilton Milberry m.Jun02, 1927.
AMORT, MARILYN JEAN & Arey, Joseph William m.Sep22, 1948.
ANDERLINI, ELLA TERESA, Miss & Bennett, Curtis Morton m.Nov25, 1911.
ANDERLINI, ANITA & Box, Reuben P. m.Feb24, 1915.
ANDERSON, CORA & Neely, William Warren m.Mar14, 1916.
ANDERSON, MARY E. & Jackman, Charles E. m.Mar05, 1922.
ANDREWS, GLADYS & Walters, John Ulrich m.Apr02, 1938.
ANGEL, ALICE V. [Davis?] & Cleaves, Joseph m.May26, 1947.
ARBUCKLE, ELIZABETH MARVELL & Cruson, Earl Leslie m.Feb27, 1946.
ARBUCKLE, GENEVIEVE, Miss & Brown, Stanley B. m.Feb22, 1923.
ARGUELLO, IRENE I. & Senger, George W. m.Dec03, 1903.
ARMENTROUT, EFFIE BELL & Specht, Richard Charles m.Nov08, 1913.
ARMSTRONG, LILY, Mrs. & Knowles, H. L. m.Dec03, 1902.
ARNANDOS, TOMASSO & Botiller, Joe m.Jan17, 1921.
ASHBAUGH, IMOGENE & Lederer, Lester m.Aug02, 1930.
ASPLUND, CLARA BELLE & Burwell, George Raymond m.Mar06, 1948.
ATKINS, ETHEL F. & Enos, Thomas M. m.Apr09, 1902.
ATKINS, LULU & Caton, John m.Sep04, 1900.
AVERITT, MARGARETTE PAULINE & Roberts, Francis Niblo m.Feb20, 1934.
BABCOCK, JOSEPHINE MAY, Mrs. & Hayward, Lysander Whetman m.Mar10, 1916.
BACON, MATIE & Duncan, William C. m.Jan31, 1906.
BAILEY, EMMA LOU & Smith, Douglas N. m.Jul03, 1946.
BAILEY, ALICE DENICE & Boudreaux, Jules Edward m.Dec20, 1946.
BARBER, BESSIE & Blaney, John J. m.Oct11, 1907.
BARBOUR, MADELINE E., Miss & Carr, Otis m.Jul30, 1923.
BARKLA, ELLA & Fry, James m.Sep02, 1900.
BARKLEY, GLADYS MARIE & Irvine, Claude Robert m.Jun18, 1949.
BARNICKEL, DETTA, Miss & Lee, B. F. [in San Francisco] m.Jan03, 1905.
BARNICKEL, JOHANNA & Levy, Phil Morton m.Jun18, 1902.
BARR, ANNA & Speich, George M. m.Oct19, 1930.
BARTLETT, MARY ALICE & Taylor, Edward Milton m.Jun06, 1917.
BARTLETT, DORIS & Madsen, Lawrence m.Jun02, 1934.
BECKETT, DOROTHY MAY & Buhlman, Rudolph Robert m.Dec28, 1938.
BENNETT, VIVIAN E. & Leavitt, Horace J. m.Jul09, 1933.
BENNETT, IDA C. & Reid, Laten P. m.Sep04, 1900.
BENNETT, MARY I. & Iverson, Horace G. m.Jun26, 1909.
BENNETT, ANNIE MAY & Hodson, Henry m.Feb18, 1902.
BENNION, DOROTHY DOUGLAS & Johnson, Darrel James m.Dec06, 1936.
BENTON, EDNA E. & Reynolds, John B. m.Dec01, 1914.
BERGIN, EVELYN ALAFAIRE & Mazzetta, Angelo James m.Mar05, 1938.
BIGELOW, VIRGINIA MAUDE & Schlotter, Jack Woodward m.Dec27, 1948.
BIGELOW, LEILA MAUD, Miss & Henry, Benjamin Harrison m.Jun19, 1920.
BIGELOW, ELIZABETH PEARL & Langworthy, John Robert m.Jul24, 1945.
BIGELOW, MASIE ELONIA & Gilzean, Warren Mayhew m.Aug10, 1916.
BIGGERSTAFF, ROSE & Meyer, Charles William m.Mar30, 1941.
BILLMEYER, LUCY A., Mrs. & Kise, Commodore C. m.Jun04, 1925.
BISHOP, VEDA & Cowan, Jack m.Dec26, 1946.

BLACK, ANNABELLE & White, William W. m.Nov22, 1936.
BLAIR, LUELLA & Vaughn, Charles Raymond m.Mar03, 1917.
BLAKEMORE, VIVIAN V. & Holland, H. H. m.Oct01, 1910.
BLANEY, HONORA & Fields, David Blackstone m.Aug07, 1908.
BLERY, SARAH ELIZABETH & Brackett, Albert James m.Nov05, 1907.
BOEHM, ELMA GLADYS & Shimmin, Homer Louis m.Dec22, 1939.
BONCE, LOUISA & Hitchcock, Charles m.Sep12, 1901.
BOWERMAN, ELSIE ANNA & Goodrich, Guy E. m.Jun24, 1915.
BOWERMAN, AMY E. & Greenwell, Wm. Ernest m.Feb26, 1914.
BOYCE, CLARA E. & Goetze, William Adolph m.Jan26, 1905.
BRADBURY, THERISA & McDonald, John A. m.Nov26, 1908.
BRAGDON, ORA GLADYS & Heath, Charles Jesse m.Jun26, 1918.
BRAMLET, JESSIE LENA & Randolph, Benjamin H. m.Aug01, 1915.
BRANNAN, EDNA TERESA & Leach, Earle N. m.Jul12, 1914.
BRAY, ADA LEE & Nachand, Raymond Andrew, Jr. m.Jan01, 1946.
BRESLER, STELLA PEARL & Wellock, George Walter m.Dec18, 1937.
BRICE, RUTH ADELLE & McCann, Earl James m.May09, 1918.
BRIGGS, BESSIE IRENE & Ladine, Roy R. m.May23, 1937.
BRILEY, MYRL & Needham, Carl m.Sep22, 1934.
BROWN, MAUDE F. & Kibler, Herbert Lee m.Sep03, 1938.
BROWN, HELEN MEDORA & Brearcliffe, Abraham Lincoln m.Dec21, 1921.
BROWN, MARY LUVENE & Noblet, F. I. m.Aug01, 1945.
BROWN, MARY MERRISSA & Munsell, Lester J. m.Nov11, 1936.
BROWN, FRANCES BERDEEN & McFadden, James Patrick m.Dec30, 1936.
BROWN, KATHRYN & Karolski, Harry Joseph m.Jul22, 1944.
BROWNE, EDNA K. & Boring, Carthel F. m.Sep30, 1942.
BRYAN, BETTY & Fisk, George B. m.Jan29, 1946.
BUCK, BARBARA JANE & Ross, William Wayne m.Feb14, 1938.
BURGER, ELIZA & Kern, Harry m.Jun27, 1907.
BURGER, JULIA & Clark, Arthur R. m.Jun03, 1903.
BURNER, LODA & Moore, John Edgar m.Nov30, 1900.
BURNS, DOROTHY & Tardiff, Leonard m.Dec09, 1946.
CALHOUN, AUDREY BEVERLY & Foote, Charles Arthur m.Oct19, 1946.
CALVERT, MARIE KATHLEEN & Clarke, Russell O. m.Nov20, 1941.
CAMPBELL, IDA GRAZILLA & Laffell, Joseph E. m.Dec18, 1900.
CAMPBELL, LILLIAN & Taylor, Paul Clement m.Nov25, 1926.
CANTRALL, GERALDINE E. & Blaney, Robert James m.Sep04, 1948.
CANTWELL, ADALINE & Brossard, William J. m.Jul28, 1939.
CARPENTER, MATTIE T. & Hawksley, H. H. m.Feb08, 1901.
CARR, MILDRED I. & Fehr, Jacob Peter m.Dec03, 1918.
CARR, ROSE & Grigsby, Pleasant m.May07, 1902.
CARTER, EVELINE F. & Sanburn, Charles R. m.Dec03, 1903.
CARTER, ELIZABETH M. & Williams, Frederick H. m.Aug23, 1905.
CARTER, ELLA JANE & Tatham, William Francis m.Dec25, 1918.
CARTER, ENID MERLE & Hawk, Howard Clinton m.Jul16, 1912.
CATON, ALICE GERTRUDE & Bonney, M. Pierce m.Nov26, 1921.
CATON, MARGARET LOUISE & Borden, William Russel m.Aug17, 1946.
CHAMBERS, JUANITA HORTENSE & Hanover, Alton Dale m.Jan01, 1928.
CHANCELLER, CLARA ELIZABETH & Pictow, Lester Wayne m.Feb15, 1941.
CHAPMAN, EVELYN & Tuck, Raymond m.Sep13, 1950.
CHAPMAN, BONNIE LOUISE & Carr, Frank Willis m.Mar07, 1921.
CHESBRO, EMMA & Carpenter, Elmer B. m.Sep23, 1922.
CHESEBRO, LUCY & Martin, Robert B. m.Dec29, 1922.
CHETWOOD, GLADYS & Blankenship, George D. m.Jul10, 1939.
CLARK, LINNIE ALICE & Testy, Charles Jerome m.Dec18, 1926.
CLARKE, INA MARIE & Dunlap, George A. m.Jul13, 1946.
CLARKE, MARIE KATHLEEN & Trusty, Robert L. m.Oct24, 1950.
CLEAVES, MARGARET JANE, Miss & Brown, Charles Leroy m.Jul20, 1920.
CLEAVES, HARRIET MARIE & Cuff, Lester L. m.Mar03, 1932.
CLEMENT, EDNA ROSE & Arbuckle, Harvey Woodrow m.May18, 1934.
CLEMENT, MINNIE DeCORA & Lorenz, John Nicholas m.Aug26, 1915.
COLBERT, MARGARITA M. & Shaw, Harry R. m.Jan22, 1902.
COLLINS, ANNIE MARGARET & Putnam, James B. m.Jul14, 1929.

MARRIAGES 1900 - 1950

COLLINS, GERALDINE & Biggerstaff, Talbert James m.Jun28, 1932.
CONDON, ANNIE & Bush, Chauncey Carroll m.Oct09, 1901.
CONLAN, VIRGINIA & Marshall, Edward E. m.Apr01, 1939.
CONNER, GRETA MAE & Smith, Bradley I. m.Dec16, 1946.
CONNER, MYRTLE RUTH & Forslund, Dero Bradford m.Jan01, 1940.
COOK, ROBERTA & Norman, Kenneth m.Dec22, 1941.
COOLEY, BLANCHE, Miss & Dunn, Samuel Allen m.Nov16 , 1925.
COPELAND, LENNIE LEA & Mills, Raymond Leroy m.Nov28, 1947.
CORNETT, LOUISE & Hutchinson, Edgar Ernest m.Sep08, 1945.
COSTA, ELVA & Miller, Alvin Richard m.Jan07, 1934.
COTTRELL, LOYOLA GENROSE & Barnickel, Bernhard m.Jun06, 1904.
COUMBS, ELIZABETH M. & Reid, George Briton McClellan m.Jan15, 1902.
COUNTS, ALICE ELIZABETH & Baird, Charles Francis m.Aug13, 1906.
CRABTREE, JANE & McKnight, Jas. N. m.Nov24, 1914.
CREWDSON, DAISY & Hylton, Kenneth P. m.Sep21, 1934.
CREWS, MAUD MARY MABEL & Montgomery, Earl Houston m.Nov09, 1917.
CREWS, MATTIE & Wigton, James m.Nov14, 1915.
CRISS, BERTHA & Murray, Bernard m.Oct23, 1937.
CROCKENBERG, JOAN MARIE HARPER & Scott, Edward Ray m.Oct22, 1947.
CROTZER, ESSIE GRACE & McGovern, Percy Tolley m.May27, 1918.
CRUM, PEARL LOUISE & Russell, Clarence Odell m.Nov13, 1930.
CRUME, HELEN FAYE & de Generes, Harold Erwin m.Aug06, 1940.
CUSSINS, OLIVE & Marcus, James E. m.Jul05, 1901.
DABBS, LADESSA ELAINE & Jones, Benjamin Clayton m.Aug26, 1938.
DACT, ESTHEL & Burns, Thomas m.Jun05, 1929.
DANFORTH, MYRA & Danforth, Richard S. m.Nov09, 1936.
DANIELSON, NEVA IDA & Campbell, Harold Hardin m.Jun16, 1944.
DANNENBRINK, ELEANOR C. & Edwards, Charles H. m.Jul07, 1915.
DAWSON, NANCY M. & Gilzean, James Albert m.Mar29, 1931.
DAWSON, BEULAH ISABELLE & Ferguson, James Ralph m.May10, 1921.
DAWSON, RUTH & Cussins, Adellbert E. m.May01, 1901.
DAWSON, EMMA NORINE & Henderson, William V. m.Jan07, 1920.
DAY, EVELYN JUNE & McClintock, Glenn Richard m.Jul10, 1949.
DAY, MARY & Taylor, Lyle Samuel m.Jan27, 1943.
DAY, GEORGIA ALICE & Olsen, William V. m.Jun18, 1929.
DAY, MARY, Mrs. & Matthews, William m.Nov28, 1901.
DEDRICK, AGNES REBECCA & Rourke, Charles James m.Jul31, 1913.
DeFOREST, ALICE JUNE & Quimby, Byrhl Dean m.Aug14, 1947.
DELLAIRE, MARY D. & French, Richard A. m.Oct22, 1942.
DENNING, IRENE E. & Jennings, Frank m.Aug01, 1946.
DICKERSON, NELLIE MAY & Brazenall, Wm. m.Oct26, 1908.
DICKEY, CATHERINE IRENE & Carr, Frank Willis m.Mar03, 1931.
DICKEY, EMILY & Gribble, Richard m.Jul06, 1904.
DILLON, PHYLLIS LORAINE & Whitney, Charles Leo m.Nov11, 1938.
DIX, EMELINE MARY & Samuelson, Wesley m.Jul25, 1936.
DOEBELIN, FANNIE, Mrs. & Bennington, Richard C. m.Apr13, 1906.
DOMENICI, EMILY MARIE & Endicott, Samuel Partridge m.Apr05, 1912.
DOMENICI, JULIA E. & Molin, James A. m.May10, 1905.
DOUGLAS, EILEEN & Hoskins, Albert m.Jun10, 1930.
DOUGLAS, IRENE & Buys, Hiram Edward m.Jan18, 1901.
DRISKELL, EDYTHE E. & Wert, William Dale m.Oct17, 1934.
DUNCAN, LOUISA & Burgard, James J. m.Jul06, 1905.
DUNCAN, SHIRLEY EVELYN & Story, Stanley Edward m.Apr17, 1949.
DUNCAN, JANE & Crabtree, Fred m.Sep15, 1906.
DUNLAP, NELLIE & Johnson, Fred m.Mar22, 1902.
EBENSPECHER, EILEEN & Rice, Keith m.Aug27, 1934.
EBERSPECHER, KATHERINE & Wold, Henry m.Mar15, 1947.
ELDRIDGE, HAZEL ALLEEN & Hunter, Joseph Edgar m.Sep01, 1918.
ELLERY, MINNIE MYRTLE & Aldrich, James E. m.Jul05, 1905.
ELLERY, CARRIE P. & Crocker, Harry m.Sep16, 1906.
ELLIS, MARGARET & Tarpley, J. W. m.Dec24, 1910.
ELLIS, MIRIAM MARIE & Lessing, Earl Preston m.Aug07, 1926.
ELLISTON, ELLA LEE & Mantague, H. E. I. [Montague?] m.Mar21, 1906.

ETTLINE, JEAN E. & Jensen, Lyle H. m.Jul28, 1947.
FARLEY, AGNES M. & Montgomery, Earl H. m.May29, 1942.
FERGUSON, MARY RUTH & Chaney, Sidney T. m.Jan09, 1929.
FETZER, MAY ELAINE & Moran, Samuel Alexander m.Jan01, 1928.
FETZER, LOUISE & O'Neill, Michael m.Apr22, 1903.
FfOULKES, JEAN A. & Ffoulkes, Thomas C. m.Jul07, 1926.
FfOULKES, RUTH CATHERINE PEARSON & Hughes, Everett Lisle m.Jun05, 1929.
FIELDS, ANNA ELVIRA, Mrs. & Langstroff, Adolph Joseph m.Aug06, 1916.
FLAGG, CLARA MAY & Weinheimer, Henry D. m.Aug10, 1904.
FLAGG, SADIE A. & Day, Walter A. m.Sep18, 1905.
FLICKINGER, ROXIE M. & Powell, Henry J. m.Jul09, 1934.
FLOWERS, HATTIE & Murphy, Albert E. m.Apr07, 1901.
FLYNN, DOLLIE & Dewey, Arthur O. m.Nov02, 1903.
FORD, FRIEDA FAY & Carr, Harrin Stanley m.Feb17, 1933.
FORRESTER, MARION KATHERINE & Jackson, Melvin Clarence m.May06, 1950.
FOSTER, EVELINE & Meyer, James m.Jul19, 1933.
FOWLER, MABEL SUSAN & Reeves, Bele B. m.Nov08, 1943.
FOX, BETTY JEAN & Seward, Lloyd Scott m.Oct28, 1941.
FOX, ELIZABETH H. & Gehm, G. F. m.Apr06, 1909.
FOX, ISABEL JOHNSON & Tourtellotte, Jesse Francis m.Jul23, 1902.
FRANK, HELENA, Mrs. & Roberts, Peter m.Nov28, 1903.
FRATES, EVA EVELYN & Efau, James Henry m.Dec24, 1915.
FREEMAN, HELEN LEOTA & Terrill, Raymond Dillon m.Jun14, 1949.
FRIEND, MARGUERITE & Derrick, Grant, Jr. m.Jun10, 1931.
FRIEND, MARY EVA & Campbell, Thomas H. m.Aug08, 1905.
FRIEND, VIOLA B. & Mead, Harland E. m.May20, 1915.
GAGEL, FRANKIE & Hammack, Lee m.Nov01, 1947.
GAINES, MAYBELLE MADELINE & Cherry, Obie Ronald m.Nov17, 1926.
GASSAWAY, LILLIAN BEATRICE & Burgess, Zera Edward m.May07, 1907.
GATES, DELIA & TRELOAR, E. W. m.Apr29, 1915.
GATES, CORDELIA, Mrs. & Shules, William m.Aug31, 1923.
GEORGE, ABBIE & Zosel, Earle L. m.Dec09, 1943.
GEORGE, LUCY & McKay, John m.Dec17, 1919.
GIBSON, HELEN ELIZABETH & Cahoone, William Muir m.Aug23, 1935.
GILZEAN, ANNA E. & McGovern, J. J. m.May09, 1900.
GILZEAN, MARVEL LOUISA & Gates, Dewey Ralph m.Feb17, 1921.
GISER, ELSIE HEDWIG & Paulson, Frank V. m.Mar31, 1936.
GIUMELLI, JOSEPHINE & McDaniel, Fred A. m.Oct10, 1931.
GOODRICH, LEOTA BELLE & Steel, Sidney Allen m.May01, 1908.
GOODYEAR, BARBARA, Miss & Thomas, Brigham m.Feb29, 1924.
GOODYEAR, JANET ELSIE & Weinheimer, Norman F. m.Dec31, 1939.
GOODYEAR, VERA A. & Senger, Milan A. m.Oct30, 1903.
GOODYEAR, IRMA & Miller, Francis Marion m.Mar18, 1914.
GOSSETT, MILDRED & Carr, Clarence m.Oct15, 1930.
GRANT, GLADYS M. & Tingley, William Leroy m.Jul11, 1950.
GRAY, ELIZABETH CAROLYN & Anderson, Richard Arthur m.Jun10, 1950.
GRAY, _____, Miss & Cox, Solomon m.Sep25, 1901.
GREATOREX, DOROTHY L., Miss & Scribner, Richard G. m.Jan01, 1923.
GREEN, VIOLET & Bailey, John Wesley m.May31, 1938.
GREENLIEF, ANNIE & Lewman, George F. m.Sep03, 1906.
GREENWELL, CLARA GERTRUDE & Kinyon, James Earle m.Sep22, 1921.
GREENWELL, AMY ELEANOR & Moran, John Garfield m.Nov06, 1921.
GREENWELL, EMMA AGNES & Miller, Samuel Calvin m.Nov21, 1907.
GRIBBLE, MARY, Mrs. & Smith, Henry Carroll m.Jan10, 1911.
GRIFFITH, MAE ELLEN & Algar, Robert Clair m.Jun09, 1935.
GRIFFITH, HELEN MARY & Desmond, Ambrose Jackson m.Jun03, 1929.
GRIGSBY, FLORENCE I. & Walker, W. N. m.Jun07, 1903.
GRILLS, MYRTLE MEEKER & Irving, Harrison L. m.Sep16, 1936.
GUGLIELMETTI, ESTHER VIRGINIA & Guespari, Bruno John m.Jun29, 1937.
GUILL, MILDRED I. & Carr, Fred Elmer m.Dec01, 1914.
HABERKAM, MAUDE ALLEN & Harry, Robert Merit m.Oct19, 1946.
HACKLER, WILMA CLARICE & Wheat, Arthur Lloyd m.Jun17, 1939.
HAFLEY, MAIDA HAZEL & Costa, Frank m.Dec24, 1939.

MARRIAGES 1900 - 1950

HAGERTY, EDITH LORETA, Miss & Locklin, George R. m.Jan12, 1920.
HAILSTONE, NANCY A. & Farmer, George H. m.Oct23, 1901.
HAILSTONE, DIANA WEBSTER & Coumbs, Walter Scott m.Feb28, 1913.
HAILSTONE, MERISSA & Platz, Martin J. m.Feb07, 1905.
HAILSTONE, ETHEL PAULINE & Switser, Truman Grant m.Mar09, 1935.
HALE, ALICE & Knaggs, Orville m.Mar24, 1938.
HALE, IDOLENE H. & Ewell, Rathborne E. m.Jun25, 1932.
HALE, BETA ISABELLE & Hunt, Rowland Merritt m.Apr11, 1938.
HALLEY, THELMA FRANCES & Fetherton, William Henry m.Sep29, 1927.
HAM, MAUD & Lynch, Fred m.Nov06, 1906.
HAMMOND, ANNIE V. & Williams, William Orange m.Feb20, 1907.
HAMMOND, LETHA L. & Schnellbacher, Braxton B. m.May13, 1900.
HANOVER, JUANITA HORTENSE & Leonard, Horace Lester m.Apr05, 1931.
HARRIS, ELIZABETH ANNE & Guthrie, Hugh Delmar m.Mar04, 1950.
HARVEY, CLARA & Howard, E. H. m.Sep28, 1903.
HAYLEY, ALTEA ORAVELLA & Lindley, George William m.Apr08, 1950.
HAYS, OPAL & Herrick, Vernon m.Aug07, 1936.
HEATH, LOIS FERN & Perdue, Harley Jene m.Dec30, 1949.
HEATH, FLORENCE J. & Noonan, Harry H. m.Jul05, 1901.
HEATON, BILLIE LAVONNE & Coumbs, Merle m.Oct21, 1935.
HENDERSON, LEONA M. & Todd, John A. m.Jul13, 1901.
HENDERSON, JANE & Jackson, Alfred Stewart m.Sep03, 1939.
HENDERSON, LEOLA VIOLET & Testy, Charles J. m.Mar21, 1906.
HETRICK, KATHERINE MAGGIE & Dawson, Harold Edward m.Jun16, 1947.
HIETT, MABEL SARAH & McKeever, Lawrence Lee m.Aug07, 1936.
HILL, ETHEL A. & Jackson, Nathaniel J. m.Nov28, 1928.
HOOKER, AGNES, Mrs. & Schaffer, Arthur A. m.Mar02, 1923.
HOSTLER, MARJORIE & Leach, Ruel Paul m.Jul29, 1946.
HOWELL, MARJORIE JOY & McGain, Roy m.Oct30, 1941.
HUESTIS, MARY HELEN & Bowman, Charles Elmer m.Apr28, 1919.
HUESTIS, IDA L. & Everest, Harry m.Apr19, 1903.
HUGHES, NAOMI MITTEN & Walker, John P. H. m.May14, 1949.
HUGHES, KATHERINE & Condon, J. J. m.Nov17, 1904.
HUNT, DOROTHY BELLE & Coumbs, Rollin William m.Aug14, 1938.
HUSSEY, CAROL IRENE & Olsen, Norman Trimble m.Jun17, 1938.
HUTCHENS, SUSIE GLADYS & Brinkman, Lester m.Dec12, 1917.
HUTCHINS, VERA & Noble, Jackson m.Apr14, 1919.
HUTCHINS, AIMEE & Cleaves, Forrest m.Dec22, 1910.
HUTCHINS, ADA C. & Spratt, Stephen T. m.Aug20, 1912.
IRVING, ANNIE & Wallen, Frank m.Jun29, 1930.
IVERSEN, ALECIA & Osgood, Frank A. m.Nov05, 1903.
IVERSON, CAMILLA G. & O'Keefe, Thomas M. m.Sep18, 1902.
JAYNE, LULU & Bouery, Pierre m.Mar23, 1903.
JEANS, AGNES F. & Jobe, Maurice G. m.Jun07, 1918.
JEANS, ALICE MARGUERITE & Canfield, Ross Doe m.Oct07, 1913.
JENKINS, BETTY LOU & Nilson, Harry Ferd m.Aug30, 1950.
JESSEE, MILLICENT GLOW & Ou, Robert Ray m.Nov06, 1949.
JOHANSSON, MARY S. & Bunch, Porter J. m.Aug27, 1945.
JOHNSON, LAURA NELL & Quinn, George Arthur m.Sep27, 1938.
JONES, ROSE W. & Blerews, Archie m.Sep25, 1946.
JORDAN, NELLIE M. & McPhetres, D. M. m.Jan12, 1910.
JORDAN, SARAH A. & Trimble, Frank L. m.Jul15, 1922.
JOSEPH, FANNY & Thoza, Manuel Silva m.Jun15, 1911.
JOSEPH, ADALINE & Hanover, Frank m.Dec19, 1900.
JOSEPH, ANNIE & Stofer, H. C. m.Dec02, 1905.
JOSEPH, MARIE & Van Cleave, Carl V. m.Jul27, 1901.
JUNKANS, ELFRIEDA & Shaw, Joseph J. m.Jun12, 1901.
JUNKANS, KARLYN HELEN & Van Matre, Walter John Peter m.Nov29, 1928.
KAPUSTA, ANNIE & Siligo, Edward J. m.Dec24, 1914.
KAPUSTA, AGNES AVELINA & McGovern, John James m.Oct04, 1919.
KASK, OLGA LOUISE & Hoelling, Frank William m.Sep10, 1938.
KAUFMAN, VELMA MAY & Langdon, Horace Joseph m.Jul25, 1934.
KAY, ALAFAIRE CADEMARTORI & Bergin, Geo. m.Dec16, 1914.

KIEFER, JERRINE, Miss & Wood, Donald Thomas m.Aug06, 1920.
KIVETT, ELMA O. & Oswill, Don C. m.Nov03, 1933.
KNAPP, BILLY JUNE & Jackson, Samuel Ballan m.Sep27, 1931.
KOELLE, MARIE & Welsh, Michael m.May05, 1905.
KOLL, WINNIE C. & Harrington, Joseph J. m.Jul09, 1927.
KOPP, IDA & Jackson, Edwin Merle m.Dec18, 1932.
LAFFRANCHINI, IRENE MARTHA & Dockery, James Edward m.Oct22, 1921.
LAINGOR, ANNE & Boyce, Jesse m.Oct09, 1906.
LAMBERT, LORETTA NEVADA & Ellingwood, John E. m.Apr14, 1934.
LAMPERT, BERTHA MAE & Johnson, Donald Lewis m.Jul24, 1950.
LANKTREE, ELEANOR M. & Simmons, William H. m.Oct11, 1937.
LARGE, ALICE, Mrs. & Haacke, Julius m.Aug07, 1911.
LARSEN, MARGARET L. & Ellery, Elias K. m.Aug23, 1914.
LARSON, HILMA O. & Wolf, Fred m.Jan09, 1942.
LATTARI, ANITA & Hancock, Thomas Dennis m.Jul20, 1949.
LAUGHLIN, LEONA LOUISE & Lowder, Emil Oliver m.Apr15, 1940.
LAYMAN, MARY AGNES & Gates, Calvin Andrew m.Apr09, 1914.
LEAVITT, NETTIE M., Mrs. & Brunken, Ludwig R. m.Dec22, 1903.
LEAVITT, WILDA MAE & Dockery, John Henry m.Jun14, 1917.
LEE, LENA ELIZABETH & Wong, Frederick S. N. m.Jan15, 1921.
LEHMAN, FRANCES VIOLET & Hanover, Harvey Hilton m.Apr25, 1934.
LEIGHTER, ELLARENA A. & Stetter, Victor Joseph m.Jul20, 1937.
LEMMON, HENRIETTA & Johnson, Robert Lee m.Oct29, 1926.
LEONARD, VIRGINIA L. & McKee, Malcolm D. m.Jun26, 1927.
LEONARD, SADIE ELENORE & Paulsen, Albert L. m.Oct16, 1901.
LEWIS, MARJORIE & Fisher, Juarez Cuidad m.Jan07, 1946.
LEWIS, MARGUERITE & Meacham, Justin A. m.Nov21, 1918.
LEYRER, NELDA & Hawkey, Otho E. m.Aug17, 1914.
LIM, EPP LUCILE [she was 100 in 1997] & Louie, Kee m.Dec25, 1918.
LINDSTROM, MARIE WILHELMINA & Gratton, Frederick Christopher m.Aug20, 1914
LOCK, EVA LENA & Russell, Benjamin F. m.Aug18, 1915.
LOCKWOOD, GERALDINE YOUNG & Betterton, Chalmer m.Feb03, 1947.
LONG, JEAN & Rais, Fred m.Apr05, 1947.
LOOMIS, ELSIE CATHERINE, Miss & Hayward, John D. m.Sep16, 1925.
LOVEN, HELEN HILDA & Woods, Mark Herbert m.Jun01, 1941.
LOWDEN, ARTIE LENORA & Moore, John Wesley m.Jan08, 1905.
LUCKIE, JESSIE & Loomis, Walter m.Oct05, 1915.
LUDDEN, HELEN & Stewart, James P. m.Sep21, 1934.
MABIE, JENNIE D. & Harvey, William L. m.Aug03, 1908.
Mc - names beginning with this prefix are alphabetized as if spelled MAC..
McCAMPBELL, MABEL RENA & Arguello, Harold Eugene m.May03, 1919.
McCLINTOCK, ELMA LOUISE & Johnson, Frank Daniel m.Dec22, 1924.
McDONALD, ETHEL W. & Hailstone, Zachariah m.Jul26, 1913.
McDONALD, IDELL BARBARA & Rourke, John Donald m.Apr28, 1919.
McKAY, LUCY & Maker, George I. m.Oct10, 1907.
McKAY, MARY & Pattison, Thos. m.Oct08, 1997.
McKAY, EDITH DELIA & Vaughn, Harry Benjamin m.Apr19, 1915.
McKAY, ANNIE & Ralph, Louis F. m.Sep30, 1903.
McKENZIE, LOLA MAY & Lung, Robert L. m.Nov20, 1937.
McKEW, AGNES B. & Lee, Thomas L. m.Jun14, 1926.
McKNIGHT, AMANDA KATHRYN & Salsbury, Devillo A. m.Apr07, 1912.
McKNIGHT, MARY JANE & Dailey, George J. m.Mar18, 1931.
McMILLAN, MARTHA G. & Van Matre, Judson C. m.Dec02, 1933.
McMULLEN, AMELIA H. & Rodgers, John F. m.Nov20, 1901.
McMURPHY, ISABELLA LORETTA & Penning, Henry Fred m.Jun18, 1937.
McNAMARA, EUNICE L. & Howell, Bud Percy m.Apr25, 1917.
McNAMARA, MATTIE BELLE & Upton, J. D. m.Mar15, 1907.
McNEILL, VIOLET PERMILLA & Spindler, Harold Albert m.Jun18, 1932.
McNEILL, MINA ADELINE & Avera, Harry Lavelle m.Nov19, 1936.
MACY, CRANSOLIA & Hall, Geo. A. m.Sep13, 1910.
MADSEN, ESTHER & Trimble, Raymond Alexander m.Nov12, 1919.
MALONEY, MARY AGNES & Layman, Lowell J. m.Nov22, 1905.
MANN, BONNIE & Cunningham, Paul Joseph m.Oct31, 1936.

MARRIAGES 1900 - 1950

MARARA, ANNA & de Reis, Manuel C. m.Mar29, 1913.
MARINGER, MARY BERNICE & Crews, Wilbert L. m.Nov14, 1913.
MARKHAM, RITA MARION & Betterton, Edward Lee m.Jun09, 1936.
MARSEN, RUBY & Pritchett, Warren S. m.Nov16, 1932.
MARSHALL, VERNA E. & Reynolds, Rodney F. m.Jun22, 1922.
MARTIN, ELEANOR ALBINA, Mrs. & Hayward, Oscar Horace m.Aug29, 1917.
MARTIN, SUSIE ELIZABETH & Mead, Corydon Jewett m.Dec01, 1912.
MATHEWS, VIOLA B. & Friend, Thomas m.Dec14, 1903.
MAYFIELLD, NEVA & Spindler, David m.Apr07, 1934.
MEAD, SUSIE ELIZABETH & Ownby, William Adolph m.Aug17, 1944.
MECKEL, ANNA MARIE & Young, Van Brunt m.Jun17, 1903.
MEEKS, LOUANN EUNICE & Wilson, Ward Thomas m.Oct23, 1950.
MEYER, GLADYS RAE, Miss & Fisher, Carlos O. m.Sep02, 1924.
MILLER, NAOMI CATHERINE & Lorenz, Floyd Hoffman m.Jul10, 1938.
MILLER, GERALDYNE ELOUISE & Johnson, Charles Alford m.Nov03, 1949.
MILLER, ELVA COSTA & Young, Lawrence George m.Jun29, 1938.
MILLER, EVA B. & Davis, Robert W. m.Jul20, 1936.
MILNE, GERTRUDE & Mansfield, Harold H. m.Dec22, 1915.
MONTGOMERY, HAZEL B. & Noble, Joseph F. m.Feb23, 1929.
MOREIRA, MARIA LOARES & de Reis, William Wilford m.May31, 1913.
MORGAN, LULA BELLE & Ransom, Joe Kurt m.May30, 1946.
MORRIS, PANSY ELIZABETH & Zachary, John Lyman m.Nov08, 1927.
MORRIS, KATHLEEN, Mrs. & Clarke, William Nelson m.Oct30, 1924.
MORWOOD, GERTRUDE ALICE & McClendon, John m.Oct19, 1935.
MOSER, BERTHA M. & Carlson, Herbert William m.Nov06, 1939.
MUNSTER, AUGUSTA & Montgomery, Nathaniel Esau m.Apr12, 1915.
MYERS, HATTIE & Hoaglin, William m.Apr31, 1913.
NALTON, GRACIE & McKibbon, Frankie m.Oct10, 1920.
NEILSON, JOY & Steele, Merton E. m.Apr09, 1939.
NEUSSE, BERTHA & Urban, Eugene m.Jul28, 1906.
NEWELL, CARRIE & Davis, Griffith T. m.May27, 1905.
NEWELL, MYRTLE & Hafley, F. H. m.Sep27, 1907.
NEWLAND, MAUD & Dean, Samuel T. m.Mar04, 1903.
NEWMAN, MARY K., Miss & Jenkins, L. B. m.Feb22, 1911.
NICHOLSON, ELIZABETH & Carr, Frank Demaunt m.Jun26, 1902.
NIGHTINGALE, CATHERINE JOSEPHINE & Schmitt, Fred William m.Oct05, 1943.
NOBLE, HAZEL BERNICE & Froloff, Albert Stephen m.Aug06, 1939.
NOONAN, ADELYNE FRANCES & Clark, Claude E. m.Dec14, 1904.
NORWOOD, LETHA & Schaffer, Arthur August m.Jun29, 1940.
NYE, HARRIET F. & Lattin, Franklin m.Sep04, 1934.
OLSEN, BERTHA FRANCES & Finnicum, Max L. m.Jun26, 1934.
OLSEN, SADIE & Hailstone, Zach m.Feb25, 1903.
OLSEN, MARY JANE & Childers, Fred Newton m.Feb26, 1922.
OLSEN, LAVERNE EMELINE & Laffranchini, Allen Charles m.Aug20, 1927.
OREWILER, STELLA & Shearer, Joseph M. m.Aug28, 1906.
ORRELL, DOROTHY LOUISE & Verburg, Edward Donald m.Dec05, 1934.
OSBORN, EVELYN MILDRED & Foster, Joseph Melvin m.Aug02, 1935.
OWEN, EDNA MARIE & Boyd, Harold George m.Dec21, 1930.
OWINGS, NORA L. & Scott, W. I. m.Jan31, 1910.
PACKARD, JESSIE M. & Grigsby, Calvin m.Jul25, 1912.
PARSONS, DONNA JEAN & Andrews, Robert Frank m.Dec20, 1947.
PATTISON, ANNA MAY & McLeod, Edward O. m.Jun20, 1942.
PAUL, MAY, Mrs. & Reid, Hans C. m.Jul29, 1925.
PAULINA, MARY & Smith, Peter D. m.Jun12, 1907.
PAULSEN, EDNA E. & Benton, Emerson J. m.May07, 1901.
PAULSEN, HANNA PAULINE & Hall, Daniel J. m.May17, 1900.
PEARSON, JEAN A. & Ffoulkes, Wade H. m.Jun25, 1915.
PECK, MINNIE ANNA & Butler, Lucius F. R. m.Jan27, 1921.
PEIRCE, CAROLINE & Culbertson, David E. m.Feb14, 1939.
PENNINGTON, MURIEL N. & Warkentin, Theodore N. m.Jun28, 1932.
PERKINS, LOUISE OLIVE & Muncy, Kenneth E. m.Jul12, 1948.
PERRY, CLARA BULEAH & White, Edward Otto m.Sep19, 1906.
PETERSON, DORA & Bassham, Albert m.Sep28, 1902.

PHILBROOK, SUSIE & Radcliff, Royal E. m.Oct08, 1922.
PHILLIPS, MARJORIE, Miss & Brown, Melville Harrison m.Jun30, 1920.
PIERCE, PATRICIA & Bartlett, Lance Taylor m.Oct07, 1932.
POST, FRANCES VOTHIER, Mrs. & Domenici, Domenico m.Apr29, 1916.
POST, ISABELLE & Malloy, Robert Watson m.Jul16, 1906.
POST, LUBERTHA E. & Hayden, Frank M. m.Nov28, 1907.
POTTER, VANCE RHOM & Fraser, William Thomas m.Jul30, 1933.
POTTER, BERTHA T. & De H'arcourt, Harry J. m.Jul31, 1939.
POWELL, FRANCES LOUISE & Ledford, Melvin Leroy m.Jul16, 1935.
PRICE, INEZ H. & Jackson, Francis O. m.Mar14, 1942.
PRINDLE, ELIZABETH ALOHA & Smith, Robert Willard m.Jun01, 1936.
PRINDLE, GEORGIA MARIAN & Laughlin, Jay Lawrence m.May31, 1941.
PROW, MAUDE L. & Foss, Martin W. m.Oct11, 1950.
QUIGLEY, MARY, Mrs. & Morgan, A. B. m.Oct13, 1901.
RAIS, MARIA SOARES & Rais, M. m.Dec27, 1930.
RALPH, LUELLA Mrs. & Van Cleave, John W. W. m.Jul02, 1900.
RALPH, RAY M. & Lowden, Eugene E. m.Mar20, 1902.
RAUZI, MYRA, Miss & Wagner, Bud m.Jun09, 1924.
RAYBURN, JENNIE C. & Schole, William m.Dec31, 1934.
RECORDS, JENNY MAY & Lowrey, Clarence W. m.Aug25, 1906.
RECORDS, NANNIE & Hutchins, H. C. m.Jun10, 1910.
REED, ALICE JOSEPHINE & Spratt, Howard Coddington m.Oct20, 1941.
REIMERS, ALIDA K. & Brown, Bowyer B. m.Aug03, 1913.
REMICK, RACHEL SUZANE & Flannery, Patrick m.Jan06, 1943.
RILEY, BETTY & Riley, Evert m.Mar20, 1947.
RILEY, EVELYN & Schurrer, Joe m.Mar09, 1934.
RINGLE, SHIRLEY RUTH & McKay, Horace m.Dec28, 1949.
RITCHIE, HALLIE BUELAH & Nightingale, Marcus m.Jun20, 1945.
ROBINSON, MARY & Young, Henry J. m.Nov25, 1909.
RODGERS, JOSEPHINE E., Miss & Simpson, Thomas J. m.Nov22, 1911.
ROGERS, KATIE & Clark, W. W. m.May25, 1915.
ROGERS, FLORA & Cordoza, Frank m.May27, 1900.
ROGERS, FANNIE C. & McKnight, Joseph Flavius m.Jul20, 1902.
ROSS, HELEN LOUISA & Bartlett, Thomas F. m.Jun21, 1931.
ROURKE, VERA PATRICIA & Griffith, James R. m.Jun02, 1934.
ROURKE, MARY AGNES & Marshall, Robert Laws m.Jun01, 1935.
ROURKE, SOPHIA AGNES & Egan, William Martin m.Apr11, 1948.
ROURKE, DOROTHY CAROL & Goodyear, Hal Eugene m.May17, 1944.
ROUSSELOTT, SARAH M. & Kentemeyer, Henry F. m.May03, 1909.
ROVELLI, VIOLETTE & Valentine, James m.Aug11, 1934.
RUCKER, RUBY & Rose, John Lester m.Feb27, 1932.
RULE, MATTIE I. & Monroe, Charles m.Nov14, 1901.
RULE, CARRIE W. & Buckley, John F. m.Jul02, 1900.
RUSH, MATTY LAVINA, Miss & Back, William Walter m.Aug18, 1923.
RUSS, GRACE W. & McDonald, John David m.May05, 1921.
RYAN, MARIE TERESA & Craft, George Jewell m.Feb06, 1918.
RYAN, CLAIRE & Barrett, James F. m.Apr10, 1947.
RYAN, KATHERINE MARY & Taylor, James Orion m.Feb22, 1948.
SAMUELS, DOROTHY J. & Hamilton, Ira C. m.Sep20, 1912.
SANBURN, DELIA MARTHA & Blake, Frank Tilden m.Dec27, 1904.
SAXIE, ELLEN & Chesbro, James m.Dec29, 1922.
SCHAFFER, ZITA & Perenin, Frank J. m.Sep05, 1904.
SCHALSKY, ANNA & Brown, David Dudley m.Jun21, 1926.
SCHENKEL, LEONA MAY & Palmer, Victor M. m.May22, 1939.
SCOTT, CLARA MAY & Richards, William m.Mar02, 1904.
SCOTT, ADELINE & Johnson, Edward Russ m.Jun16, 1939.
SCOTT, BONNIE JEAN & Cantrall, Donald Dean m.Jul17, 1949.
SELBY, WILDETH JEAN & Layman, Walter Lawrence m.Jun11, 1950.
SELLARS, BERNICE F. & Biancalana, Alessandro J. m.Jan04, 1936.
SEVENSEN, THEODORA OTILLE & Neisingh, Alfred Jerome m.Jul23, 1921.
SHADLEY, MADELINE GRACE & Raymond, Fracer D. m.May13, 1939.
SHARER, ANNA & Olsen, Emil M. m.Apr15, 1900.
SHERMAN, GERTRUDE & Hawk, Hilton Alexander m.Mar16, 1936.

MARRIAGES 1900 - 1950

SHERMAN, PAULINE & Swain, Robert Bruce m.Mar27, 1948.
SHERMAN, LOVENIA & White, Jordan Herbert m.Sep30, 1925.
SHOCK, CORA & Meyers, B. F. m.Oct31, 1915.
SHOCK, SADIE E., Mrs. & Olsen, John James m.Jun11, 1911.
SHOCK, NORA IRENE, Miss & Robinson, David H. m.Mar09, 1920.
SHOCK, ILA MAY, Miss & Reed, Royal Wallace m.Mar04, 1920.
SHOCK, CLAUDIE & Franck, Antonius Norgard m.Mar06, 1916.
SHOUP, ELSIE C., Miss & Goodyear, Eugene Merritt m.Dec20, 1911.
SILIGO, ANNA ELIZABETH & Iversen, Adolph Leffren m.Sep05, 1918.
SILIGO, BARBETTA, Mrs. & Leas, George W. m.Jun22, 1905.
SILVA, MARIAN & Gilzean, James Albert m.Jul01, 1902.
SILVA, ROSA & Flowers, W. F. m.Apr10, 1900.
SIMMONS, VIOLET, Mrs. & Carr, Charles A. m.Oct31, 1925.
SMITH, NELLIE & McKay, Robert m.Oct05, 1915.
SMITH, MARY KATHERINE & Ryan, Richard Henry m.Nov27, 1937.
SMITH, ATHA & Schneider, William m.Nov20, 1946.
SMITH, VERA & Booth, Eugene V. m.Mar16, 1947.
SPENCER, RUBYE EUGENIA & Smith, Loyal T. m.Jun29, 1946.
SPRATT, LOICE ELEANOR & Mathews, Ralph Bertram m.Feb15, 1948.
STANFIELD, BERNICE & Reese, Thomas E. m.Aug19, 1938.
STEELE, VIRGINIA LEE & Pettis, William Turner m.Jun28, 1933.
STEIN, GLADYS & Smith, Max F. m.May28, 1936.
STENBIT, ADELE GRACE & Spratt, Henry Thayer m.May01, 1935.
STEVENS, ELLA & Pratt, Asa m.Dec16, 1930.
STODDARD, FANNY FREDRICA & Messner, Henry m.Aug11, 1900.
STONE, LUBERTA & Taylor, John H. m.Apr17, 1947.
STURDIVANT, OPAL & Barse, Walter E. m.May02, 1948.
SULLIVAN, CARRIE & Spears, William m.Feb22, 1900.
SUPAN, THELMA MARIAN & Duncan, James Henry m.Apr29, 1944.
SWAIN, IRENE MARION & Buntain, Hubert Earl m.Oct21, 1934.
SWAYZE, CORA MAE & Coumbs, Walter Scott m.Apr14, 1935.
SWEATT, MAE E. & Hype, Lawrence P. m.Mar27, 1942.
SWITZER, PAULINE & Green, Stanley m.Jan04, 1947.
TALLMAN, DOROTHY JANE & Valentine, Charles Eugene m.May03, 1949.
TERRY, FLORENCE & Learoyd, Walter Rutledge m.Sep17, 1933.
THAYER, EDNA CODINGTON & Bremer, Carl William m.Jan01, 1908.
THOMAS, ISABELLA, Mrs. & Hayes, George S. m.Jul25, 1924.
THOMPSON, LEONA & Jenkins, Fallis W. m.May08, 1938.
THOMPSON, GRACE & Berglund, Torey m.Aug06, 1946.
THORNE, ALICE BURTON & Schultz, Alexander m.Jun05, 1913.
THORNE, IDA RULAND, Miss & Blair, James Russell m.Apr12,1911.
THORNE, MABEL & Collins, William G. m.Jun05, 1907.
THORP, ETHEL LOUISE & Costa, George m.Feb23, 1937.
TIBESSART, ETHEL, Miss & Chapman, William F. m.Jul12, 1920.
TINSLEY, MARY J., Mrs. & Gore, Joseph W. m.Mar01, 1917.
TINSLEY, INEZ CHARLINE & Wright, Jean Melvin m.Jan23, 1937.
TODD, AMY LUCILLE & Vick, William Bryan m.Jul12, 1929.
TODD, ZELITA, Miss & Jones, Guy P. m.Aug01, 1923.
TOMLINSON, ROBERTA LOU & Holmes, Arthur Lloyd m.Oct15, 1949.
TOWNSEND, MAMIE MARY & Farmer, Harvey Allen m.Dec01, 1928.
TRIMBLE, REBECCA E. & Vaughn, DeForest H. m.Jan19, 1922.
TRIMBLE, BELLE & Vaughn, Dan m.Apr03, 1915.
UNZICKER, ELSA MABEL, Miss & Jackson, Raymond A. m.Nov04, 1925.
VAN MATRE, CLARA EUNICE & Kreiss, Charles F. m.Jun11, 1929.
VAN MATRE, VIVIAN HELEN & Thorne, George Isaac m.Mar26, 1912.
VAN CLEAVE, DOLORES & Moore, W. C. m.Oct11, 1909.
VAN CLEAVE, DOLORES & Ford, Denis m.Sep14, 1904.
VAN MATRE, IRENE & Box, Andrew H. m.Oct20, 1912.
VANDERHOFF, IRIS & Morton, Claude D. m.Nov12, 1906.
VAUGHN, CARRIE & Adams, William m.Dec10, 1900.
VAUGHN, MAUD & Campbell, Lindsay m.Dec01, 1903.
VAUGHN, ALICE & Crews, Elmer Clair m.Jan12, 1914.
VAUGHN, EMELINE L., Mrs. & Shock, J. S. m.Oct11, 1906.

VAUGHN, LOTTIE M. & Patton, W. A. m.Feb04, 1904.
VAUGHN, BIRDIE E. & Elliston, William P. m.Oct03, 1904.
VAUGHN, CHARLOTTE & Patton, James W. m.Feb04, 1904.
VITZTHUM, NELLIE ALLEN & Brown, Jerry M. m.Aug14, 1901.
VITZTHUM, MARY ELAINE & Eugene, Joseph Kimball m.Sep01, 1928.
VITZTHUM, LENA & Tarpley, Edward Lee m.Jun25, 1902.
VITZTHUM, WILMA TERESA & Baker, Lester Willard m.Aug12, 1927.
WALKER, ALICE WINIFRED & Hawkins, Russell Buchanan m.Jul26, 1940.
WALLACE, GRACE VINEYARD & Lloyd, Walter Delmar m.Dec11, 1948.
WALSH, ALMA PEARL, Miss & Field, Milton Wayne m.Nov04, 1925.
WALTER, ESTHER & Henry, William Justin m.Mar23, 1913.
WALTON, BONITA & Lund, Adolph m.Oct03, 1946.
WARREN, ALICE & Osgood, U. G. m.Oct13, 1900.
WEGG, GRACE AILEENE & Gilman, James Herbert m.Aug05, 1948.
WEINHEIMER, MARIE & Hanna, Charles m.Jun21, 1905.
WEINHEIMER, AGNES HELENA & Junkans, Rudolph H. m.Dec07, 1904.
WEINHEIMER, CAROLINE E. & Smith, Frank M. m.Aug12, 1903.
WEINHEIMER, KATHERINE THERESA & Clark, Lawrence P. m.Oct01, 1913.
WEINHEIMER, ANNIE L. & Ryan, Edward m.Jan10, 1900.
WELLOCK, CHLOE IONE & Creeach, William Richard m.Oct05, 1944.
WESSA, BARBARA JEAN & Lea, Ralph Malcolm m.Jul12, 1947.
WESTON, EVA LILLIAN & Higgins, Frederick Ernest m.Sep14, 1913.
WHITCHURCH, LELIA OLIVE & Elliston, Thomas R. m.May13, 1906.
WHITE, GLADYS & McCleary, Marrion W. m.Nov10, 1933.
WIELAND, MAXINE H. & Dockery, Charles M. m.Sep21, 1945.
WIGGLE, MARY JANE & Lawton, Jackson Cherokee m.Feb01, 1930.
WILBURN, ZUE, Miss & Gray, Albert Fray m.Nov09, 1911.
WILBURN, SARAH GERTRUDE & Le Mar, George Kent m.May20, 1915.
WILBURN, MARY W. & McDonald, O. A. m.Aug21, 1909.
WILBURN, LILLIAN & Duncan, Ben H. m.May25, 1910.
WILCOX, IDA MAY & Checketts, La Moine m.May19, 1934.
WILLIAMS, ADELINE MARTHA & Roberts, William Thomas m.Nov11, 1912.
WILLIAMS, MINNIE & Hammond, Charles m.Sep12, 1900.
WILLIAMS, MARY & Griffith, John J. m.Apr21, 1901.
WILLIAMS, FLORENCE & Enos, Joseph m.Aug11, 1909.
WILLIAMS, LOUISA & Caton, Antone m.Aug08, 1900.
WILSON, ELIZABETH A. & Lowden, Frederick S. m.Sep27, 1903.
WILSON, NORMA LOREM & Ullom, Ellon Chase m.Jun06, 1931.
WILSON, SARAH & Trimble, John W. m.Jul30, 1903.
WILSON, HARRIETT V. & Cummings, Robert Lee m.Feb24, 1901.
WOOD, HELEN MAR & Taylor, Jesse J. m.Oct30, 1926.
WOODBURY, ETHEL CLARE & Sutherland, Henry I. m.Jun15, 1904.
WOODBURY, CORALINE KATE & Gehm, George F. m.Oct30, 1901.
WOODWORTH, ANNIE FRANCES & Hammersly, Owen Kenneth m.Jan30, 1932.
WRIGHT, EDNA MAE & Clarke, Leland Arthur m.Jun22, 1931.
WRIGHT, SHIRLEY MARDIS & Travis, William, Jr. m.Oct19, 1940.
WYCKOFF, DOROTHY EDRA & Reade, Charles Dwight, Jr. m.Aug29, 1937.
YANCEY, RUTH ANNA & Alward, Leslie Thornton, Jr. m.Mar14, 1934.
YARBROUGH, JESSIE LOUISA & Blakemore, Christian m.Jan19, 1908.
YOUNG, RUTH EDITH & McGee, Rex Cecil m.Jun21, 1949.
YOUNG, DELLA LEONA & Brown, Albert Thomas m.Oct05, 1935.
YOUNT, LUCIA R. & Jumper, Geo. M. m.Sep28, 1910.
ZWIEBEL, CATHERINE MARY & Hass, Warren Maxine m.Aug15, 1934.

END INDEX TO MARRIAGES 1900 - 1950

INDEX TO TRINITY COUNTY, CALIFORNIA, BIRTHS
1850-1900
From an unpublished manuscript by RITA M. HANOVER
in Trinity County Library, Weaverville, California
Used with permission.

NOTE: No Births were recorded in Trinity County, California, on a regular basis, until 1913. Mrs. Hanover compiled this list from the entries in the TRINITY JOURNAL, Weaverville, California, the newspaper of Trinity County, California from January 1856 to the present. Mrs. Hanover added names from other sources when she had them.

During the 1940s and 1950s many "Delayed Births" were recorded. Many Births before 1913 were recorded as "Delayed Births". These will be found in the Addendum.

Not all births were sent to the newspaper. Be sure to check each available census. For all families, also check Births 1900-1950 and the Addendum.

The author has added information to this list. These entries are in [ ].

BORN TO THE WIFE OF	SEX	BIRTH DATE
ABRAMS, F. S.	dau	Jun21, 1891
	dau	Jan11, 1893
	dau	Feb24, 1895
	(dau d. Aug24, 1895)	
ABRAHM, ISAAC	son Morris	Feb02, 1869
	dau	May27, 1870
	son	Dec31, 1871
	son	Sep07, 1873
	son	Mar18, 1875
	(son d. Nov03, 1875)	
	s. Benjamin	Nov01, 1876
ADAMS, JOHN Q.	(wife Caroline)	
	dau	May18, 1895
	son Harry A.	Dec29, 1898
AINSWORTH, LOUIS (and B.M.)	dau	Jul19, 1866
ALBIEZ, KARL	dau Selma	Mar19, 1888
ALLEN, EGBERT F.	s.[Cyrus E.]	Apr22, 1865
	dau	Aug07, 1868
ALLEN, RALPH M.	(wife Emma)	
	dau	Mar29, 1866
	dau	Jan21, 1868
[Ralph d. Sep09, 1867 in Hayfork.]		
[Emma m2) Amos Huffman Marshall.]		
ALSTAN, JOHN	son	Nov23, 1858
ANDERLINI, FRANK F.	dau Lena T.	Jun07, 1889
	son	Jul01, 1890
	son	May09, 1893
	dau	Oct19, 1894
	son	Nov05, 1896
ANDERLINI, J. A.	son	Feb28, 1897
ANDERSON, WILLIAM	(wife Clara)	

	dau	Jun07, 1859
	(dau.d. Jul24, 1860)	
ARGUELLO, JOSE	dau Lilly A.	Sep11, 1878
	dau Irene	Oct23, 1880
	son	Apr01, 1884
	(son d. Nov23, 1888)	
	son Frank	Jun22, 1886
	son Harold	Dec31, 1893
ARMENTROUT, JOHN W.	son Reverdy James	Oct14, 1873
	son Everett	Sep21, 1875
	son Loag	Mar11, 1877
	dau Jemima	Oct08, 1878
	son John Wesley	Apr26, 1880
	dau Effie	Dec04, 1883
	son	Jan18, 1887
	[son William W.	Jan16, 1886]

[Author's note: Everett d. Apr05, 1957; Loag d. Dec17, 1950; Jemima d. Feb6, 1954; John Wesley d. May10, 1929; William W. d. May17, 1938.]

ARMENTROUT, REVERDY	son Roy	Sep26, 1896
	son Frank	Dec07, 1898
ARMSTRONG, JOHN J.	son	Jun10, 1882
ARMSTRONG, WILLIAM HENRY	dau Hazel	Feb11, 1894
ASHWORTH, WILLIAM D.	dau	Oct13, 1856
BACHELDER, WILLIAM M.	son	Oct23, 1872
BADGLEY, GEORGE	dau	Sep24, 1894
	dau	Jan27, 1898
BAEHR, WILLIAM	son	Apr02, 1859
	son	Mar21, 1861
BAILEY, GEORGE L.	dau	May16, 1893
	son James S.	Jul26, 1894
	son George C.	Sep15, 1899
BAKER, THOMAS	tw. sons Willis and Walter J.	Sep10, 1859

TJ says Oct7, 1859
Family records and I.O.O.F. records say Sep10, 1859.

BAKER, WALTER J.	son	Aug13, 1885
BAKER, WILLIS E.	son	Feb08, 1889
	dau	Apr23, 1890
	dau	Aug05, 1891
	son	May07, 1893
BALBACH, LEWIS A.	dau	Nov08, 1893
	son	May11, 1895
BALCH, JAMES R.	son	Jul30, 1868
	(son d. Mar11, 1869)	
	dau	May18, 1870
	dau	Jan05, 1872
	(dau. d. Jan19, 1872)	

BIRTHS 1850 - 1900

	son Henry R.	Apr12, 1873
	son	Apr24, 1878
	(son d. Feb05, 1885)	
	tw.son & dau	Oct13, 1881
BARKLA, JAMES	(wife Elizabeth)	
	dau	Oct05, 1875
	(d. Oct26, 1875)	
	dau Virginia	May12, 1877
	dau	Mar04, 1879
BARNICKEL, JACOB	[wife Anna Junkans]	
[son John b.1872 1880 cen.]		
	dau [Kate]	Apr01, 1873
	son	Sep04, 1876
	[Bernard]	
	dau [Dora]	Jun06, 1878
BARNUM, EDWARD B. (and Alzina)		
	dau	May10, 1866
	(dau. d. Sep19, 1879)	
	son	Mar24, 1868
	dau	Oct21, 1873
BARROWS, JAMES E.	dau	Apr10, 1886
BARTHOLOMEW, MITCHELL ORLAND		
	dau	Jul04, 1867
	son	Jan07, 1869
BARTLE, FRANK M.	son	Jun14, 1878
	dau	Sep03, 1879
	son	Mar02, 1881
	son	Sep13, 1882
BARTLETT, CHARLES M.	son	Feb09, 1864
	[Charles E.]	
	dau	Sep03, 1867
	[Martha A.]	
	dau [Alice]	Aug16, 1869
	s. [George]	Sep20, 1871
	[d. Sarah	Jul03, 1874]

[+ 4 more: James W., May15, 1862; John Henry Sep22, 1865] [Thomas (n.d.); Frank b. 1879]

BARTLETT, JOHN M.	dau	Oct19, 1891
BASSHAM, GREEN BERRY	son Elbert	Oct26, 1872
	d. Florence	Nov19, 1874
	dau Ida E.	Dec31, 1876
	son	Sep02, 1879
	dau Edna	Nov29, 1881
BATES, JOHN B.	dau	Jun30, 1863
BATES, NELSON	son	Mar14, 1860
BATES, RANDALL M.	dau	Feb10, 1883
BECKETT, HENRY	son	Jun05, 1864
BEHME, M. (probably Nicholas Behme)		
	dau	Dec29, 1865

	[prob. Mary]	
BEHME, NICHOLAS	dau	Apr20, 1860
	son	Jul17, 1861
	son [Robert L.] (son d. Aug18, 1869) [dau. Mary Elizabeth age 3-1/2 yr] [dau. d. Aug25, 1869]	Mar28, 1864
	dau	Apr13, 1868
BENNER, HENRY W.	dau	Dec08, 1878
	dau	Jun11, 1880
BENNETT, DANIEL [Annie B. Bennett; b. Jan6, 1864 Weaverville d. 1940 Tiverton, R.I.; obit. says Jan. 6.]	dau	Jan09, 1864
BENNETT, JAMES	son	Oct11, 1862
BENNETT, MARCUS [and Flora E. Hughes]	dau	Aug24, 1879
	son Curtis M.	Jun09, 1881
	son Perry	Mar13, 1897
	son Bernard	Oct25, 1899
[son Harvey Squires Jun26, 1895 - Mar09, 1938] [son Louis Oct30, 1876 - Mar04, 1949]		
BENNETT, N. I.	son	Jan13, 1864
BENTON, JAMES (d. Oct22, 1895)	son Wm. M.	Sep20, 1874
	son Emerson James	Oct30, 1875
	dau	Nov26, 1876
	dau	Jun08, 1878
	dau	Dec14, 1879
BERGIN, JOHN	son Thomas F.	Aug05, 1864
	son Charles Edward	Apr24, 1868
(d. Jun24, 1871)	dau	Jun29, 1869
	dau Elizabeth M.	Nov04, 1871
BERGIN, JOHN W.	son George M.	Jun26, 1889
	dau Marian M.	May10, 1893
BERGIN, THOMAS F.	son	Jul27, 1890
	dau	Apr14, 1896
	dau	Aug06, 1898
BERKLEY, RICHARD L.	son	Apr20, 1871
BIGELOW, C. B.	son	Sep12, 1874
BIGELOW, WILLIAM RALPH	dau	Aug30, 1889
	dau Maisie	Nov04, 1890

BIRTHS 1850 - 1900

```
                                        son                     Dec27, 1891
                                         Harvey L.
                                        son Ralph W.            Oct15, 1893
                                        dau Lela M.             Mar18, 1895
                                        son                     Apr16, 1896
                                         Samuel B.

BIGGS, J. J.                            dau                     Oct20, 1865

BLAGRAVE, WILLIAM ALEXANDER [and Elizabeth Kelly]
                                        son                     Sep01, 1869
                                         James Henry

BLAGRAVE, WALTER [and Annie Laura Todd]
                                        dau Delia F.            Aug21, 1894

BLAIR, BENJAMIN M.                      dau                     Feb24, 1898

BLAIR, HUGH NEWELL                      dau                     Sep05, 1898

BLAKE, SELDON L. (Dr.)                  son                     Jan28, 1887
                                        dau                     May23, 1893
                                        dau                     Nov15, 1894

BLAKEMORE, ALBERT J. M. [and Vetura Blagrave]
                                        dau                     Feb26, 1886
(d. Feb21, 1888)                        dau                     Jan10, 1888
                                        son                     Sep12, 1889
                                        dau                     Nov08, 1890

BLAKEMORE, CHARLES L.                   son                     Nov10, 1885

BLAKEMORE, THOMAS J. [and Ursula]
                                        son                     Oct03, 1881
                                        son                     Aug24, 1883
                                         [J.A., d. 1942]
[dau Winifred L. (Koelle) b. Jan24, 1873;
  d Sep11, 1900]

BLANEY, HUGH
                                        dau Rose                Apr13, 1880
                                        dau Honora              Feb08, 1882
                                        son Hugh D.             Apr20, 1884
[Census, Jun03, 1880, has Blaney, John, age 1]

BLIVEN, CYRUS                           son                     Feb04, 1861

BOSHART, HENRY                          son                     Feb14, 1890

BOWERMAN, JACOB                         son                     Aug26, 1873
(d. Dec30, 1879)                        son                     Jul16, 1875

BOWERMAN, LESLIE                        dau                     Dec09, 1895
                                        dau                     Aug26, 1897

BOWERMAN, CHARLES                       dau                     Jul12, 1895

BOYNTON, ALFRED W.                      dau                     Mar26, 1869

BRADLEY, RICHARD M. and Catherine
(one d. Jun23, 1869)                    tw.dau.                 Feb27, 1867
(both d. Jul01, 1869)                   tw.son & dau            Dec23, 1868
[see Deaths; Bradley family not in 1870 Census]
```

BRADY, BERNARD   dau   Sep08, 1858
                                        dau   Jun17, 1860
                                        Lavina Rose
                                        son   Dec08, 1863
                                        Morris Augustus
[Anne Terresse Brady d. Sep10, 1862, aged 6 mo.]
[Alvina Brady b. Dec 1867]

BRADY, M. A. [Morris Augustus]
   [and Louisa Dannenbrink, m. Aug24, 1889]
                                        dau   Dec18, 1890
                                        (d. Nov29, 1891)
                                        s. [Detlef]   Sep13, 1892
                                        s. [Armand]   May12, 1898
   [dau   Aug21, 1905]
   Eleanor Ann [m.Voorhies]

BRAGDON, EDWIN M.   son   Jul31, 1893
                                        Harold M.
                                        dau Ora   Apr13, 1895
                                        dau   Feb13, 1898
                                        Carrie E.

BRAINARD, TIMOTHY A.   son   Jun24, 1857
                                        dau   Dec11, 1860

BRANNAN, HENRY WALTER   son Julius   Sep03, 1893
                                        dau Edna   Sep30, 1895
                                        son   Feb21, 1898
                                        James Edward

BRANNAN, JAMES   dau Alice   May15, 1862
                                        son   May23, 1866
                                        Henry Walter

BREMER, HERMAN   dau   Oct07, 1873
                                        dau   Mar31, 1875

BRITTON, JOSEPH   son   Mar16, 1898

BROWDER, ALFRED (black)
(d. Mar18, 1870)   dau   May18, 1867
[See Deaths for the Browder family history.]

BROWN, BOYER R.   son Dudley   Nov18, 1899

BROWN, FLEMING   son   Mar20, 1898

BROWN, GEORGE   son   Mar23, 1859

BROWN, MOSES V.   son   Sep03, 1860
(d. Apr19, 1862)   son   Mar21, 1862

BROWN, PHILLIP S.   son   Jan10, 1869
                                        Fleming Eugene

BROWN, RICHARD   son   Apr08, 1884

BROWN, WILLIAM B. and Matilda
                                        dau   Jan15, 1863
                                        dau   Mar12, 1866
                                        (d. Aug12, 1866)

BIRTHS 1850 - 1900

	son	Nov17, 1867
	dau	Feb14, 1869
BUCK, FRANKLIN A. [wife Jennie]		
	son	Aug29, 1860
	dau	Mar31, 1862
BUNKER, GEORGE M.	son	Jul10, 1860
	son	May23, 1866
BURGER, ADAM	son George L.	Aug13, 1896
BURGER, J. A.	son John Adam, Jr.	Jun13, 1876
	dau May E.	Mar23, 1878
	son	May26, 1880
	dau	Nov07, 1882
BURGESS, EDWARD	dau	Jan31, 1893
BURKE, THOMAS	son	Jan07, 1866
	dau	Jul06, 1867
BUSH, HENRY T. (d. Oct04, 1891)	dau	Sep29, 1891
	son Harold	Jul23, 1897
BUSH, RACHEL, Mrs. (From SHASTA COURIER)	son	Mar21, 1854
CADERMARTORI, FRANK	dau	Feb20, 1883
	dau	Jan31, 1885
CAHILL, JOHN	son	Apr07, 1857
	son	Jul09, 1860
(all born at Weaverville)	dau	Aug22, 1861
	son	Apr05, 1863
CAHILL, JOSEPH (born at Canon Creek)	son	Apr07, 1857
CAMP, M. C.	son	Mar20, 1898
CANNON, NEIL	son	Oct05, 1858
CANTY, MARY S.	dau	Apr26, 1859
CAREY, JOHN	son	Jul13, 1876
CARNES, DANIEL	son	Mar24, 1861
CARR, ALEXANDER C. [see also Addendum]	dau Alice M.	Mar04, 1884
	son Frank Willis	May19, 1888
	dau Jennie	Mar30, 1891
	son Louis A.	Sep13, 1893
	son Charles	Dec22, 1896
CARR, GEORGE L.	son	May07, 1891
	son	

CARR, JOHN	son	Apr03, 1857
	son, abt	Aug16, 1862
	son	Dec07, 1865
CARR, THOMAS	dau	Jun24, 1860
	son	Nov28, 1862
CARROLL, DENNIS	son (d. Dec27, 1862)	May22, 1861
	dau (d. Jan04, 1863)	Jul24, 1862
CARSON, ROBERT M.	dau	Jan04, 1899
CARTER, ASA M.	son Charles A.	May31, 1876
CARTER, GEORGE W.	son	May11, 1896
	son, abt	Dec11, 1897
CARTER, JAMES ALONZO	dau	Jul01, 1895
CARTER, JAMES M.	dau	Dec08, 1882
CARTER, JOHN W. [and Rebecca]	son Millard Fillmore	May17, 1858
	son [George Walter]	Apr01, 1860
	son Robert Lee	Nov19, 1863
	dau Florence	Apr18, 1866
	dau [Mary E.]	Dec25, 1871
	son Clement Adair	Apr07, 1875
CARTER, JOSEPHINE A.	d. Jessie W.	Dec17, 1888
	son John	Apr17, 1892

Board of Supervisors Minutes (1899) 1/2 orphan aid for children.

CARTER, ROBERT L.	son	Jun24, 1894
	dau	Oct25, 1898
CASEY, FRANK	dau	Feb01, 1874
CASTNER, LEWIS P.	dau	Jul16, 1887
	dau	Feb22, 1889
	dau	Jan25, 1891

[Moved to Shasta County.]

CATON, JOHN	(K.P.records)	Jun18, 1878
CHABAUD, A. (TRINITY TIMES)	dau	Jan24, 1855
CHADBOURNE, MATHEW	dau	Jun12, 1863
	dau	Feb23, 1870
CHANDLER, HORATIO	dau	Mar02, 1863

CHAPMAN, George P. and Sarah S.

	son	Nov05, 1882
	son	Aug16, 1885
	dau	Dec31, 1888
	(d. Mar16, 1890)	

CHILDERS, E. son Sep02, 1897
(Emmet?) son Jun19, 1899

CHILDERS, JAMES HORACE son Mar20, 1884
[Fredrick Newton]
[dau Aug28, 1885]
[Edith Irene]
son Jan07, 1888
[Walter Milton W.]
[son Jul28, 1889]
[Arthur Horace]
dau Nov04, 1892
[Sarah Elizabeth]
son Aug04, 1895
[Lawrence Leslie]
[b. Grants Pass, Ore. son Feb23, 1902]
[Herbert Calvin]

CHILDERS, NEWTON EMMET dau Nov23, 1894

CHRISTIANSEN, FREDERICK dau Apr08, 1882
dau Dec28, 1883

CHURCH, JOHN E. dau Jul02, 1859

CLAYTON, GEORGE H. and Mary
son Feb01, 1879
(d. Aug09, 1883) son Oct31, 1881
dau Dec04, 1884
dau Jun25, 1888

CLEAVES, CHARLES son Jul10, 1889
dau Jun15, 1899

CLEMENT, CHARLES E. dau Oct12, 1897
Luella P.

CLEMENT, WILLIAM HENRY dau Aug26, 1892

CLEMENT, WILLIAM [and Nancy Jane Swett]
son Aug23, 1863
William Henry
son Oct10, 1864
Charles Edwin
son June 1870
Albert Curtis

COCHRAN, JAMES [wife Ann; m2) Hugh Blaney]
son May10, 1862
"Robert E."
dau Mollie Aug06, 1864
son Sep30, 1868
[1880 census also lists son Edward, age 14; James age 11.]

COLBERT, JOHN dau Aug14, 1886
dau Jan08, 1889

COLE, CHARLES C. son Mar08, 1898

COLE, JOHN	son	Jul13, 1858
COLEMANSON, _____	son	Sep10, 1858
	son	Apr06, 1860
COLLINS, RICHARD B.	son Richard E.	Mar28, 1873
	son William Gabriel	Mar25, 1877
COLLINS, WILLIAM	dau	Jul17, 1898
COLLOPY, JOHN (wife Bridget)	son	Sep13, 1859
	son, abt (son d. June 4, 1869)	Mar16, 1861
CONDON, WILLIAM	son William, Jr.	Sep12, 1863
	son John Joseph	May12, 1865
	dau Mary Ellen	Apr11, 1867
	son Thomas	Nov17, 1870
	dau (dau. d. Sep28, 1873)	Nov27, 1872
	dau Ellen Theresa	Apr13, 1875
	dau Ann Elizabeth	Jun04, 1877
CONDON, WILLIAM, Jr.	dau	May19, 1898
	son	Oct07, 1899
[CONMY, JOHN J.	dau Ellen Alice	May14, 1853
	son Thomas C.	Jan14, 1855

According to the TRINITY JOURNAL May6, 1916, page 3, Ellen Alice Conmy was the first white child born in the County of Trinity, State of California.]

CONWAY, FRED E.	son William E.	Sep01, 1887
	dau Gertrude	Mar13, 1891
COPELAND, JOHN F. and Emeline (son d. Dec29, 1868)	tw.s.& d.	Jun18, 1862
CORBUS, A. T.	son	Jul19, 1866
	dau	Feb28, 1870
	son	Feb07, 1872
CORMONEY, EUGENE	dau	Jan16, 1898
COSTELLO, MICHAEL, Mrs.	son	Aug19, 1859
COUMBS, JOHN HENRY	dau Charlotte	May23, 1897
	son Thomas Wallace	Oct26, 1899

BIRTHS 1850 - 1900

COUMBS, THOMAS	dau	Dec05, 1877
(d. Apr06, 1899)	dau Maude	Sep30, 1881
	son	Nov05, 1884
	Walter Scott	
	dau	Sep14, 1888
COYLE, THOMAS	dau, abt	Jan12, 1867
	son	May10, 1869
	William S.	
CRAIG, C. W.	dau	Apr04, 1872
	dau	Aug19, 1877
CRAIG, JOSEPH	son	Aug28, 1862
	tw. s & d	Oct04, 1868
CRAWFORD, MONROE T.	son	Aug12, 1870
	son	Nov30, 1871
	dau	Sep07, 1873
	dau	Apr15, 1879
CREAMER, CHARLES N.	dau	Sep04, 1883
	dau	Dec31, 1884
	dau	Oct11, 1887
	son	May04, 1889
	dau	Sep08, 1891
	dau	Oct21, 1894
CREIGHTON, JOHN	dau, abt	Jan08, 1887
CROWLEY, DANIEL	son	Sep11, 1861
CRUM, WILLIAM	son	Oct11, 1888
CRUTHIS, JESSE	son	Apr05, 1876
	Ira Thomas	
(d. Jan21, 1896)	son Earnest	Jul21, 1878
(d. Aug30, 1892)	dau	Jan04, 1891
CULY, G. C.	son	Jul04, 1883
"CUMMINGS, John Henderson,		
b. Minersville May18, 1865".		
CUMMINGS, THOMAS	dau Dora	Aug31, 1858
CURRIE, ALGERNON S.		
[wife Rebecca McIlvane]	dau	Jul17, 1861
	dau	Aug29, 1865
[d. Aug29, 1866]	[Mary Ellen]	
	son	Jan07, 1869
CURTIS, E. J.	son	Sep27, 1862
DACK, ELISHA R.	dau	Mar06, 1877
	dau	May28, 1879
DAMMANN, ANDREW	son	Jul18, 1862
DAMSELL, JOSEPHUS	son	Apr04, 1896
	dau	Mar15, 1898

DANNENBRINK, CONRAD (d. Feb8, 1866)	son Henry	Aug15, 1864
	son	Jan21, 1866
	son	Jan14, 1867
	dau Louisa (Brady)	Oct27, 1868
	tw. d.&s.	Apr14, 1870
	son William Frederick	Apr14, 1870
	dau Augusta	Dec24, 1871
	dau Johanna	Aug12, 1873
	son Carl C.	Feb26, 1875
	dau Eleanor (Edwards)	Mar10, 1880
DAVIS, DAVID P.	son	Jun27, 1890
	dau	Dec16, 1896
DAVIS, DELBER D.	dau	Jun26, 1895
DAVIS, J. L.	son	Aug15, 1864
DAVIS, WILLIAM	dau	Mar02, 1893
DAVISON, H. B.	dau	Mar31, 1859
DAWSON, THOMAS	dau Mary M.	Mar27, 1899

"Hilda M. b. May 1895 - 1900 census.

DAY, J. LEVI	son	Sep27, 1866
	son Joseph David	Jul03, 1869
(from obit.)	son Walter Andrew	Sep30, 1876
DAY, JAMES D.	son	Jan07, 1891
DAY, JOHN D. C.	dau	Nov24, 1881
	dau	Nov08, 1883
	dau	May15, 1885
	son	Feb09, 1887
	son	Apr27, 1891
	son	Sep04, 1892
	son	Jan19, 1894
	son	Jan23, 1895
DAYTON, HARRISON B.	son	Apr29, 1866
	dau	Oct14, 1867
DELSWICH, GERHARD M.	dau	Nov09, 1898
DENNISON, LEWIS	dau Henrietta P.	Dec19, 1882
DICKEY, JOHN E.	dau	Sep09, 1895
DIMOCK, FRANK L.	son	Oct03, 1892
DIX, HENRY	dau	Sep06, 1881
	son Henry Eldon	Aug07, 1885
	dau Nellie	Dec05, 1887
	dau Nancy	Nov09, 1889

BIRTHS 1850 - 1900

	dau Luella	Sep23, 1891
DIXON, CHARLES W.	dau	Nov02, 1893
	son	May07, 1895
	dau	Feb26, 1897
DOBBYN, JOHN PRESTON	dau	Nov24, 1899
DOCKERY, JAMES E.	s.(19 lbs.)	Jul12, 1899
DOCKERY, JOHN	son	Dec12, 1897
DOCKERY, JOHN H.	son James Edward	Aug17, 1859
	son Michael	Nov17, 1861
DOCKERY, MICHAEL W.	dau Cecilia	Oct20, 1887
	dau Catherine	May29, 1890
	dau (dau. d. Aug14, 1892)	May23, 1892
	son (son d. Oct21, 1894)	Mar06, 1894
	son John H.	Nov01, 1895
DODGE, JOHN C.	son	Sep19, 1862
	dau (dau. d. Jan23, 1869)	Apr01, 1864
	dau (dau. d. May07, 1868)	Mar23, 1868
DOMENICI, DOMINICO	dau	Jun22, 1887
	son George	Oct27, 1891
DORR, JAMES CLARKSON	dau Annette	Jan15, 1865
	son Fred, abt	Jan12, 1867
DORSEY, MICHAEL	son Daniel James	Mar18, 1857
	dau	Jan24, 1859
DOUGLAS, GEORGE	dau	Dec26, 1879
	son Frank	Sep07, 1881
	dau Irene	Aug15, 1884
DOW, THOMAS S.	son	Jun17, 1890
DOWNHOUR, JOHN J.	son	Nov15, 1859
	son	Jul17, 1861
	dau	Jul24, 1863
DRINKWATER, WILLIAM C.	dau [Medora]	Oct10, 1875
	dau Mary E.	Oct28, 1877
[dau. Bertha age 8 mo 1880 census]		
	son	Apr23, 1886
DRIVER, JOHN R.	son George	Sep07, 1873
DUNCAN, ALFRED B. (wife Lucy Ann Murphy)		

	son William Caleb	May21, 1879
	dau Ora E.	Mar17, 1887
	son Ernest E.	Aug19, 1891
DUNCAN, CALEB	son	Mar31, 1864
	son	May06, 1866
	dau	May24, 1871
DUNCAN, LEONIDAS P.	dau (d. Nov10, 1876)	Oct27, 1875
	son	Jan24, 1896
DUNSTONE, BENJAMIN	dau	Apr24, 1886
DURKEE, C. W.	dau Addie N.	Jan25, 1860
EASTMAN, ELBRIDGE G.	son	Jan29, 1884
	dau	Dec17, 1886
EDWARDS, FARRAR T.	dau	Apr23, 1856
EHRMANN, HENRY	dau	Mar24, 1867
	dau (d. Mar25, 1870)	Jul27, 1868
	son Henry George	Apr18, 1871
	son William Frederick	Aug11, 1873
EINFALT, JOHN M.	son	Oct23, 1866
ELLERY, ELIAS	dau	Dec12, 1882
ELLIS, ELI	dau	Feb21, 1898
	son	May21, 1899
ENOS, JOSEPH	son John B.	Apr07, 1873
ENOS, MANUEL	son John Bargas	Apr13, 1873
ENOS, MANUEL	son	Jan20, 1891
	dau	Jan02, 1892
ERSKINE, ABIAL (wife Mattie J.)	dau	Mar19, 1859
	dau	Oct01, 1860
	son	Apr18, 1864
	dau	Jun25, 1866
ESTES, JOHN M.	dau	Apr19, 1857
	son	Apr15, 1859
(d. Oct04, 1875)	son	Oct14, 1867
	dau	Aug27, 1874
	infant (b,d same day)	Nov11, 1879
ESTILL, EVANDER	son	Apr18, 1891
	son	Jul14, 1892
EVERHART, MEADE	dau	Oct06, 1889

BIRTHS 1850 - 1900

EWING, GEORGE	dau	May12, 1898
EWING, JOSEPH	son	Nov25, 1856
FADER, CHRIS	dau	Oct28, 1858
	dau	May03, 1860
	son	Jun14, 1866
FARMER, GEORGE	son George M.	Jan24, 1866
FARMER, WILLIAM	son Charles Henry	Jan15, 1864
	son, abt	Mar10, 1866
	son William Grant	Dec13, 1868
FARMER, WILLIAM G.	son	Oct11, 1899
FARNHAM, M. P., Rev.	son	Jan14, 1869
	dau	Aug15, 1870
FECTEAU, PETER (wife Adiz)	dau (dau. d. Aug16, 1874)	Oct16, 1872
	dau	Apr19, 1874
FEENATY, HENRY	son	Nov20, 1865
	son	Oct24, 1869
	son (son d. Nov30, 1873)	Oct09, 1871
	dau	Sep11, 1873
	son	Oct04, 1875
FEHLEY, PATRICK	son	Jan07, 1858
FEIBUSH, LOUIS	dau	Jan18, 1871
	dau	Mar27, 1872
FELTER, ANDREW J.	son	Jul11, 1858
	son	Dec19, 1859
FENNEL, MARTIN	son	Mar17, 1860
FETZER, AUGUST	dau	Apr17, 1880
FIELDER, W. K.	dau	Nov16, 1862
FISHER, JAMES G.	son	Feb28, 1861
	son	Dec05, 1866
FISHER, JAMES M.	dau	Oct12, 1860
	son	Apr23, 1862
	dau (dau. d. Jul24, 1869)	May30, 1863
FISHER, JOHN S.	son	May17, 1859
FITCH, HORACE Y.	dau [Frances Grant Fitch]	Feb22, 1864
	dau (dau. d. May29, 1866)	Dec08, 1865
	son	Sep06, 1867

	[Frederick]	
FITZGERALD, WILLIAM	son	Dec22, 1863
	dau	Oct05, 1865
	dau	Oct24, 1867
FLAGG, AMASA ARTEMUS	son William C.	Aug24, 1885
FLAGG, EBEN S.	dau Sadie	Jun03, 1889
FLAGG, JACOB R.	dau Clara	May22, 1878
FLESHMAN, FRANK	son	Aug21, 1867
	dau	Feb28, 1871
FLETCHER, ANDREW	son	Jun25, 1894
FLINN, LADRUE M.	dau	Jul31, 1882
FLORES, JOHN	son	Mar15, 1875
FLOWERS, ELLIS (wife Amanda)	son (son d. Aug06, 1870)	Sep15, 1863
	dau	Mar26, 1865
	dau	Oct24, 1866
	son Albert Grant	Jul13, 1868
	son William Franklin	Oct03, 1874
	son (son d. Mar03, 1878)	Aug23, 1877
	dau	Sep12, 1880
	son Clarence E.	May04, 1885
FOSTER, GEORGE	son	Mar02, 1869
FOX, HARRISON	son [Volney Lee]	Apr24, 1867
	[dau [Josephine]	Apr05, 1869]
	[son [Charles C.]	Jan14, 1874]
FOX, ORSON	dau [Flora]	May25, 1862
	[son [William O.]	b.1863]
	dau [Elizabeth]	Aug23, 1866
	dau Annie	Jan26, 1868
	dau Isabella	Jul19, 1871
FRANKLIN, ELLIS	son	Aug13, 1869
FRATAS, MANUEL	dau	Jan24, 1868
FREETHY, RICHARD E.	dau Grace	Aug24, 1884
FRICK, CHRISTIAN	son (son d. Mar8, 1866)	Nov03, 1857
	son	Aug06, 1859

BIRTHS 1850 - 1900

	son	Mar02, 1861
FRIEND, A. C.	son	Nov10, 1873
GAFFNEY, MILES	son	Dec26, 1862
GALLAGHER, JAMES	son	Apr07, 1860
GALLOWAY, E. B., Rev.	son	Mar31, 1895
GALOON, PATRICK	son	Oct13, 1856
GARDINER, WILLIAM	son	Dec13, 1861
(wife Betty M.)	twin sons (one d. Jul15, 1864)	May07, 1864
GARRITY, THOMAS	dau	Oct04, 1858
"wife died October 10, 1858; remarried?"	son Thomas	Jul07, 1860
GAUM, FRED	dau	Oct19, 1859
(d. Nov30, 1868)	son	Dec28, 1862
GEHRING, JOHN	dau	Mar22, 1862
	son	Mar15, 1864
GERARD, M.	dau	May18, 1864
GIBBS, J. B.	dau	Nov21, 1897
GIBSON, DAVID	son, abt	Aug16, 1862
	dau	Apr24, 1864
GIBSON, JAMES C.	son	Jul19, 1861
	dau	Aug19, 1863
GIBSON, JOHN E.	son	May04, 1883
	son	Apr05, 1886
GIBSON, ROBERT KING	dau	Oct13, 1879
	son William Stewart	Dec14, 1881
GILZEAN, ALEXANDER	son [James Alexander]	May06, 1894
	son [Leonard Waldron]	Mar09, 1896
[dau.Vivian Lauretta	1900-1902]	
[dau.Mary Agnes	1901-1902]	
[dau. Edna Francis	1904-1905]	
GILZEAN, CHARLES E.	dau [Josephine Margaret]	Dec07, 1889
	dau [Jessamine Rose]	Feb15, 1891
	[son, b,d.	1895]
	son [Charles Eric]	Feb19, 1896
[son Harvey Waldron	1900-1952]	
[son Ronald Miles b,d.	1904]	
[son Charles Donald	1907-1948]	
GILZEAN, JAMES		

[wife Margaret Waldron;m. Nov7, 1848 New Orleans]
```
  [William, b,d.              bef 1852]
  [Margaret Jane, b,d.        bef 1852]
  [John                       1852-1852]
  [Mary Ellen                 1854-1908]
  [James Henry                1856-1902]
  son Alexander               b. Mar09, 1859
  [dau Isobel                 1861-1869]
  son Charles Eric            b. Mar13, 1863
```

GILZEAN, JAMES HENRY	dau Isabel Maude	Jun23, 1878
	son James Albert	May10, 1880
	dau Anna Elicia	Feb17, 1883
	son Warren Hayhew	Jul19, 1890
[son Lester Gerald	1902-1965]	
GIRARD, LOUIS N.	son	Jan25, 1889
GIVEN, JAMES E.	dau Alice	May03, 1895
	son	Mar04, 1897
GIVEN, WILLIAM C.	dau Carrie	Apr30, 1875
	son William C.	Apr08, 1884
GLASS, WILLIAM (wife Sarah)	dau Cora May	Dec05, 1890
	son William Walter	Apr02, 1893
GOERING, CHARLES (wife Louisa)	dau	May18, 1860
	son, abt Emil	May17, 1862
	son	Jul27, 1868
	(son d. Jul21, 1871)	
	son	Oct20, 1869
	dau Mabel	Sep15, 1875
GOETZE, WILLIAM	son	Oct11, 1880
GOODYEAR, CHARLES EUGENE	dau Vera (Senger)	Sep13, 1884
	son Merritt	Nov14, 1886
	dau Irma	May09, 1889
	son [Merwyn E.]	Dec08, 1891
	(son d. Jan06, 1892)	
	son Marvin [Paulsen]	Apr13, 1897
	dau Barbara	Oct23, 1899

[Note: Marvin P. Goodyear celebrated his 101st birthday in 1998.]

GORMAN, THOMAS	dau	Feb14, 1866
	son	Sep09, 1867
GOULD, ALLEN P.	son	Jan17, 1873
	son	Sep07, 1874
GRACEY, EUGENE	dau	Oct01, 1898

BIRTHS 1850 - 1900

GRACEY, WILLIAM E.	dau	Jun04, 1896
GRAVES, JOHN B.	son Claude	Aug01, 1894
	son John B.	Jun24, 1898
GRAVES, RICHARD BENJAMIN	son Rolla	Mar04, 1894
GRAY, DAVID BASKIN	son William H.	Jul17, 1873
	dau	May06, 1878
GRAY, LACEY	son	Oct05, 1898
GREENHOOD, HERMAN	dau	Jul01, 1858
GREENWELL, EARNEST A.	dau Mary S.	Oct15, 1889
	son William	Dec23, 1893
	son Reuben	Nov20, 1895
GREGORY, JOSEPH	son	Sep09, 1895
GRIBBLE, GEORGE	dau (dau d.Feb18,1894)	Mar26, 1892
	dau	Mar10, 1896
GRIBBLE, JAMES M.	son Arthur	Dec04, 1894
	son William	Apr19, 1899
GRIBBLE, RICHARD	son George	Jun29, 1861
	son James Henry	Jul10, 1869
	son Richard	Oct12, 1872
GRIBBLE, WILLIAM	dau Effie	Dec04, 1892
	son Milford	Apr11, 1898
GRIFFIN, MORRIS F.	dau	Mar20, 1866
	son	Jun09, 1868
	son	Feb02, 1871
	son	Jun20, 1873
GRIFFITH, Michael	dau	Oct18, 1872
	son	May13, 1877
	dau	Dec31, 1879
GRIFFITH, PATRICK THOMAS [wife Lora Pattison d.Dec30, 1893]		
[d. Mar06, 1892]	[son [William]	Oct17, 1890]
	son [Clarence]	Jul30, 1892
[d. Sep07, 1893)	son	Dec12, 1893
GRIGSBY, WILLIAM JAMES	son	Sep18, 1891
GUILL, WILLIAM	dau Myrtle	May24, 1895
	dau Mildred	Jul31, 1896
GUM, BURD and Isabel (dau d. Dec14, 1894)	dau	Sep28, 1894
	dau	Aug26, 1897

GUTHRIE, WILLIAM	[dau [Capitola]	b. 1872]
	dau [Flora]	Feb04, 1875
	[son	Nov24, 1875]
[son d. Aug17, 1878]	[Willie]	
	dau [Ada]	Mar03, 1878
	dau [Carrie]	Feb19, 1880
	dau Ruth	Mar10, 1882
	son Albert	Nov27, 1883
	[son Roy	Dec03, 1885]
	dau Violet	May21, 1888
GWIN, FRANKLIN S.	son	Feb09, 1860
HAAS, FRED G.	son	Jul14, 1881
	dau	Jul19, 1883
	dau Augusta	Mar05, 1885
	son	Feb01, 1887
	son	Feb22, 1890
HAGELMAN, JOHN	son (son d. Dec14, 1868)	Dec08, 1863
	son	May19, 1865
HAILSTONE, JOHN T.	son Pindor Franklin	Apr 1872
	dau Hettie	Mar31, 1873

"Maria born Feb1880" - 1900 census

HALL, ALBERT G.	dau, b,d.	Mar22, 1881
HALL, ELISHA	dau	Jan08, 1868
HALL, JOHN ("John P. and Nettie?")	son	Jun23, 1872
HALLEY, FREDERICK F.	son	Oct29, 1894
HAM, JOSEPH	dau Maude	Aug11, 1875
HAMILTON, DANIEL D.	son	Dec12, 1856
	dau	Oct08, 1860
HAMPTON, HARLEY	son Avilla D.	Nov09, 1897
HAMPTON, JASPER SUTTON	son	Feb24, 1872
	dau	Feb15, 1874
HAMPTON, WILLIAM	son (d. Feb09, 1898)	Oct31, 1897
HANLON, JOHN (wife Catherine)	dau Lizzie	May01, 1864
	son Eddie	Jun25, 1867
	son John	Apr10, 1869
	dau	Aug26, 1871
(d. Nov12, 1873)	dau	Nov08, 1873
HANNA, CHARLES	dau	Mar21, 1861
	son	Mar06, 1862

BIRTHS 1850 - 1900

HANNA, HUGH	son	Mar18, 1898
HANSEN, PETER	son	Oct13, 1860
HARBINE, HARDY (wife Eugenia A.)	dau Eugenia M.	Dec12, 1899
HARROW, JOSEPH S.	son	Oct12, 1898
HARTMAN, CHARLES (wife Rosa)	son	Dec02, 1864
	dau	Jun24, 1866
(d. Feb07, 1869)	son	Jan26, 1868
	son	Jun11, 1870
(d. Dec12, 1875)	son	Mar14, 1873
	dau	Feb28, 1875
(d. Feb20, 1877)	dau	Jun20, 1876
HARTMAN, CHARLES (Jr.)	son	Dec08, 1890
	son	Apr01, 1897
HARVEY, HENRY THOMAS [wife Rebecca]	son Henry Thomas, Jr.	Dec01, 1867
	dau [Lillie E.]	Mar21, 1869
[dau Dora J. b.1871]		
[dau Rebecca b. 1874]		
	dau Ada	Sep06, 1876
	dau Clara	Apr04, 1879
	son Albert H.	Jul10, 1884
HARVEY, JAMES	son Merrick	Aug22, 1876
	son Alfred	Jan03, 1879
HARVEY, W. L.	tw. s.& d.	Nov13, 1893
HAWK, JOHN and Lilly	son	Jul28, 1872
HAY, ED	son	Feb21, 1898
HAYS, HIRAM B.	dau	Mar07, 1875
	dau	Nov14, 1876
HAYWARD, JOHN D.	son John D.	May22, 1892
	son Lyander W.	Oct24, 1893
HEATH, JOHN WESLEY	dau Flora Jane	Nov19, 1880
	son Charles Jesse	Jul21, 1882
	dau	Nov19, 1895
	dau	Feb10, 1897
	dau	Mar12, 1898
HENDERSON, HENRY	son	Feb13, 1892
	son	May21, 1895
	son	Jan26, 1898
HENNESSEY, PATRICK O'MALLEY	dau [Mary]	Apr04, 1864
	son [John P.]	Aug17, 1866
	dau	Jun05, 1868

[d. May26, 1916]	[Esther]	
	son	Dec07, 1876
(d. Jun05, 1881)	[William]	
HENNESSEY, TIMOTHY	dau	Aug13, 1887
	Nellie Marguerite	
	dau Anne	Jun04, 1889
HERDLE, WILLIAM and Christine		
	dau	Jun04, 1858
(d. Jan18, 1867)	son	Apr20, 1861
	son	Dec21, 1863
HERRICK, F. A.	dau	Oct11, 1860
HICKS, ROBERT	dau Helen	May21, 1899
HIGGINS, WILLIAM	dau	Jun11, 1870
HILLS, FRANK M.	son	Dec29, 1865
	son	Feb09, 1867
	dau	Jun23, 1870
HILS, EDWARD	son	Mar16, 1860
HINDLEY, GEORGE	son	Nov05, 1867
	son	Aug28, 1870
	dau	Jun23, 1872
HINDLEY, HENRY	son	Jan24, 1858
	dau	Mar22, 1859
HIPPLER, ALBERT	son	Mar07, 1898
HITCHCOCK, GEORGE	TRIPLETS, 1 son, 2 dau	
		Apr18, 1899
HOADLEY, J. F.	son	Oct05, 1859
	dau	Sep26, 1867
	son	Mar20, 1872
HOBART, DeFORREST A.	dau	Jun23, 1869
	sonson	Oct02, 1874
	Charles Michael	
HOCKER, HENRY	dau Anna F.	Oct11, 1859
(wife Christina)	son	Feb08, 1861
	Henry G.	
	dau	Feb09, 1863
	Mary L. (E?)	
	son	Aug14, 1864
	Francis G.	
	son	Mar11, 1868
	William F.	
	dau	Mar09, 1873
	Maria (Mary)	
(also Clara d. Dec14, 1875 aged 1 yr 10 dy)		
HOLLAND, PATRICK	dau	Nov24, 1882
	dau	Apr20, 1890
	Catherine	
HORTON, RICHARD E.	dau	Jul06, 1888

BIRTHS 1850 - 1900

	Elizabeth	
	son Charles	Jan05, 1893
HOSLINGER, VALENTINE	son	Oct18, 1868
HOUGH, JOHN M. & Julia	son	Sep14, 1860
HOUGHTON, C. H.	dau	Aug16, 1898
HOWARD, WILLIAM G.	son	Dec01, 1895
	Raymond D.	
(d. Apr01, 1897)	dau	Mar26, 1897
	dau	Jul08, 1898
	Florence	
(d. June 14, 1899)	son	Jun03, 1899
HOWE, IRA	son	Dec20, 1863
	dau	Aug18, 1865
HOYT, JONATHON S.	dau Sadie	Mar17, 1875
HUBBARD, AUSTIN W.	son	Sep05, 1890
HUBBARD, THEODORE JUD	son	Feb02, 1864
	son	Apr12, 1868
HUGHES, ROBERT	dau	Jan25, 1860
	son	Nov01, 1861
	William Edward	
	son	Sep22, 1865
	dau	Sep27, 1868
	son	Aug30, 1873
	dau	Feb28, 1876
	dau	Aug19, 1880
HUGHES, THOMAS MILLER	son	Mar14, 1892
HUGHES, WILLIAM EDWARD	son	May04, 1896
	Clarence	
HULME, GEORGE	son	May29, 1867
(wife Elizabeth)	(son d. Aug25, 1868)	
HUNGERFORD, Z. N.	son	Mar11, 1869
HUNT, JOSEPH	son	Oct28, 1878
HUOTT, JOSEPH	dau	Feb18, 1874
(wife Catherine)	(dau. d. May15, 1875)	
	twin sons	Aug29, 1875
HUPP, WILLIAM I.	dau	Jul04, 1866
	Mary L. (Kraft)	
	dau	Mar30, 1868
	dau Martha	May23, 1870
	son	Mar09, 1872
	William Irving	
	son	Mar24, 1874
	James Wiley	
HUSON, CORNELIUS W.	son	Sep21, 1874
(wife Fannie)	(son d. Sep10, 1879)	

HUTCHINS, HENRY H.	dau Aimee	Jun18, 1891
	dau Ada C.	Sep16, 1892
	dau Vera F.	Oct27, 1895
	son Harold H.	Sep07, 1898
HUTCHINS, JOSEPH	son	Jul20, 1899
HUTCHINSON, JOSEPH	dau	May05, 1859
HYDE, JOHN	dau	Aug25, 1869
	son	Aug27, 1870
	son	Apr21, 1872
	son	Oct12, 1873
HYDE, MORRIS	son	Nov26, 1867
	son	Jun21, 1876
	dau	Feb20, 1879
	dau	May07, 1881
	dau	Jan02, 1883
INGRAM, WALKER	son	Jul28, 1888
	(son d. Aug23, 1888)	
	dau	Feb03, 1890
INNES, JOSEPH	son	Aug26, 1865
IRVING, GEORGE	son Harrison	Jan05, 1891
	dau Arabella E.	Apr24, 1892
	son Frank H.	Apr11, 1893
IVERSON, OLE	dau Camilla	Nov24, 1881
	son Adolph	Oct21, 1883
	dau Roella	Feb20, 1886
	son Horace G.	Nov22, 1887
JACKSON, JOHN (wife Catherine)	dau	Jul02, 1864
	son	Apr29, 1866
	dau	Mar17, 1869
JACKSON, WILBUR L.	son W. C.	May10, 1885
	son Jacob	Jul01, 1887
	dau Irene	Sep16, 1889
	son Raymond	Oct10, 1891
(see also Addendum)		
JAMES, CHARLES	son	Apr04, 1890
JOHNSON, HENRY	dau	Mar22, 1858
JOHNSON, J. C.	dau	Apr25, 1864
JOHNSON, L. A.	dau	Dec10, 1861
JOHNSON, WILLIAM	dau	Jul20, 1864
	dau	Mar06, 1866

[not Johnston, William H., below; both men are on 1860 census.]

Johnson: see also addendum

BIRTHS 1850 - 1900

```
JOHNSTON, WILLIAM H.              son                       Apr17, 1868
[born in Eureka                   son                       Dec05, 1871]
[see also Deaths 1850-1900 for more children.]

JONES, L. F.                      son                       Feb09,   1881    (wife
Nancy L.)                         Thomas (d.May1,1889)
                                  son                       Mar08, 1882
                                  son                       Feb26, 1887
                                  son                       Oct09, 1889

JORDAN, CHARLES                   son                       Apr04, 1862

JORDAN, MELVILLE C.               son                       Jun23, 1895
                                  Humphrey C.
                                  son                       Sep12, 1896
                                  Lawrence
                                  son                       Sep24, 1898
                                  Irving D.
                                  dau Elnora                Nov26, 1899

JOSE, EDWARD W.                   son                       Sep12, 1883
                                  dau                       Jul08, 1885
                                  son                       Mar23, 1887
                                  son                       Mar26, 1889
                                  son                       Mar24, 1891

JOSEPH, MICHAEL                   dau Palmela               Oct10, 1890
                                  dau Mary L.               Mar24, 1892

JOYNT, ROBERT                     son                       Sep09, 1862
(wife Catherine)

JUMPER, GEORGE B.                 son                       Nov14, 1887

JUNKANS, WILLIAM F.               dau                       Jan25, 1878
                                  son                       Aug09, 1880
                                  Rudolph Henry
                                  dau                       Nov14, 1897

KACZINSKY, JULIUS                 son                       Mar08, 1875
                                  dau                       Nov16, 1877
                                  son                       Aug15, 1879
                                  son                       Feb16, 1881
                                  dau                       Aug18, 1883
                                  son                       Nov19, 1885

KIEN, LOUIS                       dau                       Aug03, 1890

KELLOGG, ELI D.                   son                       Aug12, 1865
                                  Edward L.
                                  dau                       May31, 1870

KELLOGG, JOHN J.                  son Warren                Sep15, 1865
(wife Martha)                     son Joseph                Jan30, 1869

KELLOGG, LANGDON J.               dau                       May13, 1878
(wife Sarah)

KELTON, EDWARD A.                 dau                       Nov14, 1859
                                  son                       May28, 1861
                                  son                       Jul06, 1867
```

KENDRICK, M. (wife Abbey)	tw. s. Charles & James	Jan19, 1860 Jan19, 1860
KENNEY, ARTHUR	son son son	Jan24, 1860 Jul12, 1863 Jun29, 1867
KETWIG, U. [son Gerhard d. Mar17, 1873 age 1 yr 4 mo]	dau	Sep21, 1873
KILGORE, FELIX G.	son	Feb01, 1873
KING, FRANCIS	dau	Jan06, 1889
KING, JOHN	son son	Aug02, 1890 Jul31, 1891
KINGSBURY, WARREN W.	dau	Mar25, 1881
KINGSLEY, ALECK	dau	Jul20, 1862
KISE, JOSEPH BLOOMFIELD	son Elisha Samuel son Commodore Colonel	Nov24, 1870 Jul27, 1875
see also Addendum		
KITTRIDGE, CHARLES	son	Nov24, 1871
KLAUER, Mrs. (no first name given)	tw.dau.	May27, 1862
KLEEBERGER, GEORGE B.	son	Apr15, 1880
KLEIN, GEORGE	dau	Sep05, 1883
KNIGHT, SILAS D.	son	Dec25, 1866
KNOWLES, HENRY	son Henry Lincoln dau dau son George Earnest son Archie (son d. Aug07, 1898)	Dec05, 1865 Dec14, 1867 Jan12, 1872 Aug19, 1877 Jun25, 1880
KOHN, JOSEPH	dau dau	Jan02, 1859 Sep15, 1860
KOLL, JOHN	son John R.	Feb11, 1899
KOON, JOHN A.	son Roswell dau Cora E.	Jul01, 1892 Mar09, 1894
KRUTTSCHNITT, A. M.	son	Apr13, 1861
KUPER, CHARLES F. (wife Augusta)	son Charlie (son d. Oct22, 1875) son	Sep18, 1875 Nov23, 1876

	son Walter	Aug21, 1881
	(son d. abt May26, 1883)	
LA BAREE, WILLIAM HENRY, Dr.		
	dau Margaret	Dec18, 1895
	dau Livia	Jul19, 1898
LACHENMACHER, FREDRICK	dau	Sep27, 1867
(wife Dorothea)	Emma Augusta	
	[dau. d. Jan05, 1876]	
	dau Bertha	Mar17, 1869
	(dau. d. Dec19, 1875)	
	dau	Feb12, 1871
	son	Jun09, 1873
	Wm. Henry Harrison	
	(d. Dec25, 1875)	
(see also Stierlen)		
LAINGOR, GEORGE W.	dau	May01, 1885
LAINGOR, JOHN J.	son	Sep09, 1881
	George B.	
	dau Ida	Nov05, 1883
	son John	Jun17, 1885
	dau Idelle	Oct09, 1887
	son Lloyd	Nov03, 1889
LAIRD, ROBERT	dau	Jan10, 1896
	(d. Jan12, 1896)	
LAMEY, PHILLIP	son	Jan27, 1890
LAMPLEY, FRANK	son	Mar__, 1893
LAMPLEY, MONROE	dau	Jan05, 1893
LANDIS, JAMES S.	dau	Feb18, 1876
	[Laura M.]	
	son [John]	Oct22, 1877
LANG, MAX	son	Feb14, 1859
	son	Jul22, 1860
	son	Dec22, 1861
	son	Jun26, 1866
	son	Jan27, 1872
LANGE, WILLIAM	son	Jun26, 1863
(wife Louisa)	son	Sep20, 1869
LARGE, BENJAMIN	son	Jul01, 1866
LARGE, OSCEOLA Q.	dau	Jul23, 1892
	(dau. d. Aug16, 1893)	
	son	Jun05, 1896
LARGE, ROBERT	dau	Sep30, 1887
	dau	Dec30, 1892
LARISON, HENRY B.	dau	Jul16, 1898
LARSON, JOHN	dau	Dec01, 1878
	Mary Helena	
	dau	May16, 1881

	Anna (Yancey)	
	son John	Jan11, 1888
	son Charles	May18, 1890
	dau Margaret	May26, 1892
LAWS, GEORGE M.	son George Oscar	May16, 1856
	dau Christina	Aug03, 1860
LEACH, JOHN	son	Jan18, 1859
LEARY, EDWARD (wife Esther)	dau (dau. d. Mar27, 1893)	Sep20, 1867
LEAS, GEORGE W.	son Samuel Lee	Mar18, 1875
LEAS, JOHN C.	dau	Mar11, 1893
	son	May12, 1896
LEAVITT, GEO. WASHINGTON	son William C.	Apr21, 1888
	dau Isabelle	Jul20, 1890
(see also Addendum)		
LEAVITT, WILLIAM JOSIAH	dau. (dau d. Aug21, 1887)	Aug14, 1887
	dau Nellie	Dec20, 1898
LEE, SAM (see also Addendum)	dau	Sep15, 1898
LEIBRANDT, JACOB (wife Clara)	son	Jul28, 1876
	dau (dau d. Aug20, 1879)	Mar22, 1878
	son	Dec04, 1879
	son	Sep14, 1881
LEONARD, HENRY W.	dau Lucinda	Jul16, 1872
	dau	Apr12, 1874
	dau	Jun17, 1878
	dau Sadie	Jul22, 1881
	dau Helen	Nov26, 1894
LICHTBLAU, GOTTLIEB	dau	Feb25, 1879
	son	Mar29, 1880
	dau	Jul14, 1881
	dau	Feb20, 1883
LICHTY, WILLARD J.	son	Dec18, 1898
LITTLE, WILLIAM J. [wife Lydia F.]	son Oliver C.	May01, 1960
	dau Fanny	Aug01, 1864
[Fanny d. Charleston S.C. Oct31, 1866]		
	dau Irene May	May13, 1866
[Irene May d. Aug07, 1866]		
LOOMIS, ANDREW J.	son Judd	Jun20, 1859

(wife Minerva)	son	Nov14, 1860
	son	Oct22, 1862
	dau	Mar30, 1864
	dau	Oct11, 1865
LOOTS, JACOB	son	Jul25, 1862
LORD, GEORGE H.	dau	Apr13, 1865
LORD, JOHN, Dr.	son	Aug11, 1874
	son	Aug30, 1877
LORENZ, FRANK	dau	Mar28, 1873
LORENZ, FRANK JOSEPH	dau Anita	Jan21, 1893
	dau Fern	Sep01, 1894
	dau Ruby	Apr23, 1896
	son Joseph	Sep30, 1897
	son Frank	Apr21, 1899
LORENZ, HENRY [son Franz Joseph	1862-1937]	
(wife Susan)	dau	Aug31, 1865
	dau Mary Anne (dau d. Mar21, 1868)	Feb05, 1868
	son John Nicholas	Feb10, 1869
	dau ["Tillie"]	Apr08, 1871
	dau Susan	Aug05, 1874
	son William David	Nov09, 1876
	son George Jacob	Dec01, 1878
	dau Emma	Feb19, 1881
	son Grover Cleveland	Feb01, 1884
	son Charley (son d. Feb05, 1888)	Oct21, 1886
LORENZ, HENRY	son	Jan15, 1897
LORENZ, NICHOLAS	son	Dec27, 1870
	son	Sep03, 1875
	son	Nov17, 1879
	dau	Sep04, 1882
LORING, FREDERICK H.	son	Aug02, 1877
LOVERIDGE, MERWIN W.	son	Jun28, 1884
LOWDEN, FRANK	son	Jul09, 1889
	son	Dec18, 1895
LOWDEN, MARSHALL H.	dau	Mar09, 1876
	dau	May13, 1879
	dau	Feb07, 1884
LOWDEN, OWEN EUGENE	son	Mar18, 1868
	dau	Aug26, 1875
	son Frederick Spencer	Feb21, 1878
	son	Sep24, 1879

	son	Jan16, 1881
	Eli Eugene	
	dau Ora	Feb10, 1883
	son	Jul21, 1891

LOWDEN, WILEY M.	dau	Apr25, 1897

LOWDEN, WM. JEFFERSON	son	Apr27, 1888
(called "Perry")	Spencer William	
	son	Mar14, 1890
	Henry Lloyd	
	son	Nov02, 1897
	Perry Richard	

LOWDEN, WILLIAM S.	son	Oct06, 1857
	[Henry Larkin]	
	dau	Jul07, 1859
	[Carrie]	
	dau	Feb07, 1861
	[Mary T.]	
[son William age 7 - 1870 census]		
	dau	Nov16, 1864
	[Nellie S.]	
	dau	Mar29, 1875
	(dau d. April1, 1875)	

[Author's note: there is a wealth of information about the Lowden family in the J. J. Jackson Museum, Weaverville, California.]

LOWERY, GEORGE	dau	Jun02, 1878

LUDDINGTON, CHARLES	son	May21, 1857
("Paper says to the lady of - not wife")		

LYNCH, JAMES	son	Jun01, 1858

LYONS, HARRY H.	dau	Sep08, 1897
	Marcelle	
	son John	May22, 1899

MABIE, FRANK	son	Dec03, 1877
	Leland Stanley	
	dau	Jan23, 1880
	dau	Sep05, 1884
	son	Apr13, 1886

Mc - names beginning with this prefix are alphabetized as if spelled MAC.

McCAMPBELL, ROBERT	son	Aug18, 1889
	dau	Feb09, 1892
	Stella V. M.	
	son	Nov24, 1894
	dau	Mar20, 1897

McCLARY, DAVID R.	dau	Jul16, 1886

McCLURE, P. O.	dau	Aug13, 1865
(wife Hannah)	(dau d. Aug25, 1865)	

McDANIEL, W. R.	dau	Jul04, 1861
	(dau d. Nov17, 1861)	
	son	Oct14, 1862
	(son d. Feb1864)	

BIRTHS 1850 - 1900

McDONALD, BERNARD	dau Ellen L.	Nov28, 1887
	dau Margaret	Jul22, 1889
	son James P.	Feb29, 1892
	dau Norine	Mar09, 1894
	son Thomas	Apr30, 1898
	dau Bernice	Oct09, 1899
McDONALD, JAMES D.	dau Idell B.	Nov06, 1890
	son Albert W.	Dec24, 1892
	son Hilton	Jan05, 1895
McDONALD, PETER	son	Dec04, 1899
McGILLIVRAY, JOSEPH	son George	May25, 1858
	son	Jun29, 1859
	dau Helen	Oct19, 1862
	dau Caroline	Aug09, 1866
McGINNIS, JOHN	son	Apr05, 1864
	dau	Nov21, 186_
	dau	Sep11, 1867
McGOVERN, THOMAS	son John G.	Sep21, 1864
	son James T.	Mar24, 1867
	son Henry B.	Jul28, 1868
McGRATH, Phillip	son Phillip	Mar26, 1864
McKNIGHT, GEORGE (wife Sarah)	son	Apr09, 1864
	dau (dau d. Feb09, 1869)	Mar20, 1866
McLEAN, ARTHUR W.	son	Aug18, 1899
McMAHAN, JOSEPH	dau	Sep21, 1861
McMURRY, JOHN	dau	Sep16, 1875
	dau Ella	Apr11, 1877
	dau Adele	May07, 1879
McNAMARA, THOMAS J.	son Ellsworth S.	May03, 1883
	dau Belle	Nov28, 1885
	son	Feb01, 1891
	dau Eunice	Oct16, 1898
McVEAN, JOHN A.	son	Sep06, 1881
McWHORTER, ADAM L.	dau	Jun14, 1870
MAHONEY, WARREN AMOS	son James Wallace	Sep01, 1885
	dau Grace	Oct27, 1886
	dau Edith	Jun13, 1889

	dau Mary	Aug21, 1892
	son	Jan18, 1898
	George C.	
see also addendum		
MALONEY, WILLIAM	son	Jan27, 1857
	dau	Jun17, 1860
	dau	Oct08, 1861
	son	Oct26, 1862
MANSFIELD, ABRAHAM	son Daniel L.	Apr20, 1891
	son Raymond	Mar22, 1893
	son Harry	Jan30, 1895
MARAL, FRANK	dau	Oct31, 1878
MARKWELL, PARIS T.	dau	Dec19, 1897
MARSHALL, AMOS H.	son Robert Clark	May04, 1872
	dau	Feb13, 1874
	son Amos Jr.	Mar12, 1882
MARTIN, AUGUSTUS	[wife Mary]	
[dau. Carrie d. Feb25, 1865, aged 1 yr 8 mo 8 dy]		
	dau	Aug09, 1867
MARTIN, E.	son	Feb02, 1864
MARTIN, FRANK	dau	Jul15, 1869
	dau	Apr20, 1872
	son	Nov23, 1873
MARTIN, GEORGE	dau	Aug28, 1897
	dau	Jul04, 1899
MARTIN, HENRY	dau	Jul09, 1859
(wife Jane)	dau Elizabeth	Mar27, 1868
MARTIN, LORENZO	dau	Aug21, 1893
	son	Jun27, 1895
MARTIN, P. P.	son	Feb14, 1869
MARTIN, RICHARD	son	Aug27, 1866
MASON, E.	dau	Aug09, 1895
MATHEWS, A.	son	Dec24, 1888
MATHEWS, JAMES A.	dau Viola Belle	Dec24, 1877
MATHEWS, JOHN DeWITT	dau	Oct16, 1865
	dau	Mar31, 1868
	son	Mar02, 1870
MATZEN, CHRISTIAN	son Frank	Aug28, 1860
	dau Dora	Sep30, 1864

MEAD, CORYDON M.	son	Apr08, 1877
	son Harland E.	Jan07, 1882
MECKEL, CHRIS	son Fritz C.	Jul28, 1871
	dau Annie	Aug20, 1873
	dau	May12, 1876
	son Adolph Nicholas	Nov26, 1878
	dau	Mar01, 1881
MECKEL, JOHN (wife Charlotte)	son John W.	Mar31, 1858
	son Christian	Jun27, 1861
	son Henry W.	Feb20, 1864
	son Albert C.	Nov17, 1869
MESSNER, LOUIS	son	Aug07, 1897
MILLER, GEORGE	dau	Oct06, 1888
MILLER, WILLIAM D.	son	Sep27, 1890
	dau	Mar11, 1894
	son	Mar01, 1897
	son	Jul22, 1899
MINEAR, JOHN	son	Aug25, 1889
	dau	Dec07, 1890
	son	Mar08, 1892
	son	Apr18, 1894
MITCHELL, ARCHIBALD (wife Elizabeth)	son (son d. May04, 1863)	Apr05, 1858
	dau (dau d. Aug09, 1859)	Jun27, 1859
	son	Aug24, 1860
MITCHELL, JOHN (wife Nellie)	son	Oct21, 1860
	dau	Apr05, 1864
MITCHELL, WILLIAM W. (wife Mary A.)	dau (dau d. Jul27, 1869)	Jul09, 1869
MONTAGUE, J. C., Dr. [wife Mary Enright]	dau Mary F.	Sep23, 1871
	son Charles Edward (son d. Jan09, 1874)	Dec21, 1873
	son Joseph A. (son d. Aug08, 1899)	Mar10, 1875
	son Henry Edwin	Feb20, 1877
	son Charles	Feb25, 1879
	dau [Dollie]	Dec11, 1880
	son [John A.]	Apr23, 1882
MONTGOMERY, THOMAS J.	son	Nov03, 1893

	son	Jun01, 1896
MORRIS, JAMES J.	dau	Sep30, 1865
	son William	Dec28, 1867
	son Henry A.	Oct10, 1869
MORRIS, JOHN	son	Jun08, 1896
MORTIMER, WASHINGTON	son	Mar28, 1898
MOSS, AMOS S.	dau Edna	Jan24, 1886
MOTHERWELL, THOMAS	son	Aug18, 1857
MULLANE, JAMES	dau	Aug03, 1871
	son	Oct07, 1879
	(son d. Jul30, 1880)	
	dau	Feb14, 1891
	dau	Apr25, 1892
MULLINS, J. M.	son	Jul03, 1896
MURPHY, JOHN J.	dau Genevieve H.	Aug14, 1896
	dau, abt Zelda M.	May11, 1898
	son Charles B.	Sep18, 1899
MURPHY, PATRICK	son	Sep06, 1862
(wife Mary A.)	dau	Nov28, 1864
	son	Mar17, 1867
	(son d. Nov17, 1868)	
	son	Mar19, 1869
	son	Jan28, 1872
MURPHY, PETER	dau	Aug19, 1860
MYERS, HOSEA	son	Mar12, 1894
NEATHERY, THEOPHILUS	dau Elizabeth	Oct28, 1859
NEILSON, CHARLES	dau	Mar30, 1861
NEIMAN, JOHN	[dau Emily	abt 1862]
(wife Charlotte)	dau Bertha	Jul09, 1863
	(dau d. Nov30, 1868)	
	dau Eleanor	May16, 1866
	(dau d. Dec12, 1866)	
	son Gustavus William	Apr25, 1868
	(son d. May25, 1868)	
[dau Marie d. Jun09, 1865 aged 4 mo 18 dy]		
NEUMANN, H.	dau	Jul03, 1891
NEUSSE, CHARLES HENRY (Carl)		
	dau	Jan17, 1877
	dau, abt	May24, 1879
	son Charles Henry	Jan05, 1888

BIRTHS 1850 - 1900

NEWELL, JAMES	son	Dec27, 1898
NEWMAN, EDWARD	dau Mary (Jenkins)	Dec02, 1887
NEWMAN, JOHN	son Edward Legara	Feb03, 1858
NEWMAN, LOUIS H.F.	dau, abt son dau dau son (son d. Oct18, 1894)	May02, 1885 Aug31, 1887 Jun11, 1889 May02, 1892 Jul25, 1894
NICHOLS, WILLIAM H.	dau Matilda	Jan25, 1868
NICHOLS, WILLIAM JOHN	tw. sons Nelson E. William I. son Charles B.	 Feb19, 1896 Feb19, 1896 Oct29, 1898
NOBLE, DON	son dau	Feb29, 1895 Aug06, 1897
NOONAN, GEORGE EDMUND [wife Elizabeth] [son d. Jan30, 1886]	son Harrison Hyacinth son [George E. Jr.] son Clarence Russell dau Adeline Frances	May31, 1878 Oct28, 1879 Feb02, 1881 Jun30, 1882
NORCROSS, OLIVER H.P.	son (son d. Jun10, 1858) dau Ensie May	Apr09, 1857 Jan30, 1861
NORDYKE, BENJAMIN JAMES	son	Apr14, 1889
NORMAN, WARREN	son	Mar26, 1887
OBERDEENER, MOSES	son	Apr19, 1864
O'LEARY, RICHARD	dau	Feb17, 1869
OLMSTEAD, WILLIAM T.	dau	Apr16, 1857
OLSEN, LOUIS	dau Minnie son Louis B. dau Evalina dau Flora	Aug20, 1866 Oct31, 1868 Jan22, 1872 Dec27, 1875
OLSEN, JAMES PETER	dau Sarah Elizabeth son William son Alfred Wright	Jan18, 1878 May08, 1880 Mar24, 1889
O'NEIL, TIMOTHY	dau Nellie dau Kate	May13, 1858 Mar18, 1860

[Cornelius?]	son	Apr18, 1864
	James Nornelius	
	son	Oct09, 1866
	Timothy D.	
	dau Agnes	Jan30, 1869
	son John	Sep25, 1871
	son	Feb14, 1874
	(son d. Nov27, 1879)	
ORR, GEORGE	dau	Oct23, 1886
OSBORNE, GEORGE KNOX, Dr.	son George	Nov03, 1896
OSGOOD, HEZEKIAH C.	dau Rosalyn	Jan22, 1864
	dau Alva	Mar10, 1866
	dau Alvina	Apr26, 1868
	son Ulysses	Jun11, 1870
	son Wallie	Sep08, 1873
OSTHOFF, JOHANN HENRY	son Henry	May20, 1867
	son Charles	Oct24, 1868
	son	Oct25, 1870
	(son d. May3, 1874)	
	dau Lizzie	Oct05, 1873
	(dau. d. Jan21, 1874)	
	dau	Dec24, 1874
OVERMOHLE, HENRY	son	May19, 1867
[b.San Francisco	son	Jan15, 1878]
OWINGS, JOHN M.	dau, abt	Nov26, 1887
	Orrie F.	
PALMER, WILLIAM	dau	Jul18, 1860

Parry - see also Perry

PARRY, JOHN W.	son Allie	Jun28, 1893
	son Phillip	Feb13, 1895
PARTRIDGE, FERD LINCOLN	son	May05, 1893
	son	Jan26, 1895
PATTON, R.	dau	Feb10, 1889
PAULLIN, J. R.	tw. s.& d.	May24, 1856
PAULSEN, JACOB	son Charles	Mar28, 1871
[wife Louisa]	son Jacob	Mar18, 1873
	(son d. Jul17, 1874)	
	dau Bertha	Jun16, 1875
	(dau. d. Oct15, 1898)	
	son	Jun02, 1877
	Henry William	
	son	Jan27, 1880
	Arthur Edwin	
	son Fred R.	Oct05, 1887
(see also Addendum)		
PAULSEN, PETER		
[wife A. Barbara]		
[dau Elizabeth Sabina	1863-1935]	
	son Julius	Dec25, 1864

	dau Minnie	Jun23, 1866
	dau	Sep03, 1868
	Anna (Bush)	
	son	Aug14, 1870
(son d. Feb06, 1875)	Peter M.	
	dau	Dec19, 1872
	Hannah Pauline (Hall)	
	son	Apr23, 1875
	Albert Lincoln	
	son	May19, 1880
	Harry (d.1903)	
	dau Edna	Aug02, 1883
	son	May04, 1890
(see also Addendum)	Charles Arthur	
PAYNE, F.A.O.	dau	Jan01, 1862
PEACOCK, JOHN R. [wife Medora Childers]	dau Nellie	Jul24, 1863
PELLETREAU, ALEXANDER [wife Ellen Louisa]	son William	Jul27, 1859
	son Gilbert Whitman	Jul23, 1864
PERHAM, HIRAM M. [wife Harriet A.]	dau	Jul25, 1881
PERRY, HENRY	son	Jun04, 1871
PERRY, _____	dau	Mar24, 1887
PETERS, RUDOLPH	dau	Jan12, 1873
	son	Jan18, 1875
PETERSON, ERICK	dau Winnie	May05, 1891
	dau Nellie	Jun08, 1893
PHARES, HENRY C.	dau	Apr06, 1894
PHELPS, AMBROSE	son [Willie Homer] (son d. May27, 1863)	Dec18, 1862
PHILBROOK, JOHN W.	son John M.	Jun09, 1861
	dau Nettie L.	Jul20, 1864
	son [Frank] (son d. Jun09, 1868)	Apr09, 1868
	son Fred	Aug30, 1874
PHILLIPS, J. W.	son	Mar24, 1861
	dau	Jul22, 1863
PHILLIPS, J. W. (is this James W., son of Olney?)		
	son	Mar27, 1896
	son	Feb19, 1898
PHILLIPS, OLNEY	dau Lucy	Jul19, 1860
	dau Addie	Mar21, 1863
	son James Walter	Sep25, 1865
PHILPOT, MOSES	son	Jul03, 1891

	dau	Dec12, 1894
	dau	Mar16, 1898
PINCUS, ISAAC	dau Lena	Dec22, 1864
	son Joseph	Feb16, 1867
	dau Rosa	Sep24, 1869
	dau Martha	Mar29, 1876
	son (b.d.)	Jun26, 1878
	dau Bertha	Jul20, 1879
	son	Jun05, 1882
PLASS, WILLIAM	son	Apr24, 1891
PLOWMAN, K. P.	son	Jul26, 1860
POST, JOHN S.	dau Beatrice	Nov03, 1889
POTILLO, FRANK	son Nicholas	Dec13, 1870
POULEUR, B.	dau	Jan28, 1861
	dau	Apr19, 1865
RAAB, LOUIS	son (son d. Aug2, 1865)	May11, 1860
RAGLIN, LLOYD	son	Sep25, 1893
RAIS, MANUEL (De Rais)	son William	Feb17, 1891
[son John	Nov21, 1892]	
	son Frank	Jul01, 1895
	dau	Sep15, 1896
RALPH, JOHN	dau Cora Alice	May14, 1874
	dau	Jan22, 1878
	dau	Dec30, 1879
(dau. d. Jan17, 1898)	Gertrude	
REED, EDGAR L.	son Edgar L., Jr.	Mar10, 1883
	dau	Mar06, 1884
	dau Helen (dau. d. Jun30, 1893)	Oct07, 1887
REES, DAVID WILLIAM	son	Feb11, 1891
REID, DANIEL G.	dau	Oct12, 1888
	son	Nov03, 1889
	son (son d. Sep01, 1893)	Aug15, 1893
RICHARDS, WILLLIAM	dau Edith	Aug16, 1872
	son William	May10, 1874
	dau Adeline	Feb02, 1877
RIDDLE, J. B. (is this John Guy?)	dau	Apr22, 1897
RIPSTEIN, JOHN	son	Aug13, 1859
ROBINSON, DAVID S.	son	Apr24, 1880

BIRTHS 1850 - 1900

	William Allen son	Aug28, 1881
	(son d. Jan18, 1900) dau	Apr23, 1883
	(dau. d. Apr25, 1883) dau Mary S.	Feb08, 1887
ROBINSON, THOMAS EDWIN	dau	Mar08, 1886
RODERIC, ANTONE	son Joseph	Jan27, 1869
	son	Feb07, 1875
	son	Jul07, 1880
RODGERS, ANTONE D.	son John Antone	May09, 1882
	dau Fannie	Dec01, 1884
	son Edwin Lowell	Mar17, 1887
	son Antone C.	Jul11, 1889
	dau Margaret Margaret (m. Trimble)	Aug08, 1892
	dau Anne Lenore (m. Brady)	Jun10, 1894
	son Raymond	Mar17, 1899
RODGERS, FRANK A. (DUARTE)	son	Jun14, 1887
	(son d. May26, 1888) son Henry	Dec01, 1894
	son Martin	Aug23, 1897
ROSE, JOHN	dau Cintha	Feb26, 1872
ROSS, ANDREW JACKSON	dau Rosie M.	Nov26, 1864
	son Andrew Franklin	Feb05, 1871
ROURKE, DENNIS	dau [Mary Ellen]	Jul11, 1882
	son Dennis	Jun09, 1884
	son John [Donald]	May04, 1887
RUCH, MICHAEL	son Jesse P.	Jan10, 1855
	dau Mary Eliza	Feb06, 1857
RUCH, WILLIAM H. (wife Lavina A.)	dau	Mar16, 1879
RULE, WILLIAM JOHN	dau Elizabeth E.	Oct17, 1875
	dau	Jan17, 1877
	dau Carrie	Jun04, 1879
	dau Mattie	May07, 1881
RUMFELT, AUGUSTUS	dau Bessie	Mar27, 1877
RUTLEDGE, ARTHUR	dau (dau. d. Sep20, 1895)	Sep2, 1895

RYAN, PATRICK J.	dau Christina	Aug25, 1893
	son (son d. Nov27, 1895)	Sep29, 1894
	son (son d. Sep07, 1896)	Jun20, 1896
	dau Marie	Apr30, 1898
	dau Ethel	Sep24, 1899
RYAN, RICHARD	son Patrick J.	Aug08, 1867
(wife Mary)	dau (dau. d. Aug11, 1874)	Aug06, 1874
	dau Mary E.	May28, 1880
RYAN, RICHARD (wife Catherine)	dau (dau. d. Jun27, 1860)	Jan09, 1860
	dau Margaret	Mar29, 1861
SALADIN, EDOUARD [wife Marguerite] (see also Appendum)	dau	Jul06, 1898
SANBURN, JOHN G.	son Charles Randolph	Mar23, 1874
	dau Della	Nov06, 1877
SCHAFFER, AUGUST (wife Rosa)	dau Mary Ada	Jun27, 1874
	dau Anna	Aug30, 1876
	son Edward E.	Jan12, 1878
	son Frederick	Feb05, 1880
	son Arthur A.	Nov25, 1882
	son (s. weighed 13 lbs)	Jul06, 1886
	dau Zita R.	Jun02, 1888
SCHALL, LOUIS	son Louis Frederick	Jun05, 1872

SCHLOMER, [HARMON KARL]
[m. Miss Louisa Weinheimer Sep10, 1860 in Pekin, Illinois]

	son Charles	Oct12, 1861
[m. Adolph Hinters]	dau Barbara	Feb24, 1863
	triplets s.	May23, 1865
	son [Herman]	Sep05, 1867
(d. May10, 1869)	[Herman]	
	dau Louisa E. Louisa E.	Mar29, 1871
["Miss Lou" d. Mar14, 1957]		
	[son [Christian H.]	Jul16, 1873]

[Note: Henry Grant was one of the triplets; he d. Nov21, 1956]
[Three other sons, Christian, Cord, and John are buried in the Schlomer plot at Helena Cemetery.]

SCHMIDT, WILLIAM	son	Jul16, 1895
SCHNEIDER, HENRY	dau	Aug26, 1867

	Caroline son Henry Otto	Dec08, 1872
SCOFIELD, TRACY	son Frederick	Mar10, 1863
	son Charles	Mar09, 1865
SCOTT, J. W.	dau	Sep18, 1882
SCOTT, WILLIAM JASPER	dau Nellie	Jul25, 1884
	son William Irvin	Feb02, 1887
	son Stanford L.	Sep22, 1889
	son Edwin M.	Nov14, 1892
	son Linton	Jun27, 1896
[see also Addendum]		
SEAMAN, HENRY J.	son Harry	Jan18, 1859
	dau [Lulu]	Mar21, 1861
SEARLES, JOHN	son Frank E.	Mar24, 1860
	tw. dau	Mar11, 1868
SEGALIA, ANTONIO	dau Martha	Jun29, 1868

SENGER, JACOB [wife Antoinette] (sometimes written Singer)
   [dau. Mary L. d. Apr02, 1863, aged 2 yr 5 mo]

[1880 census]	[dau Josephine	1862]
[1880 census]	[son Henry	1863]
	tw. s.&d. Jacob Adams & [Madeline]	Aug21, 1865
	dau [Amelia]	Apr24, 1867
	dau [Catherine]	Mar27, 1870
	son Peter	Feb23, 1872
	son George W.	Feb26, 1876
	son Milan Arthur	May14, 1878
	dau	Dec30, 1880

[note: Trin.Co.Marriages also lists dau. Alice & Nettie]

SHANKS, JACOB	dau	Sep17, 1862
SHAW, ISAAC B.	son	Feb02, 1867
SHAY, DENNIS	son	Oct13, 1862
SHOCK, GEORGE	son	Jun02, 1890
	dau	May14, 1895
SHOCK, JOHN PRESTON	dau	Apr09, 1895
SHOCK, ZINA L.	dau Elsie M.	Jul11, 1894
	son Harold J.	Jun16, 1896

SHOLES, THEODORE FREDERICK			
	dau	Mar04, 1894	
	son	Jun19, 1895	
SHUFORD, JOHN W.	son	Jan13, 1888	
[see also Addendum]	dau Edna	Jun21, 1892	
	dau Nellie B.	Mar26, 1894	
	son John	Aug05, 1895	
SHURTLEFF, NATHANIEL B.	son Minert	Oct18, 1892	
SILIGO, LOUIS	dau	Dec03, 1899	
SILVA, ANTONE	dau	Jun20, 1887	
SILVA, AUGUST	son	Nov30, 1873	
SILVA, FRANK	son	Dec04, 1871	
SIMMONS, C.	son	Sep06, 1858	
SKINNER, ROBERT ALEXANDER			
	dau Myrtle	May15, 1891	
	son Robert E.	Jun17, 1893	
	dau Jennie E.	Mar03, 1895	
[see also Addendum]			
SLEIGHT, H.	dau	Jan25, 1859	
SLOAN, CHARLES	son	Sep03, 1859	
(wife Ellen)	son [John] (son d. May30, 1861)	Feb04, 1861	
	dau (dau. d. Dec06, 1864)	Oct14, 1862	
	son	Oct13, 1864	
SMITH, ABIAL W.	dau Lucilia	Jan20, 1877	
	son Frank	May12, 1879	
SMITH, DANIEL LINZY	son	May29, 1882	
	dau	May17, 1894	
	dau	May09, 1896	
SMITH, J. W.	son	Sep14, 1893	
SMITH, J. W.	tw.sons	Dec04, 1871	
SMITH, JOHN H.	dau	Aug15, 1872	
SMITH, JOSEPH	son	May27, 1872	
SMITH, JOSEPH	son	Sep09, 1889	
SMITH, JOSEPH W.	dau (dau. d. Oct08, 1892)	Nov25, 1886	
SMITH, SYDNEY	dau	Oct30, 1871	
SMITH, THOMAS B.	dau	Feb17, 1876	

BIRTHS 1850 - 1900

SNYDER, DANIEL	son	Dec19, 1856
	dau	Oct06, 1858
	dau, abt	Mar30, 1861
	son	Mar06, 1863
	son	Jun29, 1865
SPARKS, GEORGE	dau	Oct13, 1894
SPENCE, JOSEPH	dau	Jan15, 1860
	son	Mar03, 1864
	son	Sep15, 1865
SPIERS, JOHN	dau	Jul15, 1896
SPRATT, CHARLES W., Dr.	son Stephen T.	Aug02, 1889
	son [Earle C.] (son d. Feb12, 1894)	Nov04, 1892
(son d. Sep30, 1894)	son [Charles C.]	Jun23, 1894
	son Lloyd D.	May28, 1896
SQUIRES, HECTOR T.	dau Lille E.	Jan12, 1870
STACKPOLE, FRANK L.	dau Avis G.	Feb18, 1894
	son Morris	Feb20, 1895
	dau	Jan23, 1896
[see also Addendum]	dau Doris	Apr16, 1899
STAFFORD, JAMES A.	dau Stella A.	Oct26, 1875
STEIGLISTS, HERMAN	dau	Sep06, 1862
STIERLEN, FRED (wife Medora)	dau (dau. d. Mar16, 1865)	Jul01, 1864
STILLER, ALEXANDER A. [wife Louisa]	dau Augusta (dau. d. Dec10, 1899)	Aug04, 1857
	dau Matilda (dau. d. Jun09, 1884)	Sep04, 1858
	son Alexander Frederic (son d. Aug15, 1861)	Oct11, 1859
	son Theodore (son d. Apr29, 1869)	Dec28, 1860
	son Richard W.	b. 1862
	son Frederick Andrew (son d. May13, 1865)	Jan15, 1865
	son William David (son d. Aug01, 1866)	Apr10, 1866
	son Charles Emil	Jan15, 1868
	son	Sep10, 1871

	Albert J.	
	(son d. Dec19, 1871)	
[also son John b. May 1856 Prussia; 1860 Census]		
STILLER, RICHARD W.	dau Mary M.	Nov30, 1889
[wife Mary Montague]	[dau d. 1911]	
	son Raymond	Dec19, 1898
	[son d. Oct23, 1904]	
STODDARD, JOHN R.	dau Inez	Mar30, 1874
[wife Inez]	[dau Clara	1875]
	[son John	1877]
	[dau Fannie	1878]
	dau	Jan06, 1880
	Mary Rosalie	
	(dau. d. Aug10, 1885)	
	dau	Apr11, 1888
[see also Addendum]		
STOFFER, FRANKLIN B.	son	Jul29, 1867
	Franklin	
	dau Marian	Feb26, 1869
	dau	Feb07, 1871
	Addie B.	
STONE, RICHARD M.	dau	Aug16, 1866
	son Richard	Nov07, 1868
STONE, T. N.	dau	Dec07, 1860
STOPEL, ANTON	son	Mar18, 1879
SUDSWORTH, WRIGHT	son	Oct19, 1861
SWEET, ALONZO	dau	Jan16, 1864
	dau	May25, 1865
SWEET, DAVID WARREN	son	Apr18, 1889
TAPIE, EMILE	dau	Oct22, 1895
TARPLEY, HARVEY J.	son	Mar10, 1871
	Edward Lee	
	son	Apr20, 1879
	dau	Feb06, 1883
TAYLOR, ARTHUR J.	son	May28, 1891
TAYLOR, DAVID G.	dau Carrie	Jul16, 1868
	son Charles	Aug20, 1870
[not on 1880 census]	son	Aug15, 1872
	dau	Apr07, 1874
	Elizabeth	
	dau Mary	Sep29, 1878
TAYLOR, HOLMES	dau	Aug30, 1855
(from TRINITY TIMES)		
TESTY, JOSEPH	son	Dec5, 1861
(wife Sarah)	[Joseph Edward]	
	(son d. Dec12, 1875)	
	son	May17, 1863
(son d. Feb22, 1873)	[Edward]	

	son	Aug06, 1865
	William Bernard	
	son	Jan31, 1867
	Charles Jerome	
	dau	Aug07, 1868
[1880 census]	Marie Emily	
[unreadable 1880 cens.)	son	Jan31, 1874
THAYER, STEPHEN I.	dau Maud	Feb08, 1868
	dau	Jan24, 1872
	Jessie E.	
	dau Mary I.	Jul29, 1873
	dau Edna	Nov18, 1880
THOMPSON, GEORGE W.	son, abt	Jan25, 1857
THORNE, EDWARD	son	Feb22, 1894
	dau Edna	Jan10, 1898
THYNGE, JOHN	son	Sep26, 1888
TINSLEY, ALEXANDER	son	May22, 1857
	James Franklin	
	son	Dec25, 1859
	William Henry	
	son	Nov20, 1864
	George Washington	
	son	Nov18, 1866
	John Thomas	
	son	May14, 1869
	Elijah Samuel	
	dau	Feb20, 1871
	Daisy C.	
	son Eddy	Jan20, 1874
[not in 1880 census]	son	Nov27, 1875
	son	Jan05, 1878
	William Norman	
	dau	Jun19, 1880
TINSLEY, JAMES A. [son Charlie Albert]		
[d. Sep19, 1879 age 2 yr 9 mo 22 dy]		
[wife Mary J.]	son	Mar21, 1878
	Augustus A.	
TODD, EDWARD N.	dau Beryl	Nov03, 1894
	dau Altha	Sep19, 1896
	dau Zelita	Oct27, 1898
TODD, GEORGE W.	son	Jan15, 1868
	William Dayborn	
	dau	Jan10, 1876
TODD, LOUIS O.	son L.E.P.	Aug01, 1892
TODD, WILLIAM	[son	b. 1852]
[wife Eliza]	[Alexander]	
	[d. Jun16, 1869 age 17]	
	son John A.	Dec27, 1858
	dau Mary J.	May26, 1861
	son	Mar12, 1863
	Louis Owens	
	son	Dec30, 1864
	Edward N.	

	dau Emma A.	Jul25, 1868
TODD, WILLIAM D.	son William	Jun10, 1895
	dau Ruth	Jun24, 1897
TOURTELOTTE, JESSE H.	dau Mary	Apr21, 1860
	son	Apr09, 1867
	son Jesse Francis	Apr01, 1873
	son	Apr01, 1874
TOWER, FRANK B.	dau Essie D.	Jan10, 1893
	son Charles	Sep01, 1894
	dau Marian K.	Dec14, 1895
	son Henry	Jan18, 1898
TOWER, J. O.	son	Jun02, 1856
TRASK, BENJAMIN F.	son	Aug27, 1865
	(son d. Mar4, 1869)	
	son George Nelson	Jan23, 1868
	[dau Minerva]	
TRASK, EDWARD, Dr.	dau Mary B.	Aug20, 1859
TRASK, MADISON N.	dau	Nov28, 1872
	son	Dec23, 1875
TRELOAR, THOMAS	son Thomas Jr.	Jan29, 18661
(wife Salina)	son William	Nov18, 1862
	(son d. May31, 1868)	
	son Edward Warmington	Jul28, 1864
	[son Charles	b. 1866]
[son d. Mar7, 1868 age 14 mo]		
TRIMBLE, BRICE A.	son Royal A.	Aug02, 1893
	dau	Dec23, 1894
	son	Mar31, 1896
	dau	Oct25, 1897
	dau	Oct11, 1899
TRIMBLE, PIERCE	son John Wesley	Feb10, 1875
	son	Mar10, 1880
(son drowned Jun25, 1897)	dau Maggie M.	May09, 1882
	son	Jul06, 1884
	(son d. Aug16, 1892)	
	son James A.	Apr09, 1890
	son Francis	Mar21, 1893
	son Frederick	Feb13, 1899
TURNER, JOHN WILLIAM	dau	May25, 1887

BIRTHS 1850 - 1900

TWAMBLEY, CHARLES W.	son George	Apr30, 1866
	dau Carrie	Jan05, 1868
[d. Vina, CA Feb17, 1885]		
	son	Oct15, 1871
	dau	May09, 1874
	son John	Mar05, 1876
[d. Vina, CA Mar5, 1885]		
	[son Lyman	1882]
[d. Vina, CA May27, 1883 aged 9 mo 14 dy]		
TYE, WILLIAM	son	Nov26, 1862
	(son d. Dec1, 1862)	
	dau	Feb14, 1864
VAN CLEAVE, JOSEPH	dau	May06, 1890
	tw.dau.	May18, 1897
VANDERHOFF, JOHN H.	son	Apr05, 1884
	dau	Oct25, 1886
	dau	Apr22, 1889
	dau	Oct27, 1891
	dau	May05, 1894
	dau	Jan15, 1897
VAN MATRE, ADRIAN JUDSON [wife Alice Kellogg]		
	son	Oct01, 1887
	son	Jul20, 1890
	dau	Feb01, 1895
	dau	Mar06, 1897

VAN MATRE, JOHN CHANDLER [wife Bertha Koll]
see Addendum for the complete list of children.

VAN MATRE, MORRIS LORD (Mart) [wife Mary]		
	dau	May30, 1872
	son Bert B.	Apr03, 1874
	[son d. Jan6, 1890]	
VAN MATRE, PETER	[son Fordyce	1854]
[d. Sep6, 1857 aged about 3 yr]		
	dau Caroline	Feb07, 1858
	son John Chandler	May29, 1859
	son Walter G.	Apr29, 1861
	dau Almira	Jan01, 1863
	[dau Lou S.	b. 1865]
	dau [Minnie]	Jul28, 1867
VAUGHN, WILLIAM	son Nicholas	Apr29, 1872
VAUGHN, WILLIAM DAVID	dau	Dec26, 1886
	son Charles Raymond	Jun25, 1892
	son William Roy	Oct05, 1895
VAUGHN, WILLIS	son	May13, 1887

	dau	Dec20, 1891
VITZTHUM, GEORGE	[wife Theresa Marie]	
[dau. Bertha d. Mar06, 1867 aged 2 yr 6 mo]		
	son George Julius	Aug15, 1868
	son Charles William	Nov02, 1872
	son William President	Mar04, 1874
	son Henry H.	Jul20, 1875
	dau	Sep24, 1877
VOGEL, ERNEST	son	Sep11, 1863
VOLLMERS, OTTO	son William	Sep08, 1858
	son Otto (son d. Dec26, 1863)	Nov18, 1860
	son (son d. Aug17, 1880)	Nov12, 1862
	son Henry	Jan16, 1866
VOLLMERS, WILLIAM	dau Artela	Nov01, 1881
	son Otto R.	Mar02, 1883
	dau Alberta E.	Apr23, 1885
	son Jefferson	Mar18, 1887
	dau Ardella L.	Mar27, 1890
	son Shelby A.	Oct30, 1895
VON KRUZE, G. A.	son	Apr08, 1897
WALDORFF, EARNEST A.	dau Elsie May (Tye)	May05, 1890
WALDORFF, JACOB THEODORE	dau Matilda	Feb14, 1857
	son Jacob T.	b. 1858
	son Earnest Anderson	Dec__, 1861
	dau Mary M. (drowned May05, 1878)	b. 1864
WALDORFF, WILLIAM HENRY	dau Lulu Belle	Mar10, 1878
	dau Mollie June	Feb26, 1880
	son George Francis	Oct09, 1882
	son William Wesley	Feb10, 1884
	dau Annie May	Aug20, 1886
	son (TJ) Albert C.	Mar13, 1889
	dau Lillian Elizabeth	Apr11, 1894

	dau Gladys Marie	Apr29, 1896

[see also Addendum]

WALKER, GEORGE W.	son	Oct15, 1880
WALKER, JAMES M. C.	dau	Dec15, 1879
	dau	Oct05, 1881
WALKER, JAMES	dau	Jun28, 1863
WALLACE, EPENETUS L. [wife Susan]	son Charles (son d. Nov24, 1862)	Apr01, 1861
	son	Nov21, 1862
	son	Jan24, 1865
WALLACE, JAMES ADDISON	son Shirley	Dec20, 1896
	dau Rita	Oct19, 1899
WALLACE, JAMES C.	son James A.	Feb08, 1862
	son (son d. Dec25, 1871)	Feb10, 1869
WALLACE, J. M.	son	May14, 1866
WALLACE, THOMAS (wife Mary Ellen)	son William O'Connell	Jul02, 1874
	dau Mary Elizabeth	Oct01, 1875
	son Thomas	Oct08, 1877
	son David	Jul04, 1879
WALTER, FREDERICK	son	Dec09, 1859

[Victor Emanuel Walter on gravestone; d. Aug24, 1860]

	son	May08, 1862
	son	Jun10, 1864
	dau Flora	Apr24, 1867
WALTERS, HENRY AUGUSTUS	son	Oct06, 1891
WARREN, ARCHIE	dau Alice	Apr24, 1878
WARREN, CHARLES	son Emerson	Sep22, 1899
WATERS, J. W.	son	Mar11, 1866
WEBSTER, GEORGE	dau	Sep22, 1897
WEEKS, EDWARD EVERETT	dau Margaret	Jul12, 1899
WEEKS, F.	son	Feb24, 1861
WEINHEIMER, HENRY [wife Catherine Dockery]	dau Cecelia	Apr15, 1872
	son [Johnnie] (son d. Dec19, 1875)	Jan07, 1874
	son Henry W. Jr.	Nov12, 1875
	dau Anna Louise	Sep13, 1877

	dau Katherine T.	Oct14, 1879
	dau Caroliine	Jun04, 1881
	tw.dau. Agnes & Mary	Jan07, 1883
[see Addendum; see also Ryan]		
WELLS, JOHN W.	son	Mar13, 1861
WELLS, LUKE FORD	son Walter S.	Jun05, 1869
	dau May	May24, 1871
	dau Martha Varney	Mar19, 1873
WEYAND, ZACHARIAH T. (wife Amelia)	son Budd	May24, 1890
	son Clabe	May29, 1897
	son Babe	Sep30, 1898
WHEELER, NATHAN (wife Elizabeth A.)	dau (dau. d. Jun12, 1880)	Mar27, 1871
WHITE, CHARLES	son	Mar18, 1881
WHITE, CHARLES W.	dau Mary Eva	Oct14, 1882
(dau. d. Sep27, 1885)	dau [Nellie May] [Nellie May]	Mar16, 1884
	son Charles	Aug29, 1886
	son John	Nov24, 1887
WHITEBREAD, ADOLPH	dau	Oct27, 1875
WHITMORE, HENRY M.	(wife Naomi) dau Minnie	Jul31, 1868
WHITMORE, JOHN [Catherine Ryan]	son John R.	Mar18, 1891
	dau Helen	Oct19, 1892
	son Leonard S.	Oct10, 1895
[see also Addendum]		
WILLBURN, AARON	dau	Apr07, 1894
	dau	Sep23, 1895
	son	Oct10, 1896
WILLBURN, HIRAM DAVID	dau	Feb23, 1898
	dau	May21, 1899
WILLBURN, SIDNEY	dau (dau. d. Mar11, 1893)	Mar02, 1893
	dau	Mar07, 1894
[see also Addendum for Willburn births]		
WILLIAMS, ANTONE	son, abt	Nov09, 1889)
WILLIAMS, CHARLES E.	dau	Dec21, 1860
	dau	Feb07, 1864
	dau	Jan07, 1866

BIRTHS 1850 - 1900

WILLIAMS, ELISHA B.	son Delma H. (Delmer?)	Dec16, 1876
WILLIAMS, GEORGE	dau Carrie	Mar29, 1858
	dau Emma	Apr21, 1860
	son	Sep17, 1861
	dau	Aug17, 1867
WILLIAMS, JOSEPH W.	dau	Nov04, 1895
	dau	Sep02, 1897
WILLIAMS, MANUEL	son Samuel	Aug16, 1868
	son Manuel Jr.	Apr24, 1870
	dau Maria	Feb19, 1872
WILSON, BENJAMIN BOEN	son	Oct19, 1887
	son	Dec28, 1892
WILSON, EDGAR EVART	son	Mar13, 1898
WILSON, JAMES (wife Hattie)	dau Jean	Feb25, 1888
	tw.son Isaac J. & Homer B. (Homer d. Jan. 1891)	Jul06, 1890
	son Elmer (son d. Dec27, 1891)	Jun22, 1891
	son Charles Nelson	Mar09, 1896
	son Harold John	Oct05, 1898
WILSON, RUFUS COLLINS	dau	Oct07, 1889
	son	Nov04, 1891
	dau	Sep23, 1893
WILSON, VITRUVIUS VIVIAN	dau (dau. d. Nov29, 1873)	Aug31, 1873
	son Charles B. Charles B.	Jan29, 1877
(paper said "daughter" - in error)		
WILSON, WILLIAM, Dr.	son	Mar04, 1865
WOLFF, NICHOLAS	son George	Jan04, 1872
	dau Kate	Jan05, 1874
	dau Mary	Jan06, 1876
	son William	Feb01, 1881
WOOD, CHARLES L.	dau	Aug17, 1890
	dau	Jul23, 1892
WOODBURY, DAVID	dau Flora	Jun23, 1872
	son [Willie] (son d. Nov26, 1876)	Aug27, 1874
	son Fred	Mar06, 1878
	son Ray	Apr11, 1880
	son Clyde	May21, 1885
	son Earl	Mar25, 1893
WOODBURY, ISAAC	dau Louisa	Mar27, 1868

	dau Cora	Nov22, 1870
	son Franklin Isaac	Jan20, 1874
	dau, abt Ethel	Aug12, 1876
WRIGHT, ARTHUR	son	Jul18, 1880
ZEIGLER, CYRUS W.	son Levi E.	Mar23, 1897
	dau Cora W.	Mar31, 1898
ZUVER, JOHN BARTLEY	dau	Oct12, 1898

END TRINITY COUNTY, CALIFORNIA BIRTHS 1850-1900

Compiled by **Rita M. Hanover**, used with permission

INDEX OF BIRTHS IN TRINITY COUNTY, CALIFORNIA
1900-1950

Note: this Index is from the TRINITY JOURNAL, *January of the following year, except 1946-1950, which are from Official Records. For the earliest records, double-check with the Census; for later records, check Official Birth Records; even then, some names are mis-spelled. If a record is not in Trinity County, check in Shasta County (Redding), esp. for Births after 1940.*

Sometimes births were not recorded, but the infant showed up in the summaries of deaths. Check both births and deaths for children in a family. It is advisable to check the TRINITY JOURNAL for a week or two after the event as well as Official Records. Be sure to verify dates and spellings of names.

BORN TO THE WIFE OF	SEX	BIRTH DATE
ABERNATHY, GEORGE ASBURY	see Addendum	
ABERNATHY, HARRY E.	son,	Aug25, 1912
ABERNATHY, W. A.	daughter,	Jul15, 1911
ADAMS, AUSTIN A.	son,	Jan18, 1934
ADAMS, AUSTIN DECATOR	daughter,	Mar05, 1931
ADAMS, J. Q.	daughter,	Mar08, 1901
ADAMS, JOSEPH	daughter,	_____, 1946
ADAMS, W. J.	son,	Apr12, 1902
ADAMS, W. J.	daughter,	Feb22, 1904
ADAMS, W. J.	daughter,	Apr09, 1905
ADAMS, W. J.	son,	Aug02, 1909
ADAMS, W. J.	son,	Jan21, 1913
ADAMS, W. J.	son,	Apr19, 1914
ADAMS, W. J.	son,	Jul01, 1916
ADAMS, WM.	daughter,	Sep17, 1919
ADAMS, WILLIAM JESSE	daughter,	Feb11, 1926
ADAMS, W. J.	daughter,	Jul29, 1924
ADDISON, JACK	daughter,	Apr22, 1946
AH SON, CHARLES	son,	Nov29, 1911
ALBIEZ, GEORGE EDWIN	son,	Jun13, 1930
ALBIEZ, KARL	daughter,	Jan31, 1904
ALBIEZ, KARL	see Addendum	
ALWARD, LESLIE THORNTON	son,	May20, 1934
AMMON, CHAUNCEY LeROY	see Addendum	
ANCHARD, RALPH	daughter,	Mar10, 1923
ANDERLINI, J. A.	daughter,	Oct25, 1903
ANDERLINI, J. A.	daughter,	Jan24, 1910
ANDERLINI, T.	son,	Nov25, 1900
ANDERSON, H. E., Rev.	son,	Apr12, 1917
ANDISON, JACK	tw.dau.,	Jan26, 1947
ARBUCKLE, ARCHIE ANDREW	daughter,	Aug06, 1934
ARBUCKLE, CHAUNCEY O.	daughter,	Jul14, 1936
ARBUCKLE, CHAUNCEY O.	daughter,	Oct05, 1940
ARBUCKLE, HARVEY WOODROW	son,	Aug13, 1937
ARBUCKLE, T. C.	daughter,	Sep03, 1928
ARBUCKLE, TACITUS CHARLES	daughter,	Jun28, 1930
ARBUCKLE, TACITUS CHARLES	daughter,	Oct06, 1938
ARBUCKLE, T. W.	son,	Sep01, 1914
ARGUELLO, H. E.	son,	Mar15, 1920
ARGUELLO, HAROLD E.	daughter,	Dec31, 1923
ARMENTROUT, JOHN WILLIAM	see Addendum	
ARMENTROUT, R.	daughter,	Oct11, 1906
ARMENTROUT, R. J.	son,	Apr10, 1914
ASHCRAFT, EARL JOSEPH	daughter,	Jan07, 1949
ATHERTON, CHARLES L.	daughter,	Sep18, 1933
ATTERBERRY, PAUL JOSEPH	son,	May18, 1949

ATTERBURY, FRANK D.	son,	Nov10, 1944
AUGUSTINE, ROBERT LAWRENCE	daughter,	Jun07, 1941
BABCOCK, D. W.	son,	Oct01, 1913
BAILEY, GEO. L.	daughter,	Jul14, 1901
BAILEY, G. L.	daughter,	Apr04, 1903
BAILEY, JOHN	son,	Jul16, 1934
BAILEY, JOHN W.	daughter,	Dec16, 1943
BAILEY, WM. A.	daughter,	Sep22, 1923
BAILEY, WILLIAM A.	daughter,	Apr03, 1926
BAILEY, WM. ARCHIE	daughter,	Sep10, 1927
BAILEY, WILLIAM A.	son,	Jan22, 1929
BAILEY, WILLIAM A.	son,	Nov29, 1932
BAILEY, WILLIAM ARCHIE	son,	Mar05, 1934
BAILEY, WM. A.	son,	Jan30, 1936
BAILEY, WM. A.	daughter,	Jul30, 1937
BAILEY, WILLIAM A.	son,	Jul28, 1939
BAIRD, BILL	son,	Mar06, 1934
BARKER, FOWLER D.	son,	May15, 1925
BARKER, F. D.	daughter,	Apr24, 1928
BARKER, FOWLER DAVID	see Addendum	
BARKER, GEORGE ALBERT	daughter,	Nov07, 1945
BARKER, HOWARD D.	son,	Mar07, 1923
BARKER, LESTER CUTTER	son,	Aug25, 1946
BARKER, LESTER CULTER	daughter,	Oct27, 1947
BARTLETT, THOMAS F.	son,	Jul07, 1932
BARTLETT, THOMAS F.	daughter,	Jan17, 1940
BARTON, GEORGE E.(Dr & Mrs)	daughter,	Oct25, 1936
BASSHAM, E. A.	son,	Jun03, 1914
BASSHAM, E. A.	daughter,	Sep27, 1928
BASSHAM, RUSSEL B.	son,	Aug23, 1936
BATES, RANDALL M.	see Addendum	
BATHAM, ROLLAND	daughter,	_____, 1946
BAUMGARDNER, ALVIN R.	son,	Oct05, 1939
BEAN, HERBERT O.	son,	Dec12, 1920
BEAN, R. P.	son,	Jun02, 1908
BEARD, ROBERT NEAL	daughter,	Mar17, 1948
BEATTIE, EDWARD	daughter,	May10, 1947
BECK, E. L.	daughter,	Nov06, 1912
BEEM, THOMAS ALFRED	daughter,	Dec15, 1949
BENNETT, C. M.	daughter,	Jul15, 1913
BENNETT, C. M.	son,	Sep22, 1915
BENNETT, C. M.	daughter,	Dec06, 1917
BENNETT, GRANT	son,	Aug09, 1918
BENNETT, GRANT	daughter,	Oct04, 1919
BENNETT, GRANT	daughter,	Mar12, 1927
BENNETT, GRANT	daughter,	Apr20, 1929
BENNETT, HARVEY S.	daughter,	Oct10, 1937
BENSON, OSCAR	son,	Feb05, 1913
BENTON, E. J.	son,	Sep10, 1903
BERGIN, GEO. H.	daughter,	Aug13, 1915
BETTS, C. E.	son,	Apr11, 1922
BETTS, CHARLES E.	daughter,	May21, 1923
BETTS, CHARLES EDWARD	daughter,	Apr18, 1927
BETTS, CHARLES E.	daughter,	Aug25, 1929
BETTS, CHARLES ED	son,	Mar01, 1944
BETZER, R. R.	daughter,	Sep14, 1913
BIGELOW, SAMUEL JAMES	son,	Feb28, 1934
BIGELOW, SAMUEL JAMES	daughter,	Oct13, 1935
BIGELOW, W. R.	son,	Feb16, 1900
BIGELOW, W. R.	son,	Nov29, 1901
BIGELOW, W. R.	son,	Mar29, 1903
BIGELOW, W. R.	son,	Dec25, 1906
BIGGERSTAFF, ARDEN EDWARD	son,	Jul18, 1931

BIGGERSTAFF, CROSBY R.	daughter,	Dec18, 1939
BIGGERSTAFF, CROSBY RICHARD	daughter,	Nov07, 1941
BLACKMORE, BENJAMIN A.	daughter,	Jun11, 1940
BLAGRAVE, GEO. H.	daughter,	May11, 1910
BLAGRAVE, GEORGE H.	son,	Jun03, 1912
BLAGRAVE, JAMES	son,	Sep01, 1905
BLAIR, B. M.	daughter,	Sep01, 1900
BLAIR, B.	son,	Sep24, 1903
BLAIR, HUGH NEWELL	see Addendum	
BLAIR, JAMES R.	son,	Sep14, 1912
BLAKE, F. T.	daughter,	Apr09, 1906
BLAKE, F. T.	daughter,	Jan04, 1908
BLAKE, F. T.	daughter,	Jul17, 1909
BLAKE, F. T.	daughter,	Jun26, 1910
BLAKE, FRANK TILDEN	son,	Aug28, 1912
BLAKE, F. T.	daughter,	Aug22, 1914
BLAKE, F. T.	daughter,	Oct28, 1918
BLAKEMORE, THOMAS JEFFERSON	see Addendum	
BLAND, FLOYD E.	daughter,	May27, 1924
BLANEY, J. J.	son,	Jun24, 1908
BLANEY, J. J.	daughter,	Apr21, 1918
BLANEY, J. J.	son,	Jan27, 1920
BLOOD, BARNEY MARCEL	daughter,	Nov26, 1950
BLUE, JOHN STUART	daughter,	May29, 1941
BOMMELYN, AUGUST L.	son,	Apr09, 1933
BOSTROM, E. C.	daughter,	Aug18, 1946
BOUDREAUX, JULES EDWARD	daughter,	Apr20, 1948
BOUDREAUX, JULES EDWARD	daughter,	Aug04, 1949
BOUDREAUX, JULES EDWARD	son,	Dec28, 1950
BOUERY, PIERRE	son,	Jan30, 1913
BOWMAN, ELMER	daughter,	Dec08, 1922
BOX, ANDREW	daughter,	Feb11, 1915
BOX, REUBEN P.	daughter,	Aug27, 1916
BOX, REUBEN P.	son,	Jul06, 1918
BRADBURY, GEO. H.	daughter,	Jun23, 1916
BRADY, M. A.	daughter,	Aug21, 1905
BRAGDON, E. H.	son,	Jul10, 1903
BRAMLET, ALBERT E.	son,	Aug21, 1942
BRAMLET, ALBERT E.	son,	Oct17, 1940
BRAY, C. V. D.	son,	Jun29, 1928
BREMER, C. W.	daughter,	Jan08, 1915
BREMER, GEORGE SHELDON	son,	Sep28, 1945
BREWER, C. E.	daughter,	Dec07, 1908
BREWER, CHAS. E.	daughter,	Oct04, 1912
BRINKMAN, LESTER W.	son,	Aug06, 1918
BRISCOE, ISSAIC MERRITT	daughter,	Jul04, 1935
BRITTON, JOS.	son,	Jul31, 1900
BRITTON, JOS.	daughter,	Apr13, 1903
BRITTON, JOS.	daughter,	Sep09, 1906
BRITTON, JOSEPH S.	see Addendum	
BROSSARD, WM. J.	son,	Jun21, 1942
BROWN, B. R.	son,	Mar12, 1901
BROWN, B. R.	daughter,	Dec28, 1902
BROWN, B. R.	daughter,	Feb23, 1905
BROWN, B. R.	son,	Dec27, 1915

Note: Boyer R. and Mary I. Brown had 4 children on the 1910 census, including 1 born in 1899.

BROWN, CHARLES LeROY	son,	May16, 1921
BROWN, C. L.	son,	May09, 1922
BROWN, CHARLES L.	daughter,	Dec04, 1923
BROWN, CHAS. L.	daughter,	Jul28, 1925
BROWN, CHARLES LEROY	daughter,	May07, 1930
BROWN, CHAS. L.	son,	Oct27, 1934

BROWN, CHARLES LEROY	daughter,	Apr24, 1950
BROWN, DANIEL	son,	Mar09, 1909
BROWN, DAVID DUDLEY	son,	Apr01, 1935
BROWN, DOLPHN G.	son,	Mar28, 1923
BROWN, ELLIS	daughter,	Jun23, 1942
BROWN, FLEMING	daughter,	Jan09, 1901
BROWN, F. E.	son,	Jun06, 1903
BROWN, FLEM.	daughter,	Jul05, 1905
BROWN, E. F.	son,	Sep21, 1907
BROWN, E. F.	son,	Feb17, 1910
BROWN, FLEMING E.	daughter,	Feb03, 1912
BROWN, FLEMING	son,	Aug27, 1913
BROWN, FLEMING E.	daughter,	May05, 1915
BROWN, F. E.	daughter,	Sep14, 1917
BROWN, F. M.	son,	Feb28, 1920

Note: Fleming E. Brown had 6 children on the 1910 census, one born in 1898. Be sure to double-check the father's name for these children, but it looks like they all belong to Fleming E. and Louise E. Brown.

BROWN, HAROLD AMBROSE	son,	Oct21, 1943
BROWN, JOHN OTTO	daughter,	Jul15, 1926
BROWN, MILTON	daughter,	Mar30, 1922
BROWN, STANLEY BENTON	daughter,	May13, 1933
BROWN, WM. A.	son,	Sep12, 1911
BRUISE, CHARLES FOREST	daughter,	Apr17, 1926
BUCKLEY, J. F.	son,	Jul12, 1903
BUCKLEY, J. F.	son,	Aug03, 1905
BUNTAIN, BENJAMINE E.	son,	Nov13, 1934
BUNTAIN, BENJAMIN E.	daughter,	May24, 1936
BUNTAIN, WILLIAM CLINE	son,	Nov08, 1948
BURGARD, J. J.	son,	Nov05, 1906
BURGARD, J. J.	son,	Sep20, 1909
BURGESS, G. R.	daughter,	Feb04, 1910
BURGESS, GEORGE R.	son,	Aug15, 1911
BURGESS, G. R.	daughter,	Nov14, 1912
BURGESS, G. R.	daughter,	Jan22, 1916
BURGESS, G. R.	daughter,	Feb22, 1917
BURGESS, GEORGE RALPH	daughter,	Feb24, 1918
BURGESS, GEORGE R.	son,	Mar25, 1920
BURGESS, GEORGE RALPH	son,	Apr16, 1921
BURGESS, GEORGE RALPH	daughter,	Jan25, 1924
BURGESS, J. E.	son,	Jun12, 1908
BURKS, JOHN LESLIE	son,	May16, 1949
BURNETT, JAS.	son,	_____, 1946
BURNS, DOROTHY MAE	daughter,	Feb06, 1940
BURNS, THOMAS	son,	May16, 1934
BURNS, THOMAS	son,	Feb18, 1930
BURNSIDE, T. M.	daughter,	Mar30, 1913
BUSS, HARRY FREDERICK	son,	Aug17, 1950
BUTLER, JESSE R.	daughter,	Oct02, 1911
BUTZ, WALTER	son,	Apr14, 1923
CALVIN, GEORGE J.	son,	Apr04, 1939
CAMPBELL, LEN	daughter,	Apr19, 1905
CAMPBELL, LEN A.	son,	Jun14, 1921
CAMPBELL, R.	son,	Mar22, 1900
CAMPBELL, T. H.	son,	Aug27, 1908
CAMPBELL, THOS. H.	daughter,	Mar03, 1912
CAMPBELL, THOS. H.	daughter,	Nov02, 1918
CAMPBELL, T. H.	son,	Jul27, 1920
CANCES, JULES A.	son,	Jun21, 1916
CANNON, LOY EUGENE	daughter,	May26, 1949
CANTRELL, FLOYD HERSHAL	son,	Aug09, 1947
CARLSON, HERBERT WM.	daughter,	Aug07, 1941

CARPENTER, C. W.	daughter,	Jun18, 1915
CARPENTER, CHAS. W.	son,	Sep02, 1916
CARPENTER, CHARLES W.	daughter,	Jun27, 1920
CARR, A. C.	son,	Aug14, 1900
CARR, A. C.	son,	Jan31, 1902
CARR, A. C.	son,	Jul03, 1903
CARR, A. C.	daughter,	Jun09, 1906
CARR, A. C.	daughter,	Oct13, 1908
CARR, A. C.	son,	Feb15, 1910
CARR, A. C.	son,	May19, 1911

Note: Alexander Constantine Carr had 2 families; see also Births 1850-1900 and Addendum.

CARR, F. E.	son,	Sep27, 1915
CARR, FRED E.	daughter,	Oct03, 1916
CARTER, C. A.	daughter,	Oct03, 1902
CARTER, C. A.	daughter,	Sep20, 1907
CARTER, J. A.	son,	Jan02, 1903
CARTER, J. A.	son,	Jan25, 1905
CARTER, M. G.	son,	Nov07, 1901
CARTER, M. G.	son,	Sep14, 1906
CARTER, ROBERT MARSHALL	daughter,	Mar11, 1921
CARTER, S. A.	daughter,	Jul13, 1910
CATHER, _____	son,	Oct16, 1946
CATON, ANTONE	son,	Apr30, 1901
CATON, ANTONE	son,	Oct30, 1902
CATON, ANTONE	daughter,	Dec20, 1912
CATON, JOHN	son,	Apr19, 1901
CATON, JOHN	daughter,	Jan03, 1903
CATON, JOHN	son,	Dec28, 1911
CHAMBERLAIN, C. A.	daughter,	Dec14, 1910
CHAMBERLAIN, C. A.	son,	Oct25, 1914
CHAPMAN, EVERETT LEE	son,	Jul17, 1950
CHAPMAN, GEORGE F.	daughter,	Oct27, 1920
CHAPMAN, GEO.	son,	Nov27, 1904
CHAPMAN, G. P.	daughter,	Jan01, 1906
CHAPMAN, GEO. P.	son,	Oct08, 1910
CHAPMAN, GEORGE	daughter,	Oct20, 1911
CHAPMAN, GEO. P.	son,	Sep12, 1913
CHAPMAN, GEO. P.	daughter,	Jul01, 1915
CHAPMAN, GEORGE P.	daughter,	Nov23, 1917
CHAPMAN, GEORGE P.	daughter,	Nov16, 1925
CHAPMAN, GEORGE PHELPS	see Addendum	
CHAPMAN, RAY C.	daughter,	Dec12, 1919
CHESEBRO, JAMES	daughter,	Dec02, 1912
CHESBRO, JAMES	daughter,	Jan31, 1916
CHESTER, W. M.	son,	Apr17, 1918
CHILDERS, F. N.	son,	May20, 1922
CHILDERS, FRED N.	son,	May07, 1924
CHILDERS, FRED NEWTON	son,	Apr14, 1927
CHILDERS, FRED N.	son,	Sep14, 1929
CLARK, C. E.	son,	Dec30, 1906
CLARK, A. R.	son,	Feb27, 1904
CLARK, RALPH ISSAC FRANKLIN	daughter,	Jul25, 1941
CLARKE, ARTHUR	son,	Jun04, 1905
CLARKE, C.	son,	Jul06, 1908
CLAUSEN, HERALD L.	son,	May06, 1933
CLEAVES, C. D.	son,	Sep13, 1912
CLEAVES, C. D.	son,	Dec27, 1914
CLEAVES, C. D.	daughter,	Dec01, 1915
CLEAVES, FORREST	daughter,	Aug06, 1911
CLEAVES, HAROLD	tw.dau.,	Dec14, 1946
CLEAVES, JOSEPH	daughter,	Jan30, 1948
CLEAVES, JOSEPH	unknown	Dec21, 1948

CLEAVES, JOSEPH	daughter,	Jul27, 1950
CLEMENT, A. C.	son,	May22, 1900
CLEMENT, RANDALL ALBERT	daughter,	Nov13, 1950
CLEMENTS, CHAS.	son,	Nov09, 1901
COCHRAN, H.	daughter,	Jul25, 1903
COFFENBERRY, LLOYD GEORGE	son,	Mar16, 1948
COFFENBERRY, LLOYD GEORGE	daughter,	Jul19, 1949
COGBURN, EARL JAMES	daughter,	Nov13, 1950
COKER, WILLIAM A.	son,	Apr23, 1932
COLE, CHARLES H.	son,	Nov19, 1932
COLEMAN, OTIS FRANKLIN	daughter,	Oct12, 1950
COLLINS, M. W.	son,	Sep06, 1903
COLLINS, MAURICE WILLIAM	see Addendum	
COLLINS, W. A.	daughter,	Mar09, 1911
COLLINS, W. G.	daughter,	Apr21, 1908
COLLINS, W. G.	daughter,	Oct13, 1914
CONNELLY, R. C.	daughter,	Oct21, 1910
CONNOR, JOHN	son,	Feb22, 1904
CONNOR, J. B.	son,	Feb05, 1905
CONNER, J. B.	daughter,	Feb08, 1907
CONNER, J. B.	son,	Oct03, 1910
CONNOR, J. B.	son,	Aug20, 1911
CONNOR, J. B.	son,	Nov24, 1913
CONNER, J. B.	daughter,	Apr11, 1916
CONNER, JOHN B.	daughter,	Jun16, 1919
COOK, CLARENCE E.	daughter,	Nov08, 1935
COOKE, EDWARD FRANKLIN	son,	Apr08, 1933
COOLEY, FAYE, Mrs.	son,	Sep15, 1946
COPE, DANIAL ALBERT	daughter,	Apr27, 1950
COPELAND, JASON PAUL	see Addendum	
COPLEY, R. W.	son,	Oct31, 1919
CORBETT, MELVIN BOYD	daughter,	Jun19, 1944
CORDOZA, F.	tw.son,	Mar03, 1908
CORDOZA, FRANK	daughter,	May24, 1901
COSTA, ANTONE	son,	Jul02, 1913
COSTA, JESSE	son,	Apr07, 1902
COSTA, JESSE	son,	Jul02, 1903
COSTA, JESSE	son,	Jul02, 1904
COSTA, JESSE de	daughter,	May17, 1914
COSTA, JESSE	daughter,	May18, 1916
COSTA, JESSE	son,	Jun06, 1919
COUMBS, JOHN	son,	Jun21, 1903
COUMBS, J. H.	son,	Jan27, 1908
COUMBS, J. H.	son,	Nov11, 1909
COUMBS, J. H.	daughter,	Jan10, 1912
COUMBS, J. H.	son,	Sep02, 1915
COUMBS, THOS.	daughter,	Jul24, 1905
COUMBS, W. S.	son,	Dec22, 1914
COUMBS, WALTER	son,	Mar05, 1916
COUMBS, WALTER S.	son,	Mar12, 1919
COUMBS, WALTER SCOTT	daughter,	Nov13, 1935
COUMBS, WALTER S.	son,	Sep12, 1940
COX, JESSE MADISON	daughter,	Mar11, 1947
COX, SOL	son,	Nov28, 1903
CRABTREE, FRED	son,	Jul03, 1910
CRAFT, GEORGE	daughter,	Mar07, 1920
CRAFT, GEORGE JEWEL	son,	Nov20, 1921
CRAFT, GEORGE JEWEL	son,	Feb23, 1923
CRAFT, GEORGE JEWEL	daughter,	Aug04, 1924
CRAMER, CLIFF JAMES	son,	Oct11, 1950
CRAMPTON, GENE ARTHUR	son,	Aug11, 1949
CREAPEAU, HOWARD JAMES	daughter,	Dec15, 1933
CREPEAU, HOWARD JAMES	daughter,	Sep12, 1935

Name		Date
CRESPO, SACHARI	son,	Apr 19, 1922
CREWS, CHARLES	son,	Sep 18, 1946
CREWS, ELMER C.	son,	Jul 24, 1918
CREWS, ELMER C.	daughter,	May 15, 1920
CREWS, FLOYD HARVEY	daughter,	Sep __, 1927
CREWS, HOWARD M.	daughter,	Sep 06, 1933
CREWS, MELVIN ARNOLD	son,	Dec 13, 1935
CREWS, MELVIN	daughter,	Dec 25, 1939
CREWS, ROBT.	son,	Apr 10, 1904
CREWS, VERNON R.	daughter,	Dec 07, 1933
CREWS, VERNON ROBERT	daughter,	Jan 16, 1945
CREWS, WILBERT	daughter,	Sep 04, 1914
CROSS, GROVER P.	daughter,	Jan 29, 1939
CROUSE, DARRELL J.	daughter,	Jun 28, 1940
CROUSE, LAKE M.	daughter,	Oct 12, 1936
CROUSE, MARION CORNELL	son,	May 08, 1935
CRUSON, EDMOND V.	son,	Dec 19, 1937
CRUSON, ORVILLE RAY	daughter,	Nov 18, 1949
CUFF, LESTER L.	son,	Feb 17, 1932
CUFF, R. W.	son,	Feb 12, 1910
CUFF, RICHARD WILLIAM	see Addendum	
D'ANTONIA, RAFFAEL	son,	Aug 15, 1946
DAILEY, J. J.	daughter,	Sep 30, 1905
DAILEY, J. J.	son,	Jun 02, 1907
DAILEY, J. J.	son,	Jan 01, 1915
DAILY, JOHN J.	son,	Aug 20, 1919
DAILEY, JOHN JACOB	daughter,	Feb 06, 1921
DAILEY, ROLAND W.	son,	Jan 05, 1939
DALLAIRE, THOS.	daughter,	Nov 26, 1946
DAMSELL, JOSEPH	son,	Jan 14, 1900
DAVENPORT, DEAN	daughter,	Dec 25, 1937
DAVENPORT, DEAN	daughter,	Dec 06, 1946
DAVENPORT, WALTER FRANKLIN	son,	Jan 20, 1950
DAVIDSON, JOHN B.	son,	Mar 31, 1929
DAVIS, G. T.	son,	Dec 07, 1906
DAVIS, G. T.	daughter,	Mar 03, 1908
DAVIS, VIRGIL LEE	daughter,	Nov 24, 1948
DAWSON, S. R.	son,	Nov 27, 1900
DAWSON, T. R.	daughter,	Mar 15, 1906
DAWSON, T. R.	daughter,	Mar 15, 1908
DAWSON, THOMAS	daughter,	Apr 11, 1911
DAY, JAMES LEVI	see Addendum	
DAY, W. A.	son,	Feb 12, 1907
DAY, W. A.	daughter,	Feb 13, 1908
DAY, W. A.	daughter,	Sep 22, 1910
DAY, W. A.	son,	Sep 19, 1914
DAY, W. A.	son,	Dec 02, 1915
DAY, W. A.	son,	May 25, 1918
DAY, W. A.	son,	Sep 07, 1919
DAY, WALTER ANDREWS	daughter,	Apr 02, 1921
DAY, W. A.	son,	Dec 14, 1922
DAY, WALTER A.	daughter,	Mar 06, 1924
DAY, WALTER ANDREWS	daughter,	Jun 17, 1930
DAY, WALTER A.	son,	Jun 10, 1933
DAY, WALTER ANDREW	see Addendum	
DAY, U. G.	son,	Jun 15, 1910
DAY, ULYSSES GRANT	son,	Aug 21, 1912
DE HAVEN, ROY O.	son,	Sep 08, 1935
DEAN, H. G.	daughter,	Feb 19, 1901
DEAN, SAMUEL T.	daughter,	Sep 10, 1912
DEAN, SAMUEL THEODORE	see Addendum	
DENISON, LEWIS	see Addendum	
DENNISON, LEWIS N.	daughter,	Feb 27, 1920

DIAMOND, RAY	daughter,	Nov17, 1930
DICK, MARVIN	son,	Mar15, 1942
DICKERSON, L. A.	daughter,	Jul06, 1900
DICKEY, JAMES CALVIN	see Addendum	
DICKEY, JAMES CRUTHIS	daughter,	Jun24, 1948
DICKEY, JOHN E.	daughter,	Apr26, 1910
DIMMICK, THOMAS WILLIAM	son,	Oct09, 1935
DIX, ALBERT FRANKLIN	daughter,	Jul12, 1947
DIX, HENRY ELDON	see Addendum	
DIXON, LESTER OBIE	daughter,	Oct02, 1935
DOBBYN, J. P.	son,	Jan30, 1902
DOCKERY, J. E.	daughter,	Jun23, 1902
DOCKERY, M. W.	son,	Sep15, 1900
DOCKERY, M. W.	daughter,	Aug09, 1904
DOCKERY, MICHAEL WILLIAM	see Addendum	
DOMENICI, GEORGE	daughter,	Jan25, 1918
DOMENICI, GEO.	daughter,	Aug11, 1919
DOMENICI, GEO.	daughter,	Aug18, 1922
DONOHO, BENJAMIN K.	daughter,	Dec22, 1934
DOSS, CARLES EDWARD	daughter,	Dec08, 1948
DOSS, CARLIS E.	daughter,	Jul12, 1950
DOTTERS, SELBY ANSEL, Jr.	daughter,	May16, 1950
DOWDAKIN, RICHARD, Sgt. & Mrs	daughter,	Nov11, 1946
DOWNING, ROBERT M.	son,	Aug13, 1920
DUNBAR, GLEN	son,	Aug31, 1938
DUNCAN, ERNEST E.	son,	Aug07, 1924
DUNCAN, ERNEST EDMOND	son,	Aug24, 1926
DUNCAN, ERNEST EDMOND	daughter,	Jul02, 1930
DUNCAN, ERNEST E.	son,	Jan25, 1932
DUNCAN, L. P. Jr.	son,	May24, 1916
DUNCAN, L. P.	daughter,	Oct30, 1918
DUNCAN, L. P.	daughter,	Jan26, 1922
DUNCAN, LEONIDAS P.	daughter,	Jan09, 1925
DUNCAN, LEONIDAS P.	son,	Sep02, 1929
DUNCAN, R. F.	son,	Jul11, 1922
DUNCAN, ROBERT F.	daughter,	Oct11, 1929
DUNCAN, W. C.	son,	May23, 1910
DUNCAN, WM. C.	son,	Nov20, 1911
DUNCAN, WM.	daughter,	Dec13, 1919
DUNGAN, THOMAS FRANK	see Addendum	
DUNKLEY, L. P.	son,	Jul06, 1903
DUNN, R. H.	son,	Feb26, 1902
DUNTON, EDWARD	daughter,	Oct01, 1947
DURDLE, RICHARD A.	son,	Feb18, 1942
DURYEE, GRANT	daughter,	Jun22, 1935
DYSERT, CLIFFORD NEWELL	son,	Dec10, 1935
DYSERT, N. S.	son,	Jan21, 1911
DYSERT, N. S.	son,	Oct18, 1916
EBERSPECHER, GEO. CHRISTOPHER	daughter,	Oct07, 1938
EBERSPECHER, GEO. C.	daughter,	Jul31, 1940
EDGERTON, GILBERT HAMLIN	son,	May15, 1947
EDWARDS, C. H.	daughter,	Dec22, 1916
EDWARDS, C. H.	son,	Nov18, 1918
EFAU, JAMES	daughter,	Dec10, 1916
EFAW, JAMES H.	son,	Aug13, 1932
ELLERY, E. K.	son,	Oct07, 1920
ELLERY, ELIAS K.	son,	Mar14, 1923
ELLIS, E.	son,	Dec07, 1900
ELLIS, ELI	daughter,	Mar15, 1902
ELLIS, ELI	son,	May19, 1906
ELLIS, ELI	son,	Feb10, 1908
ELLIS, ELI	daughter,	Sep30, 1909
ELLIS, RAY JESSE	son,	Aug14, 1947

ELLIS RAY JESSE	daughter,	Jan08, 1950
ELLISTON, W.	son,	Apr20, 1908
ELLISTON, WM. P.	daughter,	Apr17, 1912
ELMGREN, EDW.	daughter,	Sep16, 1913
ELMGREN, EDWARD	son,	Feb11, 1915
ENDICOTT, S. P.	daughter,	Aug24, 1913
ENOS, THOS.	daughter,	Oct26, 1902
ENOS, T. M.	son,	Aug23, 1904
ENOS, THOMAS M.	son,	Aug15, 1933
ESLICK, IRA FRANCIS	son,	Jan18, 1931
ESLICK, IRA F.	son,	Apr30, 1940
EUER, GEORGE	son,	Nov24, 1911
EUGENE, JOSEPH K.	daughter,	Jan19, 1929
EUGENE, JOSEPH	daughter,	Apr25, 1930
EUGENE, JOSEPH	daughter,	Jul25, 1931
EVANS, BERT	son,	May13, 1913
EVANS, HECTOR ROMERO	daughter,	Jan01, 1941
EVEREST, CHARLES L.	daughter,	Dec17, 1950
EVEREST, HARRY	son,	Jan25, 1905
EVEREST, HARRY	son,	Mar22, 1906
EVEREST, JAMES P.	son,	Jul20, 1934
EVEREST, JAMES P.	son,	Jan06, 1939
EVEREST, JAMES	son,	Nov09, 1940
EVEREST, WILBUR ARISTIDES	daughter,	Jul24, 1937
EVEREST, WILBUR A.	see Addendum	
EVERETT, RALPH W.	daughter,	Sep05, 1912
EVERETT, R. W.	son,	Aug01, 1914
FARMER, CYRIL D.	daughter,	Oct17, 1921
FARMER, CYRIL	daughter,	Aug15, 1924
FARMER, CHAPPLE	daughter,	Nov24, 1949
FARMER, GEO.	daughter,	Mar16, 1903
FARMER, HARVEY ALLEN	son,	Aug11, 1935
FARMER, WALTER	daughter,	May29, 1938
FASBENDER, DONALD CURTIS	daughter,	Aug24, 1949
FEHR, JACOB P.	son,	Sep22, 1919
FELT, D.	son,	Jan09, 1917
FENNER, WILLIAM D.	son,	Jun17, 1924
FERGUSON, DALE J.	daughter,	Feb22, 1939
FERGUSON, ROY PAUL	son,	Sep03, 1947
FIELDS, D. B.	daughter,	Jul25, 1909
FIELDS, D. B., DR.	son,	Jul23, 1911
FIELDS, D. B.	son,	Oct30, 1913
FIELDS, D. B.	daughter,	Oct20, 1915
FIELDS, D. B.	daughter,	Aug12, 1923
FIFE, ANDREW RALPH	daughter,	Jan30, 1934
FINNEGAN, W. G.	son,	Jun07, 1915
FIRMIGNAC, M.	son,	Apr28, 1905
FISHER, GENE	daughter,	Nov15, 1946
FISHER, JUAREZ CUIDAD	daughter,	Jun29, 1950
FISHER, WM. JENNINGS BRYAN	daughter,	Jun03, 1948
FLAGG, JAMES JEDSON	daughter,	May31, 1934
FLETCHER, A.	daughter,	Jan26, 1901
FLOWERS, WM.	son,	Nov15, 1900
FLOWERS, WM.	son,	Sep06, 1902
FOLKEL, CH.	son,	Nov07, 1904
FONSECA, JOSEPH L.	daughter,	Apr26, 1942
FONTES, JOSEPH	son,	Apr10, 1916
FONTES, JOS. C.	daughter,	Mar20, 1922
FONTES, JOS. C.	daughter,	Jul21, 1934
FORD, HARRY EDWARD	daughter,	Nov16, 1933
FOX, ALFONSO	son,	Jun25, 1935
FOX, ALFONZO	son,	Oct19, 1943
FOX, IRA EDSON	daughter,	May20, 1914
FRATES, ANTONE		

FRENCH, SYLVESTER BYRON	son,	May14, 1948
FRIEND, T. A.	daughter,	Mar10, 1906
FRIEND, T. A.	son,	Oct02, 1908
FRIEND, THOS. A.	tw.dau.,	Sep18, 1911
FROLOFF, ALBERT S.	son,	Dec05, 1939
FROLOFF, ALBERT STEPHEN	son,	Aug08, 1941
FROMAN, CLAIRE, Mrs.	daughter,	_____, 1946
FRYE, DELMER E.	daughter,	Jan07, 1939
FULTON, RICHARD BAILEY	son,	Jul03, 1949
GALLAGHER, JACK EDWARD	daughter,	Jan15, 1950
GARRETT, B. L.	son,	Sep05, 1928
GARRETT, BALLARD L.	son,	Feb18, 1939
GARRETT, WILLIAM XENOPHON, Jr.	son,	Jan31, 1935
GASSOWAY, WILLIAM A.	daughter,	Apr27, 1923
GATES, A. R.	son,	Sep05, 1913
GATES, CALVIN	daughter,	Jan10, 1915
GATES, FRED	son,	Jul31, 1903
GATES, FRED	daughter,	Jul28, 1907
GATES, RAYMOND	son,	Jan14, 1915
GATES, VAUGHAN M.	son,	Jun28, 1936
GATES, VAUGHAN MAXWELL	daughter,	Sep10, 1938
GAY, GLENN MONROE	daughter,	May26, 1950
GIBBS, J. B.	daughter,	Apr08, 1900
GIBBS, J. B.	daughter,	Dec26, 1905
GIBBS, J. B.	son,	Oct30, 1908
GIBBS, HOWARD E.	son,	Feb23, 1939
GILMAN, H. M.	son,	Mar30, 1909
GILMAN, H. M.	daughter,	Jan24, 1912
GILMAN, H. M.	son,	Aug06, 1918
GILZEAN, ALEX	daughter,	Mar02, 1900
GILZEAN, A.	daughter,	Oct16, 1901
GILZEAN, A.	daughter,	Jul16, 1904
GILZEAN, BERT	daughter,	Jul08, 1904
GILZEAN, BURT	son,	Dec12, 1908
GILZEAN, CHAS.	son,	Jan14, 1900
GILZEAN, C. E.	son,	Jun18, 1904
GILZEAN, J. A.	daughter,	May20, 1903
GILZEAN, J. A.	daughter,	Jun26, 1917
GILZEAN, J. H.	son,	Jan09, 1902
GILZEAN, JAMES HENRY	see Addendum	
GIVAN, MERWIN JAMES	daughter,	Jun03, 1934
GIVEN, H. R.	son,	Oct12, 1901
GLASS, WALTER WM.	daughter,	Aug02, 1918
GLASS, WALTER ERNEST	daughter,	Feb28, 1949
GODSHALL, D. A.	son,	Oct01, 1920
GOODRICH, ALTON FRANCIS	daughter,	Jun20, 1948
GOODRICH, GUY	daughter,	Sep03, 1917
GOODRICH, GUY E.	son,	May10, 1919
GOODRICH, GUY E.	son,	Feb10, 1924
GOODYEAR, HAL EUGENE	son,	Nov19, 1950
GOODYEAR, MERRITT	son,	Nov25, 1912
GOULD, HAROLD G.	son,	Mar23, 1940
GOULD, HAROLD GERHING	son,	Jun22, 1941
GOVER, JOSEPH	daughter,	Mar16, 1913
GRAHAM, JAMES	daughter,	Jan11, 1901
GRAHAM, JOSEPH	daughter,	Sep25, 1933
GRAHAM, WESLEY C.	son,	May04, 1925
GRAHAM, WESLEY CHARLES	daughter,	Mar09, 1927
GRANT, MANUEL	see Addendum	
GRAVES, H. J.	son,	May01, 1917
GRAY, ALBERT FRAY	son,	Oct18, 1912
GRAY, D. B.	son,	Mar31, 1905
GRAY, DICK	son,	Jun13, 1944

GRAY, J. T.	daughter,	Oct22, 1904
GRAY, J. T.	son,	Feb03, 1911
GRAY, T. J.	daughter,	Jan11, 1908

Note: 1910 census says "John T. Gray" & wife Frances.

GRAY, HOWARD L.	daughter,	Dec23, 1938
GREEN, GEORGE	son,	Feb14, 1919
GREENWELL, ERNEST ALBERT	see Addendum	
GREENWELL, E. G.	daughter,	Aug31, 1901
GREENWELL, REUBEN A.	daughter,	May16, 1934
GREENWOOD, LUCILLE, Mrs.	son,	_____, 1946
GREGORY, JOSEPH	see Addendum	
GREIG, GEORGE	daughter,	Dec13, 1917
GREIG, GEORGE	see Addendum	
GRENSKY, FRANK J.	daughter,	Aug06, 1933
GRIBBLE, GERALD J.	son,	Jul31, 1936
GRIBBLE, J. H.	daughter,	Oct11, 1901
GRIBBLE, LEONARD R.	daughter,	Aug22, 1932
GRIBBLE, LEONARD R.	daughter,	Nov02, 1933
GRIBBLE, LEONARD R.	daughter,	Jun10, 1935
GRIBBLE, R.	son,	May26, 1907
GRIBBLE, RICHARD	son,	Oct10, 1909
GRIBBLE, WILLIAM	see Addendum	
GRIFFITH, J. J.	son,	Aug08, 1909
GRIFFITH, J. M.	daughter,	Jul24, 1903
GRIFFITH, J. M.	son,	Jun07, 1905
GRIFFITH, J. M.	daughter,	Sep27, 1906
GRIGSBY, CALVIN	daughter,	Jan07, 1915
GRIGSBY, CALVIN	son,	Jun08, 1916
GRIGSBY, CALVIN	son,	Aug15, 1918
GRIGSBY, CALVIN	see Addendum	
GRIGSBY, EARL	son,	Feb09, 1936
GRIGSBY, FRANCIS EARL	son,	Mar20, 1950
GRIGSBY, P.	son,	Oct29, 1902
GRIGSBY, PLEASANT	son,	May23, 1912
GRIGSBY, R. L.	son,	Nov14, 1900
GRIGSBY, R. L.	daughter,	Mar26, 1902
GRIGSBY, R. L.	son,	Mar23, 1906
GRIGSBY, R. L.	daughter,	Jun20, 1908
GRILLS, HARVEY LEE	son,	Sep25, 1950
GUILFORD, BERNARD B.	son,	Sep27, 1932
GURR, FRED J.	daughter,	Jan08, 1939
HAAS, FREDERICK GOTTLEIB	see Addendum	
HACKNEY, CLAUDE	son,	Dec01, 1917
HAFLEY, F. H.	daughter,	Mar02, 1911
HAILSTONE, Z.	daughter,	Jul31, 1915
HAILSTONE, Z.	daughter,	Nov07, 1916
HAILSTONE, Z.	daughter,	May25, 1918
HAILSTONE, ZACHARIAH	tw.son,	Jan25, 1920
HAILSTONE, ZACHARIAH	son,	Oct06, 1921
HAILSTONE, ZACHARIAH	daughter,	Aug23, 1923
HAILSTONE, ZACHARIAH	son,	May23, 1926
HAILSTONE, Z.	daughter,	Mar15, 1928
HALE, HAROLD PRINCE	daughter,	Jul23, 1938
HALL, D. J.	son,	May01, 1902
HALL, D. J.	daughter,	Jan01, 1905
HALL, GEO. A.	daughter,	May04, 1910
HALLEY, FRED	daughter,	May25, 1900
HALLEY, F. F. Jr.	daughter,	Mar10, 1901
HALLEY, FRED	son,	Aug25, 1903
HALLEY, FRED	daughter,	Apr01, 1910
HALLEY, F. F.	daughter,	Jul03, 1911
HAMILTON, E. R.	son,	Aug04, 1908
HAMMERSLEY, OREN	daughter,	Mar13, 1942

HAMMERSLEY, OREN KENNETH	son,	Dec10, 1943
HAMMERSLEY, O. R.	daughter,	Mar10, 1934
HAMMERSLEY, MARVIN H.	daughter,	Aug22, 1934
HAMMOND, C. E.	daughter,	Nov04, 1902
HAMMOND, C. E.	son,	Jun29, 1909
HAMMOND, CICERO BAXTER	son,	Nov07, 1947
HAMMOND, F. C.	daughter,	Jan07, 1902
HAMPTON, B. H.	daughter,	Aug29, 1904
HAMPTON, H.	daughter,	Jul28, 1900
HAMPTON, H.	son,	Jan09, 1904
HAMPTON, H.	son,	Feb12, 1907
HAMPTON, H.	son,	Nov27, 1908
HAMPTON, H. G.	daughter,	Jul20, 1901
HAMPTON, H. L.	son,	Apr10, 1900
HAMPTON, W.	daughter,	Sep05, 1900
HAMPTON, WM.	son,	Oct12, 1905
HANDLEY, JOHN GEORGE	son,	Mar06, 1949
HANLON, TOM L.	son,	Sep11, 1937
HANLON, TOM	daughter,	Jan21, 1940
HANLON, TOM	daughter,	Mar22, 1942
HANLON, TOM LESTER	daughter,	Oct26, 1944
HANLON, THOMAS LESTER	son,	Jul05, 1946
HANNA, CHAS.	daughter,	Mar03, 1909
HANNA, CHARLES	son,	Oct04, 1911
HANNON, W. J.	daughter,	Oct18, 1901
HANOVER, F. A.	daughter,	May03, 1915
HANOVER, F.	son,	Jul12, 1902
HANOVER, F. S.	son,	Oct17, 1903
HANOVER, F. S.	son,	Sep19, 1907
HANOVER, FRANK SMITH	see Addendum	
HANOVER, H. HILTON	daughter,	Dec03, 1934
HANOVER, HARVEY H.	son,	Jan26, 1936
HANOVER, ROBERT CLAY	son,	Jan08, 1944
HANOVER, ROBERT CLAY	see Addendum	
HANOVER, S. O.	tw.dau.,	Dec01, 1928
HARBINE, HARDY	son,	Jan23, 1901
HARBINE, HARDY RALSTON	see Addendum	
HARMON, GEORGE	son,	May09, 1905
HARRINGTON, JOSEPH J.	daughter,	Apr12, 1935
HARRISON, FLOYD EVERITT	son,	Jan24, 1947
HARRISON, LEROY	son,	Aug22, 1938
HARRISIB, LINDIS HUSETON	son,	Jul28, 1949
HARVEY, LELAND I.	son,	May26, 1933
HARVEY, LELAND I.	son,	Feb21, 1936
HATFIELD, LOWAIN HENRY	daughter,	Mar04, 1947
HAVER, BURTON WESLEY	son,	Feb18, 1950
HAWK, HILTON	son,	Jun05, 1939
HAWKEY, OTHO E.	daughter,	Sep10, 1914
HAWKINS, BAILEY JAMES	daughter,	Mar31, 1948
HAWKINS, ELMER	son,	Sep21, 1947
HAWKSLEY, H. H.	son,	Dec14, 1901
HAYDEN, F. M.	daughter,	Jan02, 1909
HAYDEN, F. M.	son,	Oct06, 1910
HAYDON, FRANK M.	daughter,	Jul16, 1918
HAYDON, F. M.	daughter,	Jul19, 1919
HAYDEN, FRANK MARION	son,	Mar07, 1927
HAYNES, GENE ALBERT	daughter,	Jul25, 1949
HAYS, O. O.	son,	Nov28, 1914
HAYWARD, JOHN DAVIS	daughter,	Nov30, 1927
HAYWARD, JOHN D.	daughter,	Dec11, 1929
HAYWARD, JOHN D.	daughter,	Jun30, 1932
HAYWARD, JOHN DAVIS	son,	Jan13, 1941
HEATH, CHARLES J.	daughter,	Mar05, 1919

HEATH, CHARLES JESSE	daughter,	Jul14, 1926
HEBBERT, CLARENCE WALTER	son,	Apr12, 1941
HEFFINGTON, WALTER	daughter,	Feb21, 1936
HEINSEN, NORMAN	daughter,	Sep21, 1946
HEINSOHN, NORMAN	daughter,	Oct20, 1946
HENDERSON, ALBERT E.	daughter,	Apr10, 1932
HENDERSON, ALBERT E.	daughter,	Apr02, 1936
HENDERSON, H.	daughter,	Jun17, 1901
HENDERSON, H.	daughter,	Mar02, 1906
HENDRICKS, S. C.	son,	Aug06, 1916
HENSEL, J. L.	son,	Jan29, 1900
HENSEL, J. L.	son,	Jan16, 1902
HERRICK, L. A.	daughter,	Jan22, 1916
HERRICK, VERNON	son,	Aug11, 1940
HERSHMAN, NORVIN E.	daughter,	May13, 1939
HESS, IRA DAVID	son,	Mar19, 1935
HEURTEVANT, M.	daughter,	Jul23, 1909
HEURTEVANT, M. F. M.	son,	Sep29, 1912
HICKS, ROBERT	daughter,	Nov15, 1900
HICKS, ROBT.	daughter,	Oct16, 1903
HIETT, HILTON LEE	son,	Aug08, 1935
HIETT, MARTEN G.	son,	Oct24, 1932
HILLIS, J. B.	son,	Apr13, 1901
HIPPLER, ALBERT	daughter,	Oct12, 1900
HOLTORF, OTTO	daughter,	Apr14, 1920
HOPKINS, CHARLES LESTER	daughter,	Apr19, 1948
HORTON, RICHARD EDWARD	see Addendum	
HOUCK, ERNEST	daughter,	May07, 1933
HOWARD, RAYMOND	son,	Jan18, 1932
HOWARD, RAYMOND DALTON	son,	Oct04, 1934
HOWARD, RAYMOND DALTON	son,	May02, 1941
HUESTIS, W. A.	son,	Dec16, 1901
HUESTIS, WILBUR	son,	Jan08, 1905
HUESTIS, W. A.	son,	Feb27, 1907
HUFFMAN, CLARENCE L.	son,	Apr15, 1932
HUGHES, PERRY RAYMOND	daughter,	Nov23, 1934
HUGHES, VIRGIL R.	son,	Feb27, 1933
HUGHES, VIRGIL RAYMOND	son,	Mar05, 1935
HUGHES, VIRGIL RAYMOND	son,	Oct29, 1947
HUGHES, WILLIAM EDWARD	see Addendum	
HUMPHREYS, JAMES THOMAS	daughter,	Feb28, 1949
HUNT, ELBERT FRANCIS	son,	Feb07, 1944
HUNT, HAROLD FRANKLIN	son,	Aug24, 1950
HUNT, RAYMOND STRONG	son,	Jun07, 1935
HUSSEY, IVO H.	daughter,	Mar19, 1921
HUSTON, JOHN LEROY	daughter,	Feb07, 1934
HUSTON, JOHN L.	daughter,	Jun26, 1935
HUTCHENS, H. C.	son,	Mar24, 1911
HUTCHENS, JOS.	daughter,	Apr08, 1907
HUTCHINS, HENRY	daughter,	May07, 1905
ILIFF, BENJAMIN B.	daughter,	May06, 1920
IRVING, G.	tw.son, dau.,	Jan28, 1901
IRVING, GEORGE	daughter,	Jul28, 1904
IRVING, GEORGE	son,	Oct03, 1905
IRVING, G. J.	daughter,	May20, 1908

Note: 1910 census lists Katherine Irving as a widow with 9 children.

IVAR, GUNNARD A.	son,	Mar31, 1927
IVERSON, OLE	see Addendum	
IVEY, JUNIOR DEE	daughter,	May22, 1949
JACK, ALTON A.	daughter,	Aug11, 1932
JACKMAN, EARL G.	son,	Jul13, 1923
JACKMAN, H. E.	son,	Apr07, 1922
JACKSON, J. J.	daughter,	Aug31, 1911

JACKSON, J. J.	daughter,	May26, 1915
JACKSON, J. J.	daughter,	Aug06, 1917
JACKSON, J. J.	son,	Aug16, 1919
JACKSON, EDWARD ANDREW	son,	Jul12, 1931
JACKSON, EDWARD ANDREW	daughter,	Jan02, 1937
JACKSON, EDWARD	son,	Jan25, 1942
JACKSON, EDWIN MERLE	son,	Sep26, 1933
JACKSON, EDWIN MERLE	son,	Apr03, 1935
JACKSON, FRANCIS OLIVER	daughter,	Feb03, 1945
JACKSON, FRED B.	daughter,	Dec12, 1941
JACKSON, FRED BECKER	daughter,	Dec20, 1949
JACKSON, FREDERIC HENRY	daughter,	Jan28, 1935
JACKSON, HARVEY J.	son,	Feb26, 1936
JACKSON, HARVEY	son,	Nov19, 1937
JACKSON, HARVEY J.	daughter,	Nov19, 1939
JACKSON, LEMUEL T.	daughter,	Nov25, 1936
JACKSON, MALCOLM KARNEY	son,	Jul12, 1950
JACKSON, SAMUEL, Jr.	daughter,	May04, 1938
JACKSON, SAMUEL B.	daughter,	Mar15, 1935
JACKSON, WILBERT LESLIE	see Addendum	
JACKSON, WILBUR O.	daughter,	Mar14, 1912
JACKSON, WILLIAM CHESTER	daughter,	Dec06, 1945
JAMESON, J.	son,	Sep06, 1902
JAMIESON, GEORGE E.	son,	Oct17, 1933
JEANS, A. H.	daughter,	Jun20, 1909
JEANS, ARTHUR HOWARD	see Addendum	
JEANS, H. C.	son,	Jun22, 1906
JEANS, H. C.	daughter,	Apr22, 1908
JEANS, H. C.	son,	Jan30, 1910
JENSEN, OTTO	son,	Mar04, 1903
JENSEN, OTTO C.	son,	Sep05, 1905
JENSEN, EVERETT JOHANNES	son,	Mar15, 1945
JOHNSON, F. A.	daughter,	Feb24, 1903
JOHNSON, FRANCIS EDWIN	son,	Aug06, 1948
JOHNSON, FRED	son,	Mar04, 1904
JOHNSON, FRED	daughter,	Nov04, 1907
JOHNSON, FREDERICK ALONZA	see Addendum	
JOHNSON, L. G.	son,	Feb16, 1918
JOHNSTON, RICHARD	see Addendum	
JOINER, WILLIAM WESLEY	son,	Mar01, 1948
JONES, H. S.	son,	Oct19, 1910
JONES, HARRY SHERMAN	son,	Jul08, 1912
JONES, H. S.	daughter,	Feb25, 1914
JONES, JACOB	son,	Feb15, 1949
JORDAN, CARL	daughter,	Aug31, 1908
JORDAN, M. C.	son,	Oct24, 1901
JORDAN, M. C.	son,	Aug20, 1902
JORDAN, M. C.	daughter,	Dec26, 1903
JORDAN, M. C.	daughter,	Sep21, 1911
JORDAN, IRVING	son,	Jun13, 1922
JORDAN, IRVING DAVIDSON	daughter,	Apr15, 1934
JORDON, IRVING DAVIDSON	son,	Jul23, 1937
JOTTER, E. V.	son,	Sep03, 1911
JOTTER, E. V.	daughter,	Mar11, 1914
JOTTER, E. V.	son,	Jan23, 1917
JUMPER, GEORGE M.	daughter,	May06, 1911
JUNKANS, KARL	daughter,	Aug27, 1909
JUNKANS, W.	tw.son,	May02, 1900
KAFER, P. S.	son,	May24, 1914
KAMISKY, FESTUS KARL	son,	Sep02, 1950
KAPUSTA, JOSEPH	daughter,	Jun13, 1916
KAY, CLARENCE	son,	Dec28, 1905
KAY, C. B.	daughter,	Aug04, 1910

KEENEY, WM. F. Rev.	daughter,	Dec10, 1946
KELLEY, ARTHUR JOHN	daughter,	May11, 1937
KELLY, ARTHUR JOHN	son,	May15, 1941
KELLY, FLOYD	daughter,	Sep03, 1946
KENT, A. W.	son,	Jan30, 1928
KIBLER, HERBERT LEE	daughter,	Jun06, 1939
KIBLER, LEWIS L.	son,	Mar10, 1939
KIMBALL, VIRGIL	daughter,	Mar26, 1938
KIMBALL, VIRGIL HENRY	daughter,	Aug24, 1945
KIMBALL, VIRGIL	daughter,	Aug11, 1946
KIMBALL, VIRGIL HENRY	daughter,	Sep08, 1947
KINDRED, G. W.	son,	Feb29, 1904
KINDRED, G. W.	tw.son,	Jun__, 1908
KIRACK, ELAIRD THOMAS	tw.dau., son,	Oct06, 1946
KIRKPATRICK, V.	daughter,	Jun30, 1917
KIRST, EUGENE AUGUST	son,	Oct15, 1950
KISE, E. S.	son,	Apr25, 1900
KISE, ELISHA SAMUAL	see Addendum	
KISE, JOSEPH BLOOMFIELD	see Addendum	
KLADT, ELMER EDWARD	daughter,	May05, 1948
KNIGHT, FRED GEORGE	daughter,	Nov24, 1950
KNISS, E. E.	daughter,	Sep18, 1909
KNISS, ERNEST E.	son,	Aug17, 1912
KNISS, ERNEST ELWOOD	daughter,	Feb12, 1918
KNISS, ERNEST ELWOOD	daughter,	Nov21, 1921
KNOWLTON, JESS	son,	Oct22, 1949
KOLL, J.	son,	Jun17, 1901
KOLL, JOHN	daughter,	Feb11, 1903
KOLL, JOHN	daughter,	Feb19, 1904
KOLL, JOHN	see Addendum	
KOON, GORGES LESTER	see Addendum	
KOSAK, THEODORE	daughter,	Apr11, 1930
KOSAK, FAYE MALCOLM	daughter,	Jun20, 1949
KOSAK, FAYE MALCOLM	son,	Sep16, 1950
KYES, PERRY POWERS	daughter,	Jan05, 1950
LaBAREE, W. H.	daughter,	Apr18, 1901
LACEY, LEONARD CHARLES	daughter,	Aug14, 1950
LAFFRANCHINI, CLARENCE HENRY	daughter,	Feb22, 1931
LAIRD, ROBERT	son,	Jul16, 1901
LAKE, ALBERT CHARLES	son,	Aug10, 1941
LAKEY, RICHARD JAMES	daughter,	Sep14, 1947
LAMPLEY, CHAS.	daughter,	Jul23, 1907
LANDER, CHARLES CLIFFORD	daughter,	Dec24, 1950
LANDRETH, DETMER F.	son,	Apr01, 1942
LANE, NORMAN	daughter,	Jan23, 1936
LANGBERG, ALFRED	son,	Jun18, 1946
LANGWORTHY, J. R.	son,	Sep29, 1946
LARGE, LAURENCE L.	daughter,	Aug08, 1939
LARGE, LAWRENCE L.	daughter,	Oct27, 1940
LATTIN, G. W.	son,	Oct10, 1915
LAUGHLIN, EARL WARREN	daughter,	Nov22, 1948
LAUGHLIN, FRANCIS MARION	daughter,	Jan12, 1944
LAUGHLIN, JAY LAWRENCE	daughter,	Jan12, 1948
LEACH, EARLE	daughter,	Jun29, 1916
LEACH, EARLE N.	daughter,	Sep16, 1917
LEACH, EARL	son,	Mar10, 1920
LEAS, BERNIE I.	daughter,	Feb07, 1935
LEAS, G. W.	daughter,	May12, 1906
LEAS, G. W.	daughter,	May26, 1907
LEAS, G. W.	son,	Jul20, 1908
LEAS, GEO.	son,	Jul14, 1910
LEAS, G. W.	daughter,	Mar14, 1917
LEAS, GEO. WASHINGTON	see Addendum	

LEAS, J. C.	son,	May12, 1908
LEAS, JOHN CARINGTON	see Addendum	
LEAS, S. L.	daughter,	Aug30, 1911
LEAVITT, GEO. WASHINGTON	see Addendum	
LEAVITT, W. J.	son,	Jan09, 1903
LEE, BING	daughter,	_____, 1946
LEE, SAM	daughter,	Jan27, 1911
LEES, BERNIE I. [prob.Leas]	son,	Oct13, 1940
LEHMAN, JOHN CHARLES F.	daughter,	Dec24, 1947
LEHMANN, EMIL, Jr.	daughter,	_____, 1946
LEMON, EDWARD FERDINAND	son,	Sep16, 1947
LESLIE, AUSTIN JULIUS	son,	Jun24, 1937
LEVENTON, E. W.	son,	Feb16, 1916
LEVENTON, E. W.	daughter,	Feb19, 1922
LEWIS, HOMER EDWARD	son,	Jul13, 1948
LEWMAN, G. F.	daughter,	Feb17, 1907
LIENHARD, ALBERT G.	son,	Nov09, 1940
LILIENTHAL, GEORGE	daughter,	Aug28, 1948
LILIENTHAL, GEORGE	son,	Aug11, 1950
LOCKHART, EVERETT LORANCE	daughter,	Jan23, 1949
LOGAN, LUTHER BURBANK	daughter,	Dec27, 1947
LOOMIS, LELAND JAMES	daughter,	Sep03, 1947
LOOMIS, WALTER	son,	Mar04, 1923
LORENZ, FRANZ JOSEPH	see Addendum	
LORENZ, G. C.	son,	Mar06, 1913
LORENZ, GROVER C.	daughter,	Aug16, 1914
LOUGH, WARREN LaVERN	son,	Sep02, 1949
LOWDEN, F. S.	son,	Jul17, 1907
LOWDEN, F. S.	son,	Feb29, 1904
LOWDEN, F. S.	son,	Dec05, 1905
LOWDEN, F. S.	son,	May08, 1909
LOWDEN, FRANK WILLIAM	see Addendum	
LOWDEN, OWEN EUGENE	see Addendum	
LOWDEN, W. M.	daughter,	Jun11, 1900
LOWRY, EDWIN	daughter,	Feb08, 1939
LOWRY, JEFFERSON DAVIS	see Addendum	
LUCCOCK, H. W.	daughter,	Feb17, 1905
LUDDEN, T. J.	son,	Sep27, 1907
LYON, H. H.	daughter,	Aug12, 1901
LYON, H. H.	son,	Apr03, 1905
LYON, H. H.	son,	Mar04, 1903
LYON, HIRAM HARRISON	see Addendum	

Mc - names beginning with this prefix are alphabetized as if spelled MAC.

McADAMS, ROGER TUTTLE	daughter,	Sep15, 1935
McADAMS, ROGER T.	son,	Sep18, 1936
McALEXANDER, MARION B.	son,	Jun04, 1938
McALPINE, HARRY	daughter,	Jul31, 1946
McCAMPBELL, R.	daughter,	Sep04, 1905
McCAMPBELL, ROY	son,	Aug23, 1916
McCARTNEY, CRESTON H.	son,	Jun03, 1932
McCASKILL, LEONARD CARL	son,	Mar25, 1949
McCASKILL, JOHN DEE	tw.son, dau.,	Jun30, 1947
McCLINTOCK, GLENN RICHARD	daughter,	Aug15, 1950
McCLOUD, T. B.	son,	Jul01, 1905
McCOSHUM, RAYMOND WILLIAM	son,	May16, 1948
McDANIEL, BOB	daughter,	_____, 1946
McDONALD, B.	daughter,	Sep14, 1901
McDONALD, B.	son,	Nov08, 1903
McDONALD, B.	daughter,	Jan27, 1907
McDONALD, BERNARD WILLIAM	see Addendum	
McDONALD, J. D.	daughter,	Apr28, 1901
McDONALD, R.	daughter,	Dec24, 1901
McGOVERN, J. J.	daughter,	Feb22, 1904

McGOVERN, J. J.	son,	May23, 1912
McGOVERN, J. J.	son,	Apr26, 1919
McGOVERN, J. J., Jr.	son,	Jan20, 1920
McGOVERN, JOHN J.	son,	Jul09, 1922
McKAY, JOHN J.	son,	Oct18, 1923
McKIBBIN, FRANK	son,	Jan22, 1922
McKIBBIN, FRANK F.	son,	Jan30, 1925
McKIBBIN, FRANK	son,	Apr24, 1933
McKIBBIN, FRANK	daughter,	Jan24, 1936
McKNIGHT, J. F.	daughter,	Jun05, 1903
McKNIGHT, J. F.	daughter,	Mar12, 1905
McKNIGHT, J. F.	daughter,	Sep16, 1907
McKNIGHT, J. M.	daughter,	Jul26, 1905
McKNIGHT, J. N.	son,	May05, 1917
McKNIGHT, J. N.	son,	Mar17, 1919
McKNIGHT, JIM	daughter,	May10, 1946
McKNIGHT, JAMES HENRY	daughter,	Jul04, 1947
McMORROW, D. M.	son,	Jun06, 1939
McMORROW, DONALD M.	daughter,	Oct08, 1940
McMORROW, DONALD MARTIN	daughter,	Jun12, 1948
McNEAL, BONA	daughter,	Jul02, 1931
McNEILL, LLOYD LEVINE	daughter,	Nov10, 1930
MAHONEY, WARREN AMOS	see Addendum	
MAKER, ARCHIE	daughter,	May05, 1913
MAKER, G. I.	daughter,	May07, 1908
MAKER, GEO.	son,	Jul03, 1910
MAKER, GEO,	son,	Nov08, 1912
MAKER, GEORGE	son,	Mar23, 1915
MAKER, GEORGE I.	daughter,	Apr29, 1920
MAKER, GEORGE	daughter,	May21, 1923
MAKER, GEO. I.	daughter,	Mar03, 1927
MAKER, GEORGE IRVIN	son,	Dec06, 1930
MAKER, GEO. I., Jr.	son,	Apr30, 1940
MALONE, JOHN	son,	May03, 1904
MALONE, JOHN	daughter,	Oct12, 1907
MANFORD, BEN L.	daughter,	Mar17, 1918
MANN, BERWYN A.	son,	May14, 1936
MANSFIELD, A.	daughter,	Sep17, 1906
MANSFIELD, DAVID	son,	Jul28, 1930
MANSFIELD, DAVID N.	son,	Dec17, 1932
MAR, GOOY OCK	see Addendum	
MARAVIOV, FRANK JACK	unknown	Sep04, 1948
MARCUS, J. E.	son,	Nov16, 1902
MARCUS, J. E.	son,	Feb16, 1904
MARINGER, FRANK	son,	Dec01, 1909
MARKWELL, P. T.	daughter,	Dec07, 1901
MARSHALL, R. C.	daughter,	Sep30, 1906
MARSHALL, R. C.	son,	Apr07, 1909
MARSHALL, R. C.	son,	Nov09, 1911
MARSHALL, ROBERT L.	daughter,	Mar09, 1936
MARSHALL, ROBERT LAWS	son,	Aug21, 1938
MARTIN, CHARLES	daughter,	May09, 1901
MARTIN, FRED BILL	daughter,	Sep22, 1935
MARTIN, FRED	son,	Jan18, 1939
MARTIN, J. W.	daughter,	Oct14, 1928
MARTIN, JOHN B.	son,	Feb23, 1932
MARTIN, LORENZO DOW	see Addendum	
MARTIN, ROBERT B.	daughter,	Dec18, 1927
MASTERS, JOHN WILLIE	son,	Jul26, 1950
MATHIAS, HARRY A.	son,	Apr22, 1935
MECKEL, CHRISTIAN	see Addendum	
MECKEL, F. C.	son,	Feb20, 1905
MECKEL, F. C.	daughter,	Dec06, 1906

MECKEL, F. C.	daughter,	Jul02, 1909
MECKEL, F. C.	son,	Dec08, 1910
MERRICK, JOHN HARBAUGH	son,	Jul10, 1950
METHVIN, REUEL	daughter,	Feb09, 1937
MILLER, CHARLES MARION	son,	Sep10, 1941
MILLER, EDWARD M.	daughter,	Aug17, 1941
MILLER, EDWARD	son,	Jan15, 1947
MILLER, ELVIN B.	son,	Sep10, 1936
MILLER, ELVIN B.	daughter,	Mar12, 1939
MILLER, JACOB	daughter,	Jun02, 1908
MILLER, LEE	daughter,	Mar20, 1950
MILLER, S. C.	daughter,	Apr18, 1910
MILLER, WILLIAM DANIEL	see Addendum	
MILLS, GEORGE	son,	Apr04, 1900
MILLS, GEO.	daughter,	Aug06, 1903
MILLS, GEORGE	see Addendum	
MILLS, LOUIS EARLE	son,	Apr10, 1949
MINCHER, ROBERT JOATHAN	daughter,	Dec19, 1948
MITCHELL, C. A.	daughter,	_____, 1946
MOLIN, J. A.	daughter,	Jun30, 1906
MOLIN, J. A.	son,	Aug23, 1908
MONTGOMERY, S.	son,	Mar01, 1900
MOON, J. L.	daughter,	Aug03, 1907
MOORE, J. L.	daughter,	Jan11, 1909
MOON, JAS. LUMAN	daughter,	Nov21, 1912
MOORE, LOREN	daughter,	_____, 1946
MORGAN, W.	son,	Apr03, 1908
MORRIS, ARTHUR W.	son,	Aug19, 1936
MORRIS, J. J.	son,	Apr25, 1900
MORRIS, J. J.	son,	Jun27, 1905
MORRIS, J. J.	daughter,	Jun02, 1907
MORRIS, LEONARD McKEE	son,	Jan04, 1935
MORRISON, VERNON	daughter,	Jul08, 1942
MORRISON, VERNON	son,	Nov16, 1946
MORTENSEN, EDWARD H.	son,	Apr19, 1938
MORTENSON, EDWARD HANS	son,	Feb15, 1934
MORTENSON, EDWARD H.	son,	Dec15, 1935
MOSER, C. R.	son,	Sep06, 1913
MOSER, CHAS. ROBERT	son,	Feb02, 1916
MOSER, CHARLES ROBERT	daughter,	Nov29, 1918
MOSS, AMOS	see Addendum	
MOXON, L. A.	daughter,	Nov25, 1917
MULLEN, DAVID	see Addendum	
MURDOCK, LEE WILSON	son,	Dec17, 1949
MURPHY, J. J.	son,	Jun26, 1906
MURPHY, J. J.	daughter,	Jan30, 1908
MURPHY, J. J.	son,	Dec28, 1909
MURPHY, J. J.	daughter,	Mar05, 1911
MURPHY, J. J.	daughter,	Sep16, 1914
MURRAY, JESSE JAMES	daughter,	Jun21, 1948
NEILSON, J. C.	son,	Aug03, 1904
NEVIS, MANUEL	daughter,	May04, 1904
NEWMAN, EDWARD L.	see Addendum	
NEWMAN, LOUIS HENRY	see Addendum	
NICHOLS, W. J.	son,	Aug27, 1900
NICHOLS, W. J.	daughter,	Jul23, 1902
NICHOLS, W. J.	daughter,	Jul26, 1903
NIRES, NICK MARION	son,	Apr20, 1948
NOBLE, ALBERT J.	son,	Jul12, 1932
NOBLE, ALBERT J.	son,	Sep04, 1933
NOBLE, JOSEPH F.	daughter,	May31, 1929
NOBLE, JOSEPH FRANK	daughter,	Dec15, 1930
NOBLE, JOSEPH F.	son,	Jul25, 1932

NOBLE, JOSEPH	daughter,	Dec04, 1937
NOBLE, WILLIAM	son,	Jan22, 1922
NOGARD, CHRIS [Norgaar]	son,	Jun30, 1903
NOONAN, H. H.	daughter,	Apr30, 1903
NOONAN, H. H.	son,	Aug22, 1905
NOONAN, H. H.	daughter,	Aug06, 1907
NOONAN, H. H.	daughter,	Aug21, 1909
NOONAN, H. H.	daughter,	Dec28, 1914
NOONAN, HARRISON HYACINTH	see Addendum	
NORGAAR, ANDY	daughter,	Aug06, 1929
NORGAAR, ANDY	son,	Jul13, 1930
NORGAAR, ANDY	daughter,	Feb01, 1940
NORGAAR, HELGAAR	daughter,	Oct24, 1920
NORGAAR, HELGAAR	son,	Apr25, 1923
NORGAAR, HELGAAR	daughter,	Nov12, 1930
NORGAAR, HELGAAR	daughter,	Oct11, 1940
NOWASKI, FRANK	daughter,	Jun10, 1946
NUNN, LEONARD I.	daughter,	Dec15, 1936
NUNN, LEONARD E.	daughter,	Sep02, 1940
NYHEN, JAMES E.	son,	Jan19, 1936
NYHEN, EMMETT BERNARD	son,	Dec13, 1937
O'DAY, JAMES L.	daughter,	Mar22, 1936
O'HAIR, W. B.	daughter,	Jun16, 1910
O'KEEFE, T. M.	daughter,	Sep30, 1903
O'KEEFE, T. M.	daughter,	Oct14, 1904
O'NEIL, RAYMOND EUGENE	daughter,	Jul25, 1933
ODELL, L. P.	daughter,	Feb18, 1922
OLSEN, EMIL	daughter,	Feb05, 1901
OLSEN, FREDRICK D.	son,	Jul__, 1937
OLSEN, FREDERICK DANIEL	son,	Aug30, 1938
OLSEN, JAMES R.	son,	Aug12, 1932
OLSEN, JOHN	son,	Sep23, 1900
OLSEN, J. J.	son,	Apr07, 1902
OLSEN, JOHN J.	daughter,	Sep01, 1903
OLSEN, J. J.	son,	Jun02, 1917
OLSEN, NORMAN TRIMBLE	son,	Mar14, 1941
OLSEN, W. A.	daughter,	Oct21, 1908
OLSEN, W. A.	son,	Aug13, 1912
OLSEN, WILLIAM A.	daughter,	Dec02, 1920
OLSEN, WILLIAM ALBERT	see Addendum	
OLSEN, WILLIAM X.	daughter,	Oct22, 1924
OLSEN, WILLIAM X.	daughter,	Mar24, 1930
ORDAY, GUILDA ARLEY	son,	Dec18, 1940
OSGOOD, FRANK	daughter,	Aug21, 1911
OSGOOD, FRANK A.	son,	Oct07, 1913
OSGOOD, U. G.	daughter,	Jul21, 1901
OSGOOD, U. G.	son,	Sep24, 1903
OSTHOFF, JOHN HENRY	see Addendum	
OVERHAUSER, HARRY	son,	May07, 1920
OWENS, LONNIE MARK	daughter,	Dec14, 1950
OWENS, RICHARD E.	daughter,	Jul16, 1942
OWENS, WILLIAM E.	son,	Nov10, 1936
PALLO, GEORGE EDWARD	daughter,	Jan20, 1941
PALMER, A. C.	son,	Feb08, 1907
PALMER, A. C.	son,	Sep21, 1910
PATTEN, CLARENCE	son,	Aug22, 1938
PATTISON, LLOYD C.	daughter,	Oct07, 1940
PATTISON, T. C.	son,	Oct22, 1902
PATTISON, T. C.	daughter,	Mar21, 1904
PATTISON, W. A.	son,	Apr05, 1908
PATTISON, WM.	daughter,	Jul08, 1922
PATTON, BEN	son,	Aug07, 1949
PATTON, CLARENCE ALLEN	son,	Nov23, 1935

PATTON, CLARENCE ALLEN	daughter,	Feb01, 1941
PATTON, GEORGE WASHINGTON	daughter,	May19, 1949
PATTON, J. W.	daughter,	Jan11, 1912
PATTON, J. W.	daughter,	Oct29, 1916
PATTON, J. W.	daughter,	Aug31, 1919
PATTON, JAS. W.	daughter,	Oct12, 1920
PATTON, JAMES WILLIAM	son,	Oct31, 1926
PATTON, JAMES W.	daughter,	Feb01, 1929
PATTON, JAMES WILLIAM	see Addendum	
PATTON, RALPH ALBERT	daughter,	Jan11, 1935
PATTON, RALPH A.	daughter,	Mar08, 1936
PATTON, RALPH ALBERT	son,	Sep25, 1939
PATTON, RALPH ALBERT	daughter,	Apr24, 1941
PATTON, WILLIAM	son,	Feb22, 1918
PATTON, WILLIS HARRY	daughter,	Nov11, 1931
PAULSEN, A. L.	daughter,	May13, 1902
PAULSEN, A. L.	daughter,	JULY 2, 1911
PAULSEN, JACOB	see Addendum	
PAULSEN, PETER MEINERT	see Addendum	
PEARCE, WILLIAM	see Addendum	
PERRY, ROBERT JOSEPH	daughter,	Apr09, 1944
PETCH, L. G.	daughter,	Feb04, 1914
PETTIBONE, THOMAS L.	son,	Mar31, 1938
PETTIGREW, THOMAS (Bud)	son,	_____, 1946
PHILLIPS, FRANK EDWARD	daughter,	Jan16, 1948
PHILLIPS, J. W.	daughter,	Oct10, 1900
PHILLIPS, J. W.	son,	Nov04, 1904
PHILLIPS, J. W.	son,	Feb13, 1906
PHILLIPS, J. W.	son,	May20, 1907
PHILLIPS, J. W.	daughter,	Dec03, 1908
PHILLIPS, JAMES W.	son,	Sep08, 1911
PHILLIPS, LODNER D.	see Addendum	
PLATZ, MARTY	daughter,	Jul02, 1905
POAGE, LEVI	daughter,	Oct31, 1910
POAGE, L. P.	daughter,	Oct25, 1912
POE, GERALD WARREN	son,	Oct18, 1949
POE, W. C.	son,	Nov29, 1917
POPE, FRANKIN HENRY	son,	Oct04, 1949
POTTER, F. W.	daughter,	Nov10, 1913
POTTER, JAMES E.	daughter,	Jun06, 1942
PRANDI, CHARLES	son,	Mar24, 1935
PRATT, CHARLES SELDON	daughter,	Sep01, 1947
PROUT, ALBERT H.	daughter,	Aug13, 1924
PRUETT, JAY B.	daughter,	Oct22, 1950
QUILLON, LEFFER JAMES	daughter,	Apr12, 1949
QUINN, GEORGE A.	daughter,	Feb15, 1942
QUINN, GEORGE ARTHUR	son,	Aug13, 1944
QUINT, LLOYD F.	daughter,	Apr16, 1940
RACKERBY, JOSEPH HENRY	see Addendum	
RAIS, MANUEL D.	daughter,	Dec21, 1930
RAIS, MANUEL	daughter,	Jul12, 1933
RAIS, MANUEL	son,	Dec26, 1934
RAIS, WM.	son,	Nov02, 1917
RAIS, WILLIAM	son,	Jun17, 1922
RAIS, WILLIAM	son,	Jul11, 1924
RALPH, L. D.	son,	Sep06, 1904
RALPH, LEWIS DAVID	see Addendum	
RANDALL, WM. HENRY	daughter,	Aug13, 1946
RANDOLPH, B. H.	son,	Jul16, 1916
RANDOLPH, PAYTON R.	daughter,	Mar29, 1918
RANGSUND, PHIL	tw.(?)	_____, 1946
RAUSER, GUSTAVE	son,	Apr22, 1940
REED, ROYAL WALLACE	daughter,	Mar19, 1921

Name		Date
REED, ROYAL W.	daughter,	Jul14, 1923
REED, ROYAL WALLACE	daughter,	Nov12, 1930
REESE, DIXIE FRANKLIN	son,	Jan28, 1937
REESE, JAMES D.	son,	Oct08, 1933
REESE, THOMAS E.	daughter,	Dec26, 1938
REESE, THOMAS ELBERT	son,	May02, 1945
REGAN, EDWIN J.	son,	Mar07, 1939
REGAN, EDWIN JOSEPH	daughter,	Mar02, 1941
REID, G. B.	daughter,	Dec09, 1902
REID, G. B. McC.	son,	Jul11, 1905
REID, L. P.	son,	Sep25, 1901
REID, L. P.	daughter,	Mar18, 1904
REID, W. S.	son,	Jun04, 1915
REIS, M.	daughter,	Aug09, 1902
REIWERTS, R.	daughter,	Jul17, 1919
REYNOLDS, BRUCE M.	son,	Jun29, 1940
RICE, KEITH OLIVER	daughter,	May27, 1935
RICHARDS, WM.	son,	May26, 1905
RICHARDS, WM.	son,	Mar06, 1911
RIDDLE, ALLEN OSCAR, Jr.	son,	Dec15, 1948
RIEWARTS, R. A.	son,	Jun07, 1915
RIEWERTS, R.A.	son,	Apr03, 1917
RIEWERTS, RICKMER A.	daughter,	Nov23, 1921
RIEWERTS, RICKMER A.	son,	Jan01, 1925
RIEWERTS, RICKMAN A.	daughter,	May30, 1927
RIGBY, RALPH WM.	son,	Oct05, 1937
ROBERTS, LELAND S.	son,	Jan13, 1932
ROBERTS, LELAND S.	daughter,	May22, 1933
ROBERTS, W. T.	son,	Oct11, 1913
ROBERTS, W. T.	son,	Dec25, 1914
ROBINSON, WILLIAM C.	son,	Oct05, 1935
RODGERS, ANTONE	see Addendum	
RODGERS DUARTE, FRANK	see Addendum	
RODGERS, J. F.	son,	Mar22, 1906
RODGERS, J. F.	son,	Sep15, 1902
RODGERS, JOHN FRANK	see Addendum	
ROGERS, F.	daughter,	Jul05, 1900
ROGERS, G. P.	son,	Sep28, 1946
ROSE, CHAS. FRANKLIN	son,	Jun04, 1912
ROSS, WM.	daughter,	Oct13, 1909
ROSS, W. D.	daughter,	Oct21, 1911
ROSS, WM. D.	son,	Dec04, 1917
ROSS, WILLIAM WAYNE	daughter,	Aug28, 1938
ROSS, WILLIAM WAYNE	son,	Oct08, 1939
ROSS, WILLIAM WAYNE	daughter,	Jan29, 1941
ROURKE, CHAS.	daughter,	Aug17, 1946
ROURKE, CHARLES KENNETH	daughter,	Jan11, 1948
ROURKE, DENIS	daughter,	Sep15, 1907
ROURKE, DENNIS	daughter,	Feb05, 1912
ROURKE, DENNIS	son,	Mar21, 1914
ROURKE, DENNIS	daughter,	Nov10, 1915
ROURKE, DENNIS	daughter,	May21, 1918
ROURKE, DENNIS	son,	Jul25, 1922
ROURKE, DENNIS, Sr.	son,	May16, 1932
ROWE, CHARLES B.	daughter,	Nov25, 1926
RUCKMAN, WILLIAM LEE	son,	Apr10, 1935
RUSS, GUSS	son,	Oct18, 1924
RUSSELL, DEAN LEE	son,	Oct02, 1940
RYAN, D. E.	son,	Nov15, 1901
RYAN, D. E.	son,	Apr06, 1907
RYAN, D. E.	daughter,	Apr25, 1909
RYAN, D. E.	son,	Dec12, 1912
RYAN, D. E.	daughter,	Jul29, 1916

RYAN, DAVID EDWARD	see Addendum	
RYAN, J. P.	daughter,	Aug24, 1902
RYAN, P. J.	son,	Mar05, 1904
RYAN, P. J.	daughter,	Apr06, 1905
RYAN, P. J.	son,	Nov10, 1909
RYAN, P. S.	son,	Nov10, 1910

Note: 1910 census says Patrick J. & Catherine; see also 1850-1900.

RYAN, RICHARD HENRY	son,	Nov10, 1938
RYBERG, REUBEN EMANUEL	son,	Nov24, 1947
RYBERG, REUBEN EMANUEL	son,	Nov02, 1949
SALYER, LUTHER	son,	Mar09, 1933
SCHLUETER, FREDRICK WILLIAM	son,	Nov21, 1950
SCHNEIDER, C. W.	daughter,	Jul21, 1909
SCHNELLBACHER, B.	son,	Jun18, 1901
SCHORTGEN, NICHOLAS	see Addendum	
SCHOUBLIN, NORMAN	daughter,	Nov29, 1936
SCHURER, JOSEPH A.	daughter,	Sep18, 1934
SCHURER, JOE	daughter,	Jan11, 1938
SCOTT, W. I.	daughter,	Mar03, 1911
SCOTT, WILLIAM JASPER	see Addendum	
SCOTT, WILLIE HENRY	tw.son,	Oct04, 1946
SELBY, HORACE WILLIAM	son,	Mar03, 1950
SENGER, G. A.	son,	Apr10, 1908
SENGER, GEORGE	son,	Aug22, 1911
SENGER, M. A.	daughter,	Oct11, 1904
SENGER, MILAN	son,	Apr23, 1907
SENGER, MILAN	son,	Apr14, 1910
SENGER, MILAN	son,	Jun12, 1924
SENN, JOSEPH	son,	Jul25, 1944
SETTLEMEYER, WALLACE LEON	son,	Sep02, 1950
SHAND, J. E.	son,	Feb19, 1904
SHAND, J. E.	daughter,	Jun13, 1906
SHANNON, W.	son,	Jan10, 1904
SHANNON, W. F.	daughter,	Mar30, 1906
SHANNON, WILLIAM FREDERICK	see Addendum	
SHAW, J. J.	son,	Mar17, 1902
SHAW, J. J.	son,	Nov06, 1904
SHERIDAN, W. T.	daughter,	Jan13, 1909
SHIELDS, J. A.	daughter,	Oct09, 1905
SHOCK, GEO.	son,	Mar04, 1904
SHOCK, JAMES	son,	Oct04, 1907
SHOCK, JAMES S.	daughter,	Aug13, 1920
SHOCK, JAMES S.	daughter,	Feb21, 1923
SHOCK, Z. L.	daughter,	Jan28, 1901
SHOCK, Z. L.	daughter,	May08, 1908
SHUFORD, EDWARD MARTIN	daughter,	May17, 1933
SHUFORD, J. W.	son,	Jul05, 1908
SHUFORD, JOHN WILLIAM	see Addendum	
SILIGO, EDWARD J.	son,	Apr13, 1915
SILIGO, EDWARD E.	son,	Apr19, 1918
SILIGO, JOSEPH	daughter,	Jul17, 1910
SILVA, ANTONE	son,	Apr20, 1902
SILVA, JOHN J.	daughter,	Oct05, 1915
SIMPSON, ALBERT	tw.son,	Dec13, 1941
SIMPSON, MINOR	son,	Aug18, 1906
SKINNER, ROBERT ALEXANDER	see Addendum	
SMALLEN, JAMES	daughter,	Jul31, 1924
SMITH, BRADLEY FRANK	son,	Jul13, 1947
SMITH, BRADLEY FRANK	son,	Apr28, 1949
SMITH, BRADLEY FRANK	daughter,	May03, 1950
SMITH, DALE	daughter,	Sep18, 1946
SMITH, DENZIL M.	son,	Jul17, 1936
SMITH, DOUGLAS NEAL	son,	Oct30, 1947

BIRTHS 1900 - 1950

Name		Date
SMITH, EDWARD G.	son,	Oct19, 1938
SMITH, FRANK	daughter,	Sep02, 1904
SMITH, FRANK MARION	see Addendum	
SMITH, GEORGE ROBERT	see Addendum	
SMITH, G. W.	daughter,	Sep26, 1914
SMITH, J. B.	daughter,	Nov08, 1940
SMITH, JOSEPH C.	son,	Dec05, 1949
SMITH, LYLE AVERY	son,	Nov17, 1947
SMITH, LYLE AVERY	daughter,	Feb05, 1949
SMITH, LLOYD EMMETT	son,	Oct08, 1934
SMITH, RAY C.	daughter,	Feb24, 1936
SMITH, ROBERT O'DONALD	son,	Mar24, 1947
SNYDER, JAMES H.	daughter,	Apr30, 1939
SPATZ, LEE C.	son,	Jul31, 1923
SPATZ, LEE C.	son,	Nov17, 1924
SPATZ, LEE CONRAD	daughter,	Aug31, 1926
SPATZ, LEE	son,	Sep13, 1927
SPINDLER, HAROLD ALBERT	daughter,	Jan07, 1933
SPINDLER, HOWARD ALFRED	daughter,	Oct28, 1941
SPRATT, C. W.	son,	Dec05, 1900
SPRATT, CHARLES W.	son,	Jan24, 1936
SPRATT, CHARLES WILLIAM	daughter,	Jun14, 1937
SPRATT, HENRY THAYER	son,	Dec22, 1935
SPRATT, HENRY THAYER	son,	Jan02, 1938
SPRATT, HENRY T.	son,	Jun19, 1940
SPRATT, HOWARD CODDINGTON	daughter,	Mar08, 1948
SPRATT, HOWARD CODDINGTON	son,	Jul24, 1949
SPRATT, S. I.	son,	Jan19, 1913
SPRATT, S. T.	son,	Dec26, 1915
STACKPOLE, F. L.	daughter,	May17, 1900
STACKPOLE, F.	daughter,	Apr30, 1902
STACKPOLE, F.	daughter,	Oct05, 1903
STACKPOLE, F. L.	son,	Mar31, 1905
STACKPOLE, F. L.	daughter,	Feb04, 1907
STACKPOLE, FRANK LESLIE	see Addendum	
STANLEY, A. J.	daughter,	Feb18, 1907
STANLEY, ALLAN JAY	see Addendum	
STANSELL, ROBERT FRED	son,	Nov23, 1948
STARR, KENTON CORNETT	son,	Aug17, 1947
STEDMAN, IRL	son,	May21, 1923
STEE, BYRON WAYNE	son,	Sep22, 1941
STEELE, S. A.	son,	Jun10, 1917
STEELE, S. A.	daughter,	Mar30, 1922
STEELE, S. A.	son,	Mar14, 1924
STEELE, SIDNEY A.	daughter,	Aug31, 1935
STEPHENS, JAMES WILLIAM	son,	Oct27, 1948
STEVENS, WILLIAM STEWART	son,	Jul15, 1945
STEVES, RODNEY HAROLD	daughter,	Jun10, 1947
STEVES, RODNEY HAROLD	son,	Aug17, 1934
STEWART, HARRY LEO	son,	Dec29, 1950
STILLWELL, FORREST ROY	son,	
STILLWELL, WILLIAM	see Addendum	
STOFER, H. C.	daughter,	Jan06, 1907
STOFER, H.	son,	Dec17, 1908
STOFER, H.	son,	Nov27, 1910
STRICKLAND, SANFORD ERVIN	daughter,	May26, 1949
STODDARD, JOHN ROOE	see Addendum	
STRODE, GERALD MARTIN	daughter,	Dec25, 1946
STRONG, CHARLES F.	son,	Dec28, 1932
STRONG, C. H.	son,	Mar27, 1939
STRONG, CHARLES TYLER	son,	Sep29, 1935
STRONG, CHARLES T.	daughter,	Sep17, 1936
STRONG, CHARLES TYLER, Jr.	daughter,	Feb11, 1948
STRYKER, WALLACE MAITLAND	son,	Apr23, 1941

STRYKER, WM.	daughter,	Nov02, 1946
SUN, CHARLIE	see Addendum	
SURBER, DAVID F. M.	son,	Oct21, 1939
SUTTON, C. J.	son,	Nov24, 1947
SUTTON, C. J.	son,	Jan19, 1950
SUTTON, ROY C.	daughter,	Sep07, 1919
SWANEY, WILLIAM FRANKLIN	son,	Nov24, 1945
SWITZER, TRUMAN GRANT	son,	Jun22, 1935
TARPLEY, E. L.	son,	Mar18, 1903
TARPLEY, E.	daughter,	Oct29, 1904
TARPLEY, J. W.	daughter,	Jul03, 1911
TARPLEY, J. W.	son,	Jun22, 1913
TARPLEY, J. W.	daughter,	Jul07, 1918
TAUSCH, GEORGE ELMER	son,	Oct23, 1948
TAYLOR, FRANK A.	son,	Aug03, 1920
TAYLOR, LYLE SAMUEL	daughter,	Apr05, 1947
TAYLOR, LYLE SAMUEL	son,	Aug23, 1949
TAYLOR, PAUL	tw.dau.,	Feb05, 1929
TAYLOR, PAUL	daughter,	Mar28, 1931
TAYLOR, PAUL C.	son,	Jan06, 1936
TAYLOR, WALTER EDWARD	daughter,	Dec16, 1946
TAYLOR, WALTER EDWARD	son,	Sep29, 1950
TEHAN, FRANK	son,	Feb28, 1935
TEHAN, HARRY	son,	Feb19, 1937
TESTY, C. J.	daughter,	Dec18, 1906
TEUSCHER, ROGER DAVID	son,	Aug03, 1950
THOMAS, EMMITT N.	son,	Mar28, 1939
THOMAS, PHILIP ARTHUR	daughter,	Feb19, 1941
THOMAS, PHILLIP A.	son,	Sep21, 1942
THOMAS, STANLEY	son,	Aug12, 1938
THOMAS, STANLEY O.	son,	Apr06, 1942
THOMPSON, MELVIN	daughter,	Sep23, 1946
THOMPSON, PETER S.	son,	Apr14, 1911
THORNE, JOHN	son,	Nov23, 1910
THOROUGHMAN, NORVIN EDWARD	daughter,	Sep09, 1947
THOROUGHMAN, NORVIN EDWARD	daughter,	Jan23, 1949
TINDELL, JAMES	daughter,	Jan01, 1946
TINSLEY, G. A.	daughter,	May15, 1900
TINSLEY, G.	daughter,	Nov08, 1908
TODD, E. N.	son,	Oct26, 1902
TODD, J. A.	son,	May03, 1902
TODD, J. A.	daughter,	Sep11, 1903
TODD, J. A.	son,	Nov01, 1905
TODD, W. D.	son,	Feb24, 1900
TOMPKINS, LLOYD J.	daughter,	Sep05, 1932
TORRENCE, HOMER WILLIAM	daughter,	Oct26, 1943
TOURTELLOTTE, J. F.	son,	Aug09, 1903
TOURTELLOTTE, J. F.	son,	Jul29, 1904
TOUT, CARL SHEPPARD, Jr.	daughter,	Oct19, 1948
TOWERS, FRANK	son,	Oct31, 1900
TOWERS, FRANK	daughter,	Oct18, 1904
TOWNSEND, GERALD S.	daughter,	Nov26, 1939
TOWNSEND, GERALD STEVEN	daughter,	Feb01, 1941
TOWNSEND, ROBERT AUGUSTUS	daughter,	Aug26, 1948
TRASK, BERNARD NELSON	son,	Aug14, 1921
TRASK, BERNARD N.	son,	Sep03, 1923
TRASK, GEORGE NELSON	see Addendum	
TRELOAR, E. W.	daughter,	Nov11, 1901
TRELOAR, EDWARD WASHINGTON	see Addendum	
TRIMBLE, FRANK L.	daughter,	Jul26, 1923
TRIMBLE, J. W., Jr.	daughter,	Mar29, 1904
TRIMBLE, J. W.	daughter,	Aug20, 1905
TRIMBLE, JOHN	son,	Sep30, 1907

Name		Date
TRIMBLE, J. W.	daughter,	Sep13, 1910
TRIMBLE, J. W.	daughter,	Nov25, 1913
TRIMBLE, J. W.	daughter,	Jan11, 1916
TRIMBLE, WM.	son,	May29, 1907
TRIMBLE, W. N.	son,	Jan02, 1909
TRIMBLE, W. N.	daughter,	May03, 1912
TRIMBLE, W. N.	son,	May01, 1915
TRIMBLE, W. N.	son,	Oct02, 1918
TROSPER, LLOYD H.	daughter,	Nov05, 1936
TRUBY, WM. J.	son,	May23, 1901
TUCKEY, ALFRED ROBERT, Jr.	daughter,	Sep11, 1949
TUDOR, H.	daughter,	Jan24, 1904
TUDOR, H.	daughter,	Apr19, 1908
TUDOR, HUMPHREY	son,	Mar02, 1911
TUDOR, HUMPHREY	see Addendum	
TUDOR, J.	daughter,	Apr07, 1902
TURNER, JOHN W.	tw.son,	Jul14, 1942
TYE, ARCHIE	daughter,	Nov01, 1922
TYE, ARCHIE	daughter,	May21, 1935
TYE, ARCHIE	son,	Sep07, 1937
TYSAN, JESSE ALLAN	daughter,	Jan27, 1934
UPHAM, FRANK L.	son,	Jun20, 1923
UPTON, J. D.	son,	Apr14, 1908
UPTON, J. D.	daughter,	Sep29, 1909
VALENTINE, CHARLES EUGENE	daughter,	Feb13, 1950
VAN CLEVE, C. H.	daughter,	Oct28, 1902
VAN CLEAVE, C. H.	daughter,	Jan21, 1905
VAN CLEAVE, C.	daughter,	Apr20, 1907
VAN CLEAVE, CHAS.	son,	Apr04, 1908
VAN CLEAVE, C. H.	daughter,	Feb07, 1911
VAN CLEAVE, C. H.	son,	Mar16, 1913
VAN HORN, WILLIAM EDMAN	see Addendum	
VAN MATRE, F. C.	son,	Mar21, 1904
VAN MATRE, J. C.	daughter,	May04, 1902
VAN MATRE, J. C.	son,	Apr28, 1905
VAN MATRE, J. C.	son,	Oct31, 1911
VAN MATRE, JOHN CHANDLER	see Addendum	
VAN MATRE, JUDSON CHANDLER	daughter,	Sep15, 1934
VAN MATRE, W. J.	son,	Nov12, 1917
VAN MATRE, WALTER PETER	son,	Jun14, 1933
VANCE, GEORGE S.	daughter,	Jul24, 1913
VANDERHOFF, J.	son,	Feb08, 1900
VANDERHOFF, J.	son,	Apr10, 1904
VANDERHOFF, J. H.	son,	Feb29, 1920
VAUGHN, DANIEL D.	son,	Mar16, 1922
VAUGHN, D. D.	daughter,	Oct30, 1923
VAUGHN, DeFOREST H.	son,	Oct25, 1927
VAUGHN, DeFORREST HOBART	daughter,	Oct14, 1918
VAUGHN, HARRY	daughter,	Feb24, 1922
VAUGHN, H. B.	son,	Apr20, 1923
VAUGHN, HARRY B.	son,	Nov28, 1949
VAUGHN, MERLE LEONARD	daughter,	Jan08, 1918
VAUGHN, RAY	daughter,	
VAUGHN, WILLIS HARRY	see Addendum	
VERNON, MONTE LOWE	daughter,	Jun29, 1949
VESTAL, C. A.	son,	Nov14, 1946
VILLATA, GUIDO	son,	Mar20, 1950
VINCENT, MANUEL JAMES	unknown	Oct26, 1948
VITZTHUM, W. P.	daughter,	Jul14, 1910
VITZTHUM, W. P.	daughter,	Jan12, 1915
WAGNER, BUD	daughter,	Feb14, 1925
WAGNER, BUD	son,	Jun05, 1932
WALDO, W. W.	daughter,	Oct17, 1920
WALDO, WILLIAM MARVIN	son,	Jul22, 1941

WALKER, W. M.	son,	Jan29, 1904
WALKER, W. M.	daughter,	Mar23, 1905
WALKER, W. M.	daughter,	Nov21, 1906
WALKER, WALTER M.	see Addendum	
WALLACE, A. J.	son,	May20, 1904
WALLACE, JAMES ADDISON	see Addendum	
WALSH, ASA DON	son,	Jul31, 1936
WALSH, FELIX R.	son,	Nov04, 1933
WARD, HARVEY F.	son,	Jun12, 1932
WARD, PHILIP EARL	son,	Aug26, 1949
WARE, SAMUEL NORMAN	son,	Feb10, 1948
WARREN, CHAS.	son,	Jun25, 1902
WARREN, CHAS.	daughter,	Feb21, 1904
WARREN, W. G.	daughter,	Aug02, 1900
WATSON, DUMONT	son,	Apr01, 1940
WEBB, JAMES B.	son,	Sep16, 1935
WEDEL, THEODORE	see Addendum	
WEEKS, E. E.	daughter,	Jun25, 1901
WEEKS, EDWARD EVERETT	see Addendum	
WEINHEIMER, H.	son,	Apr10, 1906
WEISGERBER, ALOYSIUS JOHN	son,	Apr22, 1948
WELBOURN, GEORGE HENRY	daughter,	Aug09, 1947
WELLOCK, BENJAMIN RICHARD	daughter,	Jul11, 1926
WELLOCK, B. R.	daughter,	Apr05, 1928
WELLOCK, BENJAMIN RICHARDS	son,	Jan01, 1930
WELLOCK, BENJAMIN RICHARD	son,	Dec18, 1943
WHITE, C. WM.	daughter,	Mar10, 1911
WHITE, C. W.	son,	Mar17, 1914
WHITE, E. O.	daughter,	Nov16, 1909
WHITE, EDWARD OTTO	see Addendum	
WHITE, EMMET ELDEN	daughter,	Apr14, 1931
WHITE, EMMETT	daughter,	Jul07, 1936
WHITE, EMMIT S.	daughter,	Mar26, 1935
WHITE, FLOYD	daughter,	Nov29, 1921
WHITE, RAYMOND E.	daughter,	Dec20, 1932
WHITELY, WILLIAM A.	daughter,	Jul06, 1922
WHITMORE, JOHN	see Addendum	
WILCOX, THEODORE ROOSEVELT	son,	Nov24, 1949
WILKINSON, LOREN J.	daughter,	Sep07, 1929
WILLBURN, A.	son,	Oct11, 1904
WILLBURN, C.	daughter,	Sep29, 1904
WILLBURN, C.	daughter,	Nov24, 1906
WILLBURN, C. D.	son,	Aug27, 1925
WILLBURN, CLARENCE ST.CLAIR	see Addendum	
WILLBURN, CHURCHMAN DIKE	daughter,	Dec05, 1927
WILLBURN, CHURCHMAN DYKE	see Addendum	
WILLBURN, H. D.	daughter,	Jan27, 1905
WILLIAMS, F. H.	son,	Apr22, 1911
WILLIAMS, JOHN	daughter,	Aug21, 1900
WILLIAMS, JOHN	son,	Feb25, 1902
WILLIAMS, JOHN	see Addendum	
WILLIAMS, R.	daughter,	Jan27, 1916
WILLIAMS, R. B.	daughter,	Nov02, 1920
WILLIAMS, S.	son,	Oct02, 1905
WILLIAMS, WILLIAM HENRY	daughter,	Oct30, 1926
WILLIAMS, W. O.	son,	May26, 1908
WILSON, ALBERT	daughter,	Nov06, 1909
WILSON, E. E.	daughter,	Jul04, 1903
WILSON, HAROLD J.	son,	Sep27, 1923
WILSON, HAROLD JOHN	daughter,	Apr17, 1926
WILSON, HAROLD J.	daughter,	Jun19, 1932
WILSON, HAROLD JOHN	son,	Mar12, 1935
WILSON, HARVEY K.	son,	Jul22, 1929

WILSON, ISAAC J.	daughter,	Apr05, 1918
WILSON, ISAAC J.	son,	Jun01, 1920
WILSON, I. J.	son,	Mar23, 1922
WILSON, JAMES	see Addendum	
WILSON, LE ROY E.	son,	Jun09, 1932
WILSON, LeROY E.	daughter,	Dec01, 1936
WILSON, LeROY E.	son,	Apr25, 1950
WILSON, ROY RAYMOND	son,	Apr22, 1902
WILSON, T. M.	son,	Aug23, 1903
WILSON, T. M.	daughter,	Oct19, 1910
WILSON, T. M.	daughter,	Jan31, 1915
WILSON, T. M.	daughter,	Nov16, 1916
WILSON, W. B.	son,	Nov08, 1905
WILSON, W. B.	daughter,	Jan25, 1908
WILSON, WILLIAM M.	daughter,	Sep20, 1933
WILSON, WILLIAM M.	daughter,	Oct25, 1936
WING, GEORGE L.	daughter,	Aug26, 1946
WISEMAN, ALONZO R.	daughter,	May10, 1940
WOOD, ROBERT WILLARD	son,	Nov24, 1941
WOODHAMS, W. H.	daughter,	May07, 1916
WOODHAMS, WILLIAM H.	son,	Apr28, 1918
WOODRUFF, LESLIE CANDRICK	daughter,	Jan18, 1948
WORTHINGTON, ED. T.	daughter,	Jan12, 1936
WRIGHT, ERVILLE ANDREW	son,	Jun08, 1943
WRIGHT, ERVILLE ANDREW	daughter,	Feb09, 1947
WRUCK, JOSEPH D.	son,	Feb02, 1929
WYATT, JOSEPH GERALD	son,	Feb15, 1950
WYATT, ROBERT EUGENE	daughter,	Dec08, 1949
WYCKOFF, ROBERT	daughter,	Mar05, 1939
YALE, FRANK LAWRENCE	son,	Mar22, 1948
YANCEY, E. W.	daughter,	Nov02, 1910
YANCEY, ELZIE W.	daughter,	Oct08, 1912
YANCEY, E. W.	son,	Jul14, 1914
YANCEY, E. W.	daughter,	Jan16, 1917
YANCEY, ELZA WILLIAM	son,	Jul12, 1918
YANCY, RALPH	son,	Aug17, 1946
YOUNG, HENRY JUNKANS	son,	Aug24, 1912
YOUNG, HENRY J.	son,	Jun25, 1915
YOUNG, CHAS.	daughter,	Feb19, 1901
YOUNG, C. W.	daughter,	May12, 1903
YOUNG, KELSO VAN BRUNT	daughter,	Nov28, 1941
YOUNG, W. W.	daughter,	Nov18, 1900
YOUNG, W. W.	daughter,	Sep27, 1902
YOUNG, W. W.	son,	Apr10, 1907
ZACHARY, J. L.	daughter,	Jun04, 1928
ZACHARY, J. L.	son,	Dec30, 1929
ZACHARY, JOHN L.	tw.son,	Sep26, 1933
ZEBROFF, NICKOLAS ANTHONY	son,	Jun04, 1950
ZEIGLER, CYRUS	daughter,	Feb12, 1900
ZEIGLAR, C. W.	daughter,	Sep29, 1902
ZIMMERLEE, DENNIS LYLE	daughter,	Jun27, 1941
ZUMWALT, ALBERT	daughter,	Nov09, 1921
ZUMWALT, ALBERT	daughter,	Jan15, 1923
ZUMWALT, ALBERT	son,	Mar13, 1924

END TRINITY COUNTY BIRTHS 1900-1950

PIONEER RECORDS OF TRINITY COUNTY, CALIFORNIA
A Century of Facts 1850-1950

ADDENDUM

Theodore Eldon Jones (1830-1907) was the Editor and Publisher of the *DOUGLAS CITY GAZETTE* at Douglas City, Trinity County, California from May 1861 to May 1862. He had been trained as a printer, and often wrote articles for the *TRINITY JOURNAL* in the years that he was Judge of the Superior Court, Trinity County, California. Births and Marriages listed in the *DOUGLAS CITY GAZETTE* (DCG) 1861-1862 are in Miscellaneous records. [also more information about T. E. Jones].

CHINESE NAMES ARE LISTED TOGETHER FOR CONVENIENCE IN READING. Sources: TRINITY JOURNAL, Index to Deaths 1873-1890, and Index to Deaths 1890-1908; some are repeated in Deaths 1900-1950.

The late Dorothy Lee (Mrs. Moon Lim Lee) said that a person would say, "Ah-h", to catch a breath, or to think of a name. It is believed that many of the following names are not the correct names of the persons who died. The accuracy of names given to "officials" is questionable. [One wonders if the name was really "Wong Back You"].

Ah Bow. Died Jun 18, 1912; aged 78 yr. (TJ Jan 4, 1913).
Ah Bow Eye. Died March 27, 1906 Junction City, Calif; age about 73; male; born China; miner; buried by Coroner at Idaho Bar. [Index to Deaths 1890-1908].
Ah Chin. Died Jan 12, 1911; aged 70 yr. (TJ Jan. 6, 1912).
Ah Chong. Died March 4, 1907 Weaverville, age 65; born China; miner. [Index to Deaths 1890-1908].
Ah Chong. Died July (n.d.) 1907 Hawkins Bar, Calif; age 46; male; born China; miner; murder. [Index to Deaths 1890-1908].
Ah Din. Died July 15, 1912; aged 70 yr. (TJ Jan 4, 1913)
Ah Dock. Died Apr 27, 1912; aged 65 yr. (TJ Jan 4, 1913).
Ah Fie. Died Feb 1, 1913; aged 86 yr. (TJ Jan 3, 1914).
Ah Gong. Died Apr. 27, 1923; aged abt 80 yr. (TJ Jan. 5, 1924).
Ah Gow. Died Sept. 28, 1924; aged 60 yr. (TJ Jan. 3, 1925).
Ah Hong. Died Dec. 14, 1894 Weaverville. Chinese miner known as "Old Hong"; came to Calif. 1849; no age given. (TJ Dec. 16, 1894 p 3).
Ah Lung. Died Aug 26, 1896, Junction City; native of China; aged about 61 yr. (TJ Sat. Sept 5, 1896 p 3).
Ah May. Died Jan. 31, 1913; aged 77 yr. (TJ Jan. 3, 1914)
Ah Ock. Died Nov. 19, 1903 Eastman Gulch, Trinity County, Cal, age 33, male; born China; miner; bedrock slide; bur. Chinese Cemetery, Weaverville. [Index to Deaths 1890-1908].
Ah Ock. Died Mar. 28, 1912; aged 64 yr (TJ Jan 4, 1913).
Ah Ock. Died May 27, 1933; age 84 yr; native of China. (TJ Jan. 8, 1934).
Ah Shuck. Died May 3, 1921; aged abt 83 yr. (TJ Jan. 7, 1922).
Ah Sing. Died Sept. 9, 1926; aged 80 yr. (TJ Jan. 1927).
Ah Sing. Died Feb 22, 1932; aged 84 yr; native China. (TJ Jan 7, 1933).
Ah Son. Died Sept. 22, 1910; aged 86 yr. (TJ Jan. 7, 1911).
Ah You. Died Dec 17, 1911; aged 70 yr. (TJ Jan 6, 1912).
Che Sing. Died Weaverville abt June 5, 1897; aka "Jo. Hamilton"; came to Calif. from China 1852 as a boy of 16; came to Weaverville about 16 years ago; in El Dorado County, he worked for Gen. Jo Hamilton, for whom he named himself; left a wife and 7 children; bur. Chinese Cem. Weaverville. (TJ Jun 5, 1897 p 3 col 2).
Chen Toy. Died Apr 1, 1919; aged 96 yr. (TJ Jan. 10, 1920).
Chew Young. Died Sep 27, 1915; aged 75 yr. (TJ Jan 1, 1916).
"Chinaman". Killed by a cave in a tunnel at Big Bar abt Feb. 13, 1894; bur. Chinese Cem. Weaverville. (TJ Feb. 17, 1894 p 3 col 6).

Chin Quong Pan. Died Oct. 19, 1923; aged 80 yr. (TJ Jan. 5, 1924).
Ching, Jim. Died Aug. 8, 1910; aged 68 yr. (TJ Jan. 7, 1911).
Chow Gee. Died Jul 10, 1915; aged 75 yr. (TJ Jan. 1, 1916).
Chue Chin. Died June 25, 1925; aged 48 yr 3 mo 10 dy. (TJ Jan. 1926).
Fon Chong. Murdered Aug. 7, 1873, Weaverville; aged 45 yr, a native of China; unknown assailant. Fon Chong has been a leading Chinaman in former years, owning several claims and employing a large number of men. Some years since he clerked for Louis Raab. Latterly he has been an interpreter in actions where members of his company were parties. (TJ Aug. 9, 1873).
Fong ah Foon. Died Oct. 19, 1905 Lewiston; age 67; male; born China; miner; buried Weaverville. [Index to Deaths 1890-1908].
Fong Thin. Died Dec. 3, 1921; aged 95 yr. (TJ Jan. 7, 1922)
Goon, Daniel. Died Jul 19, 1915; aged 78 yr 6 mo. (TJ Jan 1, 1916).
Guen Mon. Died Oct. 16, 1905 Weaverville; age 75; born China; bur. Weaverville. [Index to Deaths 1890-1908]. [see also Mon Guen].
Hong So. Died Dec 30, 1911; age 64 yr. (TJ Jan 6, 1912)
Jim Sing. Died Nov. 19, 1903 Eastman Gulch, Trinity County, Cal; age 52; male, yellow; born China; miner; bedrock slide; body shipped to China. [Index to Deaths 1890-1908].
Kim Doey. Died Sep 26, 1934, Weaverville; age 95 yr; born China. (TJ Jan 5, 1935).
Lee How. Died July 4, 1941, Weaverville; age about 90 years; born China. Informant: Moon Lee. (Trinity County BIRTHS-DEATHS 1940-1949).
LEE, MOON LIM. [Lim Bing Moon]. Died Nov 8, 1985 in Redding, Shasta Co., CA. He was born in Weaverville Jul 21, 1903, the son of Mr. and Mrs. "Sam Lee". He married Dorothy Thelma Sue [Sue Yeng] May 14, 1933 in Bakersfield, CA. Mrs. Dorothy Lee died Nov 18, 1988 in Cottonwood, Shasta Co., CA at the age of 82. Mr. and Mrs. Lee preserved Chinese customs in Weaverville and shared the customs with the people of Weaverville. Mr. Lee was responsible for seeing that the Chinese Temple in Weaverville, known as the Weaverville Joss House, became a part of the California State Park System, so that it would be preserved when he could no longer take care of it. (TJ May 20, 1933; Jul 30, 1959; Jun 3, 1971; Mar 14, 1984; Nov 12, 1985; and many other references.) [see also Lee, Sam, Mrs. and Lim Sue Kin.]
LEE, SAM, Mrs. Died Weaverville Jan. 19, 1913. (TJ Jan. 3, 1914).
Lee, Sam, infant child. Died Weaverville Jan 19, 1913. (TJ Jan. 3, 1914).
Lee Sam. Died Dec. 4, 1924. (TJ Jan. 3, 1925).
[Note: "Lee Sam" is not the father of Moon Lim Lee, whose mother, Mrs. Sam Lee, d. Jan. 19, 1913. The father of Moon Lim Lee was named Lim Sue Kin; see below.]
Lee Ying. Died May 21, 1908 Weaverville; age about 83; male; yellow; born China; miner. Informant: Charly Ah Get.
Lew Dow Chuen. Died Dec. 21, 1914; age 78 yr. (TJ Jan. 2, 1915).
Lew Tong. Died Jan 5, 1917; age 82 yr. (TJ Jan. 5, 1918).
Lim Ah Moy. Died Apr 26, 1935; age 95 yr; native of China. (TJ Jan 2, 1936).
Lim, Mary. Died Aug 16, 1914; age 72 yr. (TJ Jan. 2, 1915).
Lim Sing. Died Nov. 9, 1915; age 45 yr 3 mo. (TJ Jan. 1, 1916).
LIM SUE KIN called his store `SAM LEE', which in his See Yup Cantonese dialect means `threefold prosperity'. White people in Weaverville thought `Sam Lee' was his name, so Sam Lee he became. He was born in Dai Pai Village, Yanping District, Guangdong Province, China, April 11, 1863. His father, Lim Ock Pom (or Foon) came to America in 1867. He worked for several years, then sent to China for his son Lim Sue Kin, who arrived in the United States, California, & Weaverville in 1879. As "Sam Lee", Lim Sue Kin died at his home in Weaverville Jan 20, 1947. He was survived by four daughters, Mrs. Frederick Wong, Fall River, Mass; Mrs. Yue Joe, Taunton, Mass, Alma Fong, Redding, and Janice Lee, Sacramento, and two sons, Bing Lee, of Sacramento, and Moon Lee of Weaverville. [information from several sources, including Trinity County, Calif. Deaths 1940-1949, p 140; personal interview with Moon and Dorothy Lee Feb 10, 1980; TJ Jan 23, 1947 p 1;]

ADDENDUM

Lin Ti. Died Jan. 14, 1907 Lewiston; age about 75; male; yellow; born China; cause: murder; buried Weaverville.

Ling Sing. Died May 9, 1904 near Weaverville; age 60 years; male; yellow; foreign native. Buried Weaverville "in Chinese Cemetery by China friends".

Louie Chong. Died July 23, 1921; aged 63 yr. (TJ Jan. 7, 1922).

Mar Sing. Died Mar 11, 1912; aged 76 yr. (TJ Jan 6, 1912).

Mock Fawn. Died Sep 10, 1933; age 78 yr; native China. Also known as "Ah Fawn; Joss House Custodian; resident of Trinity County for 60 years; buried in the Chinese Cem., Weaverville. (TJ Sat. Sept 16, 1933 p 1).

Mon Guen. Died between 1903-1905 (no dates) Weaverville; about 75; male, yellow; born China. [Index to Deaths 1890-1908].

Mon La Ho. Died Jan. 12, 1908 near Junction City; age about 76; male; yellow; born China; miner; died of exposure; buried Weaverville. [Index to Deaths 1890-1908].

Ng Ching. Died April 7, 1906 Weaverville; age 63; male; yellow; born China; cook. [Index to Deaths 1890-1908].

On Lee. Died Nov. 3, 1911; age 65 yr. (TJ Jan 6, 1912).

On Lee. Died Nov. 12, 1911; age 62 yr. (TJ Jan 6, 1912). [note: check the newspaper for Nov. 1911!].

Pock Chock. Died April 25, 1906 Weaverville; age 58; male; yellow; born China; miner. [Index to Deaths 1890-1908].

Pock, Mrs. Died Chinatown [Weaverville] Sept 23, 1894; native of China, aged about 64 yr. (TJ Sat. Sep 29, 1894 p 3 col 5).

Sing Jim. Died Nov. 19, 1903 Eastman Gulch, Trinity County, Cal; age 52; male; yellow; born China; crushed in slide. (shipped). [Index to Deaths 1890-1908]. [probably Jim Sing, above].

Tung Mao Ma. Died Dec. 4, 1939; aged 88 yr 4 mo 17 dy; born Arcata, California, in 1851. Also known as Charles Lambert. (Trinity County Deaths 1937-1941).

Toy Sing. Died Mar. 30, 1922; aged 68 yr. (TJ Jan. 13, 1923).

Wah Doy. Died Nov 28, 1937; aged 95 yr; native of China. (TJ Jan 6, 1938).

Wong Back You. Died Mar. 26, 1913; aged 51 yr. (TJ Jan. 3, 1914).

Wong Doo Yuen. Died Aug 4, 1919; aged 74 yr. (TJ Jan. 10, 1920).

Wong Jon. Died May 24, 1926; aged 83 yr. (TJ Jan. 1927).

Wong Lee. Died May 8, 1934, Weaverville; aged 81 yr; born in China. (TJ Jan 5, 1935).

Wong Lin. Died Mar. 25, 1922; aged 82 yr. (TJ Jan. 13, 1923).

Ye Toy. Died Feb. 22, 1907 Junction City; age 54; female; yellow; born China; buried Weaverville. [Index to Deaths 1890-1908].

Yu Hong. Died Jul 17, 1922; aged 87 yr. (TJ Jan. 13, 1923).

DELAYED CERTIFICATES OF BIRTH, filed in TRINITY COUNTY, CALIFORNIA BIRTHS-DEATHS 1940-1949, and TRINITY COUNTY, CALIFORNIA, DELAYED CERTIFICATES OF BIRTH. All place names are in Trinity County, California.

Parents: Abernathy, George Asbury and Boswell, Rebecca Catherine.
ABERNATHY, Harry Elmar, b. Feb 18, 1882 Lewiston.
Parents: Albiez, Karl and Kessler, Katharine.
ALBIEZ, Arthur, b. Oct 06, 1890 Hayfork.
ALBIEZ, George, b. Sep 15, 1892 Hayfork.
ALBIEZ, Frieda C., b. Mar 01, 1899 Hayfork.
Parents: Ammon, Chauncey Leroy and Taylor, Ruth Edna.
AMMON, Charles, b. Sep 23, 1933 Salyer.
Parents: Armentrout, John William and Bradshaw, Harriet Eliza.
ARMENTROUT, Everett, b. Sep 21, 1875 Weaverville.
ARMENTROUT, Loar, b. Mar 11, 1877 Weaverville.
ARMENTROUT, Jemima, b. Oct 08, 1878 Weaverville.
ARMENTROUT, Effie Belle, b. Dec 03, 1883, Weaverville.
Parents: Barker, Fowler David and Vaughn, Alice Josephine.
BARKER, Harold Joe, b. Feb 08, 1931 Big Bar.
Parents: Bates, Randall M. and Briggle, Sarah E.

BATES, Belva Zelita, b. Feb 10, 1883 Weaverville.
Parents: Blair, Hugh Newell and Clanir, Eva.
BLAIR, Loraine Arabelle, b. Sep 05, 1898 Trinity Center.
Parents: Blakemore, Thomas Jefferson and Koelle, Ursula.
BLAKEMORE, Cristian, [sic] b. Nov 19, 1878 Lewiston.
Parents: Britton, Joseph S. and Dockery, Julia.
BRITTON, Frank Eeward, b. Jul 31, 1900 Weaverville.
Parents: Carr, Alexander Constantine and Gribble, Annie.
CARR, Jennie Isabelle, b. Mar 30, 1891 near Junction City. [m. J. J. Jackson].
Parents: Carr, Alexander Constantine and Decker, Hattie May.
CARR, George Washington, b. Aug 14, 1900 Douglas City.
CARR, Clarence Leamen, b. Jul 03, 1903 Weaverville.
Parents: Chapman, George Phelps and Small, Sarah S.
CHAPMAN, Earnest Gardner, b. Nov 05, 1882 Junction City.
Parents: Chapman, George Phelps and Luman, Esther.
CHAPMAN, Elsie May, b. Nov 16, 1925 Junction City.
CHAPMAN, Frank, b. Apr 24, 1927 Junction City.
Parents: Collins, Maurice William and Coady, Bessie.
COLLINS, Maurice Coady, b. Sep 06, 1903 Weaverville.
Parents: Copeland, Jason Paul and Forrester, Anna Marie.
COPELAND, Johnny Dale, b. Sep 13, 1950 Weaverville.
Parents: Cuff, Richard William and Lush, Annie.
CUFF, Monica May, b. Sep 16, 1897 Hayfork.
CUFF, Lincoln Orloff, b. Feb 12, 1910 Hayfork.
CUFF, Kermit Allen, b. Jan 16, 1912, Hayfork.
Parents: Day, James Levi and McWorthy, Grace Isabell.
DAY, Cecil Worden (f) b. Feb 19, 1898 Helena.
Parents: Day, Walter Andrew and Flagg, Sadie-Anna.
DAY, Georgia Alice, b. Feb 12, 1908 Weaverville.
Parents: Dean, Samuel Theodore and Newland, Maud Edna.
DEAN, Izora Vivian (f), b. Sep 13, 1908 Lewiston.
Parents: Denison, Lewis and Koll, Bertha [see also Van Matre].
DENISON, Henrietta Pearl (Conner) b Dec 19, 1882, Trinity County.
DENISON, Lewis Nathaniel b. Aug 2, 1884 Trinity County.
Parents: Dickey, James Calvin and Tryor, Eve Ellen.
DICKEY, Louis Albert, b. May 15, 1879 Lewiston.
Parents: Dix, Henry Eldon and Brannan, Mary.
DIX, Mary Luella, b. Sep 23, 1891 Weaverville.
Parents: Dockery, Michael William and Coumbs, Grace Cole.
DOCKERY, Kathryn Margaret, b. May 29, 1890, Weaverville.
DOCKERY, Clara Ileen, b. Aug 09, 1904 Weaverville.
Parents: Dungan, Thomas Frank and Karry, Martha Jane.
DUNGAN, Ada May, b. Apr 18, 1896 China Flat.
Parents: Everest, Wilbur A. and Shultz, Carlotta.
EVEREST, Susan Irene, b. Sep 02, 1939 Weaverville.
Parents: Gilzean, James Henry and Laws, Christine Clementine.
GILZEAN, Anna Elicia, b. Feb 17, 1883 Junction City.
Parents: Grant, Manuel and Joseph, Mary.
GRANT, Frank, b. May 29, 1873 Douglas City.
Parents: Greenwell, Ernest Albert and Todd, Emma Agnes.
GREENWELL, Reuben Albert, b. Nov 20, 1895, Weaverville.
Parents: Gregory, Joseph and Powell, Dora.
GREGORY, Jesse B. (m), b. Sep 09, 1895 Caution (nr Lake Mountain).
Parents: Greig, George and Dawson, Ruth.
GREIG, Lottie Fay, b. Apr 22, 1915 Junction City.
Parents: Gribble, William and Lorenz, Matilda.
GRIBBLE, Milfred Francis (m) b. Apr 11, 1898 nr Junction City.
Parents: Grigsby, Calvin and Baker, Jessie Maybelle.
GRIGSBY, Jessie Lucille, b. Jan 07, 1915 Hayfork.
GRIGSBY, Calvin Glenn, b. Jun 08, 1916 Hayfork.
Parents: Haas, Frederick Gottleib and Junkans, Emily Elizabeth.
HAAS, Augusta Philippine, b. Mar 05, 1885 Junction City.

ADDENDUM

HAAS, David Washington, b. Feb 22, 1890 Junction City.
Parents: Hanover, Frank Smith and Joseph, Adelene.
HANOVER, Alton Dale, b. Sep 19, 1907 Douglas City.
Parents: Hanover, Robert Clay and Duncan, Bessie Marie.
HANOVER, Jonathan Gordon, b. Ruth, Trinity Co, Jan 8, 1944.
Parents: Harbine, Hardy Ralston and Remstedt, Eugenia Alice.
HARBINE, Eugenia Myrtle, b. Dec 12, 1899, Weaverville.
Parents: Horton, Richard Edward and Harvey, Lillie Elizabeth
HORTON, Elizabeth Cathron, b. Weaverville July 06, 1888.
Parents: Hitchcock, James and Ramsey, Mary Elizabeth.
HITCHCOCK, Clyde Agustus, b. Apr 16, 1901 Harrison Gulch. [see also Births 1850-1900].
Parents: Hughes, William Edward and Senger, Katherine.
HUGHES, Clarence Edward, b. May 04, 1896 Weaverville.
Parents: Iverson, Ole and Halverson, Hannah
IVERSON, Horace Given, b. Nov 22, 1887 Weaverville.
Parents: Jackson, Wilbert Leslie and Senger, Madeline Mary.
JACKSON, John Jacob, b. Jul 01, 1887 Weaverville.
JACKSON, Irene Antonette, b. Sep 16, 1889, Weaverville.
JACKSON, Raymond Archibald, b. Oct 10, 1891, Weaverville.
Parents: Jeans, Arthur Howard and Fish, Gertrude Daisy.
JEANS, Ivan Rupert, b. Ruth, Trinity County, Jan 19, 1915. [d. Feb 5, 1998].
Parents: Johnson, Frederick Alonza and Dunlap, Nellie.
JOHNSON, Vernon Vernie, b. Mar 04, 1904 Weaverville.
JOHNSON, Edith, b. Nov 04, 1907 Weaverville.
Parents: Johnston, Richard and Shock, Claudie Whipple.
JOHNSTON, Flora, b. Aug 14, 1925 Hayfork.
JOHNSTON, Belle, b. Jul 16, 1930 near Hayfork.
JOHNSTON, Joan Emily, b. Aug 06, 1932 Hayfork.
Parents: Kise, Joseph Bloomfield and Wifley, Angeline.
KISE, Commodore Colonel, b. Jul 25, 1875 Lewiston.
Parents: Kise, Elisha Samual (sic) and Rule, Elisabeth Emma.
KISE, Earle Rule, b. Apr 25, 1900 Weaverville. [d. Feb 6, 1998 Redding, Shasta, California.]
Parents: Koll, John and Joseph, Louise Regina.
KOLL, Winnie Claudine, b. Feb 11, 1903 Lewiston.
Parents: Koon, Gorges [sic] Lester and Hendricks, Mattie Myrtle.
KOON, Meskyl Elnora (f) b. Mar 29, 1915 Salyer.
Parents: Leas, George Washington and Goetz, Babette.
LEAS, Meta Alfrieda (f), b. May 26, 1907, Lowden's Ranch, nr Lewiston.
Parents: Leas, John Carington and Biggs, Elizabeth
LEAS, Phillip Alton, b. May 12, 1908 Deadwood.
Parents: Leavitt, George Washington and Gilzean, Mary Ellen.
LEAVITT, Isabelle Emma, b. Jul 20, 1890 Deadwood.
Parents: Lorenz, Franz Joseph and Gilbert, Annie Margaret.
LORENZ, Anita Margaret, b. Red Hill (near Junction City) Jan 21, 1893.
LORENZ, Frances Phyrne, b. Red Hill (near Junction City) Sep 01, 1894.
LORENZ, Ruby Mildred, b. Weaverville Apr 23, 1896.
LORENZ, Joseph Henry, b. Weaverville Sep 30, 1897.
LORENZ, Frank Decatur, b. Weaverville Apr 21, 1899.
Parents: Lowden, Frank William and DeLong, Minne
LOWDEN, Hettie Selena, b. Mar 04, 1891 Hayfork.
Parents: Lowden, Owen Eugene and Dack, Lucy Lowe.
LOWDEN, James Edgar, b. Jul 21, 1891, Lowden's Ranch, nr Lewiston.
Parents: Lowry, Jefferson Davis and Philpot, Lydia.
LOWRY, Maud Myrtle, b. Aug 29, 1893 Hayfork.
Parents: Lyon; Hiram Harrison and Grazie, Jeannette Andre.
LYON, Norbert Lucien, b. Weaverville Apr 03, 1905.
Parents: McDonald, Bernard William and Cochran, Mary Ellen.
McDONALD, Norine Genevieve, b. Mar 09, 1894 Weaverville.
Parents: Mahoney, Warren Amos and Wallace, Margaret OraFina
MAHONEY, Mary Robb, b. Aug 21, 1892 Dedrick.

MAHONEY, George Campbell, b. Jan 18, 1898 Weaverville. [Note: Margaret OraFina Wallace was born in Oro Fino, Siskiyou Co, CA].
Parents: Mar, Gooy Ock and Mother: Gook Ying Jang.
MAR, Harold Gong-Yuen, (m) b. Mar 30, 1898 Weaverville.
MAR, Grace, (f) b. Jul 21, 1903 Weaverville.
MAR, Howard Quong-Yuen, (m) b. Oct 08, 1905 Weaverville.
Parents: Martin, Lorenzo Dow and Thauwald, Annie.
MARTIN, Naomi Hilda, b. Aug 20, 1893 Weaverville.
Parents: Meckel, Christian and Hall, Helena Josephine.
MECKEL, Helena Elizabeth, b. May 12, 1876 Helena.
MECKEL, Adolph N., b. North Fork (Helena) Nov 26, 1878.
MECKEL, Emilie Katharine, b. North Fork (Helena) Mar 01, 1881.
Parents: Miller, William Daniel and Trimble, Sarah Jane.
MILLER, Edmund Kenneth, b. Mar 01, 1897 near Hyampom.
Parents: Mills, George and Millsap, Jessie.
MILLS, William LeRoy, b. Apr 04, 1900 near Junction City.
Parents: Moss, Amos and Senger, Alice Florence.
MOSS, Ednah Antionette, b. Jan 24, 1886 Weaverville.
Parents: Mullen, David and Smith, Lizzie.
MULLEN, Grace Eleanor, b. Jun 17, 1900 Weaverville.
Parents: Newman, Edward L. and Morris, Elizabeth Jane.
NEWMAN, Mary Katherine, b. Dec 03, 1887 Hayfork.
Parents: Newman, Louis Henry and Ehrmann, Katherine.
NEWMAN, Maud, b. Jun 11, 1889 Weaverville.
Parents: Noonan, Harrison Hyacinth and Heath, Flora Jane.
NOONAN, Nellie Hyacinth, b. Aug 06, 1907, Weaverville.
Parents: Olsen, William Albert and Trimble, Margaret Mae.
OLSEN, Myrna Mae, b. Dec 02, 1902 Hyampom.
Parents: Osthoff, John Henry and Schneider, Katrina Elizabeth.
OSTHOFF, Elizabeth Mary, b. Dec 25, 1874 Junction City.
Parents: Patton, James William and Vaughn, Charlotte Maria.
PATTON, Ben, b. Nov 16, 1923 Peanut (near Hayfork).
Parents: Paulsen, Peter Meinert and Kruttschnitt, Anna Barbara.
PAULSEN, Charles Arthur b. Weaverville May 04, 1890.
Parents: Paulsen, Jacob and Goetze, Louisa Sofia.
PAULSEN, Frederick Roy, b. Weaverville Oct 5, 1887.
Parents: Pearce, William and Johnson, Arminda Pearl.
PEARCE, Margaret Geraldine, b. May 23, 1915, Weaverville.
Parents: Phillips, Lodner D. and Tingle, Bird Estelle.
PHILLIPS, Lucille Wila, b. Jun 29, 1897 Weaverville.
Parents: Rackenby, (sic) Joseph Henry and Curnew, Sarah Jane.
RACKERBY, Vesta, b. Feb 07, 1899 Trinity Center.
RACKENBY, (sic) Frank Gerhart, b. Jul 04, 1902 Trinity Center. [Note: 1900 & 1910 Census say Rackerby. See also the 1900 Census for the names of children born in Oregon].
Parents: Ralph, Lewis David and McKay, Annie Dora.
RALPH, Kenneth David, b. Sep 06, 1904 Lewiston.
Parents: Rodgers, Antone and Caton, Mary Magdalene.
RODGERS, Antone Caton, b. Jul 11, 1889 Indian Creek (nr Douglas City).
RODGERS, Annie Lenora, b. Jun 09, 1894 Indian Creek.
Parents: Rodgers Duarte, Frank and Enos, Mary.
RODGERS DUARTE, Mary, b. Jul 07, 1880 "Trinity County".
Parents: Rodgers, John Frank and McMullen, Amelia Harriett.
RODGERS, Merle Johnnie (m), b. Sep 15, 1902 Douglas City.
RODGERS, LeRoy Francis, b. Dec 29, 1903 Indian Creek.
Parents: Ryan, David Edward and Weinheimer, Anna Louise.
RYAN, Edward Vernon, b. Nov 15, 1901 Weaverville.
Parents: Schortgen, Nicholas and Wood, Mary Elizabeth.
SCHORTGEN, Earl Milford, b. Aug 28, 1901 Island Mountain.
Parents: Scott, William Jasper and Koelle, Anna.
SCOTT, Nellie J., b. Jul 26, 1884 Lewiston.
Parents: Shannon, William Frederick and Bailey, Gertrude.

SHANNON, Marian Adele, b. Jan 07, 1912 Hoaglin.
SHANNON, Robert Lee, b. Mar 16, 1916 Zenia.
SHANNON, George Henry, b. Oct 16, 1918 Zenia.
Parents: Shuford, John William and Olsen, Louisa Isabelle.
SHUFORD, Edna May, b. Jun 21, 1892 Junction City.
[Louisa Olsen's mother, Ellen Olsen, was b. Feb 7, 1843; d. Dec 21, 1926; info. from Ed Shuford abt 1991; he d. Mar 9, 1992 Weaverville. Ellen Olsen was the midwife for the Van Matre children].
Parents: Skinner, Robert Alexander and Olsen, Minnie Ann.
SKINNER, Myrtle May (Luhmann) b. Weaverville May 15, 1891.
SKINNER, Jennie Evelyn, b. Coleridge, Trinity Co. Mar. 03, 1895.
Parents: Smith, Frank Marion and Weinheimer, Caroline Elizabeth.
SMITH, Frances Marian, b. Sep 02, 1904 Weaverville.
Parents: Smith, George Robert and Heffington, Nollie Cornelia.
SMITH, Loyd Emmit, b. Kenefick, Caddo, Oklahoma May 13, 1913. (Recorded in Trinity County, CA June 5, 1943).
Parents: Stackpole, Frank Leslie and Jordan, Lydia Grace.
STACKPOLE, Avis Gertrude, b. Feb 18, 1894 Douglas City.
STACKPOLE, Doris Loann, b. Apr 16, 1899 Indian Creek.
STACKPOLE, Clarice Elaine, b. May 17, 1900 Douglas City.
Parents: Stanley, Allan Jay and Stanley, Grace Amy Baker.
STANLEY, Jerome Nelson, b. Oct 22, 1900 Carrville, Trinity County.
Parents: Stillwell, William and Stillwell, Marsha.
STILLWELL, Del Rio Jean, b. Jan 01, 1945 Zenia.
Parents: Stoddard, John Rooe and Tourtellotte, Inez Fredericka.
STODDARD, Nellie Blanche, b. Jan 21, 1885 near Carrville.
Parents: Sun, Charlie and mother: Sally Sun
SUN, Lilly Elsie, b. Mar 11, 1905 Lewiston.
SUN, Rosie Virginia (Yip), b. Dec 5, 1913 Lewiston.
SUN, Ernest Wilbert, b. Feb 9, 1916 Lewiston.
Parents: Trask, George Nelson and Kamoules, Mary Eliza.
TRASK, Bernard Nelson, b. Mar 07, 1894 Hayfork.
Parents: Treloar, Edward Washington and Flagg, Jennie Alice.
TRELOAR, Delia Bernice, b. Nov 11, 1901 Weaverville.
Parents: Tudor, Humphrey and Vanderford, Nettie.
TUDOR, Edna Owen, b. Apr 07, 1902 Weaverville.
TUDOR, Nettie Edith, b. Jan 24, 1904 near Weaverville.
TUDOR, Gwendolyn, b. Apr 19, 1908 Weaverville. [Gwendolyn Tudor Isham d. Oct 1995 Salinas, Monterey County, CA, age 87; lived in Salinas from 1962 to 1995; her husband Lloyd Isham d. 1993; survived by 2 sons, Evan Isham of Fremont, Brian Isham of Oakland, and one grandson. (Monterey County Herald Oct 9, 1995).]
Parents: Van Horn, William Edman and Johnson, Julana Nevada.
VAN HORN, Nevada Julana, b. Sep 05, 1898 Island Mountain.
Parents: Van Matre, John Chandler and Koll, Bertha.
VAN MATRE, Edna May (Browning) b. Aug 9, 1891 Minersville.
VAN MATRE, Irene Maud (Box) (Vollmers); b. 24 Oct 1895 Minersville.
VAN MATRE, Ernestine Anita; b. Sep 26, 1897 Minersville.
VAN MATRE, Bertrum Lloyd b. May 9, 1899 Minersville.
VAN MATRE, Loda Ethel (Foster) b. Jan 17, 1901 Minersville.
VAN MATRE, Ernest J. b. Apr 25, 1905 Minersville.
VAN MATRE, Walter John Peter b Jul 3, 1906 Minersville.
VAN MATRE, Judson Chandler b. Oct 31, 1911 Minersville.
[see also Dennison].
Parents: Vaughn, Willis Harry and Greenleaf, Maria.
VAUGHN, George Parson, b. May 13, 1887 Hayfork.
Parents: Walker, Walter M. and Grigsby, Florence Ida.
WALKER, Monroe Lafayette, b. Jan 29, 1904 Hayfork.
WALKER, Mary Edith, b. Mar 23, 1905 Hayfork.
Parents: Wallace, James Addison and Woodbury, Nellie Louise.
WALLACE, Rita Woodbury, b. Oct 19, 1899 Weaverville.
Parents: Wedel, Theodore and Hiebert, Elizabeth.
WEDEL, Benjamin Henry, b. Mar 01, 1942 Zenia.
Parents: Weeks, Edward Everett and Dix, Caroline Olive.

WEEKS, Mary Olive, b. Jun 25, 1901 Weaverville.
Parents: Weyand, Zackery Taylor and Weyand, Amelia Rose.
WEYAND, Clare Cecil (m) b. May 29, 1897 Weaverville.
Parents: White, Edward Otto and Perry, Clara Beulah.
WHITE, Lois Aletha, b. Nov 13, 1909 near Hoaglin.
WHITE, Wilbur Otto, b. Mar 21, 1911 "Trinity County".
WHITE, Helen Lovina, b. Nov 19, 1912 near Hoaglin.
Parents: Whitmore, John and Ryan, Catherine Theresa.
WHITMORE, John Ray, b. Mar 18, 1891 Weaverville.
WHITMORE, Helen Frances, b. Oct 19, 1892 near Weaverville.
Parents: Willburn, Churchman Dyke and Duncan, Lulu Florence.
WILLBURN, Marilyn Bernice, b. Feb 06, 1931 Long Ridge.
Parents: Willburn, Clarence St. Clair and Campbell, Irene Minnie.
WILLBURN, Carlos Lee, b. Aug 30, 1929 Hoaglin Valley.
WILLBURN, Faye, b. Mar 09, 1932 Caution (nr Island Mountain).
Parents: Williams, John and Rodgers, Mary.
WILLIAMS, Alice Magdalena, b. Aug 21, 1900 Indian Creek.
Parents: Wilson, James and Jones, Hattie.
WILSON, Amy Jean, b. Feb 25, 1888 Trinity Center.
END DELAYED CERTIFICATES OF BIRTH, TRINITY COUNTY, CALIFORNIA.

MISCELLANEOUS INFORMATION from various sources:
ANDERSON. Birth: at Sacramento Jan. 7, 1862, the wife of Wm. Anderson, of Trinity County, of a son. (DCG Wed. Jan. 29, 1862).
ANNEY. Married at the residence of A. J. Loomis, in Weaverville, Jan. 16, 1862, by Rev. Thos. Chivers, Mr. Tracy Scofield to Miss M. E. Anney. New York and Illinois papers please copy. (DCG Wed. Jan. 22, 1862).
BATES, FORDYCE. "The merchant of Minersville for many years; left Friday (Jun 2, 1899) for Massachusetts to end his days with relatives. He was a Pioneer of Trinity County." (TJ Jun 3, 1899 p 3 col 2).
BAYLES. Married at the residence of the bride's father in this county Nov 21, 1861 by Hon. E. J. Curtis, County Judge, Frank W. Young, Esq. of Weaverville to Mary E. Bayles, daughter of A. D. Bayles. New York and Rhode Island papers please copy. (DCG Nov 27, 1861).
BLAKE. Married at Douglas City Sept 22, 1861 by Hon. E. J. Curtis, Mr. Rankin Thompson to Mrs. Mary S. Blake. (DCG Sep 25, 1861).
BRETON, ARNE. Biographical information. (TJ Oct 30, 1897).
CANFIELD, ELIZABETH (d. 1902); husband Albert Canfield; dau. Sara Elizabeth Canfield m. Jason Charles Henderson; had sons: Alonzo Abner; Charles; Jeloma. (Pat Lanini, Turlock, CA Oct 1996).
CARR, GEORGE L. Biographical information. (TJ Oct 30, 1897).
CASTNER, LEWIS. Biographical information. (TJ Oct 30, 1897)
CLIFFORD. Married in San Francisco Oct. 1, 1873, by Rev. Father Kelly, Mr. John Clifford to Mrs. Julia Spear. (TJ Oct. 18, 1873).
FOGG. Married At Smith's Flat (near Douglas City) on July 3, 1861 by M. W. Personette, J.P., Mr. Calvin P. Fogg to Miss Elizabeth C. Hood, both of Smith's Flat. Maine and Missouri papers please copy. "Our best wishes attend our friend Cal, and his fair young bride in their journey through life. May their path ever be gilded with the sunshine of happiness and prosperity." (DCG Jul 10, 1861).

THE GARRETT FAMILY OF HYAMPOM
GARRETT, WILLIAM XENOPHON, Sr. came to Hyampom 1890; he had served in the Spanish American War in Cuba, and later in the Medical Corps during the Phillippines Insurrection; m. Nellie Ward of Blue Lake, Humboldt Co., 1902; one of first forest rangers in Trinity Co.; d. 1959 aged 93 yr. Mrs. Nellie Garrett d. 1960 aged 81 yr. [story by Edith Garrett pp 56-59]. [Great Register of Voters: reg. Aug 4, 1896, Hyampom; farmer, age 28, b. Virginia; 6'2", light complexion, light blue eyes, dark brown hair.]
Three children: Ballard Lee, William, Jr. "Billy", and Nellie.

ADDENDUM

1. Ballard Lee Garrett, b. Sep 21, 1903 Ward Ranch, Humboldt Co.; d. Feb 20, 1972. m. Edith Maud Patton Dec 9, 1927, Redding, Shasta Co.; b. Dec 25, 1908 Peanut, Trinity Co.; dau. of J. W. and Charlotte [Vaughn] Patton; one of 14 children; d. Mar 7, 1998 Hyampom, Trinity Co.

Children: Walter, Dorothy, David, Van Patton Garrett.

2. William Xenophon Garrett, Jr. b. Aug 5, 1905 Eureka, Humboldt Co. d. Mar 15, 1981 Hyampom, Trinity Co. m. Louise Mason Jun 1930.

Children: Florence (Mrs. Earnest Houchins), Robert, and Fern (Mrs. Harley Erskine). (MEMORIES OF HYAMPOM 1990, Louise Garrett, pp 76-77, 79).

3. Nellie; d. 1979; m. Edward H. "Slim" Mortensen in 1933; he d. 1981. Children: Virgil, Eugene, Milton. [Note: there is information about other Hyampom families in MEMORIES OF HYAMPOM 1990.]

GORDON. Married in Weaverville Sep 2, 1861 by the Hon. E. J. Curtis, Mr. David E. Gordon of Weaverville to Miss Laura E. Webb, formerly of Portland, Maine. (Note: D. E. Gordon was the publisher of the TRINITY JOURNAL at this time.) (DCG Sep 4, 1861 and Sep 14, 1861).

GORDON, WILL L. m. Miss Edith Dexter at Fruitvale, Alameda Co. (abt Oct 1899). Will is son of David E. Gordon. (TJ Nov 4, 1899 p 3 col 1).

HOOD. Married at Smith's Flat near Douglas City on July 3, 1861 by M. W. Personette, J.P., Mr. Calvin P. Fogg to Miss Elizabeth C. Hood, both of Smith's Flat. Maine and Missouri papers please copy. (DCG Jul 10, 1861).

JONES, THEODORE ELDON. b. Dec. 30, 1830 Frankfort Hill, Herkimer Co., N.Y.; d. Oct 3, 1907 San Jose, Santa Clara, Calif. m. 1) Sarah Jane Puterman Mar 28, 1867 Weaverville, Calif. b. May 10, 1839 Illinois; d. Feb 6, 1868 Sacramento, Calif. mother of Sarah Theodora Jones, b. 1867/8, prob. in Sacramento.

m. 2) Mrs. Mary (Willey) Barnes Apr 4, 1877 Weaverville, Calif. b. May 10, 1839 Illinois; d. Mar 12, 1886 San Francisco, Calif.

m. 3) Miss Clara I. Huggins Oct 17, 1887 San Francisco CA. b. Nova Scotia; d. after 1907.

(see Hicks, Patricia J., STORIES OF A GOLD MINER, for the writings of T. E. Jones, a picture, biography, and genealogy.)

KELTON. Birth: at Douglas City May 28th 1861, the wife of E. A. Kelton, of a son. (DCG May 29, 1861).

McLEOD, R. R. Biographical information. (TJ Oct 30, 1897).

MAHONEY. Married at the "Weaverville House", Douglas City, Dec 2, 1861 by the Rev. Father O'Reilly, Mr. Eugene Reardon to Miss Margaret Mahoney. (DCG Dec 4, 1861).

MOREY. Married at Weaverville May 13, 1861 by M. W. Personette, J.P., Mr. S. B. Morey of San Francisco to Miss Maggie Ruch of Weaverville. (DCG May 15, 1861).

THE OLSEN FAMILY OF HYAMPOM

I. OLSEN, JAMES PETER m. Rosa Lee Dec 22, 1864; one son: Jimmie Olsen.

m. 2) Mary Jane Adams (b. Sonoma Co.) Sep 10, 1874; seven children: John James, Mary L., Sarah Elizabeth, William Albert, Josephine Theresa "Josie", Alfred Wright and Frederick.

OLSEN, MARY JANE ADAMS m2) Abraham Lincoln Bush (Abe) Jun 14, 1901. Abe Bush b. Jun 17, 1864 Hayfork; d Jan 21, 1934; bur. Olsen Cem. Hyampom; they raised the children of son John Olsen: Robert (Bob), William (Bill, Little Will), and Mary Jane, "Tootsie".

II. Josephine Theresa Olsen, b. Jun 10, 1882 [Hyampom, Trinity Co.] m. Samuel Theodore Jackson Mar 11, 1903 Eureka, Humboldt Co., CA. He was b. Feb 8, 1878 nr Crescent City, Del Norte Co., CA.

10 children: Edward A., Lemuel T., William C., Francis (Frank), Samuel B., Harold W. (Bud) and his twin, a girl, stillborn, Donald (Dude), Fred B., and Steward A. [MEMORIES OF HYAMPOM 1990, stories by Samuel B. Jackson, pp 1-6].

PATTISON, WILLIAM, A. Sr. Died Big Bar Mar 12, 1923; b. Chautauqua Co. New York Dec 11, 1832; came to Calif. 1853, landing at San Francisco Mar 4, 1853; came to Trinity Co. May 1853; several children, all bur. in the little cemetery at Big Bar. The surviving member of the family is William A. Pattison, Jr., of Big Bar. (TJ Mar 24, 1923, p 1). [1880 Census: Pattison, William, Cox Bar, Jun 1, 1880, age 47, miner, b. New York; Sally (Indian), age 40, b. Calif.; Mary, age 15; Lora, age 13; Josephine, age 11; Thomas, age 9; William, age 6; Charles, age 1]. [see also Marriages and Deaths 1850-1900, Births: Griffith]. [Great Register of Voters 1892: Pattison, William Alanson, reg. Aug 22, 1892 Cox Bar Precinct; age 59, b. New York, miner; 5' 7-1/4", light complexion, blue eyes, brown hair; res. Big Bar; P.O. Big Bar; note: this name is often spelled "Patterson" in early records.]

PATTISON, WILLIAM A., Mrs. Died Cox Bar Feb 19, 1910, native of Calif., aged abt 67 yr. (p 2). Mrs. William C. (sic) Pattison, born in Calif. abt 67 yrs ago, leaves husband, 2 sons, Thomas C. Pattison, and W. A. Pattison, Jr. both of Cox Bar, and a granddaughter, Elsie M. Waldorff. (TJ Feb 26, 1910 pp 2 & 3). [note: the Trinity Journal index lists Mrs. Pattison as Mrs. Wm. C.; should be Wm. A. see 1892 Great Register note, above]. [Her marriage record gives her name as Sally McCollum. She and Mr. Pattison were married Dec 22, 1864]. [see also Waldorff].

PORTER, J. H. Biographical information. (TJ Oct 30, 1897).

RABUT, ODETTE SALADIN. Died Breuilly, France, Apr 27, 1989 at the age of 96. She was born Aug 11, 1892 in France, the daughter of Edouard and Marguerite Saladin. Mrs. Rabut and her daughter Marguerite came to Weaverville for a visit in Sept. 1978.

REARDON. Married at the "Weaverville House", Douglas City, Dec 2, 1861 by the Rev. Father O'Reilly, Mr. Eugene Reardon to Miss Margaret Mahoney. Our best wishes are given to the prosperity of the young couple, who in the midst of their happiness remembered the printer. May their journey through life be prosperous and happy. (DCG Dec 4, 1861). [Note: "remembering the printer" meant that cake and other delicacies were given to the printer, who usually expressed his appreciation with a flowery tribute.]

RUCH. Married at Weaverville May 13, 1861 by M. W. Personette, J.P., Mr. S. B. Morey of San Francisco to Miss Maggie Ruch of Weaverville. (DCG May 15, 1861).

SALADIN. Mrs. E. Saladin, who d. Junction City Jul 7, 1898, was Marguerite Camille Estelle Jaehle Koehler, the wife of Edouard Saladin, General Manager of the Compagnie Francaises des Hydrauliques mine (called the "Cie Fse Mine" by Trinity Co. residents). Mrs. Saladin and 2 dau. Odette (3-1/2) and Germaine (3-1/2 mo) and 2 nurses came to US from Paris in 1896. Mr. Saladin met them in Chicago. They left Chicago Feb 1, 1896, arrived Junction City (via Sacramento and Weaverville) Sat. Feb. 8, 1896. After Mrs. Saladin's death, Mr. Saladin, his mother-in-law Mrs. Koehler, his 3 little daughters (Odette was 6), and servants accompanied Mrs. Saladin's body back to France for burial. The TRINITY JOURNAL tells of Mr. Saladin's return to Trinity County in 1898 to settle his affairs, then he left for France, not intending to return to Trinity County. The Journal for Apr 15, 1899 says, "E. Saladin, formerly superintendent of the Cie Fse mine at Junction City, is now the general manager of a large steel trust in France." see also Deaths 1850-1900. [see also Rabut, for daughter Odette.]

SALADIN, EDOUARD. Died New York City 1917 at the age of 50. (letter from granddaughter, Marguerite Rabut 1979).

SCOFIELD. Married at the residence of A. J. Loomis, in Weaverville, Jan. 16, 1862, by Rev. Thos. Chivers, Mr. Tracy Scofield to Miss M. E. Anney. New York and Illinois papers please copy. (DCG Wed. Jan. 22, 1862).

SEAMAN. Married in Bethlehem, Northampton Co., Penn Jan 19, 1858, Henry J. Seaman, Esq., formerly of Trinity County, to Miss Maria A. Luckenbach, of Bethlehem. (TJ Feb 27, 1858 p 2). [Note: Seaman was Trinity County Clerk in 1854, one of the proprietors of the TRINITY JOURNAL in 1856, and owned the Weaverville Drug Store Jun 1859 - Apr 1862. He and his family left Trinity County in June 1862 for Bethlehem. Seaman died there Sep 11, 1874.]

THE SHERWOOD FAMILY OF NEW RIVER (near Denny)
SHERWOOD, miscellaneous information.
Trinity County, California Probate File P-121 (Willis Sherwood, dec'd). 24 August 1894, notice of hearing of will Oren P. Sherwood, Weaverville, Calif., applicant for letters testamentary or of administration. Abstract of Oren P. Sherwood's proof of eligibility: Stephen Sherwood died 24 Jun 1894 at Coeur in

Trinity County, California. In a letter to his attorney James W. Bartlett, Esq., he named Oren P. Sherwood, his son, as executor of his estate. His next of kin were listed as: Henry S. Sherwood, a son aged abt 58 yr, Sand Lake, Lake County, Illinois; Oren P. Sherwood, petitioner, son of deceased, aged 54 yr, residing at Weaverville, Trinity Co., Calif.; Wm. H. Sherwood, aged abt 50 yr, and John F. Sherwood, aged abt 41 yr., both sons of deceased, residing at Richville, Apache Co., Arizona; Hattie L. Sherwood, aged abt 30 yr, and Mary R. Sherwood, aged abt 25 yr, both of whom are daughters, and reside at Sand Lake, Lake County, Illinois; The Will was executed 11 Jun 1894, filed Aug 9, 1894. [This document was typed, and is about 7 pages long.]

Sherwood, Stephen appears in the Trinity Co. California Great Register of Voters first in 1879; he registered Jun 24, 1879 in New River, Trinity County; born Penn, age 68, blacksmith.

The Great Register of Voters 1892 has descriptions: Sherwood, Stephen, light complexion, gray eyes, light hair, miner, born Penn., reg. White Rock, precinct New River, P. O. Coeur, registered Sep 26, 1892.

In 1894, Sherwood, Oren Parker was registered: age 54, 5'11", light complexion, gray eyes, brown hair, scar on forehead, miner, born Illinois, resident, precinct and post office: Weaverville; he re-registered in New River in 1896. Oren Parker Sherwood d. Jan 2, 1905, Weaverville, Trinity, CA. [Family history research by Patricia J. Hicks].

SUDWORTH. Births at Douglas City Oct 19, 1861, the wife of Wright Sudworth, of a son. (DCG Oct. 23, 1861).

THOMPSON. Married at Douglas City Sept 22, 1861 by Hon. E. J. Curtis, Mr. Rankin Thompson to Mrs. Mary S. Blake. (DCG Sep 25, 1861).

THOMPSON CHILDREN. Board of Supervisors report - what to do with orphan children of late Mrs. Sophie Thompson. The Grass Valley Asylum will take 2 children: Rebecca, age 12, and James age 4; they left last Saturday, arrived there safely. The other children are taken care of in Trinity County except Anna, who is at the County Hospital. A family is needed to take her as she is old enough to at least earn her support. (TJ Feb 19, 1898 p 3). (not in 1880 or 1900 census; it might be possible to find more information in the Board of Supervisors Minutes for February 1898 in Trinity County Courthouse, Main & Court Streets, Weaverville CA 96093). [see Deaths 1850-1890].

TOURTELLOTTE, JESSE HARRISON. b. Sep 13, 1827 Thompson, Connecticut; m. Miss Fannie E. Francis of Canterbury, Conn. 1850. more information available. (TJ Oct 30, 1897).

WALDORFF FAMILY INFORMATION.
Trinity County, California Great Register of Voters Oct 5, 1872:
Waldorff, Jacob, age 46, b. Germany, miner, res. Weaverville, naturalized May 6, 1867 Trinity Co., Cal; first reg. May 6, 1867. [age 46 in 1867].
Waldorff, William, age 22, b. Germany, clerk, res. Junction City, proves citizenship Aug 3, 1871. William H. Waldorff's home in Hyampom burned Mar 17, 1890. The family moved to Humboldt County, and later spelled the name Waldorf. Here is information about this family:
I. Jacob Theodore Waldorff m. Maria Louisa Eicke (aka Marie Elise).
    1. William Henry Waldorff b. 11 Aug 1850. (see II).
    2. Matilda Waldorff, b. 14 Feb 1857 Douglas City, Trinity Co., Calif. d. 11 Feb 1863.
    3. Jacob Theodore "Johnnie" Waldorff; b. 1858 Douglas City; d. 4 Apr 1926.
    4. Earnest Anderson "Bend" Waldorff; b. 1861 Weaverville; d. 8 Jun 1920.
    5. Mary Matilda Waldorff b. 1864 Weaverville; d. 5 May 1878.
II. (1) William Henry "Billy" Waldorff came to America with parents in 1853, age 3 yr. b. 11 Aug 1850 Bremen, Niedersachsen, Germany. m. 13 Nov 1876 Douglas City, Trinity, California; d. 29 Oct 1936 Eureka, Humboldt, CA; wife: Elizabeth Addie Trimble, dau. of John Wesley Trimble & Eliza; b. 18 Jun 1857 Sedalia, Mo.; d. 19 Jan 1932 Eureka, Humboldt, CA.
III-(1) 1. Lulu Belle Waldorff b. 11 Mar 1878 Hyampom; d. 1936; m. Ed Johnson; no children.

2. Mollie Jane Waldorff, b. 26 Feb 1880 Hyampom; d. 11 Sep 1874.
3. George Francis Waldorff, b. 9 Oct 1882 Hyampom; d. 8 Oct 1912; unmarried.
4. William Wesley Waldorff, b. 10 Feb 1884 Hyampom; d. 16 Jan 1950; m. Martha Wolf abt 1920.
5. Annie May Waldorff, b. 20 Aug 1886 Hyampom; d. 1962; m. Roderick Gillis, of Aberdeen, Washington.
6. Albert Carey Waldorff, b. 13 Mar 1889 Hyampom; d. 12 Feb 1960 Calistoga, CA; m. Hazel Alice Schwartz 6 Apr 1914. [Eureka, CA].
7. Lillian Elizabeth Waldorff, b. 11 Apr 1894 Elk River, Humboldt, CA; d. 1971; m 1) Charles Kressman; 2) Sig. Johnsen; no children.
8. Gladys Marie Waldorff, b. 29 Apr 1896 Elk River, Humboldt Co. d. 1972; "married many times; no children".
IV. (III-6). Harry Albert Waldorf (one f), b. 14 Jan 1915 Napa, Napa, CA; son of Albert Carey Waldorf and Hazel Alice Schwartz (b. 22 Nov 1891, dau. of Harry Augustus Schwartz and Ida Poe); m. Alta Eleanor Briggs 25 Aug 1938 Oakland, Alameda Co.
1. Kenneth William Waldorf b. 12 Dec 1938 Long Beach, Los Angeles Co. m. Kelo Ann Thraitkill.
2. Kristine Beth Waldorf, b. 23 Nov 1944 Oakland, Alameda Co.
3. Marcia Jane Waldorf, b. 13 Aug 1950 Quantico, VA
V. (IV-1) Kenneth William Waldorf and Kelo Ann Thraitkill.
1. William Keith Waldorf, b. 11 Sep 1962.
2. Kirk Briggs Waldorf, b. 25 Aug 1963. (source for descendants of William Henry Waldorff: Harry Albert Waldorf, resident of Walnut Creek, CA Oct. 1993).
II. (I-4). Earnest Anderson Waldorff b. 1861 Weaverville; drowned in Trinity River nr. Prairie Creek 8 June 1920. m. Josephine Pattison 3 Jul 1889 at Cox Bar, Trinity Co.; dau. of William A. Pattison and Sally McCollum. She d. Nov 29, 1890, aged 22 yr 9 mo 2 dy.
1. Elsie May Waldorff. (1890-1981).
III. (II-1) Elsie May Waldorff. b. 5 May 1890 Cox's Bar, Trinity, CA. d. 22 Apr 1981 Weaverville, Trinity, CA. m. Fred Setti (Tye) 23 Dec 1922 Redding, Shasta, CA; son of Setti Jim, b. 1860 and Georgie Ann Smith; b. 15 Aug 1890 Hayfork, Trinity, CA. d. 22 Jan 1975 Weaverville, Trinity, CA.
1. Vivian Tye
IV. (III-1) Vivian Tye b. 1 Jul 1931 Arcata, Humboldt, CA. m. Wallace Simpson 29 Mar 1980 Weaverville, Trinity, CA. (he d. 20 Mar 1988 Walnut Creek, CA); no children.
[Waldorff family researched by Patricia J. Hicks in Trinity Journal, Official Records, and family information from Elsie Waldorff Tye and others.]
VAN MATRE, JOHN C. Biographical information. (TJ Oct 30, 1897).
VOLLMER, WILLIAM. Biographical information. (TJ Oct 30, 1897).
WEBB. Married in Weaverville Sep 2, 1861 by the Hon. E. J. Curtis, Mr. David E. Gordon of Weaverville to Miss Laura E. Webb, formerly of Portland, Maine. (DCG Sep 4, 1861 and Sep 14, 1861).
YOUNG. Married at the residence of the bride's father in this county Nov 21, 1861 by Hon. E. J. Curtis, County Judge, Frank W. Young, Esq. of Weaverville to Mary E. Bayles, daughter of A. D. Bayles. New York and Rhode Island papers please copy. (DCG Nov 27, 1861).

END ADDENDUM
PIONEER RECORDS OF TRINITY COUNTY, CALIFORNIA

PIONEER RECORDS OF TRINITY COUNTY, CALIFORNIA

ABOUT THE AUTHOR

Patricia Johnsen Hicks is a fifth-generation native Californian. She is a graduate of the University of California at Berkeley where she majored in English and History. Mrs. Hicks has a solid background in historical research. She has been researching Trinity County records since 1966 and is the author of several books on Trinity County History [see Bibliography]. She also is a Columnist for the TRINITY JOURNAL, the weekly newspaper of Trinity County, California, in the mountains of Northern California.

Mrs. Hicks is the wife of Frank Enochs Hicks, Jr., R.Ph. The Two Hicks Own the Weaverville Drug Store, California's Oldest Pharmacy. The Town of Weaverville was founded in the summer of 1850 and the Weaverville Drug Store has been in continuous business since July 1852.

For over twenty years, Mrs. Hicks shared information with Rita M. Hanover, who was the Reference Librarian at Trinity County Library until she retired. The two historians exchanged facts about Trinity County history and people. Mrs. Hanover has given permission for Mrs. Hicks to use her Trinity County Births, 1850-1900, from all available sources, and Trinity County Marriages 1850-1900 from the earliest books of marriage records. An Index to Mrs. Hanover's Births and Marriages appears in this book. The original manuscripts are in the Reference section of Trinity County Library, Main Street, Weaverville, California.

BIBLIOGRAPHY

Anon., JOURNALS OF THE PROBATE COURT, Trinity County, California 1852-1877, Index, Trinity County Courthouse, Weaverville, California.

Anon., MEMORIAL and BIOGRAPHICAL HISTORY of NORTHERN CALIFORNIA, Chicago, The Lewis Publishing Co., 1891, pages 289-291.

Anon., PERSONAL ANCESTRAL FILE, Release 2.1 for MS-DOS Computers, Salt Lake City, Utah, The Church of Jesus Christ of Latter-Day Saints, 1988 date calculation utility (and updates).

Anon., INDEX TO DEATHS 1873-1890, Trinity County, California, Recorder's Office, Courthouse, Weaverville, CA. *This is the earliest Official Record of Deaths in Trinity County, California. It is sketchy and incomplete. The best record of deaths before about 1913 is the TRINITY JOURNAL, the major reference for this book.* [author's note].

Anon., INDEX TO DEATHS 1889-1908, Trinity County, California, Recorder's Office, Courthouse, Weaverville, CA. *This index is sketchy and incomplete. The information from both books "Index to Deaths" has been added to the alphabetical text of deaths.*

Anon., TRINITY COUNTY, CALIFORNIA Official Records: Births-Deaths, Marriages, 1936-1950, Recorder's Office, Courthouse, Weaverville, CA.
In the 1940s, there were many Delayed Certificates of Births. These births are included in the Addendum. The Index for Births, Marriages, Deaths 1946-1950 is from Official Records.

Bauer, Elmer A., and Barnes, Floyd E., FAMILIES, A Pictorial History of Round Valley (CA) 1864 to 1938, Covelo, California, The Friends of Round Valley Public Library, 1997, 338 pages. *People looking for data from Southern Trinity County will want to check references in this book. Write to Round Valley Public Library, P.O. Box 620, Covelo, CA 95428 for information.*

DOUGLAS CITY GAZETTE, Jones, T.E., Editor and Publisher, May 1861-April 1862; microfilm copy in Trinity County Library, Weaverville, Calif.

Carr, John, PIONEER DAYS IN CALIFORNIA, Eureka, California, Times Publishing Company Book and Job Printers, 1891. Copyright 1982 by Frank B. Foster. Printed by Mid-Cal Publishers, Fresno CA 93706.

Cox, Isaac, THE ANNALS OF TRINITY COUNTY, 1858. "The First California County History", Annotated by James W. Bartlett; Eugene, Oregon 1940. Copy in Trinity County Library, Weaverville CA.

Garrett, Edith M., Garrett, Louise, & Moss, Frances V., MEMORIES OF HYAMPOM 1990, photocopies of stories, facts & pictures, 200 pages; sold as a fund-raiser 1990 in Hyampom, Trinity County, California.

Goodyear, Hal Eugene, former Trinity County Clerk and Recorder, personal interview Dec. 30, 1997.

Hanover, Rita, TRINITY COUNTY BIRTHS 1850-1900, unpublished Mss., Trinity County Library, Weaverville, California. Index to Births 1850-1900, used with permission.

Hanover, Rita, TRINITY COUNTY, CALIFORNIA CENSUS: 1852, 1860, 1870, 1880, unpublished Mss. in Trinity County Library, Weaverville, Calif.

BIBLIOGRAPHY

Hanover, Rita, TRINITY COUNTY, CALIFORNIA, GREAT REGISTER OF VOTERS, 1872-1898; unpublished Mss and microfiche, in Trinity County Library, Weaverville, California.

Hanover, Rita, TRINITY COUNTY MARRIAGES 1850-1900, unpublished Mss., Trinity County Library, Weaverville, California. Index to Marriages 1850-1900, used with permission.

Hanover, Rita, TRINITY COUNTY PIONEERS 1850-1900, reference file in Trinity County Library, Main Street, Weaverville, Calif.

Hicks, Patricia Johnsen, SOME CALLED IT `WEAVER',Weaverville, California, I COLLECT FACTS, P.O.Box 370, Weaverville, CA 96093, 1996.
Much family information in the Chapter "The Fire on Court Street"; some family information in "The Naming of Weaverville"; Bennett family biography with much family information in "Pioneers of Weaverville"; some family information in "The Quest for Mr. Weaver".

Hicks, Patricia Johnsen, STORIES OF A GOLD MINER, 2nd edition, Picture, Biography, and Genealogy of Theodore Eldon Jones, I COLLECT FACTS, P.O. Box 370, Weaverville CA 96093-0370.

Hicks, Patricia Johnsen, TRINITY COUNTY CEMETERIES, unpublished Mss., Weaverville, California.

Hicks, Patricia Johnsen, TRINITY COUNTY FACTS, reference file, Weaverville, California.

Hicks, Patricia Johnsen, WEAVERVILLE, A JEWEL OF A TOWN, Weaverville, CA I COLLECT FACTS, P.O.Box 370, Weaverville, CA 96093, 1993, has information about Pioneer Women in 1852; the Pioneer Ewing Family; and a biography of George Edmund Noonan, druggist, also known as "The Weatherman". There is family information about the Weinheimer-Ryan family in "Christmas Memories".

Hicks, Patricia Johnsen, WEAVERVILLE, Trinity County, California, Weaverville, CA, I COLLECT FACTS, P.O.Box 370, Weaverville CA 96093, 2nd printing 1994. Family information about Luke Wells Ford, The Miner's Poet, and "charge purchases" of a young miner, Willis Sherwood. [see also Addendum].

Morris, Leonard M., former Trinity County Clerk & Recorder, personal interview December 1997.

Satorius, Veronica, BETWEEN THE LINES, The Catholic Church in Shasta County, California 1853-1977, Redding, California 1978. This book has a map of Shasta County showing Roads and Place names as they appeared on Maps prior to 1900. It can be a helpful reference for Catholic families that moved between Trinity and Shasta counties, and is a wealth of information about the history of the Catholic Churches of Shasta County.

Trinity County, California, MARRIAGES, Book H page 180, March 28, 1867, and other references.

TRINITY 1966, Yearbook of the Trinity County Historical Society, P. O. Box 333, Weaverville, CA 96093-0333, pp 4-10, "The Lynching of the Ruggles Brothers".

TRINITY 1995, Yearbook of the Trinity County Historical Society, P. O. Box 333, Weaverville, CA 96093-0333, "Early Mining Along Indian Creek", pp 18-28, by Harold William Rodgers, gives a lot of family relationships of the several families, mostly from the Azores Islands, such as Rodrigues (Rodgers), Guillermo (Williams), Freitas (Fratus), & Joseph.

TRINITY 1996, Yearbook of the Trinity County Historical Society, P. O. Box 333, Weaverville, CA 96093-0333, "The Settlement of Indian Creek", pp 23-35, recollections of the late Harold Williams Rodgers (d. Apr 29, 1995), compiled by Alice Goen Jones.

TRINITY JOURNAL, Weaverville, Trinity County, California, published weekly Jan. 26, 1856ff: All available issues of the TRINITY JOURNAL from Jan. 26, 1856-present, especially Jan. 1856 - Dec. 1900.

TRINITY JOURNAL, Weaverville, Trinity County, California November 27, 1897 page 3 column 1: "The publishers of the Journal would be obliged for a report of the births, marriages and deaths as they occur in the county. As there is no official record, it is impossible for the Journal to properly publish the same, unless interested parties keep the paper advised."

TRINITY JOURNAL, "Births, Marriages, & Deaths in Trinity County", index found in one of the issues for January of each year from 1901 - 1946.

TRINITY TIMES, various editors; Dec. 1854 - Sept. 1855, bound volume in private collection in Weaverville, California.

Wong, H. K., GUM SAHN YUN (Gold Mountain Men), San Francisco, California Oct 1987, 315 pages.

END BIBLIOGRAPHY

www.ingramcontent.com/pod-product-compliance
Lightning Source LLC
Chambersburg PA
CBHW080408300426
44113CB00015B/2441